ECONOMICS AND SOCIAL PROBLEMS

ECONOMICS AND SOCIAL PROBLEMS

MAX E. FLETCHER

UNIVERSITY OF IDAHO

HOUGHTON MIFFLIN COMPANY   BOSTON

DALLAS   GENEVA, ILLINOIS   HOPEWELL, NEW JERSEY
PALO ALTO   LONDON

CHAPTER OPENER ILLUSTRATIONS BY DEBORAH T. SHOTWELL

PRINTED IN THE U.S.A.

Library of Congress Catalog Card Number: 78-69590

ISBN: 0-395-26508-8

❙ CONTENTS ❙

PREFACE xi

ONE
ECONOMICS: WHAT IT'S ALL ABOUT 1
THE MAJOR ECONOMIC PROBLEMS 3
The circular flow 3 ❙ What to produce 5 ❙ How to produce 5 ❙ Who gets what? 6 ❙ When to produce 7
RELEVANCE OF THE FREE MARKET MODEL 10
PITFALLS IN ECONOMIC THINKING 11

TWO
FOOD AND POPULATION 19
MALTHUSIANISM 20
THE MALTHUSIAN CHECKS 24
AGRICULTURAL ECONOMICS 25
Farmers in the labor force 25 ❙ The law of demand 27 ❙ The price elasticity of demand 30 ❙ The law of supply 33 ❙ The equilibrium price 35

GOVERNMENTAL REGULATION OF AGRICULTURE 36

WHAT'S PAST IS PROLOGUE 40

The American breadbasket 40 I The population bomb 42

THREE

THE NATIONAL INCOME: ACCOUNTING AND CONTROL 48

MEASUREMENT OF THE NATIONAL INCOME 49

Aggregate measurements 49 I Price indexes and real gross national product 55

NATIONAL INCOME MANAGEMENT 59

National income determination 59 I The multiplier process 63 I Employment and income stabilization 65 I Prices and income stabilization 68

FOUR

MONEY AND BANKS 75

THE ROLE OF MONEY 76

Money in the United States 77 I The equation of exchange 78 I The crude quantity theory of money 79 I The modern quantity theory of money 79

COMMERCIAL BANKS AND THE MONEY SUPPLY 80

THE FEDERAL RESERVE SYSTEM 86

Structure and operation 86 I Monetary management 89 I Monetary policy: some pros and cons 96

FIVE

GOVERNMENT IN THE ECONOMY: SPENDING AND TAXES 103

GOVERNMENT SPENDING 104

The growth of government spending 104 I Why governments have grown 107 I Current patterns of government spending 112 I The control of public spending 115

TAXES 119

Criteria for evaluating taxes 119 I Taxes by level of government 122 I Who pays the taxes? 127 I The gentle art of tax avoidance 130 I The taxpayers' revolt 135

SIX

INFLATION 139

THE HISTORICAL RECORD 140

THE PRICE OF INFLATION 143

CAUSES OF INFLATION 144

Demand-pull 144 I The Phillips curve 147 I Deficit finance and inflation 148 I Changes in the money supply 150 I Sellers' inflation: wage-push 152 I Sellers' inflation: profit-push 156

SEVEN

GOVERNMENT AND BIG BUSINESS 165

HOW MUCH GOVERNMENT? 166

THE GROWTH OF BIG BUSINESS 168

Forms of business organization 168 I The age of the "robber barons" 170 I The antitrust movement 174

CONTENTS

THE ECONOMICS OF LARGENESS 175
Economies of scale 175 | Pricing and big business 183
RECENT TRENDS 188
Conglomerate mergers 188 | Multinational corporations 191

EIGHT
INEQUALITY AND POVERTY 197
THE EXTENT OF INEQUALITY 198
Measuring inequality 198 | International comparisons of income distribution 200 | Wealth and inequality 201 | How much income inequality is ideal? 202
POVERTY AND NATIONAL COMMITMENT 209
The elimination of poverty 209 | The definition of poverty 209 | Progress against poverty 211 | Who are the poor? 213
THE ATTACK ON POVERTY 216
Where we are 216 | A guaranteed annual income 218 | The negative income tax 219 | Government as employer of last resort 221 | A living minimum wage 222 | Conclusion 223

NINE
INEQUALITY AND EDUCATION, RACE, AND SEX 226
THE ECONOMICS OF EDUCATION 227
Investment in human capital 228 | The personal investment decision 230
TROUBLED TIMES FOR EDUCATION 233
Increasing costs 233 | Inequality and school finance 234 | Inequality and education 237 | Too many diplomas? 241
RACIAL AND SEXUAL DISCRIMINATION 245
Education and discrimination 245 | Costs of discrimination 247 | Discrimination and "crowding" 248 | Progress against discrimination 249

TEN
ENERGY, ENVIRONMENT, AND GROWTH 257
OVERLAPPING PROBLEMS 258
ENERGY USE 261
The price of cheap energy 261 | An energy policy for America 265
ENVIRONMENTAL POLLUTION 270
The growing danger 270 | Control of pollution 272 | How pollution-free a world do we want? 276
ECONOMIC GROWTH 279
The historical record 279 | A no-growth society? 281 | The advantages of growth 283

ELEVEN
HEALTH CARE 288
THE SPIRALING COSTS OF HEALTH CARE 289
The historical record 289 | Causes of rising prices 290
HOW GOOD IS AMERICAN HEALTH CARE? 292
Some measures of achievement 292 | Therapeutic nihilism 293 | The American health care system 296 | Individual responsibility for health 298

CONTENTS

ORGANIZATIONS AND HEALTH MAINTENANCE 301

Fee-for-service system 301 | Prepaid medical service plans 302

NATIONAL HEALTH INSURANCE 304

Goals 304 | The future of national health insurance 308

TWELVE

THE WORLD OF WORK 311

THE WORKER IN AMERICAN HISTORY 312

Workers and the early unions 314 | Labor and the Great Depression 318 | Labor since World War II 321

THE IMPACT OF THE UNION 324

UNEMPLOYMENT 326

COLLECTIVE BARGAINING 328

ON MAKING WORK MEANINGFUL 331

Attitudes toward work 331 | Changes in the workplace 338 | Limitations of job reform 340

THIRTEEN

CITIES IN TROUBLE 345

THE ECONOMICS OF AGGLOMERATION 347

CITY EXPENDITURES 351

Diseconomies of scale 351 | The cost of labor 353 | Population shifts and new programs 354

CITY REVENUES 355

WHAT IS TO BE DONE? 356

Bankruptcy 356 | Reducing expenditures by local action 357 | Increasing state and local revenues 358 | Federal action 359

FOURTEEN

AMERICA IN THE WORLD ECONOMY 363

THE CASE FOR UNRESTRICTED INTERNATIONAL TRADE 365

THE CASE FOR FREE TRADE CHALLENGED 368

The tariff in American history 368 | Nontariff protection 373 | The recent history of protection 374 | The effects of protection 375

THE AMERICAN TRADE PATTERN 376

INTERNATIONAL FINANCE 381

Balance of payments accounting 381 | Determining the exchange rate 386 | Floating exchange rates 386 | The international gold standard 389 | The international monetary fund system 392

FIFTEEN

THE PLIGHT OF THE THIRD WORLD 397

THE POVERTY SYNDROME 399

Life expectancy 401 | Literacy 403 | Economic growth 403 | Population growth 405 | Energy and resource use 410

THE PROBLEM OF ECONOMIC DEVELOPMENT 412

Efforts to aid development 412 | Growing unemployment 415 | Growing inequality 417

SIXTEEN

GOVERNMENT IN THE ECONOMY: REGULATION, PLANNING, AND DEFENSE 424

REGULATION AND THE PUBLIC UTILITIES 426

Identification of public utilities 426 | Task of the regulatory commissions 429 | New approaches in public utility regulation 431 | Regulation and the "unregulated" industries 433

A PLANNED ECONOMY? 435

Western European planning 436 | Planning in the United States 441

THE DEFENSE INDUSTRY 442

Military spending 442 | The international war economy 446 | Military exports 447

SEVENTEEN

MARXISM AND THE SOVIET SYSTEM 450

CLASSIFICATION OF ECONOMIC SYSTEMS 451

KARL MARX AND SCIENTIFIC SOCIALISM 452

Historical materialism 453 | The labor theory of value 454

THE BOLSHEVIK REVOLUTION 456

THE STALINIST PLANNING PERIOD 457

The planning process 459 | Control of the planning system 463 | The pricing process 463

AGRICULTURE 466

Collective and state farms 466 | Private farms 468

LIVING STANDARDS 468

POST-STALINIST PLANNING: THE 1965 REFORMS 470

INDEX 479

I PREFACE I

Most students enrolling in a one-semester or one-quarter course in economics for nonmajors will take no further work in economics. What they look for, therefore, is a broad overview and understanding of what economics is all about: what the major problems and issues are and how economists go about attempting to solve or resolve them.

The general approach of this book is to identify the major current problems, both macro and micro, and then bring to bear on them those economic tools and principles — and only those — that illuminate the problems under discussion. Where there are problems economists have not been able to handle, the book surveys the issues and then acknowledges that there are no agreed-upon solutions. I believe, also, that critics of the American system should have their innings on occasion, along with mainstream supporters of the system.

Consideration is given to the major contemporary social issues of our time, including some usually slighted in introductory books: the plight of the cities, overhaul of the health and medical system, worker discontent, and the growing world of government regulation, planning, and control.

Every effort has been made to keep the exposition simple. The easier word has been chosen in preference to the more complex on every possible occasion. The economist's technical jargon has been employed sparingly. Words rather than mathematical expressions have been used whenever possible. When the materials demanded the use of mathematical analysis, the latter was introduced in its least sophisticated form. On no occasion is an understanding of anything beyond ninth-grade algebra or geometry required.

Except for the first three chapters, the order in which the various topics are taken up for discussion is to some extent arbitrary. There is no compelling reason, for example, that urban problems should be dealt with as late as Chapter Thirteen while inflation comes in Chapter Six. It could be the other way around. This means that the instructor, if he or she chooses, could repackage the topics in a different order. It would be possible, for instance, to develop a fairly broad unit on government in the economy by pulling together Chapter Five ("Government in the Economy: Spending and Taxes"), Chapter Seven ("Government and Big Business"), and Chapter Sixteen ("Government in the Economy: Regulation, Planning, and Defense"). Similarly, Chapter Fourteen ("America in the World Economy"), Chapter Fifteen ("The Plight of the Third World"), and Chapter Seventeen ("Marxism and the Soviet System") could be put together as an international economics unit.

Chapters One through Three, though, were designed to be taken up first. Chapter One, as its title indicates, introduces the reader to the economic way of thinking and to the major economic problems. It furnishes an overall setting for the more specific problems to follow. Chapter Two, along with a discussion of the related problems of food and population, provides an introduction to the basic microeconomic tools of analysis: demand and supply, market equilibrium, price elasticity. Several of the later chapters start with the premise that the reader has already mastered the rudimentary supply and demand models developed in Chapter Two. Chapter Three is the basic macroeconomics chapter. It covers national income accounting, national income determination, income stabilization, and overall price movements related to income stabilization efforts. After mastering the materials covered in Chapters Two and Three, readers will have at least the minimal micro and macro background required to handle any of the following chapters.

During my months of researching and writing I've accumulated obligations I can never repay. My thanks to two extremely competent secretaries: Candy Smetana and Diane Leaverton. My colleagues at the University of Idaho have also been helpful in taking the time and trouble to read and criticize chapter drafts in their areas of expertise. I am grateful to several manuscript referees — Professors John J. Rapczak of Rhode Island Junior College, John M. McGuire of Parkersburg Community College, Warren St. James of Nassau Community College, Angela Nation of Santa Fe Community College, and James W. Wightman of State University College at Potsdam — who saved me from some awkward slips. The responsibility for any remaining errors or omissions I must bear as best I can. Holders of copyrights have been generous in permitting use of their materials. And finally, my wife, Ann, has provided sympathetic support and encouragement by her careful and critical reading of the manuscript.

M. E. F.

ECONOMICS AND
SOCIAL PROBLEMS

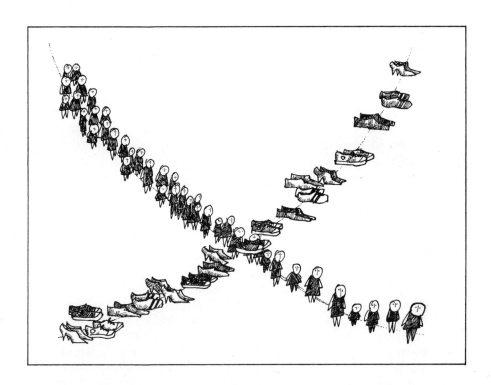

I ECONOMICS: WHAT IT'S ALL ABOUT I

When our economic system is working well we tend to take it for granted. We find other things more interesting — even more important — than the way we go about producing and distributing our material goods. But when things go badly we are forced to realize that perhaps nothing is more fundamental to a way of life than the reliability of the supply of goods and services. Even religion or the glory of a sunset will be pushed aside if people are hungry and do not know where their next meal is coming from or how they are going to get the gasoline to take them to work the next day. This suggests that at least a minimal satisfaction of basic economic needs must be achieved before much consideration can be given to other problems. The science and practice of economics, then, like the science and practice of dentistry, should help put us in the position of being able to take for granted the fundamental things, leaving us free to concentrate on more important concerns.

The basic concern of economics, as the above indicates, is with *scarcity:* the disparity between human wants and the means of satisfying them. In fact, the term *economics* suggests "economizing": deciding what we will have when we can't have everything. In many countries of the world today such economic choices are indeed agonizing, based as they are on rudimentary survival needs. But just because most of us in the United States can more or less take it for granted that our fundamental needs will somehow be satisfied, it does not follow that scarcity has been eliminated and the basic economic problem solved. We still do not have sufficient economic goods and services to satisfy all our needs — to say nothing of our mere wants. And we undoubtedly never will, since those needs and wants grow more rapidly than any conceivable increase in what is available to satisfy them. Who could have guessed a hundred years ago that the availability of goods and services today, after doubling every generation, would still fall so far short of our requirements?

Perhaps we have gone at things the wrong way. Possibly we would be better satisfied today had we learned to emphasize not the increase in our holdings of material things but the control of our desires. This has not been the "American way," however, although we can at times be forced into it. Nor has it been the objective chosen by most other economic systems. For better or worse our economic salvation is believed to lie in ever-expanding production. The road to paradise is paved with automobiles and color television sets and ski vacations.

the small society   by Brickman

I   THE MAJOR ECONOMIC PROBLEMS   I

Taking as a starting point the premise that the basic economic problem is scarcity and the essential goal of any economic system is the provision of the material things of life, we will see that there are many different ways of organizing for this mission. Whatever the economic system used, however, it must provide arrangements for resolving several major economic problems related to scarcity.

Given the availability of productive resources (conventionally identified as labor, land, and capital), some way must be found to decide *what* is to be produced. Should the system use available resources to produce yachts or baby carriages? Milk or whiskey? Schools or private swimming pools? Then, having decided somehow what to produce and how much, the decision must be made as to *how* to produce. Assuming that we are going to dig ditches, should we use picks and shovels or trenching machines? Are automobiles to be made in small shops or large factories? Of steel, or of aluminum and plastics? Then comes the most fundamental decision of all: How are the goods to be parceled out? *For whom* is production to take place? Share and share alike would be one solution — but one that is rarely found anywhere. More likely it will be decided that some will get more, others less. How are we to decide who gets more? On the basis of greater needs? Greater political clout? Greater individual contribution to production?

Finally, since we can normally assume that population will expand and needs increase, every economic system must be able to make provision for economic growth. This is primarily a *when* decision with two time options: (1) we can produce and enjoy consumer goods now or (2) we can take some of the resources that might be used in consumer goods production at this time and use them instead to construct additional factories and equipment, which will permit us to enjoy an enlarged supply of consumer goods in the future. Essentially the question is one of something now as opposed to more later.

The circular flow

An outline of these problems, and the way solutions are provided in a complete market economy, can be presented with the use of a *circular flow diagram,* which pictures the flow of goods, resources, and money through the economy (Figure 1.1).

We start with a two-part economy, divided into a production sector made up primarily of business firms and a consumption sector comprised of households (families). It is the function of business firms to turn out the consumer goods necessary for the maintenance of households (upper outside loop), drawing its productive resources from those same households (lower outside loop).

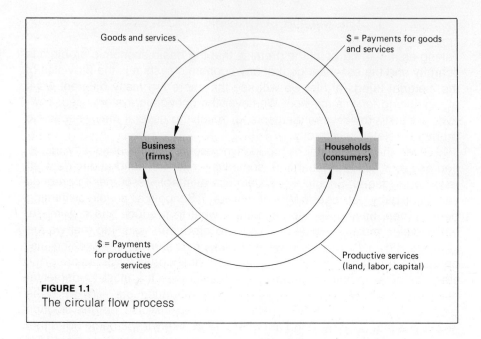

FIGURE 1.1
The circular flow process

These productive resources, as we saw earlier, are categorized as labor, land, and capital. *Labor* is routine human effort used in the production process. *Land* includes much more than we usually think of when we use the term, since it includes all unimproved natural resources — in the words of the early economists, "as received from the hand of God." *Capital* (or *capital goods*) means real capital or productive goods (not their financial values, as in Wall Street usage). It consists of a stock of things (factories, equipment, houses, inventories) built in the past and accumulated for use in further production.

All labor, it should be obvious, must be drawn from the household sector, since all workers are members of households. Similarly, the owners of land and capital are members of households, at least in a private-enterprise market economy, so we must look there also for our productive property.

Business firms, then, exist for the purpose of securing supplies of productive resources (or *productive factors,* as they are sometimes called) and converting them into consumer goods necessary for the maintenance of households, which permits the latter to continue to supply productive resources, which permits businesses to produce more, and so the flow goes — round and round and round.

It is the inner circle of the circular flow diagram that provides the clue to the governance of this economic activity by showing how money moves. In a market economy the extent and direction of the flow of money tell us what will be produced, how it will be produced, and for whom it will be produced. It also provides a time frame for answering the question of when it will be produced.

What to produce

In a private enterprise economy, the ultimate test of the success of the system is whether or not adequate provision is made for the household sector — the effectiveness with which consumption demands are met. Consumption is the ultimate end of all economic activity. This is so because the basic economic decisions are private, individual decisions, and each individual is expected to maximize his or her own satisfactions. Such satisfactions are gained through the use of consumer goods and services.

Only in centrally planned or centrally guided economies, or in a private-enterprise economy with a growing government sector, will other objectives (defense, national power, and so forth) be able to challenge consumption, now or in the future, for the right to use productive inputs. So what will be produced in a completely private-enterprise market economy will be what the consumer wants. The consumer is sovereign. Whether the consumer is an absolute monarch, governed only by personal desires, or a constitutional monarch, with desires shaped and programmed by advertisers, is by no means a trivial question. But discussion of this question must be deferred for the moment.

Assuming *consumer sovereignty,* what should be visualized in the *circular flow process* are business firms standing ready to turn loose a flood of consumer goods, awaiting only the signals from the marketplace before deciding what to produce. When the signals come, they take the form of prices, which tell businessmen how consumers are casting their "dollar ballots." A shift of dollar ballots from one product or service to another drives prices down in the industry losing consumer votes and up in the one benefiting from the swing in consumer sentiment. Lower prices, in turn, are in effect an order to cut production in an industry because opportunities for profit are becoming meager. Production is increased in the industry with rising prices, however, because higher prices promise larger rewards. So the answer to the question of whether to produce yachts or baby carriages, whiskey or milk, is made by producers responding to the call of the market. Consumers act and suppliers react.

How to produce

Once they have decided what they are going to produce, businessmen have to determine how to make their product. Two stages are involved in this decision: an engineering step and a financial step.

The engineering considerations hinge on technological factors. What alternatives are available, for example, in the way of interchangeable materials in the construction of an automobile? To what extent can light-weight aluminum replace heavier, but stronger, steel? Once the engineers have come up with alternative ways of manufacturing a soundly engineered automobile, then the costing specialists take over. Fiberglass might be beautiful in car bodies, but its cost could push the price of a car out of the mass-purchase market. Given the projected market price of automobiles and the range of engineering options available, financial considerations suggest adopting whatever production techniques and materials usage will minimize cost. This is so because, for a given level of sales, profits can be increased only by reducing costs. Thus the ditch we had to dig in our earlier example will be dug by hand if that is the cheaper way, and by trenching machine if that method promises lower costs than the pick-and-shovel gang.

In theory, then, first businessmen get their sales revenue possibilities by studying their markets and next they decide how to produce by determining what will be an adequate product for their customers and what method will turn out that product at minimum cost. Remember, though, we are still discussing a theoretical pure market economy, marked by nearly complete rationality of decision making and universal price competition — not necessarily today's approximation of that economy.

Who gets what?

In the process of deciding how to produce, businessmen in a market economy also decide who is to get what from the production flow. A vast and enticing array of consumer goods and services is available in the marketplace to all buyers with the purchase price. Those with the greatest amount of purchasing power are those able and willing to provide the largest amount of the labor or property services most in demand for current production. Skilled workers will have high incomes and will be able to enjoy large amounts of consumer goods if businessmen have decided to use a great deal of skilled labor in the manufacture of their products. Landowners will be similarly blessed if large amounts of land are required in current production. In brief, those providers of labor or property services who contribute most to production (as measured by the total value of their services) are able to command a relatively large portion of current consumer goods output; those whose labor or property services are less in demand will get less; and those without property and whose labor no one wants have no claim on current production. Thus the ethics of distribution in a completely free market economy: "From each according to his or her ability and the capability of his or her property, to each according to his or her production and that of his or her property."[1]

_____

[1] In a sense the "property" qualification is unnecessary, or would have been thought so at an earlier time, since property was regarded as the fruit of past labor. With the accumulation over the years of large inherited fortunes, however, the qualification is very much to the point.

When to produce

The free market model   From the foregoing it should be evident that what is being described is a completely self-governing economy. No one is charged with planning what to produce, establishing controls for the production process, or setting up guidelines for the allocation of goods and services. It is necessary, of course, to have well-established rules of the game (a legal system) and an umpire (government) to detect and punish those who violate the rules. It is also necessary to provide some necessities (such as national defense) not readily forthcoming because they cannot be produced and marketed profitably. But the vital core of economic activity is carried out with no overt coordination or control: It regulates itself, seemingly as if guided by an "invisible hand."

What promotes and regulates economic activity is the attempt of each individual to advance his own welfare. "Self-interest" — that most powerful of motives — is paradoxically the balance wheel. In order to maximize their consumption, individuals work hard, improve their skills, and save to accumulate productive property. And in order to maximize their earnings, businessmen make an effort to give the consumers what they want while producing as efficiently as possible. In the process resources are attracted into uses where they can make the greatest possible contribution to production, and products are distributed to those who most deserve them. Since every individual knows best what he or she wants and where his or her contribution is apt to be greatest, any attempt by government to improve on the process is bound to be self-defeating. Only if competition among buyers and among sellers is thwarted does the whole process become unstrung — but this is contrary to the rules of the game, and government is supposed to see that it does not happen. To talk of *national* economic goals under this system, it follows, is meaningless. Individuals choose and pursue their own goals; what all this adds up to on a national scale is a matter of little consequence.

This model, or set of theoretical assumptions underlying the operations of a free market economy, was first set forth in detail in the writings of the "father of economics," Adam Smith, especially in his *Wealth of Nations.* Published in 1776, the *Wealth of Nations* outlined the general case for economic freedom just as the Declaration of Independence, published in the same year, did for political freedom. To an important degree, the development of economic thought from Adam Smith's time to our own has centered on the refinement and elaboration of his ideas.

But surely, you may insist, this self-regulating model doesn't apply to economic growth? Surely if the national economy is to grow, somebody must plan and direct the growth process. Not so. The overall economy, under this system, may or may not expand its output-capability levels from year to year. If growth does take place (and it did routinely take place during the late nineteenth and early twentieth centuries, when national economies most closely approached the free market model), it will occur because a multitude of individual decisions to save and invest add up to an expanded national production capability, not because government decision makers decide that growth is in the national interest.

The production-possibilities curve   The framework within which growth takes place in a free market economy is pictured in Figure 1.2. Since this diagram uses a geometric device that will reappear many times in later chapters, it is appropriate to describe its construction. The economist's "curves" are simply shorthand ways of showing relationships between any two economic variables. A number series representing different possible values for one of the economic categories, in this case production levels for capital goods, is arrayed along the horizontal (x) axis. The other is ranged along the vertical (y) axis, as are possible levels of consumer goods production in Figure 1.2. Any point lying in the main field of the diagram, in the area between the x- and y-axes, therefore, brings together two figures: some particular value from the x-axis and some particular value from the y-axis. Point b, for example, tells us that production of an amount 0f of capital goods is possible in combination with consumer goods production in the amount 0e. All other points lying on the curve for year 1 give us other possible combinations of the two types of production — and thus the label *production-possibilities curve.*

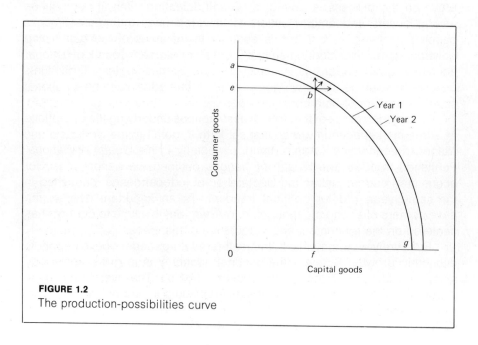

FIGURE 1.2
The production-possibilities curve

For a particular curve to make economic sense, of course, the assumptions underlying its construction must be spelled out. Such assumptions for Figure 1.2 are particularly important. One, following the logic of the circular flow concept, is that all current production takes the form of either consumption goods or capital goods. The former are goods or services of immediate usefulness to households, such as food, clothing, and permanent waves; the latter are new business plant and equipment and new houses, which will enable us to produce more consumer goods or services in the future.

The second assumption is that at any point in time a particular economy has a certain accumulated stock of capital goods and technology, or know-how, which it can apply to production with a certain level of efficiency. Point *a* says that if the economy under discussion efficiently applies all of its production capacity and technology to turning out consumer goods, it can produce an amount 0*a* of such goods. Alternatively, if it uses all its production facilities and know-how to produce capital goods it will turn out an amount 0*g* of factories, machines, and new houses. In fact, of course, no economy could operate long at point *g* since it is impossible to get along without new consumer goods. The actual point of production will, it is hoped, be somewhere out along the production-possibilities curve for year 1, say point *b*. At point *b,* as we saw earlier, the economy will produce a combination of 0*e* consumer goods and 0*f* capital goods.

Now, what the economy does by moving from point *a* to point *b* is give up or trade off a certain amount of consumer goods production (*ae*) in order to shift those resources into the production of capital goods (*fg*). In a fully employed economy, therefore, the *opportunity cost* of producing more capital goods is the loss of that much consumer goods production: Producing more capital goods means giving up the opportunity to make a certain amount of consumer goods, and vice versa. Some of the poorest countries can't move very far to the right of point *a*. They simply can't afford to lose even part of their already inadequate food supply.

If, however, families (even some of them) are sufficiently far above the subsistence level that they need not use all their incomes to buy consumer goods, then by not spending (by saving) they release resources that otherwise would have gone into making consumer goods for use in the production of capital goods or in the improvement of technology. Human resources, for example, can be used during a given period of time either to manufacture shoes or to build shoe factories — but not both. Not producing consumer goods, therefore, makes possible an increase in capital goods production. The benefit of this is that it shifts the production-possibilities curve outward, signifying that next year it will be possible to produce more consumer goods, or more capital goods incorporating superior technology, or some larger combination of both, as suggested by the arrows in the diagram.

We still haven't answered the question of why families in a position to save, to postpone consumption — thereby permitting an enlargement of the capital stock — do so voluntarily. In some cases it might simply be the result of an income flow so large that spending all of it is burdensome. But this is rarely the case. More commonly an inducement is necessary to encourage saving. That inducement takes the form of interest payments. Businessmen who need funds to take advantage of some new opportunity, which requires a new plant or other facilities, will be willing to pay a premium in the form of interest for such funds, on the assumption that their future earnings will enable them to repay both the loans and the accumulated interest. Thus will the individual decisions of investors be matched with individual decisions to save: Not spending on consumer goods leads to spending on capital goods. And if thriftiness is considered a virtue, as it is in a market system, and investment promises large rewards, as tends to be the case, then the economy will feature high savings rates, high levels of investment spending, and consequently rapid economic growth — all without the intercession of government planners and controllers — or so the story goes.

I RELEVANCE OF THE FREE MARKET MODEL I

In the face of big business, big labor, and especially big government today, it might appear that time spent on the foregoing free market model — which assumes that none of these exist — has been time wasted. Adding to this attitude is the acknowledged fact that no economy has ever worked entirely in accordance with specifications of the model. Even in Great Britain and the United States during the few decades of the late nineteenth century when the closest approximations to the model were achieved, government was not as quiescent as the self-regulating system requires nor was free competition always present.

Why, then, study a system that never was and, given present trends, never will be? One reason is that while we may never see such a system in action, we will continue to make use of parts of it. The impersonal nature of markets, as contrasted with the very personal nature of government regulation and control, suggests that whenever markets can appropriately be employed, they perhaps should be. On this basis a more thorough examination of market processes is provided in Chapter Two.

An even more compelling reason for examining the free market system is that it comes close still to being the official American economic ideology — possibly because we have not yet come up with anything more adequately descriptive of current reality. James B. Conant insisted that "it takes a new conceptual scheme to cause the abandonment of an old one."[2] Or maybe we have a simple case of cultural lag: Our institutions have changed more rapidly than our ideas. The economist John Maynard Keynes best expressed this thought:

The ideas of economists and political philosophers, both when they are right and when they are wrong, are more powerful than is commonly understood. Indeed the world is ruled by little else. Practical men, who believe themselves to be quite exempt from any intellectual influences, are usually the slaves of some defunct economist. Madmen in authority, who hear voices in the air, are distilling their frenzy from some academic scribbler of a few years back. I am sure that the power of vested interests is vastly exaggerated compared with the gradual encroachment of ideas. Not, indeed, immediately, but after a certain interval; for in the field of economic and political philosophy there are not many who are influenced by new theories after they are twenty-five or thirty years of age, so that the ideas which civil servants and politicians and even agitators apply to current events are not likely to be the newest. But, soon or late, it is ideas, not vested interests, which are dangerous for good or evil.[3]

Whether the situation is as Keynes describes it or not, when American presidents and their advisers laud the virtues of private enterprise and economic individualism, deplore the growth of government, and refuse to see the necessity of planning to accompany the inescapable growth of controls, they likely base their position on something similar to our model of the self-regulating market system.[4] And when businessmen talk the language of free enterprise they usually have something similar in mind, not the current reality.[5] If this self-regulating system is still such a general frame of reference, it is worth knowing about — even if we think it is not an adequate description of the economic situation today.

I PITFALLS IN ECONOMIC THINKING I

The study of economics is subject to particular difficulties in getting at and disseminating "the truth." Economics is, first of all, a social science — a

---

[2] James B. Conant, *On Understanding Science,* Yale University Press, New Haven, Conn., 1947, pp. 89–90.

[3] John Maynard Keynes, *The General Theory of Employment, Interest and Money,* Harcourt, Brace, New York, 1936, pp. 383–384.

[4] For support of this point of view, at least as far as one recent president is concerned, see Garry Wills, *Nixon Agonistes,* New American Library, New York, 1970.

[5] See Francis X. Sutton et al., *The American Business Creed,* Harvard University Press, Cambridge, 1956.

science of human behavior — which means that it is concerned with developing general principles governing human action. The trouble is that individual actions are extremely difficult to predict on the basis of any general principles yet formulated. Economists, for example, continue to assume that individuals rationally and single-mindedly pursue their own self-interests. In fact, the self-regulating market concept, as we have seen, is built on this premise. But self-interest is a slippery concept. So long as it can safely be interpreted narrowly in the traditional sense to mean maximum individual accumulation of economic goods with minimum effort, a firm foundation is provided on which to build elaborate economic models. But does it have to mean only this? If individuals were to act on the premise that helping others and cooperating with them is the way to maximize their own welfare, even though it brings them a smaller share of goods and services, wouldn't they still be acting on the basis of self-interest? In a market society, behavior of the latter sort finds little encouragement. But if it ever becomes widespread, much of conventional economics will have to be recast.

Another problem raised in the social sciences is the limited possibility of conducting controlled experiments. Chemists can run their compounds through their test tubes over and over again to check results. But people can't be run and rerun through the economic test tubes. Historical data can be used as a check, but time changes things and history never repeats itself exactly.

All is not lost, however. A great deal can be done if adequate amounts of current data are available. In recent years there has been a literal explosion in the development of sophisticated techniques designed to analyze numerical data: econometrics, linear programming, input-output analysis, and others. With the help of the computer, these permit the extraction of far more information from economic processes than was ever before possible. But because the economic world is so complex and changes so rapidly, there are always nagging questions as to whether the right data were collected, whether truths or nontruths were extracted from the data ("garbage in, garbage out"), and whether or not the truths, if any, will help us to predict or control the future.

If you are beginning to suspect that all this leaves room for considerable disagreement among economists, you are right. And even if economists come up with findings and conclusions on which they can agree, they face a problem not encountered by the natural scientists: The public already knows a good deal about the economic world. New findings in chemistry and biology may be readily accepted because nonspecialists have little knowledge on which to base their rejection. But everyone is or has been a member of a family and knows all about economic problems. The earliest use of the term *economics,* in fact, was by the ancient Greeks, for whom it meant the study of household management. However, ap-

proaching economics from the point of view of the household leads to
some conclusions that are incontestably false when applied to the wider
world. It was on this basis that one of the great economists, Frank Knight
of the University of Chicago, insisted that perhaps the most important task
of the economist was to convince the public that much of what it "knew"
was simply not so. He would likely have agreed with the American humorist
Josh Billings that "it is better to know nothing than to know what ain't so."
And it is easy to set up a fairly long list of common economic beliefs that
simply "ain't so."

Some representative examples include:

1 Everyone knows that if a person works hard and intelligently and
produces more she or he is bound to be better off. Therefore if farmers
work hard, if nature cooperates, and if they produce more they will be
better off. *Fact:* The first part of the statement is probably correct, because
somewhat larger production by an individual will not affect the market for
his or her output, and this would be true for an individual farmer. But if *all*
farmers produce more, their market will not be unaffected. In fact larger
agricultural production is quite apt to drive farm prices down sufficiently
to bring about a fall in total farm income (because of price inelastic
demand — see Chapter Two). This incidentally, is a nice example of the
fallacy of composition — which is the assumption that what is true for a
part will be true for the whole, or the reverse.

2 Everyone knows that a family is better off if its members spend
carefully and save as much as possible. A penny saved, after all, is a
penny earned. It follows that a frugal nation will be better off than a
spendthrift nation. *Fact:* Ben Franklin's maxim may be good economic
policy for the long run, since saving makes investment and economic

the small society   by Brickman

growth possible. But an excessive frugality at any particular point in time is likely to be disastrous, since one person's spending creates income for others. Saving (nonspending) can thus mean weakened demand and fewer jobs. A recession is ordinarily little more than a fall in overall spending, as we will see in Chapter Three.

3 Everyone knows that when we buy foreign-made goods that could be produced at home we are supporting foreign workers at the expense of our own workers. To protect and create American jobs we should have high import duties on foreign goods. *Fact:* If we buy from foreigners, we provide them with dollars that will likely be used to purchase American goods. If we curtail imports in order to protect American industries that have proved their inability to compete in world markets, we handicap the more efficient export industries and destroy jobs in those industries, as Chapter Fourteen describes.

In addition to the fallacy of composition, economics is marked by the frequent use of a number of other fallacies in reasoning. One of these is the common resort to post hoc conclusions (*post hoc, ergo propter hoc,* "after this, therefore because of this"). Because one event follows shortly on the heels of another, the inclination is strong to believe that the first causes the second. We don't really believe the rooster crows the sun up, but most of us are quite ready to believe that rising prices are always the result of previous wage boosts. They undoubtedly sometimes are, but both may be the result of other forces — rapid increases in demand, for example, as we will see later.

Another common error is the proneness to see things in terms of extremes ("Everybody on welfare is a bum"), whereas the usual situation is somewhere in the middle ("Some of the people on welfare are bums"). A similar tendency is to becloud the issue by the use of *colored words* — those that are emotion laden ("But that's socialism"). When emotion comes in the door, clear thinking goes out the window.

These latter two barriers to clear economic thinking are part of a more general problem: the difficulty of divorcing the scientific method from ideology. Use of the scientific method, in brief, demands a single-minded commitment to reason and factual analysis. Ideological belief, on the other hand, substitutes zeal for reason since an *ideology* is "any system of beliefs publicly expressed with the manifest purpose of influencing the sentiments and actions of others."[6] Ideas, according to the title of one of Max Lerner's books, are weapons. Ideologies and the scientific method need not conflict, but if they agree, it is a matter of pure happenstance. Sutton and his collaborators identify the characteristics of ideology that contrast markedly with the characteristics of science as follows:

---

[6] Sutton et al., *The American Business Creed,* p. 2.

Ideologies, whatever their content and whoever their adherents, possess certain common features. They are selective in subject matter and in use of empirical evidence and logical argument. . . . The institutionally defined objective of science is to seek understanding. . . . The ideologist seeks to influence action and attitude. . . .

[Ideologies are] simple and clear-cut even when their subject matter is complicated. . . .

[Ideologies are] expressed in language that engages the emotions, as well as the understanding, of their readers and listeners. . . .

[The] content [of ideologies] is limited to what is publicly acceptable. . . . The orientation of ideology subjects it, to a greater measure than science, to control by its audience. . . .[7]

All of this is very much to the point in economic discussion because economic systems are "isms" (capitalism, socialism, communism), even though they may be disguised under other labels (free enterprise, public ownership) — and "isms" are ideologies. What we think about an economic system, then, may be the result of critical examination; it may be a matter of purely emotional attachment; or more likely, it will be some mixture of the two. And because the economic world is so complex, it is rarely possible to determine precisely what parts of the analysis are based on reason (*positive economics* — "what is") and what parts are the predictable outcomes of the value system held by the analyst (*normative economics* — "what should be").

No part of economics is entirely free of the subtle influence of ideology. Even our view of the past is colored by what we would like to see in the present, as George Dalton demonstrates in his description of the various interpretations of the consequences of the Industrial Revolution:

For almost a hundred years now, intelligent men have disagreed about the early consequences of the British Industrial Revolution; did it make the working classes better or worse off? . . .

Disputes between professors of economic history are almost never academic. When intelligent men disagree heatedly over what happened 200 years ago, it is usually because they disagree heatedly over what should be done today. The Left assess the Industrial Revolution as a social catastrophe in part because they want to reform or socialize the capitalism of their own day. The Right assess the Industrial Revolution as a progressive development for mankind, in part because they want to conserve the capitalism of their own day which they regard as superior to socialist alternatives. When economic argument is heated, economic policy is at stake.[8]

---

[7] Sutton et al., *The American Business Creed,* pp. 3–6.
[8] George Dalton, *Economic Systems and Society: Capitalism, Communism and the Third World,* Penguin, Baltimore, Md., 1974, p. 39.

A word to the wary may be scant protection because ideological views come cloaked with layers of professional credentials, wrapped in a covering of sophisticated analytical devices. But take to heart the advice that where values are strongly held, as they are in the area of economic and social policy, ideas should be subjected to especially critical examination — even when the writers are professional economists!

I SUMMARY I

Economics focuses on the way society goes about producing and distributing its goods and services. Its concern is with scarcity, which implies a necessity to economize: to choose what we are in fact to have if we can't have everything.

Every economic system, whatever its particular institutional arrangements for producing and distributing economic goods and services, must find some way of solving the four major economic problems: deciding (1) *what to produce* with available resources (land, labor, and capital), (2) *how to produce* those goods and services, (3) *for whom* production is to take place (who is to get what), and (4) *when* the fruits of production are to be enjoyed (a certain amount of consumer goods now or more later through investment in economic growth).

In our society these economic problems are still largely resolved through reliance on market processes. Relative prices and costs, coupled with the search for profits and the maximization of consumer satisfactions, push or pull productive resources into certain channels and determine how production is to be structured. Relative rewards in production create differential incomes, enabling some to consume a lot, others only a small amount. Finally, market considerations determine the possibility and desirability of postponing consumption in order to use productive resources to create capital goods (new production capacity) so that more consumer goods will be available later.

The early classical economists, especially Adam Smith, were the first to recognize that all these problems could be solved without governmental guidance and control. Their model of market behavior came close to describing the economic realities in some of the late nineteenth-century capitalistic economies, such as those of the United States and Great Britain. Since that time the development of big business, which necessitated the growth of big labor and big government, has made the self-regulating market model unworkable on an overall basis. But the underlying concepts still describe large parts of our economy and are believed to be basic truths by many influential persons.

Since economics is a social science — a science of human behavior — it is extremely difficult to formulate general laws describing how our economy actually operates. Experimentation to determine whether or not a hypothesis is true or whether an economic model really works is rarely possible. Perhaps more important, everyone already has some conviction — however correct — as to how the economy does and should operate. Even professional economists have difficulty separating positive economics — what is — from normative economics — what should be.

| IMPORTANT TERMS AND CONCEPTS |

scarcity	fallacy of composition
circular flow diagram	post hoc fallacy
capital (capital goods)	colored words
consumer sovereignty	ideology
circular flow process	positive economics
opportunity cost	normative economics
production-possibilities curve	

| QUESTIONS, PROBLEMS, AND EXERCISES |

1 Even if population growth levels off and economic growth continues, why will we never have all we need?

2 Can you think of any current economic problem that you would rank with the four labeled as the major economic problems?

3 Why is equal sharing inconsistent with the free market solution of the "for whom" problem?

4 It is said that consumers in the Soviet Union are free to exercise consumer choice but not consumer sovereignty. What is suggested by the distinction?

5 What is the difference between positive economics and normative economics? How would you go about eliminating the normative element from positive economics?

6 Set up a production-possibilities curve for your own "production" of course-work versus leisure activities. Can you demonstrate that moving along the curve represents a type of opportunity cost or "trade-off"?

7 Show how a major depression would be pictured in the production-possibilities framework of Figure 1.2.

8 Show what would happen to the production-possibilities curve of Figure 1.2 if a country suffered major industrial damage, say by bombing during a war.

| SUGGESTED READING |

Cheit, Earl F., ed. *The Business Establishment.* Wiley, New York, 1964.

Dalton, George. *Economic Systems and Society: Capitalism, Communism and the Third World.* Penguin, Baltimore, Md., 1974.

Friedman, Milton. *Capitalism and Freedom.* University of Chicago Press, Phoenix Books, Chicago, 1962.

Galbraith, John Kenneth. *Economics and the Public Purpose.* Houghton Mifflin, Boston, 1973.

Heilbroner, Robert L. *The Economic Transformation of America.* Harcourt, Brace, Jovanovich, New York, 1977.

———. *The Worldly Philosophers: The Lives, Times and Ideas of the Great Economic Thinkers,* 4th ed. Simon and Schuster, New York, 1972.

Polanyi, Karl. *The Great Transformation: The Political and Economic Origins of Our Time.* Beacon Press, Boston, 1957.

Silk, Leonard. *Capitalism: The Moving Target.* Praeger, New York, 1974.

TWO

I FOOD AND POPULATION I

If a person had to choose one of the many economic problems confronting the world today for top billing, there would be good reasons for assigning that role to the food "crisis." We can, if necessary, learn to live with a deteriorating environment. Nations have found ways of adjusting to *inflation* — a constantly rising price level. Periodic unemployment is uncomfortable but not disastrous. The presence of significant pockets of poverty in a society is unseemly, but the poor we have always had with us. Even the energy situation may prove to be less a crisis than a demand for changes in life styles. But the relationship between available food supplies and growing population is literally a race between survival and catastrophe.

In light of conditions during the past few centuries, this statement may seem too strong. Even a casual reading of American history makes it appear that our most urgent concern has been finding outlets for super-abundant foodstuffs. Until only a few years ago, thanks to the extraordinary advances in agricultural technology, we assumed that the *Malthusian spectre* — population outrunning the available food supply — had been permanently laid to rest. We should have known better.

Only gradually and somewhat grudgingly are we coming to recognize how exceptional the past couple of hundred years have been. It is no exaggeration to say that all previous civilizations, with rare exceptions, existed on an economic shoestring. Rather than being able to take for granted an abundance of food, even highly civilized populations existed on the edge of starvation. And unless we find some way of curbing world population growth, the future promises to look more like the distant than the immediate past — not, perhaps, in the United States, but surely for many parts of the world.

| MALTHUSIANISM |

If this comes to pass, one person, more than any other, would have every right to say, "I told you so." That person is Thomas R. Malthus, an eight-eenth-century Englishman who in 1798 first formally elaborated his "dismal theorem" in *An Essay on the Principle of Population.* Put most simply, the "dismal theorem" states that if nothing checks the growth of population except misery and starvation, then the population will grow until it is miserable and starves.

Malthus wrote *The Principle of Population* in direct response to William Godwin's *Enquiry Concerning the Principles of Political Justice, and Its Influence on General Virtue and Happiness,* published in 1793. An extreme individualist and anarchist, Godwin opposed private property, economic and political inequality, and all coercive action by the state. Voluntary goodwill and the sense of justice of the individual person, guided by human reason, assured a future full of unprecedented happiness.

In opposition to this vision of the perfectability of humanity and the possibility of unlimited economic progress, Malthus posed one insuper-able obstacle: Population, *when unchecked,* increases in a geometric ratio, doubling every generation, while the means of subsistence increase at most in an arithmetic ratio, rising by an equal, absolute amount each generation. In Malthus's own language:

Taking the whole earth ... and, supposing the present population equal to a thousand millions, the human species would increase as the numbers, 1, 2, 4, 8,

16, 32, 64, 128, 256, and subsistence as 1, 2, 3, 4, 5, 6, 7, 8, 9. In two centuries the population would be to the means of subsistence as 256 to 9; in three centuries as 4096 to 13, and in two thousands years the difference would be almost incalculable.[1]

Here we have the hare and the tortoise in a desperate race, but with a hare that runs ever faster after it leaves the starting point.

Malthus finds support for his assumption of a geometric increase in population in statistics drawn from the American colonies and states: "In the northern states of America . . . the population has been found to double itself, for above a century and a half successively, in less than twenty-five years."[2]

Statistical support for the assumption of an arithmetic increase in the means of subsistence, Malthus concedes, is not so easy to come by: "The rate according to which the productions of the earth may be supposed to increase, it will not be so easy to determine." Failing to find actual production figures to employ, Malthus falls back on an intellectual argument — on what later came to be called the *law of diminishing returns.*

This law refers to the amount of extra output obtained when we add more and more of some one input to a fixed amount of other inputs. If we have, say, 10 acres of wheat land (our fixed input), it may be possible for one worker (our variable input) to come up with a harvest of 100 bushels of wheat. If, at the beginning of another crop season, we put two workers on the land, the two by combining their efforts could conceivably double

---

[1] Thomas R. Malthus, *An Essay on the Principle of Population,* Irwin Paperback Classics in Economics, Irwin, Homewood, Ill., 1963, p. 6. What Malthus illustrates with his population growth series is the spectacular growth possibilities of any number series increasing at a compound, or exponential, rate — that is, one where the increase of one period is included as part of the growing total during the next and all subsequent periods, as with a savings account where interest is added to principal and itself earns interest thereafter. Simple arithmetic tells us that anything growing at a 1 percent compound rate doubles in size in just over seventy years. If a country starts with a population of 100 million and increases the number of people year in and year out by 1 percent, seventy years later that country will have a population of 200 million. And if the rate of population growth is 2 percent rather than 1 percent, it reaches the 200 million mark not in seventy but thirty-five years. These relationships give us a very handy little rule of thumb, which we call the Rule of Seventy: To find the number of years it takes a growing number series to double, simply divide the percentage growth rate into 70. Malthus found the American population doubling in a little less than twenty-five years; therefore, that population was growing at about a 3 percent rate. The Rule of Seventy, incidentally, is useful in analyzing many other economic problems. If pollution increases by *only* 2 percent a year, for example, in thirty-five years the pollution level doubles. And if the use of aviation fuel increases by 6 percent a year, twelve years from now we will need twice as much aviation fuel.

[2] Malthus, *An Essay on the Principle of Population,* p. 3.

the production of wheat, as shown in Table 2.1. To this point, then, we have doubled our labor supply and doubled our food supply. No Malthusian problem at this juncture. Subsistence has increased as rapidly as population. But is it likely that if we once again double our labor force, to four workers, that our production of wheat would double? All the empirical evidence we now have available suggests otherwise. The extra (*marginal*) production of wheat associated with the third man-year of labor is quite likely to be less than that of the second, and the marginal output of the fourth worker is almost certain to be less than that of the third as suggested in Table 2.1. The reason we can be so sure of this is that, given 10 acres of land to work with, when we have three workers on the land, each works with $3\frac{1}{3}$ acres, and with four workers, each works with only $2\frac{1}{2}$ acres. If there is any doubt about this, extend the example to the point where we have ninety-nine workers on the 10 acres and add the one hundredth. Now each worker has only one-tenth of an acre to work with. It is entirely possible that crowding one more worker on the plot would actually reduce total output. The law of diminishing returns asserts, then, that in any production process, as the input level of one resource is increased unit by unit while those of other resources are held constant, beyond some point (the point of diminishing returns) the resulting *increases* in output will become smaller and smaller, unless an improvement in technology ("know-how") is incorporated in the productive process.

For those who find pictures better than words or numbers, the marginal output of successive units of labor is shown visually in Figure 2.1. Figure 2.1 tells us several interesting things about the population problem. First of all, diminishing returns are not in evidence in diagram A so long as the curve is rising at a constant rate (up to point *a*). Only when the curve

TABLE 2.1
Showing how returns in terms of output diminish when successive units of labor are added to 10 acres of land

Number of man-years of labor	Amount of product (bushels wheat)	Extra (marginal) output added by additional unit of labor
0	0	100
1	100	100
2	200	50
3	250	20
4	270	10
5	280	

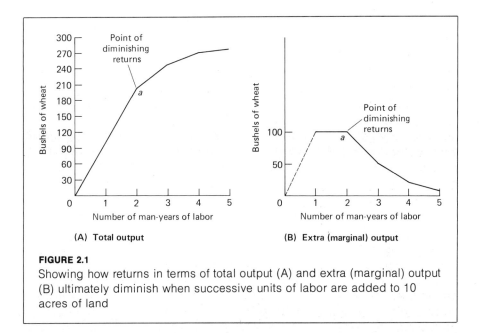

(A) Total output **(B) Extra (marginal) output**

FIGURE 2.1
Showing how returns in terms of total output (A) and extra (marginal) output (B) ultimately diminish when successive units of labor are added to 10 acres of land

begins to rise at a diminishing rate (beyond a) do we have diminishing returns to additional effort — thus the reason for labeling point a the point of diminishing returns. Similarly, diagram B, which merely pictures the changes in A from one input-output level to the next, shows no diminishing returns so long as each additional worker adds the same amount of wheat production as the previously added worker. When we add an extra worker whose contribution to output is less than the previous worker's, we know we have passed the point of diminishing returns. Second, though, we should not assume that it is never worthwhile to add additional resources (in this case in the form of more workers) once we pass the point of diminishing returns. In the case of our 10 acres of wheat land, if we stop with two workers, we are limiting the production of wheat to 200 bushels. The extra 50 bushels of wheat associated with the third worker's effort is quite likely to be more than ample to provide subsistence for the worker and his or her family, with something left over for the landlord. And rather than starve, even the fifth worker would undoubtedly be willing to work for a significant share of the meager 10-bushel addition to output. Finally, it is evident that if it were not for the law of diminishing returns, there would be no Malthusian "dismal theorem." If we could go on adding workers to the land, with each additional worker boosting food production in proportion to the increase in the work force, no one would ever have to starve. God would truly provide for willing hands. Unfortunately, however, as evidence sifting in from many parts of the world today tells us, this is not the world in which we live.

I THE MALTHUSIAN CHECKS I

All is not lost, though. Remember, Malthus insisted that his two growth ratios would diverge only if population were *unchecked.* And if the law of diminishing returns is at work in agriculture, population growth at a 3 percent rate cannot long be sustained. Malthus saw two sorts of checks coming into operation to keep population growth in line with the growth of foodstuffs: the preventive checks and the positive checks. *Preventive checks* are those that serve to control the birth rate, such as abortion, infanticide, and birth control. Since the actual growth in population is merely the difference between birth rates and death rates, the *positive checks* are those that come into operation to increase death rates — war, famine, pestilence — if birth rates are not sufficiently reduced by the preventive checks.

Inasmuch as he was a minister of the Church of England, the "gloomy parson" could scarcely advocate abortion, infanticide, or artificial birth control, all of which he considered vice. Thus, the "dismal theorem" of the first edition of the *Principle of Population:* The pressure of population against available food supplies must mean misery and starvation. Critics were quick to point out, however, that there was obviously something wrong with the theorem. Working men and women in the civilized parts of the world — and remember, this was the world that concerned Malthus — were maintaining themselves well above the level of subsistence, without the benefit of either the preventive or positive checks as Malthus had defined them. Something had been overlooked.

In the second edition of the *Principle of Population,* Malthus conceded that population restraints were not entirely reducible to vice and misery; that the preventive checks could be enlarged to include "moral restraint," which he limited to postponement of the age of marriage, accompanied by strict sexual continence before marriage. In view of the "passion between the sexes," though, this did not induce him to give up his pessimistic outlook. But it did give him and the upper classes who eagerly bought his argument a handy defense of the existing system of highly unequal property and income distribution. It was not the greedy employers who ground the workers into poverty. Instead, the workers themselves were responsible for their own unhappy conditions. By restraining their drive to procreate, workers could reduce the size of the labor force, bring a better balance between claimants and the available-wages fund, and improve their living standards. In sum, "It is not in the nature of things that any permanent and general improvement in the condition of the poor can be effected without an increase in the preventive check."[3] Unions and strikes are unavailing, and the rudimentary welfare system of the period, the Poor Law, was

---

[3] Malthus, *An Essay on the Principle of Population,* p. 282.

pernicious because it encouraged procreation without forethought. If we compare this argument with the ones presented today when proposals are brought forward to aid the overpopulated, poverty-stricken nations of the world, how modern it all sounds!

Malthus, of course, proved to be quite wrong — at least for the next century and a half. It almost appeared, in fact, that his two number series were mislabeled: population growth, instead of advancing geometrically, slowed down in the advanced nations to a nearly arithmetic series; on the other hand, the rate of increase in available food supplies exploded at close to a geometric rate.

What Malthus failed to foresee was that when living standards rise to some critical point, families find a way somehow — even in the absence of artificial birth control devices — to limit family size in order to avoid jeopardizing their rising affluence. For failing to take this into account Malthus need not be blamed, because it began to appear for the first time only around the middle of the nineteenth century. Since he lived in an ongoing agricultural and industrial revolution, however, it is difficult to see how Malthus could have failed to recognize the possibility that the law of diminishing returns as applied to agriculture would be negated by technical progress. Largely because of technical advance and the opening up of new farm lands, the agricultural problem of the first post-Malthusian century became that, not of striving to keep up with population growth, but of attempting to restrain the growth of agricultural production so that farmers would not flood the market and pay the consequences in reduced income. This was a matter of no little concern in America since most Americans have been farmers or farm workers over much of our history.

| AGRICULTURAL ECONOMICS |

Farmers in the labor force

In the absence of solid figures we can only guess about the distribution of our labor force at the time the Constitution was adopted. Most such guesses place around 90 percent of the labor force age ten or older in agriculture. Knowing what we do about agricultural productivity at the time, it makes sense to assume that it would have taken nine families engaged in farming to support one family off the farm. Agricultural techniques were so primitive that most farm families could barely produce enough to provide for their own subsistence. And even where surpluses were possible, limited means of transportation made it difficult at best and impossible at worst to get them to market.

After the beginning of the nineteenth century, agricultural techniques began to improve, along with transportation. By the time the first reliable figures became available around 1810, the farm-employed proportion of the labor force had declined to approximately 84 percent — which means that 84 farm families could now support 16 off-the-farm families in addition to providing for their own needs.

From this point the decline in the proportion of the population engaged in agriculture, as Figure 2.2 shows, was rapid until the middle of the nineteenth century, at which point it just about leveled off with just over half of the labor force employed in agriculture. The decade of the 1880s marked the dividing line between a population more than half of whom were engaged in agriculture and one with less than half its members so engaged — though it took another thirty years before the actual number of farmers and farm workers began to decrease.

In a market-directed free enterprise economy — which ours was for the most part in the nineteenth century and is so labeled today — decisions as to where people live and work are made on the basis of personal considerations. No one ordered families in the nineteenth century to take up the business of farming, and no one ordered out of farming the millions of families that have moved into other employment — or unemployment. Instead, the push and pull of market forces have brought about changes in the distribution of employment. In a nutshell, when farming is more attractive on an overall basis than other ways of making a living, many families will take up farming; and when families can no longer make a go of it in farming or when other occupations promise a better livelihood, families will move out of farming.

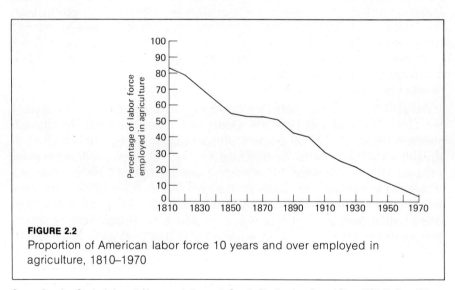

FIGURE 2.2

Proportion of American labor force 10 years and over employed in agriculture, 1810–1970

Source: Based on Stanley Lebergott, *Manpower in Economic Growth: The American Record Since 1800*, McGraw-Hill, New York, 1964, p. 510, and *Historical Statistics of the United States*, 1975, p. 127.

Cheap land, lack of alternative employment opportunities, and rising demand for farm products resulting from rapid population and industrial growth attracted many hundreds of thousands of additional families into farming in the first part of the nineteenth century and held them there. In the second half of the century, however, America discovered that it had a farm problem: Farmers were so numerous that it required a large aggregate farm income to give each farm family a decent income, one that would compare with the income of a nonfarm family. But the flood of farm products from the virgin public lands converted into private production — close to a billion acres in the first 150 years of our existence as a nation — proved too much for the American population to absorb at prices attractive to the farmers, especially after the population growth rate began to decline at midcentury. The consequence was a growing gap between farm and non-farm incomes and rising demands for the government to do something — bound up in the insistence of one farm spokesman that farmers "should raise less corn and more hell." The government proved unwilling in the nineteenth century, however, to do anything that would interfere with the free working of the market system — laissez faire ("leave the marketplace alone") had become an American religion, so government interference was regarded as not only wrong but downright sinful.

Some of the farmers and those who spoke for them realized, as the above quotation suggests, that by working together farmers could improve their situation. They had come to recognize how supply and demand operated against the interests of farmers working as individuals and how farmers working together could temper the laws of supply and demand. There proved to be too many farmers for a united course of action, so a common course was not achieved until the laissez-faire attitude weakened and government came into the agricultural marketplace in the 1920s. When government finally acted, it did so with full recognition of the unique characteristics of supply and demand in agriculture.

The law of demand

The law of demand as applied to agricultural staples has two special characteristics: Demand tends to be highly price inelastic (unresponsive), and the demand for farm products tends to increase less rapidly than does the demand for industrial products. The *law of demand* itself is a very simple proposition. It asserts only that consumers of any product will buy more of that product at a lower price than at a higher price. In other words, consumers buy larger quantities as prices fall, smaller quantities as prices rise. Such a situation would be described by Table 2.2, picturing a single family's demand for sirloin steak during a particular week. The table shows that the Smith family would be priced or rationed out of the market for sirloin steak at $3.50 per pound. The *opportunity cost* (what they would have to give up in the way of alternative purchases) is so high that they

TABLE 2.2
Smith family's demand schedule for sirloin steak,
week of May 1–7

If price per pound is ($):	Then Smith family will plan to buy (pounds):
3.50	0
3.00	2
2.50	4
2.00	6
1.50	9
1.00	12

must forego the purchase of sirloin steak in order to use their money for things they consider more vital to the family's welfare. If the price of sirloin were $3.00, the table suggests the family would find it worthwhile to divert $6.00 from other purchases and use the money for a steak dinner. Two steak dinners would be planned if the price fell to $2.50, and at $1.50 a pound or less the Smith family would plan to have sirloin just about every day.

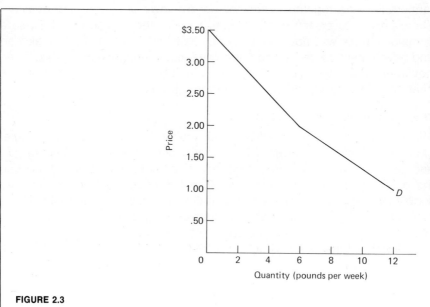

FIGURE 2.3
Smith family's demand curve for sirloin steak, week of May 1–7

We can turn the above schedule into a picture by constructing a demand curve, measuring prices along the vertical axis and the quantities related to the various prices on the horizontal axis, as in Figure 2.3. Each paired point along the demand curve represents a combination of a price and the quantity the Smith family will be prepared to buy at that price. Linking these paired points gives us a continuous curve.

The Smith family is unlikely to provide the total demand for sirloin steak in the community. But other families can be brought into the picture by simply adding the quantities they plan to buy at each price to the quantities the Smith family will buy. Our community demand for sirloin steak might then look something like the curve portrayed in Figure 2.4. What we see once again is a demand curve that slopes downward from upper left to lower right, telling us, in accordance with the law of demand, that greater quantities will be demanded at lower prices, smaller quantities at higher prices.

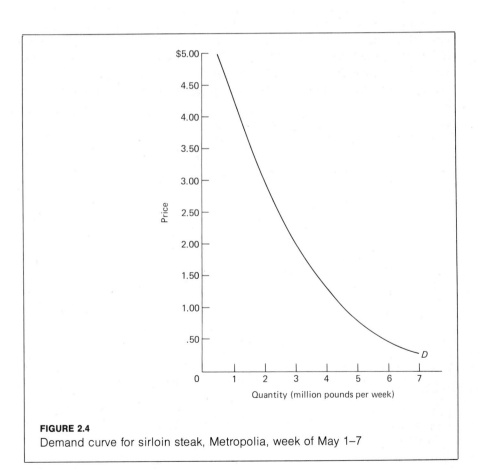

FIGURE 2.4
Demand curve for sirloin steak, Metropolia, week of May 1–7

The price elasticity of demand

What the law of demand does not say, though, is how much less consumers will be willing to buy at higher prices, how much more at lower. All it says is that less will be demanded at higher prices, more at lower. To get an idea of how much purchases will change with higher or lower prices, we need to supplement the law of demand with the concept of the *price elasticity of demand.* In broadest terms, a product with a high price elasticity of demand is one for which the demand curve tends to approach the horizontal, as in Figure 2.5(A), and one with a low price elasticity of demand is one where the demand curve tends to approach the vertical, as in Figure 2.5(B). Notice that when price comes down from $10 to $9 in diagram A, quantity demanded stretches a great deal — in fact, it doubles. Conversely, when price rises from $9 to $10, quantity demanded contracts by half. In diagram B, on the other hand, when price drops from $10 to $9, quantity demanded barely stretches at all, and when price returns to its original position, quantity demanded contracts scarcely at all. We say, then, that the demand for commodity A is relatively price elastic *because* the quantity demanded stretches or contracts greatly with price changes and that the demand for commodity B is relatively price inelastic *because* the quantity demanded stretches or contracts only slightly with price changes. More precisely, we compare the percentage changes in prices and quantities demanded. If the percentage change in price is less than

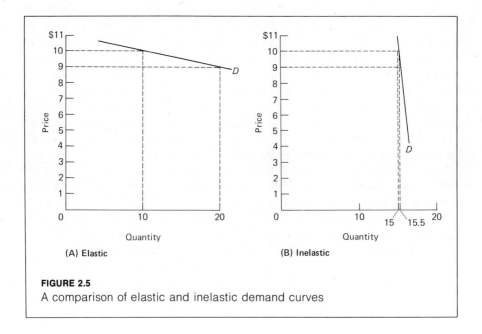

FIGURE 2.5
A comparison of elastic and inelastic demand curves

the resulting percentage change in quantity demanded, the demand is price elastic; if the percentage change in price is greater than the percentage change in quantity demanded, the demand is price inelastic; and if the percentage change in price exactly matches the percentage change in quantity demanded, the demand is of unit price elasticity:

$$e = \frac{\text{percentage change in quantity}}{\text{percentage change in price}} = \frac{\%\Delta q}{\%\Delta p}$$

With equal changes in numerator and denominator, the coefficient of demand elasticity has to be exactly one, or unity. If the numerator is greater than the denominator, as it is in the case of a relatively price elastic demand, the coefficient of elasticity is greater than one — and as much as infinity when the "curve" is completely horizontal. And if the denominator is greater than the numerator, as in the case of a relatively price inelastic demand, the coefficient of elasticity will be less than one — and will shrink to zero when the demand curve is completely vertical.

Now, the peculiarity of the demand for staple farm products such as wheat or corn, as pointed out earlier, is that demand is highly price inelastic. These are necessities for which there are no adequate substitutes, on the one hand, so we willingly pay a higher price rather than go without them. But at the same time our stomachs are limited in size, so we will not get much extra satisfaction from additional purchases. Price, therefore, has to come down a great deal to entice us into buying more. Low prices are attractive to us because they enable us to buy our usual amounts plus maybe a little bit more with a smaller money outlay, while high prices are disastrous because we are paying more for less. For farmers, just as the opposite holds: High prices are attractive and low prices are disastrous. To drive this point home, it must be recognized that if the demand curve is price inelastic, *more sells for less* and *less sells for more.* That is the whole clue to the importance of inelastic demands in agriculture. This can easily be seen from Figure 2.5(B), assuming that it represents the demand for wheat. When price comes down from $10 to $9 (a 10 percent reduction), quantity demanded barely edges upward at all (little more than a 3 percent increase). If only a small amount more means selling everything for a much lower price, it follows that wheat growers end up selling more for less — $150 at the higher price ($10 × 15), $139.50 at the lower price ($9 × 15.5). If farmers recognized their own interests, they would make sure that production of wheat would not be allowed to expand past 15 — but how do you get several million wheat growers to act as one?

We have been looking at a given demand schedule, though, one representing perhaps a single crop year. Over a longer period of time the demand for wheat should increase. The population continues to grow, and consumer incomes rise more or less steadily over time. What we should

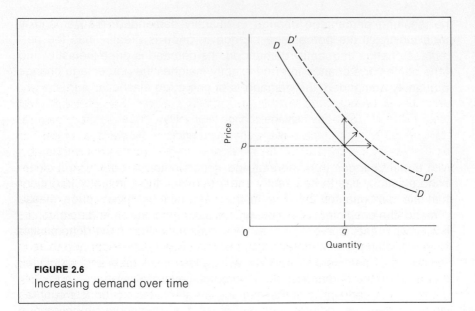

FIGURE 2.6
Increasing demand over time

expect then is a steady shift of the demand curve to the right, as in Figure 2.6. Curve *D'D'* represents an increased demand because it says that consumers of the product are more eager to buy. Comparing the new with the original curve we see that customers are willing to buy more even if prices are not reduced (the horizontal arrow), that they will continue to buy the same amount at even higher prices (the vertical arrow), or that they are willing to buy somewhat more even if prices are higher (the 45° arrow). A downward, leftward shift in the demand curve, by the same reasoning, would signify a fall in demand.

Even if they are faced with price inelastic demand curves, then, wheat farmers would not be in bad shape if the demand schedule were shifting steadily to the right. But here comes Catch-22. The demand curve will shift to the right only if the population is growing, if customer tastes do not shift away from farm staples, and if consumers are willing to spend a considerable portion of their rising incomes on farm products — none of which, down to the most recent period, happened to be true. The American population is today barely growing, and growing populations in the rest of the world have not helped the American farmer as much as we might expect because the population growth is concentrated in the poverty-stricken countries of the world. As for the tastes of American consumers, Americans have become weight conscious and have cut down their use of starchy foods, most of which are the very farm staples we have been discussing. The impact of these developments is summed up in the third point, that the demand for farm products is income inelastic: demand increases less rapidly than consumer incomes.

The law of supply

So far we have said nothing about the supply side of the marketplace, and until this is brought into the picture, nothing definite can be said about what price will actually be. The demand curve, after all, simply pictures the various quantities that consumers would be willing to buy at each of a number of different prices. The price at which the customers will be able to buy can be ascertained only if suppliers make known their requirements. The law of supply gives us part of the information we need: It stipulates that larger amounts of any commodity will come into the market at higher prices, smaller quantities at lower. Or, substituting a picture for words, the law of supply says the supply curve will generally slope upward from lower left to upper right, as in Figure 2.7. When we look at the supply picture of agriculture and compare it with nonagricultural production and supply, we find again, as with demand, that there are marked differences. In the first place, the overall agricultural supply curve is likely to be highly price inelastic; that is, it too tends to approach the vertical and represents a situation where large changes in price are likely to bring about only small changes in amounts agricultural producers are willing to supply the market — at least in a single crop period. When he expects high prices, the farmer is likely to say, "I've got to pull out all the stops and plant fence to fence in order to take advantage of high prices while they're here." And if she or he expects low prices, the farmer will say, "I've got to pull out all the stops and plant fence to fence so I can pay my taxes and the note at the bank."

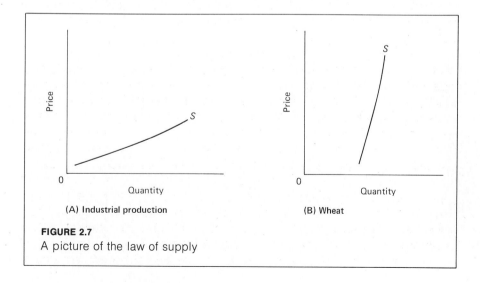

(A) Industrial production   (B) Wheat

FIGURE 2.7
A picture of the law of supply

Although they are not likely to use the technical term, farmers will behave as if they know that their opportunity cost of maximum planting is low. Their only alternative to growing crops is leaving the land idle, so they are not sacrificing much in the way of alternative uses of the land.

Finally, and of utmost importance, the supply curve in agriculture has shifted steadily over time to the disadvantage of the farmer. As additional farms come into production (the major reason for supply increases in the nineteenth century) or as each farmer becomes more productive and unit costs of production fall (the major reason for supply increases in the twentieth century), the supply curve shifts steadily downward and to the right. It appears paradoxical to describe a downward movement in the supply curve as an increase in supply, but an examination of Figure 2.8 will show that it does make sense. Supply curve $S'S'$, compared with the original supply curve SS, says that thanks to either their enlarged ability to produce or to their reduced costs of production, farmers are now willing to furnish the same quantity at a lower price (the vertical arrow), a larger amount at the same price (the horizontal arrow), or some combination of larger amounts at lower prices (the 45° arrow) — all of which adds up to a greater ability and eagerness to sell.

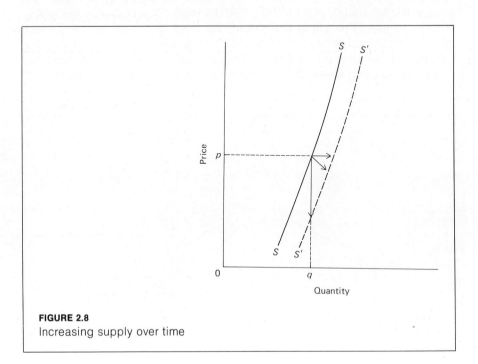

FIGURE 2.8
Increasing supply over time

The equilibrium price

Before detailing the consequences of the shifting supply curve, we need to set the stage by picturing the relationships and interactions between given supply and demand schedules. Putting together our original demand curve for a staple farm product from Figure 2.5(B) and the original supply curve from Figure 2.7 gives us the two blades of the scissors that we need to do a cutting job, as in Figure 2.9. Where the two curves cross, at a price of $5 and quantity of 1 billion bushels, we have an *equilibrium price* and quantity: Demand and supply are in balance — everyone who wants to sell at that price can find a willing buyer, and everyone who wants to buy can find a willing seller. Some buyers and sellers are rationed out of the marketplace, it is true — buyers who are unwilling or unable to pay the going price and sellers who demand too much for their product. But at that price the market clears and price is steady.

It is worth noticing, too, that no other price will be steady or will clear the market. Let us say that wheat farmers decide that $5 is an indecently low price for wheat; that it will bring them incomes well below those prevailing in other parts of the economy. They decide $7 will bring their incomes up to par with nonfarm incomes. It is obvious that unless they do something to restrain supply, the $7 price will not hold. When the price jumps from $5 to $7, a number of would-be buyers are driven from the marketplace, as indicated by the shift from a to b along the demand curve.

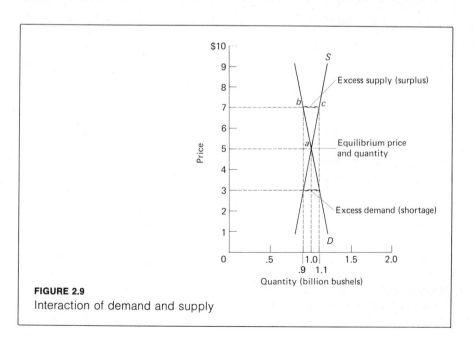

FIGURE 2.9
Interaction of demand and supply

On the other hand, a number of wheat sellers who were unwilling or unable to sell at $5 find the $7 price so attractive that they decide to bring their wheat to market, as indicated by the shift from a to c along the supply curve. A large gap opens between demand and supply, a surplus of wheat appears. Now buyers are willing to take only .9 billion bushels of wheat, but sellers want to unload 1.1 billion bushels. Some of the wheat sellers will find willing buyers, but many will find no takers at $7. Rather than holding unsold wheat, the latter will start shading the price, thereby attracting additional buyers into the marketplace. This will go on until finally the price is bid back down to the point where the surplus is eliminated, where supply and demand are in balance. And that, of course, is the $5 price from which we started. The crucial point to notice is that a surplus in an uncontrolled market is actually a surplus only in relation to an above-equilibrium price. Given the free movement of price, an uncontrolled market will eliminate surpluses — possibly, it is true, at the expense of driving some suppliers into bankruptcy.

Now let us say that the reverse situation holds — that the price of $5 is too high; that it provides too much of a windfall for the farmers and deprives too many low-income families of an opportunity to buy the bread and cereals they desperately need. So the government establishes by edict a ceiling price for wheat of $3. If this is all the government does, there is scant likelihood that the $3 price will hold. Immediately, as Figure 2.9 shows, a gap opens between demand and supply, but this time it represents a shortage. At a price of $3 buyers, attracted by the low price, will want to expand their purchases from 1 billion to 1.1 billion bushels. But the low price has driven some wheat growers from the market. Those remaining will be willing to furnish only .9 billion bushels of wheat. With a "shortage" of .2 billion bushels, it is obvious that some of the prospective buyers are going to be disappointed; they will not be able to find willing sellers. Rather than go without, they will offer more than the ceiling price (thus becoming black marketeers) and will surely find sellers willing to deliver grain to them. This bidding process will go on once again until the price rises sufficiently to close the gap between demand and supply at the equilibrium point.

I GOVERNMENTAL REGULATION OF AGRICULTURE I

What the farmers came to recognize was that whatever the advantages to others of free market prices established in uncontrolled markets, the equilibrium price brought no great benefits to themselves. Farm incomes tended to lag farther and farther behind nonfarm incomes, reaching the point in 1929 where the per capita income of the farm population averaged only $273 as compared to a national average of $750. The meager government aid provided farmers prior to the 1920s was centered on helping farmers produce more by farming more efficiently: establishment of land-grant colleges and universities under the Morrill Act (1862) to provide specialized training and education, creation of the Department of Agriculture in the federal government (1862) to act as a service agency for the farmers, formation of agricultural experiment stations under the Hatch Act (1887) to encourage scientific agricultural research, and provision of agricultural extension programs under the Smith-Lever Act (1914) for farmers outside the reach of the land-grant colleges. But the farmers had become aware that this sort of help, welcome as it was to the individual farmer, did nothing but worsen the situation of farmers collectively. More productive farmers, after all, pushed the aggregate supply curve rapidly to the right, down along a steep, price-inelastic demand curve. To their dismay farmers rediscovered, time and time again, that more really did sell for less.

The farmers and the farm bloc insisted that it was time to secure income equality, or parity, for farm families by using the federal government to rig the market, something farmers had been unable to achieve through their own cooperation. The result was two major federal bills in the 1920s, one of which was aborted by presidential veto while the other went down in the maelstrom of the Great Depression of 1929.

The McNary-Haugen bill, twice passed by Congress and twice vetoed by Republican presidents in the 1920s, was the first proposed federal legislation that explicitly recognized the peculiar economic characteristics of American agriculture. Under the bill, a government corporation was to be set up and given authority to enter agricultural staples markets and buy amounts sufficient to drive domestic prices up to parity levels. The amounts purchased would not be stored or allowed to re-enter the domestic markets but would instead be sold in foreign markets for whatever they would bring, as shown in Figure 2.10.

The other farm bill, passed in 1929 as the Agricultural Marketing Act, incorporated the major price-rigging principle of McNary-Haugen but substituted for the foreign dumping a sort of "ever-normal granary" system: The Federal Farm Board established under the act would buy grain off the market sufficient to drive price up to the established parity level, store their purchases, and release them back into the market in years of short crops. All fine in theory but the year, remember, was 1929 and the American economy was collapsing in the most severe and extended depression America had ever seen. The Federal Farm Board poured its allocated $360 million into farm markets without even slowing the decline in farm prices.

The McNary-Haugen bill and the Agricultural Marketing Act, then, were important, not for what they accomplished by way of helping the farmer, but for establishing ways the farmer might be helped. It is scarcely going too far to insist that virtually all American farm support programs down to the present time have incorporated the major principles of these

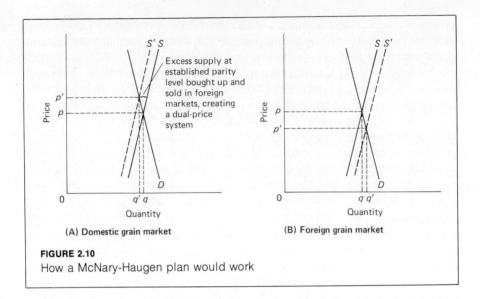

(A) Domestic grain market   (B) Foreign grain market

FIGURE 2.10
How a McNary-Haugen plan would work

two programs: Remove part of the American crop from the domestic market (soil bank, acreage restrictions, guaranteed loans, marketing quotas) so that what reaches the market will sell for a greater total amount, or find some way of getting rid of excess American supplies in foreign markets (Public Law 480, Food for Peace).

The various farm programs have not, to put it mildly, had good press. Imagine the uproar when President Roosevelt's Agricultural Adjustment Administration in 1933, to eliminate farm surpluses hanging over the market, paid farmers and ranchers for curtailing their planting, for slaughtering 6 million pigs and turning them into fertilizer, for plowing under growing cotton, for allowing peaches to rot on the trees, and for piling and burning tons of oranges — all this in a nation underfed and underclothed! The very idea, too, of paying farmers for not producing is repugnant to the American work ethic. And it has been abundantly documented that the bulk of the payments have gone to the least needy farmers. In 1969, to take a typical year, 42.3 percent of the price support benefits went to the largest 7.1 percent of the farmers, while only 4.2 percent of the benefits went to the smallest 41.2 percent of the farmers. Finally, public resentment would undoubtedly have increased had it been generally recognized that the Treasury handouts to the farmers represented only part of the total bill. As Figure 2.11 suggests, payments by American citizens as consumers in the form of higher prices about equaled payments by those same citizens as taxpayers in the form of agricultural support payments. The American taxpayer, in other words, paid higher taxes in order to drive up the prices of food. The combined transfers to farmers from consumers and taxpayers in 1969 just about equaled the total cost of federal, state, and local public assistance programs or the cost of procuring, operating, and maintaining the nation's strategic nuclear forces. Small wonder that the advocates of a permanent return to the free market system so often cite the agricultural subsidy program as a prime example of the evils of intervention.

On the other hand, it is possible to say a few kind words about the program — to find some benefits to set off against the costs. As a result of support payments, which helped to increase selling prices of farm land and thus gave farm families a sizable nest egg when they sold out, we have been able to make an orderly retreat from farming as a way of life. Our total farm population has come down without undue strain from 30.6 million in 1929 to 8.3 million in 1976. The remaining farmers are so extraordinarily efficient that one farm family, as Figure 2.2 indicates, is able to supply the foodstuffs required to feed more than twenty nonfarm families — and a significant number of families abroad as well. Thanks to the efficiency of the American farmer, the rest of us can use our talents wherever we choose without worrying about whether we shouldn't be helping out with the harvest. Whether or not the support system brought about this increasing efficiency and productivity can be argued both ways, but it clearly has not inhibited progress: During the last twenty years output per man-hour on farms went up 310 percent while the comparable output in manufacturing industries went up only 170 percent. And even if the bulk of the support payments went to the largest farmers, the family farm, as opposed to the large corporate farm, remains far and away our most important agricultural institution. Further, partly as a consequence of out-migration from farming and partly as a result of income transfers to farmers,

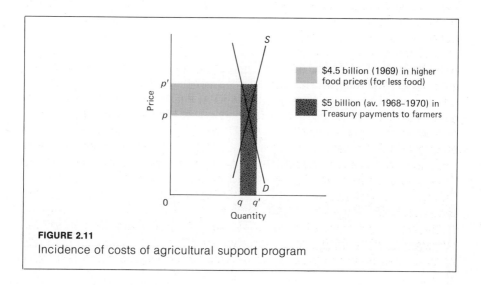

FIGURE 2.11
Incidence of costs of agricultural support program

the income gap between farm and nonfarm families has narrowed. As compared with the situation in 1929, when the average person in farming realized barely more than a third of the income received by the typical American citizen, in 1972 net income per farm ($7,089) amounted to almost two-thirds of the median American family income ($11,116). Finally, the support system has served to stabilize production and prices. The wild swings in production and prices that typify free-market-controlled agriculture have not been seen since the 1930s — not until the last few years, at least. Instead, Americans could take for granted an adequate supply of basic foodstuffs at reasonable prices, sufficient to make us the best fed nation in the world.

I WHAT'S PAST IS PROLOGUE I

The American breadbasket

No one needs to be told that the orderly world of agriculture presented above has collapsed in the last several years, and it has collapsed at the same time as, and partly as a consequence of, the re-emergence of the Malthusian spectre. As a result of poor crops in several important grain-growing countries and the migration of anchovies away from the Peruvian coast, necessitating a search for alternative supplies of protein-rich food, the demand for American foods increased dramatically. America has become the breadbasket of the world, exporting around two-thirds of its annual wheat production and over one-fifth of its total production of feed grains. The consequent rise in price delighted American farmers. They found themselves enjoying adequate incomes for the first time since World War II, all the while producing as much as they could to take advantage

© Washington Star Syndicate, Inc., permission granted by King Features Syndicate, Inc., 1977.

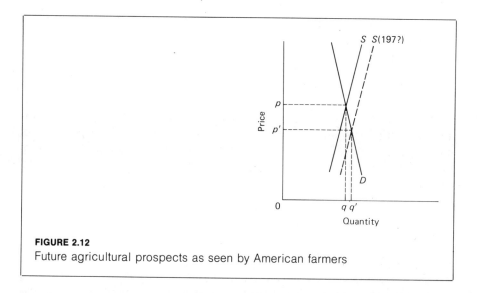

FIGURE 2.12
Future agricultural prospects as seen by American farmers

of the high prices while they lasted. But they could not help but wonder, at the same time, how long their good fortune would last. Their fears were that the foreign demand for grain was a sometime thing and that they would shortly find themselves pushing the supply of grain down a frozen, and inelastic, demand schedule, as in Figure 2.12. If this should come to pass, the consequence, as the diagram illustrates, would be drastically falling farm incomes.

To assuage these fears and encourage continued high levels of production, Congress passed the Agriculture and Consumer Protection Act of 1973. The act guaranteed growers of feed grains, wheat, and cotton government income supports if prices slipped from their 1973 high levels. It did this through a combination of price-support payments and direct payments to farmers. As pictured in Figure 2.13, three different prices were involved in the support program: the actual market price (MP), a support price (SP), and a target price (TP). When demand decreased or supply increased to the point where prices were forced down to the MP level of Figure 2.13, then the federal government entered the market and bought up AB of the crop, driving up the price to the support level (SP). In addition, the government made direct payments to farmers equal to the difference between SP and the target price (TP). With these guarantees against falling prices, American farmers have not been reluctant to push for all-out production.

During the 1977 crop year, though, it became evident that the worst fears of the farmers had been realized. Heavy production in the United States and a weak market abroad combined to tumble market prices — so far down that farmers turned increasingly to the government for help. The

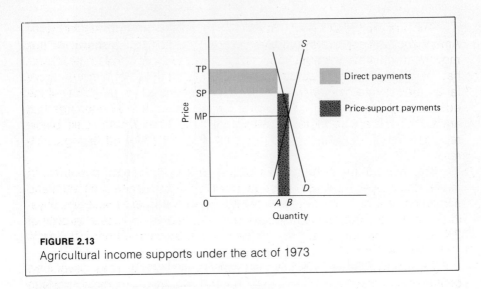

FIGURE 2.13
Agricultural income supports under the act of 1973

1973 legislation provided a sort of safety net, but one so low that farmers complained support levels were insufficient to cover their costs of production. Congress responded by revising the 1973 legislation, keeping the basic principles but raising support levels — but by no means to the point where farmers were satisfied with the help provided.

Whether or not farmers will get the guarantees they are demanding to continue with all-out production is a hot political question at the moment. That even a generous guarantee would be sufficient to protect the world against starvation, however, is more than doubtful. It may be enough to tide the growing populations of the world over the next few decades, but unless drastic steps are taken to limit the rate of population increase in the already overpopulated countries, there is little likelihood that American agriculture can meet the ever-larger demand for foodstuffs. And at this point such drastic steps appear not to be forthcoming.

The population bomb

For years a number of groups and individuals have issued warnings about the perils of uncontrolled population growth. The Hugh Moore Fund, for example, has printed and circulated hundreds of thousands of copies of a pamphlet entitled "The Population Bomb," published originally in the 1950s. It pictures graphically the growth of world population — from 1 billion in 1830 to 2 billion in 1930 — and projects further growth to 3 billion in 1965, 4 billion in 1980, 5 billion in 1990, and 6 billion in the year 2000. And it calls for a concerted effort to cope with the problem. If anything, the earlier forecasts were conservative: World population is now estimated at 3.9 billion and will reach the 4 billion level well before 1980. And little has been done to resolve the problem — perhaps because little can be done.

The vigor of the Zero Population Growth movement suggests that some Americans, at least, are aware of the problem. Unfortunately, however, this movement will have minimal impact on world population. The United States has barely more than 5 percent of the world's population, and our population growth rate has fallen to less than 1 percent, which is typical of the economically developed countries of the world. Of the 31 countries that are usually listed as highly developed, 21 now have birth rates below replacement. Falling birth rates in these countries followed falling death rates.

This has not been true, however, for the less developed countries. In these, death rates have been brought down by improvements in health and sanitation, but in many cases birth rates have held near maximum physiological limits. The consequence is a current world population growth of 2.4 percent annually and a rise in the number of people from 2 billion in 1930 to over 3.9 billion today.

Examples of what this means to the people in the less developed countries can only touch the surface, but they do provide some awareness of this human tragedy. Witness India:

At present, seventy-five percent of all Indians have no assured employment and earn four hundred rupees (about fifty-three dollars) or less a year. They cannot even count on such rock-bottom necessities for survival as one meal a day and one piece of permanent clothing, and so fall below what the government has defined in its official income profile as "the poverty line."[4]

the small society   by Brickman

© Washington Star Syndicate, Inc., permission granted by King Features Syndicate, Inc., 1977.

---

[4] Ved Mehta, "Letter from New Delhi," *The New Yorker* (October 14, 1974), 154.

And Bangladesh:

Bangladesh has a population of about 75 million which makes it the eighth most populous nation on earth. There are 1,400 Bengalis to the square mile, 2,200 to the arable mile.

The population is increasing at the rate of three percent a year. In 23 years the population will be 150 million. In 30 years, at the present growth rate, it will be 230 million.

The doubling of population by 1997 is not a horrible possibility; it is a horrible inevitability. The Bengalis already born (half the population is under 15 years of age) will assure that doubling. There will be 150 million people here even if severe birth control measures are implemented now.

As it is, there is not any effective population control program. Many millions are ignorant about birth control, and many more millions are too poor to see the value of any sort of planning. The government lacks the political commitment and courage to press for population control; the bureaucracy probably lacks the effectiveness to implement a program if it did exist. Religious and cultural factors argue against birth control. The economics of a poor farm argue for having more sons. . . .

Bangladesh already has too little food and too little land for 75 million people. It relies on food-grain imports to avert mass starvation. . . .

"It's all scary as hell — really brutal," an American population expert says. "And the worst is we see no solution." A priest working with villagers in northern Bangladesh says: "I simply have to accept it on faith that this country won't populate itself into extinction." Faith may be all there is to cling to.[5]

It is far easier to dramatize the problem, of course, than to come up with a workable solution. It would help if Americans and the citizens of Japan and the northern European countries were not such heavy eaters of grain-fed beef and poultry. As a result of this taste for meat, grain surpluses that once were diverted to poor nations are now sold to rich countries to feed their livestock. One estimate is that the livestock population of the United States consumes enough foodstuffs to feed 1.3 billion people. But if the populations of the poor countries continue to increase at a 2.4 percent annual rate, the total population of these countries will grow by more than twice 1.3 billion in less than 30 years. And besides, Americans accustomed to steaks and hamburgers are not likely to throw it all over for rice and corn. Nutritionists and sociologists point out that diet is a matter of habit, custom, and prestige. These are not easily changed.

One thing is clear: The heavily populated, less developed countries cannot look to the fertile farm lands of the United States for the long-run solution to their problem. The production capacity just will not be there.

---

[5] *Wall Street Journal* (November 26, 1974), 35. Reprinted by permission of the Wall Street Journal, © Dow Jones & Company, Inc. 1974. All Rights Reserved.

Already there are signs that the technological revolution in American agriculture may have just about run out its string. Crop production per acre in the United States increased by 35 percent in the decade 1953–1963 but rose by less than 20 percent in the next decade. And the increase in the efficiency with which inputs are converted into output (farm output per unit of total input) fell even more dramatically: a rise of 29 percent in the earlier decade, 7 percent in the latter.

For a time it was hoped that the techniques that had revolutionized American agriculture could simply be exported and applied in the less developed countries. If hybrid seeds, irrigation, insecticides and herbicides, and massive applications of synthetic fertilizer could push American agricultural output to unheard of levels, why wouldn't the same be possible in other lands? This *Green Revolution* was seen as the solution to the Malthusian spectre. The early results were indeed encouraging; many countries that experimented with the new techniques reported dramatic increases in production. But then some unanticipated side effects began to be noticed. Hybrid seeds proved to be particularly susceptible to attack by new strains of disease and insects. Irrigation required tremendous outlays of capital, always in short supply in the less developed nations. And where capital was found, failure of the monsoon rains was apt to leave the ditches and canals high and dry. Insecticides and herbicides created an ecological problem when they were washed into rivers and streams and killed the fish, a vitally necessary part of the local food supply. And the quadrupling of the world price of oil dragged the price of fertilizer up to a level beyond the reach of the poor countries. If these were not enough, the Green Revolution, where it worked, created unemployment since fewer farm laborers were required. And sometimes it could not be made to work because "landlordism" got in the way. Landless peasants obviously were unable to experiment with the new techniques, and absentee landlords had insufficient interest to make the attempt.

It is likely that reports of the spread of famine in the overpopulated parts of the world will stir the rich nations of the world into concerted action, if not for purely humanitarian reasons, then because of the threat to the "haves" of violence by the "have nots." India, after all, already has the atomic bomb, and it is within the reach of a number of other poor countries. The unfortunate fact, however, is that the developed countries cannot permanently solve this problem for the poor nations. Putting together all we know about energy limitations, environmental deterioration, and future prospects for increases in agricultural productivity leaves us with the uncomfortable realization that any rate of population growth much above zero is impossible in the long run. Whether this can be accomplished by use of the preventive checks, we do not yet know. Concerted birth control programs to this point have tended to work where the birthrate is falling anyway. But an expansion of such efforts obviously must be attempted since, as Malthus reminds us, if nothing checks the growth of population except misery and starvation, then the population will grow until it is miserable and starves.

I SUMMARY I

Of the many crises facing the world today, none is of greater long-run consequence than assuring an adequate supply of food for the world's population. This is literally a matter of life or death for millions of people.

The problem is not new. Over most of human history population has tended to outrun the means of subsistence. Formal analysis of the problem awaited the arrival of Thomas Malthus, an eighteenth-century Englishman. Combining the principle of diminishing returns to agricultural inputs with the strong "passion between the sexes," Malthus foresaw what has come to be called the Malthusian spectre: population outgrowing available food supplies. To head this off, he strongly advocated "moral restraint" in procreation.

Paradoxically, in the American nation our problem — at least from the farmer's point of view — has been, not too little food, but too much food. Farm incomes over the last one hundred years have lagged rather badly behind nonfarm incomes as a result. In the late nineteenth and early twentieth centuries federal government met the demand that something be done for the farmers by helping them to produce more efficiently. This merely aggravated the farm income problem because it led to even greater surpluses and lower prices.

Only in the 1920s did Congress take cognizance of the economics of farming — that greater aggregate farm production means less total farm income. This is the key characteristic of the price inelastic demand curve for farm products. Combined with a slowly rightward-shifting demand curve and a rapidly rightward-shifting supply curve, this is a recipe for disaster in farming.

To cope with this combination, the federal government since the 1920s has come up with a series of devices to restrict supply, all based on the premise that less production will sell for more total income: acreage allotments, soil banks, payments for not producing, marketing quotas. These were combined with devices to increase demand, such as subsidization of overseas sales of farm products, the school lunch program, and food stamps. The impact of these combined programs has been a gradual closing of the farm–nonfarm income gap.

The spectacular advances in American agriculture, however, which have assured food supplies for substantial parts of the world's population, are slowing down. This means foreign nations now dependent on American food supplies must make greater efforts to control their population growth and develop their own agriculture.

I IMPORTANT TERMS AND CONCEPTS I

Malthusian spectre

Rule of Seventy

law of diminishing returns

preventive checks

positive checks   equilibrium price

law of demand   Green Revolution

price elasticity of demand

I QUESTIONS, PROBLEMS, AND EXERCISES I

1 Why is Malthusianism described as a race between survival and catastrophe?

2 Does it make sense to say that we should expand production up to the point of diminishing returns but never beyond that point?

3 Why do improvements in technology tend to invalidate the law of diminishing returns?

4 How did government assistance to farmers in the late nineteenth century compare with what has been done for them in the twentieth century?

5 Will the Green Revolution save mankind from starvation?

6 If our use of oil and natural gas increased annually by 5 percent, how many years would it take to double our current consumption? To quadruple current consumption? To increase it by eightfold?

7 It is sometimes said that if the demand for farm products were price elastic there would be no farm income problem. Can you demonstrate why? (*Hint:* What happens to total farm income when production increases?)

8 Set up a typical demand and supply diagram and show the final impact on price and amounts clearing through the market of two concurrent developments: (1) Consumer interest in the product increases sharply at the same time that (2) wages paid workers in the industry rise considerably.

I SUGGESTED READING I

Balz, Daniel J. "When Better Farm Policy Is Made, Who Will Make It?" *Working Papers* (Spring 1977), 62–67.

"Bumper Crop of Controversy Over Farm Aid." *Business Week* (April 18, 1977), 110–118.

Heilbroner, Robert L. *An Inquiry into the Human Prospect.* Norton, New York, 1974.

Malthus, Thomas. *An Essay on the Principle of Population,* 1789 and later editions. Republished by Irwin, Homewood, Ill., 1963.

Pirages, Dennis C., and Paul R. Ehrlich. *Ark II: Social Response to Environmental Imperatives.* Freeman, San Francisco, 1974.

"Research to Multiply Food Production: Was Malthus Right?" *Business Week* (June 16, 1975), 64–72.

Wilkinson, Richard G. *Poverty and Progress: An Ecological Perspective on Economic Development.* Praeger, New York, 1973.

Woodham-Smith, Cecil. *The Great Hunger: Ireland 1845–1849.* New American Library, Signet Books, New York, 1964.

THREE

THE NATIONAL INCOME: ACCOUNTING AND CONTROL

For the greater part of our history as a nation we neither knew nor apparently cared what our total annual output was. Individuals knew that they were getting better off year by year. Companies were aware that their output capacity and earnings were growing (or not growing). We had a lot of "micro" information — knowledge about individuals, families, and business firms — but no one was charged with the responsibility of collecting the bits and pieces of economic data and combining them into a picture of what the whole economy looked like. *Macroeconomics* had not yet been born. Finally, in the 1920s a private research agency, the National Bureau of Economic Research, became seriously enough concerned with overall economic performance to begin studying the ways we could and should go about determining how the economy was performing on an overall basis. The Great Depression spurred government efforts to find out how sick the national economy really was, and during the 1930s the United States Department of Commerce, in cooperation with the National Bureau of Economic Research, undertook a study of national income. Preparation for World War II pushed the project ahead, and the war itself forced its completion. By early 1942 the Department of Commerce had reached the point where it could collect, organize, and present data in such a fashion as to show how much Americans, in the aggregate, were producing and earning. The era of national income accounting had arrived.

I   MEASUREMENT OF THE NATIONAL INCOME   I

Aggregate measurements

One way to understand the strengths and weaknesses of the national income accounts, to gain an insight into how they can inform us and how they may misinform us, is to work through some of the problems faced by the pioneers in the development of the accounts.

Gross national product   An estimate of total production is one bit of information the accounts are required to divulge. But before we can talk about total production, we must decide what we mean by *production*. Some things we can agree on without much difficulty: New cars are obviously part of annual production, as are new houses, new dresses, and new office buildings. There is little argument here. From the beginning economists have agreed that the creation of material things represents production. Material things are wealth. But what if people are busy performing activities from which nothing material results? For example, is a violin teacher productive? A school teacher? A police officer? Since no direct creation of wealth takes place, earlier economists were inclined to believe that such activities are nonproductive. Later, however, it was decided that workers who produce things require a whole range of services, and the providers of those services have to be considered part of the productive process. So today production is represented by a flow of both goods and services.

But how do we add up these goods and services? Obviously we cannot simply list them — here a haircut, there an automobile, and over there a ton of bricks. Even if we grouped by category, we would still end up with thousands of interminable lists. Adding apples and oranges presents a simple problem compared with the task of adding the whole range of goods and services turned out by a modern economic system. What we need is a common denominator — something by which we can measure this huge array. And in a pecuniary economy, what could be more logical than using the measuring rod of money value? This creates one minor problem (our measuring rod keeps changing size), but it solves our major dilemma. A dozen apples cannot be meaningfully added to a dozen or-anges, but a dollar's worth of apples can very well be added to a dollar's worth of oranges — as every shopper knows.

But who decides how many dollar's worth of production has taken place? In a market society, the answer to that is easy. We let the market decide. A new product or service is worth whatever it will bring in the marketplace. So having decided what constitutes new production (in a nutshell, whatever people will pay for), we in effect run this new production through the market to get a value placed on it. A new automobile represents $5,000 worth of new production because buyers are willing to pay that amount for it. A school teacher's services are worth $9,000 because some school board is willing to pay that amount for a year of work. And by this test the services of American housewives are worth how much? Not a cent, because the services are not allocated by way of the marketplace (but a hired housekeeper is worth what she is paid). The same is true for all do-it-yourself activities: making your bread instead of buying it, constructing your stereo set from a kit rather than purchasing it already assembled, giving yourself a permanent wave at home in preference to making an appointment at the beauty shop, making your dress in preference to se-lecting one off the rack.

So is any newly produced good or service that clears through the market part of annual production? Well, almost. A few things that move through the market are left out of our estimates, either because it is im-possible to get a reliable total of market clearances, or because the activ-ities are illegal or immoral, or both: services of prostitutes, illegally pro-duced alcoholic beverages, and the services of gamblers where gambling is outlawed. And there are a few things that so obviously represent pro-duction or productive activity that they are given an "imputed" (estimated cash) value and included in our estimates of production even though they are outside the market network: food and fuel produced and used on the farm; wages and salaries paid in kind; services provided by banks to their customers in lieu of interest payments; and the rental services provided by owner-occupied homes.

After collecting all these data (corporation reports and tax returns are the main sources) and screening and adjusting them as described above, we have our estimate of total annual production, which we call *gross national product.* It is apparent that the judgment of the marketplace is final. A fifth of whiskey represents about fifteen times as much production as a quart of milk because it is fifteen times more valuable in the market. A doctor produces five times as much in a year as a school teacher since his services sell for five times as much. In these and all other cases social value judgments are beside the point. And so are the smoke and noise and wastes created by industrial operations. Further, as national income accountants we care neither how burdensome the work or how many hours are put into production nor how equally the goods and services are distributed. Our mission is only to measure production, not to moralize about it. Little reflection is needed, though, to suggest that gross national product is a very imperfect measure of social welfare, quite aside from the basic question as to whether or not the availability of more "things" represents an increase in welfare.

It means something, on the other hand, to be able to report with some assurance that in 1976 the American nation turned out $1,691.6 billion worth of new goods and services. Further, the way we have collected and organized our data makes it possible to identify the major components of total production. Our gross national product in 1976 represented $1,079.7 billion of new goods and services delivered to families for their sustenance and enjoyment (consumption goods); $239.6 billion of additional production capacity acquired by businessmen and homeowners (gross private domestic investment — new plant, new equipment, new homes, and additions to inventory); $365.6 billion of new goods and services turned over to various levels of government, federal, state, and local (government purchases); and $6.6 billion of new goods and services delivered net to foreign buyers (*net exports:* exports minus imports).

Net national product   This is new production we have been describing, but it is not "net" new production. A fairly substantial portion of it represents new capital goods (goods produced to be used in further production) destined to serve as replacements for production facilities used up in the

the small society　　　　　　　　　**by Brickman**

productive process. Once we make an allowance (most of which is depreciation) for using up of capital and subtract our capital consumption allowance ($179.8 billion) from the total of gross national product, we have a measure of net production, *net national product* ($1,511.8 billion), all of which can safely be used up without worrying about "living off our capital." Conceptually, net national product is a useful measure; practically, it is not so useful because it is not very reliable. The estimates of depreciation are based heavily on tax considerations and vary with the particular write-off techniques being used.

National income   We could gain assurance in the reliability of our measures of production if we could check them against figures collected from different sources and organized differently. It turns out that we not only can do this, but the Department of Commerce routinely does so. In addition to using the final-market-value approach just described, the Department of Commerce also uses an income, or expenditure, approach. We can measure a baker's cake production either by counting the number of cakes turned out or the hours of labor, the amount of electricity, the vanilla, eggs, flour, and so on that went into the cakes. Similarly, we can measure aggregate national production at the point where new goods and services flow out of the production pipeline into the hands of final users or at the point where things go into the pipeline. Allowing for what remains in the pipeline (inventory changes), what goes in must equal what comes out. What goes into production, as we saw previously in the circular flow analysis, is in final analysis the services of land, labor, and capital. Trace any product far enough back in the production process and it will ultimately resolve itself into some combination of these productive factors. Measuring what the owners of these productive factors earned, then, is one way of estimating how much they provided in the way of services and what total production took place, which is the same thing as saying that what we are looking for is the total cost or expenditure involved in the acquisition of these services.

It has long been customary in economics to pair the use of each productive factor with a particular type of payment: labor earns wages, land earns rent, and capital generates interest and profit. This is the general approach used by the national income accountants, but their results are somewhat less tidy than this suggests. Labor, far and away the largest cost of production and the leading source of earned income, presents no particular problem except for the inclusion of "fringe benefits," or supplements to wages and salaries (paid vacation time, retirement provisions, sick leave, and so forth). A figure can readily be secured for corporate profits and business interest payments, but we must exclude government interest payments since they primarily represent the costs of servicing the national debt — and the national debt is identified with military borrowing and spending, not borrowing to expand production facilities. The treatment of land is more of a problem since modern land is no longer the simple natural resources of the classical economists. Instead, farms and forests today, after receiving large doses of economic resources generation after generation, come close in totality to being capital. We pick up part of the cost of their use under interest, part under proprietors' income, part under corporate profits. What remains under the rent category, paradoxically, is primarily the rent that families avoid paying because they own their own homes — the rental value of owner-occupied homes. Proprietorships are single-owner or family businesses, the earnings of which are difficult to break down into the categories described above. Take a family farm: How much of the family's earnings represents the use of family time and effort, how much is a return to what they have in the land, how much is payment for risk and enterprise? No one, not even the family itself, can say with any assurance. So the Department of Commerce throws up its collective hands and refuses even to try, using in place of any breakdown of income the category "proprietors' income."

When we put these various income measures together we have our estimate of aggregate production, this time from the income side, thus the label *national income.* And a trap, if we are not careful. We sometimes speak of any attempt to measure aggregate production or income as national income accounting. Now we have a specific measure of national income. In which sense the term *national income* is being applied is usually clear from the context of its usage.

In 1976, national income — all incomes earned in the process of production — came out as shown in Table 3.1. When we compare national income with net national product, we see that the totals do not agree, even though both are supposed to measure net production. Is something wrong with our procedures? No, our approach is all right. It's merely that net production at market prices includes all costs of production, not just the costs of productive services. One major cost does not find its way into

TABLE 3.1
National Income, 1976 ($ billion)

Compensation of employees	1,028.4
Corporate profits, before taxes	117.9
Net interest	82.0
Rental income of persons	23.5
Proprietors' income	96.7
National income	1,348.5

national income but must be included in market prices: indirect taxes — sales taxes, excise taxes, license fees, and so forth. When we add these indirect taxes and other minor adjustments ($163.3 billion in 1976) to national income, we come up with a figure very close to net national product.

Personal income In addition to providing an alternative measure of national production, national income is useful in its own right as an estimate of total annual earnings. Usually, though, we — and especially businessmen — are less concerned with how much people earn than with what they actually receive. Luckily, it turns out there is another measure designed specifically to provide that information. It is called *personal income,* and our national income account, with some subtractions and some additions, will lead us to its computation. Since personal income is all income received, whether earned or not, and national income is all income earned, whether received or not, to get to personal income from national income we need to subtract income earned but not received then add income received but not earned. The subtractions consist of those parts of corporate profits not paid out to stockholders (corporate profits taxes and withheld earnings) plus social insurance contributions; the additions are all forms of *transfer payments* (by definition income received but not earned in the current year: G.I. bill payments, retirement pension payments, welfare payments) plus net interest paid by government and consumers. Making these adjustments to the 1976 national income results in a figure of $1,375.3 billion for personal income.

Disposable personal income But we are still not talking about net spendable income because we have not yet fully settled up with the tax collector. Indirect business taxes have been allowed for, and we pulled out corporate profits taxes and social security payroll taxes in the step above, but personal income still lists income gross of personal income taxes (which suggests that the national income accounts have never been brought into the withholding era). When we pull individual income tax payments ($193.6 billion in 1976) out of personal income, we are left finally with *disposable personal income* ($1,181.7 billion in 1976), which can either be spent or not spent on consumption goods. What is spent is equal to the consumption expenditure figure in gross national product ($1,079.7 billion in 1976) plus consumer interest payments ($25.5 billion in 1976); what is not spent is by definition personal savings ($76.5 billion in 1976).

Relating the measurements Combining these five different accounts, with their constituent parts, gives us the array shown in Table 3.2. The table confirms a fact mentioned earlier — that several of our accounts have a two-sided nature. Gross national product can be estimated either by adding up the final market value of all newly produced goods and services (consumption goods, gross private domestic investment, net exports, and government purchases), or by adding up the expenditures incurred in producing those goods and services (national income payments, indirect business taxes, and capital consumption allowances). Similarly, net national product can be estimated either by adding up the final market value of all newly produced goods and services less capital consumption allowances (consumption goods, net private domestic investment, net exports, and government purchases) or by adding up the expenditures incurred in producing those goods and services (national income payments and indirect business taxes). (Net private domestic investment, cited above, is equal to gross private domestic investment minus capital consumption allowances. It represents, therefore, the net addition to our capital stock during the year.) Finally, national income is either the market value of all newly produced goods and services minus capital consumption allowances and indirect business taxes or income generated in the production of these goods and services. On the basis of these considerations we can, and will, use the terms *national production, national expenditure,* and *national income* pretty much interchangeably. What is an expenditure by one person is obviously an income receipt to another, and the market value of a product has to be equal to its costs of production if we include profits, as we do, as one of those costs of production.

Price indexes and real gross national product

We were able to come up with a composite picture of production in 1976 because we could convert all production into dollars and then add the dollars. But what if we want to compare the 1976 GNP, measured in 1976 dollars, with the 1950 GNP, which was measured in 1950 dollars? In today's world of spiraling prices, no one buys the old adage "a dollar is a dollar." There is a way out of this predicament, though, if we recognize that GNP consists of a real component (the goods and services themselves) and a price component. If we can hold the price component constant, we can isolate the change in the volume of actual goods and services; we will have *real* GNP for each year. Using a special price index called the *implicit price deflator,* we can get an estimate of the extent of price change, adjust for it, and isolate real GNP changes.

Now, a price index is just what its name suggests: a series of numbers representing the price level in each of several years in comparison with the price level of the base year of the index, with the price level of the base year represented by the number 100. Although the collection, organization, and analysis of price data present some challenging problems for the statistician, the concept of a price index is fairly simple: If it takes a certain amount of money to buy a particular bundle of goods and services

TABLE 3.2
Relation of GNP, NNP, NI, PI, DPI, and saving, 1976 ($ billion)

Personal consumption expenditures				1,079.7
Durable goods			156.5	
Nondurable goods			440.4	
Services			482.8	
Gross private domestic investment				239.6
Fixed investment		227.7		
Nonresidential		160.0		
Structures	55.3			
Producers' durable equipment	104.7			
Residential structures		67.7		
Change in business inventories			11.9	
Net export of goods and services				6.6
Exports			162.7	
Imports			156.0	
Government purchases of goods and services				365.6
Federal			133.4	
National defense		88.2		
Other		45.2		
State and local			232.2	
Equals: **Gross national product**				**1,691.6**

	Gross national product		**1,691.6**		
Less:	Capital consumption allowance		179.8		
Equals:	**Net national product**		**1,511.8**	1,028.4	Compensation of employees
Less:	Indirect business taxes (and other minor adjustments)		163.3	96.7	Proprietors' income
Equals:	**National income**		**1,348.5** =	23.5	Rental income of persons
Less:	Corporate profits	117.9		117.9	Corporate profits
	Contributions for social insurance	122.8	240.7	82.0	Net interest
Plus:	Government transfer payments	184.2			
	Net interest paid by government and consumers	38.5			
	Dividends	35.1			
	Business transfer payments	7.1			
	Other minor adjustments	2.6	267.5		
Equals:	**Personal income**		**1,375.3**		
Less:	Personal tax payments		193.6		
Equals:	**Disposable personal income**		**1,181.7**		
Less:	Personal outlays		1,105.2		
	Personal consumption expenditures	1,079.7			
	Consumer interest payments	25.5			
Equals:	**Personal saving**		**76.5**		

Source: Survey of Current Business (March 1977), 6–8.

at one point in time and twice that amount of money to buy the same bundle at a later time, then since prices have doubled, our second index number should be twice as great as the first (200 compared with 100). It follows that the purchasing power of the dollar in the second period was only half as great as it was in the first period since it took twice as many dollars to buy the same amount of goods and services. A real-world example: In the base year 1967, it took a certain amount of money to buy the standard package of goods and services represented in the consumer price index compiled by the Bureau of Labor Statistics. In 1976, it cost 170.5 percent of whatever the 1967 amount was to buy that same package, so the overall cost of living must have risen by 70.5 percent (from an index of 100 in 1967 to an index of 170.5 in 1976). By this same token the value of the consumer's dollar fell by 41 percent (the difference, not between the two index numbers, but between the reciprocals of the two numbers: $100/100 - 100/170.5 = .41$ or 41 percent). Compared with 1967, consumers in 1976 were spending 59-cent dollars.

For the "deflation" of the gross national product we will need the broadest index number series possible, one that covers not only consumer goods, but also all the other goods and services making up GNP. This is exactly what the GNP implicit price deflator series is: an index of average prices of all things going into GNP. We can take the reciprocal of each year's index number to find the purchasing power of the GNP dollar in that year, then multiply the output of goods and services for a particular year by this adjusted dollar to find real GNP for the year — one for which changes in purchasing power have been eliminated. In actual practice, the process is simpler even than this. If we divide each year's GNP as measured in current dollars (dollars of the year in question — the way GNP is usually reported) by the implicit price deflator index number for that year, we automatically convert current dollars into constant dollars: dollars with purchasing power equal to that of the dollars of the base year of the

TABLE 3.3
Gross national product ($ billion)

	1929	1933	1941	1950	1973	1974	1976
In current dollars	103.1	55.6	124.5	284.8	1306.6	1413.2	1691.6
Implicit price deflator (1972 = 100)	32.9	25.1	31.5	53.6	105.8	116.4	133.8
In constant (1972) dollars	314.7	222.1	396.6	533.5	1235.0	1214.0	1264.7

Source: *Economic Report of the President,* 1977, p. 190, and *Survey of Current Business* (March 1977), 5.

index series. This process gives a real, or constant-dollar, GNP that differs markedly from the current-dollar GNP, as Table 3.3 shows. The near-explosive growth in gross national product from 1973 to 1974 ($100 billion) turns out, as we felt at the time, to have been explosive entirely in terms of price rather than real growth.

I NATIONAL INCOME MANAGEMENT I

National income determination

So far we have learned at least the rudiments of national income accounting and can thus say with a certain degree of assurance what was produced during some period in the form of new goods and income. But we have learned almost nothing about why our economy produces at one particular level rather than another. That is our present assignment.

Up until about four decades ago the answer to this question would have been that limitations on the supply side basically determine how much will be produced. An economy obviously cannot have an output in excess of the inputs available to it in the form of productive resources. In the face of unlimited human wants, however, it was assumed that it could be taken for granted that what we could produce we would produce, especially since the process of production creates sufficient purchasing power in the form of generated income to take all goods off the market. At a given moment there might be an oversupply of particular commodities in the market, resulting from faulty individual judgments, but on an overall basis supply creates its own demand and overproduction is impossible. For over a hundred years this maxim of Say's law — "supply creates its own demand" — was the shared belief of the world's economists; in fact, its acceptance was almost the touchstone of economic competence.

Actually, of course, at the first level of analysis Say's law is incontestable: As we have learned from national income accounting the process of production (supply) does indeed create sufficient income and purchasing power to take all produced goods off the market (potential demand). The difficulty comes at the next level of analysis, where we ask for assurance that potential demand will become effective demand: that would-be buyers will become actual buyers. And that assurance is not forthcoming, as one major depression after another during the nineteenth and first half of the twentieth centuries graphically proved. It took a revolution in economic thinking, following the lead of the English economist John Maynard Keynes in his *General Theory of Employment, Interest and Money* (1936), to see that Say's law makes better sense if we stand it on its head: Demand creates its own supply. Businessmen, after all, are interested in turning out goods and services only if they are able to foresee a sufficient demand for their production at cost-covering prices; assure them of that demand and the supply will be brought forward, up to the limit of available human and property resources. Demand means spending — any kind of spending, wasteful or other — and means that we can spend our way into prosperity; in fact, it's the only way prosperity can be gained.

This new way of looking at aggregate economics is usually presented in the form of a special diagram, sometimes called the *Keynesian cross*. It can best be visualized as a variation of the demand and supply diagrams already encountered. The major difference is that in the present case we record possible output (which is equal to income) levels on the horizontal axis, but on the vertical axis we list, not prices, but total amounts demanded. A 45° helping line is then drawn, as in Figure 3.1, to represent the supply curve. Each point along this line represents an amount producers would be willing to supply (and the total income they would create in the process) should demand be forthcoming for such an amount. More concretely, the line tells us that businessmen would be willing to supply $100 billion worth of goods and services if they could anticipate a demand for $100 billion worth (point a), that they would be willing to produce at the $200 billion level if they could anticipate a demand of that magnitude (point b), and so on up the curve.

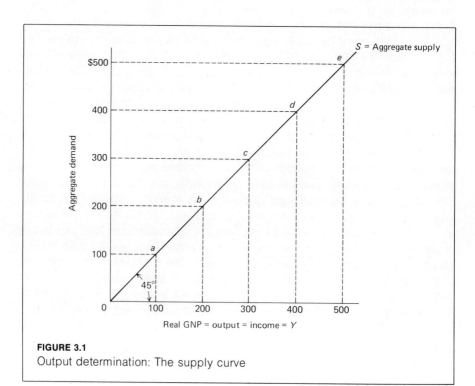

FIGURE 3.1
Output determination: The supply curve

As in the case of market analysis, to determine where the equilibrium level of output will be we must have both supply and demand curves. We build the aggregate demand schedule by adding together the demands for consumer goods, capital goods, and government purchases. Since net exports are miniscule compared with the other components of GNP, they are usually disregarded in elementary analysis.

Taking consumption spending first, since it is the largest component of overall demand, we find that consumption demand is largely dependent on the magnitude of family incomes. But family incomes, in turn, are governed primarily by the level of national production and income. On the basis of empirical studies, the general nature of this "functional relation-ship" between income and consumption spending has been determined and is portrayed by the line labeled *C* in Figure 3.2. Our 45° line, remember, represents the supply, or income-creation, line. Comparing line *C* to the 45° line gives us a picture of the relationship between potential income availability and planned spending out of various income amounts on con-sumption goods. At low levels of output and income, more than all avail-able income will be spent on consumption goods (by drawing on past savings and borrowed funds), as indicated by the fact that the consumption demand line lies above the income generation line. At the point where the

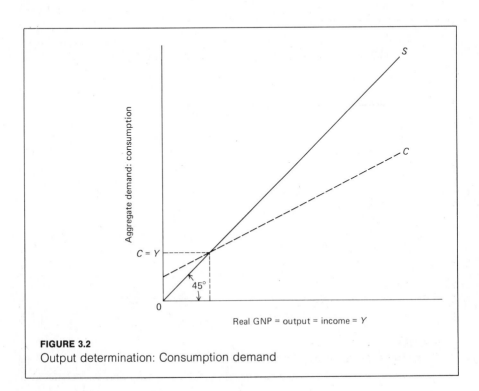

FIGURE 3.2
Output determination: Consumption demand

two curves cross (the break-even point) all income received — no more, no less — will be spent on consumption goods. To the right of this point, although consumption spending continues to rise, it does not rise as rapidly as income, so some part of income will be available for savings and tax payments.

In the present case, we make the simplifying assumption that neither investment spending (spending on new capital goods) nor government spending changes as output and income levels change. Businessmen make their capital spending plans without concern for the current or antic-ipated levels of production, and government budget makers do the same. So in both cases we have fixed levels of planned spending ($50 billion for each), which can then simply be added to the planned consumption line, giving us our aggregate demand schedule, $C + I + G$.

Having built the demand curve, we can now combine it with our supply curve (the 45° line) to determine the equilibrium level of national production and income, as pictured in Figure 3.3. At the point where the two curves cross (point *a*) we have a condition of equilibrium because everything the

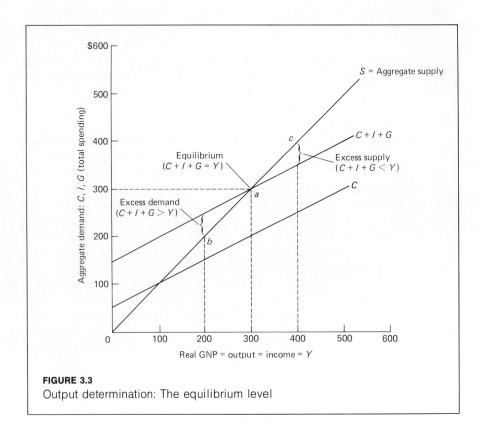

FIGURE 3.3
Output determination: The equilibrium level

producers are willing to turn out will find willing buyers. At any point to the left of this (say point *b*) we have an unstable condition because of *excess demand,* the amount by which demand exceeds supply. Buyers are clamoring for more goods and services than businessmen had planned to turn out, inducing the businessmen to increase their production levels to satisfy the insistent demand. This interaction between buyers and producers continues to operate and push up output levels until the equilibrium point is reached. Conversely, at any point to the right of the equilibrium level of output (say point *c*) buyers will not be willing or able to take all projected supplies off the market, as indicated by an excess supply gap between aggregate demand and aggregate supply. Businessmen will be left with unsold goods on their hands and will cut back on production until the equilibrium point is reached.

One point needs stressing in connection with our determination of the equilibrium level of national income. Usually we think of equilibrium as a desirable condition; we look askance at someone who has "lost his equilibrium," for example. But the national income equilibrium level may be a thoroughly undesirable one, perhaps one with extremely high unemployment. All that equilibrium means in the present connection is that demand and supply have come into balance, not that they have come into balance at a desirable level of output. The groundwork has been laid, though, for changing this equilibrium level if we do not like it. All we need do is force a shift in the demand line, giving us a new point of intersection with the supply curve, hopefully this time at the desired level of output.

The multiplier process

One feature of this shift in demand deserves special consideration. Notice in Figure 3.4 that when the demand curve moves upward by a relatively small amount (*ab*), the equilibrium level of production and income increases by a much larger amount (*cd*). We put an additional $100 billion into investment or government spending and out comes $200 billion in new goods and services. Jack pot! Well, not quite. What really happens does not depend on the laws of chance; it can be fairly reliably predicted on the basis of knowledge of the chain of developments set in motion by an injection of new spending into the income stream.

Let us say that during this income period the federal government decides to spend an additional $100 billion for cleaning up the environment (the result would be exactly the same, for present purposes, if businessmen decided to put an additional $100 billion into new plant and equipment or if consumers decided to spend $100 billion more on food, cars, and clothing). When the government actually spends the $100 billion, it will be paid out to those providing the cleanup services. But that is not the end of the matter. The money will not just sit there. Instead, with $100 billion of additional income, the providers of the cleanup services are

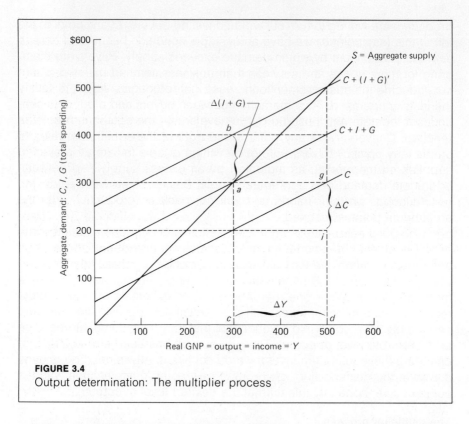

FIGURE 3.4
Output determination: The multiplier process

certain to spend part of their additional income on consumer goods. If they spend half of their new income, as we are assuming in this case, they will encourage the production of $50 billion worth of new consumer goods. But then the suppliers of these consumer goods will have $50 billion of additional income, half of which they will spend on other new consumer goods. So some other group has another $25 billion of income, half of which they will spend on consumer goods. Then another group will have $12.5 billion of income, half of which they will spend on consumer goods . . . and part of the original $100 billion is still in motion. When the "multiplier" process finally comes to an end, new goods and services in the amount of $200 billion will have been created ($100 billion of environmental cleanup services and $100 billion of new consumer goods):

$$\$100 \text{ billion} + \frac{1}{2}(\$100 \text{ billion}) + \frac{1}{4}(\$100 \text{ billion})$$

$$+ \frac{1}{8}(\$100 \text{ billion}) + \frac{1}{16}(\$100 \text{ billion}) + \cdots$$

$$+ \frac{1}{n}(\$100 \text{ billion}) = \$200 \text{ billion}$$

In terms of the diagram, the original rise in government demand (ab) induces a secondary rise in demand for consumer goods (ig), and the two together bring about an equal rise in supply (ab + ig = cd).

Since the initial rise in demand generates some multiple increase in production and income, the whole process is called, not surprisingly, the *multiplier process*, and the ratio between the final increase in production and income and the initial change in demand is called the *multiplier*. The extent of the multiplier process and the final size of the multiplier depend on the willingness of income receivers to spend new income, measured in terms of what is called the *marginal propensity to consume* (which is equal to change in consumption spending/change in income). The greater the willingness to spend new income (the higher the MPC), the larger the multiplier; the weaker the willingness to spend new income (the lower the MPC), the smaller the multiplier. (Those with a mathematical turn of mind will already have noticed that the MPC is nothing more than the slope of the consumption demand schedule.) Expressed algebraically,

$$\text{Multiplier} = \frac{1}{1 - \text{MPC}}$$

Empirical evidence suggests that in the United States the marginal propensity to consume out of gross income is about two-thirds. This means that each additional dollar of new investment or government spending will ultimately generate a total of three dollars' worth of new production and income.

Employment and income stabilization

The stage has now been set for the *income stabilization process*. This consists of the selection of some target level of output and the manipulation of demand so as to achieve this target level. But what should the target level be? A reasonable answer is that we should attempt to achieve the maximum level of output consistent with the current availability of resources. And since the most important of those resources is labor, the level of output that will provide jobs for all who desire to work suggests itself as the optimum position. In fact, under the Employment Act of 1946 Congress and the president are charged with the responsibility of achieving maximum employment.

This assumption of responsibility by the federal government for the achievement of something approaching full employment would have been considered unnecessary in an earlier era because it was believed that market processes would automatically move the economy toward full employment. In part this belief was based on Say's law, as we have seen. The other part was the conviction that unemployed labor was simply overpriced labor. At some wage rate the labor market would clear through into jobs all who wanted to work at that wage rate — just as lower prices

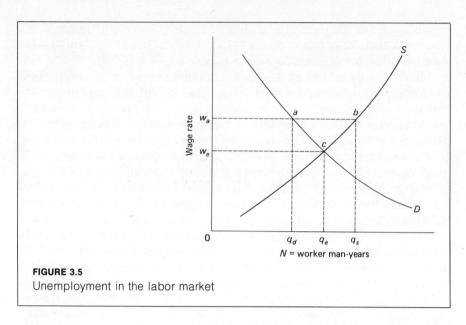

FIGURE 3.5
Unemployment in the labor market

for cabbages would remove all unsold stocks of cabbages. Such a situation can be described with the usual demand and supply diagram, with wage rates representing prices and worker man-years representing quantities, as in Figure 3.5. At a wage rate of ow_a, oq_s workers will offer their services for employment, but only oq_d will be worth hiring at such a high wage rate, so we have unemployment of ab (which is equal to $q_s - q_d$). Workers — or their unions — have simply priced themselves, or at least a large number of their members, out of the market. But given this diagnosis, the cure is simple: Let workers reduce their asking price, and more

the small society   by Brickman

will be worth hiring (while at the same time some would-be workers will drop out of the labor force because they will choose leisure over labor at lower wage rates). As wages come down employment goes up, until finally at the wage rate of ow_e all who want to work will be able to find jobs. Unemployment has been eliminated without the intervention of government.

The fact that wages did come down in major depressions at the same time that unemployment was increasing, however, suggests that something crucial may be missing from the analysis. Keynes put his finger on the missing part. The above analysis looks on wages entirely as costs of production. This leads to the conviction that labor services are overpriced if unemployment is present. But Keynes pointed out that wages, in addition to being costs, are also income and purchasing power. An overall cut in wages therefore implies a reduction in businessmen's costs, but it also means that the demand for their products may decline, leading to a reduction in their demand for workers. The actual situation may well be, not the above, with demand remaining constant, but something like that portrayed in Figure 3.6, with demand moving down with the wage rate. Instead of a wage reduction to ow_e bringing about full employment, it has instead brought about a downward shift in the labor demand schedule (to D') sufficient to offset the positive aspects of the wage reduction. The economy is as far from full employment as ever. Along the way, though, something

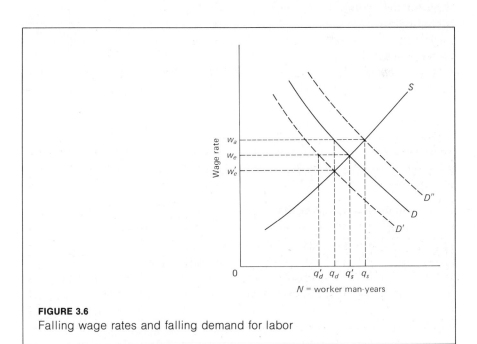

FIGURE 3.6
Falling wage rates and falling demand for labor

may have been learned: It may not be possible to achieve full employment by cutting wages, because demand will decline; but given an established wage rate (ow_a), it is possible to achieve full employment by shifting the demand curve to the right, to D'' — which is the approach used in modern stabilization analysis and policy.

This, however, involves government intervention in the economy, a course of action barred by adherence to free market principles. Many economists, therefore, simply refused to buy the Keynesian analysis because it meant buying government as part of the package. They continued, and some still continue, to argue that labor and cabbages are basically alike: Overpricing means excess supply. And the rapid growth in the power of labor unions since the 1930s helps to buttress their position. Curiously, though, although they see substantial wage cuts as a solution to unemployment, they never advocate wage increases as a cure for overfull employment and inflation.

In the face of some opposition, the Employment Act of 1946 became the law of the land, committing the federal government to take action to bring about maximum levels of production and employment. The free operations of markets were believed no longer capable of achieving such levels without government assistance. The Employment Act, however, carefully avoided committing the federal government to achieving full employment (as passage of the Full Employment Bill of 1945 would have). Notice the careful working of the 1946 act:

Section 2. The Congress hereby declares that it is the continuing policy and responsibility of the Federal Government to use all practicable means, consistent with its needs and obligations and other essential considerations of national policy, with the assistance and cooperation of industry, agriculture, labor, and State and local governments, to coordinate and utilize all its plans, functions and resources for the purpose of creating and maintaining, in a manner calculated to foster and promote free competitive enterprise and the general welfare, conditions under which there will be afforded useful employment opportunities, including self-employment, for those able, willing, and seeking to work, and to promote maximum employment, production, and purchasing power.[1]

Prices and income stabilization

The wisdom of leaving the federal government some maneuvering room has become apparent since the act was passed. Although price changes are left to operate behind the scenes, the Keynesian cross analysis more or less assumes that until full employment is reached all increases in aggregate demand will increase real output, not prices; after full employ-

---

[1] 89th Congress, Second Session, Joint Economic Committee, *Employment Act of 1946, as Amended, with Related Laws and Rules,* U.S. Government Printing Office, Washington, D.C., 1966, p. 1.

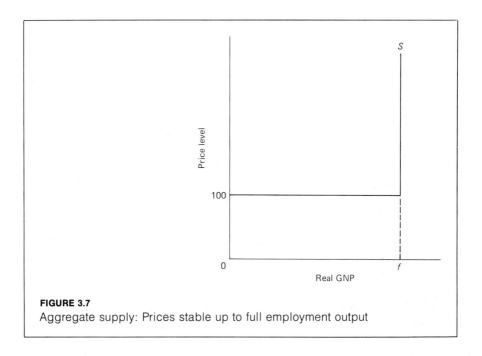

FIGURE 3.7
Aggregate supply: Prices stable up to full employment output

ment is reached all further increases in demand will increase prices only, since no additional labor resources are available further to increase real output. A somewhat different approach to the construction of the aggregate supply schedule may serve to make the point clearer. Let us break GNP into its two separate parts, listing the real-product component on the horizontal axis and putting the average-price-level component on the vertical axis. Picturing the assumption of stable prices until the full employment level of real output is reached (price increases only past that point) gives us something like Figure 3.7.

Analysis of the post–World War II period, as well as reanalysis of earlier periods, suggests that the aggregate supply schedule in the United States cannot be graphed as in Figure 3.7. Instead, the relationship between aggregate supply and demand must look something like that portrayed in Figure 3.8. Here we can see that if we start from a very low level of output, demand can be increased substantially (from D_1 to D_2) with no upward pressure on prices. This is consistent with the original Keynesian analysis and is founded on the observation that with idle resources of all sorts business firms can secure at constant prices all inputs necessary to expand their output levels. When demand is increased further, however, from D_2 to D_3, this analysis parts company with the Keynesian supply curve. Now, even though there is still insufficient demand to put all resources to work, demand is pressing hard enough against supply to create bottlenecks in certain parts of the economy, driving prices up in those

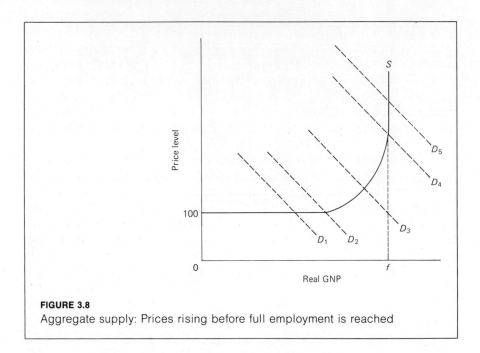

FIGURE 3.8
Aggregate supply: Prices rising before full employment is reached

sectors. Take the years 1936 and 1937 as an example. After several years of major depression the economy was on the move to full recovery but was still far short of it (unemployment averaged 16.9 percent in 1936 and 14.3 percent in 1937). While unemployment was still high, though, machine tool manufacturers looking for metalsmiths and patternmakers found there were almost none to be had, since few had been trained after the depression began in 1929 and many of those trained earlier had died or retired. The attempt of some machine tool makers to bid skilled workers of this sort away from other toolmakers did nothing to increase the supply of skilled workers, at least in the short run; it merely drove up their wages and increased the costs and prices of machine tools. And similar things were happening elsewhere in the economy, resulting in a fairly rapid upward drift in the price level. The closer the full employment level of output is approached, the more general do bottlenecks become (as indicated by the shift from D_3 to D_4), and with the rise of demand to D_5 the whole economy becomes one large bottleneck. Output can increase no further (as with the vertical part of the supply curve in Figure 3.7), but prices can increase without limit. We have reached the point of pure inflation.

This analysis suggests, then, that the extent of price level increase associated with rising demand will depend on how much slack there is in the economy. With substantial slack, prices will go up modestly, if at all; with little or no slack, prices will rise dramatically. It further suggests that if prices rise rapidly with increasing demand near the point of full employment, they should fall rapidly with any fall in demand. This has proved by no means to be the case. On the contrary, during most of our severe postwar recessions prices actually rose in the face of weak overall demand. The supply curve is apparently irreversible, as pictured in Figure 3.9. With falling demand the economy falls back, not along the original supply curve S_1, but along a completely new supply curve S_2. Businessmen react to falling demand by cutting production and employment, not prices, resulting in a new equilibrium at point b rather than point a.

Various reasons are given for this. Some economists insist that, since wages cannot be reduced because of union resistance, businessmen cannot reduce their costs and thus cannot reduce their prices. Other economists argue that the fault lies with the businessmen, not the unions. Giant corporations, in particular, are in a position to administer or dictate prices, and they know that if prices come down there may be resistance to pushing them back up. On the other hand, if workers are let go and production levels cut, it will be a simple matter to rehire workers and boost production once demand reverses itself. At this point other economists bring in the Employment Act of 1946. Businessmen know that the federal government now has an obligation under the act to respond to falling levels of output and employment by boosting demand. With an extended period of slack demand, wages and prices might slip, permitting a fall in the supply curve from S_2 to S_1 and encouraging an increase in output. But the federal government cannot wait for this; it has the responsibility of taking action

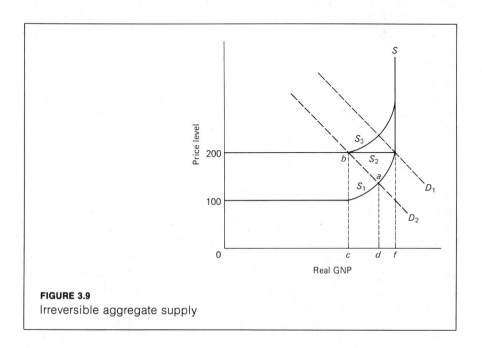

FIGURE 3.9
Irreversible aggregate supply

right away. Even in the absence of the Employment Act it is likely that such action would take place: Unemployed workers do not vote for do-nothing incumbent politicians. So demand will be enlarged, permitting a rise in production and employment, but also a rise in prices. Demand will thus move to the right, not along supply curve S_2, but along a rising supply curve S_3. Prices seemingly are governed by a ratchet process: They can rise without limit with rising demand, but falling demand brings no price relief. In the face of this combination of big labor, big business, and a national commitment to maximum output and employment, only a confirmed optimist looks for a falling — or even a stable — price level.

In principle, then, guiding the economy to high levels of production and employment appears deceptively simple. In practice, especially if much concern is felt for stable prices, bitter experience has proved that it is extremely difficult. As in so many other cases, we have learned that we cannot have the good we would like without some of the bad. If we want high levels of production and employment, we must apparently be prepared to live with high and rising prices. If we want stable prices, we seem to be faced with the necessity of putting up with more unemployment and less production than we would like. More and more, economic policy making consists merely of deciding which particular trade-off is least undesirable.

Nonetheless, for better or worse, we have a national commitment to achieve maximum levels of output and employment, primarily through the control of aggregate demand. That control is exercised by the use of fiscal policy (changing the levels of government spending, taxes, and transfer payments) and monetary policy (changing the amounts of money in circulation). We will next go on to examine the mechanics of these operations.

I SUMMARY I

Only since the early years of World War II have we had official national accounts that tell us the amounts of goods and services produced annually and the amounts of income generated in the process.

Our measuring rod for such production is the dollar, and estimates of production are based on the dollars we pay for newly produced final goods and services. This means that the "worth" of a product or service is what someone is willing to pay for it. Because of market biases and the fact that many goods and services do not clear through the market, gross national product — our most widely used measure of production — is an inadequate measure of national welfare.

National production can be, and is, measured by what comes out of the production pipeline (consumer goods and services, capital goods, goods and services bought by government, and goods and services provided foreigners less what they provide us) or by what goes into the pipeline (costs of productive services plus indirect taxes and depreciation).

Subtracting the capital goods used up in the production process from gross national product leaves us with net national product. Measuring production by the cost of productive services used (wages, rent, interest, and profits) gives us national income. Adding transfer payments to national income actually paid out provides us with a measure of personal income. And when we deduct personal tax payments from the latter we have disposable personal income.

Because the value of the dollar changes as the price level shifts, we must hold the price level constant if we are to detect fluctuations in real GNP. This we do by dividing current-dollar, or money, GNP by a special price index — the implicit price deflator series.

Although earlier economists assumed that the economy would operate at or near its full employment level because supply creates its own demand, the British economist John Maynard Keynes demonstrated that an uncontrolled economy could come into equilibrium at any level of output. To achieve the desired level of output and employment, demand must be increased or decreased by government action, thereby inducing the appropriate changes in supply.

A major problem with the Keynesian analysis is that increasing demand in a slack economy raises prices as well as production, whereas reductions in demand in an inflationary period more and more lead, not to reductions in prices, but only to cuts in production and employment.

I IMPORTANT TERMS AND CONCEPTS I

macroeconomics	real GNP
gross national product	Say's law
net national product	multiplier
national income	multiplier process
personal income	marginal propensity to consume
transfer payments	income stabilization process
disposable personal income	

I QUESTIONS, PROBLEMS, AND EXERCISES I

1 Why doesn't a hard day's work at the beach building sand castles count as part of the gross national product?

2 How adequate is the gross national product as a measure of economic welfare or well-being?

3 When the price level is rising, will real (constant-dollar) GNP be greater than or less than money (current-dollar) GNP?

4 Why is it that the expressions *gross national product, gross national expenditure,* and *gross national income* can be used more or less interchangeably?

5 Why is the aggregate supply curve today irreversible? That is, why does the aggregate demand curve shift up along one supply curve but fall back along a different supply curve?

6 Given the definition of national income as all income earned but not necessarily received and personal income as all income received but not necessarily earned, what additions and subtractions are necessary to convert national income into personal income?

7 Sometimes the distinction between gross private domestic investment and net private domestic investment is made in terms of a bathtub theorem. Water running into the tub from the open faucet represents gross investment (total annual production of capital goods), and water running out of the open drain represents depreciation, or capital consumption (the using up of capital goods during the year). Where in the bathtub would we find the example of net investment? (*Hint:* The initial water level in the tub may be taken to represent the total stock of capital goods with which the economy starts the year.)

8 Given consumption spending of $660 billion, indirect taxes of $120 billion, government spending of $170 billion, depreciation of $60 billion, gross investment spending of $130 billion, and net exports of $30 billion, can you construct totals for GNP, NNP, and NI?

I SUGGESTED READING I

Chase, Richard X. "The Failure of American Keynesianism." *Challenge,* (March–April 1976), 43–52.

Denison, Edward F. "Welfare Measurement and the GNP." *Survey of Current Business,* (January 1971), 13–16, 39.

Heilbroner, Robert L. *The Worldly Philosophers,* 4th ed. Simon and Schuster, New York, 1972.

Lekachman, Robert. *The Age of Keynes.* Random House, New York, 1966.

Lindert, Peter H. *Prices, Jobs, and Growth: An Introduction to Macroeconomics.* Little, Brown, Boston, 1976.

Mishan, E. J. "How Real Income and Its Growth Are Overstated." *Challenge* (March–April 1977), 56–59.

Robinson, Joan. "The Age of Growth." *Challenge* (May–June 1976), 4–9.

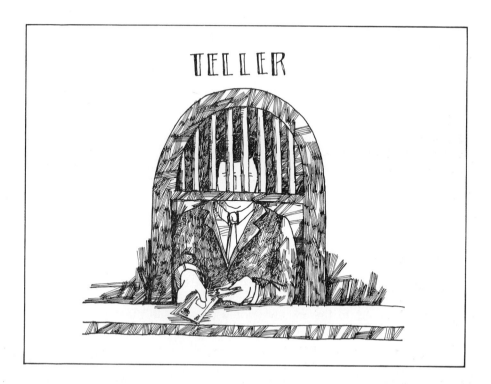

FOUR

| MONEY AND BANKS |

No topic is more central than money to an understanding of how a modern economy operates, but on no other topic is there more disagreement as to how an institutional arrangement actually works. An exchange economy today is necessarily a money-using, or pecuniary, economy. When exchanges are rare, they can be conducted as barter transactions without too much inconvenience. As an economy grows, however, individuals tend more and more to specialize, to become less self-sufficient, and to be forced into trade to satisfy the needs they can no longer supply for themselves. Before long, arranging for all the necessary swaps distracts from the primary specialized activities of individuals. Imagine the difficulties a violin teacher would have if he had to swap violin lessons for his clothing, his food, his housing, his transportation. . . .

I THE ROLE OF MONEY I

These difficulties are neatly sidestepped with the introduction of money as a medium of exchange. The violin teacher simply sells his services for money and then exchanges the money for the whole range of goods and services he needs. Money thus serves as a lubricant for trade.

If this were all that money did, we could define it quite simply: Money is a *medium of exchange*; anything generally accepted in payment of a debt is money. From this point of view, money for us today is coins, *currency* (paper money), and *demand deposits* (checking account balances).

Coins, the oldest medium of exchange, have been used for many centuries. Paper money joined coins in the Middle Ages. Demand deposits added importantly to the money supply only in the nineteenth century. Many other things have served as money at different times. Even a partial list is impressive: tobacco, wampum, cowrie shells, hides, furs, dried fish, wine, cattle, slaves, wives.

It is obvious that tobacco or wampum or furs could substitute for coins, but cattle? Slaves? Wives? That cattle did at one time serve as money cannot be denied. *Pecuniary,* which means "of or pertaining to money," is derived from the Latin *pecunia* (money), which in turn stems from *pecus* (cattle). But we can be reasonably sure that daily bills were never paid with cattle, slaves, or wives. These were money of a different sort — money serving primarily as either a *store of value* (a way of accumulating wealth) or a *standard of value* (something against which the worth of other things could be compared). In other days it meant much to say that a person owned a herd of 50 cattle, or 100 slaves, or a dozen wives, even though these were rarely used in exchange transactions. And, even though money didn't change hands when, say, a boat was exchanged for weapons, it helped in arranging the swap to know how valuable both were in terms of cattle. Today, we routinely accumulate much of our wealth in the form of money, just as we routinely set dollar values on our "valuables."

The point of this discussion is that money is a complex concept. Obviously, since money serves so many different purposes, the simple definition of money as anything generally accepted in settlement of a debt won't do, since it describes money only as a medium of exchange. Awkward as it is, we have to say that money is anything that serves generally as a medium of exchange or as a store of value or as a standard of value. The word *or* rather than *and* is used advisedly, since sometimes money used for one purpose does not serve for another. We saw that cattle were earlier utilized as a store of value and standard of value but not as a medium of exchange. Today, the United States dollar is our universal unit of account and standard of value, but dollars in one form constitute our primary medium of exchange and dollars held in another form are preferred as a store of value.

Money in the United States

If we concentrate only on money as a medium of exchange, it is relatively simple to reckon the American money supply. It consists of the dollars with which we pay our daily bills, either pocketbook money (coins and currency — paper bills) or checkbook money (dollars in the form of demand deposit balances). The Federal Reserve measures the money stock monthly and publishes the figures in the *Federal Reserve Bulletin.* Table 4.1 gives the latest available count.

This is money by anybody's reckoning — dollars immediately available for spending. A small part of the money supply, not included in Table 4.1, consists of the coins manufactured by United States Mints and distributed to the public by way of Federal Reserve and commercial banks. Currency is paper money, which today is made up entirely of Federal Reserve notes — paper IOUs issued by the Federal Reserve banks and circulated by commercial banks. Far and away the largest part of our money supply, as we have defined it, is demand deposit balances — amounts that stand to our credit in checking accounts at commercial banks. The fact that, with minor exceptions, only commercial banks can handle checking accounts is what distinguishes them from other types of financial institutions, such as savings and loan associations, savings banks, insurance companies, and investment banks.

Demand deposits are a very curious type of money. Coins and paper money can be seen and felt. But no one has ever felt or seen demand deposits. They are called demand deposits because they are available immediately upon demand. When you write a check, you order your bank to give over possession of some of the money in your checking account balance to the person to whom you write the check. What the bank gives over, though, is simply a certain amount of credit it previously recorded in

TABLE 4.1
The money stock, June 1977 ($ billion)

Currency	84.0
Demand deposits	238.0
Total	322.0

your favor on its books. Part of what has been your credit becomes someone else's credit. What the bank owed you, it now owes someone else. If
you write a check to "Cash," on the other hand, you are merely converting
a claim against the bank into currency. And when you deposit paper
money, you are converting currency into a claim against the bank. More
simply, you are converting a Federal Reserve paper IOU into a bank open-
book IOU.

Demand deposits may be strange and mysterious, yet they are the
most important part of our medium of exchange money supply. Table 4.1
shows that in amounts outstanding they exceed currency roughly three to
one, but even this ratio understates their importance. Coins and paper
money turn over or change hands frequently, but their velocity of turnover
is much less than that of demand deposits. As a consequence of their
working harder, demand deposits are involved in far more monetary transactions than currency. Well over 90 percent of the exchange transactions
in this country, according to the best guesses, involve the use of demand
deposits. Small wonder, then, that when the Federal Reserve authorities
set out to control the money supply, they concentrate their efforts on
demand deposits, leaving as much or as little currency in circulation as
the public wants.

The equation of exchange

Following the lead of one of their early-twentieth-century predecessors,
economists have long attempted to identify the role of money in an exchange economy by inserting it into an *equation of exchange.* In symbolic
terms this reads:

$$MV = PQ$$

Q stands for the total of new goods and services produced during the year,
and *P* represents the average prices of these goods and services. Together
they provide a measure of the money value of all new goods and services
turned out during the year — which happens to be the definition of gross
national product, our most widely used measure of national income or
output. So *PQ = GNP. M* is the measure of the average amount of money
in circulation, and *V* is the average number of times each unit of the money
supply turns over, or is exchanged for new goods and services or GNP,
during the year.

As it stands, the equation of exchange tells us little about the actual
operation of the economy, to say nothing of money's role in that operation.
It says only that total spending (the left-hand side of the equation) equals
total receipts (the right-hand side). No great revelations here. But by making certain assumptions, it is possible to turn the equation of exchange
into an hypothesis about the impact of changes in the money supply on
the annual production of new goods and services.

The crude quantity theory of money

Let us first make two assumptions: (1) that the velocity with which money turns over (V) is constant or changes very slowly and (2) that the amount of new goods and services turned out (Q) is determined by nonmonetary considerations — say that it is governed by the real production capabilities of the economy. We are, therefore, left with only one variable on each side of the equation, M and P. It has to follow that any change in the money supply will result in a proportionate change in the price level. Increase the money supply and prices go up, reduce the money supply and prices come down. This is the _quantity theory of money_ in its simplest form.

We have considerable evidence that the quantity theory of money in this simple, or crude, form helps to explain some price-level movements. Explosive rises in the price level (hyperinflations) have uniformly been accompanied by extraordinary increases in the money supply. And long-term movements in the price level also can be meaningfully related to parallel movements in the money supply.

When it comes to explaining short-term, moderate changes in the price level, though, the quantity theory of money in this crude form tends to break down. Since this is the world in which we live (as Keynes pointed out, in the long run we're all dead), this is a matter of some moment. Most importantly, changes in M, we have learned, affect Q as well as P. The assumption that the real output of goods and services is unaffected by the rate of change in the money supply is invalid.

The modern quantity theory of money

Revising the equation of exchange after World War II, one school of economists, led by Milton Friedman of the University of Chicago and calling themselves monetarists, came up with the following formulation:

$$M = PQ = GNP \quad \text{or} \quad \Delta M \rightarrow \Delta(PQ) = \Delta GNP$$

The assumption is still maintained that V can be disregarded, so it is, in effect, left out of the equation; but many economists now recognize that the real output of goods and services (Q) as well as average prices at which they sell (P) are very much affected by rates of change in the money supply. In fact, the monetarists come close to saying that it is _only_ changes in the money supply that affect gross national product. Whether a change in M will affect GNP by changing Q (the amount of goods and services produced) or by changing P (the prices at which they sell) is a matter of no little consequence, however, and one on which monetarist theory and predictions have been less than overwhelming. At least it is now generally recognized that changes in the money supply do matter where the national income is concerned. Since (1) we are concerned with national income stabilization, (2) changes in the money supply affect national income, (3) commercial banks create the most important part of the money supply, and (4) the Federal Reserve is able to control this process of money creation by controlling commercial bank reserves, it is time to take a closer look at how money is created and how that process is regulated.

I COMMERCIAL BANKS AND THE MONEY SUPPLY I

At a later point, when we come back to the discussion of money as a store of value, we will need to look at financial institutions other than commercial banks. But for the moment we are still concentrating on money as a medium of exchange, the most important form of which is demand deposits. And since only commercial banks, with minor exceptions, have the legal capability of creating demand deposits, we need to get better acquainted with them.

One way to get better acquainted with the commercial banks is to group them all together — all 14,633 of them — and take a financial snapshot. Fortunately, we don't have to get the banks together to take their picture. The banking authorities do that for us and publish their results monthly in the *Federal Reserve Bulletin*. The picture for July 1977 is reproduced in Table 4.2.

Luckily for the banks it appears that they are in good shape: Their books balance; every dollar's worth of liabilities is matched by a dollar's worth of assets. Actually, all this proves is that the banks' bookkeepers can add. All balance sheets (the banks like to call them *statements of condition*) are designed in such a way that they must balance. Total *assets* (what the banks own) minus *liabilities* (what the banks owe to outsiders) gives some figure, positive or negative, for the *capital accounts* (the net claim of banks' owners against assets) that balances the total account. If the total assets are matched dollar for dollar by claims (liabilities) held by persons outside the banks, the books will still balance — even though the net worth of the banks to their owners, the stockholders, is zero. In the situation described in Table 4.2, this is obviously not the case. Collectively the banks' stockholders have a large positive claim against the banks' assets, although their share is fairly modest when compared to that of the outside claimants.

Assets and liabilities have more than a balance-sheet relationship. They are closely connected with the efforts of the bank managers to earn profits for the bank owners, thereby increasing the net worth of the owners. Briefly, banks attract or create deposits (liabilities) with zero or low interest charges in order to make loans or acquire securities (assets) with higher interest charges. The difference between what they pay as interest and what they receive in interest payments represents their gross profits.

Even though the above consolidated statement of condition is highly condensed, it will be necessary to strip it down even further to see clearly

TABLE 4.2
Principal assets and liabilities — all commercial banks, July 1977
($ billion)

Assets			Liabilities	
Cash assets		124.7	Demand deposits	313.8
Loans		612.5	Time deposits	522.7
Securities		253.7	Borrowings	90.6
U.S. Treasury	99.5		Other liabilities	41.4
Other	154.2		Capital accounts	78.9
Other assets		56.5		
			Total liabilities	
Total assets		1047.4	and capital	1047.4

the process of how banks create money. On the liabilities side we will drop out everything except demand deposits. *Time deposits* must go because they are not money as we have narrowly defined it — a medium of exchange. They get their name from the fact that legally they are not available on demand. Banks can insist on advance notice of intent to withdraw funds from time and savings accounts (passbook savings, certificates of deposits, time deposits open account). More important, money in these accounts cannot be spent directly. It is impossible to pay your bills with a savings passbook. Ordinarily, you must first convert your funds into the form of either currency or additions to your checking account balance. Time and savings balances, then, are money as a store of value but not money as a medium of exchange.

We will leave out everything on the assets side of the account except cash assets and loans and leave in the cash assets account only two items: vault cash (currency held by the banks for public issue) and bank deposits with the Federal Reserve banks. We will then have to juggle our books a bit to make our accounts balance, since we have left out a number of balancing items, and round-off our figures to make them easier to work with. What we have left is the hypothetical picture shown in Table 4.3.

What we have retained of our cash assets and labeled *cash reserves* is without question the single most important account on the whole consolidated balance sheet — at least where money creation and control are concerned. By controlling this account and its relationships to the other accounts, the Federal Reserve authorities are able to manipulate the size of the money supply. Commercial banks that belong to the Federal Reserve system satisfy their legal *reserve requirement* by keeping minimum balances in the two reserve accounts. If the legal reserve requirement is 20

TABLE 4.3
Simplified consolidated statement of condition — all commercial banks
($ billion)

Assets			Liabilities	
Cash reserves		20	Demand deposits	100
Vault cash	5			
Deposit with F.R.	15			
Loans		80		
Total assets		100	Total liabilities	100

percent, this simply means that the banks must keep their combined
reserve accounts at a figure at least 20 percent as great as their total
demand deposits. In the case described in Table 4.3, demand deposits
are $100 billion, so cash reserves must amount to at least $20 billion,
which they do. Another way of looking at this is to say that with a 20
percent reserve requirement, each dollar of reserves "supports" five dollars
in demand deposits. The banks may, of course, hold more than 20 percent
in reserve balances, but they are in violation of the law if they hold less
than 20 percent.

The banks are not likely to hold more than their required reserves,
however, because balances in their reserve accounts earn no interest. This
is obvious in the case of vault cash. It is just as apparent in the case of
deposits with the Federal Reserve banks once we recognize that these are
simply checking account balances that the banks maintain with district
Federal Reserve banks, and under the current banking laws no interest
may be paid on checking account balances. Balances in these accounts
are not dead losses, though, since they are working accounts, as are all
checking accounts. The banks make deposits in the accounts, write checks
against them, and clear checks against them. They can be regarded as
ordinary checking accounts for the banks, but with the added provision
that minimum balances must be maintained — minimum balances specified by the Federal Reserve authorities. To repeat, though, the banks will
not willingly hold more than the required minimum balances because
excess reserves earn no interest. Whenever excess reserves accumulate,
the banks will promptly convert them from nonearning assets into earning
(interest-bearing) assets. In the present context, this means into loans. We
can visualize this process if we pull a single bank, say the First National
Bank of Troy, out of our consolidated balance and set up its own balance
sheet or T-account, as we do in Table 4.4.

If the legal reserve requirement is 20 percent, the First National Bank of Troy T-account meets the letter of the law: With demand deposits of $100 million, it is required to have, and it has, $20 million in its reserve balances. Now let's say that the Troy Optical Company gets a $10 million payment from the Pentagon in the form of a check drawn by the United States Treasury. Troy Optical deposits the check in its account at the First National Bank of Troy, and the First National Bank of Troy clears the check by sending it on to the Federal Reserve Bank of New York for deposit to First National's reserve account. After all entries have been made, First National's T-account reflects the accumulation of excess reserves, as shown in Table 4.5.

Since its demand deposits have increased by $10 million, First National needs an additional $2 million in reserves (20 percent of $10 million). But its present reserves are $8 million in excess of the $22 million required (20 percent of $110 million). It will therefore want to convert the $8 million of excess nonearning assets into $8 million of earning assets, which it can do by increasing its loans by that amount. When a creditworthy customer comes along, the bank has the borrower sign a note for $8 million, adds the IOU to its loan portfolio, and credits the borrower's checking account with $8 million. The transaction, which is shown in Table 4.6, affects both sides of the bank's T-account equally.

To this point, though, there has been no effect on the bank's reserve balances — and the idea was to convert excess reserves into loans. The conversion takes place as soon as the borrowed money is used. Let's say that Troy Optical took out its loan to pay for new machines, which it ordered from the Syracuse Tool and Die Company. It now writes a check for the full amount of the loan, sends it to Syracuse Tool and Die, which deposits the check in its account at Syracuse National Bank. Syracuse National credits Syracuse Tool and Die's account and clears the check by sending it on to the Federal Reserve Bank of New York for credit to its reserve account. The Federal Reserve Bank of New York transfers the money from the First National Bank of Troy to Syracuse National Bank by crediting Syracuse's reserve account and debiting First National's account. The net effect of this series of transactions is that demand deposits in the First National Bank of Troy are reduced by $8 million and the bank's reserve account is reduced by the same amount. The bank's books reflect this, as shown in Table 4.7.

First National Bank of Troy has eliminated its excess reserves by expanding its loan portfolio. It can now make new loans only as rapidly as old loans are paid off or new deposits come in. One thing that may not have been noticed along the way, though, is that the bank created new money in the process of expanding its loans. It granted the loan, remember, by writing up its demand deposits by $8 million. It's true that this created money didn't long remain with the bank. When the loan proceeds were

TABLE 4.4
T-account for First National Bank of Troy (I) ($ million)

Assets			Liabilities	
Cash reserves		20	Demand deposits	100
Vault cash	5			
Deposit with F.R.	15			
Loans		80		

TABLE 4.5
T-account for First National Bank of Troy (II) ($ million)

Cash reserves		30	Demand deposits	110
Vault cash	5			
Deposit with F.R.	25			
Loans		80		

TABLE 4.6
Lending transaction, First National Bank of Troy ($ million)

Loans	+8	Demand deposits	+8

TABLE 4.7
T-account for First National Bank of Troy (III) ($ million)

Cash reserves		22	Demand deposits	110
Vault cash	5			
Deposit with F.R.	17			
Loans		88		

TABLE 4.8
Deposit transaction, Syracuse National Bank ($ million)

Deposits with F.R.		+8	Demand deposits	+8
Required	+1.6			
Excess	+6.4			

drawn down the money left the bank. But it didn't disappear. After being used to pay off a debt, it ended up in Syracuse National. As a consequence, if Syracuse National's reserve balance was previously just sufficient to satisfy minimum legal requirements, it is now in excess of that requirement, since only part of the funds transferred to the bank needs to be held as reserves. This is shown in Table 4.8.

Syracuse National will now expand its loans by the amount of its newly acquired excess reserves ($6.4 million), creating in the process demand deposits of equal amount. When the loan proceeds are drawn down, some other bank will end up with demand deposits of $6.4 million and excess reserves of 80 percent of that amount ($5.12 million). That bank, in turn, will expand its loans in the amount of its excess reserves by creating additional demand deposits of a similar amount — and yet another bank will end up with additional demand deposits, additional excess reserves, and additional lending capacity. The process goes on and on, with additional money (but ever-decreasing amounts) being created at each step of the process.

$$(1) \qquad\qquad (2) \qquad\qquad\qquad (3) \qquad\qquad\qquad\qquad (n + 1)$$
$$(\$8\text{ million})(1) + (\$8\text{ million})(.8) + (\$8\text{ million})(.8^2) + \cdots + (\$8\text{ million})(.8^n)$$

Working this series out to its ultimate conclusion would be more than tedious, because we have an infinite progression series. But it is not necessary to work the series out. We can use a mathematical short cut. To get the final figure for total demand deposits created, we simply divide the amount of excess reserves we start with in the first bank by the required reserve ratio or percentage. Since we have been working with a reserve ratio of 20 percent and the First National Bank of Troy started out with excess reserves of $8 million, we know that ultimately the money supply will expand by a total of $40 million.

$$\text{Change in demand deposits} = \frac{\text{excess reserves}}{\text{reserve ratio}} = \frac{\$8\text{ million}}{.20} = \$40\text{ million}$$

It is apparent from the formula that reserve dollars are high-powered dollars, how high-powered depending on the reserve ratio set by the Federal Reserve. The Federal Reserve authorities are in the unique position of being able to control both the numerator and the denominator of the equation. They can lend the banks excess reserves. They can create excess reserves by purchasing United States Treasury securities in the securities markets (open market purchases), thereby putting in motion funds that will end up as bank deposits and additions to bank reserve balances. They can increase the money expansion capabilities of any existing excess reserves by reducing the reserve requirement, which also directly creates excess reserves and additions to the money supply. And they can reduce the money supply by reversing any or all of these actions. Since the Federal Reserve authorities have this great power, it is time to take a closer look at this peculiar institution.

I THE FEDERAL RESERVE SYSTEM I

And a peculiar institution it is. The name suggests that it should be part of the federal government. In a certain sense it is; in more important ways it isn't. The close relationship of the system to the federal government is indicated by the fact that Congress legislated the system into being in 1913 — and could, of course, eliminate the system at any time by a stroke of the pen. If such a step were considered too drastic, Congress could stop somewhat short of wiping out the system and merely change the rules of the game under which the Federal Reserve operates. But while Congress holds the power of life and death over the Federal Reserve system, it has exercised this power very circumspectly — far too cautiously, according to the critics of the system.

The system that exists today is basically the system that was set up in 1913, except for some tinkering here and there along the way, especially during the banking crises of the 1930s. None of the changes have altered the fundamental view that the Federal Reserve authorities, in directing the day-to-day operations of the system, should be exempt from pressures exerted both by members of Congress and by the executive branch. Neither have the power under current legislation to order the Federal Reserve authorities to do anything.

Structure and operation

The Federal Reserve system is made up of five parts: member banks, Federal Reserve banks, Federal Open Market Committee, Federal Advisory Council, and the Board of Governors. The member banks are those commercial banks that have chosen or have been required to join the system. All national banks[1] (those commercial banks whose charters were issued by the United States Treasury Department) must join the Federal Reserve system. They do this by buying a certain amount of the stock of the Federal Reserve bank in whose district they are located. As member banks they have all the rights and privileges of membership, of course, but are also

---

[1] Having a national charter does not give a bank the right to operate anywhere in the nation, as is often supposed. State banking laws bar this. Instead, all banks, whether national or state, are restricted in their operations primarily to the state in which they are headquartered.

TABLE 4.9
Selected items from consolidated statements of condition of all Federal
Reserve Banks, July 31, 1977 ($ billion)

Assets		Liabilities	
Gold certificate account	11.6	Federal Reserve notes	86.7
Loans: Member bank borrowings	.8	Deposits	
		Member bank reserves	26.9
U.S. government securities	96.4	U.S. Treasury	8.8
		Foreign	.5
Other assets	23.3	Other liabilities and capital	9.2
Total assets	132.1	Total liabilities and capital	132.1

Source: *Federal Reserve Bulletin* (August 1977), A12.

subject to Federal Reserve control and supervision. State banks (the commercial banks with charters issued by individual states) have the right to
join the system by the same route if they so choose and can meet the
minimum requirements. Some state banks have chosen to join the system;
more have not. In mid-1977 barely more than 1,000 state banks were
members. Over 8,500 had opted to stay out. Adding the 1,000-plus state
member banks to the 4,700 national member banks gives a total figure of
something over 5,700 member banks — out of the 14,633 commercial
banks in the United States. Since nearly all the largest banks in the country
are national banks, though, and the largest of the state banks are members
of the Federal Reserve system, the influence of the Federal Reserve authorities is greater than this 5.7:14.6 ratio suggests. Total deposits in
member banks typically amount to about 75 percent of total commercial
bank deposits. This means that the Federal Reserve authorities have direct
control over 75 percent of the total money supply. And since their most
important monetary control instrument, open market operations, affects
deposits in nonmember as well as member banks, they have indirect
control over the total money supply.

Rather than set up one central bank, as is typical in many countries,
our Congress so feared centralized banking power that it established
twelve central banks and scattered them and their twenty-four branches
across the country. Within their districts, the Federal Reserve banks operate in some ways much like ordinary commercial banks. As Table 4.9
indicates, they hold deposits, make loans, and buy securities, as do commercial banks. An examination of these deposits, loans, and securities, as

well as the other items on the statement of condition, however, suggests that these are far from being ordinary commercial banks.

Under liabilities we see listed no deposits of the public. Instead, we find the member bank reserve balances discussed earlier, United States Treasury checking balances, and foreign deposit balances, mainly those of foreign central banks and governments. These tell us that the Federal Reserve banks are bankers' banks and banks for the government. The assets side tells us the same thing. The banks make loans exclusively to member banks and hold as securities only United States Treasury securities or federal agency obligations. These two are very important accounts. Although the total of member-bank borrowings was not large on July 31, 1977, the availability of loans from the Federal Reserve banks can play a significant role in the life of a commercial bank. Should such a bank fall into difficulties and desperately need a financial transfusion, it can always turn to the Federal Reserve if loans are not available elsewhere. The Federal Reserve banks thus serve as lenders of last resort for member banks. The Treasury securities account is important for a different reason. As mentioned previously, open market operations are the most important of the Federal Reserve's monetary control devices; purchases for and sales from the United States government securities account constitute *open market operations.*

The remaining two accounts only serve to confirm the role of the Federal Reserve banks as bankers' banks and banks for the government. Although no longer required by law, claims against the Treasury's gold stock are held as partial backing for the paper money issued by the Federal Reserve banks in the form of Federal Reserve notes. By issuing this paper currency to the commercial banks, the Federal Reserve banks have assumed part of the constitutional mandate that Congress should assure the country of an adequate money supply.

Once the Federal Reserve authorities recognized the power of open market operations, which they did in the 1920s, it was perhaps an inevitable next step to set up a separate committee to control such operations. The Federal Open Market Committee has exercised such control since the 1930s. The committee is made up of all seven members of the Board of Governors plus five of the Federal Reserve bank presidents. With a majority of the membership on the committee, the Board of Governors is able effectively to make the decisions concerning the extent and timing of open market operations.

The Federal Advisory Council needs little attention. It is ordinarily made up of twelve bankers selected by the district Federal Reserve banks and represents the formal channel through which the banking community gets the ear of the Board of Governors. How often or how attentively the Board of Governors listens to the Federal Advisory Council is not generally known, but all public information suggests that the council's influence is not great.

Finally, we come to the capstone of the system, the Board of Governors. Here is where all the important decisions are made concerning the achievement of the Federal Reserve's major objectives: "to help counteract inflationary and deflationary movements, and to share in creating conditions favorable to a sustained, high level of employment, a stable dollar, growth of the country, and a rising level of consumption."[2] The board is made up of seven members appointed by the president of the United States and confirmed by the Senate. Members serve fourteen-year, staggered terms, so that one member of the board is ordinarily replaced every two years. This means that a president during a four-year term in office will rarely have the opportunity to appoint more than two members of the Board of Governors, although he does have the authority to designate the chairman and vice-chairman. And while he has the power to appoint new members to fill vacancies on the board, the president has no authority to remove members once appointed. Nor does Congress. Further, since the Federal Reserve generates far more funds than are necessary to finance its operations (through receipt of interest payments on the United States government securities it holds), it cannot be controlled "by the purse." By design, it has been thoroughly insulated from direct influence by Congress and the executive branch.

Monetary management

Monetary policy is the attempt to influence the level and direction of economic activity by controlling the size and availability of the money supply. Congress and the executive branch may advise and make recommendations, but as has been suggested, the determination and implementation of monetary policy are the responsibility of the Board of Governors of the Federal Reserve system. We have already reviewed the mechanics of money creation. It is necessary now only to examine more carefully the levers that the Federal Reserve Board pulls and the cranks it turns in determining the size and availability of the money supply. The flow chart presented as Figure 4.1 shows the board at work.

The chart identifies the three important tools that the Federal Reserve uses to control the size and rate of growth of the money supply: changes in reserve requirements, open market operations, and changes in the discount rate. Notice that all of them make their impact on the money supply by way of the reserve accounts of member banks.

---

[2] Board of Governors of the Federal Reserve System, *The Federal Reserve System: Purposes and Functions,* 5th ed., U.S. Government Printing Office, Washington, D.C., 1963, p. 1.

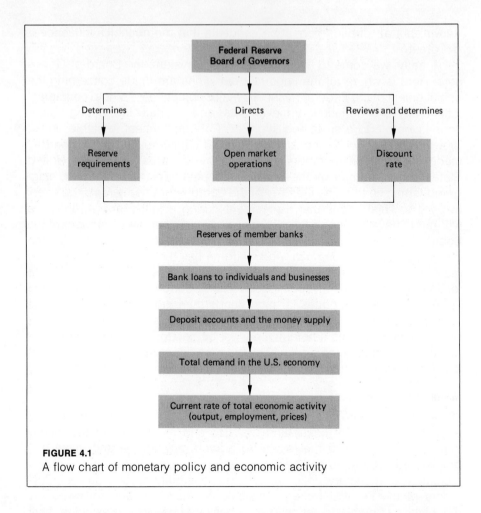

FIGURE 4.1
A flow chart of monetary policy and economic activity

Changes in reserve requirements Changes in reserve requirements affect the money supply by creating excess reserves or by forcing member banks into a situation where they have deficient reserves. Such changes also alter the size of the *money multiplier.* Let's say that the reserve requirement is 20 percent and the banks are fully loaned up, as in Table 4.10.

To create a situation of "easy money," the Federal Reserve Board now reduces the reserve requirement to 15 percent. By this action alone, a substantial portion of what were required reserves are converted into excess reserves. With a 20 percent reserve requirement, the banks needed to maintain reserves at the level of $20 billion (.20 × $100 billion). When the reserve requirement comes down to 15 percent, only $15 billion is needed in the reserve accounts (.15 × $100 billion). The banks now have

$5 billion in excess reserves, which they will promptly convert into loans and demand deposits. But the denominator of the money expansion formula, as well as the numerator, is affected by the board's action:

$$\text{Change in demand deposits} = \frac{\text{excess reserves}}{\text{reserve ratio}} = \frac{\$5 \text{ billion}}{.15} = \$33.3 \text{ billion}$$

Because of the change in the denominator, the banks expand the money supply, not by $25 billion ($5 billion/.20), but by $33.3 billion ($5 billion/.15). As this illustrates, reducing the reserve requirement can powerfully augment the money supply. In the present case, reducing the reserve requirement from 20 to 15 percent expanded the money supply by 33 percent, as shown in Table 4.11.

TABLE 4.10
Banking system consolidated statement of condition with reserve requirement set at 20 percent ($ billion)

Assets		Liabilities	
Cash reserves	20	Demand deposits	100
Loans	80		

TABLE 4.11
Banking system consolidated statement of condition after change in the reserve requirement to 15 percent ($ billion)

Assets		Liabilities	
Cash reserves	20.0	Demand deposits	133.3
Loans	113.3		

TABLE 4.12
Banking system consolidated statement of condition after change in the reserve requirement to 25 percent ($ billion)

Assets		Liabilities	
Cash reserves	20	Demand deposits	80
Loans	60		

But let's move the reserve requirement in the other direction, just to be sure that our vehicle has a reverse gear. The Federal Reserve Board, instead of reducing the reserve requirement to 15 percent, increases it to 25 percent. The banks suddenly find themselves with deficient reserve balances. With the 25 percent requirement they need $25 billion in reserves (.25 × $100 billion), but they only have $20 billion. They must, therefore, either somehow increase their reserves to $25 billion or reduce their demand deposits sufficiently to give them 25 percent coverage of their deposits. A moment's thought will tell us that they are not likely to find an additional $5 billion of reserves. The Federal Reserve banks won't lend them the reserves — not when the Federal Reserve authorities are trying to reduce the money supply. And sales of securities from the bank's portfolios fail to add to overall bank reserves. What one bank gains as a payment must come from some other bank's deposits and reserves. The only route open to the banks is, therefore, to reduce their deposits by reducing their loans. This is what a "tight money" policy is all about. Banks call in their callable loans and refuse to make additional loans as old loans are paid off. Loans are ordinarily paid off by the borrowers writing checks against demand deposits. The bookkeeping consequence is that both demand deposits and loans fall by equal amounts when loans are repaid. Within a short period of time, without any change in the actual size of reserve balances, demand deposits fall to the point where they can legally be supported by the available reserves. This can be seen in Table 4.12.

More than this, should the banks now gain excess reserves, they can expand their loans and demand deposits less than formerly because the size of the money multiplier has decreased.

$$\text{Change in demand deposits} = \frac{\text{excess reserves}}{\text{reserve ratio}} = \frac{1}{.25} = 4$$

It is apparent, then, that changes in reserve requirements do work symmetrically: Reducing the reserve ratio expands the money supply; increasing the ratio forces a contraction of the money supply. Nevertheless, Federal Reserve authorities in recent years have rarely used this powerful instrument. Reserve requirements have been changed only rarely in the immediate past and then by only small amounts. One reason for this is that changes in reserve requirements are too powerful and too clumsy a tool. Changing the reserve ratio by a fraction of a percent causes a multi-billion dollar swing in the money supply. Also, the banks don't like to make the adjustments required when the ratio changes. Further, the Federal Reserve Board has authority to set reserve requirements only for member banks, and these banks fear that they will be placed at a competitive disadvantage relative to nonmember banks when requirements are changed. Most importantly, though, everything that changes in the reserve ratio can do, open market operations can do better. And nonmember banks will be affected equally with member banks in the process.

Open market operations   The mechanics of open market operations are simple. When the Federal Reserve authorities want conditions of *easy money* — loans readily available at moderate interest rates — they order the Open Market Committee to *buy* United States government securities in the open market to add to the holding of the Federal Reserve banks. When they want *tight money* — loans hard to come by and at high interest rates — they order the Open Market Committee to *sell* part of the Federal Reserve banks' holdings of United States government securities. Let's trace through each of these transactions to see the impact on the banking system and the money supply.

First, let's imagine the banks in a fully loaned-up position and then have the Federal Reserve buy $10 billion of Treasury securities in the open market. If the Federal Reserve is buying, then someone else is selling. We'll assume it is Metropolitan Life that is selling off part of its Treasury securities portfolio. The Federal Reserve Bank of New York, which handles all these open market transactions for the whole Federal Reserve system, pays for the securities by writing a check against itself. Metropolitan Life promptly deposits the check in its account at the Chase Manhattan Bank. When the check clears at the Federal Reserve Bank of New York, the commercial banking system has gained both demand deposits of $10 billion and also additional reserves in the amount of $10 billion. The public's money supply has already been increased by $10 billion. Of even greater importance, the banking system is now in a position to further expand the money supply because it has gained excess reserves. If the reserve requirement is 20 percent, Chase Manhattan will need to hold only $2 billion in reserve against Metropolitan Life's $10 billion deposit. The other $8 billion can be worked off by loan expansion and deposit creation. As we saw earlier, this gives some other bank or banks new deposits, excess reserves, and additional lending capacity in the amount of $6.4 billion. And on and on the process goes. Ultimately, the excess reserves created when the Federal Reserve Bank of New York bought the $10 billion of Treasury securities will permit a total expansion of the money supply by $40 billion, for a total increase in the money supply of $50 billion

$$\$10 \text{ billion} + \frac{1}{.2} (\$8 \text{ billion})$$

A very powerful monetary operation indeed and one that can be expanded virtually without limit since outstanding Treasury securities available for purchase amount to hundreds of billions of dollars (this is part of the public debt, remember) and the Federal Reserve banks can buy them simply by writing checks against themselves.

Now let's turn the whole operation around. The Federal Reserve authorities have decided that the economy is overly exuberant, and they want to slow it down by creating tight money conditions — loans hard to come by at higher prices. This calls for open market sales. The Federal Reserve Bank of New York now looks for buyers for $10 billion of Treasury securities held by the Federal Reserve banks. You might wonder what would happen if no buyer could be found, but this can't happen. The Federal Reserve banks are in the unique position of not needing to show a profit in their operations; they are not ordinary profit-oriented banks. Since their primary function is to stabilize the economy, they are prepared to do this at a loss if necessary. (With around $100 billion worth of interest-bearing United States government securities in their combined portfolios, of course, they can stand a considerable number of loss-incurring sales and still show net earnings for the year.) At some price, surely, a buyer for these securities will come forward. And ordinarily they are able to sell securities at around their face value.

In the present case, Prudential Life decides to buy the Federal Reserve's offering. Life insurance companies have discovered over the years that Treasury securities, which pay a reasonably attractive rate of interest and are virtually risk-free, are an excellent form in which to hold part of their accumulated life insurance reserves. Prudential, therefore, writes a check for $10 billion in favor of the Federal Reserve Bank of New York against Prudential's account in Citibank. When the check clears, Prudential loses $10 billion from its deposit account and Citibank loses $10 billion from its reserve account. Another way of saying this is that the public's money supply has already fallen by $10 billion and the banks have yet to reckon with an $8 billion deficiency in reserve balances (only $8 billion, not $10 billion, because reserves no longer have to be held against the now-departed $10 billion in demand deposits). Failing to secure additional reserves, the banking system must now reduce demand deposits by the amount that the lost reserves previously supported — by $40 billion (again, $1/.2 \times \$8$ billion). As we saw earlier when examining the consequences of increasing reserve requirements, they do this by reducing their outstanding loans and carefully rationing new loans at higher interest rates to selected customers. The awesome power of open market sales can only be fully appreciated when we recognize that each dollar's worth of open market sales reduces bank reserves by a dollar. Should the Federal Reserve dump its entire holding of United States government securities in one massive sale, it would be more than sufficient to wipe out all bank reserves, those of member as well as nonmember banks — the latter because the deposit accounts against which checks are written in payment for the securities could just as easily be in nonmember as member banks.

Changes in the discount rate Having described changes in reserve requirements and open market operations, it comes as somewhat of an anticlimax to report that changes in the discount rate are today a minor monetary control device — a capgun among shotguns. But first, what is the discount rate? A discount is a special form of loan on which interest is deducted (discounted) before it is earned — that is, when the loan is made, rather than when it is repaid. The interest rate charged is called the *discount rate.* The term is a carry-over from the early days of the Federal Reserve, when loans to member banks typically took the form of discounts or rediscounts. It survives in an age when most such loans are of the ordinary commercial variety where interest is paid when the loan is repaid. According to present practice, then, the discount rate is nothing more than the interest rate charged member banks when they borrow from the Federal Reserve banks.

We have already seen, though, that member banks do little borrowing at the "discount window." In fact, the Federal Reserve discourages member bank borrowing except when absolutely necessary. Then how does changing the discount rate affect the money supply when banks so rarely borrow? The discount rate today serves mainly as a signal by which the Federal Reserve tells member banks of a change in the financial climate. When the Federal Reserve Board raises the discount rate, it is signaling a shift in the direction of tight money. Knowing that if they are forced to go to the discount window they will pay more for loans, member banks will cover themselves in advance by charging their own customers higher interest

the small society   by Brickman

© Washington Star Syndicate, Inc., permission granted by King Features Syndicate, Inc., 1977.

rates. The higher cost for bank loans serves to check loan expansion, and the check in loan expansion, as we have seen, restricts the expansion of the money supply. Exactly the reverse process sets in, of course, when the discount rate is reduced. Usually used in conjunction with open market operations pointed in the same direction, changes in the discount rate continue to play a role, though a fairly minor one, in the implementation of monetary policy.

Monetary policy: some pros and cons

Use of monetary policy to stabilize the economy has had its ups and downs in the period since the establishment of the Federal Reserve system. During the Roaring Twenties, it appeared that the Federal Reserve could guide the economy into a period of everlasting prosperity. Then came 1929, the Great Crash, and more than a decade of depression in which monetary policy seemed to be impotent. Going by the book, the Federal Reserve generated larger and larger amounts of excess bank reserves. But the banks failed to work off their excess reserves and increase the money supply because they couldn't find willing, credit-worthy borrowers. It was decided that the Federal Reserve couldn't "push on a string." It could create excess reserves but could not force the public to borrow. Fiscal policy, however, an alternative economic stabilization device, adequately proved its effectiveness when massive government spending during World War II and the consequent large federal deficits quickly brought the economy to the full-employment level of production. Fiscal policy (changes in the level of government spending and tax rates), therefore, largely supplanted monetary policy as a stabilization device.

In the years after World War II, though, fiscal policy proved that it too had feet of clay. Fighting a depression by the use of fiscal policy is easy, since everyone likes lower taxes and most people, especially the recipients of the government checks, like more government spending. When inflation succeeds depression as Public Enemy Number 1, on the other hand, fiscal policy calls for an increase in taxes and a reduction of government spending. These, to put it mildly, are not so popular. Moreover, during a good many of the postwar years the United States has been engaged in military adventures of one sort or another, making it next to impossible to reduce the federal budget. Logic and necessity both suggested a shift back from fiscal to monetary policy, and the latter has come into its own again during the last decade.

The results of using monetary policy in recent years have been mixed. Careful control of the monetary reins by the Federal Reserve during the early 1960s helped to provide the economy with both nearly stable prices and steadily falling levels of unemployment. But no one who has lived through the years since the late 1960s needs to be told that things have not been so well managed: For the first time in our history we have suffered through a number of years marked by both inflation and high levels of unemployment — from what we describe with the ugly word *stagflation.*

We are by no means sure why monetary policy (fiscal policy too, for that matter) apparently cannot control upward movements in the price level except at the expense of intolerably high levels of unemployment. There are grounds for believing that the economy has changed sufficiently in recent years that the assumptions on which the quantity theory of money and the flow chart of Figure 4.1 are based are no longer valid. This is especially true of the premise that the economy is marked by a high degree of competition and minimal amounts of power in the hands of individuals or groups.

The normal assumption of both quantity theorists and the flow chart illustration is that inflation calls for a reduction, or at least a reduced rate of growth, of the money supply. If M increases more rapidly than Q in the equation of exchange [$\Delta M = \Delta(PQ) = \Delta GNP$], then the consequence has to be rising prices (ΔP). Reducing the rate of increase of M to that of Q should eliminate any possibility of price-level increases. The strategy is based, then, on the premise that reducing the rate of growth of the money supply may somewhat cut the rate of increase of real output (Q), but that its primary impact will be on the price level. If the American marketplace is characterized by vigorous competition, the premise makes sense. Slowing down the increase in Q creates slack in both commodity and labor markets by reducing demand for both goods and workers. In the face of slack demand, how can wages be forced up, necessitating higher prices? How can businessmen demand — and get — higher prices when markets are weak?

The presence of strong labor organizations and gigantic, highly concentrated business firms permits both of these things to happen. Labor unions have proved over and over that they can indeed force up wages during periods of recession and high unemployment. And while recession will restrain prices in the competitive part of the business world, it may actually aggravate price-level increases in the oligopolistic sector — as described in Chapter Six. A moderate reduction in the rate of growth of the money supply, then, may bring on a recession but little relief from inflation. A major reduction in the growth of money, it is true, or an actual reduction of the amount in circulation would surely curb price-level increases. With an actual fall in the money supply, there just wouldn't be money available to pay higher wages or higher prices. But our recent experience suggests that the deep recession accompanying such a drastic step would be socially and, especially, politically unacceptable.

One major reason such a step would be unacceptable is that a tight money policy has an uneven impact on different sectors of the economy. Tight money, remember, means fewer bank loans and higher interest rates. When credit rationing is necessary, though, it takes little imagination to guess which bank borrowers will be rationed out of the market first and which last. Small businessmen and families with weak credit ratings go first; big business firms last, if at all. And the credit extended to small businessmen and families with weak credit ratings is apt to carry much higher interest charges. Finally, big businesses are quite likely to escape the consequences of tight money completely by staying away from the banks. They typically generate nearly all the funds they need by plowing back profits.

Even if monetary policy could be based explicitly on the monetarist and flow chart models, there would still be difficulties for the Federal Reserve authorities. One is bound up with the question of what M we have in mind when we assume that $\Delta M \rightarrow \Delta(PQ)$. We have been assuming up to this point that M means demand deposits since the use of demand deposits means spending on new goods and services. But spending is a consequence of a willingness to spend, and the willingness to spend may be as much affected by holdings of store-of-value money (near money) as by medium-of-exchange money (actual liquidity). It makes sense to assume — and empirical studies back up the assumption — that the larger our savings balances the more willing we are to spend a high proportion of our monthly pay checks. If the Federal Reserve authorities are really concerned about regulating the rate of spending in the economy, then, they must concern themselves not only with what they call M_1 (currency and demand deposits) but also with M_2 (M_1 plus savings deposits, time deposits open account, and certificates of deposit), something that can be controlled only with less certainty and more difficulty.

In fact, the problem doesn't end with M_2. Wealth can be accumulated in many other forms and still affect our current spending decisions as importantly as do our savings balances. Large amounts of near-monies accumulate routinely in mutual savings banks, savings and loan associations, and credit unions — none of which are directly under the control of the Federal Reserve. And once we've opened this door, what about Treasury securities and even stocks and bonds and the cash or loan value of life insurance policies? While admitting their difficulties here, the Federal Reserve authorities argue the presence of all these store-of-value monies does not make their task of monetary management impossible. All these other monies are more or less directly tied to the medium-of-exchange money, M_1. Increase demand deposits and part will spill over into savings accounts and other store-of-value holdings; reduce demand deposits and you also reduce store-of-value holdings. Even so, neither the monetarists nor the Federal Reserve authorities have yet decided whether the M to be controlled is M_1, M_2, or one of the several other Ms that the Federal Reserve now keeps track of.

And even if the Federal Reserve authorities could make up their minds as to which M to control, they would still face major problems in timing their actions. The fact is that in this complex economy we rarely know for sure exactly where we are in the business cycle — whether the economy is still expanding, for example, or whether we have begun a downward slide. Some statistical series of economic activity may still be rising at the same time that others are falling. The National Bureau of Economic Research provides some help here with its *leading indicators*. These are the statistical series — such as stock market prices — that typically change direction in advance of the rest of the economy. The trouble is that these are not entirely reliable. As one wit said, the leading indicators have predicted all nine of the last three recessions. There is inescapably, then, a recognition lag in the application of monetary policy — or any other countercyclical policy.

Once the change in the direction of the economy is generally recognized, of course, the Board of Governors can alter policies quickly. But then another problem: How long will it take for the policy measures to take hold? How long will it take for banks to work off excess reserves by expanding their loans and increasing the money supply? How long will it take banks to contract their lending and the money supply if they are confronted by deficient reserves? Unfortunately, this reaction lag, according to empirical studies, is both long and variable. This may be fatal for the successful implementation of monetary policy. Increased open market purchases undertaken to cure a recession may bear fruit in the form of increased spending over a year later, just when the economy may have recovered of its own momentum and entered a period of excessive spending and consequent inflation. "Fine-tuning" the economy by the use of monetary policy thus appears to have more than its share of problems.

Whether or not the Federal Reserve authorities will ever be able to guide the economy along a stable-price, full-employment path is still open

the small society   by Brickman

to question. That they are determined to try, however, is subject to no doubt whatsoever. In fact, they would be remiss in their duties if they failed to make the attempt. In the process they will undoubtedly make mistakes — mistakes that will be paid for by everyone in the form of depreciating dollars or enforced idleness or both. Most important, the decisions made by the Federal Reserve, despite the fact that they will affect every American, will be made in secret without any pretense of democratic control or accountability. If the president of the United States makes a decision that leads to inflation or rising unemployment, we can vote him out of office. But if the Federal Reserve Board does the same, there is no way the public can hold the members of the Board accountable for their actions. Many critics of the Federal Reserve see this as an intolerable situation.

On the other hand, how could we make the Federal Reserve Board accountable without at the same time turning the system into a political football? The condition of the economy clearly affects the chances of public officials to be re-elected. Give them the power to control the Federal Reserve, and monetary policy might follow the election returns. Even as things are now, Federal Reserve Board Chairman Arthur Burns was accused of heating up the economy to assure President Nixon's re-election in 1972. Maybe there is some intermediate point between complete autonomy for Federal Reserve officials and all-out political control of the system. But if there is, we haven't found it yet.

All of which brings us full-circle, back to the proposition with which this chapter opened: Money is vitally necessary for the successful functioning of an exchange economy, but it is difficult in the extreme to understand fully and control effectively.

I SUMMARY I

Money is anything that serves generally as a medium of exchange, store of value, or standard of value. Medium-of-exchange money in the United States at the present time consists of coins, currency (paper money), and demand deposits (checking account balances). Of these, far and away the most important are demand deposits.

The role of money in an exchange economy is usually pictured in terms of the so-called equation of exchange: $MV = PQ$. The left-hand side of the equation represents the average amount of money in circulation multiplied by the number of times each money unit is used, or turned over, during the period (velocity of circulation). This total has to equal total spending on new goods and services (Q) multiplied by the average prices of these goods and services (P) — which is GNP.

By assuming that V and Q are constants, the equation of exchange is turned into a crude quantity theory of money: Changes in M must shortly be followed by proportionate changes in overall prices. If Q is free to vary but V is not, we get the modern quantity theory: Changes in M must be followed by roughly equal changes in P or Q or both — in current-dollar *GNP.*

If changes in the money supply lead to changes in the national income, it is important to know who creates money in the United States and how its creation is controlled. The answer is that the commercial banks create most of the money (the demand deposits) through their lending and investing activities, and they are controlled in these activities by the Federal Reserve authorities.

The Federal Reserve exercises its influence by controlling the amount and effectiveness of the legal reserves held by commercial banks against their demand deposits. By engaging in open market buying of Treasury securities, reducing reserve requirements, or reducing member bank discount rates, the Federal Reserve Board of Governors permits and encourages an expansion of bank lending, which leads to an increase in the money supply; by engaging in open market selling, increasing reserve requirements, or increasing the discount rate, it does the opposite. This is what monetary policy is all about.

Monetary policy has been less than completely effective in the United States. Although a change in M will change *GNP,* it may do this through influencing P or influencing Q — but to this point we have not been able to predict accurately the avenue or magnitude of influence. There are also problems in determining how long it will take changes in the rate of growth of the money supply to influence economic activity.

I   IMPORTANT TERMS AND CONCEPTS   I

medium of exchange	reserve requirement
currency	money multiplier
demand deposits	open market operations
equation of exchange	monetary policy
quantity theory of money	discount rate
time deposits	

I   QUESTIONS, PROBLEMS, AND EXERCISES   I

1 Are checks money?

2 Why do banks make an effort to hold the bare minimum of reserves required by law?

3 Since with a 20 percent reserve requirement one dollar in reserves supports five dollars in demand deposits, why can't a *single bank* in a multibank system make loans and create deposits up to five times the amount of any excess reserves it holds? Why, in other words, is it safe for an individual bank to loan only an amount equal to its actual excess reserves?

4 Why do we no longer assume that there is a direct and proportionate relationship between changes in the money supply and changes in the price level?

5 Assume that unemployment has fallen to low levels and inflation is getting out of hand. How would the appropriate monetary policy be described and what would you call for by way of possible changes in reserve requirements? Open market operations? Discount rate?

6 Are the Federal Reserve banks branches of the federal government?

7 Why is it that when the Federal Reserve changes the level of its open market operations the consequences are felt throughout the banking system, but when it changes reserve requirements it affects the member banks almost exclusively?

8 The current reserve requirement is 20 percent and the *banking system's* balance sheet shows the following:

Reserves	22	Demand deposits	100
Loans and investments	78		

(a) What is the amount of required reserves? (b) What is the amount of excess reserves, if any? (c) If there are excess reserves and the banks work them off by expanding their loans and demand deposits, what does the balance sheet look like when this process is completed? (*Hint*: Each dollar of reserves, with a 20 percent reserve requirement, will support five dollars in demand deposits.)

I SUGGESTED READING I

Bach, G. L. *Making Monetary and Fiscal Policy.* Brookings Institution, Washington, D.C., 1971.

Federal Reserve Board. *The Federal Reserve System — Purposes and Functions.* Board of Governors of the Federal Reserve System, U.S. Government Printing Office, Washington, D.C., 1974.

Friedman, Milton. *An Economist's Protest: Columns in Political Economy.* Thomas Horton, Glen Ridge, N.J., 1972.

Galbraith, John Kenneth. *Money: Whence It Came, Where It Went.* Bantam, New York, 1976.

Maisel, Sherman. *Managing the Dollar.* Norton, New York, 1973.

Ritter, Lawrence S., and William L. Silber. *Money.* Basic Books, New York, 1970.

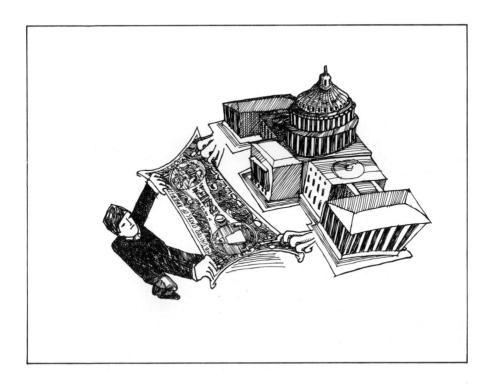

FIVE

GOVERNMENT IN THE ECONOMY: SPENDING AND TAXES

No one today needs to be told that government plays an important role in our lives. The evidence is all around us. Whether doctor, lawyer, merchant, or chief, it's a rare day that a person's life is not affected in some degree by the actions or rules of some governmental unit: the federal government, one of the fifty state governments or agencies, or one of the 78,218 local governments. We continue to call ours a private-enterprise economy, but it is always difficult, sometimes impossible, to tell where private enterprise leaves off and government begins. We have a thoroughly mixed economy.

Other chapters describe government in action: stabilizing the economy, controlling the money and banking system, setting the terms for foreign trade and finance, attempting to control big business and big labor, and laying down rules and regulations under which we all live. This chapter has a different focus: to describe the size of government and identify some of the reasons government has grown so large; to describe the functions government performs and for which it spends our money; and to identify the ways government extracts our money from us in the form of taxation. Out of this, we hope, will come some ideas as to how we can set rules for rational government spending and how tax collections can be improved so the necessary money can be raised with minimal disruption of our lives.

I GOVERNMENT SPENDING I

The growth of government spending

A quick way to picture the increase in government spending is to compare snapshots of government expenditures then and now. For the federal government, financial records are excellent, all the way back to the first years under the Constitution. It is more difficult for state and local governments, because there are so many of them and their records are less complete. The term _local governments_ covers a multiplicity of spending units, ranging all the way from counties, cities, and towns to school districts, highway districts, cemetery districts, sewerage districts, and port authorities, among others. And although we tend almost automatically to think of _government_ as the federal government, over most of our history state and local governments have played the more important role in our lives in terms of both spending and taxation as well as regulation. Only in the last half-century has the federal government come to the fore as the most important unit, both in terms of size and in terms of control over our daily lives.

By 1821 the federal government had already experienced a considerable amount of growth. Its total outlays during that year amounted to almost $16 million — $1.59 for every man, woman, and child in the country. To administer an undertaking of this size required, in addition to a modest army and navy, a civilian staff of 6,914, of whom 4,766 were Post Office employees.

Only with the beginning of the twentieth century are companion figures available for state and local governments. Putting them together with the federal figures gives a combined expenditure in 1902 of $1,660 _million_ — $21.71 for each American: $7.45 spent by the federal government, $1.78 by state governments, and $12.48 by local governments. This $1,660 million represented 7.7 percent of the year's gross national product of $21.6 billion. To administer its spending of $572 million, the federal government required 239,476 civilian employees (in 1901), over half (136,192) employed by the Post Office. Even before the age of big government, then, we find a steady growth of government. On a per capita basis, federal spending doubled and then doubled again during the years 1821–1902. And although we don't have the figures to document it, we can be reasonably sure that state and local spending did the same.

Even so, the really explosive growth in expenditures came in the twentieth century, in particular during the half-century from 1930 to the present. By 1974 the three levels of government had combined expenditures of $480 *billion*: $254 billion federal, $86 billion state, and $139 billion local. This $480 billion made up just over one-third (34 percent) of the year's gross national product. For every person in the country the federal government spent $1,203; the state and local governments combined, $1,068. Total government civilian employment had risen to 14,628,000, or 16 percent of the country's civilian labor force. Putting it another way, we had reached the point by 1974 where 1 worker out of 6 drew a government paycheck. Lest the impression be left that the bulk of these government workers were concentrated on the banks of the Potomac, it should be pointed out that the federal government had under employment only 2.9 million of these civilian workers, and not all of these were in or even near Washington. State and local governments hired the balance, 11.7 million.[1] So insistent was the demand for government spending that it consistently outran available revenues, resulting in a sharp rise in indebtedness. In 1975 the combined public debt reached $741.2 billion, of

the small society   by Brickman

I'LL TELL YOU WHAT I LIKED ABOUT THE GOOD OLD DAYS —

FOR ONE THING, BIG SPENDERS SPENT THEIR OWN MONEY!

Washington Star Syndicate Inc.

BRICKMAN

11-4

---

[1] These figures from the *Statistical Abstract of the United States,* 1976, pp. 248, 284.

which $446.3 billion was owed by the federal government, $78.8 billion by federally sponsored credit agencies (such as the Federal Home Loan Banks, Federal Land Banks, and the Federal National Mortgage Association), and $216.1 by state and local governments.[2]

In case you got swept away in the flood of statistics, the key figures are highlighted in Figures 5.1, 5.2, and 5.3. Figure 5.1 pictures the dramatic rise in the share of gross national product taken by government during the course of the twentieth century: from 7.7 percent in 1902 to 35 percent in 1975. What this meant for the average citizen of the United States is portrayed in Figure 5.2, which shows per capita spending at all levels of government literally exploding between 1902 and 1974. Finally, Figure 5.3 identifies one of the major reasons for this rise in government spending — the extraordinary increase in government payrolls.

Figures compiled by the international Organization for Economic Co-operation and Development (OECD) suggest that American developments

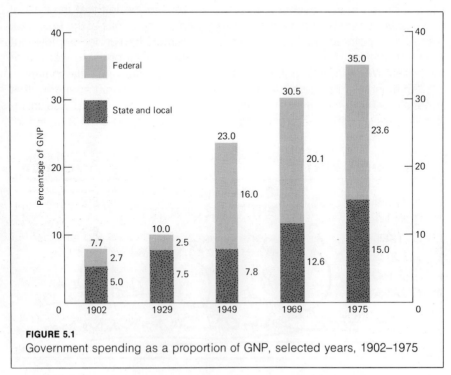

FIGURE 5.1

Government spending as a proportion of GNP, selected years, 1902–1975

Source: *Economic Report of the President, 1977,* and *Historical Statistics of the United States, 1975.*

---

[2] *Economic Report of the President,* 1977, p. 265.

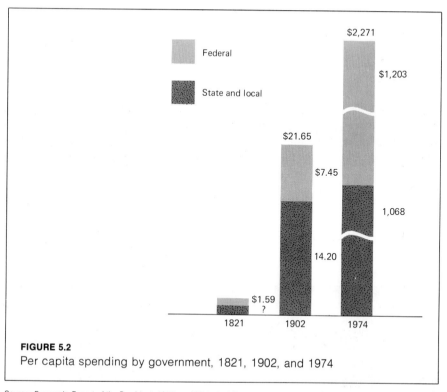

FIGURE 5.2
Per capita spending by government, 1821, 1902, and 1974

Source: *Economic Report of the President*, 1977, and *Historical Statistics of the United States*, 1975.

are not out of line with those in other parts of the world. Table 5.1 gives their figures, which are somewhat different from those just cited because they have been adjusted to allow comparison of one country with another. Except for Japan overall government spending represents about the same share of national income in all the major non-Communist nations. And even Japan is not that far out of line when account is taken of the fact that the country has almost no defense establishment to support and that social security is provided primarily by private employers.

Why governments have grown

Even if no additional duties had been taken on by the government sector over the past couple of centuries, the costs of government would have grown. In overall dollar terms, costs would be greater simply because there are now more people to be served. But we saw that this fact doesn't take us very far because costs have increased markedly even on a per capita basis. One thing we didn't take note of when we put forward the per capita figures is that 1821 dollars are not 1902 dollars, nor are 1902 dollars the same as 1974 dollars. To take just the latter period, wholesale prices

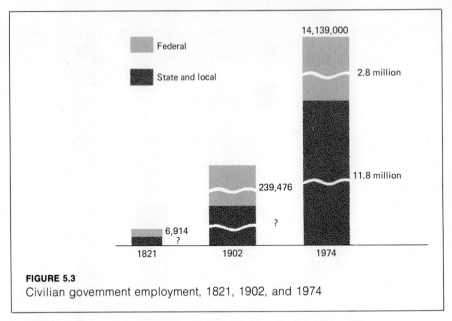

FIGURE 5.3
Civilian government employment, 1821, 1902, and 1974

Source: *Economic Report of the President*, 1974, and *Historical Statistics of the United States*, 1975.

were only 30 percent as high in 1902 as they were in 1967, and in 1974 they were 60 percent higher than they had been in 1967. Another way of putting this is to turn these figures into purchasing power equivalents: a 1902 dollar had 3.3 times the purchasing power of a 1967 dollar; a 1974 dollar would buy only 62.5 percent as much as a 1967 dollar. Overall government expenditures therefore would have had to rise by over 400 percent just to enable governments to continue doing in 1974 what they were doing in 1902.

But government expenditures rose far more rapidly than this would necessitate, as indicated by the fact that government-sector spending rose from less than 8 percent of the 1902 GNP to 35 percent of the 1975 GNP. The rise of government's share of national income, in fact, had been noticed long before the end of the nineteenth century. A German analyst, Adolf Wagner, writing in the 1880s, tied it to the shift in the United States and the western European countries from a predominantly rural-agricultural economy to an urban-industrial society. Farmers don't need too many government services — or at least they didn't use to. But city dwellers do. They need police departments and fire fighters and sewers and sidewalks and piped-in water. And industry adds significantly to the list with its demands for a sophisticated transportation system, an elaborate monetary network, and, especially, educated and trained workers.

A notable advance in the analysis of the growth of government came after World War II, in the form of studies of British and American patterns

TABLE 5.1
Total government outlays as a percentage of gross domestic product, 1975

United States	33.9
United Kingdom	41.3
West Germany	41.7
France	38.9
Italy	39.7
Canada	37.1
Norway	41.9
Belgium	41.6
Denmark	43.0
Japan	20.8

Source: Based on Organisation for Economic Co-operation and Development, *National Accounts of OECD Countries*, Vol. II, Paris, 1975.

of change in public expenditures. Alan T. Peacock and Jack Wiseman, for the United Kingdom, and M. Slade Kendrick, for the United States, demonstrated that in both countries public expenditures did not expand at a uniform rate. Instead, they increased, at least at the federal level, in a series of jumps, from one plateau to the next higher level. This can be seen for the United States in Figure 5.4, where total federal outlays are shown for the last year immediately prior to beginning of a major war, the last year of the war, and the year ten years after the end of the war. The uniform pattern is a sharp rise in spending during the war and a fallback after the war — but never to anything like budgeted outlays during the year before the war began. The Peacock-Wiseman thesis is that war encourages governments to find new sources of tax funds and to raise old taxes to extraordinary levels, all of which the public tolerates in the name of patriotism. By the time the war ends, taxpayers have adjusted to the new levels of taxation, and civilian projects requiring government spending replace the military programs that are cut back. Until the next war government spending rises only as rapidly as the civilian tax base grows, then it jumps to another, higher level.

Military spending, of course, need not rise only in wartime. With only a couple of "police actions" to worry about since the close of World War II, national defense expenditures rose from a postwar low of $12 billion in 1948 to $90 billion in 1976.

That defense-related spending makes up a substantial part of government outlays is an old story. Over the whole of the nineteenth century, defense spending averaged around one-half of the total federal budget.

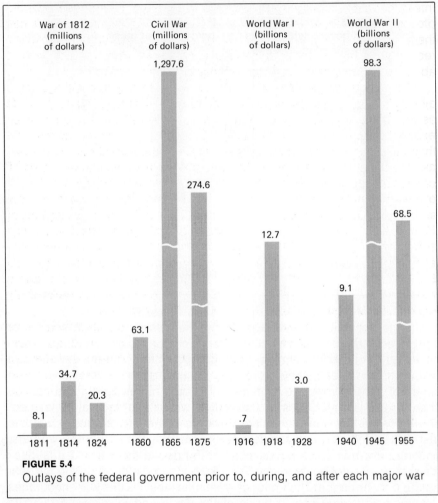

FIGURE 5.4
Outlays of the federal government prior to, during, and after each major war

Source: *Historical Statistics of the United States*, 1975, pp. 1114–1115.

What is new are additional functions that are carried out by government. Many of these stem from the activist New Deal government of Franklin Roosevelt. Governments during the nineteenth century never quite limited themselves to providing police, army, courts, and public education — all the government was allowed to do according to the strict capitalist manifesto — but they made some attempt to. The watchword according to a latter-day exponent of this point of view, President Herbert Hoover, was that while the people are expected to support the government, no one should expect the government to support the people. The Great Depression of the 1930s, however, brought home the fact that many individuals in an interdependent, industrial economy do not always control their own employment and cannot make their way unaided. If government won't help them, who will? The most spectacular growth in government outlays in recent years has been the income-support spending associated with inability to find any other satisfactory answer to this question.

Some see this development as mere humanitarianism. Others see it, along with an increasing number of other government spending projects, as the result of a basic flaw in the mechanism that controls government expenditures. According to Allan H. Meltzer, "The government grows faster than the private sector whenever the costs of government can be diffused and the benefits concentrated. Diffusing costs while concentrating benefits creates incentives for expansion and disincentives for reduction in the size of government."[3] All taxpayers pay for government programs, but the major share of the benefits typically goes to only a few individuals. By organizing into pressure groups, those few individuals can provide effective political support for adoption and continuation of their programs, while only feeble and widely dispersed resistance comes from the taxpayers in general. Ever-expanding government, from this point of view, is an integral part of representative government — a badly flawed part say opponents of the growth of government, who are most apt to hold this view.

From the other side of the spectrum comes the rebuttal that whatever the present size of the government sector, it's too small. And the system is rigged to keep it that way. According to John Kenneth Galbraith, we continue to have a problem of *social imbalance* — too little government spending, so pressing social needs are not met; too much private spending, so we're glutted with trivial consumer goods and services. The reason for this is that the most effective pressure group in the country, the advertising industry, operates exclusively on behalf of private wants. Compared with the impact of the advertising industry on the demand for privately produced goods and services, the efforts of groups organized to promote better schools or public health or garbage collection seem puny indeed. The consequence, according to Galbraith, is private glut and social squalor:

The contrast was and remains evident not alone to those who read. The family which takes its mauve and cerise, air-conditioned, power-steered, and power-braked automobile out for a tour passes through cities that are badly paved, made hideous by litter, blighted buildings, billboards, and posts for wires that should long since have been put underground. They pass on into a countryside that has been rendered largely invisible by commercial art. . . . They picnic on exquisitely packaged food from a portable icebox by a polluted stream and go on to spend

---

[3] Allan H. Meltzer, *Why Government Grows,* International Institute for Economic Research, Original Paper 4, Los Angeles, 1976, p. 7.

the night at a park which is a menace to public health and morals. Just before dozing off on an air mattress, beneath a nylon tent, amid the stench of decaying refuse, they may reflect vaguely on the curious unevenness of their blessings. Is this, indeed, the American genius?[4]

Whether too large or not large enough, the government sector is now of sufficient size that we need be concerned with its cost effectiveness. It is of some importance, then, to see where our money goes and to see if rules can't be devised to ensure that it is effectively spent.

Current patterns of government spending

Federal Perhaps the first thing to notice about federal spending is that the bulk of it today, as Table 5.2 indicates, does not involve active federal participation in the marketplace. Of the $378.7 billion it is estimated the federal government spent in fiscal 1976, barely more than one-third ($130 billion) represented purchases of goods and services that otherwise would have been available for private use. (While it is true that you may not have wanted the military tank the Defense Department bought, it is entirely possible that you would have liked the car — or the several of them — that could have been built with the materials and manpower that went into the

---

TABLE 5.2

Federal expenditures in the national income accounts, 1960 and 1976 ($ billion, for years ending June 30)

	1960	1976 (est.)
Total expenditures	91.3	378.7
Purchases of goods and services	52.7	130.0
National defense	45.0	86.7
Nondefense	7.8	43.3
Transfer payments	22.4	158.7
Grants-in-aid to state and local governments	6.8	57.8
Net interest paid	7.0	26.0
Subsidies less current surplus of government enterprises	2.3	6.2

Source: *Statistical Abstract of the United States,* 1976, p. 229.

---

[4] John Kenneth Galbraith, *The Affluent Society,* Houghton Mifflin, Boston, 1958, p. 253.

tank.) Almost two-thirds of federal spending today represents merely re-distribution of a significant portion of the national income. The federal government serves as a primary agent for picking up funds here and putting them over there.

In the case of transfer payments, it collects the funds from taxpayers and makes gifts of them to selected recipients: for food stamps ($4.6 billion), subsidies to education and training ($2.8 billion), veterans benefits ($14.7 billion), unemployment benefits ($18.1 billion), retirement pay for military ($7.2 billion), and supplemental security income ($4.7 billion). In many programs the recipient has already paid for a substantial part of the benefits he or she now receives. This is true for social security (OASDI — $70.3 billion), railroad retirement ($3.5 billion), civil service retirement ($8.3 billion), and Medicare ($16.5 billion).

The earmark of a transfer payment is an outlay for which the government gets no good or service in exchange during the current accounting period. It is obvious that in all the cases listed above the federal government gets no current direct exchange of a good or service. For all intents and purposes grants-in-aid to state and local governments could be called transfer payments. Most of this $57.8 billion took the form of categorical grants, by which the federal government helped state and local governments fund certain designated programs, such as highways, urban renewal, special education programs, medical aid to the poor (Medicaid), and public assistance. An increasing amount, however, takes the form of *revenue sharing* ($6.3 billion in 1976). These are no-strings-attached disbursements to state and local governments from the general revenues of the federal government. It may seem odd to take money from state and local residents and then return it to their governments by way of Washington, D.C. But the procedure is justified on the grounds that (1) the federal tax system does a fairer job of collecting the money than would the state and local systems and (2) the money never goes back to exactly the same communities from which it comes. The system was designed to provide for some redistribution away from richer communities to poorer regions.

The figures of Table 5.2 suggest that the role of the federal government has been changing in recent years. Table 5.3, which breaks down federal spending by function, confirms this impression. National defense, which in 1960 claimed far and away the largest single part of the federal budget, one dollar out of every two available, had by 1975 been pushed into second place. This did not mean that defense expenditures had declined in absolute amount. On the contrary, the defense outlay more than doubled between 1960 and 1975. But other items in the budget increased at a truly extraordinary rate: general science, space, and technology by six times; natural resources, environment, and energy by seven times; education, manpower, and social services by almost nineteen times; health by an unbelievable forty times; and income security by seven times. The eminent

TABLE 5.3
Federal budget outlays, by function, 1960 and 1975 ($ billion, for years ending June 30)

Function	1960	1975 (est.)
Total outlays	92.2	373.5
National defense	45.2	92.8
% of total	49.0	24.8
International affairs	2.9	5.7
Gen. sci., space, and technology	.7	4.3
Agriculture	2.6	2.9
Natural res., environ., and energy	1.7	11.8
% of total	2.0	3.2
Commerce and transportation	5.8	9.5
Community and regional dev.	.4	3.9
Educ., training, employ., and soc. serv.	1.0	18.9
% of total	1.0	5.0
Health	.8	32.1
% of total	.8	8.6
Income security	18.3	128.5
% of total	19.8	34.4
Veterans benefits and services	5.5	19.0
Law enforcement and justice	.4	4.3
General government	1.1	3.5
Revenue sharing and general purpose fiscal assistance	.2	7.4
Interest	8.3	34.8

Source: *Statistical Abstract of the United States*, 1976, p. 232.

historian Henry Steele Commager sees this as merely the continuation of a long-sustained pattern:

The fact is that for a century and a half almost every major reform in our political and social system has come about through the agency of the national government and over the opposition of powerful vested interests, states and local communities. . . . [A]s the problems we face are inescapably national, they cannot be solved by local or voluntary action. Pollution is a national problem, no one state can clean up the Mississippi River or the Great Lakes, regulate strip mining, or cleanse the air. Civil rights, medical and hospital care, drugs and mental health and crime, the urban blight, education, unemployment — these are not local but national in impact, and they will yield only to national programs of welfare and social justice.[5]

State and local   The fact that many functions are being federalized does not mean that there is little left for state and local governments to do. Because the spending functions of the state and local governments are so similar, they are lumped together in Table 5.4. As this shows, their expenditures have increased about as rapidly in recent years as those of the federal government — three and two-thirds times from 1960 to 1974, as compared with four times for the federal government. And the major reason for the rise in spending is the extraordinary increase in educational costs, easily the leading claimant of state and local funds. This, incidentally, also explains the otherwise mysterious rise in employment by state and local government, to a total of 11.8 million in 1974. Of that total, education accounted for 6.3 million — 3.5 million of whom were teachers in public colleges, universities, and schools.

Public welfare was a distant second to education in 1974, followed closely by costs of building and maintaining highways. After this came health and hospitals and police protection.

Table 5.4 also shows that there is a considerable amount of "gas and water socialism" at the local level. Many cities own and operate their own water supply, electric power, transportation, and gas supply systems, while the liquor stores are state-owned in a number of states. In part this public ownership is a matter of design. States and municipalities saw a sure source of revenue and simply took over private operations. At least as commonly, though, public ownership was the result of pure happenstance. Private companies were unable to make a go of it, the community needed and demanded the service, so the local public body was forced into business.

The control of public spending

Our experience of the last several decades teaches us that there is no fixed limit to government spending — no point at which we can say, once we've reached it, "This is as far as we go." The only limit to public spending in a democracy is public sentiment. If the general public feels that a social project of whatever nature is worthwhile and is willing to pay for it with taxes, there is no inherent reason that the project should not be undertaken.

---

[5] Henry Steele Commager, *New York Times* (March 4, 1973), Op-Ed. Reprinted in *Economic Power Failure: The Current American Crisis,* ed. Sumner M. Rosen, McGraw-Hill Paperbacks, New York, 1975, pp. 234, 236.

TABLE 5.4
Summary of state and local government expenditures, by function, 1960
and 1974 ($ million)

Function	1960	1974 Total	%
TOTAL DIRECT EXPENDITURE	60,999	225,691	100.0
DIRECT GENERAL EXPENDITURE	51,876	198,618	88.0
Education	18,719	75,833	33.5
Institutions of higher education	3,202	18,884	8.4
Local schools	15,166	53,059	23.5
Highways	9,428	19,946	8.8
Public welfare	4,404	24,745	11.1
Health and hospitals	3,794	15,945	7.0
Police protection	1,857	7,289	3.2
All other	13,674	54,860	24.3
UTILITY AND LIQUOR STORES EXPENDITURE	5,088	11,747	4.9
Water supply system	1,881	3,712	1.6
Electric power system	1,244	3,763	1.6
Transit system	750	1,366	0.6
Gas supply system	191	551	0.2
Liquor stores	1,022	2,355	1.0
INSURANCE TRUST EXPENDITURE	4,031	18,439	7.8
Employee retirement	1,265	10,900	4.6
Unemployment compensation	2,364	5,729	2.4

Source: *Statistical Abstract of the United States*, 1976, p. 264.

Cost-benefit analysis We can extract two thoughts from the last sentence and build them into a government-spending decision-making model. *Worthwhile* suggests benefits associated with any project, and *taxes* are costs — costs because what we pay in taxes denies us the opportunity to enjoy the consumer goods or services our money would have bought. In principle, then, we have an operating rule for setting a limit to government spending: Take on additional public projects only so long as the additional benefits provided, or *marginal benefits*, just match the additional costs incurred, or *marginal costs*. At that point we have reached the limit of increased government spending. This is so because to take on additional projects whose added benefits are less than their added costs would obviously reduce overall public welfare. The logic of our decision-making rule is portrayed in Figure 5.5, which describes *cost-benefit analysis* in the public sector. Our marginal social cost curve slopes upward from lower left to upper right because the more dollars that are taken for public spending, the more the loss of each dollar costs us. The first dollars taken from private spending for use on social goods don't bother us very much, because we are able to give up trivial private goods or services. As more dollars are taken from us, though, we have to sacrifice more and more important private spending plans. Stand this logic on its head and we see the reason that the marginal social benefits curve slopes downward from upper left to lower right. With only a few dollars available for social projects we spend those dollars on projects we urgently need, where the additional benefits to society are very great. To expand our level of spending during any period of time, however, means that we move successively to projects we need less and less, with lower and lower additional benefits.

Starting from the left-hand side of the diagram above we can see that it would be foolish to cut off our public spending at point *A*. At that point the additional benefits we gain from public spending (*Aa*) far outweigh the sacrifices involved in giving up private goods and services (*Ab*). This is true for all levels of spending up to point *B*. At point *B* we're on the fence as to whether to take on the last social project or not: Its additional benefits (*Bc*) only just match its required sacrifices (*Bc*). But surely we will not go beyond *B*, say to *C*. Rather than go to *C* we should choose to leave the purchasing power for use in the private sector since the sacrifice involved

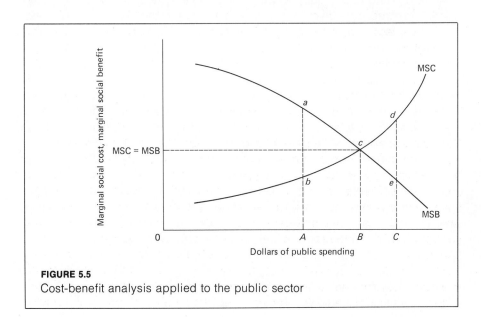

FIGURE 5.5
Cost-benefit analysis applied to the public sector

in removing the funds (*Cd*) considerably exceeds the expected benefits of the public project (*Ce*). Net social welfare is reduced by the amount of this excess (*de*).

In principle, then, we have an air-tight rule for deciding where to limit government spending. In practice the rule is not all that useful. It is one thing to talk marginal social cost and marginal social benefit, but something else to find contents for these empty boxes. Converting costs and benefits into comparable numbers is not easy. How do you measure the benefits of clean air, for example, if pollution control is the project we're discussing? How do you measure the costs of destroying an ethnic neighborhood if we're proposing to build an expressway through a run-down part of town? This latter project tells us that costs needn't be merely those associated with tax collection. And how do we compare present sacrifices with benefits that will come years from now? Somehow we must convert those future benefits into present dollars so they can be compared with the present costs. To do this requires that we use a social discount rate — and on this point there is wild disagreement among social engineers.

The planning-programming-budgeting system   During the last few decades the federal government has attempted to systematize cost-benefit analysis through adoption of a *planning-programming-budgeting system* (*PPBS*). Broader than bare-bones cost-benefit analysis, PPBS insists that federal decision makers first identify their objectives or goals, then examine alternative ways of achieving those objectives, next cost out each alternative, and finally decide which alternative is most effective in achieving the desired objectives at a given cost. What is required in the process is that all costs and all benefits be converted into dollar figures. The attempt to do this in some cases has proved impossible. The value of putting a man on Mars is one example. While the Pentagon under McNamara introduced the PPBS program and made it work, it is proving far more difficult to make it effective in other government departments. Two "scientific" studies of costs and benefits associated with a cross-Florida barge canal differed to the extent that one (by the Army Corps of Engineers) showed a prospective 20 percent excess of benefits over costs and another (by a consulting firm) could find net benefits equal to only 13 percent of total costs.[6] But even so, this may be better than flying completely by the seat of one's pants since it at least forces hard thinking about alternative costs and benefits. One analyst insists that we not "confuse the product with the process. The numbers are lousy and always will be in the civilian area. But the need to produce them pushes people in the right direction."[7]

---

[6] "Putting a Dollar Sign on Everything," *Business Week* (July 16, 1966), 128.

[7] "Putting a Dollar Sign on Everything," p. 128.

The new congressional budget process   Even if PPBS works, more or less, for government employees, what is to be done with Congress? Is it conceivable that members of Congress can be disciplined to think in terms of social costs and benefits, rather than in terms of re-election advantages and disadvantages? Unbelievable as it may be, apparently there is hope even here. In 1974, the United States Congress took a historic step forward with enactment of the Congressional Budget and Impoundment Control Act. In 1975, for the first time in history, Congress considered total federal expenditures and revenues *together,* rather than voting on the budget piece. by piece. It also attempted to determine in advance the impact of overall spending and tax collections on the level of the economy and started to focus explicitly on national budget priorities and how best to allocate total budget resources among competing purposes and programs. It may be too early to tell for sure, but it does appear that Congress may have learned that even in a $2 trillion economy we can't do everything at once.

▌ TAXES ▌

Although we continue to demand more and more government spending, no one shouts for joy when picking up the tab. While we recognize in a general way that an increase in government services must eventuate in an increase in taxes, we have a hard time relating those benefits to the taxes we pay. When we buy a sack of flour our benefits are apparent — the grocer has our money, but we have the flour. But when the tax collector takes our money, all we have is a receipt, which we find difficult to match up with specific benefits. Only a small number of taxes are levied in such fashion that the taxpayer can see the direct benefits of the use of his or her money. Public improvement assessments are one. Here the taxpayers' property values are increased by the building of sidewalks, paving of streets, or extension of sewer lines, and the special levies imposed are payments for value received. Similarly, we pay for the extension and improvement of our highway system with the gasoline tax imposed on every gallon of gasoline we buy.

Criteria for evaluating taxes

For most taxes, though, the benefits associated with tax payments are considerably more remote. This makes it far more difficult to determine whether a particular tax is "good" or "bad." And although they have struggled with the problem for over 200 years, economists are not yet in agreement as to what constitutes a good tax. They are largely in agreement, though, on what questions to ask in evaluating an existing or proposed tax. They are these:

1 *Is the tax equitable?* Paying taxes is burdensome under any circumstances, but it is especially disagreeable if we are convinced that the tax is unfair. But what does *equity* mean? As a general rule, we can agree that people similarly situated should pay the same taxes. We consider it unfair if two neighboring houses with the same market value are assessed differently for property tax purposes. But when we shift over to the personal income tax, does equity demand that everyone with the same amount of income should pay the same taxes? If this is what equity demands then we now have a highly inequitable system because we discriminate by source of income in assigning tax rates. Income from work is taxed with considerable vigor, while income from property holdings is treated much more gently by the tax collector. Earnings provided by buying property at one price and selling it later at a higher price are labeled *capital gains* and taxed at no more than half the rate of wage and salary income. And interest earnings on state and municipal bonds are taxed not at all under the federal income tax.

2 *Who bears the tax burden?* Taxes are often distinguished according to the burden they place on different income groups. We label as *regressive taxes* those that take a higher proportion of the incomes of lower-income groups than of higher-income groups. The tax burden in this case — taxes as a percentage of income — falls as income rises. A *progressive tax,* on the other hand, is exactly the opposite: one where the tax burden rises with income because the ratio of taxes to income rises. When all levels of income show the same relationship of taxes to income we say we have a *proportional tax.* Most people agree that a progressive tax is a fairer tax than a regressive tax. Take as taxes a relatively high proportion of high incomes, and you take away the opportunity to buy yachts, fur coats, and ski vacations in Switzerland; take those same dollars from the poor, and you take basic necessities. This is the primary case for levying taxes on the basis of ability to pay and adding to it the premise that ability to pay rises even more rapidly than income rises. (Even a regressive tax, after all, may require larger absolute payments as income rises, and a proportional tax surely would.)

But how much more rapidly than income does the ability to pay increase? Even fervent proponents of progressive taxes cannot agree. And in some cases economists cannot determine whether a tax is progressive or regressive. One major reason for this is that it is often impossible to determine who ultimately pays a tax — this is the problem of *tax shifting.*

The person who writes the check to the tax collector may completely escape bearing the burden of the payment because that person is in a position to shift the tax along by collecting in turn from someone else. In the case of the sales tax, for example, we take it for granted that the incidence of the tax will be, not on the merchant who remits it to the government, but on the retail buyer. Here the problems of shifting and incidence are pretty clear-cut. And because low-income buyers spend such a high proportion of their incomes on taxable items, while the rich avoid sales taxes by saving, buying stock and bonds, or taking European vacations, it is apparent that the general sales tax is regressive. But when only partial shifting takes place, the problem is extremely complex. It is widely agreed that part of the property tax on rental property is shifted forward to the renter, who is apt to be in a lower tax bracket than the property owner. To the extent that shifting does occur, the property tax is a regressive tax. But we also know that not all the tax can be shifted, and what is not shifted remains as a burden primarily on the higher-income property owner. Since we don't know what proportion of the tax is shifted, we can't say with any degree of finality whether the property tax is regressive or progressive.

The same is true of the federal corporation income tax. On paper it is progressive, since it has a two-step rate increase of 20 percent of the first $25,000 of profits, 22 percent of the second $25,000, and 48 percent of all other, and because corporation stockholders tend to be in high-income brackets. But the corporation and its stockholders may not pay the tax at all, or at least not all of it. The corporation may succeed in shifting the tax forward to the buyer of its products in the form of higher prices, or backwards to employees in the form of lower wages or to suppliers in the form of lower purchase prices. To the extent that shifting takes place, a progressive tax is converted into a regressive tax. And we simply don't know how much shifting actually occurs.

3 *What are the economic effects of the tax?*   Progressive taxes are generally thought to be fairer than regressive taxes. If this were all that mattered, we should have nothing but progressive taxes. Yet we see many regressive taxes in use. Progressive taxes must have some offsetting disadvantages. Chief of these is the assertion that since their primary impact is on the upper-income groups they destroy incentives to work hard to get ahead and to invest for the future. The rich constantly belabor the point that in taxing their industry, thrift, risk-taking, and investment at extortionate rates we are not so slowly killing the goose that lays the golden eggs. This was the argument used over and over again to bring the maximum federal income tax rate down from its peak of 94 percent in 1945 to 70 percent today.

In fact, we don't know what the net impact of high tax rates is on economic incentives. The reason we don't know is that higher taxes cut two ways. They may induce some individuals to work less hard or for fewer hours or to pass up risky investments because so much of the take is shared with the tax collector. Everyone has heard of the prize fighter who can't afford to schedule more than one championship match each year or the film actor or actress who can't afford to make more than one movie a year. But who hears of the thousands of accountants and lawyers and doctors who take on more clients or patients and work more hours to avoid a reduction of their take-home pay when taxes go up? Or the worker who takes on a second job and sends his wife to work because taxes are so high? It must be kept in mind that the marginal tax rate — that part of additional income taken by the tax collector — never exceeds 70 percent, even for the highest-income taxpayer. There is always at least 30 percent of additional income, and usually much more than that, left for the taxpayer. As a reflection of this, most of the empirical studies come to the conclusion that the incentive effects of high taxes just about balance the disincentive effects.

We looked at overall effects of tax changes on the performance of the economy in connection with fiscal policy and economic stabilization. It is important also to recognize that particular taxes influence the behavior of specific parts of the economy. By levying higher excise taxes on commodities, we increase their prices and discourage their use. Sometimes this is done deliberately and with good purpose, as with cigarette and liquor taxes. But sometimes it makes life hard for some group in the economy simply through inadvertence.

4 *Is the tax hard to collect or administer?* Tax collection in this country has been amazingly successful in terms of taxpayer compliance. We moan and complain, but we do — most of us — pay our taxes. Outright illegal evasion of taxes is still rare enough that it is newsworthy. In many other countries of the world it is so common as not even to be worth comment. On the matter of administration, some of our taxes are far better than others. Both sales and income taxes, by and large, are easy to administer. The property tax, on the other hand, is a very difficult tax to administer because of the many thorny judgments that must be made about property values.

Taxes by level of government

With some criteria to guide us, we are now in position to take a closer look at the tax system in the United States and to see which governments use what type of taxes. Table 5.5 provides us with a bird's-eye picture.

Several interesting trends are apparent when we compare 1974 with 1960. The first is the dramatic rise in tax collections at all levels of government — taxes more than tripled all along the line. In fact, state taxes increased over fourfold. This overall trend comes as no surprise since we saw earlier that government expenditures followed roughly the same pattern. The only reason taxes did not increase by quite as much as expenditures was that governments at all levels, but especially the federal government, financed more expenditures in 1974 by borrowing than in 1960.

Personal income tax Along with this spectacular rise in tax collections came some shifts in the sources of tax funds. The individual or personal income tax continued in 1974 to be the single largest source of revenue for all levels of government combined (35 percent), just as it had been in

TABLE 5.5

Tax revenue, by source and level of government, 1960 and 1974 ($ billion)

Source and year	All government Total	% of total	Federal Total	% of total	State Total	% of total	Local Total	% of total
Total								
1960	113.1	100.0	92.5	100.0	18.0	100.0	18.1	100.0
1974	395.6	100.0	264.9	100.0	74.2	100.0	56.5	100.0
Individual income								
1960	43.2	33.6	40.7	44.0	2.2	12.2	.3	1.7
1974	138.5	35.0	119.0	44.9	17.1	23.0	2.4	4.2
Corporation income								
1960	22.7	17.7	21.5	23.2	1.2	6.7	—	—
1974	44.6	11.3	38.6	14.6	6.0	8.0	—	—
Sales, excise, and customs								
1960	24.5	19.1	12.7	13.7	10.5	58.3	1.3	7.2
1974	66.2	16.7	20.1	7.6	40.6	54.7	5.5	9.7
Property								
1960	16.4	12.8	—	—	.6	3.3	15.8	87.3
1974	47.8	12.1	—	—	1.3	1.8	46.5	82.3
Payroll taxes and contributions								
1960	14.7	11.4	14.7	15.9	—	—	—	—
1974	76.8	19.4	76.8	29.0	—	—	—	—
Other taxes								
1960	7.0	5.4	2.8	3.0	3.5	19.4	.7	3.9
1974	21.8	5.5	10.4	3.9	9.3	12.5	2.1	3.7

Source: *Statistical Abstract of the United States*, 1976, pp. 230, 258.

1960. Along with its sustained use by the federal government for almost half (44.9 percent) of total revenues, both state governments and local governments pushed their use of personal income taxes. This should be a favorable situation, since we saw earlier that progressive taxes are good taxes and the individual income tax is a progressive tax. It is true that the progression in rates is not marked in state income taxes, but the federal rates range from 14 to 70 percent. What is not apparent from the table is the fact that the federal individual income tax of 1974 was not the tax of 1960, and even the tax of 1960 was far less progressive than its published rates suggested. This is because of the increasing use at the federal level of *tax expenditures,* more commonly called *tax loopholes,* a topic of sufficient importance that it will be given separate treatment later in the chapter.

Corporation income tax Along with continued, even increased, reliance on personal income taxes came a decline in reliance on taxes on corporate profits. In 1960 taxes on corporate income provided more than one of every six dollars raised in taxes by all levels of government; by 1974 only about one in nine tax dollars came from taxes on corporate profits. The primary reason for this is that corporate profits provide a major share of business investment funds, and investment spending is an important determinant of economic growth and its related increase in job opportunities. To encourage corporations to spend more on capital goods by reinvesting profits, those profits were taxed increasingly more lightly, both by reducing overall rates and by completely exempting more and more corporation earnings from taxation.

Sales tax State governments, both in 1974 and 1960, got most of their tax revenues by way of the sales tax — 58.3 percent in 1960 and 54.7 percent in 1974. In a way this is unfortunate. Sales taxes, by most reckonings, are regressive. Although sales tax rates are the same for everyone, rich or poor, sales taxes take a higher percentage of the incomes of the poor than of the rich because a larger proportion of the incomes of the poor is spent on taxable items. By turning income into savings accounts

the small society   **by Brickman**

or purchases of stocks and bonds or out-of-state travel, the rich completely escape sales taxation on most of their income. The poor are not in position to take advantage of these opportunities to escape the sales tax, so a higher proportion of their spending is subject to sales taxes and the tax/income ratio is higher for them. Many states, though, deliberately exempt purchases of some of the basic necessities, such as food and drugs, on which the poor spend a large part of their income. This necessitates an increase in the overall sales tax rate, say from 3 to 5 percent, but it makes the tax roughly proportional rather than regressive. Since only twenty-one states do this, sales taxes in general are still regressive. Yet even despite this the sales tax is a popular tax — to the extent that any tax is a popular tax. Given their choice of more sales taxes or more personal income taxes, even low-income families opt over and over again for sales taxes. We're not entirely sure why this is so. Perhaps it's simple ignorance. More likely it's because the tax is taken in many tiny bites rather than a few large chunks, so its impact is less painful.

Property tax   While the sales tax is largely the province of state governments, the property tax remains the almost exclusive bailiwick of municipal and county governments — providing them with more than four out of every five tax dollars raised in 1974. The regressivity of the property tax is very much a matter of debate, as we saw earlier in the chapter. Some analysts believe that property owners are not very successful in shifting the tax, which substantially cuts its regressivity. Others remain convinced that the tax is highly regressive. One study cited during federal hearings on property tax relief in 1973 provided the figures for Table 5.6 indicating that property taxes on owner-occupied single-family homes in 1970 were indeed highly regressive.

Whether or not the property tax is as regressive as the figures of Table 5.6 suggest is open to question. What is not even subject to debate is the fact that the property tax is a poor tax from other points of view. It is, as indicated earlier, a difficult tax to administer fairly. Tax collections are based on a complicated process. First your property is valued at market price, then it is assessed for tax purposes. If your house is appraised at $50,000 and the assessment rate is 20 percent, then your house has a tax value (assessment) of $10,000. If the tax rate in turn is 10 percent, your property tax for the year is $1,000, unless you can claim an exemption of some sort. What all this says is that property taxes are subject to change whenever the tax rate is changed, the assessment rate is changed, or the county assessor has a change of mind about the market value of your house. And the last of these is usually the most troublesome. Every time a house changes hands, a market price is established and can then be used for tax purposes. But what about a house that has remained in the hands of one family for fifty years? What is its market value? It's not going

TABLE 5.6

Real estate taxes as percentage of family income for owner-occupied single-family homes, 1970

Family income	% of family income paid in property taxes
Less than $2,000	16.6
$2,000 to $2,999	9.7
$3,000 to $3,999	7.7
$4,000 to $4,999	6.4
$5,000 to $5,999	5.5
$6,000 to $6,999	4.7
$7,000 to $9,999	4.2
$10,000 to $14,999	3.7
$15,000 to $24,999	3.3
$25,000 or more	2.9
All incomes	4.9

Source: Hearings on the Property Tax Relief and Reform Act held by the Senate Committee on Government Operations, Subcommittee on Intergovernmental Relations, 1973. Reprinted in *Dollars & Sense* (May 1976), p. 12, 324 Somerville Ave., Somerville MA 02143, a socialist magazine about the U.S. economy. $7.50 a year.

much too far to say that you will get a different answer — possibly a widely different answer — from every appraisal "expert." Property appraisal remains as much an art as a science, and there's a lot of artistic license exercised in valuing property for tax purposes.

Payroll tax Perhaps the most dramatic development in Table 5.5 is the sharp rise in payroll tax collections, from 15.9 percent of total federal taxes in 1960 to 29 percent in 1974 — in absolute terms more than a fivefold increase in collections. The reason for this is easy to find: Payroll taxes and matching employer contributions are virtually the only source of financing for the social security system, and the social security system in recent years has been both broadened and deepened — broadened by the establishment of new programs such as Medicare and the extension of coverage to additional groups, such as the self-employed; deepened by the provision of more generous benefits, especially those related to the cost-of-living escalator. Even so, with the birth rate falling and the average age of the population rising, benefits are flowing out in the form of payments more rapidly than the federal government at the moment can raise the level of tax collections. This tendency is aggravated by recognition of the fact that the payroll tax is a highly regressive tax. Low-income taxpayers pay the full tax rate on all their earnings, but high-income taxpayers pay taxes on only part of their earnings. Low incomes are typically wage or salary incomes, too, and are therefore fully subject to payroll taxes, while high incomes come in large part from property earnings, which are not subject to payroll taxes. The increasing role of payroll taxes in overall federal tax collections, therefore, coupled with a relative decline in corporate income taxes, means a reduction in the overall progressivity of the federal tax system. This, along with a state and local system that tends to be regressive overall, means that our combined government tax system has just about lost whatever progressivity it ever had.

Inheritance and estate taxes   Finally, buried under "other taxes" in Table 5.5 is one type of tax that now plays a minor role but that could play a far more important part in total tax collections. This is the inheritance tax — or, more properly, estate and inheritance taxes. Both are "death taxes," but the estate tax is levied by the federal government on the estate of a deceased person before the estate is broken up, while inheritance taxes are levied by state governments on the individual pieces of the estate inherited after break-up. In 1974 the federal government collected only $5.0 billion in estate and predeath gift taxes, and state governments only $1.4 billion in inheritance taxes. The word *only* is used advisedly since many tax experts are convinced that both levels of government could and should shift more of their tax burden to death duties. The ability to pay is clearly there. As far as inheritors are concerned this is "unearned" income. Large inheritances clearly perpetuate inequality in the distribution of wealth and impair equality of opportunity. And death taxes would appear to have considerably smaller "disincentive" effects than personal income taxes. They are, on the other hand, difficult to administer, especially as inheritance, rather than estate, taxes. This is particularly true when the estate consists primarily of a going business or farm. To pay heavy death taxes might necessitate sale of the property. There are ways of anticipating this problem, such as gifts, life insurance, or charitable trusts. But, once again, the primary barrier to wider use of death taxes seems to be strong public opposition. To protect its $5,000 inheritance the low-income family appears to be quite willing to see a high-income family receive hundreds of thousands of dollars virtually scot-free.

Who pays the taxes?

Because we continue to rely so heavily on the personal income tax, and its published rates are highly progressive, the impression is still current that we have a progressive tax system. Just how progressive the total system is we are unable to say with absolute finality because we are unable to determine the exact amount of shifting that takes place with some taxes. Whatever the incidence assumptions, our tax system is roughly

TABLE 5.7

Effective rates of federal and state-local taxes, by population decile, 1966

Population decile	Most progressive assumptions			Least progressive assumptions		
	Federal	State-local	Total	Federal	State-local	Total
First	7.8	9.1	16.8	13.8	13.7	27.5
Second	10.2	8.6	18.9	13.7	11.1	24.8
Third	13.5	8.2	21.7	15.8	10.2	26.0
Fourth	15.1	7.5	22.6	16.8	9.1	25.9
Fifth	15.9	6.9	22.8	17.4	8.4	25.8
Sixth	16.1	6.6	22.7	17.4	8.2	25.6
Seventh	16.2	6.5	22.7	17.5	8.0	25.5
Eighth	16.6	6.5	23.1	17.7	7.9	25.5
Ninth	16.7	6.6	23.3	17.6	7.5	25.1
Tenth	21.1	9.0	30.1	19.2	6.6	25.9
All deciles	17.6	7.6	25.2	17.9	8.0	25.9

Source: Table 4-11 (p. 64) from *Who Bears the Tax Burden?* by Joseph A. Pechman and Benjamin A. Okner. Copyright © 1974 by the Brookings Institution.

proportional for most families in the United States. The latest and most authoritative study, based on income and tax figures for 1966, shows the effective tax rates given in Table 5.7.

Table 5.7 identifies the tax burden borne by each income group, from the lowest 10 percent (decile) through the highest 10 percent. Even if every question of shifting is resolved by assuming that high-income groups ultimately bear the burden of the tax, state and local taxes remain regressive through the first nine income deciles. Granting the validity of these incidence assumptions does make the federal system progressive, and combining the federal taxes with state and local taxes provides a total tax system that is somewhat progressive. Notice, though, that the federal ratio of taxes to income for the highest-income decile falls far short of the 70 percent rate provided under the personal income tax. If, on the other hand, every question of shifting is resolved by assuming that lower-income groups finally bear at least a share of the burden of the tax, state and local taxes show up as sharply regressive, while federal taxes show only a hint of progression, from 13.8 percent in the lowest-income group to 19.2 percent for the highest 10 percent of the income receivers. Combining these federal rates with the corresponding state-local rates gives us an overall tax system with almost exactly proportional rates. The only major exception is that the lowest bracket pays the highest share of its income in the form of taxes.

Granted that the true effective rates of taxation lie somewhere between those of the left-hand columns and those of the right-hand columns, Table 5.7 still forces home the fact that instead of "soaking the rich" our tax system does a better job of soaking the poor. This is partially offset by paying more government benefits to the poor than to the rich out of tax proceeds, especially in the form of various sorts of welfare payments. But it does seem that if the plight of the poor is to be given serious consideration, they might be given a better break on their taxes.

The fact that our tax system has effective rates that are roughly proportional for most income groups in the country is even more apparent if rates are plotted against income on a diagram, as they are in Figure 5.6. The diagram makes it obvious that we can be absolutely sure of progression in our overall tax system only in the highest two or three percent of

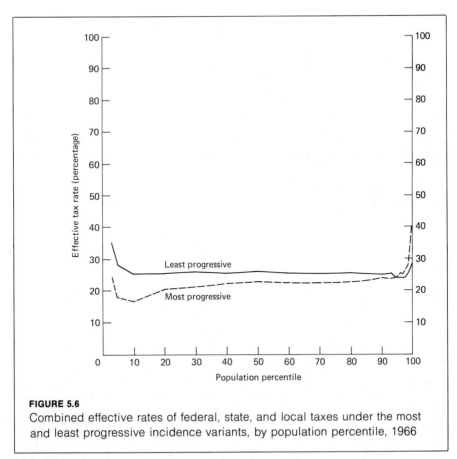

FIGURE 5.6
Combined effective rates of federal, state, and local taxes under the most and least progressive incidence variants, by population percentile, 1966

Source: From *Who Bears the Tax Burden?* by Joseph A. Pechman and Benjamin A. Okner. Copyright © 1974 by the Brookings Institution.

the income brackets — and not much even then. Equally certain is that for the bottom 10 percent of the income distribution total tax rates are regressive. Most of the rest of us pay about the same rates, all taxes combined.

The gentle art of tax avoidance

The primary reason that the federal individual income tax is far less progressive in practice than on paper is that high-income taxpayers have multiple loopholes available for escaping taxation. If you have an income of $1 million a year, you can easily afford expert advice on minimizing your tax bill. The consequence is that nobody pays the 70 percent maximum rate. Well, almost nobody. Treasury Department data for the late 1960s showed that less than 7 percent of those with incomes of $1 million and over paid an effective tax rate of 65 to 70 percent. At the other end of the distribution, 4 percent paid 0 to 5 percent — on million-plus incomes! Over 50 percent (58.2 percent) of these millionaire taxpayers paid taxes amounting to 20 to 30 percent of their incomes.[8] And since there has been no basic reform of the federal personal income tax since the 1960s, things are little changed today.

The way to minimize your tax payment is not to evade payment. According to the current practitioners' guide, evasion is doing something that, if you get caught, will mean jail or a stiff fine. Failure to report income receipts is evasion. For those on wages and salaries and subject to withholding taxes, there is no practical way to avoid reporting income anyway. Even for those with incomes not subject to withholding, it is far better to report all incomes and then take full advantage of the tax laws in avoiding payment. Tax avoidance, at worst, comes to an honest disagreement with the Revenue Commissioner; if you lose, you just pay up what you owe, plus interest.

And if you have expert counsel and a sufficiently high income you can sidetrack a huge hunk of your income without even raising a single eyebrow of the revenue commissioner. The evidence: In 1972 Americans reported adjusted gross income of $798.4 billion on their federal tax returns; after personal deductions and personal exemptions, taxable income amounted to only $446.6 billion.[9]

Over the years one loophole after another has been built into the federal individual and corporation income taxes. The estimate for fiscal 1976 is that $91,820 million in *actual taxes* — not income — slipped through one of these gaps or another. Especially for the high-income brackets, the resulting tax situation has been likened to dipping deeply with a sieve. Recognizing that providing a tax break by not collecting

---

[8] "The Basic Issues of Tax Reform," *Business Week* (February 22, 1969), 131.
[9] *Survey of Current Business* (February 1975), 34.

taxes is equivalent to spending tax proceeds for that purpose, tax experts have come to call these tax breaks *tax expenditures.* The complete list of these is impossibly long. Table 5.8 gives only those that cost the United States Treasury at least $1 billion during fiscal 1976.

Merely skimming the list of tax expenditures in Table 5.8 tells us that the tax breaks are not limited to the rich. Even modest-income taxpayers are able to take advantage of the opportunity to write off health care costs and mortgage interest and property tax payments on their homes. But most of these provisions are of little moment unless the taxpayers have substantial amounts of income against which to write off the deductions. The deductibility of mortgage interest payments, for example, reduces a 7 percent mortgage to an effective cost of 6 percent for a family making $7,000 a year, 3.5 percent for one earning $50,000 a year, and 2 percent for one receiving $400,000 a year.[10] The poor family has the same right as an upper-income family to secure its income in the form of interest payments on state and local bonds and escape paying taxes entirely. But how does it arrange to get hold of enough of those bonds to provide a living income in the first place? Alternatively, it could buy and sell property — particularly stocks and bonds and real estate — and live on the difference between the buying price and the selling price. Appreciation should provide a tidy income — and one that is sheltered from the tax collector since *capital gains* pay taxes at half the normal earned-income rate. Even some families with modest incomes are able to bring in some of their income in this fashion. This particular provision in the tax laws provided average tax savings of around 0.2 percent for those with incomes under $25,000 in 1970.[11] But for those in the $1 million and over category, "some 63 percent of total income came from net capital gains, and tax savings ran to about 20 percent of total income."[12]

Now, members of Congress don't ordinarily set about changing the tax laws with the public statement that they have some rich friends they need to take care of. That may indeed in some cases be the real reason, but the case must be publicly defended with more respectable justifications. And each of the loopholes identified above has economic logic to support it. Supreme Court Justice Marshall recognized over 150 years ago that "the power to tax is the power to destroy." The great discovery of the mid-twentieth century is that "the power to eliminate or reduce taxes is the power to create." Each tax break provided, accordingly, is supposed to accomplish some desirable national objective.

---

[10] Philip M. Stern, "Uncle Sam's Welfare Program for the Rich," reprinted in *Economic Power Failure,* ed. Sumner M. Rosen, McGraw-Hill Paperbacks, 1975, p. 205.

[11] Robert Eisner, "Bonanzas for Business Investment," *Challenge* (November–December 1973), 39.

[12] Eisner, "Bonanzas for Business Investment," p. 39.

TABLE 5.8
Selected tax expenditures of individuals and corporations, by budget category, fiscal year 1976 ($ million)

Budget category and tax expenditure provision	Amount of tax expenditure		
	Individ-uals	Corpo-rations	Total
INTERNATIONAL AFFAIRS			
Deferral of income of domestic international sales corporations	—	1,320	1,320
NATURAL RESOURCES, ENVIRONMENT, AND ENERGY			
Expensing of exploration and development costs	130	1,235	1,365
Excess of percentage over cost depletion	445	2,610	3,055
COMMERCE AND TRANSPORTATION			
$25,000 corporate surtax exemption	—	3,570	3,570
HEALTH			
Exclusion of employer contributions to medical insurance premiums and medical care	3,745	—	3,745
Deductibility of medical expenses	2,630	—	2,630
INCOME SECURITY			
Exclusion of OASI benefits for aged	2,940	—	2,940
Exclusion of unemployment insurance benefits	3,830	—	3,830
Net exclusion of pension contributions and earnings: Employer plans	5,740	—	5,740
Excess of percentage standard deduction over minimum standard deduction	1,420	—	1,420
Additional exemption for 65 and over	1,250	—	1,250

Do exports create more income for American companies and more jobs for American workers? Indeed they do, so let's encourage American businessmen to export by sheltering some of their export earnings through the establishments of DISCs (domestic international sales corporations). Do we need expanded production of natural resources, and especially oil? Of course we do, so let's encourage exploration and development by providing tax breaks to these pioneers. Are we concerned that little business cannot survive in competition with big business? Then let's exempt some of the income of small businesses from taxation. Do we want healthy Americans? Who can deny it? So let's provide the taxpayer with a break on health care costs. We need also to avoid penalizing the old and the unemployed, so we make retirement incomes and unemployment compen-

TABLE 5.8 (*continued*)

Budget category and tax expenditure provision	Amount of tax expenditure		
	Individuals	Corporations	Total
REVENUE SHARING AND GENERAL PURPOSE FISCAL ASSISTANCE			
Exclusion of interest on state and local debt	1,260	3,505	4,765
Deductibility of nonbusiness state and local taxes (other than on owner-occupied homes and gasoline)	9,950	—	9,950
BUSINESS INVESTMENT			
Investment credit	950	4,420	5,370
PERSONAL INVESTMENT			
Capital gain, individual (other than farming and timber)	4,165	—	4,165
Exclusion of interest on life insurance savings	1,820	—	1,820
Deductibility of mortgage interest on owner-occupied homes	6,500	—	6,500
Deductibility of property taxes on owner-occupied homes	5,270	—	5,270
OTHER TAX EXPENDITURES			
Deductibility of charitable contributions (other than education)	4,840	285	5,125
Deductibility of interest on consumer credit	3,460	—	3,460
NONLISTED TAX EXPENDITURES	10,505	4,025	14,530
TOTAL, ALL TAX EXPENDITURES	70,850	20,970	91,820

Source: Table 1-3 (pp. 14, 15) from *Federal Tax Reform: The Impossible Dream?* by George F. Break and Joseph A. Pechman. Copyright © 1975 by the Brookings Institution.

sation largely tax exempt. And we make it easier for state and local governments to borrow cheaply by exempting their interest payments from federal taxation. Similarly, by making their taxes deductible at the federal level, we make it easier for those governments to raise their tax rates.

Going on down the list, we encourage businessmen to invest and create more goods and more jobs by allowing them to take an investment credit against their taxes for part of the cost of their capital goods. We also encourage risky investment by taxing appreciation at the special capital gains rate, rather than the normal personal income rate. We encourage families to take out more insurance by excluding interest on life insurance savings from taxation. And we encourage those same families to buy their own homes by allowing them to deduct mortgage interest and property tax payments. We help support Goodwill, St. Vincent de Paul, and all organized religion by allowing personal and business contributions, up to very large amounts, to be charged off against the income tax. And we help poor families realize their dreams by allowing them to deduct interest payments on consumer credit from their tax returns.

For all of these loopholes — or tax expenditures, if you will — a more or less rational case can be made. Yet in the aggregate they leave us with a system that threatens to self-destruct. American taxpayers spend an extraordinary amount of time and effort trying to discover ways of sheltering their incomes from tax collectors. And they may spend even more time filling out their tax forms. Economist Milton Friedman once estimated that the human labor spent just in filling out IRS forms would be sufficient to build 40,000 new homes a year.

But what to do about it, that is the question. Reforming the federal tax system would not reduce everybody's taxes — not so long as federal expenditures continue at their present high levels. Nor would it necessarily even reduce the tax burden on the "overtaxed" middle-income groups. Today most of us are middle income. There just are not enough either rich or poor to shift much more of the tax burden to them. Besides, as we saw earlier, the middle income groups are not overtaxed compared with the rich and poor. This is one of the myths of our day.

What tax reform should do is simplify the system and get it back to its original progressivity. We might not be able to get back to a single page 1040 form, even with the elimination of all loopholes, but we could come very close. And in the process we could release an army of tax collectors, tax advisors, investment counselors, lawyers, and accountants for more productive endeavors. Coming back to earth, though, we must recognize that however attractive this prospect might be, its attainment is not very likely. *Business Week* recognized years ago that "the basic barrier to

the small society   by Brickman

reform is the simple fact that one man's loophole is another man's salvation. The beleaguered homeowner does not think of his deduction for interest and local taxes as a special privilege. He sees it as the only thing that stands between him and foreclosure."[13] Basic tax reform will come only when each favored group is willing to sacrifice its privileged position if others lose theirs. In this age of pressure politics, that day is at best some distance off.

The taxpayers' revolt

Whatever the chances of tax reform, 1978 witnessed a revolt against high and rising taxes. One part of the rebellion took the form of a broadening of the types of opposition found in the past, in particular the voting down of school levies. Ohio voters, for example, during the first half of 1978 rejected 117 of the 198 school-financing measures on the ballot in several of their major cities. Of far more significance, taxpayers began to make extensive use of an instrument of direct democracy, the voter initiative, to roll back or curb the growth of taxes. Voters in Tennessee limited the spending of their state government to an annual increase of around 10 percent. With inflation running at over 10 percent at the time the vote was taken, Tennesseans were telling their state officials that they wanted no more than a stand-still state budget in real terms.

It is not so clear what voters in California thought they were telling their representatives when by a two to one margin they approved Proposition 13 (the Jarvis-Gann constitutional amendment), thereby bringing about the most celebrated victory of the taxpayers' war. The obvious message was that taxpayers wanted a drastic cut in their property taxes and a limit to future tax growth. The case for relief was clear: Runaway increases in the price of houses had pulled property taxes up to unheard of levels, and overall housing costs had risen almost out of sight — an increase of 141 percent in southern California and 119 percent in northern California in the three years from April 1975 to April 1978.[14] The increase in the market value of a family's house did not normally bring with it an increase in the ability of the family to pay more property taxes, and by Proposition 13 homeowners expressed their unwillingness or inability to pay the higher taxes.

It is impossible to determine, though, whether or not voters were also expressing dissatisfaction with taxes in general, with the performance of their elected and appointed officials, or with the level of funding of schools, welfare programs, or other government operations. Each voter followed his or her own logic in voting for the initiative. There is no doubt about one thing: The success of the initiative was widely interpreted as a solid vote

---

[13] Milton Friedman, "The Big Drive for Tax Reform in 1973," *Business Week* (August 12, 1972), 84.
[14] *Wall Street Journal* (August 1, 1978), 1.

for across-the-board reductions in taxes. Tax reduction or tax limitation initiatives in other states, which had been languishing for lack of voter interest, suddenly had all the support they needed. Proposition 13–type initiatives were approved for the ballot in several states and more seemed in the offing. At the federal level, Representative Steiger found himself with lots of support for his efforts to force a substantial cut in the capital gains tax. And the Kemp-Roth proposal to slash personal taxes by $98 billion by means of a 33 percent cut in the federal income tax plus a $15.5 billion cut in corporate taxes, both to be phased in over three years, gained supporters in both houses of Congress.

Where the taxpayers' revolt will ultimately take us cannot at the moment be foreseen. As in so many other situations it is bound up with developments elsewhere in the economy. The revolt has to a significant degree been brought on by accelerating inflation, which has pushed taxpayers into ever-higher tax brackets and brought about an ever-wider spread between their money earnings and their real spendable incomes. This has been accompanied by falling levels of unemployment, reducing the recognized need for government support programs. If inflation is brought under control it will take some of the steam out of the anti-tax movement. And if at the same time the economy weakens, it will force recognition of the continued need for the very welfare programs now most in jeopardy.

What must be recognized — though this is not conceded by tax-cut proponents — is that substantial tax reduction, particularly at the federal level, may make it impossible to control inflation. When taxes are cut at the state or local level those governments have little option but to cut their spending. Their ability to engage in deficit financing is strictly limited. This is not true of the federal government. If its tax receipts are reduced the federal administration may choose not to cut operations and expenditures but simply to operate further in the red with borrowed money. If it does, as the economy approaches the full-employment level of output we will find that we have far too much money chasing too few goods — the classic prescription for rapid inflation.

I SUMMARY I

During our entire history as a nation there has been a pervasive tendency for government spending and taxes to increase. But what was a creeping growth during the nineteenth century has become a runaway in the twentieth. We have now reached the point where all levels of government combined take over one-third of the annual gross national product, spending well over $2,000 for every man, woman, and child in the United States.

Some of this increase in spending is explained by rising prices; some is the consequence of industrialization and urbanization; some has been occasioned by periodic emergencies, especially wars and the threat of wars; and some may be the result of pressure politics.

As for the patterns of spending, the federal budget today is dominated, not by defense spending as has been the case in the past, but by transfer payments and other forms of redistributional outlays. State and local budgets, on the other hand, are overwhelmingly given over to educational expenditures, with welfare, highway, and health spending running well behind in second, third, and fourth places.

We now recognize that there is no fixed limit to the growth of government spending. But it should be possible to do a more rational job of deciding on specific public spending projects, especially by the systematic use of cost-benefit analysis.

If public spending grows, then tax increases are not far behind. And because collections are so large we have been forced to develop criteria for evaluating taxes: equity, incidence of the tax burden, economic effects, ease of collection and administration.

The personal income tax, overall, is still our most important revenue raiser — the primary source of income for the federal government in particular. State governments rely most heavily on sales taxes, and local governments on property taxes.

As citizens we insist on believing that our combined tax system is progressive and that middle income groups pay more than their fair share of total taxes. Both of these beliefs are myths. Partly because of the increasing use of regressive payroll taxes, partly thanks to the availability of tax loopholes, our tax system is roughly proportional overall. The very poor, in fact, pay a larger share of their income in taxes than do all but the extremely rich.

❘ IMPORTANT TERMS AND CONCEPTS ❘

social imbalance	regressive tax
revenue sharing	progressive tax
cost-benefit analysis	proportional tax
marginal benefits	tax shifting
marginal costs	tax expenditure
planning-programming-budgeting system (PPBS)	tax loophole
	capital gains

❘ QUESTIONS, PROBLEMS, AND EXERCISES ❘

1 How do you explain the tremendous rise in government spending over the last century in the United States?

2 In recent years defense spending has claimed a smaller share of the federal budget. Does this mean that military spending is being squeezed downward?

3 What are the primary functions state and local governments support with their tax collections?

4 What are the earmarks of a good tax?

5 Why is it difficult in some cases to determine whether a tax is regressive or progressive?

6 If the tax loopholes are so obnoxious, why don't we simply eliminate them?

7 Estimates tell us that a new federal highway system will cost $10 billion to build — $2 billion annually for five years. Net benefits — mainly in the form of reduced transportation costs, after deducting maintenance expenses — are estimated at $300 million a year for the 50 years the highway is expected to last before having to be rebuilt. Should we build the highway?

8 A tax takes the amounts listed below from families in each of the three income brackets.

Family income (dollars)	Tax paid (dollars)
5,000	500
15,000	1,000
30,000	1,500

Is this a regressive, proportional, or progressive tax?

I SUGGESTED READING I

Advisory Commission on Intergovernmental Relations. *Trends in Fiscal Federalism, 1954–1974.* Advisory Commission on Intergovernmental Relations, Washington, D.C., 1975.

Committee for Economic Development. *The New Congressional Budget Process and the Economy.* Committee for Economic Development, New York, 1975.

Gutmann, Peter M. "Tax System: Bar to Social Mobility." *Wall Street Journal* (December 15, 1976).

Jencks, Christopher. "Rethinking Taxes." *Working Papers* (Summer 1977), 8–9, 94–96.

Meltzer, Allan H. *Why Government Grows.* International Institute for Economic Research, Original Paper 4, Los Angeles, 1976.

Owen, Henry, and Charles L. Schultze, eds. *Setting National Priorities: The Next Ten Years.* Brookings Institution, Washington, D.C., 1974.

Pechman, Joseph A., and Benjamin A. Okner. *Who Bears the Tax Burden?* Brookings Institution, Washington, D.C., 1974.

SIX

I INFLATION I

Steadily rising prices and continued erosions of the purchasing power of the dollar — alternative ways of defining *inflation* — have been facts of life over the entire lifespan of most readers of these pages. The same dollar that bought a full dollar's worth of consumer goods and services in 1955 would in 1977 purchase only 44 cents worth. Worse, the rate of decline in the purchasing power of the dollar has accelerated: 15 percent of the 56 percent fall took place during the decade 1955–1965; the other 41 percent decline occurred in the next twelve years. Is the situation desperate, or are we just living through a passing squall? The answer to this question can be neither simple nor straightforward.

Inflation, at least in the modern world, has proven to be a complex problem, and complex problems rarely have easy solutions. We must examine with a skeptical eye the one-shot cures for inflation so often put forward. Mere prudence suggests that any and all analyses and solutions be tested by common sense as well as by the evidence. To start with, inflation is not a new phenomenon. Perhaps history can provide some clues to causes and cures. On the other hand, do we really know for sure that inflation is worth worrying about? Maybe we should cease being concerned and simply learn to live with it. If we determine that we cannot live with inflation, however, then obviously some cure must be attempted. This suggests a critical examination of the current state of inflation theory and policy.

I THE HISTORICAL RECORD I

History gives us some reasons for complacency, but it also provides cause for additional concern about the prospects for containing inflation. Price data have been systematically collected, organized, and published in recent years, and price-change records are therefore much better than for earlier periods. But statisticians have pulled together the available data for earlier periods, and we now have a fairly good series covering commodity prices at the wholesale level for almost two centuries. Figure 6.1 provides a picture of such wholesale prices at five-year intervals for the period 1785–1975.

As the title indicates, prices in the above chart are represented by a price index. This is the statisticians' alternative to simply listing the raw prices, which would be next to meaningless because we would have thousands of different price quotations, some moving in one direction, some in another, and no way of getting a "group portrait." An index number is exactly that group portrait. What the statisticians do is collect a representative bundle of commodities, price them out during what they call the base period or year (1910 to 1914 in this case), and then add up the cost of buying the whole bundle during that period of time.[1] That total cost they

---

[1] The same general procedures are used in constructing all of the indexes most widely used in the United States, but each of these indexes represents a markedly different bundle of goods. The wholesale price index, as the name indicates, represents the weighted cost of commodities at the wholesale level. Since services, such as haircuts and movie admissions, cannot be wholesaled, they are excluded from the index. But services are retailed and are, therefore, picked up in the consumer price index, along with all the material goods consumers buy and

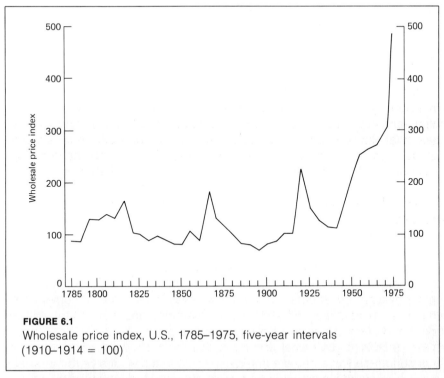

FIGURE 6.1

Wholesale price index, U.S., 1785–1975, five-year intervals
(1910–1914 = 100)

Source: Based on *Historical Statistics of the United States,* 1975, pp. 199–202, and *Federal Reserve Bulletin.*

everything else that enters into the consumer's budget. With the reservation that
the budget priced out is that of an average city wage-earning or clerical family,
the consumer price index can, therefore, serve as a measure of changes in the
cost of living. When we price everything coming out of the national production
pipeline — consumer goods and services, producers' or capital goods, goods and
services used by government — we come up with our broadest, most general
index, which we label with the inelegant title "implicit price deflator for the gross
national product." As the name suggests, this is the index we use when we want
to determine how much of our growing gross national product (the money value of
all newly produced goods and services) is made up of actual increases in the
goods and services themselves and how much is simply the result of applying
rising prices to those goods and services. In times of rapidly changing prices this
can be a very important adjustment. *Money* GNP figures for 1973 and 1974 —
current production at current prices — were $1,295 billion and $1,398 billion,
indicating a $100 billion increase in national output. Dividing through by the
implicit price deflators, which in effect holds prices constant for the two years, to
convert these current-dollar figures into *real* GNP, tells us that instead of rising by
$100 billion, national production actually fell by 2.2 percent in 1974. More than all
of the indicated rise in GNP was the result of inflation.

then designate with the number 100 — which means literally that it took 100 percent of some amount of money to buy the whole bundle of goods during the base period. Then they compare the cost of buying the same bundle of commodities during other years. If it takes twice as much money to buy the same package in some other year as it did in the base period, they indicate that fact by setting a price index figure of 200 — which means that prices are 200 percent of those in the base period, or twice as high, and also means that the purchasing power of the dollar in this particular use is only half as much. Conversely, if only half as much money is needed to buy the package in some other year as in the base period, then a price index number of 50 is assigned — saying that prices are only 50 percent as high as in the base period and that since only half the number of dollars is needed, each dollar has a value twice as great as in the base period. The mathematically inclined reader will already have gleaned from this that the purchasing power of the dollar is simply the reciprocal of the price index number for the year in question.

Tracing the pattern of price change in the chart gives us some reasons for optimism, some cause for increasing alarm. First of all, there is nothing in our history to match the disastrous runaway inflations many other countries have experienced. Prices in Germany during and immediately following World War I, as an example, rose to the point where it took 13 trillion marks in 1923 to buy what one mark bought in 1914. Toward the end of this period the value of the mark fell so rapidly that wages were paid daily and the wives of factory workers waited at the factory gates so they could turn their husbands' pay into groceries and clothing before prices rose out of sight. Of greater long-run significance, the savings of the thrifty German middle class were literally wiped out, which understandably created great animosity toward the government held responsible for the muddle and paved the way for Hitler. World War II provided even more spectacular hyperinflations. In Hungary in 1946, it took 1.4 nonillion pengoes (1.4 followed by 30 zeros) to buy what one pengo bought a few years earlier. As you've doubtless surmised, in these and many other cases the monetary systems ultimately collapsed completely and were replaced by new systems.

Price fluctuations in this country over our entire history, as the chart shows, have been modest by comparison. Further, during the first century and a half of our existence as a nation a sort of law of gravity worked in the price field: What went up was later pulled to earth. Finally, prices went up almost exclusively during wartime as a result of increased government spending on war materiel and manpower, which was insufficiently offset by tax collections, and came down and leveled off during normal peacetime years. The big price bulges came around the turn of the nineteenth century with the Napoleonic Wars and the War of 1812, during the first half of the decade 1860–1870 with the Civil War, and during the second half of the decade 1910–1920 with World War I. The interesting thing is that once the wartime demands evaporated, the price level rather promptly fell back to around its prewar average. The consequence was that the price level at the end of our first century and a half, when World War II began, was roughly where it had been at the beginning of the period. This part of our history, then, lends credence to belief that inflation is a sometime thing; that an upward price spurt will eventually burn itself out.

The right-hand side of the chart, though, representing the period from the beginning of World War II to the present, says something quite different. As far as prices are concerned, the law of gravity has apparently been repealed. In line with previous wartime experiences, the price level rose during World War II, only this time it took an even bigger jump immediately after the war once price increases were no longer constrained by wartime controls. The entire doubling of the price level between 1940 and 1950 is attributable to wartime demands inadequately offset by tax increases. But with the wartime demands behind us and with only normal peacetime spending, the price level not only refused to fall but, worse, continued to rise. Korea and Vietnam may explain part of this contrariness of the price level, but military spending, at least down into the late 1960s, was of insufficient magnitude to carry the whole burden. Prices, it is true, climbed rapidly during the rise of American participation in the Vietnam conflict — but they rose even more rapidly during the winding down of United States involvement. In all, it is evident that something has happened to the American economy since World War II to make it more inflation prone. What that something is is still a matter for debate and controversy. The principal arguments will be set forth and evaluated in a moment, but first it must be established that the effort is worthwhile. Is it really such a big thing? Does it really make a whole lot of difference whether or not we are able to reverse the inflationary process? Couldn't we just learn to live with an ever-increasing price level?

I THE PRICE OF INFLATION I

Sometimes a concise and easy answer is given to these questions: Nobody gains from inflation; everybody loses. This is simply not true. Unless inflation is accompanied by a fall in overall output — which typically has not been the case, all recent evidence to the contrary notwithstanding — Americans as a nation of people are no worse off. Production goes on increasing, the goods and services get distributed, and the *average* family gets an increasing amount of the good things of life — and the bad as well, if we want to moralize. But families live as individual units, not as mythical averages. And inflation drastically affects the distribution of goods and services. How an individual family fares depends on how its personal income responds to inflation-induced changes. A family whose income and wealth rise more rapidly than the price level increases cannot possibly be worse off in an economic sense — at least not in the short run. If accelerating inflation leads to an ultimate collapse of the economy, that's a different matter. A family whose income and wealth increase less rapidly than prices will be able to command an ever-smaller amount of new goods and services. And the family on a fixed or declining income is for obvious reasons in an utterly disastrous situation.

What it all comes down to is that while inflation will not necessarily reduce *average* welfare, it will surely redistribute incomes, and in an extremely capricious fashion. Rewards increasingly take the form of windfalls to the lucky or arbitrary exactions by the powerful, rather than payments for productive activity. Useful economic activity becomes a less sure route to financial success. Knowing the price of inflation and given the alternative of stable prices, most of us would opt for the latter. Then why don't we do it? Why do we continue to live with inflation? The reason, we will see, is complex but basically boils down to the proposition that we cannot agree on how to go about curing inflation. And where we can agree, the suggested cures may well be worse than the disease.

| CAUSES OF INFLATION |

Demand-pull

If these words were being written even as few as a couple of decades ago, the list of causes could be reduced to one: Inflation is the result of excessive aggregate demand confronted with an inadequate aggregate supply — of too much money chasing too few goods. If shoppers want to buy

the small society   **by Brickman**

more apples than are available at the current price, then the price will simply rise to the point where enough of the would-be buyers are rationed out of the market and enough additional apple supplies are drawn into the market to balance supply and demand. And if the whole national economy is visualized as simply an overblown apple market, then rising prices are a signal that demand for all goods and services is excessive in relation to available supply.

The mechanics of an individual market illustrate how excess or rising demand is likely to lead to rising prices — how demand can pull prices up. But it is scarcely necessary to point out that rising prices in one market may tell us next to nothing about the presence or absence of inflation on an across-the-economy basis. Apple prices may be rising at the same time that the price of oranges is falling. To tell what is happening in all markets we need to add together all supply and demand curves. When we do this, we come up with aggregate curves that, according to earlier adherents of the demand-pull explanation of inflation, look like those of Figure 6.2.

As in the individual market case, the aggregate demand curve slopes downward from upper left to lower right, signifying that consumers collectively will be willing to buy more of all newly produced goods and services at lower average prices, less at higher prices. The aggregate supply curve for all new goods and services, however, looks quite different from an apple supply curve. We know that the latter slopes upward, perhaps sharply, from lower left to upper right. The aggregate supply curve above, though, is flat over its entire range, up to the full-employment level of

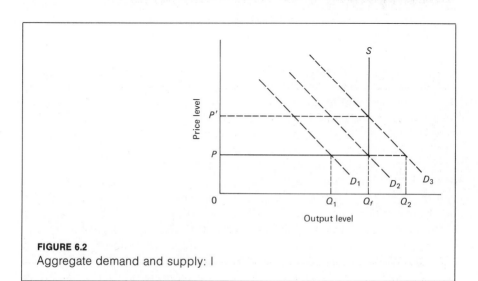

FIGURE 6.2
Aggregate demand and supply: I

output, at which point it abruptly becomes completely vertical. Free, competitive market assumptions underlie this supposed shape of the aggregate supply curve.

Assuming that $0Q_f$ is the full-employment level of output — the amount of production that will offer jobs for everyone seeking employment at current wage rates — any output to the left of $0Q_f$ is by definition a less-than-full employment level of production. This suggests that if the economy is operating at point $0Q_1$, we have idle men and idle production facilities. And since there is substantial slack in the economy, we can safely increase the spending rate, represented by a rightward shift of the demand curve to D_2, without having to worry about price level increases. Wages will not be bid up because unemployed workers will be happy to have jobs at prevailing wage rates. Production materials and facilities are also in overabundant supply, so they can be drawn into use without having to pay higher than prevailing market prices and, therefore, without the overall cost and price level rising. Either fiscal policy (tax reductions or increases in government spending) or monetary policy (increasing the amount of money in circulation) can safely be used to increase the overall rate of spending in the economy without worrying about price increases.

Once demand has been boosted to the point where the demand curve cuts the supply curve at the full-employment level of output, however, further increases in demand must be avoided since they are inflationary. At that point we will be using all of our available manpower and production facilities. We cannot produce more goods and services. If we overshoot the mark and end up with demand curve D_3 — as we almost inescapably do during wartime — we cannot avoid being confronted with inflation. With prices at an index of 100, a shift of the demand curve to D_3 opens an excess demand gap of Q_fQ_2: Too much money is chasing too few goods. And since output cannot increase, the excess demand can only be worked off by driving prices up to a higher level. Prices and wages chase each other up a vertical supply curve. Prices can be repressed and inflation bottled up temporarily by the imposition of wage and price controls. But so long as demand remains excessive in relation to supply, the forces of inflation will be waiting to take over whenever the controls are lifted. The only permanent solution is to force the demand back down at least to D_2 through a tight fiscal policy (raising taxes or reducing government spending) or tight monetary policy (reducing the money supply).

A somewhat more realistic model of aggregate demand and supply is represented in Figure 6.3. Any supply curve pictures the prices suppliers must have if they are to bring their goods and services to the market. At a minimum, suppliers must ask for prices that will cover costs of production. A lazy L-shaped supply curve, as in Figure 6.2, tells us that so long as additional supplies of labor and production materials are available at going rates, unit costs should not rise with increases in the rate of pro-

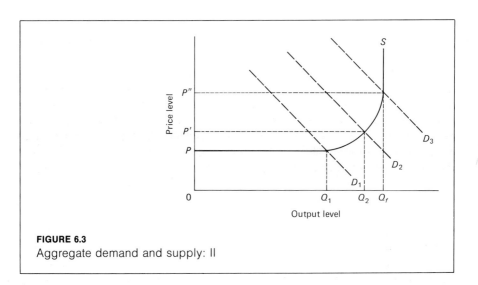

FIGURE 6.3
Aggregate demand and supply: II

duction, so there is no reason asked-for prices should rise. But we have long since discovered that it is hazardous to treat the economy as one gigantic machine, all parts of which are in perfect coordination. In fact, even though there may be a large amount of slack in the total economy when the output level is to the left of $0Q_f$, some sectors of the economy may already have reached their maximum-use levels. We may run short of a certain type of skilled worker or reach the maximum-output level of a critical raw material when other types of workers or materials are still in excess supply. The strong demand for these bottleneck workers or materials will result in rising wages or raw-materials prices, rising unit costs where they are used, and rising prices for the goods produced. The overall price level will begin to drift upward. As the full-employment level of output is approached, more of these bottlenecks appear. Increasingly, the result of boosting output is rising prices. Finally, the economy is fully employed, at which point further increases in demand are purely inflationary. The economy is one gigantic bottleneck.

An economy with an aggregate supply curve like the one in Figure 6.3 is confronted with a soul-wrenching trade-off: More jobs mean higher prices; lower prices mean fewer jobs. What are we willing to pay in terms of jobs for stable prices? In terms of inflation for full employment?

The Phillips curve

This menu of choice is usually represented by a *Phillips curve,* named after the Australian economist who examined the British historical record and found a more or less systematic relationship between the unemployment rate and the excess of wage payments over labor productivity (output per man-hour) increases. If output per man-hour rises by 3 percent, then wages can safely be boosted by that same 3 percent without increasing unit labor costs. But if wages go up by more than 3 percent, the labor cost per unit of output rises, and this will shortly be reflected in higher prices at the consumer level. The logic used to relate unemployment rates, wage increases, and prices states that if unemployment levels are high, replacement workers will be readily available and workers who have jobs will be satisfied with wage increases matching their advancing productivity. But if the unemployment rate is low, replacement workers are not available and employed workers can safely push their wage rates up in excess of any increase in productivity. Tying together the unemployment rate with the percentage annual change in the consumer price index gave us the menu of choice for the late 1960s pictured by the modified Phillips curve of Figure 6.4. During this period full employment — then defined as an unemployment rate close to 4 percent — carried a price tag of something like 3 to 5 percent in annual cost-of-living increases; stable prices could have been achieved if we had been willing to trade jobs for a slower increase in the cost of living until about 5.5 percent of the labor force was unemployed. This is also portrayed in Figure 6.3, where we see that forcing the aggregate demand curve down from D_3 to D_2 brings about a fall in the price level along with a reduction in real output and a consequent reduction in employment. We will see in a moment, however, that the choices since the beginning of the 1970s have not been this simple. Just as we made up our minds to order this much unemployment with that much price increase, management slipped in a whole new menu with higher costs all around. The Phillips curve shifted sharply upward to the right, and the aggregate supply proved to be irreversible — aggregate demand could ride up along a sharply rising supply curve toward the full-employment level of output, but when we attempted to push demand back down the same supply curve, we found that the track had been relocated and now stretched horizontally to the left from the last point at which the demand and supply curves intersected. As we discovered to our dismay, any reductions in demand worked themselves out entirely in reductions in output. Prices refused to come down. In fact, they rose with a reduction of demand. It is this phenomenon that casts doubt on two widely held demand-pull explanations of inflation: federal deficit financing and excessive money issues.

Deficit finance and inflation

There can be no doubt that on many occasions spending by the federal government in excess of its tax revenues has brought on inflation. All of our wartime price increases have resulted from the government's inability or refusal to raise taxes sufficiently to cover defense costs. To give the government the funds necessary to pay military personnel and to buy

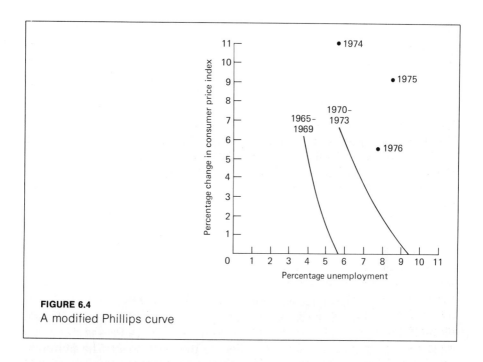

FIGURE 6.4
A modified Phillips curve

military equipment and supplies, the Treasury simply printed and sold IOUs. Little inflationary pressure resulted when these were sold to the general public, since households generally reduced their consumer spending in order to buy the bonds. Government spending for the most part replaced consumer purchases in the marketplace. The same was true to some extent when commercial banks bought the bonds or notes. The banks made loans to the Treasury rather than to their usual business customers. But a larger portion of the Treasury securities purchased by the commercial banks was bought with excess bank reserves created by the Federal Reserve for that purpose, thereby increasing the money supply. And when the Federal Reserve banks bought the Treasury securities, they created outright the money for the purchase by simply crediting the Treasury's account at the Federal Reserve. The consequence of the combined purchases by the commercial banks and the Federal Reserve was to expand the money supply by approximately the amount of the purchases. Total holdings of Treasury securities by the Federal Reserve and the commercial banks rose by a little less than $90 billion during World War II; the money supply increased by about $66 billion. Inasmuch as the economy was pushing up against full-capacity levels during the war, the consequence had to be demand-pull inflation.

Since World War II, however, operation of the economy at the full-employment level has been more the exception than the rule. If there is a significant amount of slack in the economy, the demand-pull model tells us that adding to the total available purchasing power by deficit financing need not be inflationary. The historical record, laid out in Figure 6.5, largely confirms this. During the periodic recessions in the 1950s and early 1960s we see large deficits, but the price level refused even to acknowledge them. And when we come into the late 1960s, we are back to full employment, so the large deficits of fiscal 1967 and 1968 undoubtedly contributed to the price increases of 1968 and 1969.

Demand-pull via deficit financing, however, cannot cope with the recent inflation. The surplus of 1969 failed to bring price relief, and the extent of deficit financing since then has not been sufficient to offset declines in private spending. Unemployment since the beginning of the 1970s has averaged well over 5 percent. With this level of unemployment it makes little sense to talk about demand-pull inflation, but demand-pull is the only route by which deficit financing can make its effects felt.

Changes in the money supply

Since deficit financing has its impact on the economy by way of increases in the money supply, the foregoing analysis ties directly into the present topic. And once again it is impossible to deny that changes in the rate of growth of the money supply have affected the price level. The fall in the price level from the Civil War to the end of the nineteenth century can best be explained by the growth in the money supply falling behind the growth

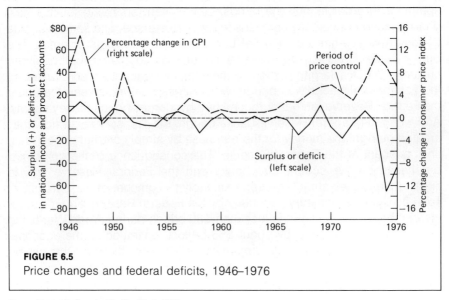

FIGURE 6.5
Price changes and federal deficits, 1946–1976

Source: *Economic Report of the President*, 1977.

of the output of goods and services — too many goods were chasing too little money, driving prices down. The relationships involved in this situation can be seen by setting them up in the form of an *equation of exchange*. This is expressed as

$$MV = PQ$$

where M represents the average money supply during the year, V is velocity or turnover (the number of times on the average that each dollar is spent), P is the average price level, and Q is the quantity of new goods and services produced during the year. The right-hand side of the equation thus represents gross national product (total production of new goods and services multiplied by their average prices), and the left-hand side represents total money spent on new goods and services. The two sides must balance since spending (the left side) must equal receipts (the right side).

Demand-pull inflation or deflation can now be described in terms of the equation. Assuming that money turnover or velocity changes slowly or not at all and that the total output of goods and services against which money exchanges is at the full-capacity level of output, an increase in the money supply must increase the price level, a reduction in the money supply must decrease the price level. The two sides of the equation must balance, so with V and Q fixed, any changes in M must lead to proportionate changes in P. By the same line of reasoning, increases in M less than increases in Q must push the price level down.

When the economy is operating with idle production capacity and idle labor resources, though, the situation becomes more complicated. Now neither P nor Q is determined in advance. Increases in the money supply, with V unchanged, must show their effects through changes in the level of gross national product. But gross national product is a composite of real goods and services and the prices at which they sell (PQ). GNP will go up if production increases, but it will go up just as surely if prices rise and output does not. Similarly, a reduction in the rate of growth of the money supply must contract the rate of growth of gross national product, but it can do this by reducing either prices or output.

This latter possibility creates particular difficulties for the demand-pull explanation of inflation, which works through changes in the rate of growth of the money supply. To take the most recent examples: The rate of growth of the money supply was slowed by deliberate Federal Reserve action from 7.9 percent in 1968 to 3.5 percent in 1969. Prices, as represented by the consumer price index, refused to fall; in fact, they rose by 5.4 percent in 1969 and by another 5.9 percent in 1970. The total output of goods and services, however, slowed from an increase of 4.7 percent in 1968 to 2.7 percent in 1969 and actually fell by 0.4 percent in 1970. The fall in demand brought about by a reduction in the rate of increase of the money supply worked itself out entirely in terms of falling output. Our most recent experience is laid out in Table 6.1. Once again, reducing the rate of growth of the money supply brought about first a reduction in the rate of economic growth and then an absolute contraction in overall production, both coupled with a rise in the inflation rate. The process can be pictured in terms of our aggregate demand and supply schedules, as shown in Figure 6.6. Here we see that the fall in demand from D_1 (1968) to D_2 (1970) moved the economy, not down along the supply curve that the demand had climbed (S_1), but back along a completely new supply curve (S_2), which sprang into existence and rose to the left of the original point of intersection with the demand curve. The economy ended up, not at point b, as the demand-pull adherents expected, with somewhat lower production and markedly lower prices, but at point c, with markedly lower production and significantly higher prices.

The difficulties encountered in applying the demand-pull logic convinced many analysts that demand-pull alone no longer provided an adequate explanation for the inflationary process; that the economy had changed so significantly in recent years that only a new, supplementary model could cast light on the process of inflation. Attention then shifted to the supply side of the market, the sellers' side.

Sellers' inflation: Wage-push

A demand-pull model of inflation is explicitly based on the assumption of active price competition in the marketplace. Prices are pulled up by eager buyers when demand is excessive in relation to supply, and sellers bid prices down when supply is greater than demand. Where price competition still prevails in the American economy, price changes do reflect the workings of these processes. No matter what happens to their costs of production, farmers have no alternative but to accept lower prices for their prod-

---

TABLE 6.1

Changes in the money supply, prices, and real GNP

Year	% change in money supply	% change in consumer price index	% change in real GNP
1972	8.7	3.3	6.2
1973	6.1	6.2	5.9
1974	4.5	11.0	−2.2

Source: *Economic Report of the President*, 1977.

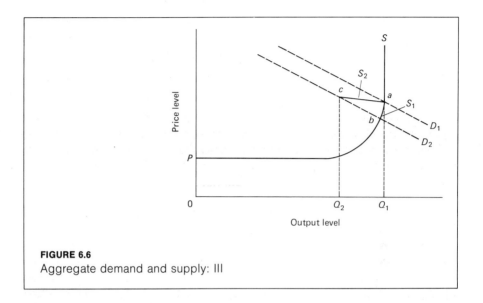

FIGURE 6.6
Aggregate demand and supply: III

ucts in years of bumper crops. They can take for granted, on the other hand, that in years of short crops or when there is a big jump in foreign orders for American crops, prices will move up sharply. The critical point to notice is that whatever happens to market prices is beyond the control of individual farmers. They are purely _price takers_. Because there are so many farmers, each producing such a tiny part of the total crop, no one farmer can influence the behavior of the marketplace. And because what each farmer produces is identical to what other farmers are producing, a

the small society   by Brickman

farmer who rejects the going price and holds out for more than other farmers are getting will find no takers. The demand curve facing each farmer is horizontal: each can sell all he wants at the going price, nothing at an above-the-market price. Farmers, then, and all other producers operating under competitive conditions — where a multiplicity of sellers turn out homogeneous products — have no option but to take the going price or let it pass by. They are in no position to set some other price.

One explanation of *seller's inflation* — the *wage-push theory* — is based on a different set of assumptions. Large sellers have sufficient control over their markets to set a new price if they do not like what the market offers. This world of the *price makers* extends beyond the product market and includes a significant part of the labor market as well. Approximately one-fourth of the American labor force is organized into labor unions, whose primary purpose is to throw the collective weight of the union membership against the employer in periodic bargaining sessions. Faced by the loss of his entire labor force, or at least a significant segment without which the others cannot continue production, the employer is not in a position to reject out of hand what he regards as exorbitant wage demands by union negotiators. And wage reductions, even in a period of weak demand for the employer's product, are out of the question. Significant wage increases, going well beyond those justified by productivity (output per man-hour) increases, are far more likely and become almost dead certain if the workers' cost of living is rising or if the demand is strong for the employer's products and profits are increasing. In the absence of unions, where workers negotiate with employers on an individual basis, wage increases are likely only when the individual workers' services are valued highly by the employer and when substitute workers are not available — which means when unemployment is minimal and demand for the employer's good or service is strong. When the opposite conditions hold, with high unemployment and weak demand for products and services, the result of individual bargaining may well be a reduction in wages or, rather, there will probably be no individual bargaining; workers will simply be notified that their wages are being cut. Since unorganized workers are typically employed by small firms operating in more or less competitive markets, the workers will accept the wage reductions, partly because they have little choice, and partly because they are aware that to do otherwise might jeopardize the continued existence of their employers.

Because big unions normally confront big business, this latter consideration rarely plays a part in wage negotiations in the industrial sector of the economy. Leaders of the large unions believe that their members' employers have the financial resources necessary to weather an economic storm and, more important, the power to "administer" their selling prices in such fashion as to pass forward to the consumer any increases in labor costs. High unemployment may bring moderation in wage demands, but almost certainly no reduction in wages. Low unemployment will almost surely mean that wages surge ahead well in advance of any increase in labor productivity, justifying an increase in prices, which will justify a further increase in wages, which will justify another increase in prices — the _wage-price spiral_ will be on.

The role of labor unions in pushing up wages in excess of productivity increases, resulting in rising prices for goods and services, has been examined in detail and has become almost an article of faith for most economists. The mechanics of the process are simple. If wages go up by 3 percent while output per man-hour remains unchanged, then unit labor costs will increase by about 3 percent, profit margins will be squeezed, and an upward pressure will be exerted on prices to restore pre-wage-increase profit margins. If wages go up by 3 percent at the same time that productivity increases by the same amount, unit labor costs remain unchanged, profit margins are unaffected, and prices need not change. If wages go up by 6 percent but productivity increases by only 3 percent, then once again, as in the first case, unit labor costs rise by about 3 percent, profit margins are squeezed, and prices are likely to rise by about 3 percent. To those already convinced that unions are responsible for inflation, the fact that wages in the recent era have systematically outrun productivity increases is proof that wage-push is an adequate explanation of our postwar inflation.

The case is really not quite that simple. First of all, the post hoc fallacy (_post hoc ergo propter hoc_: "after this, therefore because of this") may be at work. Just because wages go up and prices follow does not prove that the first causes the second. Both may be reacting to a more fundamental force. To take an example: Between 1946 and 1947, at the end of World War II, output per man-hour in manufacturing increased by 5.6 percent, but manufacturing wages including supplements rose by 15 percent and the consumer price index jumped by 14.5 percent — a classic example of wage increases in excess of the productivity rise causing a boost in the prices paid by consumers. Or was it? After several years of price controls and rationing, consumers entered the postwar era with bulging savings accounts and a willingness to spend on almost anything in sight. With demand at the flood stage, prices would undoubtedly have risen following the end of price controls, even had wages dropped. Wages were not about to drop, however, because labor markets were tight as employers attempted to hire almost anyone available in order to produce the goods and services that consumers were clamoring to buy. Given the strength of this demand, the relationship between wage increases and productivity rises was of little significance in explaining the price rise and of even less importance in showing the relationship between union power and inflation.

Prices rose in both the unionized and nonunionized sectors of the economy, as has been true whenever aggregate demand has been excessive in relation to aggregate supply.

Another reason to exercise restraint in placing sole responsibility for creating inflation on the unions is that in many cases prices have been pushed up even though unions have been moderate in their wage demands and have settled for increases well within the boundaries of rising productivity. In the spring of 1962 the president of the United States confronted head-on the chairman of the board of U.S. Steel, the country's largest steel company. This "steel crisis" followed on the heels of a publicly announced "noninflationary" wage settlement between U.S. Steel and the United Steel Workers. Although no price increase was justified by labor costs, Chairman Blough announced that profits were too skimpy, so the price of steel must rise by six dollars a ton. Because it was taken for granted that U.S. Steel's price increase would set the pattern for the industry, President Kennedy threw the whole weight of the federal government against the steel industry and forced the industry to back off — a rare undertaking, but one that suggests that in the absence of government intervention large firms have the power to set prices more or less at will.

Sellers' inflation: Profit-push

Understanding of profit-push, or administered-price, inflation begins with recognition of the fact that the American economy today is far removed from the free market economy described earlier. Some parts of our present economy, it is true, match the specifications of the market economy model reasonably well. The prime test of such an economy, remember, is that no individual seller or buyer be in a position to dictate price to the market. All are forced to make their buying or selling decisions on the basis of prices that are beyond their control. All are price takers. Individual farmers are in exactly this position. Much as he or she might like higher prices, no farmer acting alone can bring about better terms for his or her crops. And the same is true for a number of other industries typified by many producing firms all turning out similar products: lumber and wood products; processed foods and feeds; textile products and apparel; processed hides, skins, and leathers. Price behavior patterns in these industries fit the demand-pull model of inflation rather nicely over the course of the business cycle. During periods of recession, brought on by falling demand, market prices for the industry's product weaken, leaving individual sellers no alternative but to accept those lower prices. During periods of recovery and rising demand, on the other hand, prices rise as demand pushes up against limited production capacity. If all of the American economy matched the characteristics of these competitive industries, the control of inflation would be relatively simple. By increasing taxes, reducing government spending, or restricting the growth of the money supply, government authorities could make sure that too much money was not chasing too few goods and thereby driving up the price level.

Confronted by an uncomfortably rapid rise in the price level in 1969, the Nixon administration, following this logic, deliberately engineered a recession by cutting aggregate demand. Tax collections were brought in line with federal spending, resulting in a net withdrawal of $3.2 billion in purchasing power in the form of a budgetary surplus in fiscal 1969, and the rate of growth of the money supply was cut by half in calendar 1969. Farm prices responded exactly according to the script, falling by 7.3 percent from the fourth quarter of 1969 to the fourth quarter of 1970, then rising by 12.1 percent in the next year as Nixon turned the economy around in preparation for the election of 1972.

But farm prices were the only prices that did behave according to the script. In the face of weak demand, nonfarm prices rose by 5.1 percent from the fourth quarter of 1969 to the fourth quarter of 1970 and then rose by another 4.3 percent the following year. The combined result of this planned experiment in controlling inflation was a 10.5 percent rise in the consumer price index over two years and a rise in unemployment from 3.5 to 5.9 percent of the labor force. Undaunted by the sad experience of his predecessor, President Ford, counseled by the same economic advisors, repeated the Nixon program in 1974. The results of the second experiment differed from the first only to the extent that prices, instead of increasing by 10.5 percent in two years, rose by 11 percent in one year.

There were "extenuating circumstances" all along the line, of course. The Russian wheat deal and crop failures elsewhere muddied the waters; the anchovies migrated away from the coast of South America, creating a shortage of protein-rich food; the dollar was devalued, making imports more expensive; and the OPEC countries joined in a cartel to jack up the price of oil. But all of these, while admittedly important, cannot explain why prices in the United States continued to rise during these two recessions — which, by definition, were periods of weak aggregate demand. Something has obviously taken place in recent years to immunize sellers in the American marketplace against the necessity of cutting prices during periods of weak demand — in fact, to put them in a position to raise prices as demand falls.

Industrial concentration   Examining the market power and pricing practices of the large industrial corporations provides a partial explanation of the paradox of *stagflation*: inflation is a stagnant economy. Far from being passive price takers, large American corporations seem able to make a new price if they do not like what the market offers. They can do this not simply because they are large but also because there are so few firms in an industry. The mutual disadvantages of price competition are readily apparent to all, and the procedures for in-step pricing can easily be worked out.

The size of the largest American corporations truly staggers the imagination. Only a handful of countries in the world generate larger income flows or possess more wealth than Exxon, General Motors, or U.S. Steel. Small wonder that these elephants play the game by different rules than their pygmy counterparts in the price-competitive sectors of the economy. And while the pygmies far outnumber the elephants, the latter increasingly dominate the economy. To give just one example, although there are several hundred thousand manufacturing corporations in the United States, the 200 largest control over two-thirds of all manufacturing assets.

Some industries are made up of only a handful of firms, perhaps as few as four, as in automobile manufacturing. In these the existence of *oligopoly* ("few sellers") is manifest. Equally obvious is the fact that all the firms are aware of what others in the industry are doing, and no single firm will adopt a new policy without first trying to determine what the reaction of other firms in the industry will be. Pricing policy, especially, is a matter of mutual interdependence. It would be suicidal for Ford to raise prices on its new models without first having some assurance that General Motors will follow suit. Since it is a criminal offense under our antitrust laws for competing business firms to agree in advance on prices, a neat bit of strategy is required for lock-step pricing. This ordinarily comes in the form of *price leadership,* a "follow-the-leader" procedure. One firm in the industry, customarily the largest, takes the leadership in announcing prices. Once that firm makes known its prices, the other firms quickly change their prices to match. It makes little difference in this situation whether the industry is made up of four or five firms or a few dozen. All that is required is that the industry be highly concentrated; that is, that the bulk of the production is turned out by the largest producers. Faced by a multi-billion dollar concentration of power, the smaller companies are not about to risk the wrath of the price leader and its large followers.

Blair's model All this explains why prices move in tandem in highly concentrated industries, but it does not explain why prices move in only one direction, upward. For this we need more information about the mechanics of price determination. Given the power of the large business firms to set industry prices, how do they go about determining where price shall be? On the basis of the wealth of information made available to him during his many years as chief economist of the United States Senate Antitrust Subcommittee and assistant chief economist of the United States Federal Trade Commission, the late John M. Blair provided at least a partial explanation.

Blair's model is based on the premise that price in the highly concentrated industries is a function of two elements, unit costs of production and a desired profit margin. Add up the anticipated costs of producing a Chevrolet or a ton of steel, tack on a profit margin sufficient to provide General Motors or U.S. Steel with their targeted rate of return on investment, and you have what the companies consider fair prices for Chevrolets and steel. It follows that any increases in costs, such as wages that rise faster than worker productivity, will promptly be passed through to the consumer. Otherwise, profit margins would be squeezed, and the name of the game is to safeguard the interests of the owners of the business, the shareholders. But the analysis to this point suggests that falling costs would widen profit margins and provide shareholders with an unjustified windfall. Prices in this situation should come down, so that buyers of the product may share the benefits of falling costs. Since prices do not come down, something is missing in the analysis. What that something is can be determined when the complete model is presented, as it is in Figure 6.7.

Instead of being read from left to right, as in a conventional diagram, Figure 6.7 should be read from the center both ways. The central vertical line in the diagram, labeled SV 80%, represents expected unit costs and the profit margin with a standard volume of 80 percent of total capacity. Large firms ordinarily do not expect to go all out on production. A normal year for them might be one in which they produce 80 percent of their maximum capacity. Prices are therefore first set for such a normal year and adjusted if demand proves to be weaker or stronger than normal.

In some years demand might weaken to the point that only 70 percent of their productive capacity is needed. In such a situation, remember, prices in competitive industries would, and do, fall. But in the oligopolistic industries, company officials argue that prices cannot be allowed to fall because costs of production are rising. The average cost of materials used in production likely will not rise because they are bought in the marketplace and the market is weak. Labor costs are a different matter. Wages cannot be reduced because of resistance by the union. Further, large firms are reluctant to let workers go as soon as demand for the product falls. It is too hard to rehire them if the fall in demand proves to be temporary. For a time, then, labor hours available will not fall as rapidly as output, with the consequence that output per man-hour will fall and labor cost per unit of output will rise as the overall output level declines from 80 to 70 percent of capacity. With a reduction in output, fixed cost per unit will also rise.

Fixed costs, by definition, are those that do not change with shifts in the level of production. Whatever the level of operation — in fact, regardless of whether or not the firm is producing anything at all — interest costs continue, depreciation expenses run on, property taxes must be paid, the president's salary must be met, and lease and rental costs continue. If this

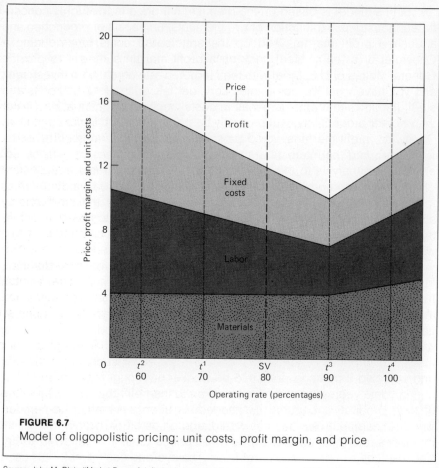

FIGURE 6.7

Model of oligopolistic pricing: unit costs, profit margin, and price

Source: John M. Blair, "Market Power & Inflation," *Journal of Economic Issues*, June 1974, p. 469.

total package of fixed costs amounts to $800 million, it will come out at $10,000 per unit if the firm is turning out a standard volume of 80,000 units. If output falls to 70,000 units, though, spreading the $800 million over the lower level of production means a rise in the unit fixed cost to $11,430.

Now the stage is set for a price boost. Higher unit labor costs and unit fixed costs have increased the total unit cost of production to the point where costs bite into the profit margin, as indicated by the vertical line t^1 [time 1] 70%. To protect the stockholder's interests, prices will be raised sufficiently to re-establish a profit margin equivalent to that of the standard volume. And the whole procedure will repeat if the operating level falls further, say to 60 percent of standard volume. A deliberately engineered recession, then, brought about by government policy designed to reduce demand so that too much money will not chase too few goods, has resulted in, not falling, but rising, prices.

But what about the right-hand side of the diagram? Here we see unit labor costs falling as the operating volume rises from 80 to 90 percent of capacity, because additional workers will not be taken on as rapidly as output increases. Output per man-hour will, therefore, rise and unit labor costs fall. Similarly, the $800 million of fixed costs can now be spread over 90,000 units, cutting the unit fixed cost to less than $9,000. With total unit costs of production substantially less than at the 80 percent standard volume, the profit margin widens and the stage is set for a price cut. Except that it never comes. Rising operating rates means that demand throughout the economy is likely strengthening. Prices are now going up in the competitive industries. With prices rising elsewhere in the economy, managers in the highly concentrated industries will be regarded as public-spirited citizens if they merely hold the line on prices, or even if they increase prices less rapidly than competitive industries do. In addition, rising demand suggests the need for additional productive capacity. Managers of the big companies can argue that only by holding on to more profits can they secure the funds necessary for additional capital formation. Finally, an individual manager will resist any temptation to cut price for fear of setting off a price war in the industry.

Putting together the two parts of the foregoing analysis gives us a picture of price changes over a typical business cycle. During the contraction phase of the cycle, prices in the competitive sectors of the economy fall in response to declining demand. But the decline in demand in the highly concentrated industries leads to price rises. And since production in the highly concentrated industries outweighs production in the competitive industries, the overall price level rises. As indicated earlier,

the small society — by Brickman

farm prices fell by 7.3 percent from the fourth quarter of 1969 to the fourth quarter of 1970, while nonfarm prices rose by 5.1 percent during the same period and the overall index rose by over 5 percent. At the beginning of the more recent recession from June 1973 to June 1974, prices in competitive industries failed to fall, thanks to strong foreign demand. In fact, they rose, but only by 1.9 percent. Prices in the concentrated industry groups, however, rose by 21.9 percent, leading to a rise in the wholesale price index of 14 percent.

During the expansion phase of the cycle, we expect to find prices rising in the competitive sectors, just as they did between December 1970 and August 1971, at which point prices were frozen. Farm and food prices during this period rose by 6.5 percent. Industrial commodity prices also rose, but at a more moderate 4.7 percent rate, in line with the foregoing analysis. Over the entire period of the 1969–1972 recession, wholesale prices rose by 6.5 percent. The terminal date of the current recession is not yet evident, but it is apparent that the upward price movement will far exceed that of the earlier recession.

Blair's model or pattern, then, appears to provide an explanation for rising prices in oligopolistic industries during recession, modest rises during the recovery period, and a failure of prices to fall at any stage of the business cycle. If he has accurately captured the essence of the pricing mechanism in the United States, several conclusions follow inescapably.

First, and perhaps most important, efforts to control inflation by deliberately restricting demand will worsen the disease rather than cure it. Recessions will, as they always do, bring unemployment and falling real incomes, but also rising prices as big businesses try to pass on rising costs to the buyers of their products.

Second, if falling demand brings falling prices in the competitive sectors of the economy but not in the concentrated industries, the thought obtrudes that perhaps the solution to inflation is to "deconcentrate" big business. Whether or not this would be possible politically, though, given the power of big business, is an open question; and whether or not the breakup of big business might not materially reduce our industrial efficiency is another.

Finally, if big business is here to stay, as it appears to be, and cannot be induced to change its pricing policies, the only long-run solution to inflation, as economist John Kenneth Galbraith has argued year-in and year-out, is to place governmental controls on prices set by the concentrated industries. Notice that this statement is not that across-the-board controls need to be established. Prices in competitive industries can safely be left to the marketplace. But given the power of the concentrated industries to control the market, there may be no escape from the necessity for government control to replace nonexistent market control. In the final analysis, if competition does not regulate, the government must — unpalatable as that would be to everyone concerned.

I SUMMARY I

The American economy has been marked by rising price levels during most of the years since the bottom of the depression of the 1930s. What was once a minor problem, though, has become a major concern. The long, historical pattern of first rising, then falling, price levels has ended in a situation where prices move in only one direction, upward.

It is not necessarily true that inflation hurts everyone. So long as the national income continues to increase, those families whose cash incomes rise more rapidly than the price level improve their lot. Only those with fixed incomes or whose incomes lag behind the inflation rate will be worse off. Thus inflation serves to redistribute real incomes, and in a capricious fashion.

The cause or causes of inflation are still a matter of debate among economists. The traditional demand-pull explanation — too much money chasing too few goods — is now suspect because prices continue to rise during periods of slack demand and recession. In fact, this is exactly what stagflation is all about. The assumption, therefore, that we can trade a given amount of inflation for a given amount of unemployment along the lines of the Phillips-curve analysis is at least questionable.

We now recognize that sellers' or supply-side conditions may result in inflation. If wages rise more rapidly than worker productivity (output per man-hour), unit labor costs rise and are passed on to the consumer in the form of higher prices. Wage-push may thus be operative even if demand-pull is absent.

Even more disconcerting, when inflation has been diagnosed as demand-pull and spending deliberately reduced through tight fiscal or monetary policies, the consequence in recent years has been rising, not falling, prices. According to the profit-push, or administered-price, explanation of inflation, falling demand reduces profit margins because of rising unit costs of production. In response to rising unit costs and the squeeze on profits, prices are pushed up in concentrated industries to re-establish desired profit margins.

Our current dilemma is that we have no agreed-upon diagnosis of inflation, but if we make the wrong diagnosis, the medicine we prescribe and administer may aggravate the disease instead of curing it.

I IMPORTANT TERMS AND CONCEPTS I

inflation

demand-pull inflation

Phillips curve

equation of exchange

sellers' inflation: wage-push

price takers

price makers

sellers' inflation: profit-push

stagflation

oligopoly

price leadership

I QUESTIONS, PROBLEMS, AND EXERCISES I

1 Inflation has been a problem all through United States history — or has it?

2 Why is it not true to say that inflation — at least in the short run — hurts everyone?

3 Why can we no longer be sure that a reduction in the rate of growth of the money supply will restrain inflation?

4 If wage increases outrun productivity increases, does this prove that excessive wage increases are the *cause* of inflation?

5 In a world of administered prices, why can't we safely assume that restraining aggregate demand will hold prices in check?

6 Compare and contrast price movements over the period of the business cycle in the competitive sectors of the economy with those in the highly concentrated sectors.

7 Money GNP was $1,413.2 billion in 1974 when measured in 1974 prices and $1,516.3 billion in 1975 when measured in 1975 prices. If the implicit price deflators were 116.4 for 1974 and 127.3 for 1975, both on a 1972 base of 100, can you specify how much of the money GNP increase from 1974 to 1975 was the consequence of price increases, how much real increases in the production of goods and services?

8 In 1967 the consumer price index stood at an even 100. Ten years later it had risen to 180. What do these figures say about the value of a 1977 dollar relative to the value of a 1967 dollar?

I SUGGESTED READING I

Blair, John M., ed. *The Roots of Inflation.* Burt Franklin, New York, 1976.

"Detroit's Dilemma on Prices." *Business Week* (January 20, 1975), 82–83.

Friedman, Milton. *An Economist's Protest.* Thomas Horton, Glen Ridge, N.J., 1972.

Lekachman, Robert. *Inflation: The Permanent Problem of Boom and Bust.* Vintage Books, New York, 1973.

Means, Gardiner C. "Simultaneous Inflation and Unemployment: A Challenge to Theory and Policy." *Challenge* (September–October 1975), 6–20.

"New Economic Weapon: Government-Prescribed Wage Restraints to Squeeze Worldwide Inflation." *Business Week* (July 26, 1976), 62–68.

Silk, Leonard. *Nixonomics,* 2d ed. Praeger, New York, 1973.

SEVEN

I GOVERNMENT AND BIG BUSINESS I

"The business of this country is business." So said President Calvin Coolidge in the 1920s. With equal justification, so could say any succeeding president down to the present time. Now, Coolidge did not mean that business is everything in the United States. As a God-fearing man, he knew well the role of organized religion. And he knew of the national effort going into education. His statement merely recognizes that business occupies the commanding heights in America; that the lion's share of our productive effort is carried out through business organizations; and that to enable business to carry out its mission, other institutions, including government, must stand aside.

Coolidge said, in his few words, that America is a capitalist nation. As in any capitalist nation, "the men who own the business, or those who are directly or indirectly their agents, have a major responsibility for decision."[1] The business system is simply capitalism at work.

I HOW MUCH GOVERNMENT? I

Granted the pivotal role of business in a capitalist system, what role should government play? There is no simple answer to this question on which everybody can agree. Nor has there ever been. Many businessmen over the years have supported the position taken by a French businessman in the age of Louis XV, who when asked by a minister of the crown what the government could do for him, replied, *"Laissez faire* [leave me alone]." But this won't do. Taken literally, it implies that business has no need for government at all. Whatever else they are, businessmen are not anarchists, as this suggests. There must be government. Even the most determined advocates of laissez faire concede this much. But how much government?

Perhaps it would be fruitful to ask not how much government there should be, but what is the minimal amount of government essential in a private-enterprise economy. Adam Smith, the master logician of the system, identified one critical role for the state, in 1776: "Avarice and ambition in the rich, in the poor the hatred of labour and the love of present ease and enjoyment, are the passions which prompt to invade property. . . . Wherever there is great property, there is great inequality. . . . The acquisition of valuable and extensive property, therefore, necessarily requires the establishment of civil government."[2] Free enterprise assumes private ownership of the means of production; government as constable or police officer is necessary as a consequence.

Capitalism is more than private ownership of property. It is also a market-directed economy, an economy of exchange and contractual relationships. Someone, obviously, must lay down the rules for these exchange transactions and see that the game is played according to them. Thus, we have another role for government, as lawgiver and law enforcer. The constable, then, plus the law, the law courts, and judges.

To round out the list of minimal functions of government we need merely recognize that just as "great property" must be protected from the avaricious rich and needy poor, so the property of a rich nation must surely

---

[1] John Kenneth Galbraith, *American Capitalism,* Houghton Mifflin, Boston, 1952, p. 4.

[2] Adam Smith, *The Wealth of Nations,* reprint ed., Modern Library, New York, 1937, p. 670.

tempt both richer and poorer nations. In the absence of private agencies willing to assume the burdens of national defense, the state must take on the chore.

For some, this exhausts the list of what government should do in a capitalist society. In the words of one contemporary advocate of this position, Ayn Rand, government is essential only for the performance of the three functions identified above: "the police, to protect you from criminals; army, to protect you from foreign invaders; and the courts, to protect your property and contracts from breach or fraud by others, to settle disputes by rational rules, according to *objective laws.*"[3] Beyond these minimal functions, government is to do *nothing.* No public education, no foreign aid, no trust busting, no consumer protection laws or agencies, no economic stabilization, no social security, no regulation of banks or stock exchanges or public utilities, no protective tariffs or subsidies of any sort, and perhaps above all, no public welfare programs. The market will provide whatever is necessary in all of these areas: What is not furnished by the market is dispensable. Social harmony and economic well-being will be achieved through the unobstructed marketplace, in other words, or will not be achieved at all.

But even Ayn Rand concedes that this stark version of capitalism has never been practiced. It has never been legislated into existence. Those who insist that the American Constitution built laissez-faire capitalism into the laws of the land are simply deluding themselves. If proof of this were needed it was graphically provided in August 1971, when President Nixon "interfered" with the marketplace to the extent of freezing wages and prices — without even bothering to ask if this was consistent with the Constitution.

What the Constitution did was make it possible to move toward a system of laissez-faire capitalism and away from the controls under which the colonists had lived and worked while subjects of the British crown. The stripping away of these controls was not a once-for-all thing. It proceeded more rapidly at the federal than at the state level. But it was never more than partially achieved, even when laissez faire came close to being a national religion during the last quarter of the nineteenth century. And laissez faire never quite meant "leave me alone" where the businessman was concerned; instead, it meant "leave me alone — except when you can help me." Multimillion-acre grants of land and low-cost federal loans to the railroad builders, protective tariffs for manufacturers, improvement of rivers and harbors, supply of navigational aids — all this government largess and more was regarded as completely compatible with laissez faire in the nineteenth century.

---

[3] Ayn Rand, *Atlas Shrugged,* Random House, New York, 1957, p. 987. (Italics in original.)

Even this limited version of laissez-faire capitalism was of brief duration. The basic logic of market-directed capitalism implies that no government regulation of the marketplace is necessary because such regulation will be provided by competition. Businessmen will provide honest goods at honest prices because if they don't, someone else will and they will be out of business. But this is true only so long as there are large numbers of businessmen in each industry competing for the consumer's dollar, no one of which is large enough to dominate the industry. Thanks to the rise of the large corporation, this market framework began to evaporate well before the end of the nineteenth century. All of which suggests that it is time to examine the various forms of business organization and see how each fits into the framework fo our American business society.

I THE GROWTH OF BIG BUSINESS I

Forms of business organization

At latest available count (1973) there were over 13 million business firms in the United States, including nearly 3 million farms (and anyone who thinks farming isn't a business hasn't been back to the farm lately). Someone with a new product or service to offer has a number of decisions to make. One that comes up immediately is what form of organization the business should adopt. Should it be organized as one of the 10.6 million individual proprietorships in the country? One of the 1 million partnerships? Or one of 2 million corporations? The fact that there are so many of each form of organization suggests that each has distinct advantages and disadvantages.

Sole proprietorship If we take a concrete case, we can see what those advantages and disadvantages are. Let's look at the John Jacobsen family and see how they went about providing the weary motoring public with the opportunity to spend the night in a clean, comfortable, no-frills, low-cost motel — the Shady Rest. The Jacobsen family had lived on their 10 acres alongside U.S. 11 for several years. They had a comfortable house, but John wanted to spend more time there instead of traveling constantly as a salesman for Consolidated Electric. The motel could be built on their own land, since there were no zoning problems. The family had accumulated some savings. John was a good amateur carpenter, and he knew exactly the sort of motel he looked for, but rarely found, in his travels. Now, a year later, the Shady Rest Motel is taking in customers. John chose to run Shady Rest as a *sole proprietorship,* where he is both owner and manager of his own business. He scarcely considered alternative organizational arrangements. From the beginning theirs was a family business — a Ma and Pa operation. They neither wanted nor needed any partners.

And they could see no point in going through the red tape and expense involved with incorporation.

They may never regret their choice of organizational form. Most of the small businesses in this country get along quite nicely as proprietorships. When one of these businesses fails, however, the owner may live to regret that choice. The fact that the average life of a small business is not much more than five years suggests that failure is not uncommon. In the proprietorship, the business and the proprietor are one and the same. This means that the assets of the business and the assets of the owner of the business are indistinguishable, and the same is true of liabilities. When the business fails, therefore, the unpaid liabilities of the business are left as liabilities for the owner. If the Shady Rest Motel fails, leaving unpaid bills for supplies or an unpaid note at the bank, the Jacobsen family savings and property will be subject to legal attachment. The sole proprietorship, thus, is subject to *unlimited liability.*

Partnership   This is also true of the *partnership,* and there it may create a more difficult problem because all the partners are owners and all are subject to unlimited liability. To make it even more serious, every partner is held responsible for commitments, however unwise, made by the other partners. But the partnership adds another dimension to the proprietorship. Additional funds can be brought into the business by taking in more partners. New managerial or technical skills can come by the same route.

At some point, though, it becomes cumbersome to attract new money or talent by taking on additional partners, although that point may be quite a distance away. The Banking Company of Aberdeen in Scotland expanded by this procedure in the nineteenth century and finally ended up with 446 partners. And the early history of manufacturing and commerce in this country, to around the middle of the nineteenth century, is the history of proprietorships and partnerships. But beyond some point in size the corporate form becomes indispensable. It was possible in the early nineteenth century to establish hundred-thousand-dollar textile mills or musket factories as proprietorships or partnerships, but unthinkable to build the $15 million Baltimore and Ohio Railroad or the $50 million Erie Railroad except as corporations.

Corporation   Where large amounts of money are involved, the corporation is the only way to go. There are two reasons for this. One is that ownership can be divided almost without limit. Ownership is conveyed by the purchase of stock issued by the corporation. Many of our largest corporations have hundreds of thousands of shares outstanding, which means that large amounts of money were raised by selling ownership blocks to large numbers of investors. Neither the proprietorship nor the partnership can avail itself of this money-raising device since neither can issue stock. The corporation can also raise money by issuing and selling bonds, long-term debt instruments. The other reason the corporation can raise large amounts of money is its *limited liability*: the investor faces a limited risk in purchasing stock. All the stockholder can lose is the purchase price of the stock. If the corporation fails leaving large unpaid debts, the stockholder cannot be held liable. The liability is that of the corporation, not the stockholder.

The stockholder's liability is limited because the corporation is a legal person, fully responsible for its own debts. With the proprietorship and the partnership, the owners are the business. But a *corporation* is a separate legal entity, "an association of human beings, given a definite and legal existence by the will of the sovereign power." By issuing a corporate charter the state breathes life into an artificial, but legal, person. As such a corporation can acquire and hold money and property, enter into contracts, sue and be sued. It may even do one thing a human being cannot: live forever.

In spite of its obvious advantages and the fact that its history can be traced back to the Middle Ages, the corporation was not widely used in business until near the middle of the nineteenth century. One reason was that most of the early businesses were small and could get along quite comfortably with the proprietorship or partnership form of organization. The corporation appeared only where the undertakings were large or were charged with carrying out public-service functions (roads, bridges, canals, banks, railroads). A second reason for limited use of the corporate form was that corporate charters were not easy to come by. Each charter required passage of a special act by a state legislature. It took time to secure a charter. And if more than one group of individuals sought corporate charters for the same undertaking, it took friends in the legislature to guarantee a charter — and friendship often came with a high price tag.

As businesses grew in size and as the delays and costs of legislative incorporation became more and more burdensome, one state after another, beginning with Connecticut in 1837, turned to free, or general, incorporation. This shifted the granting of charters from the legislature to a designated state official. It also provided that any group of incorporators who met the minimal requirements laid down for all applicants could not be denied a charter. By the middle of the century most states had adopted general incorporation laws, and the way was cleared for use of the corporate form across the whole range of American business. And use it businessmen did.

The age of the "robber barons"
The decades around the middle of the nineteenth century ushered in the take-off period of sustained national economic growth as the American Industrial Revolution got under way. Population grew rapidly and pushed

into virgin western lands, providing an insistent demand for all the things necessary to settle the frontier and to process the flood of products from the newly developed regions. Governments at all levels — municipal, county, state, and federal — proved more than willing to support completion of a transportation network that tied together the settled eastern markets with the burgeoning West. One huge national market was created. With a market of this scope there was virtually no limit to how big an American company or industry could grow. And the rest of the world, particularly England, further enlarged the market by reducing or eliminating tariffs on American goods. Rapid expansion in the number and size of American businesses was inevitable.

Economic fluctuations Shortly after the conclusion of the Civil War, however, storm clouds appeared on the business horizon. Expanding the size of business firms to take advantage of an ever-larger market proved that there were economies associated with large size. Tremendous amounts of capital could safely be embedded in the latest, most up-to-date production facilities, secure in the knowledge that when these overhead costs were spread over a very large output, the unit cost of production would be low — far lower than if more primitive production techniques and more hand labor were used. Both industrial prices and freight rates, as a consequence, fell over the course of the last quarter of the nineteenth century.

This was a boon for both the large businessman and the consumer so long as the economy was healthy. But the economy had a disconcerting tendency to stumble and fall into deep depression about once a decade. Then ensued a mad scramble for the limited amount of business available. Prices went down, and then down further, ending up in many cases well below production costs. The tendency of price cutting to end in "cut-throat competition," with prices bid down below the costs of doing business, resulted from the presence of large amounts of overhead (fixed) costs in the capital structure of big firms. If production costs are largely made up of variable costs — those that fluctuate directly with levels of production, such as wages, power, and raw materials — the firm escapes most of its costs by shutting down in a period of slack demand and waiting for the market to improve. But if a firm has invested heavily in fixed plant and equipment, its costs continue whether it operates or not. Interest on its borrowings, property taxes, and depreciation are all determined by the calendar, not by the amount of output. In bad times the manager of such a firm is irrational if he does not take on additional orders at any price that covers his variable or out-of-pocket expenses (wages, raw materials, power) and leaves anything over to apply on overhead costs. What is sound behavior for the manager of one large firm in bad times is sound behavior for all. All tended to end up doing business for less than cost-covering prices.

This was a situation to be tolerated only if nothing could be done about it. But something could be, and was, done. The big firms simply worked out arrangements whereby all firms in the industry refrained from cutting prices. This had to be done carefully because, while the federal government had no anti-price-fixing legislation until 1890, many of the states had such legislation much earlier. Further, the American legal system was based firmly on the English common (unwritten) law, under which price-fixing arrangements were regarded as conspiracies against the public. American businessmen thus had to work out their arrangements in the knowledge that their agreements were both unenforceable at law and subject to legal attack. They proved equal to the task, although it took some doing.

The gentlemen's agreement   The simplest arrangement, and one that has cropped up regularly in the hundred years since the Civil War, is the gentlemen's agreement. As its name suggests, this is simply an understanding among gentlemen (or gentlewomen) doing business in the same industry that all will maintain a certain minimum price. Its recent use came to light in the 1960s, when a grand jury indicted General Electric, Westinghouse, and twenty-seven other manufacturers of heavy electrical equipment for price fixing.

Its most ingenious, long-sustained use was in the iron and steel industry. Under the leadership of the U.S. Steel Corporation, iron- and steel-producing firms stabilized the delivered price of steel during all of the early part of the twentieth century. Known as "Pittsburgh-plus," the original system was very simple. It required only one initial meeting of managers of firms in the industry, at which all agreed that every firm asked to give an offer price for steel quoted U.S. Steel's published price at its Pittsburgh mills (the basing point) plus railroad freight from Pittsburgh to the point of destination — regardless of where the steel was actually produced and shipped. This single basing-point system was later expanded into a multiple basing-point system and extended into the cement industry. In this modified form it survived until it was weakened by legal attacks and was finally abandoned in 1948.

During its long use the gentlemen's agreement in the form of the basing-point system efficiently controlled price competition. A couple of indications of this:

1   On May 26, 1936, the Navy Department received bids from thirty-one steel companies for the delivery of a lot of rolled steel. Every company offered to deliver the steel at a price of $20,727.26.[4]

---

[4] *Temporary National Economic Committee Hearings,* Part 27, Exhibit No. 2241, U.S. Government Printing Office, Washington, D.C., 1941, p. 14548.

2 On April 23, 1936, officers of the United States Engineer Office at Tucumcari, New Mexico, opened sealed bids from eleven firms for the delivery of 6,000 barrels of cement. All eleven had submitted bids identical to the sixth decimal point: $3.286854 per barrel.[5]

The pool Sometimes price-fixing arrangements went beyond a simple understanding among business leaders and took the form of a formal written agreement among participating firms. In many of these cases not only were minimum prices agreed upon but also output quotas and the share of the market each was to have. Known as a pool, this arrangement reached its height of popularity in the early 1880s. There were railway pools, salt pools, whiskey pools, tobacco pools, powder pools, iron pipe pools, and many others. Virtually every major industry seemed to have its pool. Two weaknesses of the pool led to its demise: (1) it often broke down just when needed most, when demand was weakest — the opportunity for picking up additional business by shading the agreed-upon price proved too attractive for "chiselers" to resist — and (2) it was impossible to enforce an illegal agreement and bring the chiselers back into line. Some new device had to be found, one that would clear the legal hurdle as well as hold mavericks in check. For a time the trust device served both purposes.

The trust Gentlemen's agreements and pools can be set up regardless of whether the individual companies in an industry are organized as proprietorships, partnerships, or corporations. The trust, however, must be based on the corporate form of organization. Control of the corporation resides with ownership of the voting (common) stock, each share of which carries one vote for membership on the board of directors. Anyone who owns a majority of the common stock can control the corporation by voting in a board of directors that will carry out his or her wishes. And anyone who controls the common stock of the firms in an industry can control the industry.

This was the mechanism by which John D. Rockefeller and his Standard Oil Company controlled the oil industry in the 1880s. First a board of trustees, dominated by Standard Oil appointees, was set up. Next the board issued trust certificates, which were exchanged for the common stock — all or a majority of the shares — of the firms in the oil industry. The board of trustees was then in a position to make the pricing decisions for the industry. A recalcitrant company would shortly find itself with a new, and tractable, board of directors, voted in by the board of trustees. Recalcitrants were few, however, because the trust certificates brought participating companies a share in the sizable earnings of the industry.

[5] *Federal Trade Commission* vs. *The Cement Institute et al.,* 333 U.S. 683 (1948), cited in F. Machlup, *The Basing-Point System,* Blakiston, Philadelphia, 1949, p. 2.

After its introduction by Standard Oil in 1879, the trust device spread rapidly. Before the end of the 1880s it made its appearance in cottonseed oil, linseed oil, lead, whiskey, and sugar. But it also ran into increasing opposition, both legal and political. State courts instituted suits charging that the trust device was an illegal restraint of trade. New York courts struck down the sugar trust on these grounds in 1890, and the Standard Oil trust met the same fate in Ohio in 1892.

The antitrust movement

Of greater long-run significance was the fact that by now the American people were in a thorough state of indignation. Small businessmen demanded protection against their large, aggressive competitors. Consumers cried out against price fixing. And farmers publicly shouted their resentment against the rigging of railroad rates and prices for agricultural implements. Congress finally and grudgingly took action against the trusts — which had by now become a generic name to cover all aspects of monopoly and price fixing. Under the Interstate Commerce Act (1887), Congress established a federal Interstate Commerce Commission to police the railroads. And in 1890 it passed an even more sweeping piece of legislation, the Sherman Antitrust Act, to control monopoly and restraint of trade in all aspects of interstate commerce.

So sweeping was the Sherman Act that it came close to outlawing economic sin. Without any attempt to define the meaning of *restraint of trade,* Section 1 of the act specified that "every contract, combination in the form of trust or otherwise, or conspiracy, in restraint of trade or commerce among the several States, or with foreign nations, is hereby declared to be illegal." Section 2, without any definition of what constituted a monopoly, reads: "Every person who shall monopolize, or attempt to monopolize, or combine or conspire with any other person or persons to monopolize any part of the trade or commerce among the several States, or with foreign nations, shall be deemed guilty of a misdemeanor. . . ." Since the Sherman Act is still the basic antimonopoly law of the land, the history of the antitrust movement is largely the record of the Supreme Court's attempts to read what was in the minds of the members of Congress when they passed the act in 1890.

In the absence of explicit guidelines from Congress, the Supreme Court has had to formulate its own interpretation of what constitutes monopoly and restraint of trade. Their earliest decisions under the act set a pattern that remains largely intact. In the American Sugar Refining Company case, decided in 1895, the Court ruled that sugar refining bore no direct relation to commerce between the states — despite the fact that the sugar company, after buying up one independent company after another, had secured control of about 98 percent of United States sugar production. American Sugar was left intact. Shortly, thereafter, in the Addyston Pipe and Steel Company case, decided in 1899, the Supreme Court ruled that marketing and price-fixing agreements worked out among a group of cast-iron pipe manufacturers were clearly an illegal restraint of trade and must be dissolved.

The message of these two decisions came through clearly to the captains of industry of the period: It is illegal under the Sherman Act for independent businesses to collaborate in the assignment of markets and the fixing of prices; it is permissible, on the other hand, to achieve the same purposes by combining those same independent firms into one large organization. Small wonder that the decade around the turn of the twentieth century witnessed a vigorous merger movement. By the time it petered out in 1904, at least 318 large industrial combinations had taken place in the United States, made up of 5,200 original plants. Among the largest 92 of these combinations, 78 controlled at least 50 percent of their industries, 57 controlled 60 percent or more, and 26 controlled upwards of 80 percent.[6] When economists report that the industrial concentration ratio in the United States has not risen significantly during the last seventy years, they conveniently overlook the fact that there remained little possibility for increase after 1904.

| THE ECONOMICS OF LARGENESS |

The foregoing analysis suggests that the reason for industrial mergers is the determination to control prices. George Stigler, one of the country's leading price theorists, insists that it is close to being the only reason: "Theoretical considerations suggest that the chief purpose of merger must be to secure a monopoly position, and the history of combinations supports this presumption."[7] While this is commonly a dominant reason, it is rarely the only one. There are, first of all, large financial plums available for the promoters. The investment banking firm (J. P. Morgan) that arranged for the formation of the U.S. Steel Corporation in 1901, a corporate tent which housed two-thirds of the iron- and steel-producing capacity of the country, got $62.5 million for its efforts. Wall Street dearly loves a brisk merger movement because it leads to the issuance of large amounts of stocks and bonds, much of which has to be peddled to the American investing public.

Economies of scale

But combinations and mergers cannot be justified on the grounds that they will lead to price fixing and enrichment of investment bankers. There must

---

[6] Joe S. Bain, "Industrial Concentration and Antitrust Policy," in *Growth of the American Economy,* Harold F. Williamson, 2d ed., Englewood Cliffs, N.J., Prentice-Hall, 1951, pp. 616 n, 619 n.

[7] George Stigler, *The Theory of Price,* Macmillan, New York, 1946, p. 206.

be more respectable reasons than these. And there are, the most important of which are the *economies of scale* (*size*).

Cost advantages Among the cost-reducing factors most often cited are the ability to break labor tasks down to the performance of simple routines, thereby reducing the training required and possibly leading to the replacement of workers by tractable, reliable machines; efficient use of by-products; closing of inefficient plants; reduction of shipping costs; centralization of accounting and control functions; and more efficient use of the sales force. In addition, if the merger takes the form of *vertical integration* — the combination of firms under one management carrying on operations at different stages in the movement of the raw material through the production process — other cost reductions are possible. In steel making, for example, the blast furnace, steel converter, steel furnace, and rolling operations can be carried out in a single plant, avoiding the loss of heat entailed in moving pig iron or steel ingots between separate plants. Operations at the different stages of production, further, can be coordinated and some of the marketing costs eliminated. All of which suggests that the large firm, whether brought about by merger or by internal growth, may be able to move along an ever-falling long-run average cost curve, as pictured in Figure 7.1.

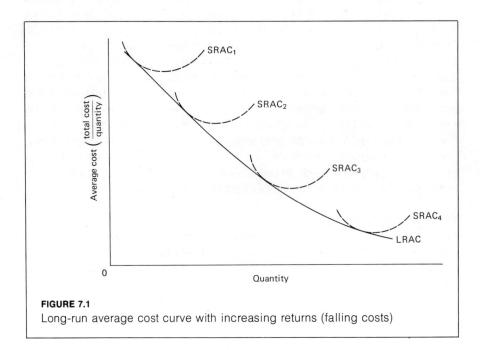

FIGURE 7.1
Long-run average cost curve with increasing returns (falling costs)

A short-run average cost curve (the SRAC's in Figure 7.1) depicts average, or unit, costs of production with a given amount of production facilities available. The company limited to $SRAC_1$ is a high-cost, high-price producer because it operates on such a small scale. It is true that it can minimize its costs within limits by choosing that level of output near the bottom of the U — at which point it is spreading its fixed costs over a relatively large volume of output but not yet encountering the diminishing returns and rising costs associated with trying to push too much labor and materials through its limited production facilities. But it cannot make the major breakthroughs associated with large size. To achieve these economies it must enlarge the scale of its operations by building or acquiring new production capacity. It then can move from $SRAC_1$ to $SRAC_2$. And then down to $SRAC_3$ and ultimately $SRAC_4$. Connecting points on each of these short-run average cost curves gives us the long-run average cost curve, LRAC.

All of this may have the appearance of an armchair exercise, but it does cast light on several real-world situations. First, it explains why companies in new industries tend to be high-cost, high-price producers and why prices usually fall as an industry grows. Companies producing new products almost always start small — sometimes in basements or garages. Henry Ford built his first automobile in a small shed behind his home. And the Ford Motor Company began business in 1903 with an investment of less than $100,000. With Ford automobiles selling in the range of $1,000 to $2,000 in 1905–1906 — several years' income for the average worker — the motor car was merely a plaything for the rich. But Henry Ford and his associates left their profits in the business, built a new factory, stocked it with the latest machines, and began their famous experiments with the moving assembly line that ushered in the mass production of automobiles. By World War I, the immortal Model T, selling for less than $600, was on the way toward putting the American public on wheels. In the mid-twenties Tin Lizzies rolled off the assembly lines at the rate of one every 10 seconds, to be picked up by buyers for an amazing $260. Similar stories could be told for many of the other consumer goods we now take for granted, all the way from ball-point pens through radios and television sets to pocket calculators and digital watches.

Monopoly and oligopoly Another aspect of the falling long-run cost curve is the problem created when the economies of scale extend so far that only one firm is needed to turn out all the products or services needed by the industry's customers. Economists call this situation one of *natural monopoly*. Dividing the business of such an industry between even two companies increases costs for both and forces customers to pay materially higher prices. Think how expensive it would be to have two telephone companies serving every community, duplicating central exchanges, utility poles, and wires. The same is true for the distribution of electricity and natural gas. In each of these cases a single company is designated as the sole supplier of services. Then, since no competitor is at hand to serve as a check to the legal monopoly, it is necessary to establish a public regulatory commission to control prices or bring the company under the jurisdiction of a previously established commission.

Finally, even if the economies of scale are not such as to lead to a situation of pure monopoly (*mono/poly* = "one/seller"), they may be present in such degree as to shrink the number of firms in an industry materially. If significant economies of scale are present, whichever firms first position themselves to take advantage of such economies by expanding their scale of operations can cut their costs, reduce their prices, and drive out of business competitors who are still attempting to get by with smaller operations. This has been the pattern in American industry. Most readers are undoubtedly aware that there are in the United States only four major automobile manufacturers, survivors of a field that at one time numbered more than 250. What they may not realize is that what is true of automobiles is true also of a large number of other industries. At some point the long-run cost curve may reach its minimum point and then begin to rise, mainly because of difficulties associated with managing and coordinating the operations of such huge enterprises. This bars the achievement of complete monopoly, but promotes something short of that. The drive to capture economies of size attainable before the cost curve turns upward reduces the number of firms to the point of oligopoly (*oligo/poly* = "few/sellers").

To identify the presence of oligopoly, economists developed a statistical measure called the *concentration ratio.* This is simply the percentage of total industry sales accounted for by a few of the largest firms in the industry (conventionally four or eight). A concentration ratio of 100 indicates that these few companies make up the entire industry. Four-firm and eight-firm concentration ratios in 1972 for selected manufacturing industries are given in Table 7.1.

What Table 7.1 tells us is that in many American industries, even though there may be many companies engaged in production, a handful of the largest account for an extraordinary share of total output. It is not going too far to insist that when the four-firm concentration exceeds, say 40, those four firms dominate the industry. What the table does not tell us, however, is how the largest firms compare with the smaller firms in terms of efficiency. If there are economies of scale possible in an industry, the long-run average cost curve, as we have seen, will be U shaped. It will slope downward to the right for a time with growth in the scale of operations, reach some minimum point where unit costs are lowest and efficiency is greatest, and then begin to rise as excessive size brings problems of management and coordination, as pictured in Figure 7.2.

TABLE 7.1

Percentage of total industry sales accounted for by the largest firms for selected manufacturing industries, 1972

Industry	Total number of companies	Concentration ratio Four-firm	Eight-firm
Motor vehicles and car bodies	165	93	99
Blast furnaces and steel mills	245	45	65
Motor vehicle parts and accessories	1,748	61	69
Newspapers	7,461	17	28
Aircraft	141	66	86
Petroleum refining	152	31	56
Electronic computing equipment	518	51	63
Commercial printing, lithographic	8,160	4	8
Tires and inner tubes	136	73	90
Meat-packing plants	2,293	26	39
Telephone, telegraph apparatus	157	92 (1967)	96 (1967)
Bottled and canned soft drinks	2,271	14	21
Farm machinery and equipment	1,465	47	61
Cigarettes	13	84	99
Soap and detergents	577	62	74
Malt beverages	108	52	70
Aircraft engines and engine parts	189	77	87
Women's and misses' dresses	5,294	9	13
Metal cans	134	66	79
Radio and television receiving sets	343	49	71

Source: *Statistical Abstract of the United States*, 1975.

The question of efficiency If efficiency were the only consideration and if it were possible to place every firm in every industry somewhere on the long-run average cost curve for the industry, the task of the antitrust authorities would be relatively simple. No company would be allowed to grow past the point of maximum efficency. Big companies already located to the right of the point of maximum efficiency would be broken up into smaller companies. Little companies located to the left of the point of maximum efficiency would be allowed, nay encouraged, to grow to the point of maximum efficiency, either through internal growth or by merger.

Unfortunately for the antitrust authorities, the economic world is not this simple. Efficiency is not, should not be, the only consideration. When

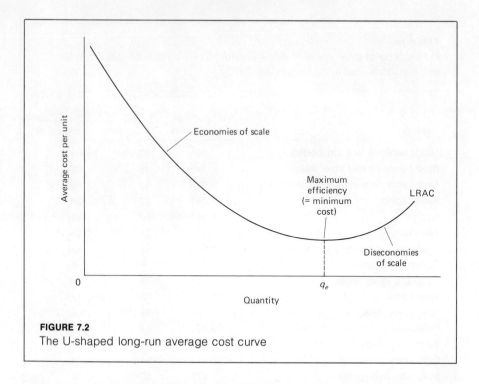

FIGURE 7.2
The U-shaped long-run average cost curve

we reach the point, as we have today, where the 200 largest manufacturing corporations control about two-thirds of all assets held by corporations engaged primarily in manufacturing, it is scarcely going too far to say that this leaves too few people with too much concentrated power — for good or ill. Assuming that each of these 200 companies is controlled by fifteen individuals (the board of directors, president, and senior vice presidents), we have a situation where something over two-thirds of a trillion dollars of annual production is controlled by 3,000 persons. The pertinent question, then, may not be whether or not these gigantic corporations are as efficient as they might be, but whether any group this size should have so much power.

Even if we grant the assumption that efficiency is the only pertinent consideration, we aren't home free. How do we measure efficiency? How do we determine whether a company is too small or too large for maximum efficiency? First of all, it may be impossible for outsiders to secure cost figures. These are closely guarded trade secrets. Second, even if such figures could be secured, their accuracy would be questionable. Most of our largest firms produce many different products. Direct labor and materials costs can be assigned fairly accurately to individual products. But the assignment of indirect costs (maintenance labor, heat, power, administration, depreciation, interest, and so forth) involves a large element of

TABLE 7.2
Ideal versus actual concentration in selected American industries

Industry	Output of an efficient firm as % of national market	Average share of market of four largest firms (%)	Four-firm concentration ratio, 1970 (%)
Typewriters	30.0	20	80
Steel	20.0	12	48
Cigarettes	20.0	21	84
Tractors	15.0	17	67
Soap	15.0	17	70
Automobiles	10.0	23	92
Rayon	6.0	20	78
Farm machinery	6.0	10	40
Metal containers	3.0	20	78
Tires	3.0	18	72
Fruit and vegetable canning	0.5	5	21
Meat-packing	0.2	6	23
Oil refining	1.75	8	33
Shoes	2.5	7	28

Source: Adapted from Joe S. Bain, *Barriers to New Competition*, Harvard University Press, Cambridge, Ch. 3. Copyright 1956 by the President and Fellows of Harvard College; and James D. Gwartney, *Economics*, Academic Press, New York, 1976, p. 391.

arbitrary judgment on the part of the company cost accountant — a judgment that is often influenced by the company's needs.

Recognizing these difficulties, some analysts have nonetheless come up with estimates, industry by industry, of the size of firm relative to the total market required for maximum efficiency. In a pioneering study, Joe S. Bain[8] provided estimates of the required output of efficient firms relative to the national market. These estimates are compared in Table 7.2 with the average market share held in 1970 by the four largest firms.

If Bain's estimates are at all accurate, some interesting conclusions about antitrust policy can be derived from Table 7.2. In some industries (typewriters, steel, cigarettes, tractors, soap) economies of scale are sufficiently important that high levels of concentration are justified on efficiency grounds. In other industries (automobiles, rayon, farm machinery,

---

[8] Joe S. Bain, *Barriers to New Competition,* Harvard University Press, Cambridge, 1956, Chap. 5.

metal containers, tires) present high concentration ratios cannot be justified on the basis of the supposed efficiencies of large size. And in the third group of industries (fruit and vegetable canning, meat-packing, oil refining, shoes) modest concentration ratios appear somewhat more than modest when matched against the economies of scale of the industry. Needless to say, if government authorities attempted to make Bain's findings the basis for antitrust policy, his figures would either be bitterly contested or be welcomed by industry spokespersons. The steel and cigarette industries, frequently under antitrust attack, would sigh with relief. Automobile, metal container, tire, and oil refining executives on the other hand, would bend every effort to prove Bain wrong.

The fact that Bain's findings are now over twenty years old and have not found general acceptance suggests some skepticism regarding his general approach. An alternative is to test efficiency by results. In a market economy, firms operating efficiently should show higher profit rates than less efficient firms. Profits, after all, are simply the difference between sales revenues and costs of operation. If large, concentrated firms do a better job in holding down costs than smaller firms, this should show up in higher profit ratios.

Since the stakes are so large, the relationship between concentration and profitability has been tested many times. In the study cited earlier, Bain examined a forty-industry sample and concluded that "there is evidently a clear association between the rate of profit earned in an industry and the degree of seller concentration in it."[9] He warned, however, that this "relation of profits to concentration may reflect the influence of concentration alone, but may with at least equal probability reflect the dual influence of concentration and the condition of entry."[10] Barriers to entry, of course, are evidence that some degree of monopolistic controls exists in the industry.

In a later study, John M. Blair, using a somewhat different approach, found that in six of the thirty industries he studied, increasing size was accompanied by increasing profitability — suggesting important economies of scale. But in eight of the other industries in his sample the reverse was true — profitability diminished with increasing size. And in the remaining sixteen there was no systematic relationship between size and profitability. Even where large size was accompanied by higher profitability, it was apt to be accompanied also by substantial monopoly power, so profit ratios were as apt to reflect monopolistic control as economic efficiency.[11] Although many other studies could be cited, the message that comes through all of them is that there is no easy way to determine with

---

[9] Bain, *Barriers to New Competition,* p. 195.

[10] Bain, *Barriers to New Competition,* pp. 195–196.

[11] John M. Blair, *Economic Concentration,* Harcourt, Brace, Jovanovich, New York, 1972, pp. 177–185.

finality the extent to which large size and concentration are related to economic efficiency. In the absence of such clear relationships the antitrust authorities are left to muddle through as best they can, pilloried by conservatives for attacking big business and its purported efficiency and by liberals for not attacking big business vigorously enough since the supposed efficiency cannot be conclusively demonstrated.

The upshot, according to Thurman Arnold, has been near paralysis: "The actual result of the antitrust laws [has been] to promote the growth of great industrial organizations by deflecting the attack on them into purely moral and ceremonial channels."[12] Galbraith's judgment is even more severe: The antitrust laws have amounted to no more than a "charade." "Modern antitrust activity," in his words,

conducts a fairly effective war on small firms which seek the same market power that the big firms already, by their nature, possess. Behind this impressive facade the big participants who have the most power bask in nearly total immunity. And since the competitive market, like God and sound family life, is something that no sound businessman can actively oppose, even the smaller entrepreneurs do not actively protest. It is possible that they do not know how they are being used.[13]

Pricing and big business

A major consideration in the recent revival of interest in antitrust is evidence available on all fronts that concentration in industry leads to a decline in price competition. When big business today talks about competition, it rarely means competition in terms of price; usually the reference is to advertising outlays or product changes. But this is not the competition envisioned in the model of a competitive market economy. This model assumes that businessmen constantly attempt to cut costs in order to reduce prices and get an edge on competitors. The main reason this rarely happens in big business is that in an industry with a few large firms a price reduction by one firm is almost sure to be matched by the other firms in the industry, leading to a situation where all may do a little more business, but at much reduced prices. Incomes for all are reduced as a consequence.

Comparison of pricing practices in concentrated and unconcentrated industries dramatizes the differences. In an industry made up of a large number of small firms, as in farming (see Chapter Two), each company is so small relative to the total market that it can do nothing about price, like it or not. It is purely a price taker. Prices are set by the interplay of supply and demand in the whole industry (diagram B in Figure 7.3) and are presented to each individual firm as accomplished facts. The demand

---

[12] Thurman Arnold, *The Folklore of Capitalism,* Yale University Press, New Haven, 1937, p. 212.

[13] *Business Week* (July 8, 1967), 71.

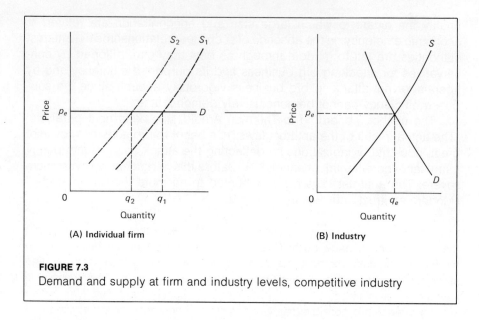

FIGURE 7.3
Demand and supply at firm and industry levels, competitive industry

curve facing each firm is completely horizontal (diagram A in Figure 7.3). Since each firm produces a product identical to that of other firms, any attempt to raise price individually is competely frustrated: Customers move away en masse because they have a perfect substitute available from other firms.

All this is changed when the product of an individual firm is distinguishable from that of other firms by a brand name and when the number of firms shrinks to the point of oligopoly. Now all the remaining firms in the industry produce similar, but not identical, products. A Marlboro is a cigarette, true, but it is not the same cigarette as a Kent (and this is true even if Marlboro smokers cannot distinguish their cigarette from others in a blindfold test. They don't, after all, buy or smoke cigarettes blindfolded). The result of this is that the manufacturer of Marlboros has some discretion in pricing. Prices can be raised somewhat without driving away all Marlboro customers, or additional customers can be attracted by cutting prices. Faced with a downsloping demand curve, as shown in Figure 7.4, the manufacturer is to some extent a price maker.

With a unique demand curve for its product — one distinguishable from the demand curve of all other producers in the industry — the seller of a differentiated product is in a position to manipulate the demand curve to the advantage of the firm. This is where advertising comes in. The role of advertising is to attempt to increase the demand for the product by shifting the demand curve upward and to the right as well as to reduce the elasticity of the demand curve by giving it a sharper downward slope, as

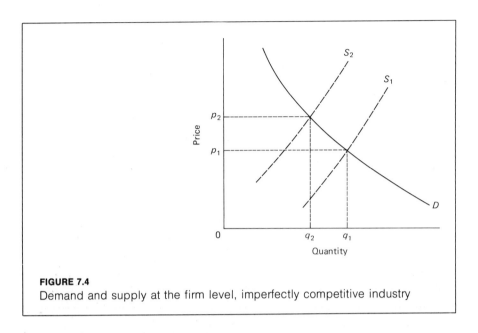

FIGURE 7.4
Demand and supply at the firm level, imperfectly competitive industry

suggested by Figure 7.5. To the extent that Marlboro smokers are convinced that Marlboros are the only cigarettes, or Kent smokers that Kents are the only cigarettes, they will willingly pay a higher price for them. Since all cigarette manufacturers are doing the same thing, however, the success of any one of them in this endeavor is usually limited. When advertising by one company is completely offset by counterefforts of others, the whole routine is a waste of time and resources. Only Madison

the small society   by Brickman

THEY SAY HIS PERSONALITY HAS SOLD THOUSANDS OF TV SETS—

MAKES SENSE. LET'S SELL OURS—

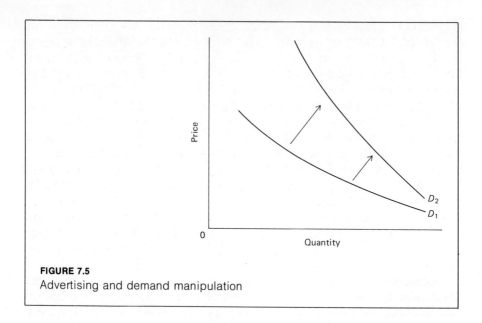

FIGURE 7.5
Advertising and demand manipulation

Avenue, the home of the advertising industry, gains — unless we count as a gain the reduction in lung cancer attendant on the reduced smoking that results from higher costs and higher prices for cigarettes.

Where the number of firms in an industry is still relatively large, each firm has some freedom of action in setting prices. Price reduction attracts customers from other companies, but not enough from any one to initiate a price war. All this is changed when there are few firms in the industry. In the automobile industry, for example, customers are shared among so few companies that General Motors will not idly stand by and allow prospective Chevrolet buyers to be bid away by a lower price for Fords. The price of Chevrolets will promptly come down to match Ford's lower price. And Ford knows this. In this situation of mutual interdependence, no one of the large companies will make any important decision — whether it's styling, prices, or terms of sale — without first attempting to anticipate reactions of other companies in the industry.

If one of the automobile companies decides to raise prices, it can expect no matching price increases by other firms. Why should Chrysler be concerned if Ford raises prices? Chrysler has good substitutes for Fords in the Plymouth or Dodge, so prospective Ford buyers are driven into Chrysler showrooms. What this means for Ford, however, is that they end up selling fewer cars for less money. In other words, their demand curve above the point of the present price is highly elastic — the quantity of Fords demanded is so sensitive (elastic) to price increases that percentage price increases are more than matched by percentage reductions in the quantity of sales. The consequence is that Ford's total sales revenues are reduced. On the other hand, lower prices for Fords, as we have seen, will be promptly matched by price reductions by General Motors and Chrysler. In effect, all automobile companies will end up moving down the *industry* demand curve, which may well be price inelastic. Percentage price reductions are not matched by equal percentage increases in the quantity of automobiles sold, which means that the whole industry ends up with reduced revenues from car sales. In diagrammatic terms, this says that the demand curve facing the individual firms in an oligopolistic industry has a "kink" at the point of present prices, as Figure 7.6 illustrates.

Examination of Figure 7.6 suggests that the individual firm is stymied as far as price changes are concerned: Higher prices mean less total revenue, lower prices also mean lower total revenue. This is the major reason cited for prices remaining constant for long periods in concentrated industries, rather than changing daily or even hourly as in competitive markets.

While the individual firm cannot change prices, though, there is no bar to price increases if all firms take action at the same time. This means that all move together up the industry demand curve. Since Ford and General Motors and Chrysler all increase prices, the automobile buyer who needs a new car has no option but to pay more. After production costs have increased to a certain point, one of the firms in an oligopolistic industry, usually the largest, takes the position of price leader and announces an increase in price sufficient at least to match the higher costs

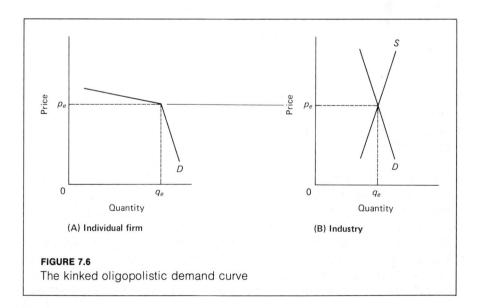

FIGURE 7.6
The kinked oligopolistic demand curve

of production. Other firms in the industry see this as a signal to raise their prices, so all end up generating greater revenues. Conversely, if costs of production fall, the firms in a concentrated industry wait for the signal from the price leader to reduce prices — a signal that rarely comes. Who can remember when the prices of automobiles last fell? Or cigarettes? Or steel?

What all the above signifies, of course, is the departure of price competition from concentrated industries. Economists are skeptical as to whether demand creation in the form of advertising and product changes carries benefits to match those provided by the now-departed price competition. What to do about it is a different matter. It is concentration and large size that drive away price competition. Attempting to restore price competition through breaking up the nation's basic industries, though, is a task that the antitrust authorities are reluctant to take on, and one that Congress is reluctant to force on them.

I   RECENT TRENDS   I

Conglomerate mergers

As if their life were not difficult enough when the antitrust authorities confronted only mergers and concentration within industries, in recent years they have been asked to deal with a flood of *conglomerate mergers* — mergers of firms doing business in completely different industries. Most economists take these conglomerate mergers lightly. After all, if Textron takes over previously independent Homelite, as it did, there is no change in the concentration ratio in the chain saw industry and little change in competitive relationships in the industry. There are as many chain saw producers as there were before the take-over. Nor do efficiency considerations provide a basis for action: Homelite, with Textron's huge resources to draw on, may be a more active and effective competitor than it was as an independent company.

Some critics refuse to be lulled by such arguments. Does it really make no difference, they ask, that thousands of independent companies have been swallowed up by billion-dollar giants? Why wouldn't it be possible for Textron to order its satellite Homelite to cut prices below costs of production, drive other chain saw producers out of business, and then raise prices to well above pre-price-war levels? Textron could easily afford to finance such a price war since it would maintain prices in its other operations and Homelite is a miniscule part of its total operations. The very possibility of competition of this sort might well deter new firms from entering the chain saw industry. Further, what is to restrain Textron from employing reciprocal purchasing leverage — informing the firms from which it buys that they will continue to get Textron's business only if the supplying firms buy their chain saws only from Homelite, their staplers from Bostitch, their airplanes from Bell Aircraft, and their radio equipment from Globe Electronics? Finally, isn't mere size itself to be feared? Would IT&T have been in a position to help subvert the Allende regime in Chile if it had been still a company of modest size in the telephone and telegraph industry?

The response of the antitrust authorities (the Antitrust Division of the Justice Department and the Federal Trade Commission) is that they have not yet seen evidence that would force them to move against the conglomerates. They have no proof of predatory price cutting, use of reciprocal purchasing leverage, or discouragement of potential entry into industries where the conglomerates operate. As for size — well, mere large size is no offense under the antitrust laws. All the antitrust officials can do at this point, they insist, is wait and see if fears about the conglomerates are realized.

The business world itself hasn't yet decided whether or not to accept these new organizations into the fold. David N. Jedelson, president of Gulf and Western Industries, one of the leading conglomerate firms, confirmed this when he related, with some annoyance, the latest definition he had heard: "A conglomerate is a kind of business that services industry the way Bonnie and Clyde serviced banks."[14]

This quotation, from a long feature article in *Business Week*, recognizes that "conglomerators often revive competition in settled industries by picking up marginal producers and energizing them with new capital, uninhibited ideas, and fresh expertise."[15] But it strongly suggests that the conglomerate movement is in large part a sideshow in a financial carnival, with conglomerators far more interested in easy pickings from financial wheeling and dealing than in prospective profits to be earned by more efficiently producing goods or services.

The scenario for a successful conglomerate take-over is built around the fact that Wall Street's investing public is far more interested in stocks with a strong potential than in those that merely pay a good dividend. Even a 10 percent dividend is piddling when compared with the possible doubling of the market price of the stock. Besides, dividends are taxable at ordinary income tax rates, while income earned by buying stocks low and selling them high is taxed as capital gains at a maximum rate of 35 percent — a vital consideration for a speculator in a high tax bracket. Generous dividends are made possible by ample annual earnings, but rapid increases in the prices of stocks occur when company earnings rise faster than the all-company average. Thus it was that in the late 1960s the stock

---

[14] *Business Week* (November 30, 1968), 74.
[15] *Business Week* (November 30, 1968), 74.

of solid, conservatively managed companies sold for 15 or 16 times annual earnings per share, while the glamour companies — those with spectacular increases in earnings per share — were rewarded with multiples as great as 50 or 60. Now let us picture two of these companies — shown in Table 7.3 — and see what financial magic results when the glamour company absorbs the conservative company.

The first thing to notice about the merger is that the Meteor Corporation need not put any of its own money into the take-over transaction (although should that prove necessary, the commercial banks have proved more than willing to accommodate with a short-term loan). Ordinarily all that is required is for the go-go corporation to print up additional amounts of its own stock certificates and offer to swap them for the shares held by stockholders of the company to be absorbed. Once a conglomerator has control of a corporation, he has a magic money machine — as the number of newly made millionaires in the country attests.

Since at the time of the merger Meteor shares were selling for twice as much as Gibraltar shares, stockholders of Gibraltar should be willing to give up two of their shares for one Meteor share, especially when they are made aware of the past spectacular increases in the price of Meteor stock. So Meteor swaps its 25,000 new shares for the 50,000 outstanding Gibraltar shares and combines Gibraltar's $1 million earnings with its own

TABLE 7.3
The financial economics of conglomeration

	Meteor Corporation I	Gibraltar Corporation
Common shares outstanding	100,000	50,000
Total earnings	$1,000,000	$1,000,000
Earnings per share	$10	$20
Market price	$400	$200
Price/earnings ratio	40/1	10/1
Market value of outstanding stock	$40,000,000	$10,000,000

	Meteor Corporation II
Common shares outstanding	125,000
Total earnings	$2,000,000
Earnings per share	$16
Market price	$640
Price/earnings ratio	40/1
Market value of outstanding stock	$80,000,000

$1 million earnings, thus doubling its annual earnings. With $2 million of earnings and 125,000 shares outstanding, earnings per share rise to $16 ($2,000,000/125,000).

At this point we assume that Meteor shares are still selling for the premerger price, $400. At a $400 price, speculators should see Meteor stock as a real bargain because this gives a price/earnings multiple of only 25 ($400/16) and the stock has been selling for 40 times its annual earnings. Recognizing a bargain, stock buyers increase their purchases of Meteor stock until its price is driven up to its former 40/1 ratio to earnings, at $640. When the stock reaches this price, its total market value will be $80 million — which means that a former $40 million company and a $10 million company now are worth $30 million more as a combined operation, all without the production of an additional nickel's worth of goods and services. Meteor has doubled its earnings, its owners are now richer by 60 percent, and the burst of activity on Wall Street has been good for stockbrokers. But the American economy has taken one more step in the direction of economic concentration.

Just possibly the business world here and there has been invigorated by this much-touted *synergism* — "the whole is greater than the sum of its parts" — but it's hard to detect it in the performance of the conglomerates. Without such evidence, and with Wall Street collapsing in the late 1960s, the magic evaporated from conglomerate mergers. After all, the success of the merger maneuver depends on maintaining a high price/earnings multiple for the conglomerate stock. If stock buyers refuse to bid the stock back up to its old multiple, the whole operation fails. The fact that something like this did happen is supported by annual merger figures: 2,407,000 in the peak year 1968, then a year-by-year decline to well under a million in 1973. Without the stimulus provided by a booming stock market, conglomerates were forced to make their way with what they had previously acquired. With those holdings they earned a return to their common stockholders in all of 1975 somewhat under the all-industry average: 11.3 percent compared with 11.8 percent.[16]

Multinational corporations

In recent years the large corporation has burst its national boundaries and spread around the world. Some American companies have conducted part of their operations overseas for many decades: General Motors in Germany, Ford in England, Chrysler in France, oil companies in the Middle East, banks with foreign branches here and there throughout the world. But what was once a rivulet has now become a flood. "Within the last ten years, global corporations have grown so fast that their combined total sales

---

[16] *Business Week* (March 22, 1976), 75, 104.

exceed the gross national product of every country except the United States and the Soviet Union. . . ."[17]

Judd Polk, formerly chief economist with the United States Council of the International Chamber of Commerce, calculates that by the turn of the century a few hundred companies will, if they maintain their present growth rates, produce goods and services amounting to four thousand two hundred billion dollars, or about fifty-four percent of the value of all goods and services.[18]

Even now, as Table 7.4 indicates, a handful of these giants can take their places alongside mid-size sovereign nations when it comes to commanding the economic resources of the world.

According to the best information available (and it's not very good), American companies now have more than $125 billion worth of direct investments abroad. Foreign global firms have another $70 billion — including some $20 billion in the United States.[19] And for American companies the overseas portion is increasing more rapidly than the domestic. In 1957 American companies invested about 10 cents abroad for every dollar they invested at home; before the mid-seventies recession they invested 25 cents. Total profits earned on these foreign investments rose from 25 percent of total profits at home in 1966 to 40 percent in 1970.[20]

The reasons for the outward thrust of American corporations are not difficult to identify. They are not the result of any conspiracy or intent to dominate the economic world but are the logical consequence of the search for profits. Briefly, American companies are reacting to (1) a rapid growth in the markets for goods in which they specialize, (2) the availability of cheaper labor, which makes it profitable to produce abroad, and (3) the threat posed by their foreign competitors' growing faster than themselves and gaining an increased share of the world market. Facilitating the building of these world empires were improvements in telephonic communications, the availability of the jet plane, better control and accountability through use of the computer, and improvements in business management. These all add up to an increased ability to control a larger volume of activity over a wider area. Had such wonderful tools been available to the rulers of an earlier era, even the Roman Empire might have been given a new lease on life.

---

[17] Richard Barnet and Ronald Muller, "Global Reach," *The New Yorker* (December 2, 1974), 53.

[18] Barnet and Muller, "Global Reach," p. 53.

[19] "Why Companies Do Business Abroad," *Readers' Digest* (November 1975), reprint.

[20] Robert L. Heilbroner, "None of Your Business," *New York Review* (March 20, 1975), 6.

TABLE 7.4
Income comparisons, selected multinational corporations and nations

Corporation	Net income from sales ($ million, 1975 except as noted)	Nation	Gross national product ($ million, 1973)
Exxon	44,748	Sweden	45,700
General Motors	35,725	Switzerland	40,900
Royal Dutch/Shell Group	32,336 (1974)	Austria	27,900
Texaco	25,100	Denmark	27,400
Ford Motor	24,000	Turkey	22,000
Mobil Oil	22,270	Norway	18,800
British Petroleum	18,345	Greece	16,300
Unilever	13,555		

Source: Corporation net income reprinted from July 14, 1975 and March 22, 1976 issues of *Business Week* by special permission. © 1975, 1976 by McGraw-Hill, Inc.; gross national product reprinted from *Statistical Abstract of the United States*, 1975.

Regardless of the intent of our modern-day empire builders, some analysts wonder if we are not reaching the point where the world's important economic decisions are made in the corporate headquarters of these international giants, at the expense of national sovereignty.[21] Perhaps they worry unnecessarily. At the very least, though, we have already learned that domestic economic policies will be frustrated unless the reactions of multinational firms are correctly anticipated. An attempt to control inflation by reducing the rate of growth of the domestic money supply is fruitless if the global firms can turn to their foreign money holdings to replace loans not readily available at domestic banks. Tighter pollution controls are difficult to implement if American companies threaten to move their operations abroad. Balance-of-payments policies must be set in the absence of accurate foreign trade figures. A large part of our exports and imports are transferred among our large corporations and their foreign subsidiaries, with prices on goods set to suit the convenience of the companies. To the extent that such prices are juggled to minimize corporate profits and taxes (and we have much evidence that such juggling takes place), taxes will be undercollected by the American government. American unions, faced by companies that can offset the growth of labor strength by

---

[21] See Stephen Hymer, "The Internationalization of Capital," *Journal of Economic Issues* (March 1972), 91–112.

transferring production abroad, are put in a difficult situation. As an example, the United Electrical Workers in Ashland, Massachusetts, struck General Electric in the 1960s to secure a wage increase to $3.40 an hour. Six months after the strike GE announced plans to move half of its timer and clock production to Singapore, where wages were $.30 an hour. Eight hundred Ashland workers were laid off.

Finally, to bring the analysis full circle, should the American government decide that these companies have become too large to tolerate, it would be a formidable problem to whittle them down to size. The companies can argue — they have argued — that small American companies would be hopelessly outclassed in the competition for world business. Douglass Grymes, president of Koppers Company, a multinational corporation, argues that "big corporations are the only ones that can compete with big corporations in world markets."[22] UCLA Professor J. Fred Weston agrees: "If we hold on to the 18th Century idea of a nation of small shopkeepers and small farms, we will become a small nation."[23] But what if these giants refuse to compete? What if they agree on prices and divide up the world's markets among themselves, as has happened on occasion in the past? Since such agreements spill over national boundaries, they are difficult for individual countries to detect and, once detected, are difficult to act against. All of which suggests to some observers that global companies demand a global police force. But where are the police officers able and willing to take on such an assignment? And how do we gain consensus on the rules they will enforce?

I SUMMARY I

Although "the business of this country is business," government by all accounts has an important role to play: It must provide a suitable framework within which business operates. At a minimum this implies the provision of police, a legal system, law courts, and national defense. In the late nineteenth century — the period of laissez-faire capitalism — this was about all government did provide. The rise of the large corporation, however, has forced government into a more active role, especially in antitrust — the protection and promotion of competition.

While there are far more proprietorships and partnerships in the United States than there are corporations, the latter have become our leading business organizations. As a consequence of their ability to fragment ownership and thereby raise almost unlimited amounts of capital, a handful of large corporations today turn out an overwhelming proportion of our annual supply of goods and services.

---

[22] *Business Week* (March 23, 1974), 47.
[23] *Business Week* (March 23, 1974), 56.

As the corporate form of organization came to the fore in the late nineteenth century and corporations grew in size, they discovered that price competition and large amounts of overhead capital could be a disastrous combination. Since that time they have utilized a variety of devices to avoid price competition — in the face of an on-again, off-again effort by the federal government to prevent restraints of competition as directed by the antitrust laws. The key problem is that while the large corporation may inhibit price competition, at the same time it promises economies of scale. We have not yet discovered how to retain the latter while discouraging the former.

Since the close of the nineteenth century, mergers have been a favored device for avoiding price competition. In recent years the merger movement has centered on conglomerate mergers: mergers across industry lines. Whether or not the long-range consequence of such mergers will be further suppression of competition is not yet clear. To this point their primary attraction appears to be the generation of stock market profits for promoters.

In addition to growing to the point that they dominate the domestic economy, giant corporations have spilled over national boundaries and become multinational or global concerns. In the process they have created multiple problems of control, both at home and abroad.

I IMPORTANT TERMS AND CONCEPTS I

capitalism	corporation
sole proprietorship	economies of scale (size)
unlimited liability	concentration ratio
partnership	conglomerate merger
limited liability	multinational corporation

I QUESTIONS, PROBLEMS, AND EXERCISES I

1 What is the minimal role reserved for government in a private enterprise economy?

2 Why are most of the big businesses in the United States corporations and most of the small businesses partnerships or sole proprietorships?

3 What sort of case would you make for the proposition that the antitrust laws, while restraining price fixing, have promoted market control by way of mergers and combinations?

4 When the argument is made that breaking up large corporations is necessary to promote effective price competition, it is promptly rebutted with the claim that this would entail heavy costs for the consumer. On what grounds does this counterargument rest?

5 Why isn't the level of profits earned by a company a sufficient measure of that company's efficiency of operations?

6 A single company in an oligopolistic industry may find unilateral price increases unwise, yet be effectively barred from unilateral, potentially profitable price reductions. Why? And what are the consequences?

7 By what route is a conglomerate merger expected to benefit the consumer?

8 Why have American corporations "gone global"? What problems has this created for the American economy?

I SUGGESTED READING I

Andreano, Ralph L., ed. *Superconcentration/Supercorporation: A Collage of Opinion on the Concentration of Economic Power*. Warner Modular Publications, Andover, Mass., 1973.

Barnet, Richard J., and Ronald E. Muller. *Global Reach: The Power of the Multinational Corporation*. Simon and Schuster, New York, 1974.

"Conglomerates." *Business Week* (November 30, 1968), 74–84.

Fusfeld, Daniel R. "The Rise of the Corporate State in America." *Journal of Economic Issues* (March 1972), 1–22.

"Is John Sherman's Antitrust Obsolete?" *Business Week* (March 23, 1974), 47–56.

Leonard, William N. "Mergers, Industrial Concentration, and Antitrust Policy." *Journal of Economic Issues* (June 1976), 354–381.

Simons, Henry C. *Economic Policy for a Free Society*. University of Chicago Press, Chicago, 1948.

Solo, Robert. *The Political Authority and the Market System*. South-Western, Cincinnati, Ohio, 1974.

EIGHT

I INEQUALITY AND POVERTY I

No topic of discussion in the field of economics produces violent disagreement quite so readily as the "proper" amount of inequality to be tolerated or promoted in the distribution of income and wealth. *Income inequality* is a pocketbook issue in every aspect, and where our pocketbooks are concerned we get touchy very quickly. Reasonable people may hold different opinions as to the best way of deciding what an economy is to produce and how production is to be organized and conducted, yet still be able to compromise and agree on working arrangements. But when it comes to the distribution of what is produced — who gets what slice of the pie that all have shared in making and baking — no division yet discovered commands anywhere near universal assent.

Some of the disagreement centers on narrow economic considerations — on the difference it makes to the efficient performance of the economy when the distribution of its output is changed in the direction of either more or less inequality. Does greater inequality, in other words, promote or impair economic efficiency? Since economics, to the extent that it can claim to be a science, is the science of efficiency, economists should be able to speak with some authority about the relationship between inequality and the effective use of productive resources.

Even if economists could agree on this relationship, however, which they cannot, they would still face the fact that inequality is far more than simply a technical economic problem. So many and diverse are its ramifications that it quickly pushes beyond the realm of economics into philosophy, social psychology, sociology, education, political science, even theology. A pattern of income and wealth distribution that is entirely acceptable on purely economic grounds may be completely unacceptable when broader social criteria are brought to bear, and vice versa. While we will be concerned in this chapter with the economics of inequality and poverty, it will be necessary at times to consider these broader social implications.

I THE EXTENT OF INEQUALITY I

Measuring inequality

With the wealth of data available from censuses and tax returns, the federal government has the information necessary to portray the distribution of income in the United States. These facts are now published regularly in a number of different forms. The breakdown that economists find most useful is family groupings by fifths or quintiles, as shown in Table 8.1. The way to read Table 8.1 is to visualize all the families in the United States, ranked in order of annual incomes. Count up from the bottom of the distribution until you have 20 percent of all the families and then add up the income those families receive. Table 8.1 tells us that the families making up the lowest fifth of the 1975 array got 5.4 percent of the total incomes received by all American families. Conversely, the 20 percent of the families at the top of the array received 41.1 percent of total family incomes.

Actually, Table 8.1 substantially understates the extent of inequality in the distribution of income, especially for the later years, because the concept of income on which it is based is quite narrow. Three major sources of income in particular are excluded: capital gains, undistributed corporate profits, and employee fringe benefits. Capital gains are the incomes made by buying such assets as stocks, bonds, and real estate at

TABLE 8.1

Percentage of aggregate family income received by each fifth, United States, selected dates

Fifths ranked by family income	1929	1935–1936	1947	1975
Lowest fifth ⎱	12.5	4.1	5.0	5.4
Second fifth ⎰		9.2	11.8	11.8
Third fifth	13.8	14.1	17.0	17.6
Fourth fifth	19.3	20.9	23.1	24.1
Highest fifth	54.4	51.7	43.2	41.1
	100.0	100.0	100.0	100.0

Source: *Historical Statistics of the United States, Statistical Abstract of the United States.*

one price and selling them later at a higher price. Undistributed corporate profits are the profits left after payment of taxes and in effect kept at work in the corporation. They are part of the stockholders' earnings but are not paid out as dividends during the current year. Employee fringe benefits are forms of compensation other than what ends up in the pay check: use of a company car, paid vacations, employer payments for group medical and dental insurance, use of the company expense account, company payments for country club memberships, and so forth. Although lower-income families receive some capital gains, have some claims to undistributed corporate profits, and enjoy part of the employee fringe benefits, it is obvious that the major shares of all three go to the high-income groups.

Even adding these types of excluded income wouldn't provide a complete picture of income inequality because we would still be overlooking other types of income — especially nonpecuniary or psychic income. The fact is that the best-paying jobs in the United States are the most pleasant and the most satisfying. Part of what they pay takes the form of high cash income, but another substantial part — the part we don't, perhaps can't, measure — takes the form of power, prestige, challenge, pleasant surroundings, and a feeling of accomplishment. For the low-paying jobs, on the other hand, the psychic income is minimal or perhaps even negative: no power, no prestige, no challenge, unpleasant or dirty surroundings, and little or no feeling of accomplishment. Comparing the job of a corporation president with that of a garbage collector is more than a matter of seeing how much each is paid.

With the above reservations in mind, Table 8.1 tells us that while there has been a movement toward greater equality in the distribution of American income during the past half-century, that movement virtually ceased with the end of World War II. Property incomes (corporation profits, rent, interest), received for the most part by families in the top fifth, were hard hit by the depression (corporate profits were actually negative in 1932 and 1933), whereas wages and salaries, the primary sources of income for the lower fifths, fell by a smaller proportion. In the next decade, the booming economy and full employment during World War II benefited the wage earner more than the property owner, partly as a consequence of the cumulative effect of the progressive personal income tax and excess profits taxes. Any further impact of progressive taxes on the distribution of income since the war, however, is hard to detect in the figures of Table 8.1. And the War on Poverty of recent years fails to show any material results as well. If we desire greater equality in the distribution of income, it is obvious that we are not going to get it with present programs. Some form of new initiative will be required.

International comparisons of income distribution

It may be helpful in deciding whether or not to move toward greater equality in income distribution to know where other nations stand. Table 8.2 provides the data for some of the other market-oriented economies. Table 8.2 reveals that, with minor exceptions, the distribution of income in economies similar to the United States differs little from our own. This is somewhat surprising when we recognize that Britain and Sweden are usually thought of as socialist countries. Apparently their socialism is more in label than

TABLE 8.2

Percentage of gross personal income received by each fifth of people, four market-oriented economies, 1964

Fifths ranked by income	United Kingdom	West Germany	Sweden	France
Lowest fifth	5.1	5.3	4.4	1.9
Second fifth	10.2	10.2	9.6	7.6
Third fifth	16.6	13.2	17.4	14.0
Fourth fifth	23.9	18.0	24.6	22.8
Highest fifth	44.2	52.9	44.0	53.7
	100.0	100.0	100.0	100.0

Source: Data from United Nations, *Incomes in Post-War Europe: A Study of Policies, Growth, and Distribution*, Geneva: United Nations, 1967. The figures represent the number of taxpayers, except for France, where unit is the household. (The non-French figures therefore understate the lowest fifth: persons with incomes too low to pay taxes are excluded.) Reprinted from Philip A. Klein, *The Management of Market-Oriented Economies, A Comparative Perspective*, Wadsworth, Belmont, Calif., 1973, p. 69. For details of data and calculation, see original source.

in fact. West Germany and France show a larger proportion of income accruing to families and individuals in the highest bracket, and France has a conspicuously smaller proportion captured by the lowest brackets. Otherwise, similarities are more apparent than differences.

Wealth and inequality

Inequality in the distribution of income leads directly to inequality in the distribution of wealth. High-income families, with more money than necessary to satisfy their immediate needs, are able to convert substantial parts of their current income into the forms of assets that we call wealth. Some of these are homes, household goods, pleasure boats, and cars, but, especially for the highest-income families, the more substantial part of the assets takes the form of investment assets: money put to work making more money. Thus high incomes lead to large holdings of earning assets, which in turn lead to even higher incomes.

The last comprehensive study of wealth holdings in the United States was conducted in 1962 by the Federal Reserve Board of Governors. It documented, as Table 8.3 shows, the direct relationship between annual incomes and wealth accumulations.

The study, in addition, confirmed the fact that wealth holdings are much more unequally distributed than are income receipts: the top 18.7 percent of all families owned 76.2 percent of all the privately held wealth, while the bottom 25 percent had none (which compares, remember, with

TABLE 8.3
Average amount of wealth held by income groups, 1962

Income category ($)	Average wealth holdings ($)
0– 2,999	7,609
3,000– 4,999	10,025
5,000– 7,499	13,207
7,500– 9,999	19,131
10,000–14,999	28,019
15,000–24,999	62,965
25,000–49,999	291,317
50,000–99,999	653,223
100,000 and over	1,698,021

Source: Dorothy Projector and Gertrude Weiss, *Survey of Financial Characteristics of Consumers*, Federal Reserve Technical Papers, U.S. Government Printing Office, Washington, D.C. (August 1966), 110.

the top fifth of income receivers getting only a little over 40 percent of all income). A later partial study conducted in 1969 provides an even more dramatic picture of the concentration of wealth: Those with wealth accumulations of over $5 million (the top 0.008 percent of the population) had as large total asset holdings as the entire bottom half of families.[1]

One final survey completes the picture of wealth holdings by showing what forms the wealth holdings of the richest 0.5 percent and 1 percent take, as shown in Table 8.4. Although Table 8.4 casts considerable light on many aspects of the perennial question of who owns America, two pieces of information are especially noteworthy. Corporate stock represents the ownership of the corporation, and a disproportionate share of American business is conducted under the corporate form of organization. Table 8.4 tells us that 1 percent of the population owns well over half of this most important form of American business. In more global terms, this same 1 percent has a free and clear claim (indicated by the net worth line) to just over one-quarter of all assets in the United States. Who owns America? Well, 2 million individuals out of the more than 200 million citizens of the country own a very significant chunk of it.

How much income inequality is ideal?

To say that one country's income is more equally distributed than another's is not necessarily to say that the position of the former is to be preferred to that of the latter. One country may have excellent reasons for preferring more equal incomes, but another may find the arguments for less equality

the small society   by Brickman

INSURANCE? ARE YOU KIDDING?

BEFORE A BURGLAR COULD STEAL ANYTHING FROM HERE, HE'D HAVE TO BRING SOMETHING IN—

Washington Star Syndicate. Inc

BRICKMAN

1-2

---

[1] Internal Revenue Service, "Statistics of Income 1969: Personal Wealth," Publication 482 (October 1973), 19. Cited in Lester C. Thurow, "Popular Mechanics: The Redistribution of Wealth," *Working Papers* (Winter 1976), 25.

TABLE 8.4

Shares of richest 0.5 percent and 1.0 percent of persons in national wealth, 1972

Asset	Total value ($ billion)	Value ($ billion) held by richest		Share (%) held by richest	
		0.5%	1.0%	0.5%	1.0%
Real estate	1492.6	150.9	225.0	10.1	15.1
Corporate stock	870.9	429.3	491.7	49.3	56.5
Bonds	158.0	82.5	94.8	52.2	60.0
Cash	748.8	63.6	101.2	8.5	13.5
Debt instruments	77.5	30.3	40.8	39.1	52.7
Life insurance (cash surrender value)	143.0	6.2	10.0	4.3	7.0
Miscellaneous and trusts					
Trusts	99.4	80.3	89.4	80.8	89.9
Miscellaneous	853.6	95.5	83.3	6.8	9.8
Total assets	4344.4	822.4	1046.9	18.9	24.1
Liabilities	808.5	100.7	131.0	12.5	16.2
Net worth	3535.9	721.7	915.9	20.4	25.9
Number of persons (millions)		1.0	2.1		

Source: *Statistical Abstract of the United States*, 1976, p. 429.

more compelling. Although they seem to suggest the same thing and in fact are often confused one with the other, the concepts of equality and equity are by no means identical. The meaning of equality we have already discussed. It is simply equal shares in the dividing-up process. Equity is something quite different. *Equity in the distribution of income* means fairness or justice in the division of income, and therefore involves an ethical judgment. Equal sharing, for some, is the very essence of fairness; according to others, equal sharing would be extremely unjust.

It is sometimes assumed that communism (philosophical communism, that is, with a small *c*, not Russian Communism, with a capital *C*) calls for complete equality in distribution. This is not quite true. According to the Marxian framework of analysis, a large step will be taken in the direction of equality when socialism (worker ownership of the means of production) replaces capitalism (capitalist ownership of the means of production). Capitalism is bound to lead to highly unequal incomes both because ownership of the means of production is highly concentrated and because the owners of productive property are able to command high prices for the services of their property. Broadening of the base of ownership under socialism to include all workers (which means everybody) will lead to a substantial move in the direction of income equality. But substantial inequality will still remain, according to Marx, since socialism will continue to reward workers according to their production. Property ownership will no longer justify differences in reward, but workers will still differ in ability and therefore differ in income receipts. When the final evolution from socialism to communism takes place, Marx agrees that a further step in the direction of equal shares is in order. But absolutely equal shares will never be justified. Communism replaces the distribution ethic of socialism, "to each according to his or her production," with "to each according to his or her needs." Needs will always differ — a common laborer needs more food than a bookkeeper, an artist needs more esthetic surroundings than a laborer — so incomes will never be completely equal.

A common strand in the writings of the advocates of socialism has always been the condemnation of the extremes of inequality found in capitalist economies and the necessity of socialism as a vehicle for moving in the direction of equality. Few socialist writers, however, make the case so forcefully and in such extreme fashion as the great Irish-English dramatist George Bernard Shaw. For Shaw — who was a great dramatist in important part because he was a pre-eminent social philosopher — socialism meant first of all "an equal share to everybody." His case for equal shares crops up here and there in his writings but is made most fully in *The Intelligent Woman's Guide to Socialism and Capitalism*.[2]

Shaw first examines alternative plans of distribution "at present advocated or practiced."

1. To each what he or she produces. 2. To each what he or she deserves. 3. To each what he or she can get and hold. 4. To the common people enough to keep them alive whilst they work all day, and the rest to the gentry. 5. Division of society into classes, the distribution being equal or thereabouts within each class, but unequal as between the classes. 6. Let us go on as we are.[3]

Shaw finds major deficiencies in each of these; he proposes equal shares as the best solution to the problem of who is to get what. He recognizes that the principal drawback to his proposal is the impact of his scheme on incentive — unless a person can earn more than another by working harder, he or she cannot be expected to work harder or longer — but his counterarguments are not convincing. His first point has some validity. In

---

[2] American edition published by Garden City Publishing, Garden City, N.Y., 1928.

[3] George Bernard Shaw, *Intelligent Woman's Guide to Socialism and Capitalism*, Garden City Publishing, Garden City, N.Y., 1928, p. xv.

the mass production industries, extra exertion is not possible since the work pace is established for the whole group of workers. But what about the slacker, whose object is to avoid work at any cost while still drawing his or her equal share? Shaw concedes that in this case there is no solution but direct compulsion — the solution that has been forced on countries, such as Cuba, that have made a serious effort to implement equal shares.

Repelled by the thought of stick-wielding, most analysts today prefer the carrot of unequal shares for unequal work. But that merely puts us back on square one: How unequal should the shares be? For one group of advocates, the believers in unrestricted market capitalism, this question is not basically a matter for *social* concern or policy. According to writer Ayn Rand, "Only individual men have the right to decide when or whether they wish to help others; society — as an organized political system — has no rights in the matter at all."[4] Redistribution from the rich to help the poor, from this point of view, is immoral unless it takes the form of private charity. Implicit in this outlook is the conviction that the rich have *earned* everything they possess and that it is therefore unethical, at the least, to take anything from them.

But how does one demonstrate that all high incomes are earned — that individual effort is the sole factor explaining income differentials? Doesn't luck play a part? Bad luck in the form of ill health surely explains why many people are poor. Couldn't good luck in the form of being in the right place at the right time contribute to the receipt of large incomes? And isn't it possible that successfully flouting the law has in many cases been rewarded with high incomes? This is individual effort, it is true, but not the sort that should make the fruits of the effort immune to challenge.

How much individual effort is involved, also, in acquiring high incomes and large wealth holdings from family gifts and inheritances? Some estimates attribute up to half of the largest fortunes in the United States to inheritance.[5] To suggest that the holders of these fortunes showed great individual initiative in choosing their parents carefully is to be merely flippant.

Finally, and most important, in a complex society such as ours, where most production is collective production, it is usually impossible to identify the contribution of an individual. Individuals do matter in production, of course, but how much they matter can rarely be determined in a particular situation. This being the case there is every reason for doubting that what an individual is currently paid is closely related to what he or she produces. The assumption that middle managers in a production plant are paid three

---

[4] Ayn Rand, *The Virtue of Selfishness*, Signet Books, New American Library, New York, 1963, p. 80.

[5] See Lester C. Thurow, "Popular Mechanics: The Redistribution of Wealth," *Working Papers* (Winter 1976), 25.

times as much as assembly-line workers because they produce three times as much is purely that — an assumption. Although the assumption may be accepted by all concerned, and may have been standard practice for generations, there is no way of proving its validity. Nor can it be convincingly demonstrated that the top 10 percent of the income receivers in the United States, who collectively get around fourteen times as much total income as the bottom 10 percent, contribute fourteen times as much to the generation of that income.

Nevertheless, the market system remains the prevalent American ideology, and the supporters of that system insist that it does, with all its imperfections, distribute rewards more or less on the basis of individual contributions. If this is indeed the case, only minimal interference with the distribution process is justified. All men are not created equal where economic performance is concerned, no matter what our Declaration of Independence asserts, and it is ridiculous to assume that they are. And if men are unequal in ability and performance, it is the essence of fairness that they be treated unequally. Provide a fair field and equal opportunity, then let the marketplace distribute its rewards unequally on the basis of unequal performance. In broad outline, this is, in fact, the way we usually justify the extent of inequality that our income distribution shows.

This justification, however, is wearing rather thin. At the very least, it by no means calls for accepting whatever distribution the market offers. First of all, the market system does not automatically provide for equal opportunity. It was earlier assumed that a businessman could not afford to discriminate against competent women and members of minority groups, because if he did he would be forced to pay more for male workers. This would leave him at a disadvantage with his competitors who did not discriminate. There seems to be sufficient slack in our competitive system, however, to tolerate the alleged inefficiencies of discrimination. Only a systematic government affirmative action–equal opportunity program is apparently sufficient to make headway against discrimination. Also, the mere fact that a child is born into one family rather than another is enough to give that child a long head start in the economic race. This goes beyond the unequal inheritance of wealth and recognizes the presence of unequal family environments derived from unequal family incomes. Being born into a family able to provide culture, travel, education, and a sense of individual responsibility almost guarantees a person a long leg up the economic ladder, and just the reverse for the child of a family unable to provide these amenities. Further, the premise that the market system proportions rewards to effort is based on the assumption that the system is thoroughly competitive — that it cannot be rigged to the advantage of some and the disadvantage of others. This assumption becomes ever more difficult to document as our economy moves steadily in the direction of domination by big business and big labor.

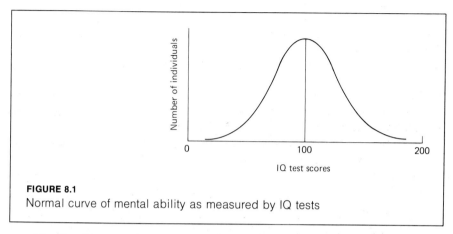

FIGURE 8.1

Normal curve of mental ability as measured by IQ tests

Finally, if incomes were actually distributed in accordance with the ability of individual income receivers, the pattern of income distribution should at least roughly take the shape of the normal, or bell-shaped, curve. If we use IQ tests to measure mental ability, for example, we find as in Figure 8.1 that most individual scores cluster fairly closely around the average of the group. About as few persons fall below the average as above the average.

When we plot the current distribution of income in the United States, though, as shown in Figure 8.2, we find that our bell-shaped curve is sadly misshapen. The left tail of the curve is shrunken while the right tail, representing families with high incomes, is greatly elongated. This strongly

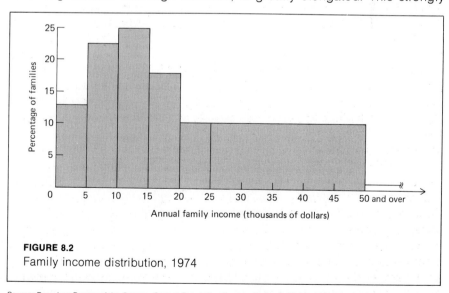

FIGURE 8.2

Family income distribution, 1974

Source: Based on Bureau of the Census, *Current Population Reports*, Series P-60, No. 101, January 1976, p. 1.

suggests that something more than mere ability must be called on to explain why so many families are able to enjoy the luxuries associated with high incomes. And the wealth distribution curve, of course, is even more thoroughly skewed because wealth, as we have seen, is far more unequally distributed than income.

One last argument for unequal income distribution on the grounds of efficient economic performance is now extremely shaky. This is the macro argument, concerned with the long-run growth of the whole economy. Growth, from this point of view, comes from investment in productive capital — in machines and factories to produce more goods and services in the future. But investment requires nonconsumption. The same economic resources cannot be used to produce both capital goods and consumption goods; the same workers cannot build shoe factories and turn out shoes at the same time. Workers will be released from manufacturing shoes and turned to building shoe factories, though, only if consumers spend less on shoes and turn their purchasing power over to the builders of factories. Low-income families cannot afford to reduce their consumption. They have so little income that all of it must go to provide vital necessities. Only high-income families have sufficient room in their budgets for a substantial amount of nonconsumption — for the savings necessary to finance the investment essential for rapid economic growth. Take these incomes from the rich, then, and all progress will stop because investment will have no pool of savings to draw from.

But the savings of the rich are a double-edged sword. They represent nonconsumption as well as investment. But that investment will take place only if there is an assured market for what the capital goods — the factories and machines — will turn out. In the example above, why will investors build new shoe factories if the demand for shoes is falling? Too much saving will thus destroy the incentive to invest. This, in fact, has been a perennial problem in the United States. Too little consumption spending has been a barrier to investment spending as often as has a shortage of savings to finance investment. The very fact that the poor spend almost all of their incomes on consumption goods is therefore as compelling an argument for providing them with additional income as the argument for tolerating high incomes because they facilitate saving.

What all the foregoing boils down to is that "scientific" analysis does not take us very far in justifying one particular pattern of income distribution in preference to another. In large part we are forced to conclude that distribution is a matter of ethical social judgment. In the words of one recognized authority:

Distributional equity is nonmechanical in principle. It implies that the distribution of income, wealth or whatever is being distributed will be in accordance with principles of justice; therefore, my personal view is that the concept of distributive equity is largely, if not completely, a subjective matter. This implies the impossibility, in principle, of objectively judging whether something called maldistribution exists in a given society and whether one distribution is better than another.[6]

❘ POVERTY AND NATIONAL COMMITMENT ❘

The elimination of poverty

If distributive equity is a subjective matter, there is no reason that poverty cannot be eliminated through redistributing income from the upper-income groups to those living in poverty. This is true at least in the United States. Our average income is so high that after redistribution all families would still be relatively affluent. It would not be true in the less developed countries of the world. Sharing the limited wealth there would mean that everyone would live in poverty. In the United States, though, all we need are the will and the way.

The will seems to be there. This is indicated by all the attention we have given to the problem of poverty in recent years and by the vast number of programs now in existence designed to deal in one fashion or another with the problem. The fact that there is general dissatisfaction with our "welfare mess," however, suggests that we are a long way from finding the ideal solution to the problem. The appropriate way is yet to be found — or at least agreed upon.

The definition of poverty

Finding the proper way starts with recognition of the fact that we haven't yet come to complete agreement on the most basic issue of the problem: What is poverty? Since, as the saying goes, the poor have always been with us, it would seem that we should long ago have found a way of distinguishing between the poor and the nonpoor. Nevertheless, we still aren't quite sure where to draw the line.

We have more or less agreed that we should start with the approach suggested by Ernest Hemingway in one of his conversations with F. Scott Fitzgerald. Fitzgerald is reported to have remarked, "You know, Ernest, the rich really are different from everyone else." Hemingway's laconic reply was, "Yes, they have more money." If the rich are rich by virtue of the fact that they have more money, then the poor are surely poor because they have less money. But how little money is required to secure a position in the ranks of the poverty group? Most important, does poverty mean *absolute poverty* or only *relative poverty*? The distinction is vital. If a certain amount of real purchasing power is all that is required to lift a family out

---

[6] Martin Bronfenbrenner, "Equality and Equity," *The Annals of the American Academy of Political and Social Science* (September 1973), 10.

of the poverty ranks, we have a fixed target and can, without excessive cost, abolish poverty. If poorness is relative, however, not only must we make an initial transfer to the poor, but we must continually increase the size of the transfer as everyone else's income rises.

Nonetheless, a significant group of economists argue that the real burden of being poor is that you fail to benefit from the rising affluence provided by a more or less steadily growing American economy. Equity in the distribution of income requires not only that the poor get a larger share of the pie now but that this share be maintained as the pie grows. They would achieve this by tying the poverty support level to some fixed proportion of the overall family median income. The most common figure cited is half the median income. As the median income grows, the support level automatically rises, and those at the bottom of the income distribution come in for a share of the benefits of economic growth.

The battle for this approach to setting an income support level, however, appears at the moment to have been fought and lost. Those agencies of the federal government concerned with establishing the *official poverty level* have opted for an absolute support level — a target that, if achieved, would permit everyone to live at a fixed level that somehow has been determined to be minimally decent. The objective here is to provide sufficient income for a family to hold body and soul together: a certain amount of food, a particular amount of housing, minimal clothing, and so on. Once this minimal package is agreed upon, and adjusted for differences in family size and location, it needs to be changed thereafter only as the cost of buying the package fluctuates.

Although other government agencies have taken a hand at defining a minimally decent standard of living, the principal burden has fallen to the Social Security Administration. Theirs are the figures now carried in official government publications and cited in the newspapers. Although we speak of *the* poverty level, the Social Security Administration found that there are many poverty levels, each dependent on family size, composition, and location. This diversity is brought out in Table 8.5, which shows the minimum amounts necessary in 1963 to maintain families with the characteristics identified.

Some adjustments to these pioneering efforts to define poverty levels have proved necessary. The differential between farm and nonfarm families, based on the premise that farm families produce a substantial part of their own food, proved on later investigation to be too wide and has been narrowed by bringing up the poverty level for farm families. By and large these are the poverty levels that guide government policy today. The nonfarm family of four, for example, is usually taken as the representative family in the United States. The official poverty level for such a family in 1975 was $5,500. This is simply the 1963 figure adjusted upward to reflect the subsequent rise in the consumer price index. Parenthetically it might

TABLE 8.5
Some Social Security Administration poverty lines,
1963 prices

Members in family	Poverty level ($)
1 under 65, nonfarm	1,580
1 under 65, farm	960
1 over 65, nonfarm	1,470
1 over 65, farm	885
4 nonfarm	3,130
4 farm	1,925
7 or more nonfarm	5,090
7 or more farm	3,055

Source: Mollie Orshansky, "Another Look at the Poverty Profile," *Social
Security Bulletin,* Social Security Administration, Washington, D.C., January
1965.

be noted that had the relative, rather than the absolute, approach been
adopted in defining the poverty level and set at half the overall median
family income, the poverty level for a representative family in 1975 would
have been $6,886 (half of $13,772).

Progress against poverty

Had the relative approach to the definition of poverty been adopted, however, the reduction of the poverty group would have been considerably
less rapid than it has been under the absolute definition. As the figures in
Table 8.6 indicate, recent progress in reducing poverty, as officially defined, has been significant. Table 8.6 tells us that the poverty group in the
United States was cut just about in half from the late 1950s to the mid-
1970s. To some extent this was a consequence of all the government
programs we group loosely under the label of the War on Poverty —
housing subsidies, Medicare and Medicaid, food stamps and school
lunches, scholarships for higher education, economic development assistance, and manpower training. Even more it was the result of sustained
economic progress. While the American population increased by 4.2 percent between 1970 and 1975, real gross national product rose by 10.8
percent. The sensitivity of poverty numbers to fluctuations in overall production is suggested by changes in the poverty group from 1973 to 1975:
a fall of 3.5 percent in real gross national product was sufficient to increase
the numbers in poverty by 2.9 million and to drive the percentage of those
in poverty up from 11.1 to 12.3. The poor obviously bear a significant part
of the burden of fighting inflation by pruning the national income.

TABLE 8.6
Persons below poverty level, 1959–1975

Year	Number below poverty level (millions)			% below poverty level		
	All persons	In families	Unrelated individuals[a]	All persons	In families	Unrelated individuals[a]
1959	39.5	34.6	4.9	22.4	20.8	46.1
1965	33.2	28.4	4.8	17.3	15.8	39.8
1969	24.1	19.2	5.0	12.1	10.4	34.0
1973	23.0	18.3	4.7	11.1	9.7	25.6
1975	25.9	20.8	5.1	12.3	10.9	25.1

[a] Persons 14 years or older not living with relatives.
Source: *Statistical Abstract of the United States*, 1976, p. 415.

The leveling off in the size of the poverty group after 1969, though, suggests that further progress in the attempt to eliminate poverty will be hard to come by if we continue to rely solely on economic growth and the programs now in place. A large portion of the poverty group is not in a position either to benefit from growth in the overall level of output or to be removed from poverty by present programs. Why this is so we can understand better if we first take a look at the persons making up the poverty group.

Who are the poor?

A reasonably complete profile of the poor can be secured by abstracting data from current government publications. Table 8.7 shows how the likelihood of poverty is affected by race and sex.

Perhaps the best way to interpret Table 8.7 is to compare the percentage below the poverty level for all groups listed with that of the average

TABLE 8.7
Persons below poverty level, by family status, and race and sex of head, 1975

Family status, race, and sex of head	% below poverty level		
	All persons	In families	Unrelated individuals
All persons	12.3		
In families		10.9	
Unrelated individuals			25.1
White	9.7		
In families		8.3	
Unrelated individuals			22.7
Black and other races	29.3		
In families		28.0	
Unrelated individuals			40.9
In families with male head	7.8		
In families		7.1	
Unrelated individuals			19.9
In families with female head	34.6		
In families		37.5	
Unrelated individuals			28.9

Source: *Statistical Abstract of the United States*, 1976, p. 415.

for all Americans — 12.3 percent. This tells us immediately that the like-lihood of poverty is much greater than average for unrelated individuals, anywhere from somewhat more than twice as likely to almost four times as likely for black and other races. This makes sense because unrelated individuals — those not living with relatives — tend to be the very young and the very old. For these groups high-paying employment, in fact em-ployment of any sort, is apt to be difficult to obtain. The impact of race and sex in pushing individuals below the poverty level is also manifest. Blacks and other non-Caucasians are almost three times as likely as the average American to find themselves in the poverty group, and members of a family headed by a female just above three times as likely. This should not be read to mean, incidentally, that black and other races and female-headed families make up most of the poverty group. Most Americans are white and most white families are headed by a male, so despite the fact that the poverty percentage is low for these groups, most of the poor in the United States are white (17.8 million out of the total 25.9 million), and more than half of the poor families are headed by a male (13.6 million compared with 12.3 million female-headed families).

Where a person or family lives is apt to have a bearing on the inci-dence of poverty, as selected poverty figures in Table 8.8 on a state-by-state basis for 1969 show. The significance of these figures is great for

TABLE 8.8
Persons and families below the poverty level,
selected states, 1969

	% below poverty level	
	Persons	Families
United States	13.7	10.7
Connecticut	7.2	5.3
New Jersey	8.1	6.1
Massachusetts	8.6	6.2
Nebraska	13.1	10.1
Montana	13.6	10.4
Idaho	13.2	10.9
Alabama	25.4	20.7
Louisiana	26.3	21.5
Arkansas	27.8	22.8
Mississippi	35.4	28.9

Source: *Statistical Abstract of the United States*, 1976, p. 419.

policy purposes. Since some states have four and five times as great a proportion of their populations living below the poverty level as do other states, it may be asking for the impossible to insist that these states solve their poverty problem with their own resources, especially since incomes in these states are lower to begin with.

By this point the flood of statistics has undoubtedly become a bit wearisome, so let's conclude with one or two summary statements. Families headed by those young in years or over 65 have a much better than average chance of ending up in poverty. This is the case also for those headed by someone with eight years or less of schooling. And poverty is not restricted to the urban ghetto. In fact, a much higher proportion of the rural population ended up in poverty in 1975 than of the metropolitan area population (15.4 percent compared with 10.8 percent). And this is true whether we are talking about whites (12.6 and 8.2 percent) or blacks (42.4 and 27.6 percent). This should come as no surprise when we recall that Table 8.8 suggested that the highest incidence of poverty is in the more rural states, the lowest incidence is in the highly industrialized, highly urbanized states.

Finally, the question of the employment status and employability of the poor must be addressed. The stereotype we carry in our heads pictures the poor as able-bodied but lazy, far preferring to stay home and receive a dole than to work. The facts fail to provide much support for this view. Well over half (61.5 percent) of the male heads of families below the poverty level in 1975 actually worked year-round full time, as did more than a third (36.5 percent) of the female heads of families. Of the male heads of households not working, an even 50 percent were ill or disabled, as were 20 percent of the female heads of families. Many of the remainder of these were women with small children, who felt they could not leave

the small society   by Brickman

© Washington Star Syndicate, Inc., permission granted by King Features Syndicate, Inc., 1977.

their children at home while they worked full time. The figures differ only slightly for blacks alone: 53.4 percent of black, male, poverty-level family heads in 1975 worked year-round full time, and of those not working 56.4 percent were ill or disabled. When we couple these figures with the incidence of high unemployment in recent years, which means that many members of the poverty groups who are more than willing and able to work are unable to find jobs, there is not much support left for the stereotype of the irresponsible, nonworking, publicly supported poor. The fact is that an overwhelming majority of the American population prefer work to idleness and public support — as is strongly suggested by the fact that over 60 percent of the male heads of families in the poverty group are at work in jobs paying less than a poverty-level wage.

| THE ATTACK ON POVERTY |

The very diversity of the poor makes it extremely difficult to attack the problem of poverty on an across-the-board basis. Many of the poor are young, many are old; many live in rural areas, but even more live in cities; many are able-bodied and willing to work, while many are ill or disabled and incapable of work; many are eager to work but are barred from employment by high general unemployment or because of racial or sexual discrimination or lack of education; many are at work but are unable to earn a poverty-level wage. The only thing the poor seem to share is insufficient income.

Where we are

Although there were many strands in the Great Society War on Poverty of the 1960s and it is perilous to make a general statement about the program, its main thrust was an attempt to raise the productivity of the poor to enable them better to make their way in a market economy. The 1960s — the late 1960s in particular, thanks in large part to Vietnam War spending — was a period of general prosperity and high employment. It was felt that good jobs were available for everyone adequately qualified. Unfortunately, it was believed, the working poor were qualified only for bottom-rung jobs — those calling for no skills and little education, and there were too few of these to provide employment for all of the poor. Upgrade the education and training of the poor, then, and the vicious circle of poverty could be broken. Some help would still be needed, it is true, for those unable to work, but current programs could be expected to take care of them.

This logic provided the impetus for a vast range of new programs, many but not all lodged under the Economic Opportunity Act (1964): Job Corps, Headstart, adult education, Volunteers in Service to America

(VISTA), Manpower Development and Training Program, and assorted area development programs. The list suggests a more all-embracing national effort than was actually the case. Total expenditures on the combined programs never exceeded 1 percent of gross national product, and in 1967 totaled less than 10 percent of what was being spent on the war in Vietnam. Even so the consensus by the early 1970s was that the program had been a costly failure. As is the case for all new comprehensive programs, red tape, confusion, and jurisdictional squabbling limited progress. When worker education and training were actually upgraded, at considerable expense, the result was often only unemployment in a different labor market. Although parts of the program showed some successes and are still in operation, the major effort was written off as a failure and quietly allowed to die.

When the life went out of the Equal Opportunity movement, the nation did not, of course, go back to no poverty program at all. Over the years a large poverty apparatus had been built up, piece by piece. Federal expenditures under these various programs grew rapidly in the 1970s, from $17.8 billion in 1970 to $27.0 billion in 1974. Table 8.9 illustrates the diversity of these federal expenditures and the magnitude of each. In addition to federal expenditures, state and local governments conduct programs that increase the total cost of maintaining the poor.

There are those who argue that the present combined poverty support system has been too severely criticized — that it is basically a sound system in need of only minor repairs. No one starves in the United States, after all, and most individuals deserving of support can find it one place or another. Critics of this point of view find the rub right there, in the phrase "deserving of support." To qualify for aid under most of these programs, an applicant must survive a *means test* — an exhaustive examination by public authorities of his or her eligibility for assistance and inability to live without government aid. Many of the worthy poor pass up the opportunity for public assistance because they are unwilling to undergo this demeaning scrutiny. Further, once the aid is granted, it is not provided without strings. If it takes the form of cash payments, the spending of the cash is supervised or at least audited by an assigned social worker. And even though the aid recipient might prefer cash, he or she is often forced to take the aid in the form of assistance in the purchase of specifically designated products or services: food, shelter, medical services. In both of these cases, the point of view is that the poor are somehow different from everyone else — that they lack a sense of responsibility and must be monitored at every step.

The present system exhibits two other major deficiencies. Most parts of the program were never designed to cope with sustained poverty. With few exceptions, they were set up to aid individuals only temporarily in need. If poverty does indeed breed poverty, breaking the vicious circle is

TABLE 8.9
Federal outlays benefiting poverty-level persons, 1974

Item		Expenditures ($ billion)
TOTAL		27.0
CASH PAYMENTS		12.0
Social security and railroad retirements	6.3	
Public assistance payments	3.8	
Veterans pensions and compensations	1.0	
Unemployment benefits	.6	
Other	.2	
IN-KIND TRANSFERS (FOOD AND HOUSING)		3.2
Food stamps	1.6	
Housing subsidy payments	.8	
Other	.8	
HEALTH		6.2
Medicaid	3.2	
Medicare	1.8	
Veterans medical care	.3	
Other	.9	
EDUCATION		1.8
MANPOWER		2.0
Skill training	.9	
Other	1.1	
OTHER		2.0

Source: *Statistical Abstract of the United States*, 1975, p. 405.

apt to require a long-term effort. More important, support is available, with minor exceptions, only to the nonworking poor. Those who work but are still unable to earn a poverty-level income are helped but little by the present system.

A guaranteed annual income

Recognizing the drawbacks of the present system, sentiment seems to be growing for some sort of a guaranteed annual income. Whatever form this guaranteed income takes, it would start with the premise that the United States is now wealthy enough to provide at least a minimal income for all its citizens.

Progress in the provision of a guaranteed annual income, though, is bound to be slow. We are moving into virtually unexplored territory and do not yet have complete answers to such questions as cost, impact on incentive, or superiority of one approach to others or of alternative forms of the same approach.

At first glance, the cost of lifting everyone out of poverty appears to be very modest. The official government estimate of the *poverty gap* — the aggregate shortfall of the incomes of all those in poverty below the poverty-level income — was just over $14 billion in 1973. For comparative purposes, this was less than one-sixth the national defense spending for that year. But it is recognized that it would take more money than is included in the poverty-gap estimate to eliminate poverty in the United States. First of all, we are not sure what a guaranteed annual income would do to the incentive to work, since any guaranteed income plan would provide an alternative to working. Pilot guaranteed income programs conducted here and there in the country suggest that the impact would not be great. It may come as a surprise to many critics of government support programs, but the poor apparently aren't all that different from the rest of us. Given the choice between idleness on a dole and a useful job, almost all Americans, rich or poor, choose to work.

But we would push that willingness to work awfully hard if we guaranteed a payment up to some support level and then took it all away when someone in the family accepted a job paying slightly more than the support level. This would be what the economist calls a 100 percent marginal rate of taxation — higher than that levied on even the highest incomes in the United States. Every dollar earned takes away a dollar in support payments. The work ethic would have to be extremely strong to induce a member of a family to take a job paying, say, $5,500 if the family were guaranteed $5,500 when no one works. To promote the incentive to work, the family must be assured that income from work will not lead to dollar-for-dollar loss of support payments. The marginal rate of taxation, in other words, must be less than 100 percent. But how much less? Every reduction in the rate, while increasing the incentive to work, increases the cost of the program. And the adoption of any rate under 100 percent means that the total cost of the program will exceed the $14 billion poverty gap.

The negative income tax

The most widely supported guaranteed income plan is the *negative income tax*. It has the backing of economists ranging all the way from the far right to the far left. In fact, its earliest and most vigorous proponent is Professor Milton Friedman of the University of Chicago, Senator Goldwater's economic advisor in the presidential campaign of 1964. His enthusiasm is based on the view that "the negative income tax is more compatible with the philosophy and aims of the proponents of limited government and maximum individual freedom than with the philosophy and aims of the proponents of the welfare state and greater government control of the economy."[7]

A negative income tax program would indeed limit government participation in the welfare system and free individuals to spend their government aid in any fashion they chose. It would take for granted that the poor, except for their limited incomes, are just like everyone else — and just as capable of making good decisions in the spending of their incomes. And it would abolish the hated means test, along with an army of social workers presently overseeing the welfare system.

The negative income tax proposal is really the essence of simplicity. It would require only that everyone file a federal personal income tax return. Those with income above the support level would of course pay taxes at the usual rate. Those with total income below the support level, though, instead of paying taxes would get a payment from the Treasury in the amount of the difference between their income and the support level — a negative tax payment. The means test is therefore none other than the one faced by all Americans now paying taxes to the Internal Revenue Service.

Two problems, however, immediately complicate the negative income tax scheme: Where should the support level be set and what should be the marginal tax rate? As indicated earlier, how these questions are answered will affect both work incentives and the cost of the program. These different implications are developed in the two hypothetical programs outlined in Table 8.10.

In one way program A is much less generous than program B. Its support level is only half that of program B. In another way, it is more generous. In order to maximize the incentive to take productive employment, beneficiaries under the program lose only 33 cents in supplementary payments for each dollar earned ($333 is "taxed away" for each $1,000 earned). The price of this, though, is that supplementary payments continue until the family hits an income three times as high as the support level. In the United States today, this would mean that if the support level were set at the 1975 poverty level for a family of four, $5,500, payments would continue until the family was earning over $16,500 — well above the median income for all families. Payments would taper off and cease much more rapidly if the marginal tax rate were increased. Under program B, with the marginal tax rate twice as high as in A, payments cease when earned incomes reach a point only half again as high as the support level. But what would this do to the incentive to work? How willingly would

---

[7] "The Case for the Negative Income Tax: A View from the Right," Paper prepared for the National Symposium on Guaranteed Income, Chamber of Commerce of the United States, December 9, 1966, p. 49.

TABLE 8.10
Hypothetical alternative negative income tax proposals

Program A ($) Guaranteed support level: $2,000 Marginal tax rate: 33%			Program B ($) Guaranteed support level: $4,000 Marginal tax rate: 67%		
Earned income	Income supplement	Total income	Earned income	Income supplement	Total income
—	2,000	2,000	—	4,000	4,000
1,000	1,667	2,667	1,000	3,333	4,333
2,000	1,333	3,333	2,000	2,667	4,667
3,000	1,000	4,000	3,000	2,000	5,000
4,000	667	4,667	4,000	1,333	5,333
5,000	333	5,333	5,000	667	5,667
6,000	—	6,000	6,000	—	6,000

individuals seek work if they knew that every dollar of earned income would lead to the loss of 67 cents in supplementary payments?

Setting the support level and the marginal tax rate, however, are more or less mechanical problems. They could be resolved by trial and error and compromise. A more serious concern is the underlying philosophy of the program — the conclusion that millions of Americans are destined for life on the dole. President Nixon's version of the negative income tax proposal, the Family Assistance Plan, went down to defeat for this reason as well as the opposition of welfare workers who feared the loss of employment and Southern senators and representatives who were repelled by the thought of white taxpayers supporting blacks in idleness.[8] The Southern members of Congress, in fact, were not alone in viewing with alarm the prospect of a permanent dole for a significant part of the population. Many critics support the idea of income maintenance but believe that income should come from employment. There are two main versions of this idea, one advocating a government guarantee of employment and the other proposing that private employers be forced to pay at least a minimum poverty-level wage.

Government as employer of last resort

Those supporting the idea of guaranteed government employment buttress their argument by pointing out that many of the poor remain poor through no choice of their own. The American economy simply fails to provide

---

[8] See Daniel P. Moynihan, "Annals of Politics: Income by Right," *New Yorker Magazine* (January 13, 20, and 27, 1973).

employment for all who would like to work and fails to provide jobs at more than poverty-level wages for many who find employment. During the whole decade of the 1930s the unemployment rate averaged out at around 19 percent. And while the average unemployment rate since World War II has been much lower than in the 1930s, in fewer than one-third of the years since World War II has unemployment dipped below the full-employment level (4 percent). Even this overstates the performance of the economy, since most of the years of full employment came during the boom times immediately following the war. Only four of the twenty-three years from 1954 to 1977 featured full employment. Moreover, as we have seen, when the economy provides jobs for some of the poor, it provides them at such low wages as to leave families in poverty: Over half of the male heads of poverty-level families worked full time in 1975.

As an alternative to unemployment, then, or private employment at less than poverty-level wages, the proposal is to guarantee government employment at more than poverty-level wages. Either private business can supply enough jobs at a living wage or government will furnish them. Every American would have the right to work at a living wage.[9]

Prospects for adopting this scheme are not bright. The news media are already filled with protests over the growing size of government. Guaranteed government employment further swells the size of this sector. Moreover the prospect of competing with government for the services of low-skilled workers in particular is not attractive to businessmen. Many businesses, particularly small businesses, can continue to exist only because they are able to hire workers at less than poverty-level wages. Forcing them to compete and pay higher wages would push many of them into bankruptcy. And a great many Americans, faced with higher costs for garbage collection, car parking, restaurant meals, laundry services, mail delivery, and so on, would undoubtedly join the small businessmen in their protests.

A living minimum wage

The proposal to force up the minimum wage to at least the poverty level is not a substitute for guaranteed government employment. It takes such guaranteed employment as its starting point and goes on to add three other provisions: (1) maintenance of a full-employment level of aggregate demand through vigorous fiscal and monetary policies, (2) enlarged government education and training programs, and (3) a requirement that all employers pay a living wage, "defined as one that would enable a worker to maintain an urban family of four in health and decency."[10] In 1972, this

---

[9] See Arnold H. Packer, "Employment Guarantees Should Replace the Welfare System," *Challenge Magazine* (March–April 1974), 21–27.

[10] Daniel R. Fusfeld, "A Living Wage," *The Annals of the American Academy of Political and Social Science* (September 1973), 34.

implied a minimum wage of $3.50 an hour. Because of the rise in living costs since 1972, it would now require a wage considerably higher than this, if Fusfeld's definition of a living wage were adopted.

It is true that the present federal minimum wage is inadequate to provide a poverty-level income. With only one member of a family working 2,000 hours a year (fifty 40-hour weeks) at the present minimum wage ($2.65 an hour), the family would have a total income of only $5,300 — less than a poverty-level income.

But forcing all employers to pay a considerably higher minimum wage is no small matter. Where employers can get along with a smaller work force, the requirement to pay higher wages would lead to a reduction in employment and a rise in unemployment — thus the necessity for a guarantee of government employment. If employers were unable to operate with a smaller work force, they could quite possibly be forced out of business. Fusfeld recognizes this possibility and calls for at least temporary help for the businesses affected in the form of special tax allowances or low-cost loans.[11]

Conclusion

However compelling the logic of alternative income distribution schemes and welfare proposals, in the final analysis any alternative must be sold not only on its merits but also on its political viability. We may have to learn to live with second-best programs because we have such difficulty in organizing political support for something better. And politicians are not necessarily obtuse when they oppose change. Quite possibly their attitudes merely reflect those of their constituents. So long as some people have less than others, they will still feel poor. And the rest of us seem

© Washington Star Syndicate, Inc., permission granted by King Features Syndicate, Inc., 1977.

---

[11] Fusfeld, "A Living Wage," p. 37.

determined to have someone poorer than ourselves. In the words of one close student of the political economy of income redistribution: "The 'poor are always with us' because the low man on the economic totem pole feels poor regardless of his absolute income. The rest of us insist on having a low man, since we would not otherwise be satisfied with our own economic positions."[12]

I SUMMARY I

Inequality in the distribution of income is of economic concern because the extent of inequality affects productive efficiency. It also has important noneconomic effects.

Income inequality in the United States narrowed significantly during the depression of the 1930s and again during World War II. Since the end of World War II, though, the distribution of income has changed only marginally. The extent of inequality is roughly the same in most of the advanced market economies.

Because of the cumulative effect of unequal income distribution, the distribution of wealth is considerably more unequal than the distribution of income. The top 5 percent of income receivers in the United States get around 15 percent of all income distributed, but the wealthiest 1 percent of the population own over one-fourth of all assets.

Recognizing that income is distributed unequally does not necessarily demand condemnation of the situation. Equality and equity (fairness or justice) are not interchangeable concepts. To date, however, we have not been able to agree on the amount of inequality that is consistent with our ideas of fairness, or even with maximum economic efficiency. In fact, there appears to be no scientific way to reach such agreement.

What we in the United States have apparently decided, though, is that we should provide a larger portion of the national income to those at the very bottom of the income scale, the poverty group. To that end, we have now established an official poverty level, but we have not yet taken steps to bring all Americans above a poverty-level income. National economic growth provided benefits sufficient to cut the size of the poverty group through the 1960s, but since then we have been on a plateau.

We have now identified and catalogued those in poverty and have come to recognize that the characteristics of the families and individuals in the group will likely make it necessary to adopt new programs if we are to reduce the group further. Among the programs being considered are various devices for guaranteeing a minimum annual income: negative income taxes, guaranteed government employment, and a living minimum wage.

---

[12] Lester C. Thurow, "The Political Economy of Income Redistribution Policies," *The Annals of the American Academy of Political and Social Science* (September 1973), 155.

I IMPORTANT TERMS AND CONCEPTS I

income inequality

equity in the distribution
of income

absolute poverty

relative poverty

official poverty level

means test

poverty gap

negative income tax

government as employer
of last resort

I QUESTIONS, PROBLEMS, AND EXERCISES I

1 The New York Stock Exchange periodically claims that ownership of American corporations is widely spread. What do the actual figures of stock ownership show?

2 If you were in a position to determine the distribution of incomes in the United States, how much inequality would you permit? How would you justify your scheme of distribution?

3 What did Karl Marx envisage as the ideal logic of income distribution? Do you think it would work?

4 How far can scientific analysis be relied on to provide justification for a particular pattern of income distribution?

5 What were the main forces at work in the reduction of the size of the official poverty group in the United States between the mid-fifties and the mid-seventies?

6 Why is poverty a *national* problem? Why can't it be solved at the state or local level?

7 What do the facts show concerning the widely held view that the poor are simply lazy — that they prefer to receive a dole rather than to work?

8 If for every dollar a poverty group family earns, 60 cents is removed from the family's poverty allowance, what is the marginal rate of taxation?

I SUGGESTED READING I

Batchelder, Alan B. *The Economics of Poverty*, 2d ed. Wiley, New York, 1971.

Lundberg, Ferdinand. *The Rich and the Super-Rich*. Bantam, New York, 1969.

Okun, Arthur. *Equality and Efficiency: The Big Tradeoff*. Brookings Institution, Washington, D. C., 1975.

Thurow, Lester C. *Generating Inequality: Mechanisms of Distribution in the U.S. Economy*. Basic Books, New York, 1975.

Tuckman, Howard P. *The Economics of the Rich*. Random House, New York, 1973.

Tussing, A. Dale. *Poverty in a Dual Economy*. St. Martin's, New York, 1975.

NINE

INEQUALITY AND
EDUCATION, RACE, AND SEX

One way to reduce income inequality and poverty is to attack the problem head-on by redistributing income, taking from the haves and giving to the have nots. As we saw in Chapter Eight, however, this is not quite as simple as it appears. It can be taken for granted that the haves are not going to support such a move very enthusiastically. And even the have nots, for the most part, would prefer to earn what they get. It would be far better if a way could be found whereby those at the lower end of the income scale could work their way into the higher income brackets.

This is what is promised by the provision of education and the elimination of discrimination. Neither of these leads to complete equality in the distribution of income. Both recognize that there are inborn differences among individuals, so some are naturally going to be more productive and therefore better paid than others. What they stress is that it is grossly unfair to add to any natural differences the manmade advantage of larger amounts of education for some than for others or to impose artificial hurdles that women must leap but not men, blacks but not whites. An equal start, a fair field, no help for one that is not available to all, no hurdles for some but not for others — then the marathon of life in a competitive market economy will honestly provide exceptional rewards for those with the greatest ability who work hardest to win. And in the process everyone will gain because greater efforts and improved performance mean more of everything for all to share. This is the vision. Let us examine it.

I THE ECONOMICS OF EDUCATION I

The two assumptions just spelled out, that income inequality can be controlled by increasing the availability of education and that more education means more production and therefore more income, have played major roles in justifying the massive support Americans have provided for education. From our early beginnings as a nation we have willingly, even enthusiastically, dug into our pockets to provide tax dollars for public schools and dug even deeper to add a comprehensive private school system. We didn't stop with universal elementary schooling. We went on to assure everyone of the availability of a high school diploma. In fact, we went one step further and virtually required everyone to complete high school. And we are not too far short now of doing the same for higher education.

Measured by money outlay, we have the most comprehensive system of education of any nation in the world. In 1973 we employed over 2.3 million teachers and spent almost $90 billion providing classroom instruction for over 54 million students at all levels. The second most ambitious effort was made by the Soviet Union — the equivalent of $26.6 billion for 49.3 million students in 1971.[1]

Most of this effort has taken place with little critical assessment as to whether or not it has all been worthwhile. The benefits have seemed apparent, and the costs have been borne fairly comfortably by a national income that has doubled every generation. Only in the past few decades have we seriously undertaken the task of seeing whether costs are really matched by benefits.

---

[1] *Statistical Abstract of the United States*, 1976, pp. 874–875.

Investment in human capital

When economists finally did get around to taking a critical look at the costs and benefits of educational expenditures, their early findings solidly backed up the view that education had been and continued to be a sound investment. In fact, this was exactly the language adopted to describe the educational process. Investment, of course, is capital formation. And capital, in turn, consists of all the things we produce, not because they are immediately useful to consumers, but because they advance the possibilities of producing even more in the future. A factory as such is of no immediate use to consumers. But the additional washing machines or refrigerators it will turn out in the future will, it is hoped, more than compensate for the labor and other resources diverted into building the factory. And just as the factory will enable us to produce more in the future, so the use of resources in the "education industry" will enable us to produce more in the years ahead. We are therefore justified in treating

human resources explicitly as a form of capital, as a produced means of production, as the product of investment. . . . Laborers have become capitalists not from a diffusion of the ownership of corporation stocks, as folklore would have it, but from the acquisition of knowledge and skill that have economic value. This knowledge and skill are in great part the product of investment and, combined with other human investment, predominantly account for the productive superiority of the technically advanced countries.[2]

Investment in schooling, in building up our stock of knowledge and skills, is thus on a par with investment in factories and machinery and new houses. Both serve to advance the production potential of the economy and increase the rate of economic growth. This is *investment in human capital*. In one sense it is a pure bonus, since it is over and above any return to education as a consumption good. The latter concept refers to the fact that the educational process itself may be an enjoyable experience. More than this, it should make students better, more sophisticated consumers by developing their esthetic awareness, teaching the value of reasoned choice, and bringing awareness of available alternatives for the allocation of time, money, even votes.

In practice, it is ordinarily impossible to distinguish with any finality between education as a consumption good and education as an investment. Art majors may choose their program entirely on the basis of interest in the course-work, yet still find on graduation that they have developed a salable skill. In broader terms, the diploma itself — any diploma — is

---

[2] Theodore W. Schultz, "Investment in Human Capital," *American Economic Review* (March 1961), 3.

usually taken by employers to mean that certain skills, attitudes, and knowledge have been accumulated along the way that make the student a more productive prospective employee than someone without such a background. According to the early studies this additional productivity alone was sufficient to justify the investment in education.

Schultz and others working this vein were led to the value of education as an investment almost by accident. In attempting to explain economic growth, they looked first to the flow of additional inputs into the production process. The growth of the labor force itself proved significant in increasing the production capability of the economy, especially a labor force equipped with ever-larger amounts of land and physical capital to work with. When the growth of real national output was matched against the growth of overall inputs in the form of labor, land, and capital, however, an awkward "residual" of output growth remained unexplained. During the period 1900–1960, for example, real net national product increased at an average annual rate of 3.12 percent. A little over one-third of this 3.12 percent could be attributed to growth in the size of the labor force. The miniscule increase in the land supply explained only one-fortieth of the 3.12 percent, and expansion of the capital stock accounted for an additional one-sixth of total growth. Adding up the various parts of overall growth accounted for by expansion of the labor force (34.8 percent), land supply (2.5 percent), and capital stock (18.6 percent) left an extraordinary 44.1 percent of the 3.12 percent annual growth rate unexplained.[3]

The American economy obviously didn't grow, then, simply by drawing in larger amounts of inputs. More factor inputs became available and were indeed used — but used ever more effectively. *Factor productivity* — output per unit of input — rose substantially during the period. But according to Schultz, "To call this discrepancy a measure of 'resource productivity' gives a name to our ignorance but does not dispel it."[4] The real question was, why did productivity rise?

The economist Edward F. Denison provided the generally accepted answer. Concentrating on the period 1929–1957, during which time real national income rose at an average annual rate of 2.93 percent, he ascertained that allowing for the rise in the average quality of the labor force resulting from education went about half way toward explaining the productivity residual. He summarized those parts of his results concerned with education as follows:

1. From 1929 to 1957 the amount of education the average worker had received was increasing almost 2 percent a year, and this was raising the average quality of labor by 0.97 percent a year, and contributing 0.67 percentage points to the

---

[3] Davis et al., *American Economic Growth*, Harper & Row, New York, 1972, p. 39.
[4] Schultz, "Investment in Human Capital," p. 6.

growth rate of real national income. Thus, it was the source of 23 percent of the growth of total real national income and 42 percent of the growth of real national income per person employed. . . .[5]

The personal investment decision

Did the overall rise in the average quality of labor do anything for the individual worker? Assuredly it did. Putting together average annual earnings for American males, the United States Bureau of the Census came up with figures indicating a step increase for every upward move on the educational ladder, as Figure 9.1 shows.

The personal return to investment in education appears even more dramatic when these annual earnings figures are converted into lifetime incomes. A college education, after all, not only puts people into a higher income bracket but is likely to keep them there for the whole of their working lives. Multiplying the incomes above by the average years of working life in the various categories, as is done in Figure 9.2, gives a

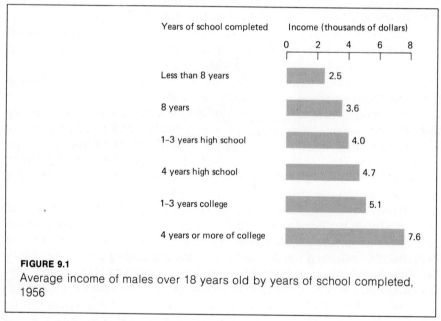

FIGURE 9.1

Average income of males over 18 years old by years of school completed, 1956

Source: *Statistical Abstract of the United States*, 1975, p. 123.

---

[5] Edward F. Denison, "Education, Economic Growth, and Gaps in Information," *Education and the Economics of Human Capital*, ed. Ronald A. Wykstra, Free Press, New York, 1971, p. 48. Reprinted from *Journal of Political Economy* (October 1962), 124–128.

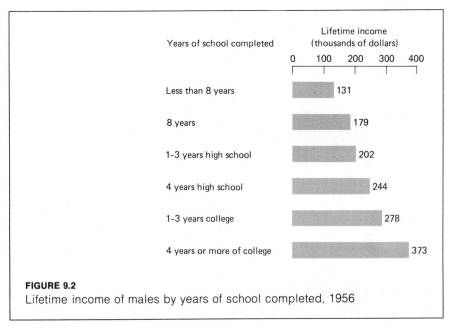

FIGURE 9.2
Lifetime income of males by years of school completed, 1956

Source: *Statistical Abstract of the United States,* 1975, p. 123.

picture of the average differences increasing amounts of education make during a lifetime of work, from age 18 to death.

Did high school pay in the 1950s? With the prospect of earning $65,000 more than someone with only a grade school education, the answer appears obvious. Was college worthwhile as a financial investment? Again, the prospect of increasing lifetime earnings by nearly $130,000 appeared to make even a very expensive college education a prudent investment.

Neither answer, however, is quite as simple as the data suggest, as critics pointed out at the time. First of all, concentrating exclusively on the comparative figures overlooks the fact that the individuals who make up each of the groups differ in more than the amounts of education they receive. Isn't it possible that college graduates are brighter, more ambitious, and come from families with better social credentials than individuals in the other categories? Answering no to any part of this question puts the challenger in direct conflict with most of the available evidence. A yes answer on the other hand means that the college graduate might have gone almost as far without the benefit of the sheepskin.

Equally important, comparing lifetime-earnings dollars against present-educational-cost dollars is no easy matter. They are not really the same dollars at all, since a dollar to be earned sometime in the future has a quite different value from a dollar presently being laid out in educational expense. The reader can see this intuitively when trying to answer the question, Which would you rather have, a dollar today or a dollar 10 years from now? Even aside from the logic of "eat, drink, and be merry, for tomorrow ye die," and disregarding the uncertainties of the future, the prospect of rising future income, and possible erosions of purchasing power resulting from inflation, a rational person must insist on taking the dollar now.

A dollar today may be worth several dollars tomorrow. Why? Because a dollar already in hand can be put to work at interest, and the original dollar plus the interest earned will amount to several dollars in a few years' time. This suggests that the premium a present dollar will carry compared with a future dollar depends on two things: income-earning opportunities for present dollars and the number of years standing between present and future dollars. Reduce the interest rate earned by present dollars and you narrow the margin between present and future dollars. Cut the earning period and you also reduce the margin. A dollar to be received 10 years from today has a present value of only a little over 46 cents if the interest rate stands at 8 percent. This has to be true since 46 cents loaned out at 8 percent with the interest compounded annually (added to the principal, that is) will grow to one dollar in 10 years. If the interest rate is 5 percent rather than 8 percent, the present value of a dollar due 10 years from today has a present value of 61.4 cents, since 61.4 cents loaned out at 5 percent will accumulate additional earnings of only 38.6 cents in 10 years. To show the powerful impact of time in all of this, if the interest rate is 8 percent, the present value of a dollar due 50 years into the future is barely over 2 cents! Put 2 cents to work today at 8 percent interest, add the interest to the principal as you go along, and in 50 years you will have a dollar.

The point to all of this is that you cannot simply compare the $100,000-plus lifetime earnings associated with a college diploma relative to a high school diploma in 1956 and assume that everything is gravy over and above the current outlay for college expenses. Some of the lifetime-earnings dollars, remember, were not going to be received until close to 50 years after graduation — they were worth only 2 cents each at the time if the alternative was to invest present dollars in, say, an 8 percent industrial bond. Moreover, the outlay for college expenses may have been only the tip of the iceberg. Many high school graduates who had worked a few years had to give up $10,000-a-year jobs to enter college. The opportunity cost of this or any other foregone employment during the period of college enrollment must be counted along with out-of-pocket expenses.

Even so, after converting future dollars of earnings into present dollars and adding the opportunity cost of foregone employment to direct, out-of-pocket expenditures, there is little doubt that additional education more than repaid its costs during the 1950s and 1960s. Economist Gary S. Becker estimated the private rate of return to a college education at about

12.5 percent in 1940 and 10 percent in 1950 for urban male whites,[6] as compared with a net return of 3 or 4 percent available on money placed in a savings account. Private rates of return on higher education in the 11–12 percent range continued to be earned into the late 1960s. Thus even with the rise in the cost of borrowing money, it appeared worthwhile for a prospective student to borrow if necessary at 8 or 9 percent interest to pay college expenses since the earnings on his college investment promised an additional 11 or 12 cents for each dollar invested. Whether or not this still holds is more open to question — but that's a topic for later discussion.

It may be objected that it is one thing to compute a private or individual rate of return to investment in education and quite another to assume that what is true for the individual is true for society as a whole. It is well known, for example, that college students rarely pay the full costs of their education. Tuition payments often — usually in the state colleges and universities — cover only a fraction of total expenses. The taxpayer picks up the tab for the balance. On the other side of the ledger, there are some differences between private or individual benefits from education and social benefits. After adjusting as best he could for these differences, Becker, in the article cited, found that although the social rate of return to investment in college education was lower than the private rate, it was still high enough in the early post–World War II period to justify the use of tax dollars. The average rates of return to business investment and to college education apparently were very close. And the consensus was that social rates of return for elementary and secondary education were considerably higher than for college.

I TROUBLED TIMES FOR EDUCATION I

The almost universal consensus of the 1950s and 1960s that education pays, both for the individual and for society at large, has collapsed in the 1970s. Just about every foundation stone on which the consensus was built has proved upon re-examination to be flawed.

Increasing costs

During the period when the economic benefits of schooling went virtually unchallenged, the American public open-handedly provided the funds for an ever-larger educational establishment, as the figures in Table 9.1 show. Although the figures are expressed in current dollars, with no adjustment for changes in purchasing power, inflation goes only a short distance in explaining the rise in expenditures. Expenditures rose by almost twenty-

---

[6] Gary S. Becker, "Underinvestment in College Education?" *American Economic Review* (May 1960), 347.

TABLE 9.1
School expenditures, public and private, 1930 to 1976 ($ billion)

	1930	1940	1950	1960	1970	1976 (est.)
Total	3.2	3.2	8.8	24.7	70.2	120.0
% of gross national product	3.1	3.5	3.4	5.1	7.5	7.5
Public	2.7	2.7	7.1	19.4	56.8	98.0
% of total	82.1	84.3	80.2	78.7	80.9	81.7
Private	.6	.5	1.7	5.3	13.4	22.0

Source: *Statistical Abstract of the United States,* 1976, p. 111.

two times between 1940 and 1970, while the consumer price index less than tripled. Moreover, the rise in educational costs far outstripped the rise in national income. Gross national product rose a little less than tenfold from 1940 to 1970. This has to mean that educational costs claimed an ever-larger part of national income. Table 9.1 shows that this was indeed the case: As a fraction of gross national product, educational expenditures rose from 3.5 percent in 1940 to 7.5 percent in 1970.

At first glance, the declining support for education is not apparent from the figures in the table. Total expenditures did after all continue to rise by a hefty $50 billion from 1970 to 1976. But most of this is explained by the erosion in the purchasing power of the dollar. With prices rising by 49 percent between 1970 and the end of 1976, it required an additional $34.4 billion just for education to do the same things in 1976 that it had done in 1970.

In part, the leveling off in real (price-adjusted) educational expenditures was the result of the fact that the wave of children from the baby boom following World War II had gone through at least the early grades. But there was more than this, as readers were informed daily in the newspapers and periodicals. Taxpayers were in full revolt against the demands of the educators. School bond issues failed with increasing regularity. Professorial salaries for the first time in several decades failed to keep pace with the cost of living as state legislators and private school boards squeezed educational budgets.

Inequality and school finance

What especially incensed low-income taxpayers was that the educational establishment, all the way from the grade schools through college, was failing to deliver on its promise to reduce the gap between children from low-income families and those from high-income families. In fact, the evidence suggested that as a consequence of the financial arrangements used to raise money for the schools, children from poor families were provided with inferior education while children from high-income families were furnished with superior schooling.

Elementary and secondary schools have traditionally secured their funds primarily from local property taxes. Federal spending for education grew rapidly in the 1960s, but well into the 1970s the federal government still paid less than 10 percent of the costs of elementary and secondary education. And none of the federal programs was designed to provide general support for the schools; all were focused on specific educational activities. In the absence of basic financial support by the federal government, the costs of financing the public schools rested on state and local governments. While the state governments could and did raise their roughly 40 percent of the funds largely through sales and income taxes, local governments had little option but to continue to use the property tax in raising their 50 percent share. Some 84 percent of locally raised school revenues come from the property tax.

Administration of the property tax is difficult at best. Establishment of the tax base through the assessment process is a judgmental process. For property not recently on the market, taxable value is a matter of guesswork. Plenty of room is left for favoritism, corruption, and careless administration.

But this is not the major problem where education is concerned. What is more important is that, however carefully or sloppily the assessment process is conducted, some school districts are going to have far more property to tax and therefore will be able to raise far more revenues than others. The range of per student property values among the school districts of California in the early 1970s, for example, was $103 to $952,156. Even within a single county the discrepancies were considerable. In Los Angeles County the tax base of Beverly Hills was $50,885 per pupil, while nearby Baldwin Park's was only $3,706.[7] Beverly Hills could tax itself at less than one-fourth the rate of Baldwin Park and still provide more than three times as much revenue for each student as the poorer district. Children of the wealthy families in Beverly Hills could with a minimal tax effort be furnished a far higher quality of education than that provided children from the less wealthy families in Baldwin Park even with a major tax effort, thereby further widening the gap between rich and poor. This appeared manifestly unfair to the low-income, low-property-value districts. And courts in California, Minnesota, Texas, and other states agreed with this judgment. The California Supreme Court found that this system of school

---

[7] "Financing Elementary and Secondary Education," *Setting National Priorities — The 1973 Budget*, Brookings Institution, 1972, p. 330.

finance "invidiously discriminates against the poor because it makes the quality of a child's education a function of the wealth of his parent and neighbors."[8]

What to do about the problem is another matter, one not yet resolved. One proposed solution is to shift the burden of financing elementary and secondary education to state governments. Some states are almost there now. In the 1970–1971 school year, the state government in Hawaii provided 89.4 percent of school funds, local school districts only 2.9 percent. The New Hampshire state government, on the other hand, raised only 9.6 percent of the money needed, leaving to local school districts the necessity of raising an additional 86.2 percent. Citing New Hampshire in this connection highlights one of the problems of this approach: The citizens of New Hampshire believe that local functions should be carried out through localized effort.

Even if this were not an issue and the financing could take place on a statewide basis, this would only relieve, not solve, the problem. The resources of wealthy school districts could be tapped to equalize educational opportunities among all school districts, but nothing would be done to equalize opportunities from state to state. And those opportunities vary almost as widely as they do within states. In the school year 1974–1975, for example, Mississippi was able to provide only $838 per pupil, while New York came up with an average of $2,005 per pupil.[9] Only the federal government with a nationwide redistribution program could rectify this situation. To do this, though, would doubly compound the problem of local responsibility raised in the New Hampshire case.

Inequality doesn't disappear when we move up to the level of higher education. Despite the financial aid available to underprivileged students, the student bodies of private colleges and universities are largely made up of children from middle-income and wealthy families. With annual tuition costs alone in these schools running to well over $5,000, it would be surprising if this were not the case. Nor do the public colleges and universities with their large student subsidies right the balance. In fact, according to one important study, they further spread apart the children of the poor and the children of the rich. In their study of the California system of higher education, Hansen and Weisbrod ascertained that children from low-income families are found in disproportionate numbers in the junior colleges of the state, those from middle-income families in the state colleges, and those from higher-income families in the state university system. Per student state expenditures in universities are considerably higher than

---

[8] *Serrano* v. *Priest,* California Supreme Court 938254, L. A. 29820 (1971), p. 1. Cited in "Financing Elementary and Secondary Education," p. 331.

[9] Ford Foundation, *Paying for Schools and Colleges*, New York, 1976, p. 2.

in the state colleges, and considerably higher in the state colleges than in the junior colleges. The consequence is that "students who complete a two-year junior college program receive an average subsidy totaling $1,440, whereas those completing a baccalaureate program at a state college receive four times as large a subsidy ($5,800) and graduates from a University of California campus receive a four-year subsidy of more than $7,100."[10] No equalization of opportunity here. No redistribution from the rich to the poor by way of public higher education. Quite the reverse.

Inequality and education

Nor was this the end. A spate of studies poured off the press in the early 1970s detailing the results of extended examination of the relationships between education and the elimination of poverty, reduction of inequality, and improvement of worker productivity. The more important of these stated flatly that the assumed relationships were very difficult to find.

Given the assignment of documenting the efficacy of the educational reform portions of the national War on Poverty, the Rand Corporation concluded that they had been little short of catastrophic: "Virtually without exception all of the large surveys of the large national compensatory educational programs have shown no beneficial results on the average."[11] Another investigator had concluded even earlier that with few exceptions the economic payoff to compensatory education was low. His conclusion, in fact, was that in the majority of the cases he studied, considerably more equalization of incomes could have been accomplished by simply giving the poor whatever money the programs had cost.[12] Too often the special educational programs, where they succeeded in attracting and holding students, led to dead-end jobs, or to no jobs at all.

Research findings of a team of Harvard investigators headed by Christopher Jencks painted a similar picture, but with a far broader brush. According to Jencks we have as a nation vastly increased the availability of education, but the consequence has been little reduction of overall inequality. The typical white person born during the decade 1895–1904 received 8.9 years of regular schooling, the typical black only 5.1 years. Whites born during the years 1940–1944, however, went on to get 12.6

---

[10] W. Lee Hansen and Burton A. Weisbrod, "The Distribution of Costs and Direct Benefits of Public Higher Education: The Case of California," *Journal of Human Resources* (Spring 1969). Reprinted in *Redistribution to the Rich and the Poor*, ed. Kenneth E. Boulding and Martin Pfaff, Wadsworth, Belmont, Calif., 1972, p. 79.

[11] Harvey Averch et al., *How Effective Is Schooling: A Critical Review and Synthesis of Research Findings*, Rand, Santa Monica, Calif., 1972, p. 125.

[12] Thomas I. Ribich, *Education and Poverty*, Brookings Institution, Washington, D.C., 1968.

years of schooling; blacks born during the same period received an average of 12.2 years.[13] The educational gap between blacks and whites has been reduced to the vanishing point, in other words, but the income gap between blacks and whites remains large. The same is true of men and women, blue-collar workers and white-collar workers.

The thrust of educational reformers to equalize opportunity and income by equalizing expenditures per pupil also received scant support from the Jencks study — almost as little as it received from the United States Supreme Court, which refused in 1973 to sustain the first of the state cases brought before it. According to Jencks, "Unequal expenditures do not . . . account for the fact that some children learn to read more competently than others, nor for the fact that some adults are more economically successful than others."[14] Jencks did find a correlation between income and schooling, but the relationship was between the *quantity* of education and earnings, not between educational *quality* and income. This makes intuitive sense. In our society, the better-paying careers are with few exceptions those that require high levels of educational attainment — medicine, the law, public accounting, and the like. "Men with extra education make more money largely because they enter lucrative occupations, not because education enhances their earning power thereafter. . . . If we compare men who not only are in the same occupations but also have similar test scores, there seems to be virtually no relationship between schooling and earnings."[15] Once people are in a particular occupation, those with additional years of schooling do not have appreciably higher earnings than others in the occupation. This suggests that "schools serve primarily as selection and certification agencies, whose job is to measure and label people."[16]

It further suggests that except for bringing someone up to the minimum threshold necessary for admission to a job, schooling does little to increase worker productivity. And Ivar Berg argues that the educational threshold level itself is capricious and arbitrary — a reflection of the "academocracy" we have become. His analysis of actual job content led him to conclude that "it cannot be argued helpfully that technological and related changes attending most jobs account for the pattern whereby better-educated personnel are 'required' and utilized by managers."[17] The Supreme Court expressed the same skepticism in *Griggs* v. *Duke Power Company* (91 S. Ct. 849, March 8, 1971). The Court held that the use of test scores and

---

[13] Christopher Jencks et al., *Inequality: A Reassessment of the Effect of Family and Schooling in America*, Harper Colophon Books, New York, 1972, p. 21.

[14] Jencks, *Inequality*, p. 29.

[15] Jencks, *Inequality*, p. 182.

[16] Jencks, *Inequality*, p. 135.

[17] Ivar Berg, *Education and Jobs: The Great Training Robbery*, Beacon Press, Boston, 1971, pp. 14–15.

educational requirements in choosing new employees violated the 1964 Civil Rights Act unless the employer could show a clear relationship between test scores or credentials and performance on the job — which this particular employer apparently could not. And if Berg is right, neither can many others.

When employers fall back on defenses other than the technical content of the job the situation is little improved. During Berg's investigations he found that:

In most industries the employers sought to justify the decision to use education as a "screening device" by claiming that educational achievement is evidence of an ability to get along with others and to make the most of opportunities. They also made references to the greater potential of better-educated workers for promotion to higher-paying, more skilled and responsible jobs.

However, when efforts were made to pinpoint the ways in which "better-educated" workers prove to be superior to those with less formal education, it was discovered that business firms typically do not collect data that would make such comparisons possible. . . .

The data . . . reveal that education is more often than not an important factor accounting for dissatisfaction among workers in many occupational categories and is related to dissatisfaction in a considerable variety of work experiences and employer policies.[18]

Some of the labor market models now being constructed start from the premise that the *cognitive skills* content of formal education — the ability to use language and make logical inferences, to use numbers easily, to absorb and retain miscellaneous information — has little direct relationship to performance on the job. The important cognitive skills are those actually developed as needed through on-the-job training programs, formal or informal. Job skills are highly specific, rather than being related to education in general. This means that the costs of training employees are shifted from the public to the employer. But some employees are more easily and, therefore, more cheaply trained than others. Only at this point does formal education beyond the three R's enter. In order to minimize the training costs for new workers in entry level jobs, employers look for employees whose background characteristics appear to make them most readily trainable. Formal educational attainment and performance have a role to play here.

Education is a form of training. The ability to absorb one type of training probably indicates something about the ability to absorb another type of training. Education becomes an indirect measure of an individual's absorptive capacity and is relevant

---

[18] Berg, *Education and Jobs*, pp. 15, 17.

to the employer even when no cognitive job skill is learned in the educational process. Through education one learns how to be trained or exhibits that one is trainable.

Education also is one way for workers to show that they have "industrial discipline." Having gone through the educational process, the worker has demonstrated an ability to show up on time, take orders, do unpleasant tasks, and observe certain norms of group behavior. These characteristics are also fundamental to the work process. Often they are more important than specific job skills.[19]

And here the labor specialist joints hands with the radical economist, who has long maintained that the primary functions of education are to instill discipline and keep the 'classes in their places. The well-documented relationship between education and earnings is not disputed. But it is argued that this relationship is one of correlation not causation. The real question is, what determines who should be educated? And the answer, according to the radical economist, is that the amount and quality of education provided a child depend very largely on the socioeconomic status of his or her parents: "If we define socioeconomic background by a weighted sum of income, occupation and educational level of the parents, a child from the ninetieth percentile may expect, on the average, five more years of schooling than a child in the tenth percentile."[20] Turning the technical jargon into common English, this says that if your parents are in the top 10 percent on this socioeconomic scale you can ordinarily expect to secure five more years of schooling than someone whose parents are in the bottom 10 percent on the same scale. Where education and future incomes are concerned, it obviously pays to choose your parents wisely. Less flippantly, what this suggests, say Bowles and Gintis, is that the school system has been deliberately rigged to assure large amounts of high-quality education for the children of the upper classes, smaller amounts of lower-quality education for the children of low-income working parents. This goes far beyond a simple reflection of different ability levels in the two groups: "Even among children with identical IQ test scores at ages six and eight, those with rich, well-educated, high-status parents could expect a much higher level of schooling than those with less-favored origins."[21]

More than this, the school system is structured in such a fashion as to service the needs of a business system and to legitimize and perpetuate

---

[19] Lester C. Thurow, *Generating Inequality: Mechanisms of Distribution in the U.S. Economy*, Basic Books, New York, 1975, p. 88.

[20] Samuel Bowles and Herbert Gintis, *Schooling in Capitalist America: Educational Reform and the Contradictions of Economic Life*, Basic Books, New York, 1976, p. 30.

[21] Bowles and Gintis, *Schooling in Capitalist America*, p. 32.

the inequalities of such a system. It does this first of all by producing many of the technical and cognitive skills required on the job. Even more important, the inequalities of the system are legitimized by perpetuation of the myth that education honestly separates the fit from the unfit and proportions rewards accordingly. In fact, the school system produces, rewards, and labels personal characteristics according to the demands of the economic system. Elementary and secondary schools, and especially those with a high proportion of low-status students, are set up and run like factories — because that is the destination of most of the students. What is needed in the factory or in factorylike jobs is discipline; what is provided first and foremost in the schools is discipline. Only at the college level, where students are prepared for managerial positions, are the restraints relaxed, because future managers need to develop their socializing and decision-making skills.

As if this were not enough, other radical critics argue that we have an overblown educational system — an academocracy — in large part because our economic system simply could not provide jobs for those who would be turned loose in the job market should the academic industry be cut back to a reasonable size. Even with almost all elementary- and secondary-school-age children taken out of the job market, along with approximately half of the college-age population, our system has come close to full employment only now and again in recent decades. Flood the job market with all those who would really prefer to work rather than go to school — if it were not for academic credentialism — and unemployment could well increase to panic proportions.

Too many diplomas?

But holding would-be workers in the education pipeline and out of the labor market may solve the job problem only for the moment. What happens when this ever-larger group of educated workers flows out into the labor market? We are getting the answer to this question daily, in the form of distress stories about unplaceable high school and college graduates, and even — perhaps especially — holders of graduate school diplomas. In collecting materials for his study of *The Overeducated American*, Richard B. Freeman put together the following evidence of supersaturation of the job market for college and university graduates:

In 1973, only 24 of 55 graduates and doctoral candidates from the University of California at Berkeley English Department searching for college teaching jobs found them; in 1974, only 15 of 62.

Of 1225 history graduates and doctoral candidates in the United States seeking jobs as academics in 1973, just 182 found them.

18% of the graduates of the 1973 class of the College of Arts and Letters at one of the "big ten" universities who entered the labor market were still unemployed

6 months after graduation. Another 15% were working as receptionists, clerks, laborers, factory workers, and janitors.

At the University of Illinois, students slept overnight in front of the placement office to sign up for interviews with firms in the spring of 1975. The job situation was so bad that the university sent out recruiters to bring in more employers.

At Harvard, students lined up outside the Office of Career Services in February 1975 for interviews with banks, with nearly twice as many seeking interviews than there were available time slots, leading one placement director to remark, "The only time I've seen more people in this building is when they're demonstrating."

A questionnaire sent to 1800 graduates at Montclair State asking about jobs they had obtained elicited a poor response, with only 289 replying that their jobs were commensurate with their education. Unemployment averaged 13% in the class of 1970.[22]

As these citations indicate, to avoid unemployment many college graduates are taking jobs foreign to their interests and training, often with financial rewards far short of what they anticipated when they began college.

For prospective teachers the situation is especially depressing. Until the 1970s, thanks to the near-explosive rise in the school population, teaching was a good "fall back" profession: If the college graduate could not find a satisfactory job elsewhere, he or she could always fall back into a teaching position. No longer. In a special section of its January 15, 1975, issue the *New York Times* reported that there were 221,000 beginning teachers competing for 118,800 jobs on the elementary and secondary level the previous fall. At the college level there were some 5,000 more new Ph.D.s than full-time faculty positions for them. Ph.D.s in physics and mathematics actively sought employment as fifth and sixth grade mathematics teachers.

And the future promises no relief. In the same issue of the *New York Times* Dr. William Graybeal, manpower specialist at the National Education Association in Washington, was reported to have said that while there were at that time 2,123,000 elementary and secondary teachers, the number was expected to decline and level off at around 2 million. As for college teachers, Professor Allan Cartter of the University of California's Higher Education Research Institute saw no increase in the inadequate number of new jobs during the 1970s and a sharp falling off of new jobs in the 1980s.

In all the gloom, there were some brights spots. As a consequence of the burgeoning of Medicare, Medicaid, and other government health care programs, the demand was brisk both for practitioners in the health care field and for teachers in the health sciences, such as pharmacology. And

---

[22] Richard B. Freeman, *The Overeducated American*, Academic Press, New York, 1976, p. 28.

as a result of the establishment of compensatory education programs, teachers, especially bilingual teachers, were in demand in the special education and industrial arts fields. At the college level there was still a shortage of teachers in some areas: finance, accounting, mining engineering, and a few others. The problem here, though, is that news of undersupplied areas gets around fast, and students flock into these fields. The beginning college or graduate student, then, can never be sure that the shortage will still exist three or four years later when the diploma is received. Freeman detects a definite cyclical pattern in employment and earnings for college graduates. A shortage of particular skills one year is reflected in high starting salaries. This pulls a large number of trainees into the field, flooding the market and driving down starting salaries four years later.[23] He relates this to the "cobweb" dynamics of the corn and hog markets, where a low price for corn one year appears to make hog raising attractive but instead virtually guarantees low pork prices when the enlarged hog supply reaches the market several years later. The overall consequence of the rapid increase in academically credentialed job candidates coupled with a slower growth in job opportunities had to mean that compensation for such applicants would at some point begin to slip relative to earnings of applicants with less impressive credentials. That point was the beginning of the 1970s. In 1969, the average income for a male college graduate was just about twice as high as that of a male grade-school graduate. By 1974 the ratio had fallen to around 1.75. For recent college graduates the decline was even more precipitous. In 1969 the typical male college graduate aged 25–34 received about 1.4 times as much annual income as the average high school graduate in the same age group. By 1974 the ratio had dropped to barely over 1.15.[24] This had to mean, of course, a fall in the rate of return on investment in a college education. Freeman's computations show such a rate of return as 11 to 12.5 percent, depending on assumptions, as late as 1968, but only 7.5 to 10 percent in 1973.[25] With the cost of borrowed money around 10 percent in 1973, the average college student obviously could not afford to borrow to go to college; his future earnings would be insufficient to justify the additional expense. And it would be foolish — if income maximization were the only reason for a college education — for a college student's parents to put up the money if they had to forego the opportunity to earn 10 percent by investing the money elsewhere.

Where does all this leave the education industry? It surely does not call for any wholesale scrapping of our school system. We still need universal literacy, to meet the demands of both democracy and a highly

[23] Freeman, *The Overeducated American*, p. 60.
[24] Freeman, *The Overeducated American*, p. 14.
[25] Freeman, *The Overeducated American*, p. 26.

technological society. And the steady increase in sophisticated technology further suggests a need for development of technical skills. But aside from general literacy and skill development, what has happened in the last few years suggests that we must question the assumption that every American needs a college diploma, or even a high school diploma. Just what is it in a salesperson's job, or even a manager's, that makes a college diploma so important? It is time that we attempted seriously to answer the question.

Some who have made the attempt argue that tying the car of education to the engine of economic progress and higher earnings was a serious mistake. The car should be uncoupled and hooked to a different engine. Going back to basics, Christopher Lasch finds merit in the ideas of our nation's founders. Jefferson, for example, "believed that the most important objects of public education were to provide for intellectual leadership and to make people effective guardians of their own liberty.... The ideal citizen of Jefferson's republic was the man who cannot be fooled by demagogues or overawed by the learned obfuscations of professional wise men. Appeals to authority do not impress him."[26] Since recent studies strongly suggest that our present educational system neither reduces inequality nor even, for the most part, imparts the skills actually required for most jobs, we have little to lose and much to gain by reorienting education in the direction suggested by the founders of the country, toward (1) "giv[ing] everybody the intellectual resources — particularly the command of language — needed to distinguish truth from public lies and thus to defend themselves against tyrants and demagogues" and (2) "train[ing]

the small society   by Brickman

A MASTERS DEGREE IN BUSINESS ADMINISTRATION... AND ALL YOU LEARNED WAS, "BUY LOW AND SELL HIGH"?

© Washington Star Syndicate, Inc., permission granted by King Features Syndicate, Inc., 1977.

---

[26] Christopher Lasch, "Inequality and Education," *The New York Review* (May 17, 1973), 24.

scholars, intellectuals, and members of the learned professions."[27] This necessarily means the abandonment of mass education and its replacement by selective, "elitist" education, available only to those — but to all of those — who are qualified for it and completely committed to it.

This solution would by no means satisfy everyone. The dream of the good life lying just beyond the college sheepskin will die hard. But the facts of life are turning this dream into a nightmare for hundreds of thousands of high school and college graduates. They, in particular, should welcome a re-examination of the premises on which we have built our system of mass education, so that those coming up behind them will not find themselves in a similar situation.

Until things are changed, of course, the person intent on maximizing his or her lifetime earnings has little choice but to complete high school and go on to college. The college diploma will not guarantee admission to a high-paying occupation, since so many fields are already oversupplied with applicants, but without the diploma chances of selection are near zero. The person who argues that this is a silly, irrational way to screen applicants into jobs has much evidence to back his or her case. But the awkward question then obtrudes, what system would be better? Selection on the basis of ability? But how do we judge ability, especially for the person without experience? Written tests of ability have proved highly unreliable. If educational credentials are disregarded and tests can't be relied on, we are back to selection on the basis of family or social connections or appearance and deportment. These have some obvious drawbacks.

I RACIAL AND SEXUAL DISCRIMINATION I

Education and discrimination

Even during the decades when the underlying logic of education as investment in human capital went virtually unchallenged, it was apparent that one important bit of evidence fit the analytical pattern very badly. Education seemed to do one thing for those with white skins and something quite different for those with dark skins, as Table 9.2, based on the 1960 data, shows.

It is evident from the table that education paid, for both whites and nonwhites. Each step increase in education brought a significant advance in lifetime earnings. But always the return to education was far higher for whites than nonwhites. The sad fact was that, for the United States as a whole, a nonwhite male college graduate was in line to receive lifetime earnings less than those earned by a white male with only an elementary

---

[27] Lasch, "Inequality and Education," p. 24.

TABLE 9.2

Estimated lifetime earnings for males, by years of school completed, region, and race, 1960

Years of school completed	United States			South		
	White	Nonwhite	% of nonwhite to white	White	Nonwhite	% of nonwhite to white
ELEMENTARY SCHOOL						
Less than 8	157,000	95,000	61	133,000	77,000	58
8	191,000	123,000	64	167,000	96,000	57
HIGH SCHOOL						
1–3	221,000	132,000	60	197,000	102,000	52
4	253,000	151,000	60	240,000	115,000	48
COLLEGE						
1–3	301,000	162,000	54	241,000	127,000	44
4	395,000	185,000	47	369,000	154,000	42
5 or more	466,000	246,000	53	455,000	213,000	47

Source: Raymond S. Franklin and Solomon Resnik, *The Political Economy of Racism*, Holt, Rinehart and Winston, 1973, p. 50. Data drawn from Bureau of the Census, *Income Distribution in the United States*, by Herman P. Miller, United States Government Printing Office, Washington, D.C., 1966.

school education. And in the South a graduate school diploma in the hands of a nonwhite male promised lifetime earnings barely greater than those of a white male high school dropout. It may reasonably be argued that a year of education in a nonwhite school was inferior to a year in a white school. No doubt schools for blacks were significantly inferior to schools for whites. But can it seriously be argued that a white elementary school education was superior to a nonwhite college education? Any reasonable person has to concede that discrimination against nonwhites must have played a part, both in the provision of inferior schools to begin with, then in the refusal to admit nonwhites into the high-paying jobs.

The economic costs of this discrimination have been and continue to be high, quite aside from the traumatic social-psychological costs. The *Wall Street Journal* recently reported the results of a study suggesting that job discrimination costs the nation $55.8 billion a year:

Library of Congress researchers sought to estimate the cost of job bias by examining the unemployment rates and earnings of nonwhite workers compared with rates for whites. If both groups had the same job skills and education in 1975, they calculated, 638,000 more minority workers would have been employed. And if wages had been equal, each minority worker would have earned $1,768 more annually.

The study concludes that such changes would generate $22.3 billion a year in additional direct wages and salaries, and $2\frac{1}{2}$ times that amount in added gross national product. . . . *Based on 1975 economic statistics, the gains would equal 3.7% of gross national product, the study says.*[28]

Costs of discrimination

As the quotation indicates there are two major economic costs of discrimination. Since nonwhites have traditionally been "last hired, first fired," they spend a disproportionate share of their time in the ranks of the unemployed, where their contribution to national production and income is obviously nil. A rough rule of thumb is that the unemployment rate for nonwhites runs at roughly twice the rate for white workers. Table 9.3 gives the figures for recent years. The table also suggests another rule of thumb: Unemployment among women averages close to one and one-half times the rate for men. This means that not only are we losing production because we fail to make use of a significant portion of nonwhite labor, but the same is true for women as well.

And just as the economy loses from failing to employ all the services of nonwhites and women, so it loses from their *underemployment* — that is, putting them to work in part-time or low-level jobs when they are qualified by ability and training for higher-level jobs. The Library of Congress

---

[28] *Wall Street Journal* (June 22, 1976), 1. Italics in original.

TABLE 9.3
Selected unemployment rates, 1970–1976, by color and sex (%)

| Year | All workers | By color | | By sex | |
		White	Black and other races	Men 20 years and over	Women 20 years and over
1970	4.9	4.5	8.2	3.5	4.8
1971	5.9	5.4	9.9	4.4	5.7
1972	5.6	5.0	10.0	4.0	5.4
1973	4.9	4.3	8.9	3.2	4.8
1974	5.6	5.0	9.9	3.8	5.5
1975	8.5	7.8	13.9	6.7	8.0
1976	7.7	7.0	13.1	5.9	7.4

Source: *Economic Report of the President*, 1977, p. 221.

study just cited provides an estimate of such losses for nonwhites. Comparable figures for women are harder to come by, but some of the studies conducted in the early 1970s show annual earnings for women averaging about 40 percent below annual earnings for men. Not all of this, of course, is "pure" discrimination. On the basis of less experience, somewhat less education, and other factors, women might be expected to earn about 20 percent less than men. The other 20 percent of the differential, then, represents "pure" discrimination against women.[29]

Discrimination and "crowding"

Why do we do this? Why do we deliberately maintain practices that systematically rob the country of a substantial portion of potential annual output? The answer appears to be that the practices continue because while the country loses certain groups gain. This can be explained by use of the *crowding* model developed by economist Barbara Bergmann. Start first with the premise that a particular part of the labor market is open to everyone with the requisite ability and training. Out of this comes a certain level of employment and wages, as shown in diagram A of Figure 9.3. Diagrams B and C show what happens when the occupation identified in diagram A is declared off-limits to women or members of a minority group. To find employment, women and nonwhites must crowd into whatever fields are still open to them, increasing the labor supply in such fields and driving down the wage rate (*w* to *w'* in diagram C). Meanwhile the white

[29] Freeman, *The Overeducated American*, pp. 163–164.

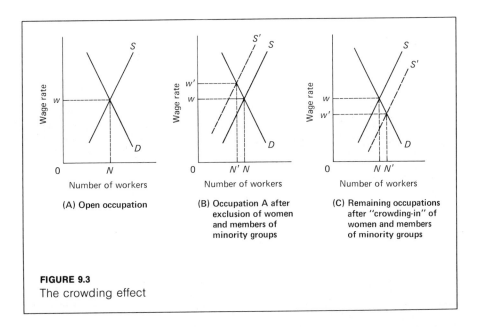

FIGURE 9.3
The crowding effect

males left to themselves in the occupation of A enjoy the higher wages
that come with a restricted labor supply (*w* to *w'* in diagram B). Discrimination, needless to say, is highly rational as far as these men are concerned — and the same is true for their wives if they have no intention of
seeking a job outside the household. And naturally the discrimination by
the employers of these men will not be identified as such. It will be cloaked
with the heartfelt conviction that women don't have the necessary aptitudes
or stamina to be truck drivers or police officers or engineers or even
doctors or lawyers, and that blacks aren't well suited for managerial positions or college teaching except at black colleges or for practicing
dentistry or medicine except in black communities. Whether or not any of
this is true is beside the point. These are — or at least have been —
articles of faith, and faith can easily surmount fact.

Progress against discrimination

But isn't this all ancient history? Haven't the rules of the game changed
sufficiently in recent years to eliminate these artificial barriers? The answer
has to be, it all depends on how we measure progress against discrimination.

If we measure progress in terms of access to jobs, we come up with
a mixed bag of improvement and regression. Unemployment among blacks
relative to whites still holds at the 2:1 ratio established at the end of World
War II. For women the recent picture is even bleaker. At the beginning of
the 1960s the unemployment rate for women was only about 10 percent

TABLE 9.4
Median money wages or salary income of year-round full-time workers, by race and sex, 1939 to 1970

	Male			Female			
Year	White (1)	Black and other races (2)	Ratio (2) to (1)	White (4)	Black and other races (5)	Ratio (4) to (1)	Ratio (5) to (1)
1939	1,419	639	.45	863	327	.61	.23
1955	4,458	2,831	.64	2,870	1,637	.64	.37
1960	5,662	3,789	.67	3,410	2,372	.60	.42
1965	6,814	4,367	.64	3,960	2,713	.58	.40
1970	9,373	6,598	.70	5,490	4,674	.59	.50

Source: Adapted from *Historical Statistics of the United States*, 1975, p. 304.

higher than for men; by the mid-seventies, as we saw earlier (Table 9.3), it was 25 to 50 percent higher. If we concentrate, not on jobs in general, but only on the best jobs, again we find a mixed picture. Black males have improved their probability of holding a job in the top 5 percent of the earnings distribution relative to that of white males from 9 percent in 1960 to 19 percent in 1973. Black females have also made progress. In 1960 there was no chance at all of a black female ending up with one of these top jobs; in 1973 the odds were merely 1,667 times as great that a white male would end up in one of these high paying jobs as that a black female would. Miniscule improvement, it is true, but movement in the right direction. For white females — women's liberation notwithstanding — movement was in the opposite direction. In 1960 white females had a probability 6 percent as great as that for white males of ending up with one of these superior assignments; by 1973 the probability had fallen to 4 percent.[30] In the latter year chances of employment in one of these high-paying jobs were 25 times greater for white males than for white females.

While overall relative employment probabilities for blacks and other minority workers have not improved since World War II, relative earnings for employed workers have, as Table 9.4 indicates.

Table 9.4 tells us that the extraordinary employment and earnings opportunities of World War II spilled over into the female and minority labor market. With unemployment down to a phenomenal 1.2 percent at the height of the war, employers had little option but to take anyone available, male or female, black or white. "Rosie the Riveter," whether black or white, took her place alongside her male counterparts.

Once the war ended blacks and other minority workers, both male and female, failed to make further gains on white male workers for a substantial period of time, but at least they held their own. Then in the late 1960s they were able to close the gap even further. This was another period of high employment, with the unemployment rate averaging just over 3.8 percent from 1965 to 1969, but it was also the period during which civil rights legislation began to take hold. This guaranteed all job applicants an *equal opportunity* for employment. Title VII of the Civil Rights Act of 1964 made it "an unlawful practice for employers to fail or refuse to hire or to discharge or otherwise discriminate against any individual with respect to his compensation, terms, conditions or privileges of employment, because of such individual's race, color, religion, sex or national origin." Executive Order 11246 outlawed discrimination by federal contractors and required *affirmative action* "to ensure that applicants are employed. . . ." A common interpretation of this affirmative action provision was that if two applicants for a job vacancy were equally qualified, then if one of them was a member

---

[30] Lester C. Thurow, "The Economic Progress of Minority Groups," *Challenge Magazine*, (March–April 1976), 21.

of a minority group or a woman the first job offer should go to that person. A number of states, sixteen in all, followed the lead of the federal government by enacting their own fair employment practices laws. And court interpretations of federal and state laws tended to favor active intervention in the employment process.

For women and members of minority groups who already held jobs the equal opportunity–affirmative action provisions had some impact but not a major one. It has proved almost impossible to undo the results of past discrimination in hiring and promotion. But for new minority entrants into the job market the results of the enforcement of these provisions were quite spectacular. By the beginning of the 1970s newly graduated black college men had attained parity with their white peers, as measured by starting salaries. And compared with white female college graduates, black female college graduates were moving into positions at an average 5 percent premium in starting salaries. If this pattern is long sustained, the gap between white and black incomes will eventually be closed. Evidence currently coming in, however, suggests that the pattern is crumbling somewhat under pressures produced by a stagnant economy. For members of minority groups the maintenance of full employment appears to be a necessity both for making jobs available and for making them available on equal terms for whites and nonwhites.

For white women, on the other hand, something more than full employment and guaranteed civil rights will apparently be necessary. Both of these were in operation during the late 1960s, yet the gap between white male and white female incomes remained at around 40 percent, as Table 9.4 indicates. In recent years, women have moved into the active labor force in ever-increasing numbers, but they have tended to crowd into or be crowded into the fields that have traditionally been regarded as "fit" for women: light factory work for the least educated, clerical work for the high school graduates and some of the college graduates, and teaching, nursing, and social work for those with professional qualifications. From 1960 to 1974 the male component of the labor force increased in numbers by 17 percent, but the number of women in the labor force rose by 55 percent. While in 1960 there were more than two men in the labor force for each woman, by 1974 the ratio had been cut to about three men for each two women. But with only minor exceptions, as Table 9.5 indicates, the new female entrants did not compete actively for men's jobs.

Some of the women did break into the ranks of the well-paid as managers and administrators, but not in sufficient numbers to keep the proportion of women employed in that category from falling. More significantly, over 7 million of the 16 million-person increase in the female labor force ended up employed where women have traditionally been employed since the invention of the typewriter, as clerical workers — and this during a period when computerization was supposed to reduce the need for clerks.

TABLE 9.5
Employed women by major occupation group, 1950 and 1974

Major occupation group	Employed women (thousands)		% change 1950–1974	% of total	
	1950	1974		1950	1974
Professional and technical workers	1,794	4,992	+178	10.3	14.9
Managers and administrators	990	1,650	+67	5.7	4.9
Salesworkers	1,443	2,265	+57	8.2	6.8
Clerical workers	4,597	11,676	+154	26.3	34.9
Craftsmen and foremen	188	511	+172	1.1	1.5
Operatives	3,336	4,331	+30	19.1	13.0
Nonfarm laborers	84	354	+321	.5	1.1
Service workers	3,850	7,156	+86	22.0	21.4
Farmworkers	1,212	957	−60	6.9	1.4
Total women	17,493	33,417	+91	100.0	100.0

Source: *Statistical Abstract of the United States*, 1975, p. 359.

Table 9.5 does show however, that women are making substantial gains in the professional and technical fields. Some of these are occupations that have long been regarded as women's fields: primary and secondary teaching, social work, entertainment. But some are professions that have been regarded as male territory. Table 9.6 identifies some of these and estimates the inroads women are making. It is obvious from the table that while women have been taking their places in the ranks of these highest-paying occupations they still have a long way to go before they are represented in proportion to their overall numbers in the labor force. And until they reach that point, their incomes will lag behind those of men.

Before closing the books on inequality of income distribution and discrimination, some mention, in all justice, should be made of the American Indian. The problem is that while we know in general terms that these are the poorest of the American ethnic groups, we don't know just how poor they are. The agency primarily concerned with the welfare of the Indians, the Bureau of Indian Affairs, has never published income figures, if they have collected them. The only data we have was released by the Economic Development Administration, based on reports from about half the Indian reservations. This indicates a median family income of $3,300 in 1969, with a range of $1,000 on several reservations to $15,000 on one reservation. This suggests an average income around one-third of that of

TABLE 9.6

Proportion of women in male-dominated professions

Occupation	Proportion of women (%)		
	1960	1970	1974
PROFESSIONAL	38.4	39.9	40.5
Accountants	16.5	26.2	23.7
Architects	2.1	3.6	—
Engineers	0.8	0.6	1.3
Law	3.5	4.9	7.0
Life and physical sciences	9.2	13.7	15.9
Pharmacists	7.5	12.0	—
Doctors	6.9	9.3	9.3
Editors and reporters	36.6	40.6	43.6
Teachers, college and university	23.9	28.6	30.9
MANAGERS			
Salaried managers	13.9	16.1	18.4

Source: Richard B. Freeman, *The Overeducated American,* Academic Press, New York, 1976, p. 172.

the typical white family. And we don't know whether even that figure is rising or declining. In the case of the American Indian, discrimination takes the form primarily of neglect.

I SUMMARY I

Measured by money outlay, the United States has the world's most comprehensive system of education. Two common justifications for this costly system have been that education controls income inequality by providing for upward mobility and that it increases production and income.

The second of these is what the economist means by investment in human capital. Studies shortly after World War II showed a net return to investment in a college education of at least 10 percent — and even higher returns to primary and secondary education. This proof that education at all levels was a good investment contributed to the rapid growth in educational outlays.

In recent years, however, we have discovered that the way these dollars have been spent may actually have widened income differentials. Children of upper-income families have benefited far more than the children of the poor.

Many scholars also have begun to question the assumed relationship between education and productivity. The notion is now current that demands for ever-higher levels of education may have little to do with improved performance on the job but everything to do with screening certain individuals into, and others out of, jobs. And this screening, according to some, takes place along distinct class lines.

Whatever function education performs, there is little present doubt that the market for holders of higher diplomas has been flooded. The rate of return to a college education, as a consequence, has fallen dramatically in the last ten years.

Whether or not education has reduced inequality may still be in doubt, but there is no question that overt discrimination on the basis of race or sex has led to greater inequality. The civil rights movement is significantly reducing overt discrimination against blacks and other nonwhites, both male and female, but has as yet done little to improve the status of white women — partly because they are flooding into the labor market in huge numbers and overcrowding their traditional fields.

I IMPORTANT TERMS AND CONCEPTS I

investment in human capital	underemployment
present dollars	crowding
future dollars	equal opportunity
education as a screening device	affirmative action

I QUESTIONS, PROBLEMS, AND EXERCISES I

1 What is the justification for classifying educational expenditures as a type of investment spending?

2 Can we credit all of the difference in lifetime earnings of a college graduate as compared to someone with only a high school diploma to the college education alone? If not, what else must be considered?

3 To what extent has education delivered on its promise to reduce income inequality in the United States?

4 On what grounds did the California Supreme Court in *Serrano* v. *Priest* find that the state's system of school finance "invidiously discriminates against the poor"?

5 Since it is difficult, perhaps impossible, to prove a relationship between the content of formal education and job performance in many occupations, why do employers in these occupations continue to insist on a college diploma for those they hire?

6 In purely monetary terms, is a college education a worthwhile investment today for the average American? What evidence can you cite for your answer?

7 What is the relationship between the maintenance of something approaching full employment and progress against discrimination?

8 If the current interest rate is 7 percent, about how much greater value has a present dollar (one in hand now) than a dollar not to be received until a year from today?

I   SUGGESTED READING   I

Berg, Ivar. *Education and Jobs: The Great Training Robbery*. Beacon Press, Boston, 1971.

Bowles, Samuel, and Herbert Gintis. *Schooling in Capitalist America: Educational Reform and the Contradictions of Economic Life*. Basic Books, New York, 1976.

Freeman, Richard B. *The Overeducated American*. Academic Press, New York, 1976.

Jencks, Christopher et al. *Inequality: A Reassessment of the Effect of Family and Schooling in America*. Harper Colophon Books, New York, 1973.

Kreps, Juanita. *Women and the American Economy: A Look to the 1980s*. The American Assembly, Prentice-Hall, Englewood Cliffs, N.J., 1976.

Franklin, Raymond S., and Solomon Resnik. *The Political Economy of Racism*. Holt, New York, 1973.

Thurow, Lester C. *Generating Inequality: Mechanisms of Distribution in the U.S. Economy*. Basic Books, New York, 1975.

TEN

I ENERGY, ENVIRONMENT, AND GROWTH I

In economics everything is related to everything else. This is especially true in a market economy, where economic activity is governed by relative prices. Economists take explicit account of this with the concept of general equilibrium. Like ripples spreading across the whole surface of a quiet pool after a pebble is thrown in, changes in one part of a market economy set off wavelike movements that ultimately spread to all other parts of the economy.

The availability and price of energy is almost a clinical case of this interrelatedness. Among other things, it is bound up with inflation, recession, and unemployment; the balance of payments; transportation; housing;

taxes; cities; economic concentration and antitrust; regional imbalances in the United States; the environment; our economic (and political) relationships with the rest of the world; architecture and the construction industry; and the possibilities for and the rate of economic growth. Everyone, in one degree or another, thus has a stake in energy policy. Unfortunately, it seems, everyone also has a stake in an energy policy different from that advocated by everyone else. This, plus the extreme complexity of the issue, goes a long way toward explaining why we have been so tardy in developing *an* energy policy.

| OVERLAPPING PROBLEMS |

But while energy is related to everything else, its ties with the environment and economic growth are among the closest. This can be seen in the fact that our major current source of energy, petroleum, has its primary use in propelling automotive vehicles (passenger cars, trucks, buses, and motorcycles), while these same vehicles are our largest single source of air pollution. It is also evidenced by the parallel growth of energy use and the national income. This relationship can be seen from the time our industrialization process began. It is especially apparent in recent years. During the 1950s and 1960s our energy use increased at the rate of 3.4 percent a year — roughly the same rate at which real gross national product grew. The fact that energy use spurted at nearly a 5 percent rate in the early 1970s while the growth of national income slowed suggests that this is the consequence of no inevitable natural law. It is now up to national economic policy to determine whether or not the relationship between economic growth and ever-increasing energy use should be broken.

Another reason for linking energy, the environment, and economic growth is that all have been subject to *compound growth rates*. Each year we add a certain percentage to our total use of energy, our total goods and services, and to our stock of pollution — and the next year we add about the same percentage to these larger totals. The result of these geometric, or exponential, increases is a doubling of all totals in amazingly short periods of time. The Rule of Seventy tells us that any statistical series growing at a 1 percent compound rate will double in seventy years (70 divided by 1). If the series is growing at 2 percent, only thirty-five years is required for the doubling (70 divided by 2). And if we continued to increase our energy use at the rate of the early 1970s, we would double our energy demands every fourteen years (70 divided by 5).

These compound growth rates (where the annual "interest," or increment, is added to the "principal" in computing the next year's increase) have a way of sneaking up on us — of turning an awkward situation into a crisis. This is pointed up by a homely little story. It tells of a farmer who one day notices a lily pad in his farm pond. The next day there are two, and the following day four. The lily pads are apparently doubling daily. The farmer doesn't worry, though. It's a big pond and there's still lots of clear water, and besides the lily pads are decorative. After a few weeks, though, the farmer begins to worry. His pond is half covered with lily pads. But his worrying comes too late — the next day his pond is completely covered over!

The story can as easily be told with numbers. A series growing at a compound (geometric) rate reaches extremely high numbers in fairly short order: 1, 2, 4, 8, 16, 32, 64, 128, 256, 512, 1024. . . . A diagram, such as Figure 10.1, conveys the same idea. The compound growth curve can be used for more than describing how crises catch us by surprise. It can convey pleasant messages, too, such as how sustained economic growth from the beginning of the nineteenth century has increased our national income by around a thousandfold. Even after allowing for population growth, this leaves us with over eleven times as many goods and services per person as our ancestors enjoyed in 1800. But when we recognize that energy use and pollution have both increased at compound rates along with national income, we realize that something will have to give in the years ahead. What was a modest demand on our energy sources halfway through the time scale in Figure 10.1 has become an all-devouring monster. Incredible as it may seem, half of the total quantity of coal ever mined has been extracted in the last thirty years, half of the total production of crude oil has been pumped in the last ten years, and with natural gas we

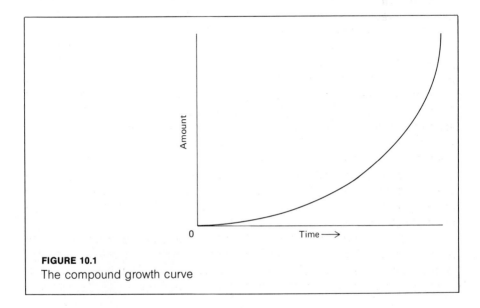

FIGURE 10.1
The compound growth curve

TABLE 10.1
United States energy consumption mix, 1973 (quadrillion Btu's)

Fuel	Residential and commercial	Industrial	Transpor- tation	Electric generation	Total consumption	% of total consumption
Coal	0.34	4.20	—	8.22	12.76	17.9
Oil	6.64	5.72	16.94	3.24	32.78	45.9
Gas	7.56	10.22	0.76	3.70	22.24	31.2
Hydro	—	0.04	—	2.74	2.78	3.9
Nuclear	—	—	—	0.80	0.80	1.1
Total primary	14.54	20.18	17.70	18.70	71.36	100.0
Electric usage	3.38	2.50	0.02	12.80[a]	—	—
Total	17.92	22.68	17.72	12.80[a]	71.36	100.0

[a] Of the 18.70 primary energy input, 12.80 became generation losses and the 5.90 is distributed to the use sectors. (Converted from million barrels oil-equivalent per day.)
Source: Reproduced from *U.S. Energy Prospects: An Engineering Viewpoint*, page 27, with the permission of the National Academy of Sciences, Washington, D.C.

have a resource that nature worked millions of years to create and that people will use up for all practical purposes in a single century. These facts, incidentally, show why it makes little sense to estimate our reserves of energy supplies and natural resources as so many remaining years at *current* rates of usage. As for pollution, what were minor pockets of foul air and water at the midpoint of the time scale of Figure 10.1 have become sufficiently widespread, to put it mildly, to take the edge off the enjoyment of our vast outpouring of goods and services.

I ENERGY USE I

The price of cheap energy

One fact borne home to us in the last few years of rising energy prices is how heavily the American economy depends on abundant supplies of cheap energy. This was true from our beginnings as a nation. The logic of production in a market economy calls for making maximum use of those resources in most abundant supply and therefore cheapest. In the early nineteenth century this meant water, wood, and wind, all of them free or extremely cheap. Water, converted into power by the use of the water wheel, was the principal "prime mover" for American industry until after the Civil War. Only with the exhaustion of good sites for water power installations and the unstable stream flows, which came with cutting the forests, did industry shift over to the steam engine. And even then the fuel for steam engines was as likely to be wood as coal. Fuel wood was more important than coal as a source of energy down to the 1880s. Wind held an important place as an energy source until late in the nineteenth century — until electricity began to replace the windmill, and the steamboat and steamship replaced the sailing ship.

With steady improvements in the steam engine and declining railroad freight costs, coal came to the fore in the late nineteenth century. In 1890 coal provided 90 percent of the energy used by industry. And, although it was being pushed by petroleum, natural gas, and hydropower, it remained the cheapest source of energy for several decades, providing at least 80 percent of industrial power into the 1920s.

The use of coal as an energy source peaked during the 1920s. Since then it has given way to oil and natural gas, slipping slowly before World War II, rapidly since then, at least down to the 1960s. By 1955 it provided less than 30 percent of total energy used in the United States. And since then, as Table 10.1 shows, it has slipped even further, and this despite the fact that our coal reserves are huge and our reserves of oil and natural gas are rapidly reaching the point of exhaustion.

What this brief historical survey of changing energy sources demonstrates is that the United States was blessed with large stocks of resources that were convertible into energy. As one source was used up — or, better, when we ran into sharply diminishing returns in one source — we could with little inconvenience move on to another. And all this was done with almost no governmental guidance. When government did get involved, as it has increasingly in recent years, the expectation was that it would simply do its best to continue what normal market processes had done in the past: guarantee the same abundant, low-cost energy supplies that normal market processes had provided all through our history. Overturning this expectation of continued low energy prices is proving to be one of the most difficult problems the federal government faces. And since energy problems in the past have in large part solved themselves, it is doubly compounded by the belief that somehow our present predicament will take care of itself if government doesn't get in the way.

The determination of the federal government to maintain low energy prices shows up in energy price indexes covering the last quarter-century. In actual dollar prices, the cost of coal, oil, natural gas, and electricity rose during this period. But so did everything else, and at a far faster rate. If energy prices are measured in dollars of constant purchasing power, as they are in Table 10.2, then we see that there has been a continuous and accelerating *fall* in the cost of energy. Underlying these figures are others indicating a fall in real (constant-dollar) coal prices of 15 percent between 1951 and 1971, a fall in real petroleum prices of 17 percent, and an unbelievable fall in real electricity rates of 43 percent.

This fall in energy prices was not entirely the result of government policy actions, of course, except to the extent that it was government policy to allow whatever happened to happen. Coal fell in real terms primarily because it was a competitive industry, and its price was held in check by

TABLE 10.2
Index of energy prices, 1950–1973

Period	Annual rate of change (%)
1950–1955	−.62
1955–1960	−.75
1960–1965	−1.31
1965–1970	−1.73
1970–mid-1973[a]	−1.87

[a] Preliminary.

Source: Edward J. Mitchell, *U.S. Energy Policy: A Primer*, American Enterprise Institute for Public Policy Research, Washington, D.C., 1974, p. 82.

the availability of low-priced alternative sources of more desirable energy, primarily oil and natural gas. But it was government policy to encourage additional coal production, and this was assisted by sympathetic tax treatment of capital goods used in the industry. Coal mine owners were also granted a generous depletion allowance, which permitted coal mining firms in effect to charge off the using up of coal stocks against their taxes rather than passing the cost forward to the consumer in the form of higher prices.

In holding down prices for the other sources of energy, the hand of government is far more visible. Oil, natural gas, electricity, and nuclear power are all regulated industries. Drilling for oil came under the control of state governments early on, to prevent the first drillers from pumping oil from a common pool underlying the property of several owners. Later the major oil-producing states of the Southwest adopted the policy of market-demand prorationing. By setting the amount of oil each owner was allowed to pump from existing wells the states in effect determined the national price of oil. When rising imports of foreign oil threatened to disrupt this control over domestic prices in the 1950s, the federal government came to the rescue by imposing mandatory oil import quotas. The price-raising tendencies of these monopolistic controls were offset until recently by federal tax measures that allowed oil producers to get their investment return from the taxpayer rather than from the buyers of gasoline and other petroleum products. Oil exploration allowances permitted petroleum companies to charge off the expense of dry holes, as well as successful ventures, to the taxpayer. Even more significant, the oil depletion allowance afforded companies an opportunity to write off mineral assets against taxes in amounts far exceeding costs. This has recently been eliminated except for small operators, but during the last years of its use, it reduced oil company income tax payments by around $1.5 billion a year, thereby providing an alternative to price rises as a source of funds for rapid exploration and exploitation of both domestic and foreign mineral reserves.

In the case of natural gas the situation is simpler. Prices for gas produced and distributed within a single state are largely left to control by supply and demand. Gas produced in one state and shipped to another for use, however, comes under the jurisdiction of the Federal Power Commission and is controlled by a ceiling price. As of September 1976 the intrastate price of natural gas in Texas was around $1.80 per 1,000 cubic feet, only slightly below the world price of oil on a Btu basis. But the average price of gas sold on the interstate market was only one-quarter of the Texas intrastate price, encouraging continued extravagant use of this rapidly depleting resource.

For electricity, state regulatory authorities have over the years adopted policies that have guaranteed bargain-basement rates, especially for large industrial users. Charged with the responsibility of allowing no more than "a fair return on a fair investment," as we will see in the section on public utility regulation, the state regulatory commissions both encouraged rapid expansion of electric generating facilities and attempted to make sure that no more than a fair price was charged to users. Since this has been an industry especially subject to increasing returns (falling long-run unit costs), prices fell steadily as the industry expanded, as Table 10.3 shows. In current dollars, and during a period when prices of almost everything else rose, the price of electricity fell by close to 80 percent for residential users and by about half for large industrial and other users over the period 1922–1970. To assure maximum demand for electricity, the regulated companies were allowed to charge off almost any amount of advertising and promotional expenses and were allowed to charge large users rates less than half those of small retail users.

The nuclear energy industry needs less attention, at least in this connection. Since costs of producing nuclear energy have been considerably higher than alternative sources, the federal government has found it necessary to subsidize the industry in various ways. Even with subsidized research and development and capital formation, the industry has barely remained competitive.

The point to this recital of energy price history is made neatly by economist Allen V. Kneese:

It seems to me at least arguable that the availability of extremely low cost energy in the first two decades following the Second World War was a disaster of substantial proportions for the nation. The reason is that there were enormous external costs associated with the massive increases in energy usage over that period. The most obvious example is air pollution, which has been shown to cause many billions of dollars of health damage annually, not to mention its many other adverse effects. In addition, cheap energy contributed at least partially to the destruction

TABLE 10.3
Average prices for electric energy, selected years

Year	Average prices, all services (¢ per kwh)	Average prices, all residential consumption (¢ per kwh)	Average prices, large users (¢ per kwh)
1922	2.83	7.38	1.80
1950	1.81	2.88	1.02
1970	1.59	2.10	0.95

Source: *Historical Statistics of the United States*, Part II, 1975, p. 287.

of our cities by permitting the generation of a dispersed pattern of residences and economic activities that ultimately made any sort of genuine urban development impossible. A corollary is that it allowed Detroit to produce enormous gas guzzlers with small, uncomfortable passenger compartments and persuade the American consumer that they were automobiles. Finally, cheap energy locked us into energy-intensive technologies embodied in very durable equipment. This now greatly limits our ability to adapt to our changed circumstances.[1]

An energy policy for America

The first point to stress in developing a workable energy policy is, as Kneese insists, that we have indeed become an energy-guzzling nation. Over and over again it has been pointed out that with only 6 percent of the world's population we consume about one-third of the world's annual energy production. And that isn't just because we have such a high standard of living to support. The standard of living in the nations of western Europe and Japan is rapidly approaching ours — in fact, in several nations it has surpassed ours, as measured by per capita national income figures. Yet, energy consumption per $1,000 of gross national product in 1972 in Switzerland, Sweden, France, Japan, and West Germany ranged from around one-third to no more than 60 percent of the American ratio. In one case, Switzerland, this is in part a consequence of relatively little development of heavy industry. But in most of these nations it is far more the result of deliberate government policy.

Sweden, for example, has adopted policies over the years that have cut its energy use/$1,000 GNP ratio to around 60 percent of the American level and has announced the intention of going beyond this to a zero-energy-growth situation. The primary, but not exclusive, device for doing this is simply high energy prices. With the Swedish economy largely dependent on oil, and with no domestic source of supply, the Swedish government foresaw and prepared for the day of declining supplies and rising prices. By 1971, two years before the OPEC nations quadrupled the world price of oil, the gasoline tax had reached 50 cents per gallon. This sharply curtailed the use of gas guzzlers. But the gasoline tax doesn't do the job alone. Automobile excise (purchase) taxes and yearly fees rise sharply in proportion to vehicle weight. The excise tax serves both to discourage the purchase of heavy cars and to provide an incentive to keep older cars in running condition longer. Supplementing these taxes are other policy measures designed to discourage automobile use and encourage travel by public transport, which is far more energy efficient. While good intracity public transportation is provided, a deliberate effort is exerted to make automobile use inconvenient and expensive: Parking tickets

---

[1] Allen V. Kneese, "A Time to Choose: America's Energy Future," *Challenge* (July–August 1975), 57.

in Stockholm begin at $12.50, and both Stockholm and Gothenburg have mazes of barriers, one-way streets, mass-transit-only lanes, and pedestrian-only streets. The upshot of these combined measures is the considerably lower weight of Swedish as compared with American cars (2425 and 3750 pounds, respectively) and the far greater use of public transportation for short trips (a private car/public transit ratio of 55/45, compared with 90/10 in the United States).[2]

What the Swedish example demonstrates is that consumers do indeed respond to higher energy prices by economizing on their use of energy — in the process reducing pollution, reducing capital requirements for energy production, and generally raising employment. Schipper and Lichtenberg suggest that "more efficient energy use will not interfere with the function of the American economy" and that "Swedish methods of energy conservation, including smaller cars, better structures, and more efficient use of process heat, would result in a savings of 30 percent of the total energy used in the United States."[3]

The real question, though, is how do we get from here to there? In the face of diminishing energy supplies, do we let the normal operations of the marketplace drive up prices, both forcing consumers to economize and accelerating the search for alternative energy sources? Or should government take a hand and control the process? It is failure to reach agreement on the answers to these questions, as much as any other single factor, that has led to the current impasse on energy policy.

Those economists who place great reliance on the normal workings of the market insist that this is not a problem over which the government should get terribly upset. As in the past, when a particular form of energy becomes scarce, its price rises, less important uses are rationed out of the market, and impetus is provided for the search for alternative supplies. Several questions are raised by this approach, however. What do we do, first of all, about low-income families who are rationed out of the market for heating oil or natural gas or gasoline? The answer is that this will be an issue with any approach. The days of cheap energy are over. If low-income families are hurt, they can be taken care of by some form of compensatory income redistribution.

A more difficult problem is that participants in the marketplace are insufficiently forward-looking. The market price largely reflects current

---

[2] These figures and the foregoing information on the Swedish energy system from Lee Schipper and Allan J. Lichtenberg, "Efficient Energy Use and Well-Being: The Swedish Example," *Science*, Vol. 194 (December 3, 1976), 1001–1013, copyright 1976 by the American Association for the Advancement of Science. In addition to the example cited above, Schipper and Lichtenberg provide many other illustrations of the imaginative Swedish approach to their energy problems.

[3] Schipper and Lichtenberg, "Efficient Energy Use and Well-Being," p. 1012.

conditions — it reacts rather than anticipates. This is not entirely true, but there is a distinct possibility that current prices will inadequately take into account the difficulties that will be encountered in making the technological breakthroughs into alternative forms of energy. Prices for oil and natural gas, for example, may not rise high enough to force us to cut our use of these products sufficiently to tide us over into the age of solar or safe nuclear energy. This is tied in with the question of what we owe future generations. Those future generations, obviously, are not represented on today's market. As economist Nicholas Georgescu-Roegen emphasizes, "Every Cadillac or every Zim — let alone any instrument of war — means fewer plowshares for some future generations, and implicitly, fewer future human beings, too."[4] Finally, market energy prices do not reflect the damage that energy production and consumption inflict on the environment — a problem to be discussed at length in the next section.

Just because market processes cannot be counted on to solve our energy problems unaided does not mean that they should be left out of the solution. A Ford Foundation study released in 1974 suggests that shortage-induced rising energy prices would cut the average annual growth rate of our energy use from its historical 3.4 percent to 2.9 percent. But, as the figures in Table 10.4 indicate, this would still permit our energy use to more than double by the year 2000. Even so, the 20 quadrillion Btu's saved is equivalent to 200,000 new oil wells, or 2,930 new coal mines, or 211 additional nuclear plants.

TABLE 10.4

United States energy consumption projections under alternative assumptions (quadrillion Btu's)

	1972	1980	1985	2000
Actual	72			
Historical growth[a]		95	115	183
Rising energy prices[b]		93	108	163
Technical fix[c]		90	96	118
Zero energy growth[d]		89	93	100

Note: Average annual growth rates: [a] 3.4 percent; [b] 2.9 percent; [c] 1.7 percent; [d] 1.2 percent (0 by end of period).
Sources: Energy Policy Project, Exploring Energy Choices, *A Preliminary Report*, The Ford Foundation, Washington, D.C., 1974, Section 7, and *Business Week* (June 1, 1974).

---

[4] Nicholas Georgescu-Roegen, "Energy and Economic Myths," *Southern Economic Journal* (January 1975), 370.

Allowing prices to rise and taking no further action would still leave us heavily dependent on unreliable sources for our oil and would also provide windfall profits for energy providers — profits that the American public is not likely to regard kindly. With returns on invested capital in recent years running well above those in the rest of American industry, the energy companies are finding it increasingly difficult to argue that lack of funds keeps them from expanding their exploration and development activities.

The *technical fix* approach takes over where the market leaves off. Prices are left to be driven up by market forces — which the study analysts assume will result in doubling energy prices within the next few years. These price rises alone should induce car buyers to shift to smaller, more efficient cars and home buyers and industry to insist on more efficient heating, lighting, and cooling. Foreigners ridicule our obsession with extremely high levels of illumination — to the point where many business buildings must be cooled even in the wintertime to drain away excess heat created by multiple banks of lights. Rising electricity prices should force us to re-examine the question of efficient lighting levels. The Ford study, in fact, suggests that every 10 percent rise in the price of electricity will result in a 6.2 percent decline in electricity use from what it might otherwise have reached. For coal the figures are 10 percent and 5.8 percent.[5]

But the technical fix requires that government go beyond simply allowing prices to rise. It also requires government to institute tax changes and regulations designed to increase load factors for aircraft; revive the failing railroad system, which is far more energy efficient than trucks or airplanes; make better use of steam in industry; encourage greater recycling of metals; promote the use of energy-saving heating and cooling systems; and concern itself generally with pockets of energy wastage where rising prices alone are insufficient to encourage more efficiency.

The amazing thing about the technical fix scenario is that while the growth in energy use is cut by half — from 3.4 to 1.7 percent — with a consequent 35 percent saving as compared with the historical growth figure, the rise of real gross national product is cut only slightly: from a projected $3,345 billion in the year 2000 to $3,219 billion. And projected employment actually increases above the historical growth level as workers shift into low-energy industries.

There is no compelling reason, of course, that price rises should be limited to those brought about by the natural working of market forces. Rather than leaving prices to be pulled up exclusively by normal market forces, the government could drive them up even more rapidly if it chose to by imposing excise (consumption) taxes. This would have the advantage

---

[5] *Business Week* (June 1, 1974), 70.

that the benefits of rising prices would accrue to the government in the form of tax proceeds, which could then be used for research and development in the energy field, for subsidizing low-income consumers who are hurt by the price rise, or to offset tax breaks elsewhere designed to improve energy efficiency (as in home insulation).

An absolute end to increasing energy use by the end of the century calls for even more drastic measures: redesigning cities and transportation systems to stress energy conservation, phasing out the use of energy-intensive products like plastics, drastically shifting economic activity toward the service sector (health and education) and away from the material-goods supply industries. Long-term planning would obviously be essential, as would dramatic increases in government regulation, subsidies, and particular taxes. In addition to a sharp slowing down of the rate of economic growth, the zero-energy-growth plan envisages a substantial change in life styles.

As for answers to questions concerning substitute sources of energy as our domestic supplies of oil and natural gas run out, the economist must tread softly. Even in the unlikely case of zero energy growth by the year 2000, our annual energy use will be running at the rate of 100 quadrillion Btu's — half again its current level — so the days of our fossil fuels are clearly numbered. But possibilities for replacement energy sources are so clouded over at the moment with scientific and engineering uncertainties that economic considerations are secondary. Can the nuclear reactors be made reliable and safe enough for expanded use? Can scientists make the breakthroughs necessary to convert the sun's ray to practical use? Is it possible to develop our one nearly inexhaustible source of fossil fuel, oil shale, in such a fashion that the extraction process will not consume almost as much fuel as it provides, as well as spew out endless mine

the small society   **by Brickman**

WHEN DEALING WITH THE OIL CARTEL...

THE TRICK IS TO CRAWL FROM A POSITION OF STRENGTH —

11-4

Washington Star Syndicate, Inc.

BRICKMAN

tailings? To these questions we simply don't have answers — but unless we make a truly determined effort to cut our energy use, we are well advised to find them in a hurry.

| ENVIRONMENTAL POLLUTION |

The growing danger

Perhaps the best reason for acknowledging that our rate of energy use must be cut is that energy production creates waste. This is one aspect of a broader problem that we will take up in a moment — the spill-overs, or externalities, apt to be associated with any type of production. As Georgescu-Roegen and Barry Commoner are forcing us to recognize, the very essence of energy production is the creation of waste. This basic fact eluded us in the past because we were blinded by the first law of thermodynamics: the principle that energy production simply involves a qualitative change, a conversion from a less useful to a more useful energy form, with no net energy loss. There is, for example, the same amount of energy in the heat, smoke, and ashes as there was in the lump of coal from which they were produced. Thus the first law of thermodynamics leaves us with the comfortable thought that we are not really using up our energy sources but simply converting them into alternative forms.

Here is where the *second law of thermodynamics* comes in. It points out the self-evident fact that energy conversion isn't simply a matter of moving energy from one form to another. It is an irreversible process. Energy is converted from an available or free form, which can be transformed into work, to an unavailable or bound form, which cannot be so transformed. Only in theory could heat, smoke, and ashes be recombined in a lump of coal. As a practical matter we are left with the heat, some of which we use, some of which escapes into the atmosphere; the smoke, which pollutes our air; and the ashes, which must somehow be disposed of.

Of these, the heat may in the long run prove most troublesome. Our "spaceship earth" has adjusted itself over the ages to make optimum use of the natural heat and energy provided by the sun. Any major supplementation of this solar heat could create enormous climatological and ecological disruptions. We have not yet reached the danger point. We add to the natural flow of solar and planetary heat only about 1/15,000 of the latter. But our heat use is growing exponentially and, as we saw with the compound growth curve, this could add up in fairly short order to a catastrophic overheating of the earth. The calculations of Robert Ayres and Allen Kneese, of Resources for the Future, dramatize the danger:

Present emission of energy is about 1/15,000 of the absorbed energy flux. But if the present rate of growth continued for 250 years emissions would reach 100% of the absorbed energy flux. The resulting increase in the earth's temperature would be about 50°C. — a condition totally unsuitable for human habitation.[6]

The measure of this bound or dissipated or waste energy is *entropy*. The entropy law says that the entropy of a closed system (spaceship earth) always increases, the change being from free energy to bound, not the other way around. Since the terrestrial dowry of unbound or low-entropy materials, both energy sources and natural resources in general, is finite, the entropy law forces us to examine carefully the relationships between process inputs and outputs (waste). For example, when the costs of exorbitant water use, fuel required for conversion, and waste disposal are added to the labor and extraordinary capital requirements, the likelihood exists that the *net* benefits of developing our oil shale deposits may never be positive. Too often, Georgescu-Roegen insists, we get caught up in a process and never stop to ask whether or not we are deriving any net benefits. He likens this to what he calls "the circumdrome of the shaving machine," which is "to shave oneself faster so as to have more time to work on a machine that shaves faster so as to work on a machine that shaves faster so as to have more time to work on a machine that shaves still faster, and so on *ad infinitum*."[7]

Recognizing the finiteness of our natural resources and convinced that solar energy is our only safe, nonpolluting source of energy but that it will require a long development period, Georgescu-Roegen lays down a "minimal bioeconomic program" for preserving their share of our terrestrial dowry for future generations:

1 Complete prohibition of production of all instruments of war.

2 Use of the productive forces released to help the underdeveloped nations to arrive as quickly as possible at a good (but not luxurious) life.

3 Reduction of the world population to the level that can be adequately fed only through organic argiculture — a burden that will fall most heavily on the underdeveloped nations.

4 Until solar energy is fully developed, imposition of strict regulations to control all waste of energy: overheating, overcooling, overspeeding, and so forth.

---

[6] Robert U. Ayres and Allen V. Kneese, *Economic and Ecological Effects of a Stationary State*, Reprint No. 99, Resources for the Future, Washington, D.C., December 1972, p. 16.

[7] Georgescu-Roegen, "Energy and Economic Myths," p. 378.

5 Regard consumption for the sake of fashion — a new car every year, keeping up with the Joneses — as a bioeconomic crime; to this end insist that manufacturers focus on durability, long life, and ease of repair.[8]

Georgescu-Roegen may in the long run prove to have a sounder diagnosis and prescription than those who insist that the energy–natural resource–environment problem is being overdramatized and that normal market processes will take care of things. As for his "minimal bioeconomic program," critics put this on a par with humorist Will Rogers' solution to the German submarine problem of World War I: Boil the Atlantic and when the submarines are forced to the surface, shoot them.

While we must wait for the future to determine whose diagnosis is right and whose is wrong on the energy issue, we have a related problem with smaller dimensions, and one we have not only diagnosed but have agreed more or less on alternative solutions. This is environmental pollution.

Control of pollution

We now have general agreement that environmental pollution in the United States — foul air, contaminated water, noise — has come about largely because of our *reward system* — the way our private market economy bestows its rewards. The object of the businessman, it must be pointed out, is not making goods but making money: more specifically, making profits. Under most circumstances, these need not conflict. More goods means more revenues, which represent both more social welfare and more profits. But sales revenues in and of themselves are not profits. Profits are what is left after all costs of production and selling are deducted:

Sales revenues ($p \times q$)	$1,000,000
Production and sales costs	900,000
Profits before taxes	$ 100,000

Given a certain amount of revenues, businesses maximize their profits by taking whatever action is necessary to minimize their costs. Not only do they make maximum use of cheap, abundant inputs — "free" air; "free" water; cheap, price-controlled natural gas rather than more expensive coal — but they take maximum advantage of any opportunity to avoid costs by spilling them over onto the public. The air belongs to no one, so why worry about exhaust fumes? Water is free, so why shouldn't the manufacturer dump wastes into the rivers and lakes? Everyone gets used to industrial noises, so why bother with quieter machinery or aircraft?

---

[8] Georgescu-Roegen, "Energy and Economic Myths," pp. 377–378.

This extends, of course, beyond the business sector. The automobile industry turns out high-polluting cars, but it's the individual operators who do the actual polluting. What we have, as ecologist Garrett Hardin points out, is a *"tragedy of the commons."* Our air and water are the property of no one; they are the common property of all, just as cattle pastures were common property in the Middle Ages. Each herder then saw his or her own advantage in adding one more animal to those already grazing the commons, and then another, until finally the commons was ruined by over-grazing or the herders saw the necessity of jointly agreeing on limitations. And this is just where we are on pollution control: "The rational man finds that his share of the cost of the wastes he discharges into the commons is less than the cost of purifying his wastes before releasing them. Since this is true for everyone, we are locked into a system of 'fouling our own nest,' so long as we behave only as independent, rational, free-enterprisers."[9]

Recognizing the origin and dimensions of the problem, however, and doing something about it are quite different matters. We lived so long in a "cowboy economy," in which we could blithely dump our wastes over the fence onto our neighbor's property, that we came close to considering this one of our inalienable rights. More than that, this presumption of the right to avoid private costs by passing them on to society in general has been built into our institutional arrangements. Forcing manufacturers, for example, to "internalize" the costs of waste disposal rather than pass them on to society in the form of polluted air or water would substantially raise private costs of production, thereby restricting both sales and production. This can be seen by use of the conventional supply and demand diagram, as in Figure 10.2.

The upsweeping supply curve S in Figure 10.2 could be taken to represent the unit costs of production in the absence of pollution restraints in any one of a large number of different situations. It could be a paper mill spilling its wastes into a passing stream, forcing downstream residents to filter their stream-supplied water or to treat it chemically before use. It could be a steel mill spewing black smoke, forcing its downwind neighbors to breathe foul air and clean their homes and clothing at frequent inter-vals. It could be an airline with noisy planes, shattering the nerves of nearby residents. In all these cases there are production *spillovers* — social costs of production external to those recognized on the income statement of the offending firms. One principle of pollution control is to find a way of internalizing these *externalities*, so that private costs of production will more adequately reflect all social costs. Two approaches, used individually or in some combination, do this: taxation (sometimes

---

[9] Garrett Hardin, "The Tragedy of the Commons," reprinted in *Pollution, Resources, and the Environment*, ed. Alain C. Enthoven and A. Myrick Freeman III, Norton, New York, 1973, p. 7.

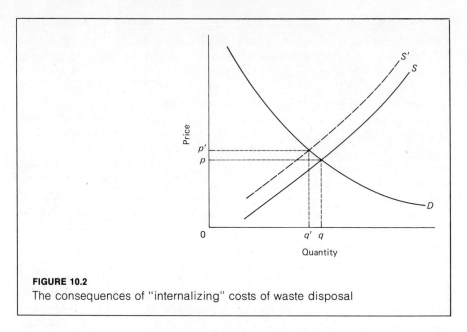

FIGURE 10.2
The consequences of "internalizing" costs of waste disposal

called *incentive pricing*) and direct regulation. The third, subsidization, solves the problem of pollution but not by internalizing it. Each of the three has its advantages, but all have drawbacks as well.

Taxation In concept at least, the simplest and most desirable approach to pollution control is a *waste*, or *effluent, charge*. A tax is levied on each offending firm in proportion to the severity of the pollution created. That firm now faces a difficult choice. Let's say this is the paper mill mentioned previously. The paper mill's manager now must decide whether to pay the tax and go on dumping its wastes into the stream, or to install waste-treatment facilities and curb its dumping. Either the tax must be added to the company's costs of production, or the costs of buying and installing waste-treatment facilities must be added to other costs. In either case costs per unit of production rise, and the supply curve shifts upward and to the left to S', which is where it should have been and would have been all along if all social costs of production had been recognized.

As can be seen by comparing the intersections of S and S' with the demand curve, however, this solution has a cost: The level of output, and therefore of employment, is lower and prices are higher. We trade off paper mill jobs and higher prices for paper for a cleaner environment. Economists argue that this is a reasonable price to pay. The consumer of the product and the producer should bear *all* costs of production. But those who speak for the poor often argue that if this is the trade-off, they'll take the pollution. They can live with it, but they can't live without jobs. When the effluent tax or regulation-set limit to pollution becomes higher than the offending firm can bear, the choice is truly agonizing — as is suggested by a typical headline from the *Wall Street Journal*, this of July 16, 1975: "Smelter's Emissions Threaten Populace, but So Does Possible Loss of 1,000 Jobs."

As suggested, by and large economists like the tax or effluent-charge approach. It provides offending firms with an incentive to clean up the pollution they create, but it neither tells them how to go about the job nor does it force all companies to respond in the same way or to the same degree. The worst offenders will find payment of the tax more burdensome than cleaning up their operations, and therefore they will clean up, thus reducing the severity of the problem; minor offenders may find it cheaper to pay the tax — at least at its current level. As this suggests, this doesn't exactly create a "license to pollute," since if we find even the reduced pollution level intolerable we can always raise the tax or charge higher and higher, to the zero discharge level if necessary. Whether or not we should insist on zero discharge is another matter, one that will be discussed in a moment.

In some cases — where monitoring is easy — the effluent charge works well. It is relatively simple to measure discharge from the smokestack of a large, coal-fueled electric plant and levy a tax proportional to the amount of solid particles and gases discharged into the atmosphere. The amount of solid wastes and chemicals dumped into the stream by our paper mill can also be fairly readily determined and penalized by a tax. But how does one monitor the discharge of the greatest air polluter of them all, the family automobile? Hang an exhaust meter on the tailpipe of each, make it a major crime to remove or tamper with the meter, and then hire an army of meter readers? In this case, as in those similar to it, outright government regulation is a simpler solution.

Direct regulation   The last paragraph suggests that we use the effluent charge in controlling waste discharge into the air and water. In fact, with rare exceptions, we don't. We have, instead, generally extended an old principle into a new area: If something undesirable is going on, pass a law against it. If stream pollution is a problem, then pass a law making it a crime to pour wastes into the streams. If the air has become filthy, then require industry to treat its exhaust air, down to some specified level, before releasing it into the atmosphere. It is of course easier to pass a law than to guarantee compliance. The problems of monitoring are still present. But Americans are law-abiding, as a whole, so substantial results can be achieved.

Perhaps more significant, regulation lacks the flexibility and incentives associated with effluent charges. Once an offending firm has reduced its pollution level to the legal maximum, it has no incentive to push on down past that point, as it would if forced to pay an effluent charge of, say, 30 cents for every pound of BOD (biochemical oxygen demand) it released into a stream. And, as with all regulatory systems, there is the ever-present risk of the regulated industries capturing the regulators and getting by with noncompliance.

As compared with subsidization, though, the chief argument against both regulation and taxes is that they force up costs of production and prices and reduce output and employment. And this is indeed true. Whether our paper mill installs waste-treatment facilities to satisfy the law or to escape an effluent charge, it will in either case be forced to move up and to the left along its demand curve. This can be avoided if subsidies are used instead.

Subsidization When subsidies are available, the polluting firm is provided with the funds to cover installation of pollution-control equipment. Its unit costs are therefore not increased, and its supply curve remains at S in Figure 10.2. This being the case, the pollution menace is removed but with no increase in the product price and no consequent reduction of production or employment. Consumers of the product will be happy, workers in the plant will be happy — only the taxpayer will be sad, because he or she will pick up the tab but perhaps consume none of the product whatever.

And there are other problems with subsidies. Perhaps of greatest significance is the fact that some firms in an industry are careful never to pollute in the first place or have sufficient public spirit to undertake their own cleanup process. The laggards and those least socially minded are thus the ones to benefit from the taxpayers' contribution — whether the subsidy comes from an outright public grant or from a reduction in the offending firm's taxes. In the latter case other taxes must be raised to cover the loss of revenues. There is the further question of the psychology of the approach: Is it appropriate for the government to go hat in hand to a polluting firm and bribe it to clean up its mess? Shouldn't the true costs simply be recognized and internalized by the imposition of regulations or taxes?

How pollution-free a world do we want?

Whichever one or combination of the three approaches outlined above is adopted, we still face the question as to how far we want to carry them. Although the easy answer is "all the way," there are compelling reasons for stopping somewhat short of that point. Pollution cleanup costs tend to rise sharply as we approach the 100 percent pollution-free level. When 30 percent of the BOD is removed from a body of water, for example, it costs around 4 cents a pound to remove the next 1 percent. But when 90 percent of the BOD has been eliminated it costs 30 cents to remove the next 1 percent, and at the 95 percent level the cost rises to 50 cents for the next 1 percent. Under the Federal Water Pollution Control Act of 1972, Congress established fairly tough standards for 1977, far more demanding standards for 1983, and zero discharge by 1985. Achieving even the 1977 standards was a challenge many industries failed to meet. But meeting the 1983 standards will require the consumption of twenty times more energy to remove a pound of pollutant than is required to meet the 1977 standards. In the chemical industry, the $800 per annual ton to remove pollutants under the 1977 requirements will jump to $6,300 for 1983. The 1977 requirements call for the steel industry to remove 96 percent of the pollutants. To reach 1983 goals will require twelve times the cost per pound of pollutants removed.[10] Although these are industry-produced figures and may be biased upwards, there is little doubt that marginal costs to society, whoever ends up paying the bill, rise precipitously as we get near completely clean water or air.

However, the marginal social benefits tend to decline as the water is made cleaner. It may be of great urgency to remove the stink and slime from a river, important but somewhat less so to clean it to the point where fish survive and it's not dangerous to fall overboard from a boat, desirable but not urgent to have it clean enough for swimming, and of limited interest to have it completely safe for drinking since other ways of getting safe drinking water are available.

When we convert these two ideas into scalar form and pair them in a diagram we get something like the relationship shown in Figure 10.3, with

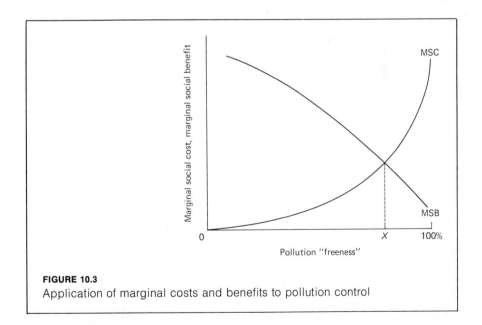

FIGURE 10.3
Application of marginal costs and benefits to pollution control

[10] Edwin A. Gee, "Rethinking the Timetable for Refreshing Our Waters," The Conference Board *Record* (April 1976), 55.

diminishing marginal social benefits to our pollution-control efforts coupled with rising marginal social costs. At any point to the left of X it is obviously worth our while to push ahead with additional pollution control measures. The additional benefits accruing to society in general are in excess of the extra costs involved, so society's net welfare is increased. Past point X, though, just the opposite is the case. Now, thanks to the rapidly rising costs of additional pollution control measures and falling marginal benefits, society reduces its net welfare by putting additional resources into pollution cleanup. Measuring net welfare by the excess of marginal social benefits over marginal social costs leaves us with a negative amount.

It seems scarcely necessary to point out that it is easier to depict MSB and MSC as smooth, determinate curves than it is to flesh them out with realistic numbers — as we saw earlier when we used the same approach to determine the limits to government spending. There is the further problem of determining just who in society is to bear the major burden of the additional costs and who gets the lion's share of the added benefits. Resolving these issues will elicit lively debate for many years to come.

There is growing consensus, though, that the federal government must lead the environmental-control effort. It isn't just a matter of money, whether coming in as taxes or going out as pollution-control expenditures, although that is part of it. More important is the fact that those polluting a community or state are often nonresidents. Rivers may be polluted well upstream, and air can be polluted at any point as it moves in an easterly direction across the United States. Only noise is generated and consumed locally and is therefore subject to local control. But even here the local control effort may be frustrated by industry threats to relocate or to locate new plants elsewhere to avoid stringent local controls. Only nationwide standards can

the small society   **by Brickman**

forestall this. This does not mean, of course, that communities and states merely sit and wait for the federal government to act. The vigorous anti-pollution effort in California and a few other states has put strong pressure on the federal government to follow suit.

I   ECONOMIC GROWTH   I

The historical record

Until only a few years ago no feature of the American economy was pointed to with greater pride than its spectacular growth record. And the record has been impressive. As we saw earlier in the chapter, our national income has increased a thousandfold since the beginning of the nineteenth century. Part of this rapid increase in output, of course, was necessary to keep up with our growing population and to take care of the millions of immigrants we admitted, especially during the nineteenth century. But even taking into account this growth in the number of claimants for the annual national output still allows us to estimate that the goods and services available per person increased more than elevenfold.

Only recently have we extended the national income accounts back into the nineteenth century. We can now say with some degree of assurance not only how rapidly the American economy grew, as measured by annual rates of change in gross national product or net national product, but where the growth contributions came from. Summary figures for both of these are presented in Table 10.5. As the table indicates, growth of output (net national product) is determined by the amounts of inputs drawn into production (land, labor, and capital) and the efficiency with which they are used (productivity). With our population growing rapidly until recently, it is not too surprising that additions to the labor force made the greatest contribution to long-run growth — 42.7 percent for the whole period. What is surprising is that the billion-plus acres of land converted from public ownership to private use during our history as a nation made such a modest contribution to economic growth. Even more remarkable is the fact that while additions to our capital stock (industrial plant, equipment, and private residences) during the last sixty years of the nineteenth century contributed significantly to that period's increase in net national product (25.9 percent), during the twentieth century the growth burden has shifted to productivity increases. Productivity means essentially technology or know-how. This suggests that if continued rapid economic growth is our objective, then the primary emphasis should not be on boosting our capital stock at a forced rate but on improving technology in order to increase the efficiency with which we use labor and capital.

The use of *if* in the last sentence suggests that something new has been added to the economic growth literature. During all of our national

TEN | ENERGY, ENVIRONMENT, AND GROWTH

TABLE 10.5
Contributions of factor inputs and productivity to the growth of net national product, 1840–1960

Contributions of	1840–1960	1840–1900	1900–1960
PANEL 1: AVERAGE ANNUAL RATES OF GROWTH (percent)			
(1) Labor force	1.52	1.88	1.12
(2) Land supply	.21	.38	.08
(3) Capital stock	.81	1.03	.60
(4) Productivity	1.02	.69	1.32
(5) Totals (growth of NNP)	3.56	3.98	3.12
PANEL 2: PERCENTAGE DISTRIBUTIONS (percent)			
(1) Labor force	42.7	47.2	34.8
(2) Land supply	5.9	9.6	2.5
(3) Capital stock	22.8	25.9	18.6
(4) Productivity	28.6	17.3	44.1
(5) Totals	100.0	100.0	100.0

Source: Table 2.12 (p. 39) by Robert Gallman from *American Economic Growth: An Economist's History of the United States* by Lance E. Davis, et al. Copyright © 1972 by Harper & Row Publishers, Inc. Used by permission of the publisher.

history, at least until the last few years, it has been taken for granted that increased human happiness depends on ever-greater availability of economic goods and services — and that is exactly what economic growth is all about. Both the American people and their economists have been infected with the virus of "growthmania." In recent years, however, this consensus on the possibility and desirability of continued rapid growth in the highly developed economies has evaporated. Substantial numbers of scientists see the world simply running out of natural resources at some time in the near future unless our use rate is sharply reduced. According to one influential group, the authors of the Club of Rome report, we will exhaust those materials most crucial to present patterns of industrial civilization within 173 years — even assuming that, somehow, five times the known reserves of needed natural resources are found.[11] A far more sweeping attack on economic growth is mounted by those who argue that economic growth itself has only the most tenuous relationship to human welfare. The costs of growth — especially those related to a deteriorating

[11] Dennis L. Meadows et al. *The Limits to Growth, A Report for the Club of Rome's Project on the Predicament of Mankind*, Universe Books, New York, 1972, Table 4, pp. 56–57.

environment — and the limited offsetting benefits suggest the idea of a no-growth society.

A no-growth society?

The proposition of a *no-growth society* has two parts: freezing gross national product at its current level and limiting population to its present size. To prevent production capacity from expanding, capital outlays would be limited to those necessary for the replacement of capital goods now in use. Gross investment and net investment would not differ. With cessation of production increases, per capita national income would have to fall if population were allowed to increase. Thus the necessity for restrictions on population growth.

Although no-growth as a policy prescription focuses on limiting gross national product and population, no-growth as an analytical critique starts from the proposition that gross national product is a completely inadequate measure of human welfare — even beyond its equation with "gross national pollution." Some of these limitations of GNP as a welfare measure were itemized in the chapter on national income and its accounting: failure to consider do-it-yourself activities and housewives' services; inclusion of any economic good or service for which people are willing to pay, regardless of doubts about the welfare contribution of many products or services (war goods, noninformational advertising, alcohol, and drugs); disregard of conditions of production and the division of time between work and leisure. Attempts have been made to convert the gross national product to a "measure of human welfare" by allowing and adjusting for the deficiencies cited. While these early efforts are extremely crude, they support the conclusion that half or more of any increase in gross national product is completely empty of any welfare content. And a substantial part of what remains might disappear if we had adequate answers to questions regarding the relationship between economic growth and the increasing crime rate, the divorce rate, drug usage, worker alienation, congestion, and general boredom.[12] Galbraith summarizes the issue graphically: "The penultimate Western man, stalled in the ultimate traffic jam and slowly succumbing to carbon monoxide, will not be cheered to hear from the last survivor that the gross national product went up by a record amount."[13]

Perhaps the whole attempt to capture human happiness in a number is doomed to failure. This is suggested when we remember that we have on average more than eleven times the goods and services available to our ancestors of 1800 and then ask the question, are we eleven times

---

[12] For an exploration of some of these issues see Tibor Scitovsky, *The Joyless Economy: An Inquiry into Human Satisfaction and Consumer Dissatisfaction*, Oxford University Press, New York, 1976.

[13] Cited in *Business Week* (April 11, 1970), 82.

happier? The answer of course has to be no. Partly this answer depends on recognition of all the clean air, quiet, pure water, and elbow room available to the typical person at the beginning of the nineteenth century. More important, as we're coming to recognize, the notion of growth itself is somewhat fraudulent. Something about the riches it promises to bring is illusory.

The illusion rests on comparing an increasing flow of wealth to one person or family while everyone else remains poor with that same flow of wealth when it is shared by everyone else. If the rich are few and the poor are many, the rich have the best of all possible worlds. They will not only be respected for their wealth, but they can readily find housekeepers, maids, butlers, and chauffeurs. But when everyone is rich, there is no one to respect their wealth or to work for them. Our basic requirements — a minimal level of food, shelter, and clothing — do not claim an extraordinary amount of material goods. Perhaps no way can this be driven home more forcefully than by recognizing that a *poverty-level income* in the United States exceeds the *average income* in Great Britain. In the United States today, this leaves most of our income to satisfy the demand for what Fred Hirsch calls *positional goods*[14] These are goods whose individual enjoyments are integrally affected by their degree of general use or availability. A Cadillac has tremendous "usefulness" if we have the only one in the neighborhood; when everyone else has one, we "need" a Mercedes or Rolls Royce. A college diploma has a large value — until everyone else has one. What it all comes down to, as Hirsch points out, is that a high proportion of our goods today are of value only when they are owned by a minority. Like standing on tiptoe in a crowd, an initial advantage works for a few but is self-defeating for all.

The concept of positional goods helps to explain why investigators fail to find a systematic relationship between national income and happiness. Richard Easterlin's studies show no margin of happiness in wealthy over poorer countries and no increase in the percentage of persons reporting themselves as "happy" over the past thirty-odd years in the United States.[15] This same approach, however, does suggest that when a society becomes engaged in a positional contest for consumption it becomes more difficult, not easier, for government to arrange for the redistribution of income. Redistribution from the rich to the poor is not likely to limit the ability of the rich to meet their basic economic requirements, but it will surely infringe on their positional consumption. They will consequently use part of their wealth to fight any and all attempts to take any of the remainder

---

[14] Fred Hirsch, *Social Limits to Growth*, A Twentieth Century Fund Study, Harvard University Press, Cambridge, 1976. Much of the discussion that follows is based on Hirsch's analysis.

[15] Richard Easterlin, "Does Money Buy Happiness?" *The Public Interest* (Winter 1973), 3–10.

from them. We seem, therefore, on a voyage to nowhere, but unable to change course.

The advantages of growth

Adherents to the no-growth position currently make up only a small part of the general public and probably an even smaller proportion of professional economists. The latter see major disadvantages to a cessation or even a major slowing-down of growth, and they see significant benefits to be derived from continued expansion of national income.

They may concede that consumers in the United States do not urgently need ever-increasing amounts of consumer goods. But the United States is part of a global economy, and scarcity remains an urgent problem in many parts of the world. By increasing its own production the United States will be in position to help the have-not nations. This assumes of course that the *will* is there to help the poorer nations and that only the *way* needs providing — a very large assumption considering the tiny fraction of 1 percent of a $2 trillion gross national product that foreign aid now represents.

Closer to home is the argument that only a growing national income will permit everyone eventually to become rich. A sizable part of our population has been left behind in the race for riches, but given a large enough increase in national income everyone can share the wealth. Again, though, this confuses *way* with *will*. As was pointed out in Chapter Eight, we could eliminate poverty overnight right now if we so chose. We seem determined to retain a large positional consumption gap.

Stand this point on its head, though, and a stronger argument against no-growth turns up. Inequalities in income distribution are at least tolerable if the national income is rising. The pie is getting larger so everyone can at least hope for a bigger slice. Freeze the size of the pie and income distribution becomes a zero-sum game: What one group gains another must lose. This is one reason among others that Kenneth Boulding advocates a growing or progressive economy. It diminishes social conflict. When "one person or group becomes richer" only when "the rest of the society must become poorer . . . this increases the payoffs for successful exploitation — that is, the use of organized threat in order to redistribute income. . . . Stationary states . . . are frequently mafia-type societies in which government is primarily an institution for redistributing income toward the powerful and away from the weak."[16]

Equally important is the historically close relationship between economic growth and increases in employment opportunities. Harvard economist Arthur Okun has put this relationship into numbers, called Okun's law. According to Okun's law, a 4 percent real national income growth is

---

[16] Kenneth E. Boulding, "The Shadow of the Stationary State," in *The No-Growth Society*, ed. Mancur Olson and Hans H. Landsberg, Norton, New York, 1973, p. 95.

necessary simply to absorb new entrants into the labor force and thus hold the unemployment rate constant. Each additional 1 percentage point increase in the income growth rate brings a $\frac{1}{3}$ of 1 percent reduction in the unemployment rate. There are ways of simultaneously reducing the rate of growth of gross national product and increasing employment — such as drastically reducing the work week and sharing the available employment — but none that has much appeal at the moment. Once again, then, reducing the growth rate would increase social tensions.

Finally, radical critics of the American economic system are convinced that economic growth, however undesirable it may be in the form it takes, *must* continue to be a major economic objective so long as our economic system retains its present form. Socialism could exist either as a stationary state or with carefully directed growth, but capitalism must grow or die. This is because capitalism is geared to the earning of profits. Profits come primarily from developing new products, building new markets, expanding production facilities. None of these activities are required in a stationary state. Economic activity would largely be reduced to routine, which doesn't justify the payment of economic profits. And without profits there is no need for the capitalist. So whether or not we really want or need more and more economic goods, the radicals insist we're going to get more because the capitalists must provide them.

Those who argue for continued growth see no inexorable conflict between growth and either depletion of energy or raw material sources or degradation of the environment. Growth, first of all, will provide the income necessary both for developing new energy sources and for taking on the massive job of cleaning up the environment. Growth, secondly, need not take the form it has taken in the past. It can be directed into less energy-intensive pathways — more services and leisure in the consumption package and fewer material goods, for example — and stripped of its wórst pollution features. And if pollution costs were internalized, the outflow of goods and services would represent a net accretion of social benefits, and its curtailment a loss of those benefits.

At this point the outcome of the growth–no-growth argument cannot clearly be foreseen. That is mainly because the focus has been on alternative policies for only the next several decades. Had it taken the next several centuries as its time frame, it would have had a different flavor. The exponential rise in resource use that we have witnessed in recent years may continue for the next several decades or even for the next couple of generations. But is it conceivable that it could continue for several hundred years? The magnitudes involved toward the end of such a period literally boggle the mind. The same is the case with the "benefits" of growth. Who would willingly take on the task of spending an income of a couple of hundred thousand dollars annually — especially when the Joneses have the same income? How many boats and cars and vacation trips and fancy restaurant meals can one family conveniently sandwich into its yearly activities?

▌ SUMMARY ▌

Energy, the environment, and economic growth are closely related. Growth demands increasing amounts of energy and at the same time contributes to environmental degradation.

Whatever our source of energy — whether water, wind, and wood as in the early nineteenth century; coal in the late nineteenth and early twentieth centuries; or oil and natural gas in the later twentieth century — the United States has been prodigal in its use. This prodigality has been deliberately encouraged by government policies promoting low energy prices.

We are now aware that our traditional sources of energy are rapidly being depleted. We are therefore faced with the necessity of either discouraging high-level usage or rapidly bringing on-stream alternative supplies. Which approach we are to use, however, and how to achieve the chosen end are as yet undecided.

One factor complicating the problem is that energy production creates pollution. This is especially true, except for solar energy, of waste created in the form of heat.

The current pollution problem is largely the result of uncontrolled production of goods and services — one of the social costs of private enterprise. In their search for profits businessmen have felt free to spill their wastes into the environment. We now recognize that these pollution costs must be internalized, either by imposing taxes on spillovers or by simply outlawing them. An alternative is to subsidize pollution cleanup efforts. All of these approaches, though, redistribute costs: to the consumer, worker, or taxpayer. This, plus the fact that marginal social benefits associated with pollution control fall as the cleanup proceeds while marginal social costs rise rapidly, suggests that we may not want to proceed to the 100 percent cleanup level.

As for growth, the love affair Americans have had with rapid economic growth has cooled in recent years. Some critics now cite growing scarcities of the resources demanded by continued rapid growth. Others point to the tenuous connection between growth and human happiness. On the other hand, growth clearly does create jobs, and the rising incomes associated with growth make less burdensome the division of national income in a socially acceptable fashion.

Given the declining benefits of growth, though, and the resource demands growth makes, it seems clear that economic growth will be more of a challenge — and will be more challenged — in the decades ahead than it has been over our history as a nation.

| IMPORTANT TERMS AND CONCEPTS |

compound growth rates   effluent charge

spillovers   private cost versus social cost

externalities   marginal social costs

second law of thermodynamics   marginal social benefits

entropy   no-growth society

"tragedy of the commons"   positional goods

| QUESTIONS, PROBLEMS, AND EXERCISES |

1 In what ways is the energy problem directly related to the problems of environmental pollution and economic growth?

2 What has been the consequence of low-priced energy over the course of American history?

3 What case would you make for the proposition that normal market processes will take care of the energy shortage? Why are some economists unwilling to rely on this solution?

4 Why do economists tend to prefer to control pollution by way of an effluent tax rather than by direct regulation or subsidies?

5 Do we — or should we — really want a completely pollution-free world?

6 Evaluate the claim that economic growth in the United States has largely been the consequence of providing workers with ever-larger stocks of capital with which to work.

7 Why hasn't the extraordinary increase of national income in the United States made us happier?

8 Use a supply and demand diagram to demonstrate how the internalization of pollution costs is almost certain to increase selling prices and reduce output and employment.

| SUGGESTED READING |

Barkley, Paul W., and David W. Seckler. *Economic Growth and Environmental Decay: The Solution Becomes the Problem.* Harcourt, Brace, Jovanovich, New York, 1972.

Commoner, Barry. *The Poverty of Power: Energy and the Economic Crisis.* Knopf, New York, 1976.

Georgescu-Roegen, Nicholas. *Energy and Economic Myths.* Pergamon, New York, 1976.

Hirsch, Fred. *Social Limits to Growth*. Harvard University Press, Cambridge, 1976.

Macrae, Norman. *America's Third Century*. Harcourt, Brace, Jovanovich, New York, 1976.

Mishan, E. J. *Technology and Growth: The Price We Pay*. Praeger, New York, 1969.

Olson, Mancur, and Hans H. Landsberg, eds. *The No-Growth Society*. Norton, New York, 1973.

| HEALTH CARE |

The American health care industry is not well. It is running an inflationary fever. Its circulation is poor, leaving some of its members starved for care and others gorged from forced feeding. Its gold plating is wearing thin in places, exposing base metal beneath. And its caretakers are suffering from an identity crisis, feeling both overworked and underloved. In short, the most expensive medical system in the world is having a hard time these days proving that what it delivers by way of health care justifies the lavish bill it presents to the American people. After examining the health services industry in considerable detail, economists Howard Bowen and James Jeffers conclude that

The industry tends to be highly inflexible; does not use resources efficiently; and is inequitable in terms of the health services made available to certain geographic areas, age groups, and income classes. The system is characterized by overuse and misuse of services; poor adjustments of the quantity of services supplied to changes in demand; and price escalation, as growth in insurance, income, and public expectations give rise to increased outlays on health. When large quantities of money are poured into such a system, as has happened during the last two decades, the results are massive price increases and significant frustrations of the objectives of the outlays.[1]

Going beyond even this gloomy assessment, some responsible critics insist the system is so bad that we would be better off with no organized medical care at all.

I THE SPIRALING COSTS OF HEALTH CARE I

The historical record

On one issue there can be no doubt: There has been a literal explosion in the costs of medical care in recent decades. During the most recent period for which figures are available, 1965–1975, overall health expenditures increased an average of 12 percent a year. Since this rate of increase far exceeded the growth of the national income, the consequence had to be a steady rise in the share of national income claimed by the health sector. Table 11.1 shows that this was indeed the case. In the early 1970s health care expenditures crossed the $100 billion mark. By the mid-seventies these expenditures claimed around $1 of every $12 generated by the economy in order to pay for the more than $500 worth of health and medical services provided the average American. So insistent was this rising demand for medical services that supply fell far short of expanding rapidly enough to accommodate the demand. According to the estimates of the Social Security Administration only about half the total increase in personal health care expenditures during the decade 1965–1975 went to pay for increased amounts of better quality services. The remainder (53 percent) represented pure price inflation.

This is borne out by comparing increases in medical care prices with overall increases in the cost of living. During fiscal year 1975 all items in the consumer price index increased by 11 percent. But medical care prices increased at a 12.5 percent rate. This 12.5 percent represented a 15.4 percent increase in hospital service charges, a 16.4 percent rise in hospital semiprivate room charges, a 12.8 percent increase in physicians'

---

[1] Howard R. Bowen and James R. Jeffers, *The Economics of Health Services*, General Learning Press, New York, 1971, p. 22.

TABLE 11.1
National health expenditures as percentage of gross national product

Fiscal year	Total health expenditures ($ billion)	% of GNP	Health expenditures per capita
1929	3.6	3.6	29.16
1940	3.9	4.1	38.83
1950	12.0	4.6	78.35
1960	25.9	5.2	141.63
1970	69.2	7.2	333.57
1975	122.2	8.4	547.03
1976	139.3	8.6	637.97

Souce: Marjorie Smith Mueller and Robert M. Gibson, "National Health Expenditures, Fiscal Year 1975," *Social Security Bulletin* (February 1976), 6, and Robert M. Gibson and Marjorie Smith Mueller, "National Health Expenditures, Fiscal Year 1976," *Social Security Bulletin* (April 1977), 4.

fees, and a more modest rise of 10.8 percent in dentists' fees.[2] Since hospital care costs represent close to 40 percent of overall medical care expenditures, their explosive rise goes far to explain why the medical-care price index advances considerably more rapidly than the consumer price index.

Causes of rising prices
The foregoing analysis suggests that rising medical care prices are the consequence of demand increasing more rapidly than it can be accommodated by supply. It takes time to train more physicians and to build more hospitals, but demand can gallop ahead overnight, forcing up prices for the services of currently available physicians and hospitals. This is not the whole story, as we will see later, but it is a significant part of the story.

Part of this rising demand is accounted for by the growth in the over-65 segment of the population. The aged have more health problems than younger persons and spend more than three times as much per person on medical care as the rest of the population. Another portion of the rising demand reflects increases in living standards. The demand for health care is income elastic: As our incomes go up, we spend more on medical services, both in absolute terms and as a proportion of total income. With

---

[2] Marjorie Smith Mueller and Robert M. Gibson, "National Health Expenditures, Fiscal Year 1975," *Social Security Bulletin* (February 1976), 3.

more money to spend we visit the doctor more frequently, put ourselves on the operating table more often, buy and use more drugs, and spend more time in the hospital.

More important than either of these factors, however, according to most analysts, is the radical shift in recent years in the way medical costs are financed. It hasn't been too many years since the time when a person got sick, went to the doctor, was sent to the hospital, and then ended up paying both the doctor and the hospital with his own personal check — likely written against borrowed money. Today this sequence is becoming almost rare. A person still sees the doctor and goes to the hospital, of course, but both bills are likely to be paid by some third party: a private health insurance company or a government bureau or agency. Such *third party payments* reached the level of half of all personal health care expenditures for the first time in 1970. By fiscal 1975 these third parties took the responsibility for paying over two-thirds of total expenditures. In the case of hospital care costs, in fact, individuals were left with direct responsibility for only 8 percent of total payments — a mere $3.7 billion of the $46.6 billion total. Private insurance footed the bill for $16.7 billion of the balance, and government at some level paid the remainder.

This shift of payment to third parties does not necessarily mean that the person provided with medical services escapes all costs. Insurance companies anticipate their own payments by collecting premiums in advance. Some insured patients will pay less in premiums than the insurance companies pay out for medical expenses, but that simply means other insured patients must pay more in premiums than the companies return to the doctor or hospital. This is broadly true, too, of *Medicare* — the federal government's expansion of the social security system to provide coverage for the costs of health services for virtually everyone over the age of 65.

the small society   **by Brickman**

I PAID MY ANALYST SO MUCH MONEY I THINK IT'S GIVING HIM A SENSE OF GUILT—

6-21

BRICKMAN

Washington Star Syndicate, Inc.

Most of this over-65 group will have paid enough payroll taxes over the years to establish eligibility under the system, thereby making at least a substantial contribution to the costs of their medical care. Only under the *Medicaid* program, jointly funded by the federal and state governments as a form of welfare, do the "medically indigent" receive medical treatment toward the costs of which they make no contribution.

While the shift of payment to third parties need not mean that medical patients escape all costs, it does contribute to rising demand and ineffi-cient use of medical care facilities — at least under current arrangements. With the physician's bill prepaid or assumed by some third party, patients are not reluctant to visit their doctor at frequent intervals. Nor is the doctor, with 92 percent of hospital costs covered by insurance or government programs, reluctant to send patients to the hospital for extended periods. Finally, since hospitals can readily pass their rising costs on to these third parties, they continually improve the "quality" of the care they provide. With Medicare and Medicaid coming into existence in 1965 and private health insurance payments tripling between 1965 and 1975, it is no acci-dent that the cost of the average hospital stay more than tripled during this same period, from $311 to $1,017. As for physicians' fees, one esti-mate is that Medicare and Medicaid in just two years boosted the annual income of an average physician some $7,000.[3]

I HOW GOOD IS AMERICAN HEALTH CARE? I

Some measures of achievement

With the most expensive health care system in the world, it should follow that we have the world's best system. The American Medical Association insists that this is indeed the case. But is it? The fact is that we can't know for sure since we have no agreed-upon standard of "goodness." There are various ways of defining good medical care: efficiency, reasonable price, friendly concern, medical competence, beautiful hospitals, numbers of physicians, general state of health. Some of these are capable of meas-urement, some are not.

Where figures are available, especially comparative figures, they sug-gest that the American health care industry does not lead the world. One commonly cited health index is the infant mortality rate. Medical progress is usually cited as the major reason for the drop in the infant mortality rate from 100 per 1,000 live births at the beginning of World War I to around 17 at the present time. But if the medical profession claims credit for this development, it must also explain why its performance falls short of that of other countries. Sweden has reduced its infant mortality rate to 10 deaths

---

[3] Cited in A. F. Ehrbar, "A Radical Prescription for Medical Care," *Fortune* (February 1977), 168.

in the first year of life per 1,000 live births, and the figure in the Netherlands stands at 11 per 1,000. According to the most recent figures, in fact, sixteen nations — most with per capita medical outlays far lower than ours — have cut their infant mortality rate to a level lower than that of the United States. And alongside an overall infant mortality rate in the United States of 17 per 1,000 must be placed a significantly higher rate for nonwhites: 30 deaths per 1,000 live births.

Another numerical measure of medical progress is the steady increase in life expectancy. The historical record here is indeed impressive. At the beginning of the twentieth century the average American could expect at birth to live barely more than 47 years (46.3 years for males, 48.3 for females). Partly as a consequence of the reduction or control of childhood diseases and the development of "wonder drugs," these figures by 1972 had risen to 67.4 years for males and 75.1 years for females. Even so, the latter figures fall short of those achieved in eight other nations. Sweden, for example, reports a life expectancy at birth of 72 years for males and 77 years for females.

But there is far more involved in both the reduction of infant mortality and the increase in life expectancy than the quality of a country's medical care system. Although we use the terms *medical care* and *health care* more or less interchangeably, there is a world of difference between the two. Ours can be more accurately described as a medical care or therapy system because its almost exclusive focus in on medicating people back to health once they become ill. Mainly by this route does it deliver health and improve the mortality figures. An alternative way to reduce mortality is to start with healthy people and keep them from getting sick. Medical science, it is true, has made some contributions here: water purification, infection prevention in midwifery, vaccination and inoculation, and a few antibacterials and insecticides.

Of greater importance than all of these, however, are the improvements in health which have come with rising economic well-being. A population that is ill-fed, ill-clothed, and ill-housed is not likely to be healthy, even with the best medical care. Largely as a consequence of rising real incomes, tuberculosis reached a peak and began a steady decline long before specific medication was available. Cholera, dysentery, typhoid, scarlet fever, diptheria, and whooping cough all peaked and started to decline outside medical control. There is a growing consensus that the primary forces that affect health are the standard of living, public health measures, and scientific progress. In developed countries, at least, the marginal contribution of medical care to reducing mortality is small indeed.

Therapeutic nihilism

There is, in fact, a fairly large group of critics who openly express disbelief in the effectiveness of medicine, and especially of organized medicine — thus the label *therapeutic nihilism*. One of them, Ivan Illich, opens his latest book with the flat statement: "The medical establishment has become a major threat to health. The disabling impact of professional control over medicine has reached the proportions of an epidemic."[4] If Illich were writing about the nineteenth century, his conclusions would enjoy wide support. There is general agreement that most medical practice of that day was completely ineffective. The medical profession itself will concede, if pressed, that it was not until after the beginning of the twentieth century that the average patient stood a better than even chance of being helped rather than hurt by a visit to a doctor.

Illich, however, is not writing about the nineteenth century. He is writing about the here and now. And he is saying that doctors still take more away from health than they contribute to it. His bill of indictment of the medical profession requires a whole book to develop, but the following points stand out:[5]

1 Doctors have taken more than their share of credit for reductions in mortality rates during the past several centuries. Rather than stemming from the actions and expertise of individual physicians, these have come primarily from improvements in the standard of living, especially as it has affected nutrition, and from public health measures, such as improved sanitation.

2 It is well known that some parts of the United States are far better supplied with physicians and hospital services than other parts, yet these differences cannot be related in any systematic fashion with variations in mortality or life expectancy or any other index of health.

3 Taking the United States as a whole, we have seen an explosion of medical care costs but have been able to observe no corresponding improvement in health. Life expectancy and mortality rates are on a plateau.

4 Clinical evidence can be found which supports the view that a number of widely accepted medical practices, often very expensive ones, may have no positive value (intensive care procedures) or may actually have an adverse effect on survival (treating diabetics with pills rather than insulin shots, inducing remissions in cancer of the prostate with estrogens).

5 The medical establishment is over-built. Too many hospitals and too many hospital beds, along with too many surgeons, lead to much unnecessary surgery. The ready availability of antibiotics and psychoactive drugs and other medications leads to overprescription and often to adverse, even fatal, complications.

---

[4] Ivan Illich, *Medical Nemesis: The Expropriation of Health*, Pantheon, New York, 1976, p. 3.

[5] Following Paul Starr, "The Politics of Therapeutic Nihilism," *Working Papers* (Summer 1976), 50–51.

6 Although good statistics are unavailable, some studies suggest that there may be several million iatrogenic (doctor-caused) injuries each year. The recent flurry over malpractice suits and insurance touches only the tip of a large iceberg.

7 In addition to this *clinical* iatrogenesis, Illich argues that medicine has created even more illness by redefining normal human experience as sickness. This medicalization of life he calls *social* iatrogenesis. Organized medicine creates illness by weakening individual autonomy and the capacity of people to "suffer their reality." In earlier days individuals stoically endured pain, anxiety, and death. Now they feel sick and expect to be made well. This Illich calls *cultural* iatrogenesis.

Convinced by the logic of the case he has made, Illich calls for a vast scaling back of the medical establishment.

A world of optimal and widespread health is obviously a world of minimal and only occasional medical intervention. Healthy people are those who live in healthy homes on a healthy diet in an environment equally fit for birth, growth, work, healing, and dying; they are sustained by a culture that enhances the conscious acceptance of limits to population, of aging, of incomplete recovery and ever-imminent death. Healthy people need minimal bureaucratic interference to mate, give birth, share the human condition, and die.[6]

While conceding the validity of some of the individual points and arguments made by the therapeutic nihilists, most critics are unable to foresee a general improvement in health that would accompany turning away from professionals toward self-care. The world of drugs today, for example, is so complex that only the professional is able to lead a person safely through it. The argument that the danger of misuse could be avoided by nonuse is not convincing. A sick person will take any help he or she can get, drugs or other. Self-prescription may be fatal. Similarly, it's easy to talk and write about stoicism and self-sufficiency, but sickness creates dependency and medicine — even a sugar pill — often relieves it. Medical care rarely makes a difference between life and death; most of it involves the relief of discomfort, disability, and uncertainty. One estimate by a chief of psychiatry at a United States Public Health Service Hospital is that between 50 and 80 percent of general practice patients come primarily for emotional reasons.[7] "The secret of patient care," physicians constantly remind colleagues and students, "is caring for the patient." It may be that there are many lapses in the exercise of this responsibility, but there is no

---

[6] Illich, *Medical Nemesis*, pp. 274–275.

[7] Stephen F. Jencks, "Who Cares?" *Working Papers* (Winter 1976), 61.

evidence today of any strong sentiment that families, friends, and organized religion are or could be better able than physicians to provide this care. It is apparent, then, that we must be prepared to live with organized medicine for the foreseeable future. But we need not live with it in its present form.

The American health care system

Our health care system reflects an uneasy balance between the tradition of intense economic individualism inherited from the past and the current need for a broad social approach to health care problems. To this point the demand for individual freedom for both consumers and providers of health care services weighs far more heavily in the balance than does any concern for an adequate overall social policy. Doctors Robert Greifinger and Victor Sidel conclude their historical survey of American medicine with this observation:

Given the history of the U.S. and the state of its current society, it is not surprising that we have a medical care system which is highly technical, disease-oriented rather than health-oriented, largely fragmented and uncoordinated, and which uses methods of organization which often seem to be based on private gain rather than on the most effective attainment of the public good.[8]

The fact is that Americans in general have been well pleased with their medical care system during most of the twentieth century. Until the beginning of this century, it is true, they had grave doubts about the efficacy of the medical profession, and with reason. But the reputation of medical practitioners benefited from a series of dramatic changes in the twentieth century, some of which they initiated, some they did not.

Improvements in health resulted both from changes in personal behavior (better hygiene and reproductive practices) and in environmental conditions (more adequate food supplies, provision of safe water and milk, and sewage disposal). Then came breakthroughs in containing germ-related diseases. Hitching its wagon to the rising star of science and technology, the medical profession could point with pride to its accomplishments.

Accompanying these developments were significant improvements in the training of physicians. Concerned about the quality of medical education, the Carnegie Commission early in the century authorized Abraham Flexner, a nonphysician, to evaluate medical education throughout the country. The Flexner Report, published in 1910, pictured such a deplorable level of training that it shocked the medical profession into action. Within

---

[8] Robert B. Greifinger and Victor W. Sidel, "American Medicine," *Environment* 18, No. 4 (May 1976), 16.

a few years many borderline schools were shut down and changes were instituted to guarantee adequate training in those that remained. The American Medical Association could then claim that its demanding requirements for medical schools, coupled with tough screening examinations for licenses to practice medicine, guaranteed Americans the services of the highest-quality medical practitioners in the world. Along with these changes came improvements in hospitals, partly as a consequence of the establishment of higher-quality standards.

This love affair of Americans with their doctors began to sour shortly after World War II. As our incomes rose and we demanded more and more medical services, we found that the determination of the medical societies to maintain quality standards for training hospitals and medical licensing boards guaranteed a doctor shortage. Average compensation for physicians rose as a consequence to over $50,000 a year. And with his time so valuable, who could reasonably expect the family physician to waste it driving the rounds of his patients' homes? To economize on this scarce resource the patients must come to the doctor. And from the doctor's office the patient was far more likely than in the past to move on to the hospital. There he or she could be looked after carefully, and the attending physician would have available the full range of sophisticated diagnostic and treatment facilities. Partly for this reason, partly because hospitalization costs were covered by third parties, we discovered we had a shortage of hospital facilities — reflected in exploding hospital charges.

To add insult to injury, the typical American shortly became convinced that he or she was not only paying more but getting less. The family physician, in addition to changing the terms on which he provided his services, appeared to be in danger of dying out entirely. Comprising around two-thirds of the total physician population in 1949, general practitioners declined to less than one-quarter in 1973. Continuation of this trend would mean the complete disappearance of the all-purpose family doctor by the year 2000. While around 60 percent of patient visits to physicians are for basic, general, or primary medical care, only 1 percent of the hospital residencies available in 1970 offered specific training in general or family practice. Although both the medical profession and the government are attempting to reverse this pattern, the fact is that both financial rewards and prestige remain considerably higher in one of the specialties than in general practice.

In addition to losing the services of the family physician, Americans discovered that their purchases of medical care were not sufficient in and of themselves to improve their overall health. Mortality figures, after declining over the century, leveled off and in some cases even began to rise. At best the allocation of more and more men and women, money, and machines affects mortality and morbidity rates only marginally. Americans are suddenly being shocked into recognizing that money not only can't buy happiness, it can't buy health either. Each individual, it appears, must bear a substantial part of the responsibility for his or her own health.

Individual responsibility for health

The relationship between individual life styles and health has long been recognized. An "unhealthy way of life" is a stock expression. But only in recent years have studies been conducted that systematically explore the relationship between the way we live and our health. Since their results are so remarkable, two of these studies in particular are worth outlining. In his *Who Shall Live?* [9] Victor R. Fuchs compares mortality figures from two adjoining states, Utah and Nevada, to show how differences in life styles relate to health. With similar levels of income and medical care in the two states, the inhabitants of Utah are among the healthiest in the country, while the residents of Nevada are at the opposite end of the spectrum. This shows up first of all in an infant mortality rate higher by about 40 percent in Nevada than in Utah. The differences in death rates are even more remarkable in some of the older age groups, as Table 11.2 indicates.

Failing to find significant differences in income, schooling, urbanization, climate, or any other variable sometimes associated with higher or lower death rates, Fuchs is forced to the conclusion that variations in life styles must be called on for an explanation. Utah is inhabited primarily by Mormons, who are discouraged by their religion from using either alcohol or tobacco and who generally lead stable, quiet lives. Nevada reverses all of these. Per capita consumption of alcohol and tobacco is high, as are the indexes of marital and geographical instability. The favorable impact of a quiet, settled life with the same marital partner shows up in health statistics over and over again. Of far greater consequence is high-level use of alcohol and tobacco. Table 11.3 shows their combined impact on death rates in the two states. The consequence of "high, wide, and handsome" living, as they define it in Nevada, appears to be a significantly shorter life.

In their studies of nearly 7,000 adults followed for five and one-half years, Breslow and Belloc [10] found that life expectancy and health are significantly related to certain basic health habits:

1 Three meals a day at regular times and no snacking

2 Breakfast every day

3 Moderate exercise two or three times a week

---

[9] Victor R. Fuchs, *Who Shall Live?*, Basic Books, New York, 1975, pp. 52–54.

[10] N. B. Belloc and L. Breslow, "The Relation of Physical Health Status and Health Practices," *Preventive Medicine* (August 1972), 409–421.

4 Adequate sleep (7 or 8 hours a night)

5 No smoking

6 Moderate weight

7 No alcohol or only in moderation

A 45-year-old man who practices none to three of these habits has a remaining life expectancy of 21.6 years (to age 67). One with six to seven

TABLE 11.2

Excess of death rates in Nevada compared with Utah, average for 1959–1961 and 1966–1968

Age group	Males (%)	Females (%)
Less than 1	42	35
1–19	16	26
20–29	44	42
30–39	37	42
40–49	54	69
50–59	38	28
60–69	26	17
70–79	20	6

Source: Table from *Who Shall Live? Health, Economics, and Social Choice*, by Victor R. Fuchs, p. 52, © 1974 by Basic Books, Inc., Publishers, New York.

TABLE 11.3

Excess of death rates in Nevada compared with Utah for cirrhosis of the liver and malignant neoplasms of the respiratory system, average for 1966–1968

Age group	Males (%)	Females (%)
30–39	590	443
40–49	111	296
50–59	206	205
60–69	117	227

Source: Table from *Who Shall Live? Health, Economics, and Social Choice*, by Victor R. Fuchs, p. 54, © 1974 by Basic Books, Inc., Publishers, New York.

of the habits can expect to live for another 33.1 years (to age 78). This suggests that relatively simple changes in habits of living can add 11 years to life expectancy — more by four times than the 2.7 years added to life expectancy at age 65 during the entire period 1900–1966. Their studies suggested to Belloc and Breslow that the health status of someone who practiced all seven habits was similar to that of someone 30 years younger who observed none.

The message conveyed by both of these studies — and of many others that could be cited — seems obvious: It would be far more humane as well as more cost-effective to concentrate on keeping people healthy instead of merely standing by with expensive and elaborate patch-up machinery and waiting for them to get ill and diseased. But our emphasis is almost entirely on the latter. Out of our nearly $150 billion annual expenditure on health, we spend only 2 to 2.5 percent on disease prevention and control measures and only 0.5 percent for health education. State and local governments spend almost nothing for environmental-health research, and the federal government outlay is only around 0.25 percent of total health expenditures. Yet there is little public complaint about the scant proportion of our health resources going into health maintenance rather than treatment. It is probably true, as Doctor John Knowles insists, that

If no one smoked cigarettes or consumed alcohol and everyone exercised regularly, maintained optimal weight on a low fat, low refined-carbohydrate, high fiber-content diet, reduced stress by simplifying their lives, obtained adequate rest and recreation, understood the needs of infants and children for the proper nutrition and nurturing of their intellectual and affective development, had available to them,

the small society   by Brickman

and would use, genetic counseling and selective abortion, drank fluoridated water, followed the doctor's orders for medications and self-care once disease was detected, used available health services at the appropriate time for screening examinations and health education–preventive medicine programs, the savings to the country would be mammoth in terms of billions of dollars, a vast reduction in human misery, and an attendant marked improvement in the quality of life. Our country would be strengthened immeasurably, and we could divert our energies — human and financial — to other pressing issues of national and international concern.[11]

But to go from there to argue that "the cost of sloth, gluttony, alcoholic intemperance, reckless driving, sexual frenzy, and smoking is now a national, and not an individual, responsibility"[12] is to find a responsibility recognized by neither the nation nor the individual. Our present health insurance programs, both public and private, are basically "disease insurance," since they do not cover either health education or other preventive measures. Doctors find it far more interesting as well as financially rewarding to treat diseases rather than to concentrate on keeping people sound and well. Hospitals would be bankrupt in short order if their flow of patients ceased. And the flow is not likely to diminish because Americans insist on the unhindered right to kill and maim themselves and make themselves sick and diseased.

The latter is partly the consequence of sheer ignorance. Doctors and medical investigators are coming to recognize the influence of life styles on health maintenance, but the message has not yet got through to the public. This suggests, at a minimum, an enlarged research effort devoted to the topic and a massive increase in health education programs, especially in the primary and secondary schools where attitudes are in the process of being formed. But it will undoubtedly be necessary to go beyond this and recast the form of the American medical delivery system.

I ORGANIZATIONS AND HEALTH MAINTENANCE I

Fee-for-service system

Many years ago the great British playwright George Bernard Shaw dramatized the dilemma of the doctor under present fee-for-service arrangements: "That any sane nation, having observed that you could provide for the supply of bread by giving bakers a pecuniary interest in baking for

---

[11] John H. Knowles, "The Responsibility of the Individual," *Daedalus* (Winter 1977), 75.

[12] Knowles, "The Responsibility of the Individual," p. 59.

you, should go on to give a surgeon a pecuniary interest in cutting off your leg, is enough to make one despair of political humanity."[13]

Although strongly suspected, it is difficult to prove that surgeons are led to perform unnecessary surgery under a fee-for-service arrangement. It is often a matter of individual judgment as to whether or not surgery is necessary. But there is good evidence to show that when doctors charge on the basis of each operation performed, they perform far more operations than they do when they have no such financial interest. Numerous studies show that patients enrolled in prepaid medical plans are only half as likely to lose an appendix or uterus or their tonsils as patients consulting private practitioners. It has also been shown that requiring a second medical opinion before proceeding with surgery reduces the number of operations. And there are data showing a strong relationship between the number of surgeons in a particular locality and the number of operations performed, regardless of the size of the local population.

Going beyond the field of surgery to medicine at large, the conviction is widespread that "under the existing system of payment for each individual service, the doctor's need to get paid inevitably conflicts at times with the patient's need to get well."[14] This was not the original reason for the establishment of prepaid medical plans, but it is now seen as one of its major attractions.

Prepaid medical service plans

What has since been formalized as the Kaiser-Permanente Health Plan began as a device to secure medical services for the employees of a major military contractor operating in isolated areas of the western United States. Under this *prepaid medical service plan*, doctors were brought in by the company, and employees contracted for their services by the payment of fixed monthly charges. The program has grown steadily in the years since World War II and is now open to noncompany participants. It currently enrolls over 3 million people in California, Oregon, and Hawaii. Its features, outlined below, have been adopted by several other plans.[15]

1 *Prepayment.* This is the unique feature of this type of plan. The barrier of a fee at the time medical services are rendered does not exist. One monthly payment entitles members to the whole array of services offered.

---

[13] Preface to George Bernard Shaw, *The Doctor's Dilemma*, Penguin Books, Baltimore, Md., p. 7.

[14] Selig Greenberg, *The Troubled Calling: Crisis in the Medical Establishment*, Macmillan, New York, 1965, p. 2.

[15] Based on Bowen and Jeffers, *The Economics of Health Services*, p. 20.

2 *Group practice.* A group of medical specialists is brought together to create a team. All members work full time. Whatever expertise or services each member of the group contributes, all income is pooled and shared on a prearranged basis. Continuing education and mutual help are encouraged.

3 *An integrated medical center.* The medical group itself is hospital-based, but there are clinics scattered throughout the area in which the patient population resides.

4 *Voluntary enrollment.* All members of the group join voluntarily. This means that the plan must compete with alternative plans and arrangements to hold its clientele.

5 *Capitation payment.* Physicians and hospitals involved in the plan are paid a flat, negotiated sum for each individual enrolled in the plan — not on the basis of the services actually provided. Since the amount to be paid is a flat sum set in advance, both physicians and hospitals have an incentive to minimize the need for their own services.

6 *Comprehensive coverage.* In addition to the usual in-the-doctor's-office and in-the-hospital consultation and treatment, patients are provided out-patient care, extended care, home health service, drug coverage, and mental health services. The doctors of the group decide in each case what type of treatment is in order and where it can best be provided.

Although it is difficult in short compass to describe in detail the advantages and disadvantages of prepaid group medical practice, one or two things do stand out. The major disadvantage is a tendency for consumers to demand more services than they contract for under fee-for-service arrangements. Offsetting this is the fact that

The group earns most net revenue when the subscribing population is least ill — not far from the Chinese custom of paying physicians only when patients are well. Thus there are tremendous incentives to control costs, efficiently utilize resources, and prevent "over-doctoring" at all times. Prevention, health education, and early detection of disease tend to be emphasized more under the prepaid system than under fee-for-service.[16]

Since the problems of American medicine are exactly those the prepaid group plans focus on — prevention as well as cure, control of costs, efficiency of utilization — it would seem that such plans should represent the wave of the future. For a time it appeared they would. The Nixon administration was sufficiently impressed by the prepaid group plans that it used them as a model for federally sponsored Health Maintenance

---

[16] Bowen and Jeffers, *The Economics of Health Services*, p. 20.

Organizations. In spite of widespread promotion, however, there has been little actual implementation of such arrangements.

With individuals less than enthusiastic about preventive health care and most members of the medical establishment wedded to the idea of fee-for-service, the moment obviously hasn't yet arrived for a comprehensive reordering of our health care priorities. Instead the demand seems to be for no more than a broadening of our present system — to the point where every individual is guaranteed his or her "right" to health care. This is taking the form of some sort of national health insurance program.

| NATIONAL HEALTH INSURANCE |

One of the foundation stones on which the present edifice of government medical care programs has been built is the principle that health is a right, not a privilege. Medicare implicitly and Medicaid explicitly start from the premise that no American should be denied health care because of lack of income. Before recognizing that this currently is a right with many exceptions, it should be pointed out that it is also a right the very existence of which is denied by many economists. Since economic resources are and always will be limited, guaranteeing some individuals now denied them their "rights" to unrestricted medical care must inevitably conflict with the "rights" of others to adequate educational opportunities or police protection or welfare payments. To this point Americans have indicated a willingness to give over more and more resources to the medical-care industry in order to subsidize low-income patients. But there is undoubtedly some limit beyond which rights to additional care simply would not be recognized — a limit imposed by competing demands for the same share of the national income. Candidate Jimmy Carter during his presidential campaign, for example, called for and promised a national health insurance program, but President Jimmy Carter early in his first year in office decided that other programs had higher priority in the federal budget and that health insurance would have to wait.

Goals

Access to all   There appears to be a consensus at this time, however, that all individuals should have access to the health care system, irrespective of their financial circumstances, and should be provided with adequate care. The fact that we are the only industrialized country in the world that provides no such across-the-board medical coverage contributes to this belief. So does recognition of the many holes in our present patchwork system. Medicaid — our primary system for delivering health care services to low-income families — entirely excluded 28 percent of the poor for one reason or another in 1973. And even among those covered, the quality and quantity of medical services provided varied widely from those available to higher-income families.

The case for national health insurance would not be urgent if the low-income families excluded from Medicaid and Medicare were adequately covered by private health insurance. This is far from being the case. According to federal government analysts, "While only 20 percent of the population under sixty-five has no private hospital insurance, a disproportionate number of the working poor, of blacks, and of people living in the South are among those uninsured. Forty percent of all black people under sixty-five and 75 percent of poor children do not have hospital insurance coverage."[17]

As the above suggests, ensuring access to medical care for all is the most commonly cited reason for a national health insurance program. But it is by no means the only reason. Two other goals commonly given for national health insurance are (1) reducing or eliminating the financial hardship of medical bills and (2) limiting the rise in health care costs.

Elimination of financial hardship   With the explosive rise in medical care costs in recent years, paying medical bills has become a problem for families well up the income scale. Public programs and private health insurance provide only a partial solution to their problem. Over a million Americans have been declared "uninsurable" by the private insurance companies and denied coverage. Another large group is self-employed or works for small businesses without group medical insurance policies. They must either go without medical insurance or pay exorbitant premiums for limited coverage under individual policies. Even when group policies are available, the coverage of medical treatment is apt to be limited. Only half the population has major medical coverage — this in the day when a terminal cancer patient can incur hospital and medical costs in the tens of thousands of dollars.

Curtailment of rising health care costs   It appears paradoxical to give national health insurance a role in limiting the rise in health care costs, when earlier a case was made that private insurance and the implementation of Medicare and Medicaid played an important role in driving up health care costs. What the heading is driving at, however, is the role of a *well-designed* insurance system in holding costs down, whereas a poorly designed one has forced them up. Insurance policies have normally provided complete coverage for short hospital stays, but limited or no coverage for alternative forms of health care service. This has encouraged

---

[17] Figures for 1970. Cited in Karen Davis, *National Health Insurance: Benefits, Costs, and Consequences,* Brookings Institution, Washington, D.C., 1975, pp. 34–35.

patients to get themselves hospitalized and remain hospitalized rather than seek out-patient treatment or nursing-home care. The guaranteed clientele has also encouraged hospital administrators and doctors to provide an ever-wider range of sophisticated services with fancy price tags attached. And since someone else is paying the bill, neither patient nor physician is much concerned about "policing" the services provided and the bills presented.

A well-designed national health care system would build in some device to encourage restraint in the provision, use, and pricing of medical services. Economists place their greatest hopes on a national health insurance plan with substantial cost-sharing provisions. It is assumed that if the patient is forced to contribute part of the cost of medical treatment, he or she will think twice before asking for hospitalization and will be concerned with services provided and their costs. There is also the possibility that patients will shop around for "best buys" in medical services, thus bringing some competition into the field. One way to bring about this cost sharing is to make some initial amount of a medical bill, say $100, deductible from the insurance proceeds. Another device often used is to have the patient share remaining costs with the government or insurance company beyond the deductible amount, say 80 percent paid by the insurance company or government and 20 percent by the patient.

A national health insurance plan could be rejected out of hand, though, even if it satisfied the triple objectives of providing access to all, eliminating financial hardship, and limiting the rise in health care costs. As Karen Davis points out, an acceptable plan must meet all these goals and also be (1) equitably financed, (2) easy to understand and administer, and (3) acceptable to providers of medical services and the general public.[18]

Equitable financing   A plan providing access to medical services to the poor would be of limited usefulness to them if they were required to pay their full share of the costs. Equitable financing thus suggests funding the program with a payment scheme that falls more heavily on higher-income than lower-income families. An actuarially sound program, where participants pay premiums in proportion to the average benefits provided for all, would obviously not accomplish this. Taking a fixed amount from each family, regardless of income, means that the poor would pay an extremely high proportion of their incomes, the rich a relatively low proportion. This would be the most regressive of all ways of financing a national insurance program. The situation is improved somewhat if the program is financed by government-collected taxes and primary reliance is placed on payroll taxes, as is done in the case of the social security system. But even payroll taxes are somewhat regressive because taxes are not levied on nonpayroll income nor on payroll income above a certain amount. Since substan-

---

[18] Davis, *National Health Insurance*, p. 5.

tial portions of higher incomes escape taxation, the taxes collected are a smaller proportion of total income than is the case for earners of low-wage incomes. Equitable financing thus almost comes down to the use of progressive taxes — and that means the federal personal income tax. This creates two problems, however. The insurance principle is lost because participants do not contribute in proportion to benefits received. And high-income families recognize that they have little to gain from the program since they will contribute considerably more than they receive back in benefits. They will get some protection for catastrophic illnesses, but at an extremely high cost.

Ease of understanding and administration   Complex as the problem is, it is possible that a group of experts could design a national health insurance program to meet all the required objectives. But it would likely be a complex plan, difficult for the average person to understand, and awkward to administer. Confusion and delays in reimbursement could lead to disappointment and disillusionment with the whole system. Every provision of the ultimate plan needs, therefore, to be tested for simplicity and workability.

Acceptability among interest groups   The American people appear willing to support some sort of national health insurance program that promises to achieve the goals already outlined. But these goals will be achieved only if the interest groups in the medical care industry — physicians, hospitals, and other providers of medical services — willingly support the program. The reluctance of the American Medical Association, in particular, to support any extension of government intervention in the medical field is well known:

Over the years, the AMA has opposed voluntary health insurance, the social security law, compulsory smallpox vaccination, public immunization against diphtheria, Federal aid to reduce infant and maternal deaths, public venereal disease clinics, school health services, government-financed medical care for dependents of men in the Armed Forces, workmen's compensation for industrial injuries, and the Red Cross blood banks. . . . It damned group-practice plans as "medical soviets." . . . It once termed Blue Cross a "half-baked scheme" that would result in "mechanization of medical practices." It has fought Federal aid to medical schools as "a back-door route to socialized medicine."[19]

Members of the AMA insist that this was reasoned opposition, based on their determination to protect the doctor-patient relationship and the right of every person to a free choice of a physician or surgeon. Critics argue that the AMA's support for the status quo can only be understood if

_____

[19] Greenberg, *The Troubled Calling*, p. 155.

it is first recognized that the medical profession as a whole leads all others in annual income of its members. In strictly economic terms, they have little to gain from change and much to lose. Whatever their grounds for opposition to change, it is recognized that their support for any alternative to present arrangements must be secured if a new program is to have any chance of success.

The future of national health insurance

Although the need for alternative arrangements in the medical care field is urgent, it is not desperate. The sentiment appears to be that it would be better to live with the present system a few more years than to rush into something that might be even worse. This is especially true since the American people face "a confusing proliferation of choices":

More than twenty national health insurance bills were introduced in the Ninety-third Congress — ranging from bills that would provide federal tax subsidies to encourage more people to buy private health insurance to plans that would replace most private health insurance with a public plan. Some plans would cover all of the population, others would exclude certain segments. Some would replace the Medicare program for the elderly, some would modify it, and others would leave it alone. Some plans would be voluntary; others would automatically provide a specified health policy to everyone. Some would incorporate special plans for different groups; others call for a uniform plan for all persons. Some cover a wide range of medical services, including preventive services, family planning, maternity care, long-term care, and mental health services; others contain only a few of these benefits. A variety of methods for paying hospitals, physicians, and other health providers is to be found in the bills under consideration. Financing of the plans relies on a varied mix of revenues from state governments, employers, patients, and federal payroll taxes and general revenues.[20]

About the only point on which there appears to be general agreement, at least among economists in the health care field, is that it would be near-disastrous to guarantee access to medical care to everyone under a national insurance scheme while doing nothing about the conditions under which those medical services are delivered. On a limited basis, this is what we did under Medicare and Medicaid, generating escalating costs. This would have been true even if there had been an abundance of physicians and surgeons, which we will have in the near future, as soon as those now in training pour out into practice. Doctors are in position both to determine how much of their own services are needed and what prices to charge for them. A national insurance program that simply guaranteed payment of medical bills and did nothing else would commit an ever-

---

[20] Davis, *National Health Insurance*, pp. 6–7.

larger part of the national income to paying those bills. In setting up its National Health Service at the end of World War II, Britain recognized the problem of controlling medical charges under a free-access system and met it by nationalizing the hospitals and setting charges for the services of family physicians. But this is clearly "socialized medicine" and would be bitterly contested in the United States. We will in all likelihood stop considerably short of such a program. How much short, only time will tell.

I SUMMARY I

The American health care industry is in trouble. Costs are escalating along with general dissatisfaction with the system. Between 1929 and 1976 total health expenditures rose from $3.6 billion to $139.3 billion — and no let-up is in sight. Yet there is strong feeling that the increase in costs has not led to significantly higher-quality health care.

Part of the increase in costs is explained by rising demand for medical services as we get richer and older. But of equal importance is the shift in recent years to third party payment of medical and hospital bills and the consequent loss of control over costs.

For the highest medical bills in the world the American people get a medical care industry not demonstrably better than that of several other countries with less expensive systems. Improvements in infant mortality rates and the average length of life lag behind those of many other nations.

Some critics argue that we are less healthy than we should be primarily because we are overdoctored. They therefore call for a scaling-back of organized medicine. The medical profession contests this approach to better health. Physicians do concede, however, that their job would be more manageable if Americans chose less unhealthy ways of living: better eating and drinking habits, less or no smoking, regular exercise, and adequate sleep.

To this point, though, we have placed far less emphasis on prevention than on cure. The primary concern is still with finding some way to guarantee all Americans their "right" to medical care. To this end, a number of prepaid medical service plans are already in operation and more are planned. The route to a national health insurance system, on the other hand, is still marked by enough disagreement as to the one best plan that its attainment appears to be some years off.

I IMPORTANT TERMS AND CONCEPTS I

third party payments	health care
Medicare	therapeutic nihilism
Medicaid	prepaid medical service plans
medical care	national health insurance

I QUESTIONS, PROBLEMS, AND EXERCISES I

1 What evidence is usually cited to demonstrate that our health care system is in need of an overhaul?

2 How good is American medical care compared with that provided in other economically advanced countries?

3 What case do the therapeutic nihilists make for scaling back organized medicine? How convincing do you think their case is?

4 Why is the family doctor — the general practitioner — apparently a dying breed?

5 What do the comparative figures for Utah and Nevada say about the efficacy of medical care in controlling mortality rates?

6 Should all Americans have the right to health and medical care, regardless of ability to pay?

7 Why should patients under a national health care system be required to pay part of the cost of their medical treatment?

8 Why is the medical profession less than enthusiastic about national health insurance?

I SUGGESTED READING I

Bowen, Howard R., and James R. Jeffers. *The Economics of Health Services.* General Learning Press, New York, 1971.

Davis, Karen. *National Health Insurance: Benefits, Costs, and Consequences.* Brookings Institution, Washington, D.C., 1975.

Fuchs, Victor R. *Who Shall Live? Health, Economics, and Social Choice.* Basic Books, New York, 1974.

Greifinger, Robert B., and Victor W. Sidel. "American Medicine." *Environment,* 18, No. 4 (May 1976), 6–18.

Illich, Ivan. *Medical Nemesis: The Expropriation of Health.* Calder & Boyers, London, 1975.

Kristein, Marvin M., et al. "Health Economics and Preventive Care." *Science,* 195 (February 1977), 457–462.

Starr, Paul. "The Politics of Therapeutic Nihilism." *Working Papers* (Summer 1976), 48–55.

Thomas, Lewis. *The Lives of a Cell.* Bantam, New York, 1974.

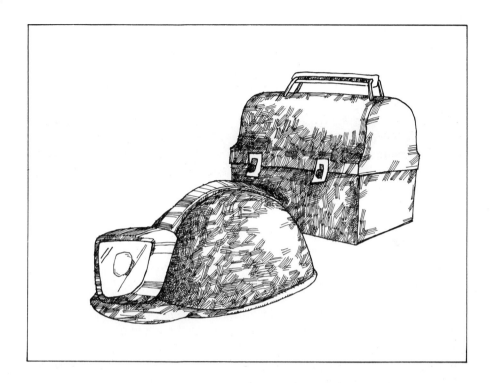

| THE WORLD OF WORK |

We live today in a consumption-oriented society. Adam Smith, the so-called father of economics, provided the setting over 200 years ago in his *Wealth of Nations* when he insisted that "consumption is the sole end and purpose of all production; and the interest of the producer ought to be attended to, only so far as it may be necessary for promoting that of the consumer." Economist Walt W. Rostow argued recently that we have reached the promised land. His premise is that nations develop through five different economic stages, culminating in the age of high mass consumption — which the United States entered early in the twentieth century.

So thoroughly are we wedded today to the idea that high consumption is the goal of life and our daily round of work only the means that we have difficulty even entertaining the notion that any other means-end relationship is possible.

But many thinkers over the years have put forward the idea that consumption is, or should be, the means, and work the end — that we eat in order to work, not that we work solely in order to eat. The fact is, though, that we don't eat only in order to work. Eating can be enjoyable in its own right. But neither need we work just so that we can eat. Work, too, can be enjoyable in its own right. Given the consumption orientation of economics since the days of Adam Smith, however, and the coupled notion that "the interest of the producer ought to be attended to, only so far as it may be necessary for promoting that of the consumer," it is not surprising that we have given far more attention to the worker as consumer than to the worker as worker — except to the extent that we have concerned ourselves with improving the efficiency of the worker so that we will all have more of the "good things of life." Work is irksome but necessary — that has been about the long and short of it.

Over the years opposition to this point of view has come from two fronts. What we broadly call the labor movement has concerned itself with improving the lot of the worker. While the notion has rarely been entertained that work might under any circumstances be made actually pleasant, the leaders of the labor movement have insisted that many improvements are possible to make work at least less burdensome: shorter hours, improved working conditions, better pay, elimination of child labor, and so on. And in recent years many persons have revived the idea, promoted by radical thinkers in the nineteenth century, that work might actually be an enjoyable experience, if only the "alienation" of the worker from his work and from his fellow workers could be eliminated. After all, adherents to this point of view argue, close to half our waking hours are spent at the workplace. Couldn't life be improved as readily by improving the work experience as by concentrating only on crowding more consumer goods and services into the leisure hours? Answering yes to this question is easier than actually improving the work experience, but we will later survey some of the recent innovations designed to do just that. But first a short survey of the earlier approach, the labor movement.

I THE WORKER IN AMERICAN HISTORY I

When we see or hear the words *labor movement,* we almost automatically think of labor unions. Unions have indeed been in the forefront of the movement to improve the lot of the American workingman — and, to a much lesser extent, workingwoman — for the last hundred years. But the almost exclusive concern of the union has been its own members, and even today only a relatively small fraction of the labor force (less than one-quarter) holds union membership. Toward the end of the nineteenth century the share of the labor force organized into unions began to rise. It reached its high point for the century just as the century closed — at less than 3 percent of the labor force. This suggests that during the nineteenth century as a whole, unions had insufficient coverage or influence to do very much for most of the American labor force.

It does not mean, however, that nothing was done to improve the life of the working person. All through the nineteenth century the possibility existed of using government at one level or another to improve the lot of the worker. Workers increased in both absolute and relative numbers during the century, and their votes, along with those of labor sympathizers, were sufficient on many occasions to secure the passage of prolabor legislation or the elimination of antilabor laws. Early in the century labor votes and influence were sufficient to eliminate property qualifications for voting, to repeal the laws providing imprisonment for failure to pay debts, to repeal the state militia laws that unfairly discriminated against workers, to broaden the scope of free public education so children of working people could get at least some schooling and would not compete with adults for jobs while in school, and to clear the way for legal suits against employers who refused to pay their workers. The first state factory acts came during this period also, reducing the hours and improving safety conditions for children employed in industry. And in 1840 the first step toward reducing the workday was taken when President Van Buren issued an executive order limiting the workday for federal employees to ten hours.

In the second half of the century, progress via the political route came more grudgingly. The only major accomplishments came during the Civil War, when labor's influence was great because its cooperation was vital for successful prosecution of the war. Shortly after the war began, labor got two major pieces of legislation it had long worked for: the Homestead Act (1862), which provided up to 160 acres of federal land free for settlers willing to clear and work the land, and the Morrill Act (also 1862), which offered grants of federal lands to states willing to establish land-grant colleges to teach "such branches of learning as are related to agriculture and the mechanic arts." In response to union pressure, Congress also restricted the workday to eight hours for federal employees in 1868 and passed a series of laws during the last quarter of the century restricting immigration.

It was hoped that the adoption of the eight-hour day for federal employees would set the pattern for private industry as well. But this was not to be the case until over half a century later. The typical eleven-hour workday, six-day workweek of 1860 was adjusted downward only to a ten-hour day by 1890. Some workers in 1890, it is true, did better than this, especially highly skilled craftsmen. But some did far worse. The steel mills, for example, operated seven days a week, twenty-four hours a day, with two twelve-hour labor shifts. The standard workweek was thus twelve hours a day for all seven days of the week — a killing eighty-four hours. And every other Sunday, when the day shifts and night shifts exchanged places, half the labor force got Sunday off but the other half worked straight through for twenty-four hours. Since it was either work or go hungry, the steel workers stuck to the job. There were always others waiting at the factory gates to replace them if they objected to the terms of employment. During the period 1890–1929 the overall unemployment rate fluctuated mainly between 5 and 15 percent of the labor force, averaging approximately 10 percent.[1]

For those who found and held a job life did improve, not primarily as a consequence of political change or union influence, but because the economy was industrializing and growing rapidly. Real gross national product grew at an average annual rate of 4.5 percent between 1870 and 1913, permitting real annual earnings of nonfarm employees (average earnings converted into dollars with constant purchasing power) to rise by something more than 50 percent from 1870 to 1900 (from 375 to 573 1914 dollars).[2]

Workers and the early unions

The foregoing account correctly conveys the idea of the relative unimportance of unions in shaping the lives of workers during the nineteenth century; it may also falsely suggest the absence of unions from the American scene. Although unions proved their long-run viability only in the second half of the nineteenth century, the whole of the century witnessed a succession of union launchings, most of which failed, but which, in the process, provided object lessons for later unions. This was the time of testing for the very idea of unionization, and many lessons were learned the hard way, lessons that condition the behavior of union leaders down to the present day. An understanding of why union leaders behave as they do is impossible without some knowledge of what has shaped their behavior patterns.

Although, as was indicated, workers were occasionally able to influence legislation by exercising their right to vote, more commonly workers found government arrayed against them on the side of the employer, especially when they attempted to promote their interests through forming and joining unions. In fact, during the first part of the nineteenth century, down to 1842, it was an open question as to whether or not unions had a

---

[1] Lloyd G. Reynolds, *Labor Economics and Labor Relations,* 3d ed., Prentice-Hall, Englewood Cliffs, N.J., 1959, p. 358.

[2] *Historical Statistics of the United States,* 1975, Part I, p. 165.

legal right to exist. The common law outlawed "conspiracies in restraint of trade," and judges of the time were quite likely to ask the obvious question: If unions are not organizations designed to control the trade in human labor, then what in the world are they? As late as 1836 twenty striking tailors were thrown into prison for jointly refusing to work. Finally, in 1842, the Supreme Court of Massachusetts decided in *Commonwealth* v. *Hunt* that so long as unions pursued legal ends the unions themselves had a legal right to exist.

A legal right, however, was a necessary but not sufficient condition for existence. Over and over again unions came into being during good economic times (when employers could be forced to pay higher wages and workers could afford to pay membership dues), flourished for a time, then disappeared in the next major depression. Not a single union remained in existence throughout the entire first half of the nineteenth century. Only during the prosperous 1850s did unions appear that are still with us today (in particular the typographers' union and some of the railroad brotherhoods).

The periodic depressions were usually sufficient to do in struggling unions, but they were helped mightily by the wide array of perfectly legal anti-union instruments available to the employer. Any employer determined to prevent the unionization of his work place could legally employ any of these devices: refuse to hire known union members; employ labor spies to circulate among the labor force and detect secret union members, who could then be fired; not only fire union members and especially union organizers but also distribute blacklists to other employers so that they could avoid hiring them; force a prospective employee to sign a *yellow dog contract,* stipulating that he or she was not a union member and would refuse to join a union during the period of employment; employ strikebreakers to take the place of workers who went out on strike; and readily secure injunctions from friendly judges, ordering union leaders under certain conditions to desist from calling strikes or to instruct workers to go back to work if a strike was under way. All of these have been declared illegal during the past half-century or their use sharply circumscribed, but labor leaders have long memories and a familiarity with labor history. Even today, when they are assured that business and labor have common interests, they are reminded of the days when the major concern of business seemed to be that of preventing labor from arranging for its own self-protection.

The successful unions in the nineteenth century were those that paid strict attention to the narrow economic interests of members — and only to those. They didn't fritter away union funds in attempting to establish labor parties — expensive undertakings, yet never capable of matching the strength of the established political parties. They didn't try to displace the businessman by preaching revolution or by establishing producers' cooperatives and going into business themselves. Those who did learned very shortly that this required more skills and resources than they possessed. And finally they not only concentrated on the narrow economic interests of their own members but also restricted their membership to those with common interests.

The Knights of Labor Proof of the wisdom of this last rule was provided by the spectacular failure of one of the more colorful unions of the late nineteenth century, the Knights of Labor. The Knights of Labor was founded shortly after the Civil War on the premise that the way to advance the interests of workers was to organize all of them into one gigantic union. What employer could withstand the concentrated power of a union that represented everybody — skilled and unskilled, men and women, blacks and whites, workers and those merely sympathetic to the workers' cause? For a time it appeared that this organized power was indeed irresistible. Union members, often in the face of opposition by the central leadership, called a series of strikes in the early 1880s to oppose depression-induced wage reductions. Their success brought a wave of new members into the union, cresting at a claimed three-quarters of a million total membership in 1886.

But the end was already in sight. Strikes are great when they succeed, but only one or two unsuccessful strikes can bring down the mightiest of unions. Flushed with success, the members of the union disregarded the go-slow pleas of the union leadership and walked off the job when their demands were not met. When a general strike was called to back up the demand for an eight-hour day and produced only the most meager of results the union's back was broken. Now one group within the union found its interests in conflict with those of other groups. The skilled workers recognized that they could promote their own welfare more effectively if they didn't have to worry about the unskilled. Withdraw unskilled workers from the job and they can easily be replaced, but take the skilled workers off the job and there is no way the employer can replace them on short notice. The upshot was that the skilled workers quickly pulled out of the Knights of Labor, leaving that organization to die a quiet death while trying to bring about change through the political process.

The American Federation of Labor Just as the Knights of Labor collapsed, a new labor organization came into being — an organization with a philosophy deliberately adopted to avoid the major mistakes of past unions, especially those of the Knights of Labor. This was the American Federation of Labor, established in 1886 under the leadership of Samuel Gompers, its first and only president for the next forty years, with the exception of one year. To maximize the strategic power of the skilled worker, only skilled craftsmen were permitted to join an AFL union. And there was one national union, and only one, for all the local *craft unions*. The AFL, then, was and is in one sense no union at all: It is, as its name indicates, a federation of national unions, with each of the latter in turn made up of all the craft locals in a particular calling (carpenters, plumbers, steamfitters, and so forth).

The individual worker typically came in contact only with the officers of his local union. But they were affected nonetheless by the AFL, since a national craft union was allowed to federate with the AFL only after agreeing to abide by common rules. The first and foremost of these has already been cited: No unskilled workers allowed (with only minor exceptions), and in the early years almost no women or nonwhites. Entrance into a skilled craft was to be by the long-traditional route, an extended apprenticeship. A hands-off attitude toward politics was mandatory; no thought of a labor party was even to be entertained. Campaign contributions were in order, though, distributed in such a fashion as to reward labor's friends and punish its enemies. Any attempt to overthrow the capitalist system was to be given up — partly on the sensible ground that such efforts were likely to be fruitless anyway. Accept the business system, then, but accept it on labor's own terms. What terms those were Samuel Gompers shortly made explicit. When asked what labor really wanted, Gompers' one-word reply was, "More." More today than yesterday, more tomorrow than today. And more meant three things: higher wages, better working conditions, and shorter hours. This, in a nutshell, is the philosophy of business, or bread-and-butter, unionism. Unions, at least in the United States, see themselves primarily as business organizations, charged with the mission of securing more bread and butter for their dues-paying members. If along the way some benefits of their activities spill over into the hands of non-union workers, that's nice, but it's no real part of their intentions.

This was obviously the union philosophy for which skilled American workers had been looking. They flocked to the AFL in ever-increasing numbers down to the 1920s: .6 million total membership in 1900, 1.6 million in 1910, and 4.1 million in 1920. In the latter year, over 12 percent of the American labor force was organized into unions, and more than four out of five organized workers were members of the American Federation of Labor. Even the unions that did not federate with the AFL tended to adopt its aims and objectives. Only now and again did a union appear with more far-reaching and radical objectives — the socialists and the spectacular "Wobblies" (Industrial Workers of the World), for example. And their successes were brief. American workers, and in particular American skilled workers, have never been much interested in revolutionary or even democratic anticapitalist unions.

Rather surprisingly total union membership fell rather sharply during the booming 1920s, just when all prior experience would have suggested further gains by the unions. This decline in union membership (from 5 million in 1920 to 3.6 million in 1929) has been attributed to a massive, successful counterattack by industry. The National Association of Manufacturers, in particular, shortly after its formation in the 1890s, undertook a "crusade against unionism" on the premise that unionism had the same aim as socialism and was therefore un-American. World War I set back the campaign, but it began to pay off handsomely in the 1920s, as union membership figures indicate. The only good union, according to this point of view, was a company union — one thoroughly dominated by company officers and therefore incapable of independent action. By 1928 around 1.5 million American workers were members of such organizations.

Labor and the Great Depression

If union leaders thought things were tough in the 1920s, they had only to wait for 1929 and the beginning of the Great Depression to realize how bad things could be. Union membership fell with every rise in the unemployment rate. Unemployment rose from 3.2 percent of the labor force in 1929 to 24.9 percent in 1933, while union membership fell from 3.6 million (7.5 percent of the labor force) to 2.9 million (5.7 percent of the labor force) in the same years. Unemployed workers can't very well pay union dues, nor do they have much incentive to stay with the union if the union is unable to deliver any wages — to say nothing of higher wages.

What may seem strange, in light of the last statement and continuing high levels of unemployment for the rest of the decade (still very close to 10 percent when war broke out in 1941), is that union membership literally exploded during the remainder of the thirties. From its low point in 1933, the trough of the depression, union membership rose to an extraordinary 10.5 million in 1941 (18.3 percent of the labor force). The primary reason for the reversal of the decline in unionization is that the federal government at long last threw its support behind the union movement.

Growing federal support   This development was under way even before the inauguration of Franklin D. Roosevelt and the New Deal. In 1932 Congress passed the Norris-LaGuardia Act, which outlawed the use of the yellow-dog contract and placed sharp restrictions on use of the labor injunction. Of far greater moment, the National Industrial Recovery Act of 1933 guaranteed workers the right to organize and bargain collectively through representatives of their own choosing, free from interference or coercion. It thereby removed the fear of joining a union, which had been inherited from the past. When the National Industrial Recovery Act was declared unconstitutional by the Supreme Court a couple of years later, this right to organize and bargain collectively was picked up in 1935 and incorporated into what is still our basic piece of labor legislation — the National Labor Relations Act, commonly called the *Wagner Act.* In addition to assuring labor the right to organize and bargain collectively, the Wagner

Act set up a policing agency, the National Labor Relations Board, to guarantee labor its rights. No longer could an employer legally hire or fire on the basis of union membership or in other ways interfere with employees in the exercise of their guaranteed rights. Further, once the employees elected a union to represent them, the employer could not legally refuse to bargain collectively with that union representative. For a time, some employers simply disregarded the Wagner Act because they were told by eminent lawyers that the act was unconstitutional. This cloud was removed when the Supreme Court upheld the act in the spring of 1937, at which time most employers recognized that unions were here to stay and re-signed themselves to working with them when their employees insisted on having them.

The Congress of Industrial Organizations   Another major reason for the sharp rise in union membership during the 1930s is that unions vastly increased the scope of their membership drive. Until the mid-thirties the focus of organizational efforts remained the skilled craft worker and the craft union. As late as 1933, 72 percent of all organized workers were members of the American Federation of Labor. Increasingly, though, it was recognized that the craft union was ill-suited for organizing industrial workers. What is the particular skill of the worker who tightens nut number 417 as the Ford chassis moves by? Some labor leaders, especially in mining and clothing manufacturing, argued that a major opportunity was being missed by not setting up *industrial unions* — organizations that bring together all employees of a particular firm or industry regardless of their particular skills. When the American Federation of Labor refused to move fast enough to suit them, the dissidents pulled their unions out of the AFL and used them as a nucleus for a completely new labor federation based on the industrial principle of organization — the Congress of Industrial Organizations. It quickly moved into the mass-production indus-tries — automobiles, steel, farm machinery, rubber, and so on — and brought millions of unskilled and semiskilled workers into unions.

Consequences of unemployment   It would be going far beyond the scope of this work to describe all of the consequences of the Great Depres-sion for American workers. But since we are still living with some of those consequences in the form of New Deal legislation, several dimensions of the Great Depression must be examined. The first thing to notice is that the official unemployment rate serves very inadequately as a measure of the severity of unemployment. In the worst year of the depression, 1933, the official count was 12,830,000 unemployed — one out of four members of the labor force. But even if this count is accurate — and there are good reasons for believing that it missed many unemployed workers — it un-derstates the unemployment problem. Many of those counted as employed worked only part time. And many others worked at jobs for which they were overqualified, having been let go from jobs for which they were highly trained and forced to work at whatever they could find.

Even if the unemployment figures were not understated, they would represent a truly great burden for the nation. Natural resources and production facilities not used in one period can always be used at a later time, but labor services not used here and now are gone forever. One estimate is that had the idle workers of the 1930s been fully employed for the entire period, sufficient earnings would have been generated to provide a new home for every American family, with enough left over for a college education for every college-age youth of the period.

But this is merely the economic cost. The psychological cost, although impossible to measure, may have been far greater — the blighted careers, the trauma of endless days at home waiting for a job to open up, the feeling of rejection and worthlessness, the necessity to beg or borrow or steal. In the introduction to his *Hard Times, An Oral History of the Great Depression,* Studs Terkel sums up the typical reaction of the unemployed to their situations:

The suddenly-idle hands blamed themselves, rather than society. True, there were hunger marches and protestations to City Hall and Washington, but the millions experienced a private kind of shame when the pink slip came. No matter that others suffered the same fate, the inner voice whispered, "I'm a failure."

True, there was a sharing among many of the dispossessed, but, at close quarters, frustration became, at times, violence, and violence turned inward. Thus, sons and fathers fell away, one from the other. And the mother, seeking work, said nothing. Outside forces, except to the more articulate and political rebels, were in some vague way responsible, but not really. It was a personal guilt.[3]

Congress responded to this situation with two pieces of legislation that affected the whole of the labor force, not just the union sector. The first and more important was the Social Security Act of 1935. The act as finally passed contained three major provisions: (1) a compulsory federal retirement program, to be financed by a joint payroll tax on employees and employers in covered employments; (2) a combined federal-state program of unemployment insurance, financed by a payroll tax on employers; and (3) federal aid to the states in the form of matching funds for the care of certain needy persons (blind and physically handicapped, crippled children, widowed mothers with dependent children). Some of these provisions, it is apparent, were only slightly related to the depression. Once Congress decided to act it took the occasion to catch up with the European

---

[3] Studs Terkel, *Hard Times, An Oral History of the Great Depression,* Pantheon, New York, 1970, p. 5.

nations, several of which had set up comprehensive social security pro-grams many decades earlier. The Social Security Act established the rudiments of our present social security system, but the system has been much expanded since 1935.

Three years later, in 1938, Congress concerned itself with the terms under which labor could be employed, in the Fair Labor Standards Act. It is usually called the Wages and Hours bill because one of its major provisions established a national minimum wage (a floor under wages) and another set the forty-hour week as the maximum that could be worked without the payment of overtime wages (a ceiling over hours). A third section of the bill outlawed the use of child labor in establishments pro-ducing goods for interstate commerce.

Labor since World War II

As with all wars, World War II strengthened the hand of labor and increased the influence and drawing power of the unions. Union membership as a consequence jumped sharply during the war, from 8.9 million members (15.5 percent of the labor force) in 1940 to 15 million members (22 percent of the labor force) in 1950. From there the percentage of the labor force organized into unions inched upward to 25.5 percent in 1953, and then gardually slipped to a little less than 22 percent at the present time.

The primary reason for this slippage is fairly evident: major intersec-toral shifts within the economy. During the postwar period our output of manufactured goods has increased substantially. But thanks to labor-saving technology, employment in manufacturing and other goods-related industries, as Table 12.1 indicates, has come close to leveling off com-pletely. The significance of these figures lies in the fact that the goods-related industries provide most of the jobs for blue-collar workers, the most

the small society   by Brickman

TABLE 12.1
Nonagricultural employment, by industrial classification, 1950–1975

Year	Total nonagricultural employment (thousands)	Employment in goods-related industries (mining, construction, and manufacturing) (thousands)	% of total	Employment in service-related industries and all others (thousands)	% of total
1950	45,222	18,475	40.9	26,747	59.1
1955	50,675	20,476	40.4	30,199	59.6
1960	54,234	20,393	37.6	33,840	62.4
1965	60,815	21,880	36.0	38,936	64.0
1970	70,920	23,507	33.1	47,412	66.9
1975 (prel.)	76,080	21,950	28.9	54,130	71.1

Source: *Statistical Abstract of the United States,* 1975, p. 353.

easily organized. The service-related industries, on the other hand, are largely staffed by white-collar workers: teachers, government employees, clerks, salespeople. These historically have been the most difficult to organize. The unions have had success in organizing some groups of white-collar workers, especially government employees, but not enough to keep the overall percentage of the labor force that is organized from falling.

Another contributing factor could be the shift in emphasis of postwar labor legislation. Congress read the sentiment of the American people, probably correctly, as a conviction that the New Deal labor legislation went too far in the direction of guaranteeing labor's rights while restricting management's rights. As a consequence the only major piece of labor legislation passed since World War II, the Taft-Hartley Act, added safeguards against union encroachment on management's rights and set limits on certain types of union activities.

The Taft-Hartley Act (Labor Management Relations Act, 1947) modified the Wagner Act in a number of directions. One provision narrowed the form union representation could take. Until Taft-Hartley, union representation could take either of two major forms: closed shop or union shop. Both require union membership as a condition of continued employment where a union represents the workers. The *closed shop* however, requires union membership *before* an individual employment contract can be signed; the *union shop* requires it only *after* the signing of the contract. This appears to be a distinction without a difference, but employers argue that restricting their potential labor pool entirely to those already members of a union in effect makes the union, rather than the employer, the hiring agent. By outlawing the closed shop, the Taft-Hartley Act restored to management its historic right to hire. But the act went beyond this and placed even the union shop in jeopardy by stipulating that the union shop arrangement was permitted only where there were no state laws to the contrary. A not too subtle signal was thereby sent to state governments, encouraging them to pass "right to work" laws, which outlaw union shop contracts and guarantee that union membership cannot be a condition of employment. A number of states, mostly in the South, promptly did so. The Taft-Hartley Act also revived the hated labor injunction and authorized its use by the federal government to call off strikes, at least temporarily, where the public health or safety is threatened. Other provisions of the act sharply limited the use of the strike as a union weapon and set up a number of safeguards to protect members against their union leaders. The combined impact of all these provisions cannot be determined, but for union leaders the effects were sufficient to justify their referring to Taft-Hartley as the "slave labor law."

Another piece of post–World War II labor legislation, the Landrum-Griffin bill (Labor-Management Reporting and Disclosure Act of 1959), took one further step in the direction of labor reform. Far less sweeping than Taft-Hartley, its primary purpose, as its official name suggests, was to protect union members from corrupt union bosses by laying down stricter rules within which union leaders were forced to operate and requiring detailed reports of certain union procedures.

I THE IMPACT OF THE UNION I

After this tour through labor history, it is worth stopping to ask the question, What have been the consequences of the union movement? The question is not easy to answer. First of all, one of the major results of unionization cannot be measured. Throughout their history unions have sought not only economic gains for members but security against oppression by foremen and employers, protection against discriminatory discharge, and the establishment of a limited "right to the job" that can be challenged only on the grounds of inefficiency or insubordination. The labor contract — the collective bargaining agreement — lays down the ground rules for delivering this personal security package and also provides a local union representative in the form of the shop steward to see that the rules are observed by foremen and employers. The feeling of isolation and individual helplessness that came with the growth of big business has thus been reduced for union members. As Kenneth Boulding points out, "Much of the drive which leads people to join labor unions is the desire to be able to look the 'boss' squarely in the eye as an equal. . . ."[4]

But what about the material benefits delivered by the unions? Can't they be measured? They can in principle, but in practice the task has proved to be extremely difficult. It is not possible merely to compare wages and other benefits in companies or industries that are organized against similar compensation packages where no unions exist and assume that the presence of the union explains the entire difference. Some jobs would be high-wage jobs, and others would be low-wage jobs — whether or not the workers were represented by unions. This is because some workers are simply more productive than other workers, thanks to better training or better equipment and technology provided them. The fact that they produce more makes it possible for employers to pay them more — union or no union. Over the long haul of American economic development, in fact, it is this increase in labor productivity, as measured by output per man-day or man-year, that goes further than any other single factor in explaining the rise in labor's real income. The old saw about blood out of a turnip applies fully here.

---

[4] Kenneth E. Boulding, *The Organizational Revolution: A Study in the Ethics of Economic Organization,* Quadrangle, Chicago, 1968, p. 205.

But it doesn't explain everything. Just because an employer is in a position to pay higher wages does not mean that higher wages will actually be paid. The employer may simply let the rising worker productivity ride through in the form of higher profit margins. Only if the union is there with the power to demand that the workers' share of rising productivity be paid in the form of higher wages will there be reasonable certainty that wages will indeed rise. In a recent study economist H. G. Lewis attempted to identify the wage differential attributable to the exercise of union power. He found the difference extraordinary in some industries at certain times (50 percent in bituminous coal mining in 1956–1957) and quite modest at other times (less than 5 percent for common labor in building construction in the late 1950s). On the whole, Lewis surmises, union wage rates exceeded nonunion rates as follows:[5]

Period	Percentage
1923–1929	15–20
1931–1933	Over 25
1939–1941	10–20
1945–1949	0–5
1957–1958	10–15

If we take a midpoint of the 10–15 percent range of advantage for union wages over nonunion wages, say 12 percent, and multiply the average wage for 1957–1958 by that figure, we come up with an income differential of around $600. Average union dues at that time were around $50. So for a $50 investment the average union member got a return of $600.

This is not the whole story, of course. Unions in many cases have forced wages up, not just by the amount that labor productivity has increased, but far beyond the rise in output per man-hour. This has to mean that the labor cost per unit of output must rise — as indeed it has, as Table 12.2 shows. During the period 1947 to 1969 output per man-hour just about exactly doubled, compensation per man-hour somewhat more than tripled, and the labor cost per unit of output was forced up by a little over two-thirds. To keep their profit margins from falling as unit labor costs rose, employers simply passed the rising labor costs on to the buyers of their products. We have here, then, at least a partial explanation of the post–World War II rise in the price level.

And this is not all. To the extent that employers cannot pass wage costs forward, they may have to let workers go, increasing the overall unemployment rate. Union leaders must therefore be careful lest they price their members out of jobs. Even if rising labor costs can be passed forward

[5] H. G. Lewis, *Unionism and Relative Wages in the United States,* University of Chicago Press, Chicago, 1963, p. 193. © 1963 by The University of Chicago. Cited in Davis et al., *American Economic Growth,* Harper & Row, New York, 1972, p. 227.

TABLE 12.2

Indexes of output per man-hour, compensation per man-hour, and unit labor cost, 1947 and 1969

Year	Output per man-hour (1958 = 100)	Compensation per man-hour (1967 = 100)	Unit labor cost (1967 = 100)
1947	68.7	36.2	70.6
1969	136.4	115.6	118.9

Source: *Historical Statistics of the United States,* 1975, pp. 162–163.

in the form of higher prices, employers are provided with a further incentive to replace their now higher-priced labor with machinery of some sort. Such technological unemployment is often cited as one explanation for the gradual rise of the unemployment level since World War II.

I UNEMPLOYMENT I

Unions and their wage policies may have to shoulder some of the blame for unemployment in the United States, but the overall performance of the economy is of far greater consequence. Long before unions rose to a position of influence, the American economy delivered enough jobs to go around only on rare occasions. During the seventeen years immediately preceding our entry into World War I, unemployment dropped below 4 percent of the nonfarm labor force only once. It averaged over 10.5 percent for the period as a whole.[6] Armed with more sophisticated analytical and control tools and the determination to maintain high levels of employment, we have done a far better job in limiting unemployment in the years since World War II than in any earlier period. Even so, unemployment has been at or below the 4 percent full-employment level in only ten of the thirty-two postwar years through 1977. And so long as inflation remains a problem and we must trade employment for price stability, the future promises no improvement over the past.

Because unemployment has been and will likely continue to be a problem, it is worthwhile to spend a moment seeing how we go about measuring it. We will see that it is no simple matter to get a measure that commands anywhere near universal agreement. In fact, the federal government has not yet found such a measure. Some economists insist that the official count considerably overstates the true dimensions of the un-

[6] *Historical Statistics of the United States,* 1975, p. 126.

employment problem, while others argue at least as convincingly that the official count includes only a fraction of the unemployed.

Each month the federal government provides a numerical breakdown showing what each member of the working-age population (sixteen years and older) did during the previous month. Each person in this noninstitutional population is grouped into one of the categories listed in Table 12.3. The accuracy of the specific numbers is not a major issue, in spite of the fact that they are sophisticated guesses. Less than a moment's thought tells us that the numbers cannot represent actual counts. A monthly count would be an impossible undertaking. What the Bureau of the Census, the federal agency charged with collecting the numbers, actually does is take a scientific sample each month. Someone in one out of about every 1,300 households in the country is asked about the activities during the previous week of all members of the household. How many in school? How many working? How many out of work? How many not interested in outside employment? One in 1,300 households seems like a very small sample, but it is up to fifty times larger than that used by the national public opinion polls. Carefully handled, a very small sample can accurately describe a very large population.

The controversy surrounding the employment survey, then, does not center on sampling techniques. It is concerned primarily with the pigeonholing process. The logic of the classification scheme laid out in Table 12.3 appears sharp and clear-cut. Those who neither work nor look for work are not in the labor force (housewives, students, retired and disabled persons). Those at work are employed. And those out of work and looking for work are unemployed. But things are not really this clear at all. Is a housewife who is not actively looking for work but who would willingly take a job if one were offered really not in the labor force, as the Census Bureau

TABLE 12.3
Employment status of the population, June 1977
(millions of persons 16 years old and older)

(1) Total noninstitutional population	158.5
(2) Less: Not in labor force	58.7
(3) Total labor force	99.8
(4) Less: Members of armed forces	2.2
(5) Civilian labor force	97.6
(6) Employed	90.6
(7) Unemployed	7.0
(8) Unemployment rate (7 divided by 5)	7.1%

Source: *Federal Reserve Bulletin* (August 1977), A47.

enumerator classifies her? Is a man who works a single hour for pay during the census week really employed, as the Census Bureau says? Isn't he more like $\frac{39}{40}$ unemployed? Is a person no longer either unemployed or in the labor force because after pounding the pavements for months he decides no jobs are available and quits looking? On the other side of the ledger, should we not at some point reclassify from unemployed to not in the labor force the worker who draws unemployment compensation and refuses as unsuitable every job that comes along? And what if he, a skilled machinist, out of desperation takes a job as floor sweeper? Is he now fully employed?

There are no easy answers to these questions. Just listing them, however, suggests that it is easy to find fault with whatever the Census Bureau does. Those who oppose a more active government role in promoting employment can argue that because we should really be concerned with the employment status of the male breadwinner in the family, we therefore should not be unduly alarmed if the unemployment rate rises as a result of housewives and teenagers coming into the labor market in ever-increasing numbers to supplement an already high family income. Those who favor vigorous government action, on the other hand, ask the obvious question, why should anyone in the United States who for any reason wants to work be denied the opportunity to do so? And they are equally concerned with the systematic undercounting of the unemployed. Officially recognizing the discouraged unemployed worker and the unemployment reflected in part-time jobs or unskilled jobs for skilled workers would raise the unemployment rate by several percentage points. And even that rate, because it is an average, would provide scanty indication of the true severity of the unemployment problem for many groups in the economy. The official unemployment rate of 7.5 percent in February 1977 did not show that 13.1 percent of the members of minority groups were unemployed. Or that 18.5 percent of teenagers were unemployed. Or that 8.7 percent of blue-collar workers were unemployed, compared with only 4.6 percent for white-collar workers.[7] Nor that — to put it in terms of a recent *Wall Street Journal* headline — "To Many Ghetto Blacks a Steady Job Becomes Only a Distant Hope,"[8] with one consequence of this a soaring crime rate.

| COLLECTIVE BARGAINING |

The major function of the union is to secure a better bargain with the employer for workers than the workers could secure for themselves individually — this is the function of *collective bargaining*. This does not mean

[7] *Survey of Current Business* (March 1977), 5–13.
[8] *Wall Street Journal* (November 15, 1976), 1.

that some workers at some times might not do better for themselves than the union contract provides. But it must mean, if the union is to be supported by its members, that workers in the aggregate must feel that the union delivers more than it costs. A simple majority of the workers is all that is required to vote in a union as a collective bargaining representative, and that same majority can always vote it out in favor of either individual bargaining or some other union. This necessity of union representatives to keep their members satisfied is probably the single most important constraint on union leaders in the collective bargaining process.

With over a hundred unions negotiating thousands of labor contracts each year, it is obviously impossible in brief compass to describe the ins and outs of the bargaining process. All that is possible is to outline the general framework and provide some of the flavor of that process. And the first thing to notice is that the collective bargaining agreement is indeed collective, in two different senses of that term. On the basis of the principle that "in union there is strength," the union bargains in the name of all the workers. It offers the employer or employers an all-or-none arrangement: Take all the workers on terms to be negotiated or take none at all. And when those terms are arranged, they are arranged for all workers collectively. No individual worker can opt out of the terms if he or she doesn't like them or attempt to do better on a solo basis.

The collective bargaining agreement, then, is a joint labor contract for all the workers in the bargaining unit. That unit may include only some of a company's workers, where different groups of workers are represented by different (usually craft) unions; all of a company's workers; or all of several companies' workers in the case of industrywide bargaining. Contracts may be for any chosen period of time, but they are usually for a single year, although two- or even three-year contracts are not uncommon.

Many months before the contract expires both the unions and management start preparing for a replacement contract. Union meetings focus on the inadequacies of the current contract, and by the time negotiating sessions begin the union negotiators have a firm idea of what their membership will accept. Management negotiators confer with company officers and decide on the limits within which an agreement can be reached.

Negotiations begin early enough to permit reaching agreement on all issues before the old contract expires, although there appears to be a tendency for deliberations to be rather slow-paced until the strike deadline approaches. The issues on which negotiations take place can be extremely diverse, since union negotiators see the field as wide open for discussion of every managerial action that directly affects the welfare of their membership or the strength and security of the union. Management representatives, needless to say, insist that there are certain rights and privileges that have always belonged to management and are therefore nonnegotiable. What usually comes out of the bargaining session is agreement on each of the following points:

1 The basic structure of the agreement: duration of the contract and method of extending or renewing it, prevention of strikes for the life of the agreement, handling of grievances arising under the contract

2 Status and rights of the union and management: recognition of the union, voluntary or compulsory union membership, company participation in collection of union dues, union activity on company time or property, rights reserved for management

3 Job tenure and job security: handling of hiring and discharge, promotion and transfer, layoff and re-employment, calculation and application of seniority (length of service) rights

4 Work routines: standard workday and workweek, payment for overtime, provision for holidays and vacations, work speeds, working conditions (health, safety, sanitation, heating and lighting, ventilation), production methods

5 Amount and method of compensation: basic wage schedule, changes in the schedule, method of wage payment, indirect or supplementary wage payments (pensions, health and welfare funds, supplementary unemployment benefit plans)

Although we usually think that a struggle over money lies at the heart of the collective bargaining process, the list suggests that issues other than money may dominate the deliberations. It is often far easier to agree on the financial terms of the contract than on rights and privileges of the two parties involved. The union usually knows pretty well how much management can afford to pay and can be forced to pay, and management negotiators usually are well aware of what the membership is demanding of the union negotiators. But rights and privileges — such as union security and management's right to hire and fire — are entirely nonpecuniary, yet may be defended to the last ditch since each side may see them as necessary to its very existence.

And what if agreement cannot be reached? Then, of course, comes the strike, labor's ultimate weapon. Just as it is said that war is diplomacy continued by other methods, so the strike is bargaining continued by another means. Without the strike threat unions might continue to exist, as they do in the Soviet Union, and carry out a sort of combined personnel management and grievance function, but their efficacy in collective bargaining would drop to near zero. Without at least the threat of a complete and concerted withdrawal of their labor force, employers would have little incentive to concede to the demands of the unions.

The very threat of a strike, which is costly both for union members and the employer, is usually enough to bring agreement during the time allowed for collective bargaining. Sometimes the two parties start so far apart that the gap cannot be completely narrowed by the strike deadline. A strike and its financial drain are necessary to make compromise possible. And sometimes strikes result from simple miscalculation. Bargaining, after all, involves bluff and deception, threat and counterthreat. With all the strategies of gamesmanship involved, it is easy to make irretrievable mistakes.

But when all is said and done, an amazing proportion of collective bargaining sessions are successfully concluded without resort to strikes. During the seven years 1967 through 1973, for example, there were an average of a little over 5,000 work stoppages in the United States, lasting about three to four weeks. In no one of these years, however, did these involve as many as 5 percent of all employed workers or cause the loss of as much as one-half of 1 percent of a year's working time.[9] In all, not a very high price to pay for an integral part of the American collective bargaining system.

I   ON MAKING WORK MEANINGFUL   I

What goes into the collective bargaining process is determined to a large degree by the attitudes of workers toward their jobs and toward their employers. These attitudes in turn are closely related: The more satisfied workers are with their jobs, the more kindly disposed they are likely to be toward their employers and the more moderate the demands they will make of them. Recognizing this, employers have devoted an extraordinary amount of time and money in recent years trying to find out what makes workers dissatisfied with their jobs and what can be done about it. From these studies have come a significant number of experimental programs, some of which have been so successful in improving worker satisfaction and performance that they have far more than recovered their costs. A few of these will be examined later. Other studies, though, suggest that in many cases there is little the individual employer can do to alter the way the worker regards his employment. Either necessary changes in employment conditions would be so expensive as to be prohibitive, or it is determined that the attitude of the worker is conditioned more by the way society views work than by the worker's on-the-job experience. This latter point is bound up with the questions as to whether or not the work ethic is disappearing.

Attitudes toward work

General attitudes toward work have indeed changed over the centuries. We have little evidence from the workers themselves in earlier periods as to what they thought about the world of work. Workers don't write histories. But the histories that have been written agree that work and the role of

---

[9] *Statistical Abstract of the United States,* 1975, p. 373.

workers were not highly regarded in earlier eras. Speaking for the Greek world in which he lived, Aristotle recognized the necessity of work to satisfy survival needs but insisted that the ideal life was one of leisure. Leisure meant, not idleness, but activity pursued free of compulsion — music, for example, or contemplation. Those forced to work, by contrast, were rewarded for their efforts by being placed at the very bottom of the social order. Work was the mark of a slave.

The world of early Christianity appears at first glance to mark a departure from this point of view. Christian writings stress the dignity as well as the necessity of work. But there was far more of the latter than the former. The New Testament is a prolonged incitement to "work with your own hands." And St. Paul laid down the rule that if any man would not work, neither should he eat. Of greater significance, however, in indicating the true attitude toward work during this period is the fact that toil, according to the Bible, was a curse imposed upon men and women as a symbol of their banishment from God. There was no work, after all, in the Garden of Eden. And the work of this life was of little consequence compared with the spiritual work of preparing to face God. This world was only a passage to a better one, in which there would be no work.

All this changed with the Renaissance and Reformation. The ferment of new ideas associated with the Renaissance helped to alter the curse-of-work concept. The right of a few to enjoy a life of leisure supported by the many began to be questioned. The possibility of altering the world for the better through systematic effort encouraged a more positive attitude toward work. But it was the Protestant Reformation that had the most profound impact in replacing the view that work was solely a temporary curse with the idea that it was the important first concern of life. Work became the rightful duty of all, and leisure, now defined as idleness, became the worst sin. This is the concept that has come down to us as the *work ethic* or the *Protestant ethic*. From John Calvin down through Benjamin Franklin, John Wesley, and Horatio Alger, workers have been constantly reminded of their duty to labor for God and their brother men.

From many sources today, however, comes word that the Protestant ethic is dead, or at least dying. Absenteeism, labor turnover, the call to drop out of society, early retirements — all these and more are taken as indications that workers no longer see productive effort as their first concern. Yet it is entirely possible that the announced demise of the work ethic is premature. First of all, there is the distinct possibility that the hold of the work ethic in the past has been exaggerated. When it was a matter of working in order to eat, it required no ethical code to explain why men worked, and worked hard. Working less today, and working less hard, may simply be a function of rising affluence. Since it is no longer necessary to labor so long or so hard to provide for basic necessities, workers are not subject to the same compulsions as previously.

On the other hand it is possible that the incentive to work is still as strong as ever but the rewards of working are less. Most commonly cited in this connection is the "dehumanization" of an increasing number of jobs as a consequence of greater and greater specialization and division of labor. *Division of labor* in the form of distribution of tasks, crafts, or specialties of production has been known through all recorded history. What the Industrial Revolution added to this social division of labor, or division by occupation, was a manufacturing or workshop division of labor. The difference between these two can perhaps be made clear by citing Adam Smith's classical example of pin making. Having a group of workers specialized in the making of pins would, of course, be an example of social division of labor. But even by 1776, as Adam Smith makes clear, pin making had gone far beyond this in the division of labor:

In the way in which this business is now carried on, not only the whole work is a peculiar trade, but it is divided into a number of branches, of which the greater part are likewise peculiar trades. One man draws out the wire, another straights it, a third cuts it, a fourth points it, a fifth grinds it at the top for receiving the head; to make the head requires two or three distinct operations; to put it on, is a peculiar business, to whiten the pins is another; it is even a trade by itself to put them into the paper; and the important business of making a pin is, in this manner, divided into about eighteen distinct operations, which, in some manufactories, are all performed by distinct hands. . . .[10]

The consequence of this manufacturing or workshop division of labor is a vast "improvement in the productive powers of labour, and the greater part of the skill, dexterity, and judgment with which it is any where directed, or applied, seem to have been the effects of the division of labour."[11] In the case just cited, Smith doubts that a worker laboring alone could turn out as many as 20 pins a day; as a specialized member of a pin-making team, though, his share of a day's production was around 4,800 pins.

Smith accounts for this spectacular increase in output resulting from the detailed division of labor by citing three consequences of such division of labor: (1) the increase in dexterity that comes with "reducing every man's business to some one simple operation, and . . . making this operation the sole employment of his life"; (2) the saving of time commonly lost in shifting from one type of work to another; and (3) the impetus provided for the invention of machines to facilitate the application of labor or reduce the amount of labor time required.[12] To this, need be added only

---

[10] Adam Smith, *The Wealth of Nations,* reprint ed., Modern Library, New York, 1937, pp. 4–5.
[11] Smith, *The Wealth of Nations,* p. 3.
[12] Smith, *The Wealth of Nations,* p. 7.

one additional factor and we have the whole logic of the division of labor carried to its natural conclusion in modern factories and offices. This is the opportunity provided the employer of purchasing only the precise quantities of skills or muscle power necessary for each process. Economist John R. Commons showed how this applied in the first American assembly-line (or perhaps better, disassembly line) industry, the meatpacking conveyor:

It would be difficult to find another industry where division of labor has been so ingeniously and microscopically worked out. The animal has been surveyed and laid off like a map; and the men have been classified in over thirty specialties and twenty rates of pay, from 16 cents to 50 cents an hour. The 50-cent man is restricted to using the knife on the most delicate parts of the hide (floorman) or to using the ax in splitting the backbone (splitter); and wherever a less-skilled man can be slipped in at 18 cents, $18\frac{1}{2}$ cents, 20 cents, 21 cents, $22\frac{1}{2}$ cents, 24 cents, 25 cents, and so on, a place is made for him, and an occupation mapped out. In working on the hide alone there are nine positions, at eight different rates of pay. A 20-cent man pulls off the tail, a $22\frac{1}{2}$-cent man pounds off another part where good leather is not found, and the knife of the 40-cent man cuts a different texture and has a different "feel" from that of the 50-cent man.[13]

While there can be little doubt that this detailed division of labor both vastly increased production and reduced costs and prices, it is an open question still as to what it did to the workers involved. Adam Smith, all the while lauding the value of division of labor in terms of increasing production, had grave reservations about what it would do to the workers employed:

The man whose whole life is spent in performing a few simple operations, of which the effects too are, perhaps, always the same, or very nearly the same, has no occasion to exert his understanding, or to exercise his invention in finding out expedients for removing difficulties which never occur. He naturally loses, therefore, the habit of such exertion, and generally becomes as stupid and ignorant as it is possible for a human creature to become.[14]

The nineteenth-century writer John Ruskin put the case far more dramatically:

We have much studied and perfected, of late, the great civilised invention of the division of labour; only we give it a false name. It is not, truly speaking, the labour

---

[13] John R. Commons, "Labor Conditions in Meat Packing," *Quarterly Journal of Economics*, 19 (1904–1905), 3.

[14] Smith, *The Wealth of Nations*, p. 734.

that is divided; but the men: — Divided into mere segments of men — broken into small fragments and crumbs of life. . . . the great cry that rises from all our manufacturing cities, louder than the furnace blast, is all in very deed for this, — that we manufacture everything there except men.[15]

And from there it's but a short step down to Lordstown, Ohio, and the General Motors Vega plant:

It was boring, monotonous work. I was an inspector and I didn't actually shoot the screws or tighten the bolts or anything like that. A guy could be there eight hours and there was some other body doing the same job over and over, all day long, all week long, all year long. Years. If you thought about it you'd go stir. People are unique animals. They are able to adjust. Jesus Christ! Can you imagine squeezing the trigger of a gun while it's spotted so many times? You count the spots, the same count, the same job, job after job after job. It's got to drive a guy nuts. . . .

The guys are not happy here. They don't come home thinking, Boy, I did a great job today and I can't wait to get back tomorrow. That's not the feeling at all. I don't think he thinks a blasted thing about the plant until he comes back. He's not concerned at all if the product's good, bad, or indifferent.

Their idea is not to run the plant. I don't think they'd know what to do with it. They don't want to tell the company what to do, but simply have something to say about what *they're* going to do. They just want to be treated with dignity. That's not asking a hell of a lot.[16]

This was Lordstown, and the eruptions among the younger, better-educated workers there made headlines across the country. But does this necessarily mean that discontent with work is becoming general, or was Lordstown a special case? A conclusive answer is not easy to find. Evidence can be cited to support either point of view. Gallup pollsters found some decline in worker satisfaction in the early 1970s, but as late as 1973, as Table 12.4 indicates, over three-quarters of workers polled were satisfied with the work they did, and only 11 percent were dissatisfied. And even the small proportion of those polled who were dissatisfied may have been taking out on their jobs the frustration they felt when, in a period of high inflation, their jobs in many cases failed to deliver additional earnings as rapidly as prices were rising.

Scattered evidence from a wide variety of other sources, however, tells a different story from the Gallup Poll results. Rising absenteeism,

---

[15] John Ruskin, *The Stones of Venice, Vol. II: The Sea-Stories,* Merrill and Baker, New York, n.d., pp. 165–166.
[16] Studs Terkel, *Working,* Avon Books, New York, 1975, pp. 258–259, 264–265. Report of an interview with president of Lordstown local, United Auto Workers.

TABLE 12.4

Work satisfaction according to the Gallup poll

(QUESTION: "ON THE WHOLE, WOULD YOU SAY YOU ARE SATISFIED OR DISSATISFIED WITH THE WORK YOU DO?")

Year	Satisfied (%)	Dissatisfied (%)	No opinion (%)
1949	67	20	13
1963	85	11	4
1965	82	13	5
1966	86	8	6
1969	87	7	6
1971	84	9	7
1973	77	11	12

Source: *Congressional Record* (daily edition), April 30, 1973, p. S7942.

tardiness, disciplinary problems, increased willingness to strike, even sabotage — all of these are reported with ever-greater frequency in accounts of blue-collar workers' behavior. And these examples can be matched with symptoms of discontent among white-collar workers, particularly clerical workers. During the period 1960–1972, for example, while overall union membership increased by 15 percent, white-collar union membership increased by 57 percent.[17] Some interviewers and pollsters have attempted to get a measure of this dissatisfaction in a roundabout fashion. Instead of the question, "Are you satisfied with your job?" — which inevitably suggests a counter question, "Satisfied relative to what? Unemployment?" — workers are asked whether or not they would choose similar work again. The answers to such a question, as Table 12.5 shows, disclose a good deal of dissatisfaction among both blue-collar and nonprofessional white-collar workers.

Follow-up studies have indicated that while *extrinsic factors* — pay, vacation time, and working conditions — have some role to play in explaining worker dissatisfaction, the nature of the job itself is the most important determinant of worker satisfaction. The competence of supervisors, the amount of on-the-job independence, and the opportunity fully to use and develop skills are all related closely to overall job satisfaction. In essence, these suggest that the idea should be to design work to fit people, rather than the other way round, as has been the case since the early days of scientific management.

---

[17] *Statistical Abstract of the United States,* 1975, p. 371.

aximum
337
ON MAKING WORK MEANINGFUL

TABLE 12.5
Percentage of workers saying they would choose similar work again

Occupation	%	Occupation	%
PROFESSIONAL AND WHITE-COLLAR		SKILLED TRADES AND BLUE-COLLAR	
Urban university professors	93	Skilled printers	52
Mathematicians	91	Paper workers	42
Physicists	89	Skilled auto workers	41
Biologists	89	Skilled steelworkers	41
Chemists	86	Textile workers	31
Firm lawyers	85	Blue-collar workers	24
School superintendents	85	Unskilled steelworkers	21
Lawyers	83	Unskilled auto workers	16
Journalists (Washington correspondents)	82		
Church university professors	77		
Solo lawyers	75		
White-collar workers (nonprofessional)	43		

Source: Robert L. Kahn, "The Work Module: A Proposal for the Humanization of Work," in *Work and the Quality of Life: Resource Papers for Work in America*, ed. James O'Toole, M.I.T. Press, Cambridge, 1974, p. 204.

And this is exactly what personnel engineers have been arguing at least since the 1950s. Perhaps the most renowned proponent of this point of view has been Abraham Maslow. In his *Motivation and Personality,* published in 1954, Maslow insisted that all workers, simply because they are human beings and not machines, have needs going far beyond mere maintenance. They do have the latter, of course, since anything else would be of no moment if physical and survival needs — food, shelter, clothing — were not met. When these needs are satisfied, however, higher-order needs come into play. These are the social needs, such as recognition and acceptance by peers. And when these are satisfied yet another layer of needs appears: self-realization and spiritual development. Frustration and discontent come with failure to satisfy needs at any level in the hierarchy; the most enduring satisfaction can be achieved only by providing for the basic, social, and higher-order individual needs simultaneously.

Maslow's ideas, and similar ones proposed by other industrial psychologists, have been extended and tested in numerous experimental settings during the last several decades. They are the basis for a wide variety of work reform proposals. Especially in the form of Douglas McGregor's "Theories X and Y," they have provided practical alternatives for managers. In his *The Human Side of Enterprise,* McGregor labeled the traditional management style *Theory X.* This holds that workers inherently dislike work; can be motivated only by coercion, control, and punishment; like security; and prefer limited responsibility. *Theory Y,* not surprisingly, assumes just the opposite: that workers naturally desire work and responsibility and are best motivated by being assigned challenging work that uses their capabilities fully. From the latter and similar systems comes a basic model for improving work:

1 Jobs should give each individual the opportunity to use broad and varied skills, and tasks of meaningful size.

2 Jobs should allow the individual as much responsibility and autonomy as is feasible, without imposing too much rigid supervision.

3 Workplaces should offer an integrated social environment with room for personal interaction.[18]

Changes in the workplace

Carried into the workplace, these operating principles have led to many possibly irreversible changes in the relationships of workers to their jobs and of management to workers. The changes are too numerous to describe in detail, but they can be grouped under these headings:

Participative management   Management has suddenly discovered that workers have capabilities and knowledge that go untapped when orders simply come down from on high. Not only this. Taking advantage of these capabilities and knowledge ties the workers into the company's goals. Their self-realization is achieved in the process of their identifying themselves with the company's success. Everybody gains.

Many techniques have been tried with various degrees of success. The oldest and simplest is the suggestion box. One step beyond this are organized efforts where, through exhortation or classroom orientation or discussion, an attempt is made to force a closer identification between individual and company interests. One way to show that the company cares is to relabel foremen or supervisors as team leaders — as near-equals. The ultimate extension of this idea is to establish autonomous work groups. Here small production units are formed and given authority within established limits to set their own quotas, work methods, job assignments, and even pay rates. Typically workers have responded to this grant of autonomy by enlarging their output — partly to prove that they are worthy of the company's trust, partly because their jobs are more interesting and challenging.

---

[18] Sar A. Levitan and William B. Johnston, *Work Is Here to Stay, Alas,* Olympus Publishing, Salt Lake City, Utah, 1973, p. 124.

Job and career enrichment   In a sense, all the innovations described above with the exception of the last are still basically devices to fit the worker to the job. Job enrichment suggests the reverse: to adapt the job to individual interests and capabilities. One way to do this is to reverse the drive of the last 200 years to achieve the greatest possible division of labor. The end of that road has too often been boredom and, as Adam Smith feared, stupid and ignorant workers — not stupid and ignorant by nature, but made stupid and ignorant by lack of challenge. The final stage in the division of labor is the assembly line, which often brings, as Table 12.5 suggests, the greatest degree of worker dissatisfaction. A gradual, halting move is now underway away from assembly-line manufacture toward benchwork or team assembly. Both of the two leading Swedish automobile manufacturers, Saab and Volvo, now merged into one company, are in the process of giving up the assembly line. The assembly work is being taken over by teams or groups, each of which is given considerable leeway in deciding how to allocate and rotate work among its members, as well as to set the pace at which the work is performed. Each worker has the opportunity to learn and do several jobs and to identify his or her effort with a larger segment of the completed automobile.

In non-assembly-line jobs a rearrangement of tasks is taking place. Instead of assigning workers to perform one simple task day after day, work assignments are now being rotated. One day a worker may have a boring and undesirable assignment, but he or she can look forward to a more pleasant and creative assignment shortly. Along with this task rotation often comes job rotation. Under this arrangement workers are urged to continue learning new jobs, even to the point where they have mastered all the jobs on the floor and can shift readily from one to another. Starting as a carburetor specialist in a motor manufacturing plant, for example, a worker can end up being a motor specialist, competent not just in carburetor work but in all other aspects of motor manufacture. This general principle is now being applied on a more limited basis as highly specialized, simple jobs are converted into broader, more complex career opportunities. What is lost in the division of labor, it is hoped, will be more than regained through greater worker satisfaction and consequently greater worker effort.

Humanization   A wide variety of experiments in workplace conditions are now under way, based on recognition, finally, of the fact that the worker is a responsible human being. To give the worker more discretion in the performance of his or her duties, rigid rules and standards are going by the boards. The hated time clock is disappearing. The physical separation of workers from management is being eliminated by the establishment of common dining, lavatory, and parking facilities for management and workers. In some cases workers are put on the same pay basis as management, with salaries replacing hourly wages. And the old rules against talking with fellow workers during working hours are now being dropped. In fact, in some cases workplaces are deliberately being rearranged to permit and encourage social interaction — by the installation of circular benchwork arrangements, for example.

The area of greatest activity at the moment in matching jobs to worker interests is the overhaul of the standard workweek. A number of variations in the eight-to-five, Monday-through-Friday pattern are being tried. In some companies workers are working ten-hour days but only four days a week. This gives them a three-day weekend. In other cases workers still must put in eight-hour days, but they are given considerable flexibility in when they begin and end their days. This has some spillover benefits for urban communities since rush-hour congestion is reduced. Finally, management is taking a more tolerant position today when workers want to take time off for personal reasons. Excused absences increasingly take the place of unexcused absences.

Limitations of job reform

The foregoing may suggest a far greater scope for the *job enlargement* or *job enrichment* movement than is currently the case. To the present point no more than just over 150 American firms have been engaged in any sort of comprehensive program of job revision. Reports from these firms, however, are strongly positive. In most cases, worker productivity has shot upward, permitting savings not only in labor costs but ultimately in capital costs as well because fewer workers need to be employed and less space is necessary to house them. But the skeptics insist that *ultimately* may be a long time coming: that the short-run fruits of change may not be harvestable in the long run. What may be at work here is a *Hawthorne effect,* in which workers show a burst of enthusiasm for work reform, improve their performance, but gradually slip back to the old level as new routines become standard routine.

The term *Hawthorne effect* comes from experiments in work redesign conducted at the Hawthorne plant of the Western Electric Company, starting in 1927. In order to study the incidence of fatigue and monotony associated with the assembly of telephone relays, five women workers were selected and observed carefully under different working conditions. A number of the modern innovations were tried: variation in the length of the working day and the number of working days in the week, introduction of rest pauses, changing the temperature of the work space, encouragement of conversation, and so on. When the experiment was concluded in 1932 and performance results analyzed they "illustrate[d] the futility of attending exclusively to the economic motivation of workers, or to their physical conditions of work. These things are of high importance; but no group of workers can be expected to remain satisfied, or to co-operate effectively unless their social organization and sentiments are also protected."[19] What the study showed in particular was a sharp spurt in productivity, almost regardless of physical working conditions, when management demonstrated an interest in a group of workers. The increase in productivity, however, was short-lived, and the workers soon slipped back to their former pace. In this case, though, changes were imposed on the workers, who had no hand in the decision-making process. If job redesign involves worker participation in decision making, there is at least the hope that productivity increases will be long lasting. It is too early to tell. If the early productivity improvements are not sustained, it is reasonable to expect a drift back to previous conditions. Business firms, after all, are not in business to make workers' lives more satisfying; their primary purpose remains that of increasing their profits, in this situation by reducing their labor costs. Some failures of the new departures have already been reported, leading to their abandonment. Many others may prove less auspicious on second examination than on the first: There is a human tendency for experimenters to overestimate positive results and disregard negative consequences.

Finally, there is a limit to changes in work procedures possible in a technological, mass-production society. In the first place, a huge capital investment is required in most cases to change manufacturing jobs significantly, since the nature of those jobs has been determined by the plant and equipment accumulated over the years. Even beyond this, at some point, as we have seen, the logic "of enlarging jobs, increasing skills,

the small society   by Brickman

© Washington Star Syndicate, Inc., permission granted by King Features Syndicate, Inc., 1977.

[19] L. J. Henderson et al., "The Effects of Social Environment," in *Papers on the Science of Administration,* ed. Luther Gulick and L. Urwick, Institute of Public Administration, New York, 1937, p. 149.

lengthening job cycles, or rotating tasks runs head on into the logic which dictated division of labor in the first place. . . . Specialization may be costly in terms of satisfaction, but it is cheap in terms of production."[20] Unions have yet to throw their weight behind the work reform proposals, perhaps put off by the fact "that 80 percent of 150 firms currently conducting experiments designed to 'enlarge' and 'enrich' work were nonunion."[21]

One personnel specialist, after surveying the whole field of worker discontent in a highly industrialized, mass-production society, comes to a rather gloomy assessment of the more-or-less cosmetic changes that have so far been made to cope with the problem of worker discontent:

A boring job is a boring job, but some adjust to it more easily than others. All of a sudden, businessmen, economists, and politicans have begun to talk about job enrichment as the remedy for a host of maladies — even as a means of improving our balance of payments. It is not clear that all workers want job enrichment or that job enrichment alone, without increased wages, increased promotional opportunities, and a higher social status for blue-collar work would resolve the blue-collar dissatisfaction that does exist. Job enrichment may also require redesigning production processes and may reduce technological efficiency. Further, it may necessitate a revamping (inevitably upwards) of our pay scales, restraining of management, and possibly a reduction in the rigidity of our seniority rules. After these costs are deducted, the net advantage of job enrichment, either to our economy or to our remaining society, may be low.[22]

I SUMMARY I

In a market society the focus of economic activity is on the end product — consumer goods and services. Workers and their needs are given consideration only to the extent that this leads to increased production. Recent years, however, have seen the growth of concern with workers as workers.

Labor unions, of course, have always been concerned with the interests of their members. But unions in the United States developed slowly. As late as the beginning of the twentieth century no more than 3 percent of American workers were organized into unions. Membership grew rapidly once the right to organize and bargain collectively was guaranteed by law, but even today fewer than one worker in four is a union member.

---

[20] Levitan and Johnston, *Work Is Here to Stay, Alas,* p. 147.

[21] Ivar Berg, "The End of the Protestant Ethic and All That," in *Work and the Quality of Life,* ed. O'Toole, p. 38.

[22] George Strauss, "Is There a Blue-Collar Revolt Against Work?" in *Work and the Quality of Life,* ed. O'Toole, p. 65.

Evaluation of the impact of the union is difficult, partly because unions provide some noneconomic benefits, such as greater personal security. As for the purely economic benefits, in particular higher wages, studies show that unions likely provide benefits that considerably exceed membership dues.

One thing unions cannot deliver is a guarantee of continuous employment. And the record of the American economy in providing jobs for all is not impressive. This is especially true at the present time for young and nonwhite workers.

Unions deliver their benefits to members mainly by way of the collective bargaining agreement. By presenting employers with a choice of hiring all workers in the collective bargaining unit on specified terms or hiring none at all, the union is able to exert far more pressure for a better contract than would a typical individual worker bargaining alone.

Whereas in the past the emphasis was on forcing workers to adapt to the job as best they could, in recent years a number of efforts have been made to adjust the job and working conditions to the needs and interests of the workers. This arises, in part, from evidence of growing worker dissatisfaction. It is also the result of studies showing that reducing this dissatisfaction may greatly increase worker productivity. How meaningful most jobs can be made in a mass-production, high-technology society, though, remains to be seen.

I   IMPORTANT TERMS AND CONCEPTS   I

Commonwealth v. *Hunt*   union shop

craft union   open shop

business unionism   collective bargaining

industrial union   work ethic

Wagner Act   division of labor

closed shop   Hawthorne effect

I   QUESTIONS, PROBLEMS, AND EXERCISES   I

1 To what extent were unions responsible for improvements in the lot of the working man or woman in the nineteenth century in the United States?

2 Compare and contrast the philosophy of the AFL with that of the Knights of Labor.

3 Why did union membership rise so rapidly during the Great Depression, when all previous experience had been for union membership to decline sharply during depressions?

4 What has been responsible for the leveling-off of the percentage of the American labor force organized into unions?

5 Why do union leaders argue that measuring the impact of the union only in terms of union–nonunion wage differentials leaves out a key function of the union?

6 To what extent can we rely on the official unemployment figures as an accurate measure of true unemployment?

7 Is the work ethic disappearing in America?

8 How far can changes in work procedures go toward reducing worker discontent?

I SUGGESTED READING I

Braverman, Harry. *Labor and Monopoly Capital: The Degradation of Work in the Twentieth Century.* Monthly Review Press, New York and London, 1974.

Lacy, Dan. *The White Use of Blacks in America.* McGraw-Hill Paperbacks, New York, 1972.

Levitan, Sar A., and William B. Johnston. *Work is Here to Stay, Alas.* Olympus Publishing, Salt Lake City, Utah, 1973.

O'Toole, James, ed. *Work and the Quality of Life: Resource Papers for Work in America.* M.I.T. Press, Cambridge, 1974.

Pelling, Henry. *American Labor.* University of Chicago Press, Chicago, 1960.

Terkel, Studs. *Working, An Oral History of the Great Depression.* Avon Books, New York, 1975.

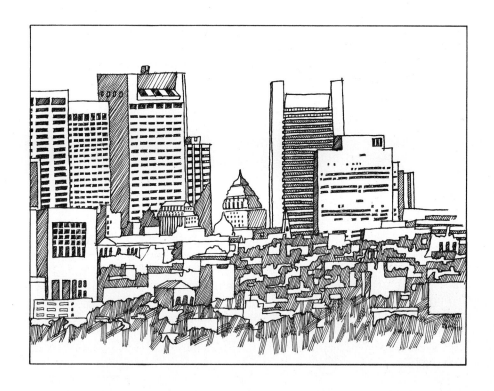

| CITIES IN TROUBLE |

During our 200 years as a nation the population of the United States has not only grown extraordinarily, from less than 4 million in 1790 to around 220 million today; it has also redistributed itself, from east to west and from rural areas to the cities. We tend to picture our forebears of 1790 clustered in a few cities along the east coast. In fact, it stretches things to say they were clustered anywhere. There were only twenty-four towns or cities of 2,500 population or more in that year, and altogether they claimed barely more than 5 percent of the total population. The remaining 95 percent was scattered all up and down the eastern seaboard, some in villages and hamlets, but most on farms.

During the next several decades the westward migration picked up momentum while urbanization failed to keep pace. It is true that the number of towns and cities increased substantially, from twenty-four in 1790 to ninety in 1830, but the proportion of the population housed in these urban areas increased only from 5.1 to 8.5 percent. It was at about the latter time, though, that the American Industrial Revolution shifted into high gear. Its impact on the rural to urban shift of the population can be seen in Figure 13.1. At the close of the period covered by the diagram, 1970, the cities of America claimed close to three-quarters (73.4 percent) of the total population — which they housed on a bare 2 percent of the land area of the United States.

We are apt to visualize this depopulation of the rural areas as leading to the demise of small towns. To an extent this is true. The number of farm-based towns has indeed declined sharply with the fall in the farm population and the substitution of cars and trucks for horses and mules. But with every farm shopping center lost, as Figure 13.1 attests, has come the birth of several new small towns — satellites of the huge urban centers. During the period when the farm population was declining most rapidly, in the decades following World War II, the total number of cities in America doubled, reaching a total of 7,062 in 1970.

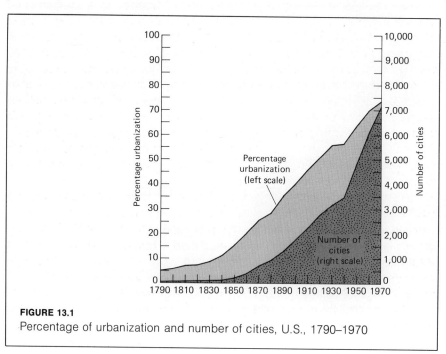

FIGURE 13.1

Percentage of urbanization and number of cities, U.S., 1790–1970

Source: Based on *Historical Statistics of the United States*, 1975, pp. 11–12.

With this development we are coming close to the heart of the "urban crisis." The problem obviously is not that the number of cities in America is declining. It is instead that many of our largest cities, in particular those in the Northeast and Central States, have ceased growing. In fact, several have been losing both residents and industry to their suburban bedroom communities and satellite cities. Worse than this, they have lost many of their most prosperous residents to the suburbs, to be replaced with far less prosperous in-migrants. With the loss of the affluent goes much of their revenue-producing capacity, and with the gain of the poor come new problems calling for increased governmental expenditures. The result is a budgetary or fiscal crisis, perhaps best exemplified by the near-bankruptcy of New York City.

I THE ECONOMICS OF AGGLOMERATION I

Since no one planned their growth, our large cities would not have become large had they not offered sufficient benefits to attract industry. The benefits they offered are identified under the label of *economies of agglomeration* — suggesting that bringing together in one central place large numbers of people and activities reduces commercial and industrial costs.

Although industrial location theory has developed into a sophisticated science in recent years, it is still concerned with one basic issue: how to situate a new business to assure maximum profits for its owners by minimizing costs and maximizing the availability of markets. The large cities offered locations that promised just this. Their growing populations were ready-made markets for the goods of commercial or manufacturing enterprises. If these markets were not sufficient, other cities could be reached readily and cheaply via the railway network. Thanks to the volume of goods handled and competition among different carriers, freight rates were considerably lower between major cities than for non-interurban routes. This was true also for *terminal costs* — the costs of loading a commodity on the carrier and getting it on its way.

More than this, the cities offered new and growing manufacturing industries other opportunities to cut their costs and accelerate their growth. They provided, for example, a large pool of labor, both skilled and unskilled. Rather than training their own skilled workers or paying premium wages to bring them to the plant site, urban industries were usually able to dip into the labor pool already available in the cities. The unskilled were nearly always on tap, too, since that supply was constantly replenished by high birth rates, the flow of workers from farms to cities, and the massive inflow of foreign immigrants — most of whom ended up in the large cities. Manufacturers also had immediately at hand in the cities a wide array of auxiliary services: a large banking and financial community, specialized repair services, replacement parts, training and educational institutions, consultants of all sorts, and so on. Finally, the low-cost rail transportation network that served well in getting goods to outside markets also was available to bring in cheaply whatever raw materials or partially fabricated inputs were needed by manufacturers but not available locally.

For all these reasons *industrialization* and *urbanization* were almost interchangeable terms until after World War I. Since the 1920s, however, suburbanization has increasingly replaced urbanization in this paired relationship. Industrialists have found that they can achieve nearly all the benefits of a central city site by locating their operations in the suburbs of a large city. They can still draw on the specialized services of the city while attracting their needed workers out into the suburbs. The motor truck is available to get their goods to the railroad or even to the final market and to bring in needed supplies. Manufacturers thus lose little by relocating just outside the big cities. And they stand to gain much. Land costs are materially lower, making it feasible to build the sprawling, single-floor manufacturing plants that have almost entirely replaced the multistory factories of earlier periods. Insurance costs may be lower because there is less danger of fire and crime. Taxes are almost sure to be less because services provided by government — crime prevention, fire protection, sewage disposal, water, even education — are less costly than in the inner cities.

The flight of business and industry from the central cities is not, of course, the only factor contributing to the more rapid growth of the suburbs than of the central cities. Increasing crime rates, pollution, congestion, and higher taxes in the cities, plus a growing desire for elbow room have played a part in attracting populations to the suburbs at a far more rapid rate than to the central cities. Table 13.1 shows the different rates of growth.

What Table 13.1 tells us is that while the urban population continued to grow rapidly during the twenty years from 1950 to 1970, it also substantially redistributed itself during the period. While barely more than 30 percent of the urban population was located in suburban or fringe areas in 1950, almost half was found there by 1970. Even this doesn't tell the whole story, since some central cities did considerably worse than others. During the period 1960–1973, for example, every one of the six largest cities in the Northeast lost population. Five of the seven largest in the Midwest lost population, and one of the other two would have, had it not annexed suburbs. Only one of the large southern cities, New Orleans, on the other hand, lost population, as did only two in the West, San Francisco and Seattle. These developments tell us that the central cities not only lost ground relative to their suburbs, but also that industry and population were pulled from the Snow Belt cities of the Northeast and Midwest to the Sun Belt cities of the South and West. It is thus the big Snow Belt cities that are now in greatest trouble.

TABLE 13.1
Urban population — total, central cities, and fringe areas, 1950–1970 (millions)

Year	Total urban population	Central cities	Fringe areas
1950	69.2	48.4	20.9
1960	95.8	58.0	37.9
1970	118.4	63.9	54.5

Source: *Historical Statistics of the United States,* 1975, p. 13.

TABLE 13.2
Urban population, by racial makeup, 1950–1970 (millions)

Year	Total urban population			Central cities			Fringe areas		
	White	Black	Ratio B/W	White	Black	Ratio B/W	White	Black	Ratio B/W
1950	62.0	7.1	.115	42.0	6.1	.145	19.9	1.0	.050
1960	83.8	11.3	.135	47.7	9.7	.203	36.2	1.5	.041
1970	101.0	15.7	.155	49.5	13.2	.267	54.0	2.5	.046

Source: Adapted from *Historical Statistics of the United States,* 1975, p. 13.

Adding to the difficulties of these cities, as mentioned earlier, is the fact that the population they lose tends to come from their middle- and high-income groups, and the people who flow in as partial replacements are in high proportion from the lowest-income categories. One way of showing this is to take the figures of Table 13.1 and break them into their racial components, as Table 13.2 does. We see from Table 13.2 that there has been a tremendous influx of blacks from the rural into the urban areas in recent years. By the close of the period covered by Table 13.2, the black population of the United States was significantly more urbanized (82 percent) than was the white (72.5 percent). But while part of the migration of blacks was to suburban areas — enough to keep them at around 5 percent of that population — the great flow was to the central cities. This was sufficient to push the proportion of blacks to whites in the population of the central cities up from 14.5 percent in 1950 to 26.7 percent in 1970. The relationship of this to the fiscal problem of the central cities is that a high proportion of the black migrants fled the rural areas, especially in the South, because of farm mechanization and declining job opportunities —

only to arrive in the northern cities just when industry and jobs were moving from the central cities. They now constitute part of the hardest of our hard-core unemployment problems.

The foregoing suggests an increasing welfare problem for the central cities, particularly for those in the Northeast and Midwest, where private employment opportunities are declining. An examination of the changing percentage of the population below the official poverty level in the large cities confirms this conclusion. During the decade 1960–1970, when the poverty group in the United States as a whole declined from 18.4 to 10.7 million, or by almost 42 percent, the percentage of the population below the poverty line in the six largest Northeast cities fell by no more than 10 percent (New York) to 30 percent (Pittsburgh). Among the midwestern cities, only in Indianapolis did the poverty percentage decline by as much as the national average. Even the largest cities in the South and West did less well by this measure than the rest of the country, although this was partly offset by the fact that the large cities in the West started in 1960 with poverty-group percentages well below the national average. In 1975 one out of eight residents of New York City received welfare payments, one out of seven in Newark and St. Louis, and one out of six in Philadelphia, Baltimore, and Boston.

As a summary on the economies of the large urban centers, "one can say of the most troubled cities that their economies are going nowhere and their people (the more productive) are going elsewhere."[1] This does not mean, however, as the next section will show, that these declining cities are low-cost cities. Population, industry, and jobs may fall, but municipal

the small society   by Brickman

© Washington Star Syndicate, Inc., permission granted by King Features Syndicate, Inc., 1977.

---

[1] David T. Stanley, *Cities in Trouble,* Academy for Contemporary Problems, Columbus, Ohio, December 1976, p. 5.

services and, therefore, municipal expenditures seem to go nowhere but up. This is one reason indeed that these cities are declining.

I CITY EXPENDITURES I

Diseconomies of scale

Whatever economies of scale may have been present in earlier periods in the provision of urban services, all the evidence today indicates that diseconomies of scale prevail over almost the entire range of such services. As Table 13.3 confirms, the cost per resident of providing municipal services rises in almost every case with each increase in city size. But it takes a huge leap upwards from the next-to-largest to the largest bracket — telling us why the largest cities are in the deepest trouble.

In a case or two the spending differential between the largest cities and all others is at least partly the result of simple mismanagement. But as a general rule the larger cities are as well managed as the smaller. The major differences lie in the greater needs and higher costs in the large cities. As indicated earlier, the larger cities have much greater concentrations of people in need of public assistance, especially the aged and the poor. Crime rates rise as city size increases. How large a gap exists between the large cities and the smaller where these factors are concerned can be detected from Table 13.4, which compares certain central-city-family characteristics and crime rates with those of the areas lying immediately outside the central cities.

In addition to the proportion of aid-dependent families and crime, density and congestion increase as the city size rises, increasing the need for such services as traffic control, street lighting, sidewalks, and street repair. Finally, some of the larger cities provide services that are either left to other governmental agencies or not provided by government at all in the smaller cities. Public higher education, for example, is almost everywhere else carried on state budgets. But New York City has insisted on providing its own city university system — as well as its own hospitals and supplementary poverty programs. Garbage collection is also in the hands of city authorities, as it is in most of the large cities; whereas many of the smaller cities leave it up to residents to contract with private sanitary companies for removal of their garbage. And in spite of what Table 13.3 suggests, overall public education costs on a per capita basis are actually higher in smaller cities than they are in the largest cities. This has to be the case since there are relatively fewer families with school-age children in the bigger cities. The spending figures for education in Table 13.3 are misleading because they include only the spending by the city governments themselves, not total educational costs. As the city size decreases, chances increase that separate school districts are in existence with their

TABLE 13.3

Total spending per capita for United States cities by population size, 1971–1972 (%)

Function	All cities	1 million or more (6)	500,000– 999,999 (21)	300,000– 499,999 (21)	200,000– 299,999 (17)	100,000– 199,999 (88)	50,000– 99,999 (231)	Below 50,000 (17,663)
Education	38.94	110.91	46.19	53.58	50.46	45.47	32.58	12.11
Police	29.86	64.57	42.50	31.29	30.19	27.25	23.54	18.02
Welfare	22.96	120.43	38.08	6.17	8.43	5.70	2.95	0.86
Fire protection	16.73	27.00	22.92	22.06	22.97	21.36	18.63	9.43
Hospitals	14.66	53.17	24.61	6.46	5.56	6.94	6.00	5.84
Highways	12.20	11.20	11.45	9.97	11.31	11.60	12.03	13.24
Parks and recreation	11.90	13.21	21.28	20.56	18.52	15.71	13.28	6.58
Interest on debt	11.57	24.73	15.30	15.55	14.44	11.13	8.41	6.75
Sanitation	10.11	19.47	13.24	10.81	13.39	10.63	8.65	6.38
Sewerage	5.60	3.91	8.03	8.05	6.16	5.95	5.36	5.22
Health	5.18	19.60	11.09	4.69	3.78	2.91	2.02	0.74
Housing	4.36	15.01	7.03	5.24	5.93	4.36	2.32	0.71
All functions	220.90	549.71	322.45	228.08	233.76	201.79	165.38	110.77

Note: Spending figures exclude capital outlays. The number of cities in each size group is given in parentheses.
Source: United States Bureau of the Census, *City Government Finances, 1971–72*, U.S. Government Printing Office, Washington, D.C.

TABLE 13.4
Family characteristics and crime rates in metropolitan areas, 1970

Item	Central city	Outside central city
Percentage of persons below poverty level	13.4	6.3
Percentage aged 25–29 with less than high school education	25.3	19.2
Percentage of population over 65	11.1	7.4
Female-headed families as a percentage of all families	17.0	8.8
AFDC families as a percentage of all families[a]	9.8	2.4
Crime rate (per 1,000 inhabitants)	45.6	21.4

[a] AFDC = Aid to Families with Dependent Children.
Source: Table 9.2 (p. 295) from *Setting National Priorities: The 1973 Budget*, by Charles L. Schultze, Edward R. Fried, Alice M. Rivlin, and Nancy H. Teeters. Copyright © 1972 by the Brookings Institution.

own taxing and spending authority, leaving only relatively small amounts of spending to be caught up in the city budgets.

With cost differentials between the largest and next-to-largest cities as great as those exhibited in Table 13.3, it can almost be taken for granted that recent spending increases for the largest cities have far outstripped those of other cities. Bureau of the Census data confirm this assumption. Between 1960 and 1972, per capita spending outlays for the combined functions listed increased by 181 percent for all cities. For the six largest, however, such outlays jumped by 269 percent.

Even if the cities had continued to do only the things they did in 1960, it would have cost them more to do them in 1972 — but not 181 percent more, to say nothing of 269 percent more. The consumer price index rose by only 41 percent during this period. There were obviously many factors at work other than the overall rise in the cost of living. One of these is suggested by the fact that the price index of goods and services purchased by local governments rose at twice the rate of the general consumer price index during the period.

The cost of labor

Among the goods and services purchased by city governments, far and away the most important single item is labor services, typically constituting at least half the total of a city's operating budget. And not only have cities sharply increased their hiring of workers, but the cost per unit of labor employed has risen spectacularly, as Table 13.5 shows.

The public employees themselves explain this rapid rise in their wages as simple catch-up. They were substantially underpaid relative to

---

TABLE 13.5
How public employee wage gains stack up against the private sector

	Average annual increase (%), 1955–1973	% increase, 1955–1973
All private industry	4.7	129.3
Manufacturing	4.6	124.0
Federal government (civilian)	5.9	182.9
State and local government	5.6	165.2

Source: Reprinted from July 21, 1975, issue of *Business Week* by special permission. © 1975 by McGraw-Hill, Inc. Data from Advisory Commission on Intergovernmental Relations.

---

private workers at the beginning of the period covered by Table 13.5, and their wages therefore had to increase faster than those of private workers to catch up by the end of the period. Catch up they did, and — in a few cases — then some. By the mid-seventies virtually all employees of the Metropolitan Boston Transportation Authority earned over $14,000 a year.[2] Similar examples can be cited for a few favored groups in other large cities. In addition to catching up in hourly wages, public employees now enjoy better pension and health insurance plans, more liberal holiday and vacation provisions, and greater job security than do comparable workers in the private sector.

It was one thing for public employees to recognize that their benefits from work lagged behind those of similar workers in private industry and quite another to close the gap. How did they accomplish this? The answer is partly a successful educational campaign to alert the public to their plight. More important, though, was a determination to increase their bargaining clout through unionization. At the beginning of the period covered by Table 13.5, fewer than 1 million public employees belonged to unions; by the end of the period the total was around 2.5 million. Give the public employees this added bargaining power, add in the fact that a high proportion of city employees are members of minority groups, throw in the racial violence of the 1960s, and you have the stage set for a dramatic rise not only in wages but in total city employment.

Population shifts and new programs

Rising labor costs, then, are the single most important reason for rapidly increasing costs encountered by the cities, especially the larger cities. But going along with this, and partly causing it, has been the shift in the

---

[2] *Business Week* (July 21, 1975), 50.

population mix of the large cities. Some of these, such as Newark and Cleveland, have been all but abandoned by the middle class, leaving behind a population heavily dependent on government services and aid. Above and beyond this has been the development and implementation by the big cities of a whole host of new programs: local programs for pollution control, consumer protection, drug rehabilitation, family planning, day care, and community colleges. Some of these were nonexistent at the beginning of the 1960s; some were already in existence but have since been drastically expanded.

One of the major reasons both for beginning new programs and for expanding old ones has been the availability of federal funds with very generous cost-sharing arrangements. Medicare and Medicaid, for example, permitted city governments to expand their municipal hospitals and enlarge their health programs, with most of the costs being picked up by the federal government. Similar cost-sharing arrangements were made available for education, pollution control, sewage disposal, welfare, and other poverty-related services. Although in many cases the cities' administrations weren't quite sure where the city's share of these cost-sharing projects would come from, they felt that they couldn't pass up this cheap money.

❙ CITY REVENUES ❙

Even though their costs and expenditures have risen dramatically in recent years, the big cities would be in no particular difficulty today had they been able to increase their revenues in step. This they have not been able to do despite heroic increases in tax rates, amounting to nearly 25 percent for the large declining cities during the period 1967–1972. In its annual study of tax burdens in the nation's thirty largest cities, the District of Columbia government found that in 1974 the heaviest tax burdens for a typical family were found in Boston, Milwaukee, New York, Buffalo, Chicago, Philadelphia, Los Angeles, and Baltimore — all of which are troubled and declining cities, with the exception of Los Angeles.[3] As one of many possible examples of these tax increases, a Boston family earning $10,000 now pays $2,000 in state and local taxes for the privilege of living in the city, compared with only $360 in Jacksonville.[4]

If cities cannot raise sufficient revenue by taxation to cover their annual outlays, the difference must be covered by borrowing — by printing IOU's (interest-bearing notes or bonds) and selling them. The real fiscal crisis arrives when a city finances a substantial part of its budget year after year

---

[3] Cited in Stanley, *Cities in Trouble,* p. 7.

[4] Thomas Muller, "Urban Growth and Decline," *Challenge* (May–June 1976), 12.

by borrowing, then finds that no one is willing to buy its offered securities. This was exactly New York City's situation in 1975. Prospective securities buyers saw no way that New York City could raise the money to cover its escalating "normal" costs and make interest payments on its ballooning debt as well. The attractive interest rates being offered meant little if New York would be unable to pay them, so investors passed them by. Only a last-minute financial infusion by the federal government kept the city out of the bankruptcy courts. And unless some way is found to reverse recent trends, New York will be only the first of several large cities lurching toward bankruptcy.

Why do cities resort to borrowing? Why don't they simply raise taxes sufficiently to cover their costs, however high? One answer is that borrowing can play an honest role in a city's budget. If large new capital projects — city halls, airports, park improvements, new roads — were built entirely out of tax revenues, then present residents would pay for these improvements, but future residents would enjoy most of the benefits. For capital improvements, then, it makes sense to borrow the funds now and have those future residents help finance the projects they enjoy by paying taxes to cover the annual interest cost and retire the securities when they mature.

This argument doesn't extend to current operating outlays, however. It is the present residents who benefit from these expenditures, so they should pick up the tab in tax payments. The brutal fact, though, is that those residents in many cases are not able to make the tax payments sufficient to cover the cost of the services provided. This is demonstrably true of the large poverty and near-poverty groups in the big cities. Beyond these groups there are others who would be able to pay higher taxes, but they have a way of opting out if higher taxes are imposed: They can simply leave the greedy city for other locations where they will be taxed more lightly. There are strong indications that for this reason tax increases in the declining cities may be counterproductive. They drive away so many businesses and middle- and higher-income families that those remaining contribute insufficient additional taxes to compensate for the loss.

I WHAT IS TO BE DONE? I

Bankruptcy

The easy answer to the question posed in the heading is nothing. When the financial burdens of the large cities become too much for them to bear, they can simply file a petition in bankruptcy court to have their debts and other financial obligations — such as overly generous pension plans for city employees — scaled down to manageable proportions. Meanwhile the city will continue doing business more or less as usual. Hundreds of thousands of Americans have discovered over the years that going through bankruptcy is a reasonably tolerable experience. And a number of our smaller cities have traveled the same route.

But, as we discovered when New York City teetered on the edge of bankruptcy, going through the bankruptcy mill as an individual or small company or small city is quite a different matter than it would be for one of our major cities. There is no domino effect in the former cases, as there would be in the latter. Since the finances of the state of New York are closely linked with those of New York City, it was realized that financial collapse in New York City would likely lead to financial collapse of the state. Also, had New York City failed, the securities of other big cities would have come under close scrutiny. Some of them may well have found it impossible to sell the paper they needed to stay afloat financially. Even as it was, New York City's troubles put the whole of the municipal securities market under a cloud, forcing some cities to delay floating securities issues and requiring all to pay higher interest charges for the money they were able to raise.

To talk about "scaling down debts and financial obligations" is simple enough, but what it really means is that those who hold the claims either won't get paid or will get paid only part of what they are owed by the city. Some of these debt holders might well afford the loss. It is doubtful that even complete default on the $1.4 billion of New York City debt held by the big New York City banks would have ruined them. But municipal securities are favored holdings for many small investors. For them default would mean at least the partial loss of lifetime savings.

When all the pros and cons of bankruptcy for New York City were considered, the cons considerably outweighed the pros. But to this point the city's troubles have merely been papered over with loans from the federal government. By no means has a permanent solution been found for its financial problems. Nor has one been found for any of the other declining cities. The solutions being put forward recognize that the cities are capable of taking some action in their own behalf, but also that many of the big city troubles are really national problems that show up in the cities. Some sort of joint action is therefore demanded.

Reducing expenditures by local action

In light of the galloping rise in city expenditures, one route to financial equilibrium would be to hold a tighter rein on city spending. Learn to tolerate more potholes in the city streets, higher pupil-teacher ratios in the schools, fewer police officers on the beat, smaller fire crews. While some possibilities exist for tightening up along these lines, they are limited. A city must hope to attract new residents and new businesses and to hold those it already has. It is not likely to do either if the level of its services is allowed to deteriorate seriously, especially when its nearby suburbs offer considerably better services.

If the services can't be cut back much, can they not be provided more efficiently and therefore at lower cost? In an attempt to do just this, many cities are experimenting with productivity programs, essentially oriented toward bringing the performance of city employees and agencies up to par with private industry. So far no major breakthroughs have occurred, but some of the new programs are quite sophisticated and will take some time to prove themselves.

Another route to reduced expenditures would be to unload some of the cities' present functions. Some services — garbage collection, for example — might be turned over to the private sector. The poor might be helped to disperse themselves throughout the metropolitan region, rather than being concentrated in the central cities. Both of these face great opposition — from the city employees and their unions in the first case, from suburban residents and the poor themselves in the second — but they might succeed if vigorously pushed.

Increasing state and local revenues

The most direct route for supplementing city revenues, levying more taxes, is almost closed, as we saw earlier. Large-city taxes are already so high that they encourage flight and discourage entry of those able to pay the higher rates. Only by finding a new group of taxpayers could taxes be raised substantially. One possibility looks very tempting: Combine the whole of the metropolitan area into one large tax district, thereby tapping the resources of the affluent suburbanites to help solve the problems of the central cities. There is justice in this approach because many of the suburbanites work in the city and use its services but escape paying for them by residing in another tax jurisdiction. Some cities have pushed through annexation plans based on this logic. More commonly, however, such proposals are resoundingly voted down by suburban residents, many of whom fled the city to avoid its rising costs.

If the cities' tax burden can't be shared with the suburbanites alone, then maybe it could be shared among all state residents by using more state revenues to subsidize the cities. Although the residents of the cities see the beauty of this arrangement, to all those outside the cities it merely looks like more of the same — more taxes, that is. And they have the votes to defeat it.

Federal action

Failing to find adequate solutions at the local or state level, once again a major problem is being dumped into the lap of the federal government. In fact, without its substantial contribution, the problems of the declining large cities would have become unbearable by this time. As mentioned earlier, only the financial lifeline thrown New York City by the United States Treasury kept the city out of the bankruptcy courts. And a great deal of financial aid flows from the federal to city treasuries by other channels, as Table 13.6 shows. As a consequence of increasing money flows from state and federal governments, city governments found it necessary to pick up an increasingly smaller fraction of their total available funds from their traditional sources — only 62 percent from taxes and charges in 1973, compared with 80 percent in 1960. What part of this intergovernmental revenue flow is state, what part federal, is impossible to determine with any precision because much of what the cities receive comes from the federal government via the state governments.

In addition to seeing the flow of money from the federal government increased, the large cities would like to see changes made in the federal support program. This program now takes two different forms: *categorical assistance grants* and *general revenue sharing,* sometimes distinguished as "strings-attached" grants and "no strings" grants. Under the former, the federal government assists the cities to provide certain categories of services — usually new or expanded beyond what the cities are currently providing — by offering funds earmarked for such services. Examples are urban renewal, urban mass transit, and public housing. The federal government not only closely monitors the spending of these funds, to see that they are not diverted to other uses, but generally requires that the cities put up substantial amounts of matching funds as well. Since categorical grants lead to a further burden on municipal budgets, the cities would prefer to see them shifted to the general revenue sharing program. If the general revenue sharing program were expanded, and if the program were tilted more sharply in the direction of assisting the beleaguered large cities, it could go far to relieve their distress.

But the federal government is being asked to do far more. One thing that the northern cities insist on is a reversal of the present net flow of

TABLE 13.6
City government finances, general revenues: 1960–1973 ($ million)

Item	1960	% of total	1973	% of total	% change 1960–1973
Total general revenue	11,647	100.0	41,243	100.0	254
Intergovernmental revenue	2,321	20.0	15,562	37.7	570
Taxes	7,109	61.0	18,477	44.8	160
Charges and miscellaneous	2,217	19.0	7,204	17.5	225

Source: Adapted from *Statistical Abstract of the United States,* 1975, p. 270.

federal dollars away from the northern states to the southern and western states. Because their aggregate incomes are still relatively high, the northern states contribute substantial amounts of federal tax dollars, more than the southern or western states on a per capita basis. Yet when it comes to spending those federal receipts, they go in disproportionate amounts to the southern and western states. The result, as Table 13.7 shows, is a net flow of income to the southern and western states away from the northern states. The northeastern and midwestern states ask that this be kept in mind when the federal government awards construction contracts, purchases its supplies, places its military contracts, builds its military bases, and awards its discretionary grants. With more money flowing into the northern states, more is bound to end up in the coffers of their troubled big cities.

A number of federal programs now under consideration, if adopted, would also help these cities. Some form of federal negative income tax scheme or other arrangement for guaranteeing at least a minimal income for all poverty-level families would take some of that burden off the cities. Federal assumption of a larger share of the national educational expense would also relieve municipal budgets. And a national health program would shift some medical costs away from the cities. Those who speak for the large cities argue persuasively that the reduction of poverty and the provision of educational and health care services are basically national concerns — or at least they should be. In the absence of adequate national

TABLE 13.7

Comparison of per capita federal spending and per capita federal taxes plus deficit

Region	Federal spending ($) per person	Federal taxes ($) per person (including federal deficit)	Difference ($) (spending less taxes)
New England	1,470	1,533	−63
Mid-Atlantic	1,325	1,594	−269
Great Lakes	1,064	1,518	−454
Great Plains	1,287	1,374	−87
South Atlantic	1,454	1,303	151
South Central	1,327	1,137	190
Mountain	1,615	1,238	377
Pacific	1,745	1,497	248

Source: Joel Havemann, Rochelle L. Stanfield, and Neal R. Pierce, "Special Report: Where the Funds Flow," *National Journal* (June 26, 1976), 881.

programs, however, the large cities will continue to attract disproportionate numbers of those most in need of income supplements and with the greatest educational and health problems. City authorities feel duty-bound to help these disadvantaged groups, but the price is a steady worsening of the cities' financial situation.

Chances of success for federal or even state programs specifically designed to aid the failing large cities are hard to estimate but must be considered not too bright at best. As many commentators have pointed out, most of us continue to regard the big cities with suspicion — dens of iniquity and all that. If they're in trouble, they deserve it. Moreover, population shifts during the last several decades have materially diluted the political strength of the large cities. Americans may have moved to the cities in recent years, but not to the large cities: only one American out of seven now lives in a large city, and fewer than one out of twenty in either Chicago or New York City, compared with one out of twelve in one of these two cities in the 1930s.[5] Clearly the residents of the large troubled cities must make a persuasive case for national assistance if it is to be forthcoming; they haven't the votes to muscle their programs through either state or federal legislatures.

I SUMMARY I

During our first fifty years as a nation our population grew rapidly, but the percentage of the population living in cities increased slowly. Around the middle of the nineteenth century, however, the situation was reversed: The population growth rate began to slow down, while the urbanized share of the population began to grow rapidly, thanks mainly to city-based industrialization.

Until recently this urban growth meant growth of the largest cities in particular. These large urban centers offered industry important economies of agglomeration. Manufacturing companies were assured of a wide range of low-cost services, sufficient to assure lower costs of production and distribution than in any other location.

In recent years the largest cities, in particular those in the northeastern and central states, have failed to provide this competitive advantage for industry. Manufacturing and distribution costs have risen rapidly in such cities — far more rapidly than in the suburbs and fringe areas. The consequence has been a flight of industry and its tax-paying capacity, along with a large share of high-income taxpayers, to the suburbs. At the same time, internal migration has brought huge numbers of the very poor to the cities. A shrinking tax base accompanied by a growing need for revenue to help the poor constitutes an urban financial crisis.

---

[5] Muller, "Urban Growth and Decline," p. 13.

Although some courses of action not yet fully tried are open to the failing cities, all signs point to the necessity for additional federal aid in solving this crisis.

I IMPORTANT TERMS AND CONCEPTS I

economies of agglomeration   general revenue sharing

categorical assistance grants

I QUESTIONS, PROBLEMS, AND EXERCISES I

1 What has been the historical relationship in the United States between industrialization and urbanization?

2 What promises of increased operating returns did cities offer in an earlier era to attract industry? Why can they no longer deliver on these promises?

3 Why have spending increases by the largest cities outstripped those of smaller cities?

4 Doesn't it appear paradoxical to cite the availability of federal cost-sharing programs as one reason for rapidly rising costs in large cities?

5 If the large cities desperately need increased operating revenues, as they claim, why don't they simply raise taxes?

6 Why doesn't bankruptcy promise the same easy way out for financially overburdened large cities as it does for business firms in a similar situation?

7 If the large cities are in financial trouble but the suburbs are financially healthy, why are the two not simply joined into one tax-paying unit?

8 Since the largest cities can't pay their own way, doesn't this suggest that they have outlived their usefulness and should simply be allowed to die?

I SUGGESTED READING I

Franklin, Raymond S., and Solomon Resnik. *The Political Economy of Racism.* Holt, New York, 1973.

Fusfeld, Daniel R. *The Basic Economics of the Urban Racial Crisis.* Holt, New York, 1973.

Joint Economic Committee, Congress of the United States. *New York City's Financial Crisis.* U.S. Government Printing Office, Washington, D.C., 1975.

Pettengill, Robert B., and Jogindar S. Uppal. *Can Cities Survive? The Fiscal Plight of American Cities.* St. Martin's, New York, 1974.

Stanley, David T. *Cities in Trouble.* Academy for Contemporary Problems, Columbus, Ohio, 1976.

FOURTEEN

∣ AMERICA IN THE WORLD ECONOMY ∣

Our discussion of economic problems to this point has for the most part been based on the premise that we have a completely free hand in solving those problems. Inequality, poverty, economic stabilization, inflation — all have been treated as if we lived in splendid isolation; as if what we did in solving these problems would be of little concern to our neighbors in the international community of nations. Now we must face up to the fact that as the largest country in the world, at least in economic terms, there is virtually nothing we do that does not have an impact on our neighbors. Since we are the world's largest trading nation, the health of our economy

TABLE 14.1
Foreign trade and the leading trading nations, 1950, 1970, and 1975 ($ billion, U.S.)

	United States			Canada 1975	France 1975	West Germany 1975	United Kingdom 1975	Japan 1975
	1950	1970	1975					
Gross national product	286.2	982.4	1516.3	158.3	337.9	423.0	228.8	491.0
Merchandise exports	10.8	43.3	107.7	32.1	52.2	90.5	43.8	55.8
% of GNP	3.8	4.4	7.1	20.3	15.4	21.4	19.1	11.3
Merchandise imports	9.1	40.2	96.9	33.8	54.2	74.4	53.3	57.9
% of GNP	3.2	4.1	6.4	21.4	16.0	17.6	23.3	11.8

Source: *Historical Statistics of the United States, 1975*, p. 886, and *Statistical Abstract of the United States, 1976*, p. 877.

is vital to the dozens of small countries that send us a high proportion of their exports: coffee, cocoa, copra, iron ore, copper, and so on. A slight fall of income in the United States has on many occasions sharply cut our imports of these products, thereby creating severe economic problems in the exporting nations, whose export earnings make up a large part of their national incomes. This is the logic that lies behind the old quip that when the United States sneezes the small exporting countries are apt to catch pneumonia. And even the large exporting nations will feel less well. During the world recession of the mid-1970s, in fact, it was recognized that only full economic recovery in the United States would enable the rest of the world to regain its economic health. Only a strong American economy could provide sufficient demand for foreign products to send the producers of those goods back to work.

Looked at from this point of view, it is apparent that many other countries are far more dependent on foreign trade than is the United States. Table 14.1 provides recent trade figures that confirm this fact. The table shows that while our merchandise exports and imports have risen in spectacular fashion during the past quarter-century, in both absolute terms and in relationship to gross national product, exports and imports as late as 1975 still represented well under 10 percent of our gross national product.

For many other nations, the role of foreign trade is far more important — in some cases close to a matter of life or death. Table 14.1 indicates that the dollar values of exports and imports for our large trading partners don't match those of the United States. But neither do their national incomes. Expressed as a fraction of GNP, exports and imports in all these countries are far more significant than they are for the United States. Export earnings make up a truly substantial portion of their national incomes, as well as providing the funds with which to buy the imports on which the countries are heavily dependent. Unable to export, and therefore unable to buy imports, the population of the United Kingdom could well starve, since Britain lost the ability to feed her people from her own fields as early as the middle of the nineteenth century. In France, West Germany, and Japan the wheels of industry would grind to a halt in short order without imported oil since no one of these countries has a domestic source of supply.

l THE CASE FOR UNRESTRICTED INTERNATIONAL TRADE l

The general case for foreign trade rests on the interdependence already demonstrated. Whether by design or by accident, most nations of the world are now in a position where a sharp reduction in foreign trade would have multiple adverse consequences, ranging all the way from some deterioration in the standard of living to an absolute collapse of the economy.

A moment's thought should be sufficient to recognize the fact that international trade is grounded on the same logic as interregional trade. Why doesn't the state of New York attempt to become self-sufficient and get along on its own production? Or California? Or Idaho? For exactly the same reason that the United States doesn't attempt complete self-sufficiency: To do so would severely reduce the standard of living of its residents. Living standards would in all cases be adversely affected for the same reasons: (1) local residents would be denied the opportunity to consume some goods and services not capable of being produced at home and (2) residents would be able to secure other goods and services only at higher prices by producing for themselves what they previously imported.

The lack of availability of many goods or services in the absence of importation is immediately apparent. Residents of New York and Idaho would find their diets much changed if they were denied the citrus fruits and winter vegetables of the Sun Belt states — just as all Americans would find their eating habits altered if they no longer had the bananas, coffee, tea, coconut, cocoa, and other foods of the tropics. The same is true for raw materials for industrial use. Without the lumber and minerals of the less industrialized states, construction and manufacturing in the industrial states would suffer — as would obviously be the case for the American aluminum industry if it were denied bauxite from Jamaica.

The case for trade when a region or country completely lacks certain vital foods or raw materials is easily made. It is more difficult to see why a region or country should bring in products that could be produced locally. One step along the way might be to start with an easy case, where the product could be produced locally but only with great difficulty and therefore only at great cost. Take the case of the foods mentioned above. It is not strictly true that New York and Idaho could not grow citrus fruits, or that bananas and coconuts could not be grown in the United States. All of these could be grown in hothouses — but at exorbitant expense. Growing conditions for oranges, lemons, and grapefruit are so ideal in Florida and California, on the other hand, that they can be grown very cheaply, as is the case for bananas in Honduras and coffee in Brazil. What we have in all these are situations of _absolute advantage_. In every case, the region or country is blessed by conditions that make it an extremely efficient producer — more efficient, and therefore lower cost, than any other region or country. Since they can produce these products so well, it makes obvious sense to concentrate their efforts on producing them. By specializing in products they can produce more efficiently and more cheaply than any other region, they can turn out more goods with the same resources than can any other region.

They will also turn out more of these products than they can use themselves, while failing to produce other things they badly need. But trade can right this situation. While they are specializing in what they can produce most efficiently, other regions are also specializing in what they do best, also producing surpluses of certain products while leaving shortages of others. Then the surpluses of the two areas are in effect swapped. The exports of one region pay for its imports from the other. Since each region does what it can do best, total production is maximized, and therefore the availability of material goods for both regions is maximized. Multiply these instances by all the cases where regions or nations have an absolute advantage in the production of one thing or another and you have a very strong argument for specialization and trade in the promotion of material welfare throughout the world.

But not a complete argument. What do we do with the region or country that apparently can't produce anything — not a single thing — more efficiently than some other region or country? Has it no place in the overall pattern of trade? The answer, perhaps surprisingly, is that it too has a role to play. The reason for this is that while this region or country may not do anything superlatively, it surely does some things better than other things. Another way of saying this is that it has a _comparative advantage_ in certain lines of activity as compared with other lines. Perhaps a country is a reasonably good shipbuilding nation but is lousy in electronics manufacturing. It will obviously get far more out of its resources by devoting them to shipbuilding than to the production of television sets.

Conversely, some other country, while it can turn out both ships and television sets more cheaply than country A, will find that it pays not to produce both. Instead, it will specialize in the manufacture of television sets, because that's where it has its greater margin of advantage over the first country. It will rely on the other country for its ships, trading television sets for them. The case is exactly parallel to that of a physician who is at once a highly skilled heart surgeon, a better filing clerk than she can hire, and a superb cook. In addition to performing surgery, will she do her own filing and cooking? Of course not — not, at least, if the filing and cooking take time away from her surgery. While she has an absolute advantage in all three endeavors, her comparative advantage is greatest in surgery. That's where she should concentrate her energies because that's what will maximize the returns to her efforts. She will therefore hire a filing clerk and a cook and concentrate on surgery — just as country B will concentrate on television manufacturing, where its comparative advantage is greater compared with country A, and country A will concentrate on shipbuilding, where its comparative disadvantage relative to country B is less than in television manufacturing.

Generalizing this case we have the basic logic for unrestricted international trade. By specializing in the production of what it does best, every country turns out the maximum value of goods and services of which it is capable. With production at a maximum in each country, it has to follow that world production must also be as large as possible. All that remains is for trade to take the excess production of one country and exchange it for the surplus products of other countries and world consumption can be maximized. This last point is crucial. Unless nations can exchange surpluses of the products they produce for the products they fail to produce, they cannot afford to specialize. Specialization and its manifold efficiencies, therefore, go hand in hand with free trade. One depends on the other.

| THE CASE FOR FREE TRADE CHALLENGED |

The argument for free trade that we have presented appears not only simple to understand but eminently logical. It equates free trade with the promotion of economic welfare. Trade restrictions thus bear a high price tag — an overall reduction of consumption possibilities and therefore of material welfare. On these grounds the case for free international trade — and free interregional trade too, of course — has borne the endorsement of virtually all professional economists. In fact, its acceptance is almost a litmus test as to whether or not an individual deserves the label of economist. Nothing is so apt to incense the economics profession as a move away from free trade.

The tariff in American history

Yet the sad fact is that absolutely free trade has never prevailed at any time throughout the world. While most countries have flirted at one time or another with free trade, their flirtation has usually been brief. A short period of time is ordinarily sufficient to dampen their enthusiasm for unrestricted international trade. The United States record of restrictive import duties — the most widely used device to control trade — is pictured in Figure 14.1. It shows that there have been few times in our history when we have even come close to absolutely free trade. Most of the time our industries have enjoyed substantial levels of protection from foreign imports.

During the nineteenth century the two major reasons for departing from unrestricted free trade were to provide the federal government with operating funds and to protect American industry. Some of the tariff acts were specifically identified as revenue tariffs, while others were protective tariffs.

Now, there is no difference in kind between revenue and protective tariffs. Any tariff may be either a revenue or protective tariff. The difference is one of degree. The purpose of a protective tariff, obviously, is to protect American industry against foreign competition by forcing an increase in the price of a foreign product to the point where it cannot undersell American goods. To the lower price of the foreign product is added an import duty sufficient to boost its price in the United States up to or beyond the

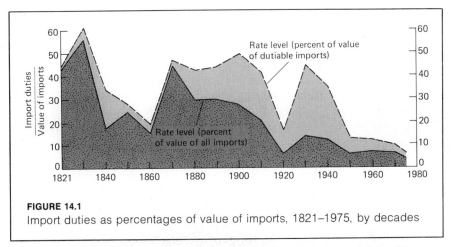

FIGURE 14.1

Import duties as percentages of value of imports, 1821–1975, by decades

Source: *Historical Statistics of the United States*, 1975, p. 888, and *Statistical Abstract of the United States*, 1976, p. 849.

price of the American competitive product. If the foreign cost of production is materially below the American cost of production, it will require a very high import duty to close off foreign competition. And if this high import duty is completely effective in shutting off the import of foreign goods, it obviously will produce no revenue for the collection agency, the federal government. _A revenue tariff,_ then, sets import duties at sufficiently low rates that they hinder as little as possible the free import of foreign goods and thereby maximize the revenue flow to the government. A protective tariff, conversely, provides import duties high enough to cut the flow of foreign goods into the United States and thereby restrict the domestic market largely to goods produced at home.

These two principles competed during the nineteenth century for priority in the determination of duty levels. Both were present in passing the first major tariff act of the century, the Tariff Act of 1816. Advocates of protection made extensive use of what has always been the single most effective argument for high import duties: the *infant-industry argument for protection.* The particular infant of concern at that time was the textile industry. With the foreign supply of textiles cut off during the War of 1812, the American industry made substantial progress. But with the coming of peace in 1814, British textiles from a much more advanced industry flooded back into the United States, underselling the brand-new and inexperienced American companies and driving many of them out of business. With some justice the American producers demanded protection for their infant industry, at least until it had an opportunity to grow up and could compete on even terms with foreign producers. The fact that the American textile industry is still demanding protection against foreign competition may suggest a weakness in their argument.

But revenue considerations also came into play in the deliberations on the Tariff Act of 1816. The federal debt had doubled during the War of 1812, and Congress was much concerned about raising the money to pay off the debt. They turned to import duties then, as they did over and over again during the century, as the most convenient way of refilling the federal coffers. In fact, during the entire century import duties were far and away the single largest source of federal revenues.

The remainder of the nineteenth century is largely a story of northern industrialists pushing for high tariff duties to protect their growing manufacturing enterprises and determined opposition from farmers in the South and West. Farmers, after all, and especially the southern cotton farmers, depended heavily on foreign markets as an outlet for their products. Without the ability to sell in our markets because of high duties, foreigners would be unable to acquire the dollars with which to buy American farm products. Recognition by southern cotton producers during the 1850s that they were losing control of Congress to northern industrialists who favored high tariff policies has been cited as a major reason — perhaps as important as slavery — for the withdrawal of the South from Congress and the beginning of the Civil War.[1]

By the beginning of the twentieth century the United States had become the leading industrial nation in the world. The infant-industry argument for protective duties was wearing a bit thin. Yet another glance at Figure 14.1 tells us that except for a brief period around World War I, when Wilson and the Democrats were in office, import duties remained high. This, too, in face of the fact that the nation had by now established both corporate and personal income taxes as revenue sources. The first third of the century thus featured very ingenious rationalizations for protective duties — during a period when all economic logic suggested that American industry had advanced to the point where it needed no protection at all.

The American farmer, first of all, was sold the argument that since the major outlet for his products was at home, not abroad, he should protect the domestic market against foreign competition. Using this line of analysis, the Hawley-Smoot Act in 1930 pushed import duties on agricultural products and provisions up from 20 to 34 percent — an increase of over 69 percent, the greatest advance of any item in the whole tariff schedule.[2] With this sort of treatment, farmers were scarcely in a position to oppose similar increases for industry.

---

[1] See Louis M. Hacker, *The Triumph of American Capitalism,* Columbia University Press, New York, 1947, Part III.

[2] Broadus Mitchell, *Depression Decade: From New Era through New Deal, 1929–1941,* Harper Torchbooks, New York, 1947, p. 66.

Another argument that gained currency during this period led to the *scientific tariff*. At first glance, this appears to be the essence of reasonableness. American industry asks only that all competitors, both domestic and foreign, in the American marketplace, get an even start. If foreign producers, for whatever reason, are able to land goods in the United States and sell them at a price less than the American producer can match, then an import duty should be levied just sufficient to equalize selling prices. Advocates of this approach did recognize that there would be some difficulties of determining unit costs of production at home and abroad and picking representative figures for equalizing purposes, but they thought these could be overcome. What they refused to recognize was that the scientific tariff effectively eliminates the entire basis for foreign trade. International trade, as we saw earlier, is worthwhile primarily because we are provided with an opportunity to buy some foreign goods more cheaply than we can buy them at home. In exchange for this, foreigners are able to buy some of our products more cheaply than they can secure them at home. If the prices of all goods were equalized by imposition of duties, it would destroy the very basis of foreign trade. Even so, the scientific tariff is a sturdy weed. It has recently reappeared in altered form in the steel industry as *reference prices* — prices based on estimated foreign costs of production, below which no foreign steel will be allowed to sell in the United States if the American industry has its way with the president and Congress.

The Great Depression of the 1930s nurtured a couple of major arguments for protection, and the two world wars brought forth another. Although it had been gaining ground earlier, the depression brought the *cheap foreign labor* idea to the forefront. In its simplest form, it is identified as the bowl-of-rice argument. How can American industry, paying the highest wages in the world, possibly compete on even terms with industry in foreign countries where wages need be no more than enough to provide a bowl of rice a day? The fact is, of course, that American industry does compete, so there must be a flaw in the argument. The flaw is that daily wages alone do not determine costs of production. What is of concern to the manufacturer is labor cost per unit of output. Workers who are paid ten times as much as foreign workers but produce fifteen times as much are really cheap labor. Thanks to our system of education and our extraordinary stock of capital equipment and technology, this has about described our situation. There is another side to this, however. Give those foreign workers capital equipment, training, and technology equivalent to ours, as increasingly has been the situation since World War II, yet keep their wages low, and there is no way American industry can compete. This is the basic reason, in fact, that one American industry after another, all the way from pottery through radio manufacturing, has either emigrated to the low-wage countries or is in the process of doing so. The consequence, of course, is usually unemployment of some duration for American workers left behind when their old industry departs.

Not surprisingly, the employment aspects of foreign trade come to the fore during each period of depression or recession in the United States. It is simple enough to argue that protection by its very nature serves to perpetuate inefficient industries (if they were efficient, after all, they wouldn't need protection) at the expense of efficient industries — those able to sell abroad if only foreigners can secure American dollars by selling their goods to us. By reducing import duties we in effect force workers out of low-productivity industries into high-productivity industries. This is all well and good if demand is strong and the efficient industries are taking on additional workers. But if unemployment is already high, laid-off workers may be forced to enjoy a lengthy vacation without pay.

The argument can be even further generalized, as it was during the 1930s, especially in the writings of John Maynard Keynes.[3] The Keynesian analysis ties foreign trade into the general logic of employment theory. It does this by recognizing that exports are job-creating and imports job-destroying. If there is an active demand for bulldozers, either domestic or foreign, then Caterpillar will take on the additional workers necessary to build the tractors. The income generated in manufacturing these bulldozers, moreover, will circulate through the economy as it is spent, so that each dollar paid out, by being spent and respent, will increase the national income by several dollars. This is, of course, the multiplier process, with which we got acquainted in Chapter Three. Conversely, if an American construction company decides to buy a Japanese bulldozer rather than a Caterpillar, then Caterpillar has one less tractor to build and will lay off or refuse to hire the workers associated with that tractor. The income lost will pull down the national income in a multiple fashion, just as it pushed it up when Caterpillar built its tractors. Much of the attention given to protection to industry in recent decades, especially during periods of recession, has centered on these employment aspects of exports and imports. It is the principal argument used by labor unions in their support of protective barriers. So far these moves have been tempered by recognition of the fact that barring imports or subsidizing exports to increase employment is a game all nations can play. An attempt to "beggar thy neighbor" by shutting out imports is apt to lead to prompt retaliation — in which case both nations will end up poorer because foreign trade and all its benefits will be reduced.

A final argument for protection to domestic industry has been around a long time but it still retains its vigor. Adam Smith — a zealot in the cause of economic efficiency — conceded in his 1776 *Wealth of Nations* that

---

[3] See John Maynard Keynes, *General Theory of Employment, Interest and Money,* Harcourt, Brace, New York 1936.

"defense is more important than opulence." This means that if an industry is absolutely indispensable for defense purposes but is at the same time inefficient to the point that it cannot compete against world competition, then it must be kept alive by special protection. Britain's maritime fleet, of crucial importance in wartime, was one specific case Adam Smith had in mind. And the American maritime fleet, particularly since World War I, has been the beneficiary of almost continual financial transfusions by the federal government. All in the name of defense. At times the argument has been carried into other industries. Could we get along without an optical industry during wartime? Who would provide us with bombsights, periscopes, and binoculars? And maybe we had better protect the bicycle industry, not because bicycles would be indispensable in wartime, but because bicycle manufacturing workers have skills that could readily be shifted and employed in war-goods industries — even in the production of bombsights. When the argument is stretched this far, however, it becomes almost ridiculous. World War III, if it comes, is not likely to be another World War I or II, in both of which we had time to gear up for a major war effort. Nuclear weapons changed all that. More to the point, when modern wars are considered, what is not a war industry? Maybe cosmetics or toys are not, but agriculture surely is, along with most manufacturing industries. If we must protect most American industries because they are helpful in wartime, then the defense argument becomes so broad as to be of little use in deciding where protection should be provided.

Nontariff protection

The analysis to this point has proceeded mainly on the assumption that protection, if it is to be provided, will take the form of import duties on foreign goods. There is justification for this, since our own history tells us that is the form of protection we have employed most systematically. But it is actually only one of many ways in which domestic industry can be favored.

The case of the American merchant fleet already cited demonstrates one alternative way of protecting American industry. Provided with government _subsidy payments_ ranging up to half of new ship construction costs, American shipbuilders are able to sell their ships at competitive prices. The subsidy, in fact, has often been advocated as preferable to import duties. Our first vigorous proponent of protection for American industry, Alexander Hamilton, took such a position in his _Report on Manufactures_ (1791). Arguing along infant-industry lines, he recommended the payment of bounties to the founders of new manufacturing companies. Such payments, he felt, would be more positive and direct than import duties. Economists have since argued that direct subsidies would also be more open to inspection by the public, since they would be listed in the annual budget and would therefore have to be rejustified every year. The fact that the maritime subsidy — both for building and for operation — quietly rides through every federal budget-making process renders this point at least questionable.

Given their preference, American industrialists and workers have usually opted for *import quotas as protective devices.* The problem with import duties, as they see it, is that foreign producers can get around them by putting on an efficiency drive and pushing down costs of production, so that even with the added duty they can undersell the American producer. Or, alternatively, American costs of production are not held in check so that domestic prices are forced above the landed price of foreign products. There is no way around a quota, though. If foreign sugar producers are allowed to send only 100,000 tons of their combined crop to the American market, then obviously the balance of the annual demand must come from domestic production. The price-competitiveness of foreign producers is of little moment.

Finally, imports can be discouraged and exports boosted by deliberately *rigging the exchange rate* (the price of a foreign currency in terms of the domestic currency). Let's say the German mark now sells for 25 cents. Our government has the power, if it chooses to exercise it, to change the exchange rate to 50 cents for one mark. This is called *competitive devaluation,* since it represents a reduction of the value of the dollar in terms of the mark. Formerly, a dollar bought 4 marks; after devaluation it buys only 2 marks. The important point is that since the dollar now buys only half as many marks as previously, the price of a German Volkswagen is effectively doubled for American car buyers. This is indeed the major reason why Volkswagen prices in the United States rose from around $2,000 in 1971 to $4,000 by 1976 — and the reason, too, for the sharp decline in Volkswagen imports into the United States. On the other hand, since he or she can now buy twice as many American cents with a mark, the German citizen should find many American goods excellent buys. The IBM computer that was previously out of the German's reach may now be a real bargain, since its price has been cut in half.

The recent history of protection

After this tour through the jungle-land of interferences with free trade, it is a distinct pleasure to report that free trade began to come back into its own again during the 1930s, as Figure 14.1 portrays. With the Trade Agreement Acts of 1934, Congress set forces in motion to reverse the high tariff levels established during the previous twelve years. It did this by giving over to the president the authority to reduce the extraordinarily high Hawley-Smoot rates by up to 50 percent — on the condition that beneficiaries of these lowered rates would reciprocate by reducing their duties on our goods. The same principle was embodied in the Extension of Trade Act of 1947. The consequence has been a drastic reduction of import duties during the last forty years — from 59 percent of dutiable imports in 1932 to a mere 6 percent in 1975. During the period since World War II, in particular, the United States has set an example in its attempts to lead the world back to free trade.

In this effort, it has been only partially successful. The less developed countries of the world see that the highly industrialized countries have everything to gain from free trade and nothing to lose. With no restrictions on the movement of industrial goods, the experienced, highly efficient industrial nations would be able to sweep the products of the new manufacturers in the developing countries completely out of the marketplace. In fact, policymakers in these countries believe this is one reason manufacturing industries in the Third World made so little progress for so long. Until they decided to give their new industries adequate protection against the more efficient, mass-production manufacturers in the industrialized countries, their own inefficient, small-scale manufacturers were buffeted by competition they couldn't match. These countries, then, are quite willing to pay the higher prices associated with protection of inefficient industries, feeling that it is only by this route that they can hope to be more than suppliers of agricultural products and minerals for the world.

And partly for the same reason the other industrialized nations have been less enthusiastic about free trade than has the United States. With no restrictions on imports the most efficient nation can take over markets anywhere in the world. Ocean shipping rates, after all, are extraordinarily low compared with overland rates and provide only a scant margin of protection to inefficient domestic producers. When the European nations moved toward free trade after World War II, then, they moved very cautiously. While they reduced the barriers to trade among themselves, within the framework of the Common Market, they carefully protected their markets against low-cost American goods by building a protective tariff wall around the whole Common Market.

The effects of protection

Lest too much be made of the powers of protection, it should be pointed out that there are strict limits to what protection of domestic industries can do. Unless a country has a potential comparative advantage in some field, no amount of protection will guarantee the success of a new industry in that area. We could easily close out Honduran bananas and Brazilian coffee, but would we thereby spawn American banana and coffee industries? Not likely. If a country does have a potential comparative advantage in some field, however, then protection can at least push a new industry along more rapidly than would otherwise be possible. In the face of vigorous and effective British competition, for example, it is unlikely that the American steel industry would have led the world by the end of the nineteenth century without the protection of high import duties. On the other hand, our advantages for making steel, in the form of readily available iron ore, coal, and limestone, were sufficiently great that free trade would not have prevented the industry from developing at some later time.

| THE AMERICAN TRADE PATTERN |

In closing this section on foreign trade, let us take a brief look at our present trade pattern. What do we import? What do we export? Who are our major trading partners? Detailed answers to these questions would fill many books, but summary figures can give us at least a panoramic view. First, a picture of our trading partners is provided in Table 14.2.

In addition to telling us where we send our merchandise exports and where we get our imported goods, Table 14.2 points up a number of other facets of our trade. First of all, it confirms one aspect of trade that has been mentioned previously: that goods largely pay for goods — that exports pay for imports and imports for exports. Obviously, there needn't be an exact one-for-one relationship here. It is possible, as we will see in more detail later when we look at the balance of payments, to find other ways of paying for imports: selling services, drawing on past savings in the form of gold or foreign exchange accumulations, borrowing, getting gifts, using inflows of foreign investment funds. But in the long run it is primarily exports that pay for imports. Exports in general, that is. Exports and imports from any one country or even any one part of the world may be far out of balance, as Table 14.2 tells us was the case in 1974. What is earned in exporting to one part of the world may always be used in buying imports from some other part of the world. This, in fact, is the well-known principle of *multi- lateral trade*.

Another thing that Table 14.2 points out is that an extraordinary part of our total trade is conducted with a handful of nations: our neighbors in the Western Hemisphere and the well-developed nations elsewhere. *Well- developed* means rich, so it should come as no surprise that we conduct close to two-thirds of our trade — both exports and imports — with rich countries. Although the developing countries have the people and the need for our goods, they don't have the money to buy them. And aside from some foodstuffs and raw materials, these poor countries produce little that we need. If there is a moral in all this, it may be that we should have an interest in seeing that these countries make economic progress, so they will have the income to take our goods and the industrial capacity to provide us with their manufactures in exchange.

Canada looms very large in the picture presented in Table 14.2, taking around 20 percent of our exports and providing us with over 22 percent of our merchandise imports. This makes it misleading to talk of our foreign trade as "overseas" trade. Over the years we have developed close economic ties with Canada, and an extensive trade is the consequence.

TABLE 14.2

United States exports and imports of merchandise, by continent, area, and selected countries, 1974 ($ million)

	Exports	Imports
Total	98,506	100,972
Developed countries[a]	63,018	60,479
% of total	64.0	59.9
Developing countries[a]	32,698	39,471
% of total	33.2	39.1
Communist areas of Europe and Asia	2,239	1,007
% of total	2.3	1.0
Africa	3,659	6,617
% of total	3.7	6.6
Asia	25,784	27,500
% of total	26.2	27.2
Australia and Oceania	2,697	1,503
% of total	2.7	1.5
Europe	30,070	24,635
% of total	30.5	24.4
North America	27,887	31,728
% of total	28.3	31.4
South America	7,857	8,974
% of total	8.0	8.9
Western Hemisphere	35,744	40,701
% of total	36.3	40.3
Canada	19,932	22,282
20 Latin American countries	14,504	13,678
Western Europe	28,639	23,745
% of total	29.1	23.5
West Germany	4,986	6,428
United Kingdom	4,574	4,021
France	2,942	2,305
Belgium and Luxembourg	2,285	1,681
Italy	2,752	2,593
Netherlands	3,979	1,453
Communist areas in Europe	1,432	891
% of total	1.5	.9
Asia	25,784	27,500
% of total	26.2	27.2
Japan	10,679	12,455
Communist areas in Asia	807	116

[a] Developed countries include Canada, Western Europe, Japan, Australia, New Zealand, and Republic of South Africa; developing countries include rest of world excluding Communist areas in Europe and Asia.

Source: *Statistical Abstract of the United States*, 1975, pp. 814–817.

TABLE 14.3

U.S. merchandise exports and imports, by selected commodity groups, 1960 and 1974 ($ million)

Commodity	Exports		Imports	
	1960	1974	1960	1974
TOTAL	20,408	97,143	15,073	100,972
% OF TOTAL				
Food and live animals	13.2	14.4	19.9	9.3
Beverages and tobacco	2.4	1.3	2.6	1.3
Crude materials, inedible, except fuels	13.7	11.3	18.3	5.9
Mineral fuels and related materials	4.1	3.5	10.5	25.1
Chemicals	8.7	9.1	5.3	4.0
Machinery and transport equipment	34.3	39.3	9.7	24.5
Other manufactured goods	18.7	17.0	30.3	27.2
FOOD AND LIVE ANIMALS	2,684	13,983	2,996	9,379
Grains and preparations	1,761	10,331		
Wheat, including wheat flour	1,029	4,589		
Corn	285	3,772		
Meat and preparations			314	1,344
Fish			308	1,499
Fruits and nuts			218	628
Sugar			507	2,256
Coffee, green			1,003	1,504
BEVERAGES AND TOBACCO	483	1,247	396	1,321
Tobacco and manufactures	477	1,193		
Alcoholic beverages			273	1,028
CRUDE MATERIALS, INEDIBLE, EXCEPT FUELS	2,805	10,934	2,752	5,915
Soybeans	336	3,537		
Raw cotton	980	1,335		
Woodpulp			305	1,088
Iron ore and concentrates			322	696

TABLE 14.3 (*continued*)

Commodity	Exports 1960	Exports 1974	Imports 1960	Imports 1974
MINERALS, FUELS, AND RELATED MATERIALS	842	3,442	1,587	25,350
Coal	354	2,437		
Petroleum and products			1,550	24,210
Natural gas			33	503
ANIMAL AND VEGETABLE OILS AND FATS	295	1,423	95	544
CHEMICALS	1,776	8,822	807	3,991
MACHINERY AND TRANSPORT EQUIPMENT	6,992	38,189	1,466	24,713
Power generating machinery	490	2,882		
Electronic computers, parts and access	100	2,198		
Power machinery and switchgear	250	1,492		
Radio and television apparatus	180	1,157		
Road motor vehicles, and parts	1,270	7,248		
Aircraft, parts, and accessories	1,024	5,766		
Engines and parts			24	1,530
Office machines			68	1,020
Telecommunications apparatus			127	2,315
Electron tubes, transistors, semiconductor devices, and parts			13	1,045
Automobiles and parts			627	10,640
OTHER MANUFACTURED GOODS	3,815	16,516	4,572	27,507
Paper and paperboard	185	1,232		
Iron and steelmill products	381	2,500	431	5,013
Textiles, other than clothing	478	1,795	562	1,629
Professional, scientific, and controlling instruments	241	1,662		
Newsprint			688	1,484
Clothing			304	2,323
Footwear			148	1,153

Source: *Statistical Abstract of the United States*, 1975, pp. 818–821.

Although Canada has become an important industrial nation, she still draws a high proportion of her manufactured goods from the United States. The fact that Michigan, the automobile center of the United States, led all states in the export of manufactures in 1972 almost tells us where Canada gets a large percentage of her automobiles. And when cars are built in Canada, a high proportion of their parts comes from the United States — as is true of many of her other manufacturing operations. On the other hand, Canada, with her large forests and natural gas deposits, provides us with a significant share of our newsprint and natural gas, as well as manufactured goods.

Judging from the daily papers and newscasts, with their constant references to détente with the Communist countries, it would seem that the results of the thaw in our relationships with them should show up in the trade statistics. They do, but it almost takes a magnifying glass to see them: 1.5 percent of our exports to the Communist areas in Europe, and only .9 percent of our imports from them; and only about half that amount of exports to the Communist areas in Asia (which means essentially the People's Republic of China), along with a miniscule .1 percent of our imports from them. Communist China is still a poor country, unable to develop much of an export surplus, especially of the goods in which we are interested. They, therefore, have difficulty getting the dollars with which to import our goods. In addition, they are still sufficiently uncertain about world opinion toward them that they are reluctant to give up their self-sufficiency. The latter point is true, to a lesser extent, of the Soviet Union and the other Communist nations of western Europe.

Now for the goods we export and import. Table 14.3 tells that story.

Although we sometimes get the impression from the daily news and our casual reading that the United States has lost its competitive advantage in manufacturing and now exports little but _extractive materials_ — products of our farms, forests, and mines — Table 14.3 tells us that this is decidedly not the case. Exports of food and crude materials have indeed grown extraordinarily in recent years — about fivefold from 1960 to 1974. But that is just about how much exports in general have increased, so the growth in our exports of manufactured products has kept pace with our exports of food and crude materials. In fact, during this period, if we lump together chemicals, machinery and transport equipment, and other manufactured goods, and call them all manufactured goods, the proportion of our exports made up of manufactured goods has increased from 61.7 percent to 65.4 percent. Rising wages and inflation in the United States have obviously not priced us out of the world's markets for manufactured goods. While our comparative advantage has slipped in some areas, such as office machines, electronics, automobiles, textiles, clothing, and footwear, it has strengthened in others: computers, paper, professional instruments, and aircraft. So long as we can continue to develop new industries that take full advantage of our sophisticated technology and skilled labor force, we will be able to pay our way in world trade.

Both the world food crisis of the early 1970s and the energy crisis show up in the trade figures. The former makes its appearance in the form of a quantum leap in our exports of wheat, corn, and soybeans (although soybeans, for some not immediately apparent reason, get listed under the heading "Crude materials, inedible"). The latter appears in the form of a 588 percent increase in the value of our coal exports — coupled with a phenomenal 1,462 percent increase in the value of our imports of petroleum and petroleum products. By 1974 these represented about one-quarter of the total value of all imports and were the major reason that the United States had an _unfavorable balance of trade_ for the year — an excess of imports over exports. This is considered unfavorable because we ended up owing foreigners more for the goods we bought from them than we earned from our sales to them. We therefore faced the necessity of finding some way of paying off the balance. All of which takes us into the mysterious world of international finance.

❙ INTERNATIONAL FINANCE ❙

Balance of payments accounting

Actually, international finance is not all that mysterious. We have, in fact, learned something about it already in our discussion of foreign trade. What we need now is a device that will fit the pieces of international finance we already have, along with others we will need to get acquainted with, into a big picture. This is the purpose of a balance of payments statement.

the small society   by Brickman

The easiest way to see what a balance of payments statement is all about is to imagine that at the beginning of the year you placed yourself on our national borders — all of them at once, somehow — so you were in position during the year to keep a record of all transactions involving American citizens with residents of foreign countries. Don't get the impression that you were primarily concerned with governments dealing with governments. These were part of your concern, of course. But of far more importance were the hundreds of thousands of deals struck by private citizens, by which Americans obligated themselves to pay foreigners or foreigners obligated themselves to pay Americans — for cars, foodstuffs, oil, stocks and bonds, tourist expenditures, iron ore, copper, and on and on and on. At the end of the year you add up the books on these international transactions and you find, perhaps to your surprise, that the books balance: Americans ended up paying foreigners exactly as much as foreigners ended up paying Americans. Well, not quite. You're a few hundred million dollars off but you know that this "statistical discrepancy" results only from the fact that you missed some transactions along the way — some money slipped into secret Swiss bank accounts without your being aware of it, for example, or some Mexican pot was successfully smuggled across the border.

The reason you know your books would balance if you had been able to record all transactions is that they're designed so that they must balance. Your own monthly income-outgo statement would balance if it followed balance of payments accounting rules. Let's say your monthly check is $1,000. Now, if you spend exactly $1,000, it is obvious that you have an even balance. But what if you spend $1,300 using your monthly paycheck, $100 from savings, and $200 from a bank loan? Then, by international balance of payments accounting rules, your books still balance: Funds made available from all sources (earnings, savings, loans) equal expenditures. Label as *credits* all the funds brought in during a year through international transactions and as *debits* all payments to foreigners, and you have a country's international balance of payments. The balance of payments must balance, then, but just as with an individual or a family, it makes a considerable difference how the balance is achieved, whether primarily by way of earnings; or in large part by drawing down past savings or by borrowing.

While the logic of national balance of payments accounting is the same as it is for an individual or a family, the earnings, savings, and loans take quite different forms, as we see from Table 14.4, the United States international balance of payments for two recent years.

Lines (1) through (3) we are already familiar with, having examined merchandise trade in some detail in the previous section. It remains only to notice that from 1974 to 1975 our trade balance swung from unfavorable to favorable. The reasons for this do not concern us at the moment, but the consequences do. Our adverse trade balance in 1974 left us owing

TABLE 14.4

United States international transactions — summary, 1974 and 1975 ($ million)

Credits (+), debits (−)	1974	1975
(1) Merchandise exports	98,310	107,133
(2) Merchandise imports	−103,679	−98,150
(3) Merchandise trade balance	−5,369	8,983
(4) Military transactions, net	−2,083	−833
(5) Investment income, net	10,227	6,007
(6) Other service transactions, net	812	2,163
(7) Balance on goods and services	3,586	16,269
(8) Unilateral transfers	−7,185	−4,620
(9) Remittances, pensions, and other transfers	−1,710	−1,727
(10) U.S. government grants (excluding military)	−5,475	−2,893
(11) Balance on current account	−3,598	11,650
(12) U.S. government capital transactions, net (outflow, −)	1,089	−1,731
(13) Change in U.S. official reserve assets (increase, −)	−1,434	−607
(14) Gold	—	—
(15) SDRs	−172	−66
(16) Reserve position in IMF	−1,265	−466
(17) Foreign currencies	3	−75
(18) Change in U.S. private assets abroad (increase, −)	−32,323	−27,061
(19) Bank-reported and nonbank-reported claims	−22,715	−14,547
(20) U.S. purchase of foreign securities, net	−1,854	−6,206
(21) U.S. direct investments abroad, net	−7,753	−6,307
(22) Change in foreign official assets in U.S. (increase, +)	10,257	4,603
(23) Change in foreign private assets in U.S. (increase, +)	21,452	8,544
(24) U.S. bank-reported and nonbank-reported liabilities	17,632	731
(25) Foreign private purchases of U.S. Treasury securities, net	697	2,649
(26) Foreign purchases of other U.S. securities, net	378	2,727
(27) Foreign direct investments in the U.S., net	2,745	2,437
(28) Discrepancy	4,557	4,602

Source: *Federal Reserve Bulletin* (July 1976), A58.

foreigners something over $5 billion, which had to be made up on the other transactions. In 1975, though, our exports far more than paid for our imports, leaving us with a nearly $9 billion credit balance to be used elsewhere.

Because we subsidize a number of foreign armies and get no subsidies in return, line (4) is always negative. It is the net total of our overseas military aid program, by which we provide foreign governments the American dollars to buy our military hardware. Since it means an outflow of dollars, it has the same consequence for balance of payments purposes as imports of merchandise, which also lead to an outflow of dollars.

Line (5) means money flowing into the country, and thus is a credit item. It is the return investors in this country received during the year on their past investments abroad. Much of this is company income — profits coming back to the United States from investment in foreign countries by American multinational firms. At the time the foreign investments were made, money drained out of the United States. Now the reverse is taking place.

Line (6) represents our net sale of services, as opposed to goods. We sell computers, earth-moving equipment, and aircraft to foreign buyers — but we also sell insurance, airline transportation, and hotel accommodations for tourists. We buy the latter, too, but in 1974 and 1975 we sold more than we bought, adding to our net claims against foreigners. In fact, when we add lines (5) and (6) to the goods accounts we find a credit balance on goods and services for both years.

Part of this credit balance — more than all of it in 1974 — went for unilateral transfers. These are in effect gifts — or at least one-way payments: money going out, but nothing coming back in exchange. Perhaps the two most important forms these transfers take are pension payments to

the small society   by Brickman

Americans retired and living abroad and government foreign aid grants. Adding these in gives us the "balance on current account," with a debit balance in 1974, a credit balance in 1975.

The federal government comes into the picture again at line (12), which represents the government's long-term loan transactions, mainly those for foreign aid. A positive balance for 1974 says the government was repaid more on past loans than it extended in new loans, a situation that was reversed in 1975.

Lines (13) through (17) are the principal forms of national savings available for international transactions. These are the different types of official *reserve assets* — assets, in other words, that are acceptable in settling foreign debts. Gold is one type of asset that has always had a place in international transactions, although for the United States it played no part in 1974 and 1975. SDRs ("special drawing rights") are funds made available to member nations of the International Monetary Fund. They can be thought of as a special type of bank money issued by the IMF, an international equivalent to checking account balances within a country. In both 1974 and 1975 we built up our account balances, in effect replenishing our savings account. And we did the same for our reserve position in the International Monetary Fund. Our reserve position in IMF is simply a certain amount of guaranteed loan funds, available on demand — much like overdraft funds available to the holder of a checking account in a domestic bank. During 1974 and 1975 our federal government reestablished its guaranteed loan position by repaying some of its past loans. Finally, the stock of foreign currencies held by the government was drawn down by $3 million in 1974 but more than replenished in 1975.

Lines (18) through (21) reflect the movement of dollars out of this country into the international money and capital markets. In both 1974 and 1975 very large amounts of dollars moved out of the United States into either foreign bank accounts or the purchase of various types of foreign interest-bearing financial obligations. To these totals were added additional dollars flowing into the hands of foreigners in payment for foreign equity (ownership) securities or income-producing property purchased by Americans (direct investments). It is these investment flows or capital flows abroad that ultimately generate the investment income of line (5).

While this was happening, a reverse flow was also taking place — foreign money flowing into the United States. Line (22) tells us that foreign governments or central banks were busy during both years converting substantial amounts of their own currencies into dollars for holding in the United States in the form primarily of bank balances — either Federal Reserve or commercial bank — or United States Treasury obligations (bills, notes, and bonds). Over the years these government treasuries and central banks have found that they are in constant need of dollars and it is wise to have large accumulations on hand.

The same is true, as lines (23) through (27) tell us, of private individuals and companies. Foreign funds come into the United States for conversion into dollars for a variety of reasons: because the rate of return on investments in the United States is better than at home, because the inflation rate is lower, because private wealth is less likely to be expropriated, to get money out of the way of the local tax collector. For whatever reason it comes, it makes that amount of foreign money available to Americans for use abroad, exactly as it does when it comes in in payment for our exports.

So the balance of payments balances — with the help of disquietingly large statistical discrepancies in both years, certifying that the mesh in the governmental statistical net is fairly coarse. In broadest terms, we can say that our exports of goods, services, and IOUs paid for our imports of goods, services, and IOUs — and in the process determined the foreign exchange rate and enabled us to make gifts as well.

Determining the exchange rate

The concept of the exchange rate is simple. It is, as we saw earlier, simply the price of one national currency in terms of another — the rate at which dollars, for example, exchange for Mexican pesos, British pounds sterling, French francs, or German marks. At any point in time there are literally hundreds of exchange rates in existence, one for the currency unit of every country against the currency unit of each country with which it trades.

Determination of each of these exchange rates, on the other hand, is somewhat more complex, since it depends on the international rules under which the trading countries of the world are operating. And these rules have on occasion changed. During most of the years between 1834 and 1933, for example, the United States operated under the provisions of the full, or automatic, gold standard. From 1934 to the end of World War II we were on a limited gold standard. With the end of World War II, exchange rates came under the control of one of the United Nations organizations, the International Monetary Fund. With the introduction of the New Economic Policy of August 1971 by then-President Nixon, the United States set aside the IMF controls and moved toward flexible, or floating, exchange rates. Since we have been living with this last system for several years now and its replacement by another system seems unlikely in the near future, perhaps we should examine its mechanics first. This approach has the added virtue of allowing us to start with the simplest system.

Floating exchange rates

In the determination of any exchange rate the first thing to be reckoned with is that an international transaction almost always involves two prices — the price of the product, service, or security in its own local currency unit, and the price of that currency unit in terms of the buyer's currency unit. Let's be specific and say we're talking about your decision to buy a British sports car, a Jaguar. What you will end up paying for the Jaguar will depend on both the factory price in Britain (so many pounds sterling) and the dollar price of the pound. Change either of these and the price you ultimately pay for the Jaguar changes. Now, the pound sterling price of the Jaguar is determined in the same fashion as are the prices of all other industrial goods, by the combined forces of demand — both foreign and domestic — and supply.

Demand and supply also determine the price of the pound sterling in the international money markets. The demand for pounds comes from all those foreigners who have bought or are contemplating buying British goods, services, or securities and need to pay for them with pounds. The British sellers will ordinarily insist on being paid in pounds, since it is with pounds that they pay their own bills. Foreign buyers of British goods, then, must take their own currencies into the foreign exchange markets, convert them into pounds, and then send the pounds to the British sellers. The intermediation of commercial banks simplifies the process but doesn't change its basic logic. At the same time all this is going on, British citizens are committing themselves to buy foreign goods, services, and securities. They therefore must take their local money, pounds, and convert it into foreign currencies to pay their foreign bills. The supply of pounds they bring into the market, it should be obvious, constitutes the demand for each foreign currency.

Let's see how all this might work out in determining a single exchange rate, that between the pound and the American dollar. Figure 14.2 pictures the exchange market in terms of the demand for and the supply of pounds. The first thing to notice about this market is that both demand and supply are a bit curious: the demand curve is simultaneously a supply curve, and the supply curve is at the same time a demand curve. This is so because the demand for pounds is made up of Americans who are in the exchange market with dollars looking for pounds into which to exchange them. Their supply of dollars constitutes the demand for pounds. Nonetheless, the demand curve, it should be noticed, has the customary slope, from upper left to lower right. This is so because if the dollar price of the pound is high, say $4.00, it takes a lot of American money to buy British goods, so not many pounds will be demanded. At a price of $1.00, though, British goods are very cheap because pounds cost so little, so a lot of dollars will be offered in exchange for pounds. Shifting to the supply side, the supply curve represents all those English citizens who have bought American goods, services, or securities and now must bring their own money, pounds, into the market and look for an exchange into dollars. The supply curve slopes upward from lower left to upper right because dollars are very expensive, and therefore American goods, services, and securities are very expensive, at a low dollar/pound exchange rate. At a $1.00

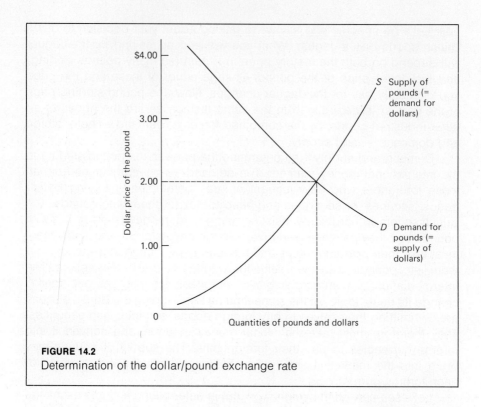

FIGURE 14.2
Determination of the dollar/pound exchange rate

exchange rate a pound buys only $1.00 worth of American goods. At the other end of the supply curve, however, a pound buys $4.00 worth of American goods, so a lot of pounds will look for conversion at that exchange rate.

It is apparent from the diagram and from the general logic of supply and demand analysis, that in a free market there will always be some price that clears the market. In this case, it is $2.00 for £1. Everyone with pounds who wants to convert into dollars at that price finds a willing seller of dollars. This is what we mean by market determination of exchange rates. And if exchange rates are free to fluctuate or float up or down, we have a *floating exchange rate.*

Floating exchange rates promise one huge advantage. Adverse developments in the domestic economy may be largely offset by favorable changes in foreign trade brought about by changes in the exchange rate. Let's say an inflationary spurt takes place in the United States, threatening to cut our exports and the jobs dependent on them because our goods are becoming too expensive for foreign buyers. If this comes about, it will be reflected, at least as far as Britain is concerned, in a leftward shift of the supply curve of Figure 14.2. Because American domestic prices are higher, British buyers want fewer American goods and will therefore bring fewer pounds forward for exchange into dollars. As the supply curve shifts to the left, however, notice that the dollar price of the pound rises, signifying that American buyers of British goods must put up more dollars for each pound. This reduces their purchases of British products, hopefully in favor of American goods. This same rise in the exchange rate for Americans, though, represents a fall in the price of the dollar for British buyers of American goods. Instead of $2.00 their pound can now buy $2.50 or $3.00. By this route American goods regain the attractiveness they lost when their domestic prices rose through inflation. What all this really means is that governments can pursue whatever domestic monetary and fiscal policies they choose without having to worry about balance of payments problems. Changes in the exchange rate will take care of those.

But this freedom for domestic economic policy comes with a high price tag attached. Fluctuations in the exchange rate may be of sufficient magnitude and frequency to disorganize world trade. During 1974, for example, the dollar fell 17.5 percent against the Deutsche mark, only to rise by 9.5 percent and then fall again to a new low by the end of the year. The normal billing period in international trade is thirty days. This seems like a short period, but there have been several occasions during which a currency has dropped in price by as much as 10 percent during a month, completely wiping out any contemplated profit on the resale of goods bought for import during the period. "'Businessmen need a modicum of stable prices in order to make long-term commitments,' says Paul Davidson of Rutgers University. 'In order to foster international trade, exchange rates cannot vary all over the lot because of random shocks.'" [4]

Even more disappointing is the growing realization that countries don't have unlimited ability to isolate their domestic economies. "'The idea that floating can isolate the domestic economy leads to policies that produce fluctuations in the exchange rates,' points out Paul A. Volcker, incoming president of the Federal Reserve Bank of New York. 'But those fluctuations feed back into the domestic economy so there is no isolation.'" [5] This disillusionment with floating exchange rates leads many economists to the conviction that ultimately the international financial community must work its way back to some system of fixed exchange rates. The only question is what the system will be.

The international gold standard

If solidity in exchange rates is desired, then the international gold standard has abundant historical evidence to prove that it can deliver it. During the entire hundred years from 1834 to 1933 the dollar price of the British pound

---

[4] *Business Week* (June 2, 1974), 61.
[5] *Business Week* (June 2, 1974), 61.

never varied by more than a couple of cents from $4.87 — not, at least, during those parts of the century when both countries were on the full gold standard.

How was this miracle performed? In fact, it was no miracle. It was an inevitable consequence of subordinating all other economic policies to the maintenance of a stable exchange rate. The full, or automatic, gold standard calls for a country to do four things:

1 Define the country's currency in terms of gold — that is, set a rate of equivalence between gold and the currency unit. During the period 1834–1933, a dollar was defined as the equivalent of about $\frac{1}{20}$ of an ounce of gold (in exact terms, one ounce of gold equaled $20.67). The pound sterling during the same period was valued at about $\frac{1}{4}$ of an ounce of gold. In terms of gold, then, the pound had a value around five times as great as the dollar (it was precisely 4.87 times as great — thus the $4.87 exchange rate).

2 Allow free convertibility from gold into the domestic currency unit and from the domestic currency unit into gold. This means simply that citizens can buy gold bars or gold coins with other types of money at the established price, and holders of gold can always sell the gold to the banks or the government at the fixed price.

3 Allow free import and export of gold.

4 Allow gold movements into or out of the country to determine domestic price levels, rather than attempting to counteract price movements by contracyclical government policies.

If these rules are established and held to unswervingly, the exchange rate cannot change by more than a few cents — the cost of shipping gold out of or into the country. Figure 14.3 shows how fluctuations of exchange rates are limited to the gold import and export points. Let's say that the dollar is worth $\frac{1}{20}$ of an ounce of gold, the pound is worth $\frac{1}{4}$ of an ounce of gold, and the exchange rate at $5.00 exactly reflects this "mint par of exchange" ($\frac{1}{4} \div \frac{1}{20} = 5.00$). Now American buyers develop a craze for British tweeds, and the demand for the pounds necessary to pay for the tweeds rises to D'. If the exchange rate fully reflected these changing market forces, it would rise to $6.00. But we have already said that the exchange rate under the gold standard cannot move by more than a few cents. What keeps it from rising? The answer is that as soon as the exchange rate rises by around 3 cents, the cost of shipping gold to London, it will pay the American buyer to purchase gold in the United States, where for $5.00 he can get a quarter-ounce of gold, ship it to London, and there convert it into a British pound with which to pay for his tweeds. With this alternative open, the exchange rate can never rise beyond $5.03. The

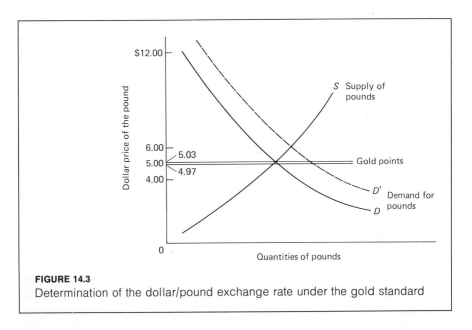

FIGURE 14.3
Determination of the dollar/pound exchange rate under the gold standard

opposite happens, of course, if the supply or demand shifts are in the other direction.

At $5.03, though, Figure 14.3 tells us that we have disequilibrium in the foreign exchange market. The quantity of pounds demanded at $5.03 is far larger than the quantity available. What closes the gap? This is where rule 4 comes into play. If the two countries do nothing to offset the outflow of gold from the United States and into Great Britain, the gold movements themselves will close the gap. This is because on the gold standard gold is money; in fact, it's high-powered money because it not only circulates as money but serves as monetary reserves for the banking system. When the United States loses gold in the situation described in Figure 14.3, its money supply contracts at the same time that Britain's money supply is expanding. Higher prices for British goods, including their tweeds, makes them less attractive to American buyers, sales fall, and the demand for pounds falls back toward its original position. At the same time, because of the fall in American prices, American goods become more attractive to British buyers, sales increase, and the supply of pounds shifts to the right. Ultimately equilibrium is regained and the gold flow ceases.

In summary, the gold standard did bring stable exchange rates. But the price was instability in domestic economies. Gold inflows brought rising prices and prosperity. Gold outflows brought falling prices and recession. And any interference with these developments on the part of the government was taboo — barred by the rules of the gold standard game. Some proponents of the gold standard today (and there are a number, including Alan Greenspan, Chairman of the Council of Economic Advisors under presidents Nixon and Ford) insist this would be all to the good, especially since governments have been less than brilliant in managing countercyclical monetary and fiscal policy. But most analysts argue still that we cannot afford to give up attempts to manage the domestic economy, no matter what the record has been.

The international monetary fund system

The beauty of the IMF system was that it promised the best of both worlds — the gold-standard world where exchange rates fluctuate not at all or only infrequently, and the floating-exchange-rate world where the domestic economy need not suffer eternally the consequences of fixed exchange rates. To deliver on this promise the IMF combined aspects of the gold standard with some features of market-determined exchange rates. From the gold standard came definition of each member country's currency either in terms of gold or of the American dollar. Because the dollar was defined in terms of gold ($35.00 an ounce), these came to the same thing. No domestic circulation of gold or domestic convertibility was entailed, but central banks and governments were guaranteed the right to settle claims among themselves with the transfer of gold. These were the remnants of the gold standard.

By defining their currencies in terms of gold or the American dollar, member countries adopted a particular exchange rate. The IMF then expected them to defend their exchange rates. If Great Britain, for instance, with an adopted $5.00 exchange rate, failed to control inflation, both the demand for pounds and the supply of pounds would be affected. Figure 14.4 indicates that the demand for pounds would decrease to D' because American buyers would no longer find British tweeds so attractive. The supply of pounds would shift to S' because American goods, thanks to their relatively lower prices, would now be more attractive to British buyers than domestic products. The consequence, as Figure 14.4 shows, would be a decline in the exchange rate to $4.00 unless British authorities did something about the situation.

According to the rules of the game they chose to play, the British authorities were requred to take action. Allowing the exchange rate to fall from $5.00 to $4.00 amounted to *devaluation* of the pound. It would provide exporters with a 20 percent price reduction and force importers to pay 25 percent more for their American goods, thus providing a strong competitive advantage for British industry. Nations during the 1930s had learned that this was a quick and easy way to pick up additional business for their industries — at least until their neighbors retaliated by devaluing in turn. This process disrupted international trade, however, and the IMF was determined to head off devaluation except where there was no alternative.

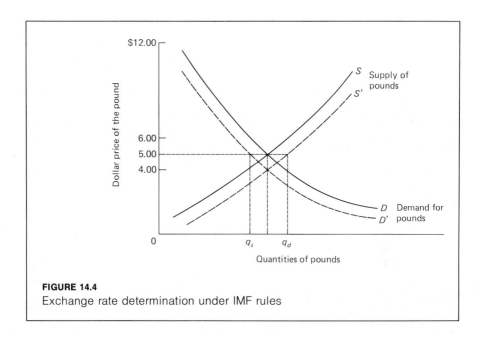

FIGURE 14.4
Exchange rate determination under IMF rules

In the Figure 14.4 situation the British authorities did have an alternative. They could take action against the inflationary condition that initially led to the shifts in the demand and supply curves. But this would take time, and in the meantime, the exchange market was out of equilibrium at a $5.00 exchange rate. There was a demand for $0q_d$ dollars but only $0q_s$ dollars were willingly supplied. To hold the rate at $5.00 an additional amount of dollars $(q_s - q_d)$ had to be put into the exchange market. If Britain's monetary authorities had such an amount of dollars, they could sell them to satisfy the unsatisfied demand. If they did not have the dollars, then the IMF would ride to the rescue, lending Britain dollars for use until the cure for inflation took hold. If for some valid reason it turned out that the inflation could not be cured, the IMF would grant Great Britain approval to devalue officially, thereby once more making its goods competitive in international markets and discouraging frivolous imports.

This was the system in existence throughout the non-Communist world from the end of World War II until August 1971, when the United States refused any longer to observe the rules of the game. Up until the late 1960s the system worked reasonably well. Exchange rates were constant for long periods of time, but they did change when it was essential. By the late 1960s, though, devaluation had come to be looked on as a sign of national weakness — an unwillingness to take the actions necessary to head off devaluation, especially an unwillingness to take a strong enough stand against domestic inflation. The dollar, in particular, was overvalued, which meant that American exports were overpriced and imports underpriced. The consequence was our first unfavorable trade balance of the century in 1971. Yet until August 1971, no American president was willing seriously to propose devaluation. With growing inflation coupled with serious balance of payments problems, signified by a massive outflow of dollars abroad, President Nixon packaged an end to the IMF system along with changed domestic policy in his August 1971 New Economic Policy: a freeze on wages and prices, suspension of the convertibility of dollars into gold by foreigners, a temporary 10 percent surcharge on imports. Both of the latter two provisions are inconsistent with IMF rules. Later in the year the United States officially devalued the dollar, the first step in a process that shortly led to a floating exchange system in 1973.

The IMF still exists, but its rules are no longer observed. Although there is considerable dissatisfaction with floating (and in some cases, deliberately manipulated) exchange rates, the world's monetary authorities have yet to decide on a satisfactory replacement. It appears that we will have to live with the present arrangements until some crisis situation forces agreement on an alternative.

I SUMMARY I

As the world's largest trading nation, the United States plays a key role in the international economy. The strength of our demand for foreign imports is a good barometer of the health of the economies of many of the nations with which we trade. And without those outside products and services the vitality of our own economy would be seriously affected. Our policies toward trade, then, as well as the policies we pursue domestically, have a critical role in determining the vigor of the American as well as the international economy.

The essential case for free international trade is relatively simple. International trade widens the market for goods and services, thereby encouraging specialization and increasing the efficiency of production. With each nation concentrating its productive efforts on what it can do best — where it has the greatest comparative advantage — world production and real incomes are maximized. Since specialization implies the loss of self-sufficiency, free trade is necessary in order that excess amounts of each nation's products can be exchanged for what the nation does not produce.

But even though free trade promises maximum efficiency and maximum production, that promise historically has never been fully realized. The modern world has never seen completely free trade. The primary reason is that while free trade benefits the vast majority, it brings adverse consequences for vocal minorities. The latter demand that their interests be protected by curbing foreign competition.

Although the United States engages in trade with nearly all the nations of the world, the bulk of our trade is with the richer countries. Study of our exports shows that we have not lost our competitive advantage in the overseas sale of manufactured goods. As is well known, our imports are increasingly dominated by petroleum shipments.

After a century during which our merchandise exports systematically exceeded our imports, giving us a favorable balance of trade, our imports in recent years have run ahead of exports. We have thus had to rely more heavily on exports of services and IOUs in our international balance of payments.

Today overall imports and exports of goods, services, and IOUs and the money movements associated with them, more or less freely determine the foreign exchange rate — the rate at which one nation's currency exchanges for that of another nation. This has by no means always been the case. For most of our history as a nation, in fact, the price we set on gold under the international gold standard determined the foreign exchange rate of the dollar. And after we gave up the gold standard and went with the International Monetary Fund system, the exchange rate was governed by IMF rules.

I   IMPORTANT TERMS AND CONCEPTS   I

absolute advantage

comparative advantage

revenue tariff

protective tariff

infant-industry argument
    for protection

scientific tariff

multilateral trade

unfavorable balance of trade

floating exchange rate

international gold standard

devaluation

I   QUESTIONS, PROBLEMS, AND EXERCISES   I

1 Why does what we do in the United States to solve our own economic problems have such a large impact on the rest of the world?

2 What role is there in world trade for a nation that cannot provide a single good or service as efficiently as some other nation?

3 Summarize in a short paragraph the basic argument for free trade.

4 Given the power of the argument for free international trade, why have so many restrictions been placed on international trade over the years?

5 Why isn't the acknowledged fact that foreign workers are paid less than American workers a sufficient reason for protecting American-made goods?

6 What makes the poorer countries less than enthusiastic about free trade?

7 Why is such a large part of the United States trade conducted with the economically advanced nations?

8 Why must our international balance of payments actually balance?

9 Use Figure 14.2 to show what would happen to the dollar price of the pound if prices of American export goods held steady while the prices of British goods rose rapidly. Then go on to describe what the change in the dollar price of the pound would do to trade between the two countries.

I SUGGESTED READING I

"At the Summit Talks: Creeping Cartelization." *Business Week* (May 9, 1977), 64–83.

Calleo, David P., and Benjamin M. Rowland. *America and the World Political Economy: Atlantic Dreams and National Realities.* Indiana University Press, Bloomington, 1973.

Canterbery, E. Ray. *Economics on a New Frontier.* Wadsworth, Belmont, Calif., 1968.

"Floating Exchange Rates: The Calm Before an Economic Storm." *Business Week* (October 3, 1977), 68–80.

Ingram, James C. *International Economic Problems,* 3d ed. Wiley, Santa Barbara, Calif., 1978.

Silk, Leonard. *Nixonomics,* 2d ed. Praeger, New York, 1973.

Wallich, Henry C. "What Makes Exchange Rates Move?" *Challenge* (July–August 1977), 34–40.

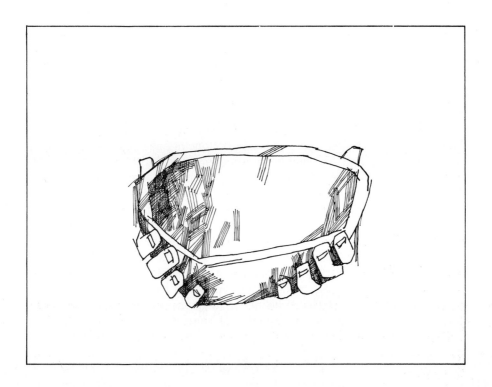

| THE PLIGHT OF THE THIRD WORLD |

Discussion has to this point focused almost exclusively on the economic problems of the industrially advanced, market-oriented nations, especially the United States. Another group of nations, associated with the Soviet Union, rely far more extensively than does the United States on government control and central planning to solve their economic problems. There is yet a third, far larger group of countries, numbering around 100 nations. This *Third World* contains over half the world's population, most of whom share one common characteristic: They are desperately poor. A study of the Third World, then, is a study of world poverty and what can be done about it.

The developed parts of the world, as we have seen, are not entirely free of the problem of poverty. But poverty is usually relative rather than absolute in these countries. It is the rare family in the United States that needs to worry about its actual survival. Poverty in Third World countries, on the other hand, is not uncommonly a matter of life or death. For example, "seventy-five percent of all [East] Indians have no assured employment and earn four hundred rupees (about fifty-three dollars) or less a year. They cannot even count on such rock-bottom necessities for survival as one meal a day and one piece of permanent clothing, and so fall below what the government has defined in its official income profile as 'the poverty line.'"[1]

Poverty is ordinarily defined as an "insufficient flow of income" — the term *insufficient* being subject in turn to definition by the appropriate authorities in each country. The official poverty-line income in India, as the above quotation suggests, is one that barely staves off disaster. And with such a large proportion of the population officially classified in the poverty group, poverty obviously could not be eliminated as it could in the United States simply by taking from the rich and giving to the poor. There just aren't enough of the rich. Poverty in most Third World countries is essentially a matter of too little national production and too many people to share this production.

This is brought home when the total world output of goods and services is divided into relative shares according to its place of production and compared with the proportion of the world's population laying claim to each production share, as shown by Table 15.1.

What Table 15.1 tells us is that the industrially developed nations of North America and Europe, along with Japan, produce more than 70 percent of the world's output and share it among less than one-fourth of the world's population. The nations of Asia and the Middle East, on the other hand, must attempt to provide for over half of the world's people with less than 10 percent of the world's output. And the African nations can lay claim to less than one-fortieth of world output in attempting to provide for more than one-tenth of the earth's population. This is indeed a world of haves and have nots.

Dividing each nation's gross national product by its total population provides a rough and ready index of how far each of the developing nations has proceeded along the path of economic growth and the probable extent of poverty in each of these nations. Everything that has been said previously about gross national product as a measure of welfare must be kept in mind in using this index, but even so we will see that a low per capita gross national product figure for a country is a fairly certain indication that the usual symptoms of poverty will be present.

---

[1] Ved Mehta, "Letter from New Delhi," *The New Yorker* (October 14, 1974), 154.

TABLE 15.1
Gross national product and population, 1972 (%)

	Gross national product	Population
North America	34.6	6.2
Europe, excluding U.S.S.R.	30.2	13.4
U.S.S.R.	10.4	6.6
Asia, including Middle East and excluding Japan	8.9	52.4
Japan	6.8	2.9
Central and South America[a]	5.3	7.9
Africa	2.4	10.1
Oceania	1.3	0.6
Total	100.0	100.0
Developed market economies[b]	67.0	17.9
Centrally planned economies[c]	18.9	32.1
Developing countries	14.1	49.9
Total	100.0	100.0

Note: In 1972, world GNP was $3.7 trillion, population was 3.7 billion.
[a] Includes Mexico.
[b] Australia, Austria, Belgium, Canada, Denmark, Finland, France, West Germany, Iceland, Ireland, Italy, Japan, Luxembourg, Netherlands, New Zealand, Norway, Portugal, Puerto Rico, South Africa, Sweden, Switzerland, United Kingdom, United States.
[c] Albania, Bulgaria, China, Cuba, Czechoslovakia, East Germany, Hungary, North Korea, Mongolia, Poland, Romania, USSR, North Vietnam.
Source: *World Bank Atlas, 1974: Population, Per Capita Product, and Growth Rates*, World Bank Group, Washington, D.C., 1974, pp. 8–10.

| THE POVERTY SYNDROME |

The figures in this section attempt to portray the meaning of world poverty. Figure 15.1 sets the stage by giving per capita gross national product in United States dollar equivalents for a group of nations at different stages of economic development. The United States, Japan, and the Soviet Union are included in the charts as representatives of the highly industrialized, well-developed world. Mexico comes in as a representative of those countries at an intermediate stage of industrialization and development. Saudi Arabia is listed partly because it is the leader of the Organization of Petroleum Exporting Countries (OPEC), partly because it can serve as an object lesson in mistaking per capita GNP for economic development. Finally, two Asian countries (Bangladesh and Nepal) and an African country (Uganda) are brought in to represent the poorest of the poor.

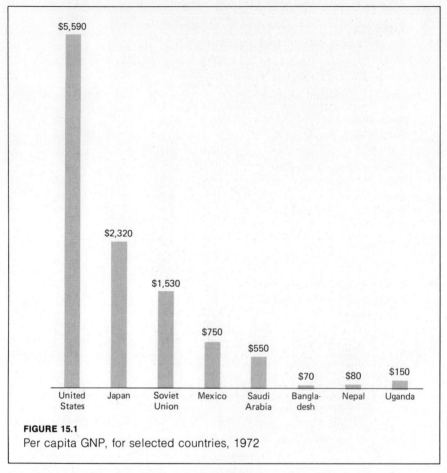

FIGURE 15.1
Per capita GNP, for selected countries, 1972

Source: Based on *World Bank Atlas, 1974: Population, Per Capita Product, and Growth Rates,* World Bank Group, Washington, D.C., 1974, pp. 8, 10.

Because it employs per capita GNP as its measure, Figure 15.1 overdramatizes the extremes of worldly wealth and poverty. It is simply inconceivable that an American has available almost one hundred times as many goods and services as a citizen of Bangladesh or Nepal. Common sense and an understanding of national income accounting suggest that the differences are great, but not that great. Gross national product, remember, measures production as it passes through the marketplace on its way to the final user — and all newly produced goods and services that command a price are considered part of that production. Close to one-quarter of our total production is automobile-related. But how much better off are we who ride in automobiles than those natives of Bangladesh who live in villages and walk to work? How much better off are we because of the billions of dollars we spend annually on cigarettes, drugs, and alcoholic drinks? On the other side of the coin, how much better off are we because our food and clothing and housing are produced by others rather than ourselves, as typically is the case in the developing nations? Since these do-it-yourself activities are outside the market, they are not caught in the gross national product net.

Life expectancy

Incontestably, then, gross national product comparisons exaggerate real differences in wealth and income. But however much distortion comes from using GNP as a basis for comparison, Figure 15.2 suggests that it remains a fact that residents of high per capita GNP nations are indeed better off where one vital aspect of life is concerned — the length of life itself. A newborn citizen of the United States, Japan, or the Soviet Union can expect to live about twice as long as a newborn child in the poorest countries.

Figure 15.3 makes it clear that this does not mean that no people live beyond their forties or fifties in Bangladesh and Uganda. There are in fact many old-timers in these countries, but they are a small proportion of the

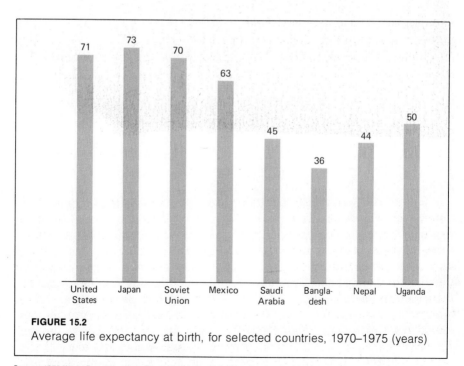

FIGURE 15.2

Average life expectancy at birth, for selected countries, 1970–1975 (years)

Source: 1975 *World Population Data Sheet,* Population Reference Bureau, Inc.; Washington, D.C. Reprinted by permission.

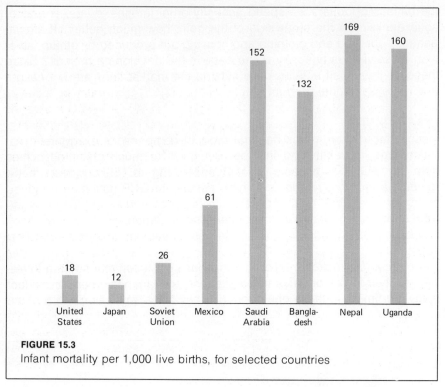

FIGURE 15.3
Infant mortality per 1,000 live births, for selected countries

Source: 1975 *World Population Data Sheet,* Population Reference Bureau, Inc.; Washington, D.C. Reprinted by permission.

army of babies born each year. Because so many of these babies fail to survive their first year or are wiped out later by one of the childhood diseases, the average length of life is quite short. After all, if two babies are born, one to die immediately and the other to live to one hundred, the average length of life of the two is fifty years.

Figures 15.2 and 15.3 together tell us that raising the income level normally increases the average length of life, especially by reducing infant mortality. Higher incomes mean healthier mothers, babies, and children because those incomes bring more and better food, clothing, and shelter, as well as better sanitation and medical treatment. Not all of this immediately, however, as the figures for Saudi Arabia show. Thanks to rapidly increased production of oil and its sale at escalating prices, along with a fairly small population (around 9 million in mid-1975), Saudi Arabia's per capita GNP hit the high level of $550 in 1972 and exploded up to around $3,000 in 1974. For the moment, however, Saudi Arabia still exhibits life expectancy and infant mortality figures common to much poorer countries. Economic development brings higher per capita incomes, but the experience of Saudi Arabia and the other OPEC nations suggests that the reverse need not be true: Income can grow without a comparable amount of economic development taking place. Development is income growth plus change — change involving the whole of society. *Modernization* is a better shorthand expression for this development than *industrialization* because the latter implies that change may be limited to the realm of industry, whereas modernization correctly suggests that development spreads across the whole of society and involves many aspects of life: economic, political, social, cultural. There can be no doubt that the economies of the OPEC nations have grown (the per capita GNP figure for the United Arab Emirates in 1974 was an unbelievable $21,000), but development in the terms specified above will clearly take some time.

Literacy

The literacy rates pictured in Figure 15.4 are both causes and consequences of the development process. Because the literacy rates in the poorest countries are extremely low, their development efforts are handicapped. Lack of the ability to read and write is no particular drawback when the people of a nation continue to do the routine things they have always done. But modernization of an economy means change and calls for workers, businessmen, and administrators who are able to read and write and at least "do figures." An insufficient educational effort thus impedes growth — and minimal growth means few additional resources to put into education. Poverty breeds poverty.

Economic growth

Figure 15.5 provides support for the adage "Them that has, gits." The countries with the highest per capita incomes tend also to be the countries with the most rapid rates of increase in those incomes. The discouraging thing about this is that the poor countries, as Table 15.2 shows, come close to matching the overall growth rate of the rich countries. But the total income growth in the rich countries is far larger in absolute terms than it is for the poor countries. Equally important, rapid population growth in the poor countries means that there is an ever-larger group of claimants for their meager increases. Both of these effects are shown in Table 15.2.

A mere *1 percent* increase in the 1970 level of gross national product in the rich countries would have meant an additional $25.7 billion for distribution among 920 million people — nearly $30 apiece. For the very poor countries, on the other hand, had their collective gross national product increased by *10 percent,* this would have given them only $23 billion to be divided among almost 2 billion people — a $10 dividend. Unfortunately for these poor nations, their collective gross national product rose considerably less than 10 percent. And fortunately for the rich nations, their collective gross national product rose by far more than 1 percent. The

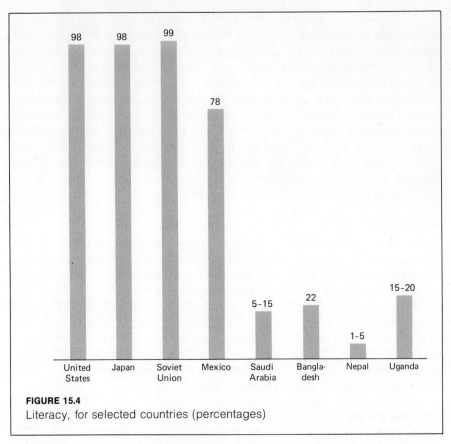

FIGURE 15.4

Literacy, for selected countries (percentages)

Source: Based on United Nations, *Handbook of International Trade and Development Statistics: Supplement 1973,* Publication Sales No. E/F. 74. II. D.7, pp. 102–115.

result was vast widening of the absolute per capita income gap separating the two economic worlds. With some significant exceptions, the people in the poor nations did not get any poorer, but they got richer at a glacial pace. The people in the rich nations significantly increased their wealth.

If trends similar to those pictured in Table 15.2 continue to the end of the century, the consequence, as Table 15.3 suggests, will be a widening of the per capita income spread between rich and poor nations from a gap to a chasm.

The widening of this income gap, as Table 15.2 shows, is not the result of an inadequate growth effort by the developing nations. In overall terms their growth performance differs little from that of the developed countries. The difference lies in their far greater population growth and the consequent necessity for dividing the meager fruits of growth among so

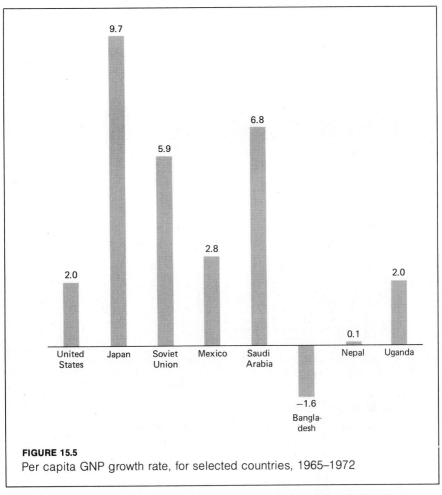

FIGURE 15.5
Per capita GNP growth rate, for selected countries, 1965–1972

Source: Based on *World Bank Atlas, 1974: Population, Per Capita Product, and Growth Rates,* World Bank Group, Washington, D.C., 1974.

many claimants. Figure 15.6 provides some of the dimensions of the problem.

Population growth

Birthrates and death rates are tied together in Figure 15.6 because between the two they determine a country's rate of population growth, if migration is disregarded. If 16 babies had been born during one of these early years in the 1970s in the United States for each 1,000 members of the population at that time and no one had died, the population would have increased by 1.6 percent. Conversely, had no babies been born but 9 persons out of

TABLE 15.2

GNP, per capita GNP and population: 1970 levels and 1969–1970 annual growth rates

	Total GNP, 1970 ($ billions)	Per capita GNP, 1970 ($)	GNP annual growth rate 1960–1970 (%)	Per capita GNP annual growth rate 1960–1970 (%)	Population 1970 (millions)	Population annual growth rate 1960–1970 (%)
Rich countries	2,570	2,790	5.5	4.4	920	1.1
Middle-income countries	270	870	6.5	4.5	310	2.0
Poor countries	155	300	6.0	3.2	520	2.8
Very poor countries	230	120	4.0	1.8	1,930	2.2
World	3,225	880	6.1	4.1	3,680	2.0

Source: Richard Jolly, "International Dimensions," in Hollis Chenery et al., *Redistribution with Growth*, Oxford University Press for World Bank and Institute of Development Studies, University of Sussex, London, 1974, p. 160.

TABLE 15.3

Estimates of per capita GNP for 1965 and 2000 (1965 dollars)

	1965	2000	Annual growth rate 1965–2000
Developing countries	145	388	2.85
Africa	144	281	1.95
Asia	118	324	2.95
South America	379	928	2.60
Developed countries	1,729	6,126	3.67
Europe	1,377	5,087	3.80
Japan	866	8,656	6.80
North America	3,023	7,921	2.80
Oceania	1,641	3,344	2.05
World	646	1,769	2.90

Source: Jagdish N. Bhagwati, "Economic and World Order from the 1970's to the 1990's: The Key Issues," in *Economics and World Order from the 1970s to the 1990s,* ed. Bhagwati, Macmillan, New York, 1972, p. 28. Copyright © 1972, The Macmillan Company.

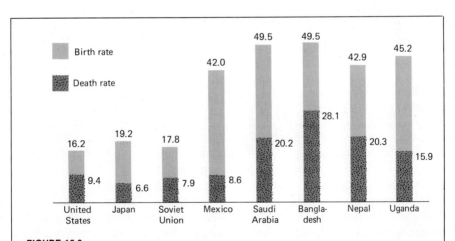

FIGURE 15.6

Birth rate per 1,000 and death rate per 1,000, for selected countries, 1970–1975 average

Source: 1975 *World Population Data Sheet,* Population Reference Bureau, Inc.; Washington, D.C. Reprinted by permission.

each 1,000 had died, then the population would have declined by .9 percent. Subtracting the death rate from the birthrate and converting into percentage terms thus gives the actual annual rate of population increase — around .7 percent. (It was actually higher than this because of immigration.)

Only a high death rate keeps the population of Bangladesh from exploding — as population is currently doing in Mexico and many of the other developing nations. Science and the advance of medical techniques have brought dramatic reductions in the death rate in many poor countries, in advance of the general adoption of parallel techniques to control the birthrate. The consequence is a population growth rate on the order of 3 percent in countries like Mexico and Uganda — a growth rate that doubles their populations every quarter-century.

Many observers believe these galloping populations to be the greatest single barrier to rapid expansion of per capita income in the developing nations — as well as the most difficult to remove. The president of the World Bank, Robert S. McNamara, puts the case bluntly: "The greatest single obstacle to the economic and social advancement of the majority of the people in the underdeveloped world is rampant population growth."[2]

The proposition was established earlier that a larger population means a larger denominator by which to divide in converting GNP to per capita GNP. But the drawbacks of a large and rapidly rising population go far beyond this, extending to a shortfall of actual increase below the potential increase in GNP itself. This is so because populations grow from the bottom upwards. The first indication of an increase in the population is an expansion of the numbers of babies and children — all of whom must be fed, clothed, housed, perhaps provided with schools. Resources that otherwise might have been used to build factories or improve farms and make the economy more productive must be given over instead to supporting children. And it will be years — as many as fifteen — before the children begin to make even a partial contribution to their own support.

Rapid population growth, further, aggravates two related problems that are increasingly coming to the fore in the developing nations: the extent of unemployment and the degree of inequality in the distribution of the national income. Mexico, with a projected doubling of its population in just over twenty years, dramatizes both of these problems. "The Mexico City newsmagazine *Proceso,* quoting government figures, predicts that 1,195,000 Mexican youths will reach the employment age each year between last year [1976] and 1982. If things go as well as expected, there will be jobs for about 300,000 of them. . . ."[3] Small wonder that the United

[2] Robert S. McNamara, *One Hundred Countries, Two Billion People: The Dimensions of Development,* Pall Mall, London, 1973, p. 31.

[3] Gene Lyons, "Inside the Volcano," *Harper's* (June 1977), 42.

States has inherited an army of illegal aliens estimated by experts at somewhere between 6 and 8 million. For the unemployed who remain in Mexico, of course, a spot is reserved at the very bottom of the already distorted income distribution.

With all the publicity that has been given the problem, it would be difficult to find any group of national authorities anywhere in the world who are ignorant of the adverse consequences of rapid population growth. Then why don't they do something about it? In a few cases they have. Birthrates in Hong Kong, Singapore, and Taiwan have fallen sharply in recent years. Even more dramatic is the case of China. With a population already in excess of 800 million at the beginning of the 1970s, China was given little chance by population specialists of substantially reducing its birthrate much before the end of the century. Unbeknownst to them, however, China's birthrate was already beginning to plummet. From a rate of 44/1,000 in 1955 it had been brought down gradually to around 37/1,000 at the beginning of the 1970s. During the next five years it averaged an amazing 26.9/1,000. But China had just about everything going for it. Infant mortality had been reduced to a fairly modest level (55/1,000 live births), and childhood diseases had been brought under control so parents need not have large numbers of children to be sure that two or three survived to maturity. A comprehensive social security system had been introduced, including both free medical treatment and retirement pensions, so parents needed no longer look to their children as a "welfare guarantee." Literacy rates had been increased to the point where written birth control information could be understood, and a successful challenge made to the tradition of large families. Perhaps most important, the omnipresent Chinese government was able to promote group pressures in favor of small families.

Whether or not other countries with large and rising populations will be able to follow in China's footsteps is still doubtful. India's attempt to do so during Indira Ghandi's administration brought down little but the government. With the second largest population in the world, India's birthrate remained at the high level of 39.9/1,000 during the first half of the 1970s. Coupled with a death rate of only 15.7/1,000, this meant a population growth rate of close to 2.5 percent — sufficient to increase the number of people in India by around 15 million a year during this period, twice the population of New York City.

There are those who still argue that to worry about population growth swallowing the benefits of economic development is to see things in an upside-down fashion: Concentrate on the economic growth process and population will take care of itself. As evidence they cite the cases of western Europe and the United States, in both of which no centralized population control efforts were necessary to bring down the birthrate. When industrialization, urbanization, and especially family incomes reached a certain level, sufficient incentive was provided families to reduce the number of children voluntarily. But those who make this argument concede that this voluntary reduction of family size and the consequent fall in the population growth did not come about until those countries were well advanced economically. The first beginnings of decline in the birthrate can be detected around the middle of the nineteenth century. One hundred years later per capita incomes in the underdeveloped countries, though, were only one-sixth to one-third of those achieved in the developed countries by the middle of the nineteenth century. Conceding that we know far less than we need to know about what determines population growth and what can be done to control it, the spokesman for the World Bank nonetheless takes a dim view of simply standing by and hoping that it will take care of itself:

Today the average birth rate for developing countries is 40 to 45 per 1,000 of population. To reduce this rate to the 17 to 20 per 1,000 that is common in contemporary Europe would require a reduction in the developing world of some 50 million births a year. To suppose that economic advancement by itself, without the assistance of well-organized family planning, could accomplish this in any feasible time frame of the future is wholly naive.[4]

Energy and resource use

One final aspect of the profile of Third World countries needs some illumination if we are to understand what underdevelopment means and development implies. Figure 15.7 concerns itself with this point by contrasting energy use in the countries we have been comparing. Not too surprisingly, the well-developed countries, because they are industrialized and urbanized, use far more energy than the less-developed countries, who are still largely agricultural. This suggests an important question: If the developing countries are to follow the development path laid out by the well-developed countries, where will the energy come from? For the OPEC countries, lying atop the bulk of the world's oil reserves, this constitutes no problem, at least for the moment. But what about India, Pakistan, and Bangladesh? And what about the African nations south of the Sahara, none of whom have any significant amount of oil? With continued growth in the rest of the world these nations will find it necessary to pay ever-higher prices to compete for the dwindling supplies of energy resources, whether oil, natural gas, coal, or uranium-produced nuclear energy.

And if this is true for energy, it is equally true for the other natural resources used in huge amounts by industrialized and industrializing countries: iron ore, copper, aluminum, tin, lead, and so on. The unfortunate fact is that today's less-developed countries, with few exceptions, are resource poor. And where they have a supply of natural resources, usually that supply is limited to one commodity. For the remainder of their needs

---

[4] McNamara, *One Hundred Countries, Two Billion People,* p. 40.

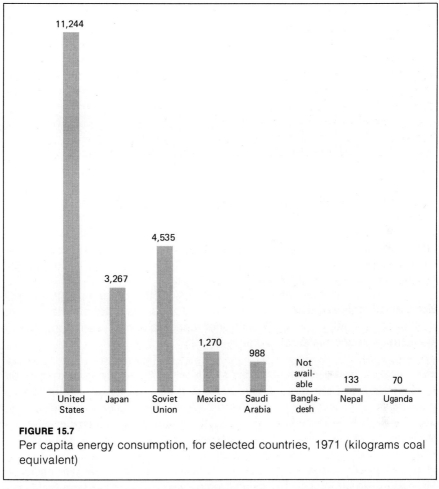

FIGURE 15.7
Per capita energy consumption, for selected countries, 1971 (kilograms coal equivalent)

Source: Based on United Nations, *Handbook of International Trade and Development Statistics: Supplement 1973,* Publication Sales No. E/F. 74. II. D.7, pp. 102–115.

they must compete in world markets, and as Dennis Pirages and Paul Ehrlich imply, that competition in the years ahead will be brutal:

Bringing *all the nations* of the world to the American level of affluence would require a much bigger resource investment than that outlined for mainland China. To accomplish this, if world population growth had halted around 1970, the world's annual production of steel would have to be increased six times. Copper production would have to be increased sixfold, and lead production would have to increase by eight times. But these annual consumption figures are dwarfed by the requirements for "catching up" — the amount of minerals that would be needed to provide all the people on the globe with the stock of equipment necessary to sustain

American production and consumption levels. To produce the per capita United States stock for the entire world would require mining 250 times the present United States annual production of tin, 200 times as much lead, 100 times as much copper, and 75 times as much zinc and iron. In theory the needed iron is still available, but its usefulness could well be limited by lack of molybdenum, which is required for the process that converts iron to steel. The needed quantities of other metals are much greater than *all* known or inferred reserves.[5]

I   THE PROBLEM OF ECONOMIC DEVELOPMENT   I

Efforts to aid development

Economists came late to the problem of economic development. It wasn't until well after World War II that it became one of the recognized specialties of the discipline. Since finding its niche, the field of economic development has been intensively cultivated. Along the way some bitter lessons have been learned, in particular the fact that the more the development process is studied, the more perplexing it appears.

This has come as rather a rude shock. In the beginning, the development process and how to accelerate it appeared rather simple. Writing in the early 1960s, Robert Heilbroner came close to summarizing the consensus economists had achieved:

From what we have learned about the strictly economic aspect of underdevelopment we know already what the core process of economic expansion must be. It must consist of raising the low level of productivity which in every underdeveloped area constitutes the immediate economic cause of poverty. This low level of productivity, as we have seen, is largely traceable to the pervasive lack of capital in a backward nation. Hence if such a nation is to grow — if it is to increase its output of food, to expand its scale and variety of manufacturing — clearly its first economic task is to build up capital. The meager productive capacities of bare hands and bent backs must be supplemented by the enormous leverage of machines, power, transport, industrial equipment of every kind.[6]

Complications relating to the control of population growth, the fracturing of long-observed customs and traditions, and the necessity for responsible political leadership were recognized, but they were considered soluble if the savings necessary to increase the investment rate were found. This is the way the advanced nations had made their "great ascent," so the less-

---

[5] Dennis C. Pirages and Paul R. Ehrlich, *Ark II: Social Response to Environmental Imperatives,* Freeman, San Francisco, 1974, pp. 232–233.

[6] Robert L. Heilbroner, *The Great Ascent: The Struggle for Economic Development in Our Times,* Harper Torchbooks, New York, 1963, p. 74.

developed countries needed but to follow the path that had already been blazed.

Since they were desperately poor — even poorer than the advanced nations had been when they began their development effort — the underdeveloped countries would have some difficulty cutting domestic consumption to release resources for investment, but that meant only that they would need some outside help. There was a well-established precedent even for this. When they had made some progress in their own development effort in the nineteenth century, the European countries and the United States turned and fed investment capital into countries less well advanced than themselves. British capital flowed into the United States in substantial amounts during the nineteenth century, as well as into Latin America and the British colonies. French capitalists helped build the European railway network, provided financing for mining ventures, and dug the Suez Canal. The American effort came later, after the beginning of the twentieth century, but then American capital moved abroad in substantial amounts.

Since World War II the counterpart of this effort has been a large flow of funds from the developed to the developing countries. The multinational corporations have put a substantial part of their investment funds into the industrialized countries, but much has gone as well into the development of manufacturing facilities and even more into the exploitation of natural resources in the poor nations. The huge international banks have been generous with their loans, to the point where they are now owed amounts estimated upwards from $130 billion. And the international agencies, such as the World Bank, and the governments of the developed countries have also helped, not only with loans and grants, but also by providing technical information and advice. Claire Sterling provides a graphic, if somewhat jaundiced, view of the latter for Nepal, one of the least developed of the less-developed countries:

At last count when I was there, about 700 missionaries of progress were racking around town in their Land Rovers and Toyota jeeps, representing some fifty donor-states and agencies, all urging assorted projects on a nation the size of Arkansas. Among the foreign benefactors are USAID, the Indian Cooperation Mission, the Chinese, Russians, British, Canadians, Australians, New Zealanders, Pakistanis, and Swiss, the Japanese Overseas Cooperation Volunteers, the German Volunteer Service, the Ford Foundation, the Rockefeller Foundation, the Dooley Foundation (using volunteer airline hostesses who take six months off for good works), Anglia University, Cornell University, the World Bank, the Asian Development Bank, the International Development Agency, the International Monetary Fund, the UN's Save the Children Fund, UNICEF (also for children), UNDP (development), UNIDO (international development), UNESCO (education and science), FAO (Food and agriculture), WFP (food), ITU (telecommunications), ICAO (civil aviation), WHO (health), WMG (weather), OTC (technical), UPU (postal), UNIC (informational), and

IMCO (Maritime), this last of the opinion that landlocked Nepal ought to own a cargo vessel moored across India, in Calcutta.[7]

The point of Sterling's article is that the advice provided by "the missionaries of progress" has been disastrous for Nepal, since it has at least gone along with an already established policy of denuding Nepal of its trees. The consequent erosion, silting, and uncontrolled flooding have been immense.

The question is now being raised as to whether or not the advice and help provided other developing nations has been any more beneficial. Growth, as measured in terms of gross national product, there clearly has been, as Table 15.2 and Figure 15.5 tell us. But along with this growth have come side effects that have denied any benefits of this growth to major parts of the populations of the developing countries. Concentration of the growth process on urbanized industry has created massive unemployment as well as marked increases in the extent of inequality in the distribution of income. One writer summarizes the consequences of the earlier policies in these terms:

The general development strategies of the 1950s and 1960s placed their bets — and therefore their incentives — on limiting consumption, raising savings and investment rates as rapidly as possible, investing heavily in the protected "modern" sector of the economy, and concentrating government expenditures on "economic" as opposed to "social" overhead projects such as education, health, housing, and sanitation. The costs to the poorest 40 percent of the population in many countries that followed this "trickle-down" strategy have now become clear. Not only have

© Washington Star Syndicate, Inc., permission granted by King Features Syndicate, Inc., 1977.

---

[7] Claire Sterling, "Nepal," *The Atlantic Monthly* (October 1976), 14.

their *relative* incomes and standards of living decreased, sometimes markedly; there is considerable evidence to suggest that the *absolute* incomes of the bottom 10–20 percent also may have fallen.[8]

Growing unemployment

As suggested earlier, one of the reasons that the benefits of growth failed to trickle down to the lower-income groups in the developing nations is that substantial portions of these groups were forced into the ranks of the unemployed. The growth in unemployment is denied by almost no one, but the extent of the increase is a matter for debate. Unemployment in the farming sector, still the primary area of employment for around 85 percent of the workers, is largely invisible. It usually takes the form of underemployment — more workers than are really necessary to operate the farms — rather than outright unemployment. Only when farms are mechanized and machines replace farm hands does unemployment rise visibly. Since the Green Revolution — the application of American-style, advanced technology to farming — is often accompanied by mechanization, pockets of actual unemployment have appeared here and there in the Third World as the Green Revolution has spread.

The common symptom of excess labor in the rural areas is a rising tide of farm workers migrating from the countryside to the cities. To give only one example of this, Mexico City, already over 10 million, is growing at a rate sufficient to double its size in six years, making it the largest city in the world.[9] Similar patterns can be seen in Quito, New Delhi, Calcutta, Manila, and most other cities of the Third World.

The tragedy is that these farm workers are fleeing a known desperate situation to enter one even more desperate. Surveys of urban unemployment in the late 1960s found the rates to range mostly from 10 to 20 percent for the urban labor force as a whole and from 15 to 25 percent for the 15–24 age group. Recent estimates put the overall average rate somewhere in the neighborhood of 25–30 percent.

The explanation for the rising unemployment couples the steady rise in populations with misdirected policies, especially those concerned with capital investment. A rise of population about three times that of the rich nations means that to maintain a given unemployment rate a poor nation must create three new jobs for every one required in a rich nation of equal size. Beyond this, an already difficult problem has been made insoluble by the adoption of wrong-headed policies. Aping the developed countries,

---

[8] Roger D. Hansen, "The Emerging Challenge: Global Distribution of Income and Economic Opportunity," in James W. Howe et al., *The U.S. and World Development: Agenda for Action, 1975,* Praeger Publishers for the Overseas Development Council, New York, 1975, p. 169.

[9] Lyons, "Inside the Volcano," p. 43.

many of the poor nations in allocating their scarce investment funds have concentrated on high-technology, capital-intensive industrial projects in urban areas. This policy skimps the rural areas and deprives them of new jobs. And there is more. The high tariffs necessary to protect the "infant industries" substantially increase the costs of what farmers and other rural residents buy. Flight from the countryside is further encouraged.

This aggravation of difficulties in the agricultural regions is by no means offset by favorable developments in the cities. Life is much better for the few additional workers employed in the new manufacturing operations, it is true. They, along with the rising businessmen and government functionaries, are the economic elite in the Third World countries. But far too few jobs are created to employ the growing flood of job applicants. This, in part, is because production processes imported from the developed nations stress maximum use of capital, because it is relatively cheap in those rich countries, and minimal use of labor, since it is expensive in the developed nations. The fact that exactly opposite conditions hold in the poor countries is commonly overlooked, as Schumacher points out:

Far more serious [than increasing indebtedness] is the dependence created when a poor country falls for the production and consumption patterns of the rich. A textile mill I recently visited in Africa provides a telling example. The manager showed me with considerable pride that his factory was at the highest technological level to be found anywhere in the world. Why was it so highly automated? "Because," he said, "African labour, unused to industrial work, would make mistakes, whereas automated machinery does not make mistakes. The quality standards demanded today," he explained, "are such that my product must be perfect to be able to find a market." He summed up his policy by saying: "Surely, my task is to eliminate the human factor." Nor is this all. Because of inappropriate quality standards, all his equipment had to be imported from the most advanced countries; the sophisticated equipment demanded that all higher management and maintenance personnel had to be imported. Even the raw materials had to be imported because the locally grown cotton was too short for top quality yarn and the postulated standards demanded the use of a high percentage of man-made fibers. This is not an untypical case.[10]

To create more employment in the Third World nations while at the same time reversing the tidal flow of workers from the countryside to the cities, Schumacher puts forward four propositions as focal points for the development effort:

1 ... workplaces have to be created in the areas where the people are living now, and not primarily in the metropolitan areas into which they tend to migrate.

---

[10] E. F. Schumacher, *Small is Beautiful: Economics as if People Mattered,* Harper & Row, New York, 1973, pp. 183–184.

2 . . . these workplaces must be, on average, cheap enough so that they can be created in large numbers without this calling for an unattainable level of capital formation and imports.

3 . . . the production methods employed must be relatively simple, so that the demands for high skills are minimised, not only in the production process itself, but also in matters of organization, raw material supply, financing, marketing, and so forth.

4 . . . production should be mainly from local materials and mainly for local use.

These four requirements can be met only if there is a "regional" approach to development, and second, if there is a conscious effort to develop and apply what might be called an "intermediate technology."[11]

By *intermediate technology* Schumacher means basing production processes neither on the primitive technology of bygone ages nor the "sophisticated, highly capital-intensive, high energy-input dependent, and human labour-saving technology" of the rich countries, but something in between. The creation of small "agro-industrial" establishments in the rural and small-town areas would not likely maximize output per worker — the touchstone of economic efficiency in the rich countries — but it would go far toward maximizing work opportunities for the unemployed and underemployed, a matter currently of far greater concern.

Growing inequality

The rise in unemployment in the Third World is associated with two different problems of income distribution, which will inescapably be of increasing concern in the years ahead: a widening of the income gap between the rich nations and the poor nations, especially the very poor nations, and a widening of the income gap between rich and poor families within these poor nations.

The UN target of a 5 percent growth in GNP in Third World countries during the decade of the 1960s was actually met, as Table 15.2 shows. And this was accomplished with minimal help from the developed countries. The richest country in the world, for example, the United States, provided development assistance in increasingly meager amounts during the 1960s. At the beginning of the 1970s its total development assistance funds in all forms constituted barely more than three-tenths of 1 percent of the nation's gross national product.

When we break this overall 5 percent GNP growth down for country-by-country analysis, though, it loses much of its significance. In fact, the 5 percent turns out to be almost a statistical delusion. Some of the countries of the Third World did very well during the 1960s; some did very badly. An average of the two groups is therefore not particularly meaningful. This

---

[11] E. F. Schumacher, *Small is Beautiful,* p. 165.

bimodal split adds credence to what has been called the first law of development: "To the person who hath shall be given." The richer among the poor countries, those halfway up the ladder, accounted for the lion's share of the progress made. The really poor failed to meet the target. And since the really poor are also the large countries of the world — India, Bangladesh, Indonesia, Pakistan — the targeted growth rate was definitely *not* reached for the poor countries as a whole if we weigh them as we should, by numbers of people involved, rather than merely by size of GNP.

What all this means for world welfare is suggested when we examine the distribution of the fruits of economic growth during the 1960s. During that period world GNP increased by $1,100 billion. Of this trillion-plus dollars, 80 percent went to countries where per capita incomes already averaged over $1,000 — and those countries had only one-quarter of the world's population. Only 6 percent of the $1,100 billion increase went to countries where per capita incomes averaged $200 or less — but they contained 60 percent of the world's people.[12]

These figures suggest that although a number of the Third World countries have made the transition to self-sustaining economic growth, about an equal number — some thirty to forty nations — and these the most populous, are still trapped in poverty. Identified as the *Fourth World,* their plight appears nearly hopeless: rapid population growth; heavy dependence on imported oil, food, and fertilizers, with prices of these tripling or quadrupling since the beginning of the 1970s; all the conditions associated with hard-core poverty — and these in a world where the rich countries seemingly care less and less. The UN's modest .7 percent of GNP target of development assistance from the rich countries to the poor during the Second Development Decade, the 1970s, is apparently going to be underachieved by half.

The situation is becoming desperate. But where it goes from here is still in doubt. These Fourth World countries insist that they cannot make it on their own and demand help from the richer nations. They claim in fact that aid is owed them. Most of them are former colonies of the rich countries, and they argue that many of their problems stem from that fact. As colonies, they insist, their economies were systematically controlled to promote the interests of the colonial nations. Resources were looted, manufacturing suppressed, and education and other social projects neglected. And they see the rich nations perpetuating something like colonial policies by rigging import duties and controls against the products of the Fourth World nations and adopting rules of the game for the international agencies to promote the interests of the rich nations at the expense of the poor. Small wonder that every opportunity is seized by the poor nations to force the United Nations actively to work for substantial changes in the international economic system.

---

[12] McNamara, *One Hundred Countries, Two Billion People,* p. 75.

Needless to say, the view is quite different from the vantage point of the rich nations. They see the Fourth World nations as crippled from their own internal problems and policies, without a change in which, outside aid and assistance would be of little help. Most of the poorest countries are military dictatorships. Why should the wealthy countries provide assistance, they ask, when the aid money will be spent to promote the interests of the ruling clique, not necessarily the interests of the people? The fact that military expenditures in the Third World countries have been rising at a rate of 8 percent a year — considerably more than the percentage increases of their national incomes — adds pertinence to this question. Equally telling, why provide aid if it must be spread so thin just to keep more and more babies and children alive? Finally, why provide aid if its benefits are claimed by only a small fraction of the population and little of it trickles down to the desperately poor?

Income distribution figures for the poor countries suggest that the latter is indeed the case. Any increases in national income, whether from internal developments or as benefits of external aid, seem to end up in the hands of a very small group within each country. Accurate income distribution figures are hard to come by, but all the available evidence says that initially unequal distributions in the Third World countries are becoming even more skewed in the direction of low proportions of total income for the poor, high proportions for the rich. In Brazil, for example, at the beginning of the 1960s, the poorest 50 percent of the population received 20 percent of the national income, the richest 10 percent took 41 percent. By the middle 1960s the share of the poorest 50 percent had fallen to 15 percent, and the top 5 percent claimed 40 percent of the total income. In the Philippines the top 10 percent took 40 percent; in Colombia, 50 percent. A major study financed by the Ford Foundation and published in the early 1970s concluded that "it is clear that the small gains of development [in

the small society   by Brickman

India] during the past decade have been very unequally distributed and the gulf between the rich and the poor has widened."[13]

What these developments suggest for some hard-nosed observers is an international policy of simply abandoning the poorest of the poor countries. Their situation is so hopeless that any attempt to help them is likely to be useless, and the inadequate aid funds available should be concentrated on countries where they could do some good. This is similar to the policy of *triage* adopted by French military doctors at the front during World War I. During major assaults they realized that they could not treat all the wounded promptly. So they divided the wounded into three groups: those who would likely survive without aid, those who needed immediate aid to survive, and those who would likely die even with medical attention. By concentrating all their attention on the second group they maximized the number of lives they could save. This is the policy now being promoted by some for the most desperate cases of the Fourth World. They in effect have been selected out as category-three triage cases.

At least so far this policy has found little support. First of all, although the countries may be economically ill, they have enough vigor and resources left to make life extremely uncomfortable for the rich countries if such a policy were openly adopted.

In addition, triage is based on premises that simply are not factual. In particular, it is not true that world resources are so inadequate that the poorest must be denied assistance. How can such a statement be justified when the two countries in the world with the largest economies, the United States and the Soviet Union, between them spend over $200 billion a year in military expenditures — an amount almost as great as the collective incomes of all the very poorest countries of the world? And how can it be justified when the richest countries, out of swollen national incomes, provide less than one-third of 1 percent of such incomes as assistance to their poor neighbors?

On the other hand, if the richer countries are to help their poor neighbors, there is every reason for insisting the development effort of the latter should not simply be more of the same that has been done in the past. Highly unequal incomes, we have seen, are closely related to growing unemployment and underemployment. And these in turn are the result of pushing development within the framework of a *dual economy*: concentrating the modernization push on large industries in the cities while leaving the agricultural regions to stagnate. A strategy of economic development that concentrated tax structures, commercial policies, and public expenditures on the development of a modern, capital-intensive industrial

---

[13] Distribution figures and quotation from Derek T. Healey, "Development Policy: New Thinking About an Interpretation," *Journal of Economic Literature* (September 1972), 777.

sector has done nothing of a direct nature to increase the development prospects for the rural poor. But there is no inherent reason why agriculture should not become a full partner in the development push, possibly along the agribusiness lines laid down by Schumacher.

For this to happen, though, and for it to benefit the poverty population, 70 percent of whom are made up of landless rural laborers or subsistence farm families, substantial changes in development planning and institutional arrangements will be necessary. A policy of *employment* maximization should be substituted for *output* maximization, or at least some better balance found between the two. Recent investigations, in fact, suggest that there may be little if any conflict between the two objectives. Within this general framework, greater employment as well as greater equity in income distribution appear to require changes in land tenure, help to small farmers, rural public works programs, and better medical and educational facilities in rural areas.

Of these the first, changes in land tenure, is recognized both as the key to the success of the rural strategy and its most formidable political obstacle. It is essential that significant amounts of land be put under the ownership or control of landless laborers and subsistence farmers. Otherwise the other parts of the rural program would go primarily to benefit the already well-off large farmers. Since the large landowners in most of these countries hold substantial amounts of political power, however, they are in position to get the parts of the program that benefit them and resist those contrary to their interests, in particular proposals for land redistribution. Some progress has been made in some countries in buying land for redistribution, but this on a limited basis. No general solution has been found.

In sum, a number of the Third World countries — Hong Kong, Singapore, Taiwan, South Korea, a number of the Latin American nations — appear to have made it over the hump in their modernization drives. But for the very poorest — the Fourth World — the situation can only be described as desperate.

I SUMMARY I

Poverty in the United States is a relative matter. Few in our poverty group face actual starvation. In many nations of the world, however — those of the Third World — poverty is not uncommonly a matter of life or death. This is suggested by the fact that a small number of relatively lightly populated nations claim an extremely high proportion of the world's production, while a large number of heavily populated nations have available only a tiny fraction of that production.

Measuring the level of economic development by per capita GNP may distort the actual spread between rich and poor nations. Nonetheless it is true that low per capita GNP figures are accompanied by others that suggest low living standards: short life expectancy, high infant mortality, low literacy rates, low per capita GNP growth rates.

Reducing their high population growth rates, which tend to perpetuate poverty, is a necessary but formidable project for the less-developed countries. But it is not the only problem they face. There appears little likelihood, for example, that they will be able to secure the resources essential to long-sustained growth.

The major effort put in by economists in studying the development process in recent years has borne meager fruits. In fact, some of the policies recommended earlier, while they may not have stalled the growth push, surely have directed it along wrong paths. Concentration of the development effort on high-technology urban industries, for instance, has created massive problems of unemployment and marked increases in income inequality. In recognition of these problems, development specialists are now giving greater attention to agriculture and intermediate technology for the rural areas.

While some of the less-developed nations have made the break-through into self-sustained economic growth, a relatively large number — some thirty or forty — appear hopelessly trapped in poverty. For these Fourth World countries desperate internal remedies are called for, along with generous assistance from outside.

I IMPORTANT TERMS AND CONCEPTS I

Third World   triage
modernization   dual economy
intermediate technology   poverty syndrome
Fourth World

I QUESTIONS, PROBLEMS, AND EXERCISES I

1 What makes poverty in a Third World nation such as India quite a different problem from poverty in the United States?

2 In 1972 per capita GNP in the United States was $5,590, in Bangladesh $70. Does this mean that the average American was almost 100 times better off than the average person in Bangladesh? If not, why not?

3 Why is economic development more than a rise in per capita income?

4 Since their collective national incomes are rising at a respectable rate, why is the income gap between the rich nations and the poor nations steadily increasing?

5 What supports the argument that the less-developed countries cannot hope to develop and industrialize indefinitely along the path blazed by the now well-developed nations?

6 Why has concentration of the growth effort in the less-developed nations on urbanized industrialization aggravated the problem of income distribution and unemployment?

7 On what grounds do the poor nations of the world insist they are "owed" substantial development aid by the world's rich countries?

8 What position do you take on the adoption of a policy of triage for the nations of the Fourth World?

❘ SUGGESTED READING ❘

Barraclough, Geoffrey. "The Haves and the Have Nots." *New York Review* (May 13, 1976), 31–41.

Franke, Richard W. "Miracle Seeds and Shattered Dreams in Java," *Challenge* (July–August 1974), 41–47.

Healey, Derek T. "Development Policy: New Thinking About an Interpretation." *Journal of Economic Literature* (September 1972), 757–797.

Maddison, Angus, *Economic Progress and Policy in Developing Countries.* Norton, New York, 1970.

Schumacher, E. F. *Small is Beautiful: Economics as if People Mattered.* Harper & Row, New York, 1973.

Wilber, Charles K., ed. *The Political Economy of Development and Underdevelopment.* Random House, New York, 1973.

Wilkinson, Richard G. *Poverty and Progress: An Ecological Perspective on Economic Development.* Praeger, New York, 1973.

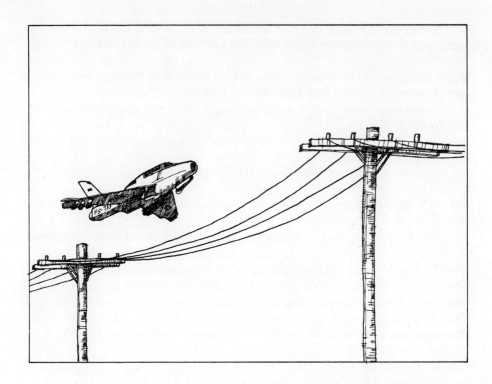

SIXTEEN

GOVERNMENT IN THE ECONOMY: REGULATION, PLANNING, AND DEFENSE

If our economy behaved today as the early economists believed it should, this chapter could be short and even sweet. Defense considerations could be described in a few words. Regulation could be reduced to a description of how market competition protects the consumer and makes government regulation and controls unnecessary, except those embodied in whatever antitrust program is required to keep the economy fully competitive. And central planning would need no description at all since in a well-functioning market economy only individuals have goals and plans. There are no national goals and therefore no need for national plans and planning.

This was the blueprint laid down in the writings of a long series of economists, starting with Adam Smith in 1776 and extending right down to a few at the present time. An earlier concern that allowing individuals complete freedom to pursue their own self-interests would not necessarily promote the public welfare was shrugged off as needless worry.

Adam Smith neatly turned the tables on those who argue that government knows best. He maintained just the opposite: The state can never effectively promote the general welfare because state servants can never know or care as much about individual desires, aspirations, and abilities as the individuals who make up the society. The free play of supply and demand in the unrestricted marketplace, on the other hand, assures that what is most wanted gets produced, that economic resources are drawn into uses where they make the greatest contribution, and that those who contribute most to production are most generously rewarded. Efficiency and equity are both served. In the pursuit of their own private interests, individuals are led "as if by an invisible hand" to promote the public interest. This being the case, a "spontaneous harmony of egoisms" is achieved if government provides an appropriate framework within which free markets can work and beyond that limits itself to carrying out only three duties: national defense, administration of justice, and the maintenance of a strictly limited number of public works and public institutions that are not profitable private undertakings.

Although it is incorrect to say that the American Constitution was designed with this generalized model of laissez faire in mind, it is a fact that the Constitution proved adaptable to this purpose. During the course of the nineteenth century the comprehensive government restraints and controls inherited from the colonial period were gradually stripped away, first at the federal level, later at the state and local level. Not entirely, however. Government never completely withdrew from the marketplace — not even to the boundaries suggested by the businessmen's interpretation of laissez faire: "Leave us alone except where you can help us."

It proved impossible, in particular, to leave one important category of business activities to regulation by the marketplace. What we have come to call *public utilities* were deemed to have characteristics that made it impossible to leave them without government regulation. They were, on the one hand, so "affected with a public interest" that it was considered imperative for government to see that their services were provided reliably. The provision of railroad transportation, as an example, was considered too important to be left to the vagaries of the marketplace. And on the other hand, it was discovered the hard way that where public utility services were provided, they were not necessarily provided at reasonable prices. Competition proved ineffective as a price regulator — either because it never appeared at all or because it destroyed itself as the industry developed.

Whatever the reason for this (and we will see later what the reason was), it left the government with only two choices: either to regulate the industry while leaving it in private hands or to place the industry under public ownership and operate it as a part of government. Either competition regulates or the government must; this was the lesson learned during the nineteenth century, and it is the guiding principle of government intervention today. While assuming regulation of the railroads in 1887, the federal government almost simultaneously launched a major effort to keep other industries sufficiently competitive to avoid the necessity of regulation. This was the major thrust of the Sherman Antitrust Act of 1890. The failure of the antitrust effort from that time to this can be seen in the spread of government regulation across the face of American business, perhaps best symbolized by the adoption of general wage and price controls during the Nixon administration.

I REGULATION AND THE PUBLIC UTILITIES I

Identification of public utilities

We all sort of know what the public utilities are. We know that the telephone company is one and our electric power company another, that the railroads are in the group, along with radio and television broadcasting. But what we don't know is where the public utilities begin and where they end. Nor do the experts.

One clue to setting boundaries for the group is to recognize that it sometimes carries other labels. One is the *regulated industries*. Standing between the privately owned competitive firms on the one side and government departments or bureaus on the other, public utilities are for the

the small society   by Brickman

© Washington Star Syndicate, Inc., permission granted by King Features Syndicate, Inc., 1977.

most part profit-oriented, privately owned firms, the regulation of which, it is felt, cannot safely be left to the operation of competitive market forces. At the same time — at least in the United States — it is believed that their continued operation under private ownership is preferable to government ownership. Since public ownership is shunned and competition is considered to be an inadequate regulator, the visible hand of government regulation replaces the invisible hand of control through market processes.

But this approach is circular. The regulated industries are public utilities because they are regulated. What we need to know is why they are regulated. Why can't their regulation safely be left to the operation of market forces? An alternative label, *public service industries,* takes us part way to an answer. In the language of the court decision, these are firms "affected with a public interest." In the case of *Munn* v. *Illinois* (92 U.S. 113, 1887), Chief Justice Waite pointed out that the right to regulate businesses affected with the public interest had existed in Anglo-American law from "time immemorial."

This settled the regulatory issue for the subject of this particular lawsuit, a grain elevator and warehouse company. And if a grain elevator is a business affected with a public interest, then surely a railroad is too. But what else? Although the public interest was the pivot upon which the setting of public constraints on private capital turned, deciding which firms qualified for regulation and which did not proved to be no easy matter. The railroads exhibited the necessary qualifications, as did telephone, electric, gas, and water companies. But among those blackballed from the club were fire insurance companies, theater ticket agencies, employment agencies, gasoline distributors, and the ice business.

Trying to make economic sense out of the court decisions has provided a major challenge for economists. One common element ran through all the decisions: the conviction that competition was inadequate in each situation as a regulatory force. Initially economists said this was because these industries were *natural monopolies,* which occur where competition is either wasteful of resources or operates under conditions that will ultimately lead to its own self-destruction.

The first of these is easy to visualize. Imagine the waste that would occur if a community were served by three competing telephone companies. This would necessitate not only three central exchanges, but also three sets of telephone poles and wires and the listing of customers in three different telephone books. Even so, the presence of three competing companies might keep service up and rates down — for a time.

Any equilibrium established among the three companies would be shaky. This is because each of the companies would recognize that there are tremendous *economies of scale* to be realized. This is basically what economists mean when they use the term *natural monopoly.* Because unit costs fall as additional customers are taken on, any one of the companies can ride down its falling unit cost curve by bidding away customers of the other companies until it simply drives them out of business. Equally as likely, each of the companies will realize that any one of them that gets the jump on its rivals has the opportunity to reduce rates for new customers and steal them from the other companies. They will therefore forestall this course of action by agreeing on rates that all will charge. In either case, what started out as a competitive situation ends up as a monopoly — a single surviving company, or three companies acting as one as far as prices are concerned.

Under conditions of natural monopoly, then, the market fails to regulate itself in such a fashion as to protect the consumer. Companies in the industry are placed under the wing of either a state or federal regulatory commission and charged with a number of responsibilities:

1 To limit their prices and profits to "reasonable" levels
2 To provide service adequate in quantity and quality at the established prices, even at peak times
3 To get advance approval for adding or dropping services
4 To protect the safety of the public.

Things are not all bad, however. In exchange for these duties, regulated firms are entitled to specific rights:

1 To "reasonable" prices and profits
2 To complete or partial protection from competition (via a franchise)
3 To exercise the right of eminent domain in acquiring property
4 To be governed by reasonable rules.[1]

How to guarantee these rights and assure the performance of the duties has been a perennial problem for the regulators, one that they have by no means solved. But more of that later. First we must recognize that the natural monopoly approach to classifying industries as public utilities proved both too broad and too narrow. Too broad because some industries subject to economies of scale were deemed to be adequately regulated by existing competition, in some cases by competition across industry lines, such as that among railroads, barges, and trucks. Too narrow because an increasing number of situations were identified where economies of scale could not be identified for sure, but competition worked badly nonetheless. In place of the natural monopoly criterion for public utility classification, economists today look for other features:

---

[1] Clair Wilcox and William G. Shepherd, *Public Policies Toward Business,* 5th ed., Irwin, Homewood, Ill., 1975, p. 333.

1 Demand elasticities that differ among the various groups of customers of the company, making it highly profitable for the company to discriminate in setting prices or rates — charging residential users of electricity far more than industrial users, for example

2 Wide swings in demand for the service provided, leaving a large part of the company's production facilities idle much of the time — and a reluctance therefore to provide a full range of facilities

3 Customers connected physically to suppliers, either by wires or pipes or other means, giving the supplier considerable control over the customer

4 A vital need by the customers for the output from this supplier. This is basically what "vested with a public interest" has come to mean.

Using this approach to classifying industries as public utilities gives us the present dimensions of the public utility sector: (1) parts of the energy complex (electric power and natural gas), (2) most of the communications industry (telephones, postal services, broadcasting, cable television), (3) much of the transportation network (railroads, urban transit, waterways, pipelines, airlines), and (4) some odds and ends (water, sewage, ports, hospitals). A moment's thought is sufficient to tell us that the economy must falter if these industries stumble. Without adequate supplies of energy and transportation services, in particular, economic advance is stifled.

Task of the regulatory commissions

It is the function of the regulatory commissions to see that these industries deliver adequate service at honest prices. How well have they done? The answer, by all accounts, is not very well. And the critics of their performance come from all points on the political spectrum, all the way from the far left to the far right. It's a rare person who has a kind word for the regulators.

But before we join this chorus of critics, let's at least recognize that the regulatory commissions are given a supremely difficult task to do and not enough to do it with. They must operate within a legal framework that provides, under both the Fifth and Fourteenth Amendments to the Constitution, that "no person shall be deprived of life, liberty, or property without due process of law." The regulated corporations have been included as persons under these amendments, and property has been broadened beyond physical property to include expected earnings on industrial property. Rate setting by a public utility commission obviously must on occasion cut the flow of expected earnings. When it does the commission can anticipate a protracted legal battle, since this is what *due process* is all about. And facing the regulators are industries with considerable political clout, armies of expert lawyers and economists, and sizable war coffers.

Determining a fair rate of return   Overshadowing all these difficulties is the fact that the regulatory bodies have never known quite what they should do to guarantee the regulated industries their rights while holding them strictly to their duties. At first glance this looks fairly simple. All that is necessary is that the regulated firm be allowed to set prices for its services that will provide a "fair" rate of return on the property it is using to provide the services. And what is a fair rate of return? One obviously which avoids both confiscating the stockholders' property and gouging the consumer.

The basic terms of the regulatory situation can be summed up in the *rate of return equation*:

$$\text{Rate of return} = \frac{\text{total revenue} - \text{total cost}}{\text{capital}}$$

Whatever the rate of return allowed, it is determined by both numerator and denominator in the right-hand fraction. Since this quite possibly will be the framework of government regulation as it spreads outward from the public utility field, it is worth pointing out that each of the four parts in the return equation are apt to be viewed differently by the regulators and the regulated industries. Total revenue, for example, is price multiplied by quantity provided. But what amount of services should a company be expected to provide? All the customers want under any and all conditions? Bus service at three o'clock in the morning? And is the price of service fair? Better, is the whole range of prices fair?

As for the total costs, how free a hand should the company have in charging off costs against revenues? What salaries should company officials be allowed to pay themselves? Should limits be set on the advertising budget? And what about contributions to worthy causes, however defined?

Capital would seem to be the least arbitrary of the four items, since it is simply a figure taken from the company's books. But it may be the most troublesome of all. What if the company has reached its present capital size by buying up a number of other companies along the way? Should it be allowed to include in its capital account — its *rate base* — whatever amount, however unreasonable, it paid for the other companies' assets? Conversely, in a world of inflation should original costs not be scaled upwards to reflect current reproduction costs?

Even if agreement is secured here, all is not settled. It is still necessary to decide what is a *fair rate of return* — whether 6 percent, 8 percent, 10 percent, or some other. The companies themselves argue that they should be allowed to receive at least as much as their capital would earn in the nonregulated industries. Aggressive regulatory commissioners respond that this is far too high since the regulated companies face much less risk. They operate in markets where they are provided with a captive clientele and little or no competition. The outcome of this encounter is most likely to be, not a rate set on the basis of economic rationality, but a compromise rate set somewhere around midpoint between the proposals of the company and the counterproposals of the commission. In recent years, it has averaged between 6 and 10 percent, or about 2 percentage points above the rate of return on riskless Treasury securities.[2]

Regulation of the "regulated" industries   Regulation today neither begins nor ends with the regulated industries. But long after regulation has spilled over into all parts of the economy, we continue to identify the public utilities as *the* regulated industries.

Regulators for the public utilities are found at all levels of government. But regardless of who ends up in charge, performance scores are rarely high. Criticisms range across a wide spectrum: greater emphasis on political loyalty than on expertness; capture of the regulators by the industries they regulate; an exceptional amount of foot dragging; an inclination to compromise and sacrifice principle in order to avoid controversy.

New approaches in public utility regulation

Identifying the weaknesses of regulation, though, is much easier than determining what to do about them. The prescriptions range widely but fall generally into three major categories: nationalization, more and better regulation, and deregulation.

Nationalization   One of the strongest supporters of the free enterprise system, the late Henry Simons of the University of Chicago, insisted in his writings that

> Public regulation of private monopoly would seem to be, at best, an anomalous arrangement, tolerable only as a temporary expedient. Half-hearted, sporadic, principle-less regulation is a misfortune for all concerned; and systematic regulation, on the basis of any definite and adequate principle, would leave private ownership almost without a significant function or responsibility to discharge. . . . Political control of utility charges is imperative, to be sure, for competition simply cannot function effectively as an agency of control. We may endure regulation for a time, on the dubious assumption that governments are more nearly competent to regulate than to operate. *In general, however, the state should face the necessity of actually taking over, owning, and managing directly, both the railroads and the utilities, and all other industries in which it is impossible to maintain effectively competitive conditions.*[3]

---

[2] Wilcox and Shepherd, *Public Policies Toward Business,* p. 344.

[3] Henry C. Simons, *Economic Policy for a Free Society,* University of Chicago Press, Chicago, 1948, p. 51. Italics in original.

Faced with the choice of regulation or public ownership, virtually all other countries have nationalized their railroads and public utilities. Sentiment against public ownership in the United States, however, is so strong that it does not appear to be a feasible alternative. The virtually complete breakdown of the eastern railway network under private ownership and regulation recently led, not to public ownership, but to continued private ownership and regulation along with a massive federal subsidy.

More and better regulation   The starting point here is to recognize that the myopic concentration of commissions on the rate of return equation bars them from seeing their industries as vital parts of the total economy. Interrelationships between one industry and another and the overall market structure are lost sight of. Little attention is given to taking advantage of existing and potential competition as a regulatory force. State commissioners, particularly, fail to see beyond the ends of their noses, which suggests that they should give up a major part of their authority to national commissions.

Equally important, greater attention must be given to improving the quality of the commissions. Technical expertise of both commissioners and staffs must be stressed. Better salaries and more operating funds need to be provided. Greater insulation from political and industrial pressures ought somehow to be arranged. Nowhere, though, does there seem to be strong enough support for these proposals to make much headway.

Deregulation   The basic difficulty with deregulation is that since regulation was called for originally because of market failure, it would be fruitless to return to the status quo ante. Two rebuttals to this point of view are offered. One is that market situations change over time. When the federal government took over regulation of the railroads in 1887, for example, railroads were indeed monopolies. Today, however, the railroads face across-the-board competition from alternative means of transportation: trucks, buses, barges and ships, airplanes. A strong argument can be made that each of these will protect the consumer of transportation services from the others if formal regulation disappears. A similar argument is that even if competition is not perfect, it is much less imperfect than regulation. Besides, regulation is not costless. To the cost of maintaining commissions must be added outlandish legal expenses and red tape, which are imposed on the regulated companies.

These considerations are sufficient to induce a great many knowledgeable Americans that we should move toward a return to regulation by the market. At the very least we should force the regulatory commissions to prove that they do more good than harm. The state of Colorado has just adopted *sunset laws* to do exactly that, and other states and even the federal government are ready to follow suit. In Colorado the life of a regulatory agency will simply be terminated after six years unless that agency can justify its existence.[4]

How seriously the legislatures will take their duties if sunset laws become general remains to be seen. Already the moves to deregulate are creating panic in some quarters. And this where it might least be expected: in the regulated industries themselves. Deregulation of the airlines, for example, would bring pricing flexibility, which they like. But it would also allow more competition, which they abhor. According to Robert F. Six, chairman of Continental Air Lines, free entry of new competitors "is liable to result in a period of initial chaos and ultimately in a situation in which most of our air system will be in the control of a few giants."[5] And if airlines do indeed operate under conditions of economies of scale, Six may well be right. The trucking industry described the Ford administration's deregulatory proposals as "the ultimate in government irresponsibility. . . . The result would be economic chaos."[6] And as other regulated industries are sounded, all the way from railroads to banks, they chime in with similar sentiments. Competition is great — for everybody else.

Regulation and the "unregulated" industries

Along with the push to reduce the amount of regulation within the public utility sector itself has come a steady extension of government "regulated" industries. Up until 1934 whether or not a particular industry exhibited the characteristics for classification as a public utility was a matter of some moment. If it did, it was subject to regulation; if it did not, it was, by and large, exempt from regulation. This was the general case, even though there were major exceptions, such as the regulations that came with the Pure Food and Drug Act (1906), the Federal Trade Commission Act (1914), and the National Industrial Recovery Act (1933).

The last barrier to the general extension of federal regulation fell in 1934. In that year the Supreme Court told members of the milk business that it really didn't make any difference that the industry didn't have the characteristics of a public utility. It was still subject to the pricing limitations established by the New York milk control board:

If the law-making body within its sphere of government concludes that the conditions or practices in an industry make unrestricted competition an inadequate safeguard of the consumer's interest, produce waste harmful to the public, threaten ultimately to cut off the supply of a commodity needed by the public, or portend the destruction of the industry itself, appropriate statutes may be passed. . . .[7]

---

[4] *Wall Street Journal* (June 25, 1976), 1, 25.

[5] "Airlines May Lose Some Protective Cover," *Business Week* (April 26, 1976), 35.

[6] Joe Sims, "On Faith and Free Enterprise," The Conference Board *Record* (May 1976), 17.

[7] *Nebbia* v. *New York*, 291 U.S. 536.

As the above suggests, all that is required for an extension of government regulation is the belief of the public (validated by five members of the Supreme Court) that competition fails to bring satisfactory regulation to an industry. Along this route have come troops of new government regulations, far more than space or patience permits listing. *Business Week,* in a special issue devoted to government intervention, provides some indexes of the rising tide of federal regulation between 1970 and 1975: growth of spending by major economic regulatory agencies from $166 million for eight agencies to $428 million for ten agencies; increase in spending by major social regulatory agencies from $1.4 billion for twelve agencies to $4.3 billion for seventeen agencies; and an increase of pages in the *Code of Federal Regulations* from 54,105 to 72,200.[8] Many of these regulations are described in other parts of this work; many the reader is familiar with through personal experience; and many more, undoubtedly, are in the offing. All have a common source: the conviction that competition fails to deliver honest goods or services at honest prices without discrimination. This means, of course, that the oft-given advice that government simply back off in its regulatory efforts can't be taken too seriously. If government does pull back, we are left with the undesirable situation that created the initial clamor for new legislation.

Other than this common characteristic, little can be said in a general way about the increasing scope of government regulation. One fact worth noting is that once we leave the public utility sector, government regulation may take a wide variety of forms. In fact there is little the federal government does that fails in some way to influence business behavior. Taxes can pull a firm this way or push it that — even into the grave, as a chief justice of the Supreme Court remarked at the beginning of the nineteenth century. And subsidies (negative taxes) can do the same. Regulatory powers need not be exercised by the government itself. They can be "farmed out" by allowing self-regulation to various private bodies, such as labor unions, trade associations, licensed professions, and agricultural cooperatives. The way governments pattern their spending influences business behavior, as does the establishment or removal of tariffs and quotas.

One final comment about this web of government regulation and control is that it has no visible pattern. The public complains, and public-spirited legislators respond with one more strand to the web — often with the apology that this is the only way to protect freedom and free enterprise. And they do have a point. Restrictions on one group's behavior are often necessary to expand freedom for another, perhaps larger, group. As economist Paul Samuelson remarks, "Stop lights are also go lights." It's an open question whether or not the extension of government controls has

---

[8] "Government Intervention," *Business Week* (April 4, 1977), 47.

reduced overall freedom. The businessman's is not the only voice that needs to be heard here.

What is not in question is that the multiplicity of regulations and controls often work at cross-purposes. They have typically been responses to emergencies, with little time available for seeing how well they fit the big picture. What is becoming evident is that slowly but surely we're being forced to consider how they do fit together and how they will work together in the future. And this is what planning is all about.

❙ A PLANNED ECONOMY? ❙

The response of many persons to the question posed in the section heading is that it is an idle question: We already have a planned economy — government is a partner in everything we do. But this misses the whole point of planning. Mere government intervention is not planning. In fact, as suggested in the previous paragraph, it is typically the opposite of planning. Planning may indeed involve government intervention, but intervention need not imply planning.

As a nation we are continually caught by surprise because we refuse to look ahead and recognize that changes underway in one part of the economy signify consequences for other parts of the economy. No one, in fact, is charged with the responsibility of attempting to see how ongoing programs will affect the total economy. Our ideology still rests for the most part on belief that the "invisible hand" will somehow force private interest to mesh with public welfare. Planning is a dirty word in the lexicon of this ideology. Not entirely, of course. Planning is not taboo for the private sector of the economy. A family that refuses to look ahead and anticipate its future needs is, like the grasshopper in the fable, considered irresponsible. A corporation president who fails to foresee developments that will impinge on his business will not long be president. The consequence is that virtually every large corporation has a planning section or division. And since fewer than 2,000 of the largest corporations turn out over half of our goods and services, it might be said that we are half way toward a national planning system — over half way if we add government commissions and agencies, which are assumed to do some planning for their sectors.

But we're not half way toward a *national* planning system. We have barely taken the first step. The proof of this is all about us. With the insistent prodding of the road transport system and the automobile companies we have over the last half-century constructed a massive highway network, tying all parts of the country together with bands of asphalt or concrete. The results of this no one anticipated: destruction of the railroads, congestion of the cities, urban sprawl, tens of thousands of deaths annually from automobile accidents, prodigal use of irreplaceable fossil fuel, pollution of the atmosphere, the shift of sex from the bedroom to the automobile, and on and on. At the same time that this was taking place we also built up an absolute dependence on natural gas and other petroleum products. As the result of these and other unanticipated developments we now live in a state of near-perpetual crisis: an energy crisis, an urban crisis, an unemployment crisis, an environmental crisis, an inflation crisis. Perhaps crisis is too strong a word. Undoubtedly it is for some of these. But at least the overall situation is serious enough to force us to suspect that the invisible hand is arthritic. Like it or not, it seems apparent the federal government will be forced to effect the overall coordination that the private planning system fails to supply. The only question is when and in what form.

When we move into central planning, we will have one major advantage over other countries. Since we're among the last of the world's countries to adopt central planning, we at least have the opportunity to benefit from mistakes already made elsewhere. We know the pitfalls and perils of *imperative planning,* where — on the basis of a tightly centralized national plan — the national government issues orders and individuals and companies have little option but to obey. The Soviet planning system has been studied in detail, and we know all about the problems of incentives and inefficiencies it creates. And yet, before we pass on to other planning systems, we might notice that Soviet planning bears a remarkable resemblance to the system we adopted during our only episode of central planning, during World War II. Should we reach a crisis situation of massive proportions, even short of war, the temptation would be strong to reinstitute the command system we employed successfully during World War II. To avoid reaching such a crisis situation we might draw some lessons from the experiences of the western European countries, nearly all of whom engage in some degree of central planning.

Western European planning

British planning   To put it most bluntly, we have little to learn from British planning, except from its problems and mistakes. The British planning system has never gotten off the ground. This is surprising, since a socialist Labour government dedicated to the idea of planning took over with an overwhelming mandate from the voters after World War II. And by 1948 all the basic elements were in place to promote the success of planning: a significant part of industry had been placed under government control by way of nationalization; through nationalization of the central bank (the Bank of England) along with the institution of modern governmental budgeting methods, the nation's finances were under control; the extensive new social welfare program cried out for coordination with other parts of the economy;

and planning councils had been set up by the government. Yet no long-range planning occurred. Any plans established proved to be empty shells.

One of the foremost experts on western European planning, Andrew Shonfield,[9] summarizes the failure as a complex mixture of the necessity to concentrate on short-run emergency problems, coupled with an intense opposition to planning itself. The most difficult of these short-run problems was the perennial recurrence of balance of payments crises. Heavily dependent on exports as a source of national income, Britain over and over again had to sacrifice long-run growth objectives to reverse a deteriorating trade balance. Recessions, it was felt, had to be created deliberately by holding down on investment and consumer spending in order to curb the price rises that were excluding British export goods from foreign markets. These stop-and-go policies proved incompatible with the achievement of long-run goals. This has been true right down to the present moment.

Even in the absence of these emergencies, however, it is doubtful that planning would have been successful. The will to plan simply wasn't there. The inheritors of the laissez-faire tradition, the members of the Conservative party, delighted in opposing planning. They insisted it was both unnecessary and wouldn't work — until they came to power and implemented their own planning system in 1962. Then they faced the same problems the Labour government had been unable to overcome. Working through their unions, workers refused to abide by any government plans that jeopardized their immediate interests. Suspicion of experts and government officials combined to give both a very small role in the planning process. Those with an abundance of practical experience were left to draw up the planning guidelines, and they proved inadequate to the task. Finally, the refusal to mix public and private power left both only half informed as to what the other was doing and intended to do.

French planning Exactly the opposite has been the case in France. There the will to plan has been strong. In fact, analysts of French planning write about a "conspiracy to plan" between senior government officials and leaders of the business world. This led to a national planning system shortly after World War II, which has been in place, with minor modifications now and then, ever since. How successful it has been is still a matter of debate, with the pros and cons largely divided along ideological lines. Supporters of the invisible hand argue that the undeniable success of the French economy since World War II has been achieved despite, rather than because of, planning. Proponents of the visible hand of government coordination feel they have adequate grounds for believing the contrary.

---

[9] See Andrew Shonfield, *Modern Capitalism,* Oxford University Press, New York, 1969.

As for the French people themselves, they believe that on the whole their planning system has been a success.

But what is the French planning system? The French describe it as *indicative planning,* as opposed to imperative planning of the Soviet variety. They drive this home with the insistence that their planners are "catalysts" rather than "commissars." What they mean by both of these thoughts is that through collaboration and pooling of information from all parts of the economy come indications of what the economy and its various parts could and should achieve during the next planning period. In the process of preparing the national plan for the next five years, for example, a steel company executive may learn that his company should reconsider its own plans to expand its production facilities. When the expansion plans of all members of the steel industry are pooled there is a strong indication that if all go ahead, the anticipated market for steel will not absorb the planned increase in output. The steel industry is thereby saved from jeopardizing its investment funds and future profits, while at the same time it is learned that those investment funds are now available for higher-priority use elsewhere in the economy. And the same learning process takes place in all other sectors of the economy. Out of this combined pooling and learning process come numbers indicating where the economy as a whole as well as its major parts will be five years hence: how rapidly real GNP will grow; how GNP will be broken down among consumption, investment, foreign, and public use; what relocation will take place in industry; what funds and resources will be available for education, and so on.

As already suggested this planning is a voluntary, collaborative effort among the members of the government planning commission, other officials of the government, and representatives from the private sector of the economy. The government planning commission (General Planning Commissariat) is a small body (around 100) of professional planners. Their primary duty is to institute the planning procedure, shepherd it along, and check for and eliminate inconsistencies so the final plan will be "coherent."

The detailed work of planning is left mainly to twenty-five (Fifth Plan) *modernization committees.* These are bodies drawn from all sectors of the economy: labor union leaders, farmers, business leaders, civil servants, trade association executives, and independent persons (university professors, members of professional groups, experts). Around four-fifths of the modernization committees are *vertical committees.* Their function is to take a single sector of the economy, say steel or transportation, slice it out of the economy, and study it top to bottom. By pooling their information and comparing notes they reach consensus on the current condition and future possibilities of their sector of the economy. The remaining one-fifth are *horizontal committees.* It is their duty to examine problems that cut across all individual sectors of the economy: labor resources, productivity, relationships between aggregate supply and aggregate demand, research, and regional balance.

It is obvious that just the process of scrutinizing all parts of the economy in detail every five years has tremendous educational value for the participants in the process — and the participants are the leaders of the French economy. Beyond this, the act of participating provides an incentive to help accomplish the targets or goals set by the plan. The French government, however, does not rely entirely on such incentives in its own efforts to achieve the national goals. French planning is by no means as indicative and so little imperative as we are led to believe. Industry leaders are not entirely left to make their own decision as to whether or not to abide by the targets indicated by the plan. The very label applied to the French economy, *synthetic capitalism,* suggesting as it does a mixture of protectionism and enlightened state intervention, conveys a different impression. Individual companies are pulled by government favors (allocation of credit, reduction of taxes, granting of location permits) and pushed by government discrimination to go along with the plan.

The long experience with planning in France suggests that we should examine it when and if we move toward central planning. There is no doubt that we could not adopt the system as it stands. Whether or not there are major differences between the French and American national characters may be a matter of debate, but that there are major differences between French and American attitudes cannot be denied. The French have never given the free market the veneration we have. Perhaps as a consequence they feel far warmer toward government and government servants. With little government–business hostility, planning comes about almost naturally.

Swedish planning   The same is true in Sweden. Otherwise it would be impossible to explain why a fully democratic country has reached the point where government collects and spends over half the national income. Although the Swedish social welfare system has many interesting features other than its sheer size, it is not our current concern. What is of more immediate interest is how the Swedish government has guided and planned the Swedish economy to the stage where it provides perhaps the highest standard of living in the world for its members.

Sweden has no comprehensive planning system to match that of France. It concentrates single-mindedly instead on the maintenance of full employment and rapid economic growth in a free enterprise economy. Although we continue to think of "socialist" Sweden, the perception is correct only if socialism is equated with the social welfare state. If socialism is public ownership, then Sweden is about the least socialistic of the European nations. Publicly owned enterprises account for less than 10 percent of total production, even if we count cooperatives in the public sector. And what public ownership exists (largely in the public utilities) for the most part predates the rise to power of socialist governments.

But the Swedish governments have by no means left all aspects of private decision-making to regulation by the market forces of supply and demand. Those concerned with investment spending and the allocation of labor, in particular, are regulated and coordinated by the government. Planning comes into the picture through recognition of the fact that a market economy is inherently unstable and that investment spending, economic growth, and employment will all be adversely affected from time to time unless institutional arrangements are set up in advance to counteract the forces of recession and inflation. Such stabilizers have long since been in place. The purpose of planning and controlling investment spending, as we saw in the chapter on national income, is to spread it out over a period of years in such a way that it will not aggravate cyclical tendencies in the economy. In the absence of government influence, businessmen are inclined to bunch their investment spending during boom times and hold on to their money when times are bad. This tends alternatively to increase inflationary pressures and worsen slumps. Effective national policy calls for slicing off the peaks and filling in the troughs by restraining some of the boom-period investment spending and releasing the funds when the economy slows down. This is exactly what the Swedish investment reserves system does. Businessmen are encouraged to hold back on at least part of their investment spending until given a green light. They do this under an arrangement whereby up to 40 percent of their pretax earnings escape all taxes if they are used for investment purposes only when times are bad. If businessmen insist on using them when inflation is a major problem, they pay the full amount of the corporate income tax — a not inconsiderable total.

The government also contributes to a stable overall flow of investment spending by planning its own use of tax funds. Thanks to the large size of the Swedish social security system, payroll taxes flow into the treasury in sizable amounts. If private demand is strong and inflation threatens, the Swedish government simply holds the funds in reserve. As soon as times turn bad, however, the government takes off the shelf a number of pre-planned public works projects and puts its accumulated reserves to work in sopping up unemployment.

Coordinating national employment policy and focusing it on effective use of the labor force is the primary function of the National Labor Market Board. This is an independent tripartite agency made up of representatives from labor, management, and the government. It not only operates a very effective nationwide placement service but also plans projects suitable to be carried out as emergency public works, keeps a constant check on labor market developments, and puts into operation the various employment-creating measures. Its effectiveness is partly attested to by the fact that overall Swedish unemployment during the period 1960–1974 ranged from a low of 1.2 percent to a high of 2.7 percent, while comparable figures for the United States, adjusted to the same basis of measurement, were 3.5 percent and 6.7 percent.[10] And during the current worldwide recession the Swedish economy has continued to expand, although slowly, and unemployment has risen only marginally.

Planning in the United States

Meanwhile, back in the United States, central planning has come to the fore as a national issue, brought on by the unsatisfactory performance of the economy in recent years. The Humphrey-Javits bill set sail as the "Balanced Growth and Economic Planning Act" and before it was even out of port metamorphosed into the Humphrey-Hawkins "Full Employment and Balanced Growth Act." The change of title is significant: We obviously have not yet reached the point where a planning bill can afford to be labeled a planning bill. Since President Carter was induced to endorse even the watered-down version during his election campaign only after much arm twisting, it is doubtful that he will push it very vigorously.

And that suits groups from both ends of the political spectrum. Conservatives see attempts to set national goals and focus all energies on achieving them as leading only to further inflation, weakening of free enterprise, and enlargement of the public sector. What we would have, from this point of view, would be planned chaos. From the political left comes the conviction that the planning apparatus would promptly be captured by and directed to the interests of big business. Workers, consumers, and taxpayers would be left to pay the bills. Only at the liberal-moderate center is central planning regarded as both desirable and inevitable. According to Galbraith: "The state . . . will take steps to effect the coordination of which the [private] planning system is incapable. It will impose overall planning on the [private] planning system. This is the next and wholly certain step in economic development. . . ."[11]

Readers of these words will have a far better vantage point than the writer has at this moment to see who is right in the current debate. Will central planning come to the United States in any form? If it does, will it strengthen or weaken the performance of the American economy? Five or ten years should be sufficient to provide at least preliminary answers to these questions.

---

[10] Robert M. Solow, "Jobs, Jobs, Jobs: How to Create Them Without Reinflation?" *Across the Board* (January 1977), 40.

[11] John Kenneth Galbraith, *Economics and the Public Purpose,* Houghton Mifflin, Boston, 1973, p. 346.

| THE DEFENSE INDUSTRY |

Military spending

It makes good sense to proceed directly from planning to a discussion of the American defense industry since the latter is the largest planned economy outside the Soviet Union. Currently budgeted at over $100 billion a year, annual spending by the Department of Defense exceeds the total annual incomes of all but a tiny handful of the world's nations. Moreover, annual military spending has risen more or less steadily since the end of World War II. Of the total national income generated during the period 1946–1976, well over $1,500 billion has been claimed by the military. Not all of this was devoted to current operating expenses. Much went into accumulating assets. By 1969 Department of Defense property holdings — plant and equipment, land, and inventories of war goods — amounted to $202 billion, making it richer than any of the smaller nations and incomparably more powerful. It owned, for example, 39 million acres of land and sufficient nuclear explosives to provide the equivalent of six tons of TNT for every inhabitant on the globe.[12] It also had close to 5 million employees — soldiers and civilians — scattered across more than 2,000 bases or locations around the world; operated the third largest distribution network in the country (its Post Exchange), ranking just after Sears and A & P; and with its contracts for military equipment kept a number of multi-billion-dollar corporations alive and several score more in economic health. In the article previously cited, Heilbroner estimates that should the Department of Defense shut down and nothing takes its place, unemployment in

the small society   by Brickman

HOO-BOY!

I SURE MISS THAT SENSE OF BELONGING I HAD WHEN THE WHOLE COUNTRY WAS GUNG-HO —

6-25
BRICKMAN

Washington Star Syndicate. Inc

---

[12] Robert L. Heilbroner, "Military America," *The New York Review* (July 23, 1970), 5.

the United States would triple. This suggests that the Department of Defense is not about to shut down. It is supported by liberals for its job-creating potential. According to Lawrence R. Klein, President Carter's chief economic advisor during the 1976 presidential campaign, "Defense spending is a significant factor in the economy. It is a very big component of total national production. It has been a large part of the whole expansion of the American economy since World War II." By his reckoning, "Every cutback of a dollar in defense will cut two dollars from overall GNP and drag down a lot of jobs."[13] Conservatives, on the other hand, are much less concerned with the economic aspects of the Pentagon budget than they are with its impact on world politics. If we allow the Soviet Union to outstrip us in military spending, they say, then we have come close to conceding world domination to the Communist cause.

A third basis of support for an increasing, high level of military spending is probably of greater consequence than either of those already listed. This is what is called the *military-industrial complex.* The label itself has impeccable conservative credentials. It derives from the late President Eisenhower's final address, in which he warned that "in the councils of government we must guard against the acquisition of unwarranted influence, whether sought or unsought, by the military-industrial complex. The potential for the disastrous rise of misplaced power exists and will persist." According to a leading student of military economics that potential has been realized. The military-industrial complex is now in the saddle, in the form of

a loose, informally defined collection of firms producing military products, senior military officers, and members of the executive and legislative branches of the federal government — all of them limited by the market relations of the military products network and having a common ideology as to the importance of maintaining or enlarging the armed forces of the United States and their role in American politics.[14]

The consequence is a separate economy within the American economy; one that operates under its own peculiar rules.

In the competitive sectors of the economy a certain minimal level of cost control and efficiency are essential for survival. Not so in the military sector. Procurement officers for the Department of Defense find the competitive marketplace unreliable and troublesome. They prefer to pick out a preferred supplier and then work with it, or consider only several familiar

---

[13] "The Impact of Cuts in Defense Spending," *Business Week* (January 19, 1976), 51.

[14] Seymour Melman, *Pentagon Capitalism: The Political Economy of War,* McGraw-Hill Paperbacks, New York, 1970, p. 10.

candidates. As a result approximately two-thirds of all military contracts are awarded with virtually no competition at all, either by extending a current contract or by negotiating with a single source of supply. Military purchasing officers know that if they do call for competitive bids, the bids are likely to be next to meaningless. Prospective suppliers practice *buying-in* — quoting an offer price far below what they know their actual costs will be, then demanding higher payments after they get the contract because of "unanticipated" costs. And the Department of Defense has little option but to pay the higher prices since to do otherwise would in many cases throw their suppliers into bankruptcy. A handful of their largest suppliers — Lockheed, General Dynamics, McDonnell Douglas, Grumman Aircraft — depend on the Department of Defense for over half of their annual sales, and the Defense Department in turn depends on these firms for a continuing flow of defense goods. They can't be allowed to fail, as was shown when the federal government rushed to the aid of Lockheed with loan guarantees when the latter fell into financial difficulties.

This mutual dependency also leads to *follow-on contracting,* which further militates against rewarding efficiency and penalizing inefficiency. In the competitive sectors of the economy a company that delivered its product at two or three times the initial contract price — common practice among military contractors — and delivered a product, moreover, inferior to that specified in the contract, would be an unlikely candidate for a second contract. But it happens routinely in the military. In military aircraft production, in particular, successive models have been timed and allotted as if they had been designed to keep the eight main private aircraft assembly lines in operation.[15] This amounts to rotation of contracts, regardless of how each company performed under its last contract.

With a system seemingly designed to promote waste and inefficiency, the near-constant cost-overruns and low quality of a substantial portion of delivered products should occasion little surprise. The question is, can we do anything about it? As far as designing a more efficient system is concerned, that is no great problem. We now have a regulated industry tightly controlled by government officials (the military) with virtually no interest in cost minimization. Simply shifting control to a government agency independent of the Pentagon, thereby breaking the incestuous relationship between supplier and user, would be an improvement. To represent much of an improvement, though, the new regulatory agency would need different guidelines from those used by the military. Less reliance on a small handful of suppliers is strongly indicated. This could be achieved by requiring far more competitive bidding and perhaps by limiting military contracts to a fixed percentage of a supplying company's

---

[15] James R. Kurth, "The Political Economy of Weapons Procurement: The Follow-on Imperative," *American Economic Review* (May 1972), 304–311.

total business — say 25 percent. Being forced to meet the market test of efficiency on at least 75 percent of its production should force a firm to become more efficient in its military production. A new approach to contracting is also required, one that provides incentives for maximizing efficiency and minimizing costs, rather than the reverse.

An alternative approach would be to nationalize the defense industry. As it is, taxpayers bear all the risks, and the owners of the defense firms get all the profits. Nationalization would but acknowledge that the defense industry is now for all intents run as part of the federal government. It would, however, remove the present determination to promote the growth of the defense sector because it provides benefits to owners of the defense firms. The counterargument that publicly owned corporations lack efficiency is not very strong, since it would be hard to find a less efficient system than we now have.

Reorganizing the defense industry would be a difficult task, at best. It would help to reduce the impact of inefficiency in the present industry by reducing its size. The problem here, as we saw at the beginning of this section, is that both liberals and conservatives, for different reasons, support a high level of military spending. It avails little that the arguments with which they support their positions are weak. It can be and has been demonstrated over and over again that military spending is a poor way to sustain the national economy and promote employment. One billion dollars of defense expenditures provides about 55,000 jobs. But spending that same billion dollars in the health care industry would provide jobs for 77,000 nurses; in education for 100,000 teachers; on the Job Corps, for 151,000 new employees; in public housing, for an additional 76,000 workers.[16] By spending on the military rather than on other government projects or on private goods and services, we actually hold down total employment.

To this some economists respond, "Nonsense." Their conviction is that without the military spending there would likely be no alternative spending. Military spending has thoroughly respectable social credentials while other forms of government spending are suspect. We have a huge pressure group promoting increased spending by the arms industry: the military contractors themselves, thousands of other firms that benefit from subcontracts or sub-subcontracts, the hundreds of communities dependent on military base spending, and the sizable numbers in our population who still see Communists everywhere. Those who are most likely to oppose a high level of overall government spending are least likely to be concerned with the high level of military spending.

[16] Marion Anderson, *The Empty Pork Barrel: Unemployment and the Pentagon Budget,* Public Interest Research Group in Michigan, Lansing, Mich., April 1975, p. 1.

The argument that increased military spending is essential to guarantee peace is not answerable on economic grounds. All the layman can do is observe that ours does not appear to be a particularly peaceful world. In fact, the arms race has spread around the globe.

The international war economy

Figures provided by the United States Arms Control and Disarmament Agency show that worldwide military expenditures in 1974 reached a total of $315 billion — $79 for every man, woman, and child on earth. While the United States and the Soviet Union combined to spend about three-fifths of the total, all other parts of the world contributed their share, as Table 16.1 exhibits.

One can be cynical and argue that the opportunity cost of military spending in developed countries is not high. What the military spends would otherwise go for frivolous projects: second and third cars for each family, more rich food when we're already fat, more clothes when our closets are full. No such case can be made for the developing countries. With a population of nearly 40 million, for example, Egypt had a gross national product in 1976 of only about $12 billion. Yet over the past twenty years, Egypt admits to spending $40 billion on imported military equipment alone.[17] The sad fact is that world military spending totals over 35 percent of the combined national incomes of all the developing nations.

TABLE 16.1
Worldwide military expenditures, 1965 and 1974

	Military expenditures					
	Total ($ billion)		Per capita		As % of GNP	
	1965	1974	1965	1974	1965	1974
Worldwide, total	160	315	48	79	6.7	5.7
% U.S. of total	32	27	—	—	7.6	6.2
Developed countries	142	260	151	254	7.2	5.8
Developing countries	18	55	7	19	4.4	5.3
NATO countries	79	136	156	246	6.1	4.9
Warsaw Pact countries	60	119	181	332	5 to 9	5 to 9
Other	21	60	8	20	—	—

Source: *Statistical Abstract of the United States,* 1976, p. 328.

[17] "Egypt: If Belt-tightening Fails, What Next?" *Business Week* (February 7, 1977), 42.

In other words, if all military spending ceased tomorrow and the released resources were the next day turned into a gigantic foreign aid program, the incomes of the developing nations could be increased by more than one-third. This is not likely to happen, of course, especially since overseas arm shipments have become a very big business, as the figures for Egypt suggest.

Military exports

As in the case of domestic military expenditures, the United States and the Soviet Union lead the rest of the world in arms exports. Over the period 1961–1974, the United States exported arms worth a total of $37 billion; the Soviet Union, $22 billion. France came in third in this morbid race, but with a total of only $3 billion.[18] And what was a race has now become a rout. Foreign orders for American weapons came in at a rate of $8.5 billion in fiscal 1976, were expected to hit $9 billion during the 1977 fiscal year, and all indications are that they will remain at this high level through 1980. And this in the face of a worldwide recession.

Looked at strictly from an economic point of view, arms sales are an excellent piece of business for the United States. With a strong foreign demand we can continue to keep our defense industry operating full-tilt. This will enable us to capture all of the economies of large-scale production. Research and development expenses amount to a high proportion of final delivery costs of new weapons systems. If we have to spread these R & D costs over just a few aircraft or missiles, unit costs will be extremely high. But if, thanks to sizable foreign orders, we can spread total costs over a large production run, then both we and foreign buyers can benefit from lower unit costs. A recent Congressional Budget Office study showed the current level of foreign arms sales is cutting the Pentagon's cost for weapons by $560 million a year.[19]

Moreover, both military spending and arms exports have a multiplied impact on the domestic economy. Eliminating all overseas arms sales would cut gross national product by around $20 billion, at a cost of 350,000 jobs.[20] Finally, we've been having troubles lately balancing our merchandise imports and exports. Without the nearly $10 billion in arms shipments, our trade balance would turn hopelessly unfavorable.

As the title of the *Business Week* article suggests, we do have a major dilemma in our foreign arms sales. We see the moral aspects of permitting — more, encouraging — the developing nations of the world to use their skimpy incomes to put on a display of our arms. But to this point we have been able to live with our consciences, comforted by the fact that if we

---

[18] Ruth Leger Sivard, *World Military and Social Expenditures, 1976,* WMSE Publications, Leesburg, Va., 1976, p. 8.

[19] "The Foreign Arms Sale Dilemma," *Business Week* (December 20, 1976), 79.

[20] "The Foreign Arms Sale Dilemma," p. 79.

don't sell arms to them, any of a number of other countries will be happy to do so.

I SUMMARY I

Increasing government regulation and moves toward central planning, common to all market economies, have been brought about by the failure of competition adequately to regulate the marketplace.

It was recognized early that one important category of industries, the public utilities, had economic characteristics that made competition expensive while guaranteeing that it would ultimately be succeeded by monopoly. They thus became the regulated industries.

The history of regulation in the public utility field has not been an illustrious one. Almost no one is happy with the current situation. But how to improve conditions is an open question. And it is a very important question since government regulation has long since spilled over into areas far removed from the public utilities.

One thing the extension of government regulation into new fields has forced us to recognize is that for regulation to be effective some coordination of the multiplicity of regulatory efforts is essential. This is part of what national planning attempts to provide.

As we move into national planning, we are fortunate in having the experiences of other nations to guide us. In particular, we may be able to learn from the Swedish and French planning systems.

In our defense industry we already have the largest planned economy outside the Soviet Union. It is not the best model of all that planning might be. But although it is easy to criticize the operations of the Department of Defense, it is difficult, in the face of multiple vested interests and hard-set attitudes, to do much about them. Defense spending creates jobs that might otherwise not exist as well as showing that we're at least making an effort to stay abreast of the Russians.

With a sharp, worldwide cutback in military spending, of course, would come the release of huge amounts of resources for peacetime uses. The really poor countries of the world, in particular, might gain if resources were not being used for the arms race. The paradox of this, though, is that those same poor countries have joined in the arms race — as witnessed by our present $10 billion level of arms exports, most of which goes to relatively poor countries.

I IMPORTANT TERMS AND CONCEPTS I

public utilities	imperative planning
rate of return equation	indicative planning
fair rate of return	military-industrial complex
sunset laws	

| QUESTIONS, PROBLEMS, AND EXERCISES |

1 Why can the telephone industry be labeled a natural monopoly? And why does this make regulation necessary?

2 Should public utility companies be allowed to earn the same rate of return on their invested capital as ordinary industrial corporations?

3 The United States is one of the few industrially advanced countries in the world to leave its public utilities under private ownership. Why would you think the other countries nationalized their public utilities?

4 Does the massive intervention by the federal government in business affairs indicate that we have a planned economy in the United States?

5 Why has Great Britain been unable to set up and operate an effective national planning system? Do you think we would have the same problems if we attempted national planning in the United States?

6 Is Sweden really a socialist nation?

7 How effective in creating jobs is military spending as compared to alternative forms of spending?

8 If our military exports are suspected of increasing world tensions, why don't we scale them back?

| SUGGESTED READING |

Anderson, Marion. *The Empty Pork Barrel: Unemployment and the Pentagon Budget.* Public Interest Research Group in Michigan, Lansing, Mich., 1975.

"Government Intervention." *Business Week* (April 4, 1977), 42–95.

"Impact of Federal Regulation." *Challenge* (November–December 1976), 34–52.

Melman, Seymour. *Pentagon Capitalism: The Political Economy of War.* McGraw-Hill, New York, 1970.

————. "Twelve Propositions on Productivity and the War Economy." *Challenge* (March–April 1975), 7–11.

Schultze, Charles L. *The Public Use of Private Interest.* Brookings, Washington, D.C., 1977.

Shonfield, Andrew. *Modern Capitalism: The Changing Balance of Public and Private Power.* Oxford University Press, New York, 1969.

Sivard, Ruth Leger. *World Military and Social Expenditures, 1976.* WMSE Publications, Leesburg, Va., 1976.

SEVENTEEN

I MARXISM AND THE SOVIET SYSTEM I

Although discussion to this point has centered almost exclusively on America, much of what has been written is descriptive of many other economies. This is especially true of the countries in western Europe. Several of these we think of as socialist nations. In fact, some of them so label themselves. But they are far more capitalistic than socialistic. In no country of western Europe is the extent of public ownership of the means of production more than 25 percent. In most of these countries markets are as free as in the United States. And the primary governor of business activity is still the more or less unrestricted search for profits. Only if socialism means either social welfare or economic planning are the western European nations socialistic. But if this is what socialism means, then France and West Germany are more socialistic than Great Britain and the Scandinavian countries.

This suggests that there is no general agreement as to what socialism really is. In the words of one interpreter, socialism

is both abstract and concrete, theoretical and practical, idealist and materialist, very old and entirely modern; it ranges from a mere sentiment to a precise program of action; different advocates present it as a philosophy of life, a sort of religion, an ethical code, an economic system, a historical category, a juridical principle; it is a popular movement and a scientific analysis, an interpretation of the past and a vision of the future, a war cry and the negation of war, a violent revolution and a gentle revolution, a gospel of love and altruism, and a campaign of hate and greed, the hope of mankind and the end of civilization, the dawn of the millennium and a frightful catastrophe."[1]

In the Western nations the self-regulating market system has progressively broken down, forcing governments to take over more and more economic functions. Any and all departures from the completely laissez-faire position have been labeled socialistic. By this benchmark, *socialism* means all of the following: social insurance, economic planning, government owner-ship, economic stabilization and control, and public education. By these standards the United States is now a socialistic nation.

Adding to the confusion is the fact that socialist parties may preach one thing and practice quite another. The National Socialist German Work-ers' Party (Nazis) in Hitler's Germany talked socialism but practiced con-trolled capitalism. And the Soviet Communist party today, by its own insistence, practices not communism but socialism. At the very least, we should distinguish between ideologies as concepts and what is done in the name of these ideologies. Some help is provided if we use small letters to designate concepts (anarchism, socialism, communism) and capital letters to designate their organizational representations (Socialist party, Communist party, International Working People's Association). Then we will know whether we are talking about a concept, an "ideal type," or whether reference is being made to expedient use of labels by political parties to mislead the public.

I CLASSIFICATION OF ECONOMIC SYSTEMS I

Historically, the characteristic most widely agreed on for differentiating the three major types of economic systems one from another (capitalism, socialism, and communism) has been the ownership of property. Under

---

[1] A. Shadwell, "Socialism — Its Origin and Meaning," *Quarterly Review* (July 1924), 2.

capitalism, all property is privately owned. Because he or she owns the productive property, the capitalist is the key figure and the hero of the system. From this point of view, socialism is capitalism without the capitalist. Ownership of the means of production is taken out of the hands of the capitalist and placed in the collective hands of the state through nationalization (public ownership). With communism the final step is taken. All property, productive as well as personal, is taken out of private and into public ownership and we have communal ownership of everything. The history of the United States is marked by the coming and going of cooperative communities with communal ownership. And the American armed forces today, paradoxically, come close to practicing communism (with a small c) since almost everything is "G.I.," government issue.

Another way of distinguishing these systems is to ask who gets what and why under each system. What is the distribution ethic of each? Under capitalism the maxim is: "From each according to his or her ability and the capability of his or her property, to each according to his or her production and that of his or her property." With the elimination of private productive property, the maxim of socialism becomes: "From each according to his or her ability, to each according to his or her production." The beauty of this arrangement, according to the socialists, is that now everybody has to go to work. No longer will anyone find it possible to live off the earnings of inherited or accumulated property. And because property earnings make up such a large share of the highest incomes under capitalism, nationalization means substantially greater equality in income distribution. Finally, communism sees the appropriate way to distribute income quite differently: "From each according to his or her ability, to each according to his or her needs." Not equal distribution, notice, since needs will differ. An artist's needs will not be the same as a steel worker's. But the assumption is that needs will not differ greatly, so something approaching equal distribution will result.

| KARL MARX AND SCIENTIFIC SOCIALISM |

Just as the Scotsman Adam Smith is credited with elaboration of the basic theoretical model of capitalism in his declaration of economic freedom, *The Wealth of Nations,* so credit for building the foundations for modern socialism is given to the nineteenth-century German, Karl Marx. The persuasiveness of the Marxian analysis is suggested by the fact that today just about half of the world's population lives in countries where the official economic philosophy is Marxism. In his writings Marx elaborated a sophisticated critique of capitalism, isolating the particular flaws inherent in the system that would ultimately lead to its collapse and replacement by socialism — which would, in turn, finally give way to communism. It is interesting to note that Marx wrote very little about either socialism or communism, even though he is called "the father of scientific socialism." The task of drawing up blueprints for those societies he left to his disciples. As the title of his major work, *Das Kapital,* suggests, Marx studied capitalism in order to identify its fundamental weaknesses. In contrast to most other economists of his time, Marx did not see capitalism as the ultimate economic system. Quite the contrary. Marx saw capitalism as just another vastly imperfect system that would shortly take its place in the dustbin of history.

Historical materialism

To reach this unsettling conclusion, Marx built or refined two powerful analytical tools: historical materialism and the labor theory of value. *Historical materialism,* sometimes called the *economic interpretation of history* or *economic determinism,* is a broad philosophy of historical change. It insists that material forces in conflict, not ideas, are the prime movers in precipitating change. Ideas merely reflect the more basic technological and economic realities, as indicated in Figure 17.1.

The bedrock on which historical movement is built are the means of production available to a society at a particular point of time: human beings themselves, identified natural resources, and know-how or technology. Energizing and further developing these means of production calls for an appropriate set of economic institutions — a "sympathetic" economic system.

For Marx the economic system was primarily a set of master–servant relationships or a way to keep the workers working. Thus, "the history of all hitherto existing society is the history of class struggles." Under capitalism the workers work because they have to. Since they are the proletariat, the "propertyless," they have no property to support them in idleness.

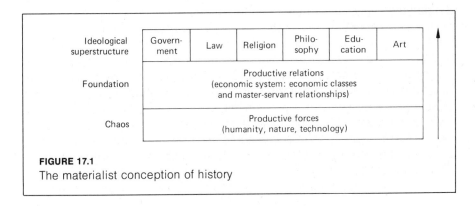

FIGURE 17.1
The materialist conception of history

So they have no recourse but to offer their labor services to the property owners, the bourgeoisie.

Out of a particular economic system springs an ideological superstructure essential to the support, defense, and maintenance of the system. Under capitalism this means a government with power to use coercion in the interests of the bourgeoisie or capitalists; a legal system to justify and direct this use of force; religion to preach resignation to the workers on the promise of "pie in the sky"; an educational system to teach the three Rs and also the virtues of free enterprise; philosophers to prove the inherent reasonableness of the tenets of capitalism; and artists to sing and picture the glories of the system. Ideas grow out of or reflect the underlying economic system in this way, but the economic system grows out of and is supported by the underlying real forces of production.

Now, all is well with these arrangements so long as the economic system is consonant with the needs and demands of the real forces of production. And during the early phases of the Industrial Revolution, Marx conceded that capitalism was the right system at the right time. Marx's *Communist Manifesto* (1848) is full of praise for the accomplishments of capitalism and capitalists during this period. But as the means of production change and expand, capitalism, instead of helping in this process of development, more and more becomes a device for throttling further expansion. The thrust of change cannot be denied, however, and finally, Marx contends, restrictive capitalism will be thrown off, the capitalists will be thrown out, and the workers themselves will take over to permit further rapid economic growth. And with them will come not merely a new economic system but also a whole new set of social ideas — a new ideological superstructure.

The labor theory of value

To show why capitalism progressively leads to the restriction of production, rather than to further expansion, Marx used his second major tool of analysis, the *labor theory of value*. Most market economists, as we have noted, see nothing mysterious in the concept of value — what a product is worth. Value is free-market price, nothing more. Along with many predecessors, however, Marx did not believe that ever-changing market price necessarily represented true value. He would have been delighted with today's quip that economists know the price of everything but the value of nothing. Value must be something more solid and constant than mere price. Marx found this constant in the form of the amount of labor embodied in a product. Measure the amount of labor time used in making a product (both present labor and past labor — that built into capital goods and later given up in the form of depreciation) and you have an objective measure of the value of the product.

Workers, not capitalists, are therefore ultimately responsible for all production, for all value creation. But workers under capitalism are not paid as if they create all value. Part of the value they create is returned to them in the form of wages, but because capitalists own the means of production, they are able to rake off a substantial part of the value created by the worker. The worker is thus systematically exploited. A diagram may help to show the process of exploitation more clearly. Figure 17.2 shows the use of a 10-hour workday, about par for the middle of the nineteenth century when Marx wrote. Part of the workday, the "necessary labor time," is, in effect, given over to the production of subsistence goods necessary for the maintenance of the workers. This is the labor time that must be paid for, in the form of subsistence wages. But since the employers are in a position to set the terms of employment, they decide on a 10-hour day and work the workers the rest of the day without pay. They have already paid the workers what their time is worth: their own cost of production — "the cost required for the maintenance of the labourer as a labourer, and for his education and training as a labourer."[2] So the workers work 6 hours for themselves and 4 hours for their employers. During these last 4 hours — the hours that are "surplus" to the number of hours necessary to produce the means of their own subsistence — the workers produce *surplus value* since all 10 hours of the day generate value. The capitalist employers see this surplus value as a necessary return to the property used (profits, interest, and rent), but the workers, since they have created all value, see it as simple exploitation.

Because they are interested in maximizing their property returns, the capitalists employ every expedient to increase surplus value: lengthen the workday, drive the workers harder to reduce the necessary labor time, or accomplish the same thing by giving the workers more machines to work with. All these may help the capitalists in the short run, only to create

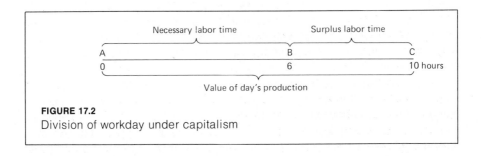

FIGURE 17.2
Division of workday under capitalism

---

[2] Karl Marx, *Wage-Labour and Capital,* International Publishers reprint, New York, 1933, p. 26.

disaster in the long run. If production increases but wages do not, who buys the output of business? Crises of overproduction become more frequent and more severe as unsold goods build up and the production process must slow down. During these crises the weaker capitalists are forced to the wall, join the ranks of the proletariat, and their businesses are taken over by the bigger, stronger capitalists. Production becomes increasingly concentrated. At the same time displacement of workers by machines not only creates a "reserve army of the unemployed" but also the rapid increase in fixed capital drives down the profit rate. Capitalism becomes weaker and weaker and finally, perhaps during a major economic crisis, the workers simply decide to improve their lot by revolution. The expropriators are expropriated.

I THE BOLSHEVIK REVOLUTION I

The message of Marxism was explicit: Capitalism was doomed by its own internal contradictions; the workers had nothing to lose and everything to gain from its ultimate demise. The message was heard most clearly in, of all places, czarist Russia, a country with only the rudimentary beginnings of capitalism and a tiny industrial labor force. The extent of the ferment created by the infiltration of Marx's ideas is suggested by the extensive discussion of those ideas in the publications of the great nineteenth-century Russian writers: Tolstoi, Dostoevsky, Turgenev. And the action was not limited to discussion. Before the end of the century a Marxist party, the Social Democrats, was founded and shortly began to recruit and propagandize for the revolution. Just after the turn of the century, in 1903, the party split, and one segment was organized as a party of professional revolutionaries, under the leadership of Vladimir Lenin, and made ready to take over when the economy collapsed.

The collapse came in 1917 when the Russian economy proved unable to meet both normal peacetime needs as well as the additional demands imposed by Russia's participation in World War I. When the leadership of Czar Nicholas II proved inadequate to the task in the spring of 1917, the czar and his family were forced out and Prince Lvov was given a chance to form a government and bring order out of chaos. He failed and the job fell to Alexander Kerensky and the moderate socialists. They failed, too, and the assignment was finally taken on by Lenin, Trotsky, and the Bolsheviks in November. Considering what had already happened and the nature of the assignment, the wonder is not so much that they had or made an opportunity to take over the government but that they were willing to take on such an apparently hopeless and thankless task.

Take it on they did, however, but on their own terms. Lenin promptly negotiated peace with Germany to get Russia out of the war, reluctantly agreeing to terms (harsher, incidentally, than those the Allies later set for Germany). Over the next three years the Communists, while fighting a civil war, nationalized the productive property of the country. The land was taken from the former nobility, many of whom had left the country, and turned over to the peasants. Factories and the public utilities were taken from their private owners and assigned to the workers, foreign trade became a government monopoly, and the banks were taken over by the state. By the end of this period of "War Communism," the government was in firm control of the commanding heights of the economy.

But the effort had been demanding. Industrial production was down to around 15 percent of its prewar level, and agricultural production was off by about half. The Communists decided they had tried to do too much in too short a period of time; a period of "rest and recuperation" was in order. This came in the form of a New Economic Policy, which to the outside observer looked much like the old capitalistic policy. Some free enterprise was permitted, foreign capital was invited into the country, control by management replaced worker control in industry, and farmers again produced for the market rather than having their crops requisitioned by government order. By 1926 the New Economic Policy had done its work. Production was back to prewar levels. Joseph Stalin, Lenin's successor, decided that an adequate foundation existed for a return to the socialist path. Under his direction the New Economic Policy was wiped off the books. With the initiation of the first five-year plan in 1928 the era of Stalinist planning began.

I   THE STALINIST PLANNING PERIOD   I

And so was launched perhaps the most massive experiment involving human subjects the world had ever known. Columbus in the fifteenth century pushed off into the uncharted Atlantic with a handful of professional seamen aboard; Stalin pushed off into an unknown economic future with the fate of millions of Russian citizens bound up with the correctness of his judgment. Many of them did not survive the experiment.[3] Further, never before had an attempt been made to guide and control a large economy from one central point — and many professional economists in the Western world were convinced it could not be done. Without the signals emitted by

---

[3] Stalin is reported to have told Winston Churchill during a World War II meeting that resistance by the peasants to collectivization cost 5 to 10 million lives.

free markets, they asserted, the government would have no accurate guidelines for steering the economy.

Whatever the price in human terms,[4] the Soviet experiment has abundantly proven the workability of central government guidance and control.

There is no doubt that this was and is a *command economy*. All the
major economic decisions are made by government command, not by the
marketplace. *What* to produce is decided by high Communist party members, government ministers, and planning officials. *How* to produce is
determined partly by planners, partly by enterprise directors (the equivalent of our company presidents); but since all prices and most wages are
set by the government, the enterprise director has far less maneuvering
room than does a company president in the United States. And, again,
since prices and wages are government controlled and there are no private
property earnings, the government largely determines *for whom* goods and
services are produced. The *when* decision, too, is made by the central
government. By laying down the dictum that only about half of current
production (compared with around two-thirds in the United States) shall
take the form of consumer goods, Moscow earmarks a very substantial part
of current resources for the production of growth-promoting capital goods.

Growth has taken place. Of that there can be no doubt. The exact
amount of growth is more debatable. In judging this question Western
observers must primarily rely on data provided by the Soviets themselves,
and quite apart from the difficulties of making comparisons among completely dissimilar economic systems, it is known that the data are manipulated. The Western observer, then, is like the gambler knowingly playing
against a crooked wheel since it is the only one in town. Even with all the
difficulties associated with collection and necessary adjustment of the
data, however, a broad consensus has been reached that the real gross
national product of the Soviet Union has grown at a rate of at least 6 percent
a year, compared with a rate of roughly half that figure in the United States.
And since GNP includes everything produced by all sectors of the economy, a bad performance in any one of these sectors — as in agriculture
in the Soviet Union — serves to force the overall growth rate down. Concentrating only on what the Soviet authorities consider most important,
industrial production, we find a compound growth rate of close to 10
percent.[5]

---

[4] Fairness demands that it be noted that Russia had never known democratic
freedoms before the Communist regime; the czarist governments were not at all
averse to using harsh measures.

[5] George Schopflin, ed., *The Soviet Union and Eastern Europe: A Handbook,* Praeger, New York, 1970, p. 286.

The planning process

Although the Western world hears most about the five-year plans of the Soviet Union, those plans have never been the most important day-to-day guidelines. The five-year projections are simply broad frameworks within which economic activity takes place. They isolate certain parts of the economy and, in effect, say that those are the areas where greatest efforts are to be made. They lay down goals ("five years from now our output of cement must be double what it is today") without much concern for the particular techniques involved in reaching the targets. The one-year plans provide the operational guidelines. If the five-year projections are to be realized (sometimes they are, sometimes they are not), it will be through the instrumentality of the annual working plans.

The five-year plans are in effect laid down from on high, and the notion is current that this is also true of the one-year plans. Formulation of the annual plans, however, is far more complex than this. It involves high government and party officials, the professional planners, administrative agencies, as well as the officials of the local enterprises.

Next year's plan starts from this year's plan. On the basis of current performance and the longer-range plans, high government and party officers work up a bill of particulars that they think next year's plan should incorporate. Is steel production adequate? If not, let's see if we can boost it by 10 percent. Is the "squawk level" too high for comfort because housing has been skimped? Give the housing industry 15 percent more materials. The government planning agency (Gosplan) is then given these overall guidelines, and others of course, and told to work them into the next plan. Gosplan starts with the current plan; adds a "growth expectation," industry by industry; adjusts for the directives it has received from the central government; and ends up with a fairly detailed set of tentative projections. These are then sent on down the production chain for a feasibility critique.

The organization of the production chain has been subject to frequent change. Typically, however, it has taken one of the two forms indicated in Figure 17.3, which shows the reorganization of Soviet industry in 1957–1958. For some years prior to 1958 production was organized on the basis of technical specialization. Each industry was separated from others for purposes of administration and control, and each enterprise was the responsibility of some industry minister in Moscow. The strength of this arrangement is that it centralizes control and accountability and promotes industrywide cooperation. Its strength is also its weakness. Centralized control means distant control, ignorance of local conditions, and possibly long-delayed decision making; industrywide cooperation may mean promotion of a strong industry headed by a powerful minister at the expense of other industries. Territorial control resolves these problems by a partial decentralization of decision making, but at the price of some loss of vertical

FIGURE 17.3
Organization of Soviet industry, 1957 and 1958

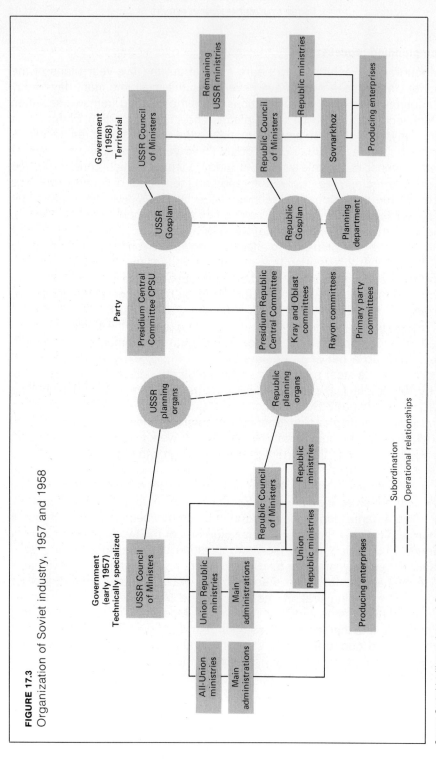

Source: Central Intelligence Agency & Department of State, *The Political and Economic Effects of the 1957 Soviet Industrial Reorganization*, CIA/RR 157, October 1958, p. 14.

communication and possibly the sacrifice of overall objectives in the promotion of local interests.

A key part of the organization, whatever form it takes, is brought out
by the diagram: the role of the Communist party. The Soviet Union, as all
readers are aware, is a one-party state. What is not so generally known is
that the Communist party is made up of relatively few Soviet citizens —
typically only 5 to 10 percent. Membership in the party is partly a matter
of personal choice, partly a matter of being chosen.[6] Sometimes individuals will opt out of joining the party, even if invited, because membership
imposes additional burdens. In addition to whatever job he or she holds,
a party member must take on duties assigned by the party: propaganda
and recruitment, attendance at meetings, and so on. Most important for
present purposes is that party members are the eyes and ears of the party.
From whatever vantage point they occupy — and they are, of course,
scattered throughout the nation — they conduct a constant surveillance of
the performance of those around them. Partly for this reason, partly because Soviet citizens are encouraged to observe and write letters for
publication in the local newspapers, the life of a public official or an
enterprise director is indeed life in a fishbowl. The secrecy with which
American firms conduct their business is simply unknown in the Soviet
Union.

If production is organized along the lines of technical specialization,
then, Gosplan's tentative plans for the industry will move down the chain
of command — from the minister to the main administrators (*glavki*) until
they finally reach the local enterprise. If a territorial basis is used for
organization, regional councils of national economy (*sovnarkhozy*) take the
place of the main administrations.

Gosplan's preliminary directive tells the producing enterprise what it
will be expected to produce next year and what will be provided in the
way of materials and labor. If the enterprise director decides he or she
can do the job with what will be provided, he or she endorses the plan
and sends it on its way back up the line. More commonly he or she will
see the task as an impossible one: too much to do, too little to do it with.
He or she will therefore make a plea for a smaller production allotment
and ask for more inputs. There is one especially urgent reason for insisting
on a smaller production assignment: whether or not the enterprise achieves
its production target will make a significant difference in the amount of pay

---

[6] "The most active and politically most conscious citizens in the ranks of the
working class and other sections of the working people unite in the Communist
Party of the Soviet Union (Bolsheviks), which is the vanguard of the working people
in their struggle to strengthen and develop the socialist system and is the leading
core of all organizations of the working people, both public and state." *Constitution
of the U.S.S.R.*, New York: American Russian Institute, n.d., Article 126, p. 36.

the enterprise director receives. The annual production assignment will be broken down into monthly quotas. In the months when the quota is not filled the enterprise director will get only the base salary. In addition, many months like this will find him or her out of a job (and in an earlier period perhaps on the way to Siberia). If the quota is met, the enterprise director will get not only his or her regular salary but a substantial bonus, ranging up to 40 or 50 percent additional pay, depending on the amount by which the targeted figure is overachieved. The enterprise director thus has a strong personal financial incentive for pushing for a small production quota and large amounts of productive resources. Added to this is the fact that if he or she decides to be a hero and accepts a high production assignment, that enlarged output will become the base for an even larger assignment the following year.

Whether the enterprise director makes a case for a lower quota and more materials or not depends on the reaction of his or her superiors in the industrial or regional administrations, the ministries, and Gosplan. After a review by the industrial or regional administrations, as the case may be, and the ministries involved, Gosplan will have the task of incorporating acceptable suggestions into a final plan. Reconciliation of the various parts of the plan, during the major part of the planning period, was done with the use of *material balances* for each of perhaps 1,000 to 1,500 key commodities, of the sort shown in Table 17.1. (Today the job is done with the computer and supplemented by input-output tables, more sophisticated versions of material balances.) The table might well represent a typical dilemma facing Gosplan in the reconciliation of the plan: 130 million tons of steel required to accomplish the aims of the plan, but only 120 million tons projected as forthcoming. The Gordian knot typically is cut by some combination of building larger production demands into the

TABLE 17.1
Material balance for steel, plan year 19___ (million tons)

Sources		Uses	
Stocks at the start of the planning period	10	Production and operating needs	65
Production	100	Capital construction	40
Imports	5	Replenishment of state stocks	5
Mobilization of internal resources	5	Exports	0
		Other needs	5
		Stocks at the end of the planning period	15
Total	120	Total	130

plans of steel-producing enterprises and scaling down the availability of steel to its users. Thus adjusted, the annual plans and input authorizations make their way down the production chain as orders, typically being received some weeks or months after the planning period has already begun.

It was indicated that reaching the production goal was all that mattered. Prior to 1965 this indeed was largely the case. Some thirty-five or forty goals, the number depending in part on the industry concerned, were actually set: level of quality, economy in the use of materials, efficiency in the use of labor and energy, and so on. Enterprise directors quickly learned, however, that they could rarely achieve all their targets. They further found that with the Soviet Union's desperate need for ever-larger amounts of output they could safely disregard almost all other guidelines if they achieved their targeted level of production. Meeting the production quota, instead of being *a* criterion of success, became *the* criterion of success. With some exceptions of course. Low-quality consumer goods were acceptable, flawed guided missiles or space vehicles were not.

Control of the planning system

A set of plans is an exercise in futility if no steps are taken to guide activity along the lines laid down in the plans. Planning and controlling, often lumped into one category, are thus two quite different steps. Recognizing this, authorities in the Soviet Union have built an elaborate control system. Parts of it have already been cited — the Communist party, the administrative bodies, and the various organs of Gosplan. The most effective day-to-day surveillance and control, however, is exercised by Gosbank, the central bank of the Soviet Union.

Gosbank has no exact equivalent in the United States, but if we merged the Federal Reserve banks with all the commercial banks, we would have something like it. For present purposes, we are concerned with its commercial banking functions. Gosbank has branches throughout the country. Every enterprise has an account with one of these local branches. Funds necessary for the operations of the enterprise, as determined by the current plan, are secured by drawing on the account, and sales receipts are cleared into the account. By checking the flows into and out of the account against the enterprise's operating plan, Gosbank officials can determine whether or not the enterprise is living up to its plan. Any departures from the script are promptly reported to the appropriate authorities. In this way the Soviet Union exercises "control by the ruble."

The pricing process

If prices were to change from day to day, even hour to hour as they do in the United States, basic relationships would shift so rapidly that the planning process would become extremely difficult — perhaps impossible —

to manage. Primarily for this reason nearly all prices in the Soviet Union are set by government authorities and changed only at their direction. The magnitude of the task of setting the millions of prices involved further suggests why prices once set have a tendency to stay there, some for periods of up to ten years.

The fact that prices are set by the government, however, does not mean that they first had to repeal the laws of supply and demand. Instead, price setting is a way of regulating the relationships between supply and demand. Pricing authorities select the prices they hope will clear the market, on the basis of their estimates of the amounts that will be made available on the supply side and the quantities that will be taken at various prices. If they are right, all who want to buy at the price set will be able to secure the quantity desired. If they guess wrong, either of two things can happen: Shortages will multiply and some would-be buyers will be turned away, indicating that the price has been set too low; or inventories of unsold goods will build up, suggesting that the price was set too high. By watching for shortages or gluts the pricing authorities, if they choose, can make the same adjustments that would be made in a free market situation — a process, incidentally, very similar to that carried out by control commissions in the United States during World War II and after the imposition of price ceilings in 1971.

Pricing of industrial products as they move through the production pipeline has a somewhat different rationale. Prices there partly serve a rationing function (given the total of his or her wage funds, for example, the number of workers an enterprise director can take on will depend on where their wages are set), partly an accounting function. The goods in process are priced out as they move from one stage of the production process to the next. Included as costs in the prices established are most of the things that would show up in American accounting practice: wages, depreciation, energy used — even a profit markup (since profit accrues to state-owned enterprises, it is permissible, even if the capitalists had made it a dirty word). Two usual charges under capitalistic production, however, were not made prior to 1965: interest charges on long-term capital and rent payments for the use of land. Both fixed capital and land were rationed, not by charging a price but by "strategic" considerations — with the undoubted result of considerable misallocation as measured by the test of economic efficiency.

Pricing in agriculture is governed by special considerations. Since government agencies are the middlemen in the Soviet distribution system — the sole buyers of bulk crops from the agricultural cooperatives as well as the operators of all retail stores — substantial amounts of government revenues can be raised by buying cheap and selling dear. And inasmuch as agriculture was far and away the major activity of the Russian people when the Communists took over, providing as much as 90 percent of total employment, in one way or another farming had to furnish most of the funds needed for industrialization. The price squeeze on the farmer — the famous (or infamous) *scissors*: low acquisition prices for farm products, high prices on everything the farmer buys — has thus provided a significant part of the growth funds for the entire economy. At the same time, of course, it came dangerously close at times to killing the goose that laid the golden eggs by severely damaging production incentives.

One of the most important uses of the pricing process is in the allocation of labor. Contrary to general impression, workers in the Soviet Union are not chained to their jobs and moved about only by government dictate. Instead, workers respond to the call of the market much as they do in the United States. High wages attract workers, low wages repel them. By setting higher wage rates the government can pull workers into a region of short labor supply or induce them to secure training in needed skills. Since all education is provided at public expense, the government does obligate recipients in some cases to take a particular job and hold it for a certain period of time, much as the armed forces do in the case of college ROTC programs in the United States. Once this obligation is fulfilled, workers in the Soviet Union are free to take or leave a job as they choose. The labor turnover rate in fact is quite similar to that of the United States.

There is one final and very important use of prices — as a macroeconomic stabilizer. Take the assumed case shown in Table 17.2. Here we see total production of 100 billion rubles, representing the creation of almost the same amount of purchasing power since wage payments constitute the largest part of production costs. It is easy to visualize the inflationary pressures resulting from turning loose nearly 100 billion rubles of purchasing power to chase 50 billion rubles worth of consumer goods. To absorb the excess purchasing power — and provide a significant amount of revenue for the government at the same time — a *turnover tax* is added to the prices of the consumer goods before they reach the market.

TABLE 17.2
Gross national product by end use, 19____
(billion rubles)

Private consumption goods	50
Capital goods	25
Defense goods	15
Government consumption	10
Total gross national product	100

The tax need not be levied at a constant 100 percent rate, as this suggests. In fact, it is not. Necessities such as food and clothing are taxed at a low rate, if at all; luxury items, on the other hand, like caviar, perfume, and furs, pay a rate of several hundred percent.

| AGRICULTURE |

Pivotal to the success of the overall economy, agriculture has been both the hope and the despair of the Soviet Union. And all the despair is not created by the malfunctioning of economic planning and control. While the Soviet Union contains a large amount of agricultural land, most of it lies north of the 49th parallel (the southern boundary of western Canada) and a considerable part of the remainder is, or was, desert. Weather, then, goes a long way in determining agricultural success or failure.

But it by no means explains everything. The necessity for the government to wring a surplus out of agriculture has presented major problems for the maintenance of work incentives. With the ever-present possibility of securing higher earnings off the farm, many of the more talented and ambitious youngsters have drifted off to industrial jobs in the cities, leaving "only the old, the shiftless, and those without initiative . . . on the farms."[7] And those who remained have faced the necessity of working under conditions not at all to their liking, quite aside from the low earnings offered.

Collective and state farms

Partly for reasons of political control, partly because of the necessity to economize in the use of scarce equipment, starting in the 1930s agriculture in the Soviet Union was forced away from family farms and into giant combined operations. These have taken the form either of collective farms (large cooperatives) or state farms ("factories in the field"). On the latter, operations are directed by government managers who hire and release workers as needs change and pay cash wages.

The collective farms, on the other hand, are ostensibly owned and operated by the members of the collective. They put their time into the operations of the farm and are paid shares out of the proceeds of sales at harvest time. Since the amount of the proceeds is established by the government acquisition price, what they earn is basically determined by government price setters. And until recent years those earnings were meager — barely more than subsistence wages.

---

[7] Allen B. Ballard, Jr., "A Barnyard View of Soviet Agriculture," *The Reporter* (May 23, 1963), 39.

TABLE 17.3
Agricultural resources and organization, United States and Soviet

Item	Year	Unit	U.S.	U.S.S.R.	U.S.S.R. as % of U.S.
Population, July 1	1975	Millions	213.5	254.5	119
Civilian labor force	1975	Millions	92.6	131.8	142
Annual average employment in agriculture	1975	Millions	3.4	34.8	1024
Farm share of the labor force (annual average)	1975	%	3.7	26.4	714
Sown cropland	1974	Millions of acres	339.5	535.0	158
Tractors on farms	1974	Thousands	4,376	2,267	52
Motor trucks on farms	1974	Thousands	2,906	1,336	46
Grain combines on farms	1974	Thousands	698	673	96

Item	Year	Unit	U.S.	U.S.S.R. Collective farms	U.S.S.R. State farms
Farm numbers	1966	Number	3,239,000	36,493	12,196
Farm size					
Land area per farm	1966	Acres	351	31,425	120,632
Sown area per farm	1966	Acres	92	6,919	18,038
Workers per farm	1966	Number	1.6	417	651
Land area per worker	1966	Acres	219	75	185

Source: U.S. Congress, Joint Economic Committee, *Soviet Economic Performance: 1966-67*, 1968, pp. 31–32; U.S. Congress, Joint Economic Committee, *Soviet Economy in a New Perspective*, 1976, pp. 115, 132, 578; *Economic Report of the President*, 1977, pp. 217, 219.

An idea of differences between Soviet and American farming can be gained from Table 17.3, which provides some of the dimensions of agriculture in the two countries.

Private farms

One of the more interesting aspects of Soviet farming is not brought out by these figures: the role of private farms. These private farms are the last vestige of family farming. They consist of small plots of land, an acre or two, surrounding farm homes and given over to the use of the family. On these small parcels the farm families keep a cow or two (thus the label "acre and a cow farming"), some pigs and chickens, and engage in intensive vegetable cultivation — partly for their own use, partly for the market. The market in this case means not the government purchasing agency, which takes the bulk product of the collective farm, but the local farmers' market. The beauty of this arrangement is that prices in the local markets are absolutely uncontrolled — the farm family can secure an honest market price for their produce. On these family plots, aggregating only about 3.8 percent of the total farm land in the country, is produced an amazing proportion of the total output of a number of farm products: 66 percent of the potatoes, 45 percent of the vegetables, 52 percent of the meat, 53 percent of the milk, 85 percent of the eggs, and 22 percent of the wool.[8]

This private farming has always been an embarrassment to the Soviet government. It diverts farm labor from the principal activity of the cooperative and at the same time says a great deal about the efficiency of free labor and free markets. Attempts to suppress the practice, however, have always grounded on the rocks of necessity. Without the family plots agricultural output would suffer, and it has been shaky at best. While the Soviet government claimed an annual rate of growth in gross national product of 9 percent during the period 1950–1964, they conceded that agricultural output during this period increased at no more than a 4 percent rate.[9]

| LIVING STANDARDS |

Since the satisfaction of consumer needs ranks well down on the list of national priorities, getting what is left after growth and defense needs have been provided for, we should expect to find living standards relatively low in the Soviet Union. For the most part this is indeed what we do find. In fact, during the first several decades of the Communist regime real per

---

[8] Jerzy F. Karcz, "Krushchev's Agricultural Policies," *The Soviet Economy: A Book of Readings,* 3d ed., ed. Morris Bornstein and Daniel R. Fusfeld, Irwin, Homewood, Ill., 1970, p. 227.

[9] Howard J. Sherman, *The Soviet Economy,* Little, Brown, Boston, 1969, p. 109.

capita consumption actually fell. As late as 1950, it was no more than about 15 percent higher than its 1928 level.[10] In the last couple of decades there has been a significant increase in the availability of consumer goods, but it is still the rare family that has an automobile or a vacuum cleaner. A laggard agriculture also means a relative scarcity of many farm products, especially dairy products and meat. And authorization for the materials and labor resources necessary to satisfy an urgent demand for more and better housing has never found its way into the annual plans — or, if it got there, was apt to be knocked out if the materials and labor were needed, as they usually were, to meet other goals. In the provision of consumer hard goods, some foods, and modern housing, then, the Soviet Union lags well behind the United States.

On the other hand, as we would expect of a socialist economy, the Soviet citizen is provided with far more free or heavily subsidized social services than is the case in the United States. Education is free all the way through graduate school, and the better students in higher education are provided with state scholarships as well. The social security system is extremely broad, covering the Soviet citizen literally all the way from the cradle to the grave: free maternity care; maternity leave with pay; special allowances for families with children; state provision of nurseries, kinder-gartens, and after-school care in primary schools of children with working parents; socialized medicine; sickness and disability coverage at state expense; old-age pensions at age 60 for men and 55 for women; and the provision of state homes for the old and disabled. All costs for these services are covered by allocations from state funds, rather than by the imposition of payroll taxes. Housing is considered a social service, too, and its cost is heavily subsidized by the state. Living quarters may not be as spacious or modern as users would like, but this is partially offset by the fact that rents are low. While the typical American family is forced to spend 25 to 30 percent of its income for housing, the average family in the Soviet Union gets its quarters for less than 5 percent of its income.[11]

While the social security system in the Soviet Union is comprehensive and reasonably generous on other counts, one program found in most other social security systems is conspicuously absent from the Soviet system: unemployment compensation. This is not the result of oversight but reflects instead an interpretation of the Constitution of the Soviet Union, Article 118 of which provides that

Citizens of the U.S.S.R. have the right to work; that is, the right to guaranteed employment and payment for their work in accordance with its quantity and quality.

---

[10] Janet G. Chapman, "Consumption in the Soviet Union," *The Soviet Economy: A Book of Readings,* 3d ed., ed. Morris Bornstein and Daniel R. Fusfeld, Irwin, Homewood, Ill., 1970, p. 325.

[11] Sherman, *The Soviet Economy,* p. 20.

The right to work is ensured by the socialist organization of the national economy, the steady growth of the productive forces of Soviet society, the elimination of the possibility of economic crisis, and the abolition of unemployment.

Unemployment compensation is considered unnecessary because unemployment has been legislated out of existence. For the most part this has reflected economic reality. A shortage of jobs is rarely a problem in an economy typified by a shortage of labor, the usual condition in the Soviet Union. On occasion, however, the necessity to cut production in one sector of the economy and turn workers loose without income to look for work in other parts of the economy has led to some unhappiness.

I POST-STALINIST PLANNING: THE 1965 REFORMS I

Until about the beginning of the 1960s the Stalinist planning and control system worked well. While all the world's market economies were struggling with the Great Depression in the 1930s, the Soviet economy pushed steadily ahead. And the planning and control techniques designed for peacetime proved to be readily adaptable to wartime demands during World War II — in fact even the market economies were forced during the war to use planning and control systems similar in many ways to those of the Soviet system.

As the Soviet economy grew and became more complex after World War II, though, the planning techniques appropriate for a smaller, simpler economy began to work with increasing difficulty. If growth is a matter of doing the same things over and over again — building more steel mills, oil refineries, truck plants — and if the production techniques and processes can in many cases be borrowed from more advanced countries, then the whole process can be reduced to routine and incorporated into relatively simple plans. But what happens when further progress depends on breaking out into new paths? When the bottleneck to rapid growth is not a shortage of steel or cement or hydroelectric power but a lack of plastics, synthetic fertilizer, and chemicals?

That the Soviet economy is capable of making new departures is indicated by Soviet space technology, which for a time led the world. But that the Soviets have been incapable of doing this across the whole economy within the framework of Stalinist planning and control techniques is indicated by the comparative growth rates for gross national product shown in Table 17.4. After coming close to leading the growth race until the late 1950s, the Soviet Union fell to an also-ran position as the decade came to a close, despite squeezing the consumer and pushing more resources into capital-goods creation. Private consumption fell from 50.6 percent of gross national product in 1955 to 46.2 percent in 1965, while investment spend-

TABLE 17.4

Comparative growth rates of gross national product

Country	Percentage of increase (annual average)	
	1950–58	1958–65
U.S.S.R.	7.1	5.3
France	4.4	5.4
Germany	7.6	5.8
Italy	5.6	6.1
United Kingdom	2.4	3.9
Japan	6.1	12.0
United States	2.9	4.4

Source: Adapted from Stanley H. Cohn, "Analysis of the Soviet Growth Model," *The Soviet Economy: A Book of Readings*, 3d ed., ed. Morris Bornstein and Daniel R. Fusfeld, Irwin, Homewood, Ill., 1970, p. 303. Reprinted by permission of the publisher, from Stanley H. Cohn, *Economic Development in the Soviet Union*, (Lexington, Mass.: D. C. Heath and Company, 1970).

ing rose from 25.3 percent to 30.4 percent.[12] The additional resources given over to capital formation were simply not being used as efficiently in the age of chemicals, plastics, and complex machinery as they had been in the days of steel and coal. As one indication of this, it took 1.5 rubles in the form of new capital goods to increase annual gross national product by 1.0 ruble during the period 1950–1958, but 2.6 rubles of additional capital goods to increase gross national product by the same amount in 1958–1963.[13]

Difficulties in the Soviet Union's planning system, of course, were not the sole reason for the growth slowdown. The easily harvested natural resources had in large part been taken, which brought about diminishing returns and rising costs in working old sources of supply and necessitated large expenditures to develop new sources. The Soviet Union faced a critical labor shortage, resulting partly from the tremendous losses of personnel during World War II, partly from the move to a shorter workweek, and partly from the fact that few additional workers were available by transfer from agriculture or from the household (women by this time made up over half of the total labor force). Investment in human capital in the form of educational expenditures had paid high dividends as the nation moved from widespread illiteracy to almost universal literacy, but once the

[12] Stanley H. Cohn, "Analysis of the Soviet Growth Model," p. 310.
[13] Serafin Pervushin, "Direction of the Main Blow," *Soviet Life* (January 1967), 5.

point of complete literacy was neared, gains in the form of increased production came more grudgingly. Whatever the reasons for the slowdown, however, the planning system was charged with responsibility for overcoming all barriers standing in the way of increasing the growth rate. To do this it obviously needed a major overhaul, and the overhaul was announced and begun in 1965.

Premier Kosygin was designated to introduce the new reform package, which he did in a speech at a plenary meeting of the Communist Party Central Committee in September 1965, along with an itemization of conditions making the reform urgent: "In recent years the national income and industrial output calculated per ruble of the fixed assets' worth has somewhat declined. The rate of growth of labor productivity in industry . . . has slowed down . . . [and] our learned economists are doing very little in the way of analyzing the effectiveness of social production and of working out ways of increasing it."[14] Perhaps of greatest importance had been a "slow introduction of scientific achievements derive[d] . . . from the inadequacy for practical purposes of a number of scientific projects and . . . from the slowness with which industry masters the highly effective technological processes, machinery and materials which have been evolved by science. . . . New technologies are not finding proper place in production."[15] In summary, "The forms of management, planning and stimulation now in use in industry no longer conform to modern technico-economical conditions and the level of development of productive forces. . . . Greater flexibility and efficiency are needed in industrial management and planning under present conditions."[16]

Comprehensive reform measures were proposed. They included an overhaul of the planning mechanism, more attractive acquisition prices and additional services for agriculture, and reorganization of industry once again (back to a modified technical specialization). The key changes, however, centered on the control framework for industry. In place of the thirty-five to forty control indexes previously used, the individual enterprise in the future need worry about only five or six: volume and assortment of output, wage fund, volume of centralized investment funds, material and technical supplies, and the amount of profit and level of profitability. And just as gross output had become the key success indicator under the old system, it was expected that overall profitability would be the primary measure of success under the new.

---

[14] United States Congress, Joint Economic Committee, *New Directions in the Soviet Economy,* Part IV, 89th Congress, Second Session, 1966, p. 1036.

[15] U.S. Congress, *New Directions in the Soviet Economy,* pp. 1038–39.

[16] U.S. Congress, *New Directions in the Soviet Economy,* p. 1040.

Profit and profitability are of course closely related. The *profitability ratio* is a broader measure of performance than profit alone because it relates profit to the amount of capital used in its generation:

$$\text{Profitability ratio} = \frac{\text{net profits}}{\text{average amount of capital employed}}$$

Use of a profitability index to measure performance would be nothing new to a production manager in American business. It amounts to little more than rate of return on invested capital — long the test of efficiency among American businessmen. For the Soviet enterprise director, though, it represented a wrenching change in direction. And it seemingly does the same for official Soviet Marxist ideology. Soviet spokespersons have been busy since the reform explaining, not entirely convincingly, that there is nothing in the new guidelines that conflicts with the writings and teachings of Marx and Lenin.

Both the numerator of the profitability ratio formula as well as the denominator represent new departures. Net profits are the difference between total sales and total costs of producing the goods sold. Total output as a measure of success thus gives way to goods actually sold, which means that the producing enterprise must pay attention to quality and deliver according to specification. A self-policing device was built into this arrangement by giving the receiving agency the right to inspect and reject goods delivered, thus making it possible for total production and total sales to mean two quite different things. Costs of production also take on a new meaning since interest charges were instituted for the use of fixed capital and rent charges for the use of land — both previously provided without cost to the enterprise. Now enterprise directors, before taking advantage of the availability of fixed capital and land, would have to assure themselves that the costs could be covered by the revenues that they generate — a type of market rationing practiced in the United States. But placing capital used in the denominator of the formula makes the situation even more demanding. Not only must the cost of borrowing capital be covered, but something over and above the interest and depreciation costs must be earned. Efficient use of capital in the search for profits becomes the order of the new day.

In the search for profits the enterprise directors were to be given greater freedom of action. For a time it looked as if they might even be given the option of changing their selling prices as market conditions changed, as many Soviet economists urged. Ultimately, however, it was decided that this right must be reserved for government price controllers, since otherwise prices would be apt to change so rapidly that planning could not possibly accommodate them. The enterprise directors, though, were given far more latitude in the use of the allocated wage funds. Within much wider limits they could experiment with new types of incentive wage payments, paying highly productive workers far more than workers who dragged their heels. In fact the latter could be fired outright. As an additional incentive for the workers, a larger share of profits earned by the enterprise was to be made available for both worker cash bonuses and welfare expenditures — expanded housing, more and better recreation facilities, and so forth. For the enterprise directors themselves, achieving the planned profit level and profitability ratio (say 6 percent) would mean, not only higher morale for the work force, but greater personal income since bonuses were now tied to the profitability index.

Kosygin's proposals became law in 1965, and the reform began in 1966 when the first 40 enterprises shifted over to the new system. By 1967 the number had increased to over 700, and by the end of 1968 the changeover had spread across industry, building construction, and transport and was moving into other sectors. And while this was going on in the Soviet Union similar movements were afoot in other Soviet-type economies: Poland, Hungary, Czechoslovakia, Bulgaria, East Germany, Rumania.[17]

How well the reforms have worked is still a matter of dispute. Perhaps it is too early to tell. There were a number of spectacular early successes — but this is likely to happen following any major change. Lately there have been increasing reports of "bureaucratic obstruction and sabotage" of the new arrangements and "continued extra-legal interference by government and Party organs in the day-to-day operations of enterprises."[18] The eighth five-year plan, spanning 1966 through 1970, projected a 6.3 percent growth rate for gross national product but achieved only 5.3 percent. For the ninth five-year plan (1971–1975) a 38.6 percent increase in national income for the period was planned, but only a 28 percent increase was achieved. And the fact that the Soviet Union has been forced to import not only wheat but also foreign technology in the form of automobile and truck and chemical plants suggests that the final reform of the system has not yet been witnessed.

Whether the next reform will be a further step toward decentralized decision-making and greater market direction of economic activity or back toward strict, centralized guidance under directives emanating from Gosplan, only time will tell. Whatever move is made will depend as much on political as economic considerations. At any rate, while the direction of change is not clear, it is impossible to disagree with the judgment that

---

[17] See George F. Feiwel, ed., *New Currents in Soviet-Type Economies: A Reader,* International Textbook, Scranton, Pa., 1968.
[18] Sherman, *The Soviet Economy,* p. 317.

"unless drastic adverse changes in the international scene occur, it seems quite likely that the winds of progress and change will continue to blow strongly in the Soviet economy."[19]

I SUMMARY I

In examining Marxism and the Soviet system we take a careful look at "the father of scientific socialism" as well as the first important economy to be restructured along Marxian lines.

Although he was an avowed socialist, Marx never laid down a detailed blueprint for his model of socialism. Instead, he spent his lifetime studying capitalism, trying to find the internal weaknesses that would lead to its demise. He became convinced that those weaknesses centered on the fact that under capitalism the workers create all value but are paid only a fraction of the value they create. This system of exploitation ends only when the workers remove the capitalists and themselves take over the means of production.

The first explicitly Marxist group to put these ideas to the test were the Bolsheviks (Communists) who took command of the Russian state and economy in 1917. While putting down opposing factions in a bloody civil war, the Bolsheviks completed their nationalization program and then went on in the late 1920s to establish the modern world's first fully planned economy.

Under Stalin, institutions and guidelines were set up whereby all important decisions in the Soviet Union are made by the central government and all important economic activities guided by a central plan. The key economic plan was not and is not the five-year plan we commonly hear about but the annual plan. A government planning agency (Gosplan) has primary responsibility for preparation of this annual plan, while the government bank (Gosbank) has a key responsibility for seeing that actual activities match planned activities. The plan is normally broken into twelve monthly installments, which tell managers in all parts of the economy what is expected of them each month of the year.

Although major difficulties were encountered from time to time in carrying out the central plans, especially in agriculture, on the whole planning worked well as long as economic growth meant primarily doing what had already been done, only on a larger scale. During the first thirty years of planning the Soviet economy grew at roughly twice the rate of the American economy during the same period.

When the Soviet economy reached the point where further expansion meant breaking into new fields — chemicals and plastics, for example — the planning system began to falter. This led to a comprehensive overhaul of the system in 1965, the primary innovation of which was the introduction of profitability or rate of

---

[19] Sherman, *The Soviet Economy*, p. 318.

return on total capital as the key control device and success criterion in the planning system. The 1965 reforms did give the economy a lift, but later reports suggest they are not a sufficient and final answer to economic problems in the Soviet Union.

| IMPORTANT TERMS AND CONCEPTS |

capitalism	surplus value
socialism	command economy
communism	material balances
scientific socialism	turnover tax
historical materialism	profitability ratio
labor theory of value	

| QUESTIONS, PROBLEMS, AND EXERCISES |

1 How can the ownership of property serve as a basis for distinguishing capitalism from socialism and socialism from communism? What distribution ethic for each economic system follows from this basis of classification?

2 Why, according to Marx, does capitalism contain the seeds of its own destruction?

3 What primary organizational arrangements has the Soviet Union used for industry? Why have they shifted back and forth, from one organizational structure to the other?

4 Under the Soviet planning system, why do enterprise directors fight so hard for low production targets and large allotments of productive inputs?

5 How does Gosbank help to control the operations of individual enterprises under the planning system in the Soviet Union?

6 If the Soviet government sets all prices, as they do, doesn't this mean that they first have to repeal the laws of supply and demand?

7 Why is there no system of unemployment compensation in the Soviet Union? Does its absence imply the same sorts of hardships as would the absence of our system of unemployment compensation in the United States?

8 Why did the rate of economic growth in the Soviet Union decline in the late 1950s and early 1960s? What did the Soviet leaders do to reverse the trend?

| SUGGESTED READING |

Bornstein, Morris, and Daniel R. Fusfeld. *The Soviet Economy: A Book of Readings,* 3d ed. Irwin, Homewood, Ill., 1970.

Congress of the United States, Joint Economic Committee. *Soviet Economy in a New Perspective: A Compendium of Papers.* U.S. Government Printing Office, Washington. D.C., 1976.

Gurley, John G. *Challengers to Capitalism: Marx, Lenin, and Mao.* San Francisco Book Co., San Francisco, 1976.

McLellan, David. *Karl Marx.* Viking, New York, 1975.

Marx, Karl, and Friedrich Engels. *Manifesto of the Communist Party.* Various present publishers, 1848.

Sherman, Howard J. *The Soviet Economy.* Little, Brown, Boston, 1969.

| INDEX |

Ability, income distribution and, 206–208
Absolute advantage, foreign trade and, 366–367. *See also* Comparative advantage
Absolute poverty, 209–210
Addyston Pipe and Steel Company, 174–175
Administered-price inflation, 156–162
Advertising, pricing and, 184–186
Affirmative action, 251–252
  income distribution and, 206
Age
  health care needs and, 290
  poverty and, 215
Agricultural Adjustment Administration, 38–39
Agricultural economics
  equilibrium price and, 35–36
  farmers in labor force and, 25–27
  law of demand and, 27–29
  law of supply and, 33–34
  price elasticity of demand and, 30–33
Agricultural Marketing Act, 37–38
Agriculture
  governmental regulation of, 36–42, 46
  Green Revolution in, 45, 415
  price supports in, 40–42
  rise in crop production of, 45
  in Soviet Union, 464–465, 466–468
  tariff protection of, 370

Agriculture and Consumer Protection Act, 41, 42
Airlines, deregulation of, 433
American Federation of Labor (AFL), 316–318
American Indians, poverty among, 253–254
American Medical Association (AMA)
  medical school requirements of, 297
  opposition to national health insurance, 307–308
American Sugar Refining Company, 174
Antitrust legislation, 174–175
  economies of scale and, 181–183
Aristotle, 332
Arnold, Thurman, 183
Assembly line, alternatives to, 339
Assets
  of commercial banks, 80
  reserve, 385
Attitudes, toward work, 312, 331–338
Automobiles, excise tax on, 265
Ayres, Robert U., 270

Bain, Joe S., 181–182
Balanced Growth and Economic Planning Act, 441
Balance of payments accounting, 381–386

Balance of trade
British problems with, 437
unfavorable, 381–394
Balance sheets, of commercial banks, 80, 82–85
Baltimore, Md.
poverty in, 350
taxes in, 355
Bangladesh, 399
life expectancy in, 401
population growth in, 44, 408
Banking Company of Aberdeen, 169
Bankruptcy, of cities, 356–357
Banks
commercial, 80–86
Federal Reserve, 87–88
international, 413
national, 86–87
state, 87
Becker, Gary S., 232, 233
Belloc, N. B., 298
Benefits, marginal, 116
social, 277–278
Berg, Ivar, 238, 239
Bergmann, Barbara, 248
Bible, work portrayed by, 332
Big business
conglomerate mergers in, 188–191
economies of scale and, 175–183
multinational, 191–194
pricing and, 171–173, 174, 183–188
Sherman Antitrust Act and, 174–175
Biochemical oxygen demand (BOD), 275, 276
Birth control, 45
Birth rate
in India, 409
population growth and, 43, 405, 408
reductions in, 409–410
Blair, John M., 182
model of inflation, 158–162
Blue-collar workers
dissatisfaction among, 336
organization of, 321, 323
Board of Governors, of Federal Reserve system, 88–89
Bolshevik Revolution, 456–457
Bonds, city financing through, 355–356
Boston, Mass.
poverty in, 350
taxes in, 355
Boulding, Kenneth, 283, 324

Bowen, Howard, 288
Bowles, Samuel, 240
Brands, product differentiation and, 184
Brazil, income distribution in, 419
Breslow, L., 298
Britain
average income in, 282
economic planning in, 436–437
foreign aid from, 413
importance of foreign trade to, 365
income distribution in, 200–201
National Health Service in, 309
Buffalo, N.Y., taxes in, 355
Bureau of Indian Affairs, 253
Bureau of the Census, unemployment figures of, 327–328
Burns, Arthur, 100
Business. See also Big business
Industry(ies)
economic fluctuations and, 171–172
flight from cities, 348
gentlemen's agreement and, 172–173
growth of, 168–195
organizational forms of, 168–170
ownership of, 202
role of, in U.S., 165–168
tight money and, 97–98
urbanization of, 347–348
Business unionism, 317
Buying-in, 444

California
school finance in, 235–236
tax revolt in, 135–136
Canada, trade with, 376, 380
Capital
definition of, 4
human, investment in, 228–230
Capital accounts, 80
Capital gains, 120, 198–199
taxes on, 120, 131
Capital goods, 4
Capitalism, 166–168, 452
income distribution under, 203–204
labor theory of value and, 455–456
Marx's views on, 453–454, 455–456
necessity for economic growth under, 284
role of government in, 166–168
synthetic, 439
and U.S. Constitution, 167, 425
Capitation payment, 303
Career enrichment, 339

Carter, Jimmy
  economic planning and, 441
  position on national health insurance, 304
Cartter, Allan, 242
Cash reserves, 81
  reserve requirements and, 81–82
Categorical assistance grants, to cities, 359
Charters, corporate, 170
Checking accounts, *see* Demand deposits
Chicago, Ill.
  population of, 361
  taxes in, 355
Circular flow process, 3–5, 9
Cities
  bankruptcy of, 356–357
  cost of labor to, 353–354
  diseconomies of scale and, 351–353
  economies of agglomeration and, 347–351
  federal aid to, 358–361
  population shifts and new programs in, 354–355
  reducing expenditures of, 357–358
  revenues of, 355–356
  sharing tax burden of, 358
  unemployment in, 415
Civil Rights Act, 251
Civil War, tariff policy and, 370
Cleveland, Ohio, 355
Closed shop, 323
Club of Rome, 280
Coal, as energy source, 261, 262–263
Code of Federal Regulations, 434
Collective bargaining, 328–331
Collective farms, 466
College
  income inequality and finance of, 236–237
  land-grant, 313
  return on investment in, 231–233, 243
Colombia, income distribution in, 419
Colored words, 14
Commager, Henry Steele, 114
Command Economy, 458
Commercial banks, money supply and, 80–86
Commoner, Barry, 270
Commons, John R., 334
Commonwealth v. *Hunt,* 315
Communism, 452
  income distribution under, 203
  Russian, 457
Communist countries, trade with, 380
Communist party, in Soviet Union, 451, 461

Comparative advantage, foreign trade and, 367, 376–377, 380–381
Competition, as regulatory force, 168, 427
Composition, fallacy of, 13
Compound growth rates, 258–259
Conant, James B., 10
Concentration ratio, 178–179
Conglomerate merger, 188
Conglomerates
  advantages of, 189–191
  dangers of, 188–189
Congress
  new budget process of, 119
  power over Federal Reserve system, 86, 89
Congressional Budget and Impoundment Control Act, 119
Congress of Industrial Organizations (CIO), 319
Connecticut, incorporation of, 170
Consumer price index, 140–141n
Consumer sovereignty, 5
Consumption, as goal, 5, 311–312
Consumption sector, 3
Consumption spending, income related to, 61–62
Contract
  collective bargaining and, 329–330
  yellow dog, 315
Coolidge, Calvin, 165–166
Corporations, 169–170
  income taxes, 124
  multinational, 191–194
Cost(s)
  of discrimination, 247–248
  of education, 233–234, 351, 353
  fixed, 159–160, 171
  of health care, 289–292, 305–306
  indirect, assignment of, 180–181
  of labor, 325–326, 353–354
  marginal, 116, 277–278
  mergers and, 176–177
  opportunity, 9, 27–28
  private and social, of pollution, 273, 276–279
  production decisions and, 6
  short-run average, 177
  social, 277–278
  terminal, 347
  of unemployment, 320
Cost-benefit analysis
  of government spending, 116–118
  and pollution control, 277–278

Craft unions, 317, 319

Credits, in balance of payments accounting, 382

Crowding, discrimination and, 248–249

Cuba, income distribution in, 205

Currency, 76, 77

Dalton, George, 15

Davidson, Paul, 389

Davis, Karen, 306

Death rates
in India, 409
population growth and, 43, 405, 408

Death taxes, 127

Debits, in balance of payments accounting, 382

Defense industry
international war economy and, 446–447
military exports and, 447–448
military spending and, 442–446
as planned economy, 442–443
protection of, 372–373

Defense spending, 109–110
size of, 113

Deficit finance, inflation and, 148–150

Demand
agricultural economics and, 27–29
excess, 63
floating exchange rates and, 387
law of, 27
price elasticity of, 30–33

Demand curve, 28–29
of industry, 186–187

Demand deposits, 76, 77–78
importance of, 78

Demand elasticity, public utilities and, 429

Demand-pull inflation, 144–147, 149–150
equation of exchange and, 151
money supply and, 151–152

Denison, Edward F., 229

Department of Agriculture, 37

Department of Commerce, 49

Depression, fiscal policy and, 96. See also Great Depression

Deregulation, of public utilities, 432–433

Deutsche mark, value of dollar against, 389

Devaluation, 392
alternatives to, 393
of dollar, 393–394

Developed nations, trade with, 376

Developing nations, see Fourth World; Third World

Diet, in developed nations, 44

Diminishing returns, law of, 21–23

Discount rate, 95–96

Discrimination, costs of, 247–248
crowding and, 248–249
and education, 245–247
elimination of, 227
and income, 245–248, 250–253
progress against, 248, 251–254

Disposable personal income, 54

Distribution, in free market economy, 6

Division of labor, 333–335

Dollar
devaluation of, 393–394
floating exchange rate and, 389
foreign need for, 385–386
gold standard and, 389–391
present and future, 231–233
purchasing power of, 107–108, 142

Domestic international sales corporations (DISCs), 132

Dual economy, in development, 420–421

Due process, 429

Easterlin, Richard, 282

Economic determinism, 453–454

Economic development. See also Economic growth
distribution of, 418
efforts to aid, 412–415, 417, 418
in free market model, 7–8
income and, 402–403
international comparisons of, 403–405
pollution and resources and, 284
of Soviet Union, 458, 470–475
stages of, 311

Economic Development Administration, 253

Economic growth. See also Economic development
advantages of, 283–285
history of, 279–281
in no-growth society, 281–283

Economic Opportunity Act, 216–217

Economic planning, 435–436
British, 436–437
French, 437–439
imperative, 436
indicative, 438
need for, 435–436
Soviet, 457–466, 470–475
Swedish, 439–441
in United States, 441

Economics
  basic concerns, 1–2
  earliest use of term, 12
  fallacies in thinking, 13–16
  free market model, 7–8, 10–11
  major problems, 3–11
  positive and normative, 15
  production decisions, 5–6
  productive resources, 3–4
  economic systems, classification of, 431–432
Economies of agglomeration, 347–351
Economies of scale, 175–176
  cost advantages and, 176–177
  efficiency and, 179–183
  and military exports, 447
  monopoly and oligopoly and, 177–178, 427–428
Education
  cost of, 231–233, 351, 353
  discrimination and, 245–247
  and employment, 238–243
  excess, 241–245
  expenditures for, 115, 227, 233–234
  of, and income inequality, financing, 234–237
  inequality of, 237–241
  as investment in human capital, 228–230
  personal investment decision and, 230–233, 243
  of physicians, 296–297
  poverty and, 215
  as screening device, 239–240
  in Soviet Union, 227, 465, 469
Efficiency, size of business and, 179–183
Effluent charge, 274
Egypt, defense spending in, 446–447
Ehrlich, Paul, 411
Eisenhower, Dwight D., 443
Electricity
  price of, 268
  regulation of, 263–264
Employer of last resort, government as, 221–222
Employment. See also Unemployment; Work
  demand-pull and, 145–147
  education related to, 238–243
  equal opportunity for, 251
  as goal of foreign aid, 421
  by government, 104, 105, 442–443
  guaranteed, 221–222
  income stabilization and, 65–68
  Phillips curve and, 147–148

poverty and, 215–216, 221–222
  in Soviet Union, 469–470
  Swedish planning for, 440–441
Employment Act of 1946, 65, 68, 71–72
Energy
  importance of, 257–258
  price of, 261–265, 266–269
  problems related to, 258–261
  replacement sources of, 269–270
  in Third World, 410
Energy crisis, foreign trade and, 381
Energy policy, for America, 257–258, 262, 265–270
Entropy, pollution and, 271
Environment. See also Pollution
  energy related to, 257–259, 261
Equation of exchange, 78, 151
Equilibrium price, 35–36
Equity
  in income distribution, 203
  in taxation, 120
Estate tax, 127
Exchange, equation of, 78, 151
Exchange rates
  determining, 386
  floating, 386–389, 394
  international gold standard and, 389–392
  International Monetary Fund and, 392, 394
  market determination of, 388
Excise tax, 122
  on automobiles, 265
  for energy policy, 268–269
Exports. See also Foreign trade
  military, 447–448
  net, 51
Externalities, 270, 273
Extractive materials, export of, 380

Factor productivity, 229
Fair Labor Standards Act, 321
Fallacy of Composition, 13
Family Assistance Plan, 221
Farmers. See also Agricultural economics; Agriculture
  in developing countries, 415
  in labor force, 25–27, 39
Federal Advisory Council, 88–89
Federal Farm Board, 37
Federal government, see Government; Government spending
Federal Open Market Committee, 88
Federal Power Commission, 263
Federal Reserve banks, functions of, 87–88

Federal Reserve Board, accountability of, 100

Federal Reserve Bulletin, 77, 80

Federal Reserve notes, 77, 88

Federal Reserve system, 86
  control of money quantity by, 80
  minimum balances specified by, 82
  monetary management by, 89–96
  monetary policy of, 96–100
  reserve requirements of, 81–86, 89–93, 96
  structure and operation of, 86–89

Federal Trade Commission Act, 433

Federal Water Pollution Control Act, 276–277

Fee-for-service system, 301–302

Fine tuning the economy, 99

Fiscal policy, 96

Fitzgerald, F. Scott, 209

Five-year plans, Soviet, 459

Follow-on contracting, 444

Food crisis, 18–20, 45
  foreign trade and, 381
  Malthusianism and, 20–25

Food for Peace, 38

Ford, Gerald, 157

Ford, Henry, 177

Ford Motor Company, 177

Foreign aid, 385
  early, 413
  military, 384
  policy for, 420–421

Foreign market, 14

Foreign trade
  balance of payments accounting and, 381–386
  British, 437
  comparative advantage and, 367, 376–377, 380–381
  and energy crisis, 381
  exchange rates and, 386–389
  importance of, 365
  international gold standard and, 389–392
  International Monetary Fund system and, 392–394
  military exports, 447–448
  multilateral, 376
  nontariff protection and, 373–374
  pattern of, U.S., 376–381
  tariffs and, 368–373, 374–375
  unrestricted, 365–368, 375

Fourth World, 418
  controversy over aid to, 420–421
  reasons for problems of, 418–419

France
  economic planning in, 437–439
  foreign aid from, 413
  importance of foreign trade to, 365
  income distribution in, 201
  military exports of, 447

Freeman, Richard B., 241, 243

Free market economy, 7–8

Free market model, 7–8, 10–11

Free trade, *see* Foreign trade, unrestricted

Friedman, Milton, 134, 219–220

Fringe benefits, 199

Fuchs, Victor R., 298

Full Employment and Balanced Growth Act, 441

Fusfeld, Daniel R., 223

Future dollars, 232

Galbraith, John Kenneth, 111, 162, 183, 281, 441

Gas industry, regulation of, 263

General Electric, 194

General Motors, 191, 335

General revenue sharing, 359

Gentlemen's agreement, 172–173

Georgescu-Roegen, Nicholas, 267, 270, 271–272

Germany. *See also* West Germany
  inflation in, 142

Gintis, Herbert, 240

Godwin, William, 20

Gold, as reserve asset, 385

Gold standard, 386, 389–392
  International Monetary Fund and, 392

Gompers, Samuel, 316, 317

Gosbank, 463

Gosplan, 459, 461, 462–463

Government. *See also* Cities; State(s)
  aid to cities, 358–361
  attack on poverty, 216–218
  and big business, 165–195
  as employer of last resort, 221–222
  extension of regulation by, 433–435
  level of, and taxes, 122–127, 355
  local, 104
  protection of domestic industries by, 373–374
  reasons for growth of, 107–112
  regulation of agriculture by, 36–42, 46
  regulation of energy use by, 262–264
  regulation of pollution by, 275–276
  regulation of public utilities by, 425–433

role of, 166–168
support of labor unions by, 318–319
unemployment reduction and, 65–68
Government spending
control of, 115–119
cost-benefit analysis of, 116–118
for education, 235
federal patterns of, 112–115
growth of, 104–107
military and defense, 109–110, 113, 442–446
planning-programming-budgeting system, 118
state and local patterns of, 104–106, 115
Graybeal, William, 242
Great Britain, *see* Britain
Great Depression
labor and, 318–321
tariffs and, 371–372
Green Revolution, failure of, 45, 415
Greenspan, Alan, 392
Greifinger, Robert, 296
Griggs v. *Duke Power Company,* 238–239
Gross national product (GNP), 49–51
definition of, 50
equation of exchange and, 78
growth of, 314
implicit price deflator for, 141n
international comparisons of, 403–405, 417–418
in measuring economic growth, 398–403
no-growth society and, 281
poverty related to, 211
price indexes and, 55, 58–59
real, 55–59
related to other national income measures, 54–55
of Soviet Union, 458
Growth. *See also* Economic development; Economic growth
compound rates of, 258–259
Grymes, Douglas, 194
Gulf and Western Industries, 189

Hansen, W. Lee, 236
Hardin, Garrett, 273
Hatch Act, 37
Hawaii, school finance in, 236
Hawley-Smoot Act, 370
Hawthorne effect, 340–341
Health care
cost of, 289–292, 305–306

current status of, 288–289
evaluation of, 292–293
individual responsibility for, 298–301
Medicaid, 292, 304–305, 308, 355
Medicare, 291–292, 304, 305–308, 355
national health insurance and, 304–309
therapeutic nihilism and, 293–296
United States' system for, 296–298
Health maintenance, 300–301
fee-for-service system, 301–302
prepaid plans for, 302–304
Heat pollution, 270–271
Heilbroner, Robert L., 412, 442
Hemingway, Ernest, 209
Hirsch, Fred, 282
Historical materialism, 453–454
Homelite, 188–189
Homestead Act, 313
Hong Kong, birthrate in, 409
Hoover, Herbert, 110
Housing, in Soviet Union, 469
Hugh Moore Fund, 42
Human capital, investment in, 228–230
Humanization, of workplace, 339–340
Hungary, inflation in, 142
Hyperinflations, 79, 142

Iatrogenesis, clinical and social, 295
Ideology
definition of, 14
scientific method and, 14–16
Illich, Ivan, 293–295
Imperative planning, 436
Implicit price deflator, 55, 141n
Imports, *see* Foreign trade
Incentive(s)
effects of taxation on, 121–122
guaranteed annual income and, 219
for pollution control, 275–276
to work, 332–333
Income. *See also* National income; Poverty
consumption spending related to, 61–62
education and, 230–233, 243
equity of taxes and, 120–121
of farmers, 27, 36, 40–41
guaranteed, 218–219
health care demand and, 290–291
life expectancy and, 402–403
national health insurance financing and, 306–307
nonpecuniary, 199

Income (*cont.*)
  personal, 54
  poverty-level, 282
Income distribution. *See also* Income inequality; poverty
  and ability, 206–208
  under capitalism, 203–209
  under communism and socialism, 203–205
  equity in, 203
  international comparisons of, 200–201
Income inequality, 197–198. *See also* Poverty
  in developing countries, 414
  and discrimination, 245–248, 250, 252
  economic growth and, 283
  educational costs and, 227–237
  educational inequality and, 237–241
  international, 404
  justification for, 202–209
  measuring, 198–200
  in Third World, 417–421
  wealth and, 201–202
Income stabilization
  employment and, 65–68
  prices and, 68–72
Income stabilization process, 65
Income support, 210
  spending for, 111
Income tax
  avoidance of, 130–131
  corporate, 121, 124
  negative, 219–221
  paid by oil industry, 263
  personal, 122–124
Indexes, *see* Price indexes
India
  income distribution in, 419–420
  population of, 409
  poverty in, 43, 398
Indicative planning, 438
Industrialization, 348
Industrial Revolution
  capitalism during, 454
  division of labor and, 333
  growth of businesses and, 170–171
  urbanization and, 346
Industrial unions, 319
Industrial Workers of the World (IWW), 317
Industry(ies). *See also* Big business; Business
  concentration of, 157–158, 178–183
  defense, 372–373, 442–448
  demand curve of, 186–187
  protection by tariffs, 368–373

·public service, 427
  regulation of, 426–427, 433–435
  Soviet organization of, 459–463
Inequality of wealth, 197–198, 201–202, 203. *See also* Income inequality
Infant-industry argument, 369–370, 416
Infant mortality
  in China, 409
  international comparisons of, 292–293
  life expectancy figures and, 402
Inflation, 139–140
  Blair's model of, 158–162
  causes of, 144–163
  control of, 162
  deficit finance and, 148–150
  demand-pull and, 144–147, 149–150
  explosive, 79, 142
  fiscal policy and, 96
  floating exchange rates and, 388–389
  history of, 140–143
  industrial concentration and, 157–158
  money supply and, 149, 150–152
  Phillips curve and, 147–148
  poor and, 211
  price of, 143–144
  profit-push, 156–162
  wage-push, 152–156
Inheritance, income distribution and, 205
Inheritance tax, 127
Insurance, health, 291, 304–309
Interest rate, *see* Discount rate
Intermediate technology, 417
International gold standard, *see* Gold standard
International Monetary Fund (IMF), 385, 392–394
  exchange rates and, 386
International trade, *see* Foreign trade
Interstate Commerce Act, 174
Interstate Commerce Commission, 174
Investment(s)
  in education, personal, 230–233
  foreign, 192
  in human capital, 228–230
  income distribution and, 208

Jacksonville, Fla., taxes in, 355
Japan, 399
  government spending in, 107
  importance of foreign trade to, 365
Jarvis-Gann amendment, 135–136
Jedelson, David N., 189
Jeffers, James, 288

Jefferson, Thomas, 244
Jencks, Christopher, 237–238
Job enrichment, 339, 340
Job reform, 340–342
Job rotation, 339
Job satisfaction
  division of labor and, 335
  extrinsic factors and, 336–338

Kaiser-Permanente Health Plan, 302–303
Kemp-Roth proposal, 136
Kendrick, M. Slade, 109
Kennedy, John F., 156
Kerensky, Alexander, 456
Keynes, John Maynard, 11, 59, 67, 372
Keynesian cross, 60
  full employment and, 68–69
Klein, Lawrence R., 443
Kneese, Allen V., 264, 265, 270
Knight, Frank, 13
Knights of Labor, 316
Knowles, John, 300
Kosygin, Aleksei N., 472

Labor
  conditions of, in American history, 312–324
  cost of, 65–67, 353–354
  definition of, 4
  division of, 333–335
  foreign, 371–372
  Soviet allocation of, 465
Labor force, farmers in, 25–27, 39
Labor Management Relations Act, 323
Labor-Management Reporting and Disclosure Act, 323–324
Labor theory of value, 454–456
Labor unions. See also names of specific unions
  business unionism, 317
  collective bargaining and, 328–331
  craft, 317, 319
  dissatisfaction and, 336
  early, 314–318
  federal support of, 318–319
  during Great Depression, 318–319
  growth of, 313
  impact of, 324–326
  industrial, 319
  job reform and, 342
  multinational corporations and, 193–194
  power over economy, 97
  for public employees, 354
  in Soviet Union, 330

  unemployment and, 325–326
  wage-push inflation and, 154–156
  since World War II, 321–324
Laissez-faire capitalism, 166
  farmers and, 27
  limitation of, 167–168, 425
Land, definition of, 4
Landrum-Griffin bill, 323–324
Land tenure, in Third World, 421
Lasch, Christopher, 244
Leading indicators, 99
Legislation
  antitrust, 174–175, 181–183
  New Deal, 318–319, 323
  sunset, 432–433
Lenin, Vladimir, 456–457
Lewis, H. G., 325
Liability(ies)
  of commercial banks, 80, 81
  limited, 170
  unlimited, 169
Library of Congress, 247
Lichtenberg, Allan J., 266
Life expectancy, international comparisons of, 293, 401–403
Life style, health and, 298–301
Limited liability, 170
Literacy, international comparisons of, 403, 409, 471–472
Living standards, in Soviet Union, 468–470
Loans
  changes in reserve requirements and, 92
  discount rate and, 95
  from Federal Reserve banks, 88
  for foreign aid, 385, 413
Local government, 104–106. See also Cities
  spending by, 115
  taxation by, 122–126, 355–356, 358
Lockheed, 444
Los Angeles, Calif., taxes in, 355
Lvov, Prince George, 456

McGregor, Douglas, 337
McNamara, Robert S., 408
McNary-Haugen bill, 37–38
Macroeconomics, 48
Malthus, Thomas R., 20
Malthusianism, 20–23
  checks in, 24–25
Malthusian spectre, 20
Management styles, 337–338
Marginal benefits, 116–118
  social, 277–278

Marginal costs, 116–118
  social, 277–278
Marginal propensity to consume (MPC), 65
Market, regulation by, 432–433
Marshall, John, 131
Marx, Karl, 452–455
Maslow, Abraham, 337
Material balances, 462
Means test, 217
Medicaid, 292, 304–305, 308, 355
Medical care, see Health care
Medicare, 291–292, 304, 305–308, 355
Medium of exchange, Money as, 76–77, 98
Meltzer, Allan H., 111
Mergers, 188–191
  reasons for, 175–183
Mexico, 399
  population of, 408
  unemployment in, 408–409
Mexico City, growth of, 415
Michigan, exports of, 380
Military-industrial complex, 443–446, 447.
  See also Defense industry
Milk industry, regulation of, 433
Milwaukee, Wis., taxes in, 355
Minimum wage, level of, 222–223
Mississippi, school finance in, 236
Modernization, in economic development,
  403
Modernization committees, 438–439
Monetarists, quantity theory of money of,
  79–80
Monetary management
  discount rate and, 95–96
  monetary policy and, 89
  open market operations and, 93–95
  recognition lag and, 98–99
  reserve requirements and, 90–93
Monetary policy
  advantages and disadvantages of, 96–100
  of Federal Reserve system, 89
Money. *See also* Monetary management;
  Monetary policy; Money supply
  definition of, 76
  easy and tight, 93
  equation of exchange and, 78
  functions of, 76, 77
  quantity theory of, 79–80
  in United States, 77–78
Money flow, 4–5
Money multiplier, reserve requirements and,
  90–92

Money supply
  commercial banks and, 80–86
  deficit finance and, 149
  Federal Reserve system and, 85–101
  inflation and, 149, 150–152
  rate of growth of, 97–98
Monopoly
  economies of scale and, 177–178
  natural, 177–178, 427–428
Morrill Act, 37, 313
Multilateral trade, 376
Multinational corporations, 191–194
  in developing countries, 413
Multiplier, 65
Multiplier process, national income and,
  63–65
Munn v. *Illinois,* 427

National Association of Manufacturers, attack
  on unions, 318
National banks
  definition of, 86
  in Federal Reserve system, 86–87
National Bureau of Economic Research, 48–
  49, 99
National health insurance, 304–309
National income
  accounting and control, 48–74
  aggregate measurements of, 49–59
  determination of, 59–63
  energy use and, 258
  equilibrium level of, 63
  growth of, 279
  multiplier process and, 63–65
  stabilization, 65–72
National Industrial Recovery Act, 318, 433
Nationalization
  of military-industrial complex, 445
  of public utilities, 431–432
National Labor Relations Act, 318–319
National Labor Relations Board, 319
National Socialist German Workers' Party,
  451
Needs, of workers, 337
Negative income tax, 219–221
Nepal, 399
  foreign aid to, 413–414
Netherlands, infant mortality in, 293
Net national product, 51–52
  related to other national income measures,
  55
Nevada, mortality in, 298

Newark, N.J., 355
  poverty in, 350
New Deal legislation, 318–319, 323
New Economic Policy
  of Nixon, 386, 394
  of Soviet Union, 457
New Hampshire, school finance in, 236
New Orleans, La., population of, 348
New York City
  population of, 361
  poverty in, 350
  services financed by, 351
  taxes in, 355
  threat of bankruptcy in, 356, 357
New York milk control board, 433
New York State, school finance in, 236
Nicholas II (czar of Russia), 456
Nixon, Richard M., 157, 167, 221, 386, 394
No-growth society, 281–283
Norris-LaGuardia Act, 318
Nuclear energy, price of, 264

Ohio, tax revolt in, 135
Oil
  regulation of industry, 263
  Sweden's policy on, 265–266
Okun, Arthur, 283
Okun's law, 283–284
Oligopoly
  and economies of scale, 177–178, 427–428
  identification of, 178
  inflation and, 158
Open market operations
  of Federal Reserve system, 85, 87, 88
  monetary management and, 93–95
  Treasury securities account and, 88
Opportunity costs, 9
Organization for Economic Cooperation and
    Development (OECD), 106
Organization of Petroleum Exporting Coun-
    tries (OPEC), 399
Overeducation, 241–245

Partnership, 169
Payroll tax, 126–127
Peacock, Alan T., 109
People's Republic of China
  birthrate in, 409
  trade with, 380
Personal income, 54

Philadelphia, Pa.
  poverty in, 350
  taxes in, 355
Phillipines, income distribution in, 419
Phillips curve, inflation and, 147–148
Physicians, training of, 296–297
Pirages, Dennis, 411
Pittsburgh, Pa., poverty in, 350
"Pittsburgh-plus," 172
Planning, see Economic planning
Planning-programming-budgeting system
    (PPBS), 118
Polk, Judd, 192
Pollution
  control of, 271–279
  economic growth and, 284
  energy use and, 258, 259, 261
  growth of, 270–272
  measurement of, 276
Pools, price fixing and, 173
Poor, composition of, 213–216
Poor Law, 24–25
Population, 20
  checks on, 24–25
  distribution of, 345–347, 348–350
  growth of, 42–44, 45, 345
  international comparisons of, 405, 408, 409
  Malthusianism and, 20–23
  problems of rapid growth in, 408–409
  in Third World, 403
  unemployment and growth of, 415
Positional goods, 282
Positive checks, 24
Post hoc fallacy, 14
Post Office, 104, 105
Pound, dollar price of, 389–391
Poverty. See also Income inequality
  absolute, 209–210
  among American Indians, 253–254
  definition of, 209–211, 398
  demographic characteristics and, 213–216
  elimination of, 209, 211, 213, 216–224
  guaranteed annual income and, 218–219
  guaranteed government employment and,
      221–222
  in India, 43
  minimum wage and, 222–223
  negative income tax and, 219–221
  relative, 209, 210
  in Third World, 398–412
  urban, 350
Poverty gap, 219

Poverty level, official, 210–211
Poverty syndrome, 398–412
Prepaid medical service plans, 302–304
Present dollars, 232
Preventive checks, 24
Price(s). *See also* Cost(s); Inflation; Price fixing
  agricultural, 152–154
  business concentration and, 175, 183–188
  control of, 97, 146, 162
  cutting of, 171–172
  of energy, 262–265, 266–269
  equilibrium, 35–36
  incentive, 274
  income stabilization and, 68–72
  of labor, 65–67
  as macroeconomic stabilizer, 465–466
  reference, 371
  Soviet regulation of, 463–466
Price elasticity, of demand, 30–33
Price fixing
  gentlemen's agreement and, 172–173
  legislation against, 172
  pool and, 173
  trust and, 173–174
Price indexes, 140–142
  definition of, 55
  implicit price deflator, 141n
  real gross national product and, 55, 58–59
  wholesale, 140n–141n
Price leadership, 158
Price makers, 154
Price supports, agricultural, 41–42
Price takers, 153
Product differentiation, 184–186
Production
  decisions concerning, 4–8
  definition of, 49
  determining value of, 50
Production-possibilities curve, 8–10
Production sector, 3
Productive resources, 3–4
Productivity
  economic growth and, 279
  education and, 229–230, 238
  factor, 229
  Hawthorne effect and, 340–341
  income related to, 205–206, 324–325
Profit(s)
  business concentration and, 182–183
  of commercial banks, 80
  corporate, undistributed, 199
  as Soviet goal, 472–474

Profitability ratio, 473
Profit-push inflation, 156–157
  Blair's model of, 158–162
  industrial concentration and, 157–158
Progressive tax(es), 120, 121, 123–124, 128, 200
Property ownership, economic systems and, 452
Property tax, 125–126
  shifting of, 121
  for support of education, 235
Proportional tax(es), 120, 128–130
Proposition 13, 135–136
Protective tariff, 368–369
Protestant ethic, 332
Public assistance, 217–218
Public debt, 105–106
Public utilities
  government regulation of, 263–264, 425–433
  identification of, 426–429
Pure Food and Drug Act, 433

Quantity theory of money, 79–80

Race. *See also* Affirmative action; Discrimination
  and income, 245–248, 250–252
  poverty and, 214
  unemployment and, 247–249
  urbanization and, 349–350
Railroads
  federal subsidy to, 432
  regulation of, 426, 427, 428, 429, 431–432
Rand, Ayn, 167, 205
Rand Corporation, 237
Rate base, 430
Rate of return, fair, 430–431
Rate of return equation, 430
Real GNP, 55–59
Regressive taxes, 120, 121, 124–127
Regulation, by government
  of agriculture, 36–40
  cost of, 434
  versus deregulation, 432–433
  expansion of, 433–435
  fair rate of return, determining, 430–431
  of military-industrial complex, 444–445
  versus nationalization, 431–432
  of public utilities, 263–264, 425–433
  of Soviet economic planning, 463
Relative poverty, 209, 210

Reserve requirements
 changes in, 90–93, 96
 maintenance of, 81–86
Residence, poverty and, 214–215
Resources
 economic growth and, 284
 productive, 4
 rate of use of, 259, 261
 in Third World, 410–412
Revenue sharing, 113
 general, 359
Revenue tariff, 369
Reward system, pollution and, 272
"Right to work" laws, 323
Robber barons, age of, 170–174
Rockefeller, John D., 173–174
Roosevelt, Franklin, 110
Rostow, Walt W., 311
Rule of Seventy, 21n, 258
Ruskin, John, 334
Russia. See also Soviet Union
 Bolshevik Revolution in, 456–457

Saab, 339
St. Louis, Mo., poverty in, 350
St. Paul, 332
Sales tax, 124–125
 shifting of, 120–121
Samuelson, Paul, 434
San Francisco, Calif., population of, 348
Saudi Arabia, 399
 life expectancy in, 402–403
Saving(s)
 consequences of, 13–14
 willingness to spend and, 98
Say's law, 59
Scarcity, 2, 3
Schipper, Lee, 266
Schultz, Theodore W., 229
Schumacher, E. F., 416
Scientific method, ideologies and, 14–16
Scientific socialism, 452–453
Scientific tariff, 371
Seattle, Wash., population of, 348
Second law of thermo-dynamics, 270
Self-interest
 concept of, 12
 in free market economy, 7
Sellers' inflation
 profit-push, 156–162
 wage-push, 152–156

Services, determining value of, 50
Sex. See also Affirmative action; Discrimination
 and income, 245–248, 250–253
 and occupation, 252–253
 poverty and, 214
 unemployment and, 247, 249, 251
Shaw, George Bernard, 204–205, 301
Sherman Antitrust Act, 174–175, 426
Shonfield, Andrew, 437
Short-run average cost curve (SRAC), size of business and, 177
Sidel, Victor, 296
Simons, Henry C., 431
Singapore, birthrate in, 409
Six, Robert F., 433
Smith, Adam, 7, 166, 311, 333, 334, 372–373, 425
Smith-Lever Act, 37
Social Democrats, 456
Social imbalance, in governmental spending, 111–112
Socialism, 452
 definition of, 450–451
 historical materialism and, 453–454
 income distribution under, 203–205
 labor theory of value and, 454–456
 scientific, 452–453
 Swedish, 439–440
Social Security Act, 320–321
Social Security Administration
 definition of poverty level by, 210–211
 estimates of health care expenditures by, 289
Social security system. See also Medicare
 in China, 409
 in Soviet Union, 469
 tax collections and, 126
Socioeconomic status, education and, 240
Sole proprietorship, 169
Soviet Union, 399
 agriculture in, 464–465, 466–468
 economic planning in, 436, 457–466, 470–475
 education in, 465, 469
 living standards in, 468–470
 military expenditures of, 420
 military exports of, 447
 socialism in, 451
 unions in, 330
Special drawing rights (SDRs), 385
Specialization. See also Labor, division of
 foreign trade and, 366–368

Spending. *See also* Government spending
regulation of, 98
Spillovers, of production, 270, 273
Stabilization. *See* Income stabilization
Stagflation, 97, 157
Stalin, Joseph, 457
economic planning under, 457–466
Standard Oil Company, 173–174
State(s)
and discrimination, 252
incorporation of, 170
and pollution control, 278–279
regulatory authorities, 263–264, 432–433
school financing by, 235–237
spending by, 104
taxation by, 122–127
State banks, 87
State farms, 466
Statements of condition, 80
Steel crisis, 156
Steel industry
price fixing in, 172–173
reference prices in, 371
working conditions in, 314
Steiger, William A., 136
Sterling, Claire, 413, 414
Stigler, George, 175
Stock, 169
conglomerate mergers and, 189–191
limited liability and, 170
ownership of, 202
Store of value, money as, 76–77, 98
Strikes
collective bargaining and, 330–331
Knights of Labor and, 316
Taft-Hartley Act and, 323
Subsidization
for pollution control, 276
to protect industries, 373–374
Suburbanization, 348
Sunset laws, 432–433
Supply
floating exchange rates and, 387
law of, 33–34
Supply curve, 33–34
Supreme Court
interpretation of Sherman Antitrust Act by, 174–175
labor unions and, 318–319
regulation of industries and, 433
ruling on educational inequality, 238
Surplus value, 455

Sweden
economic planning in, 439–441
energy use in, 265–266
income distribution in, 200–201
infant mortality in, 292–293
life expectancy in, 293
Switzerland, energy use in, 265
Synergism, 191

T-account, *see* Balance sheets
Taft-Hartley Act, 323
Taiwan, birthrate in, 409
Tariff(s)
infant-industry argument for, 369–370, 416
protective, 368–369
revenue, 369
scientific, 371
Tariff Act of 1816, 369–370
Taxation, marginal rate of, 219
Taxes, 116
avoidance of, 130–135
capital gains, 120
in cities, 355, 356, 358
collection and administration of, 122, 125, 127, 235
corporate income, 124
criteria for evaluating, 119–122
effective rates of, 127–130
for energy policy, 268–269
on energy use, 265
growth in, 122
inheritance and estate, 127
negative income, 219–221
payroll, 126–127
personal income, 122–124
for pollution control, 274–275
progressive, 120, 121, 123–124, 128, 200
property, 125–126
proportional, 120, 128–130
regressive, 120, 121, 124, 127
regulation by, 434
revolt against, 135–136
sales, 124–125
sharing burden of cities and, 358
to support education, 235
turnover, 465–466
Tax expenditures, *see* Tax loopholes
Tax loopholes, 124, 130–134
Tax reform, 134–135
Tax shifting, 120–121
Teachers, lack of jobs for, 242–243
Technical fix, for energy use control, 268

Technology
  intermediate, 417
  misapplication to Third World, 416–417
  production decisions and, 5–6
Tennessee, tax revolt in, 135
Terkel, Studs, 320
Textile industry, tariff protection of, 369
Textron, 188–189
Therapeutic nihilism, 293–296
Thermodynamics, second law of, 270
Third party payments, 291–292
Third World, 397
  economic growth, 403–405
  efforts to aid, 412–415, 417, 418
  energy and resource use in, 410–412
  and free trade, 375
  income distribution in, 417–421
  life expectancy in, 401–403
  literacy in, 403
  population growth in, 405–506
  poverty in, 398–412
  trade with, 376
  unemployment in, 414, 415–417
Time deposits, 81, 98
Trade. *See also* Foreign trade
  unfavorable balance of, 381, 394
"Tragedy of the commons," 273
Transfer payments, 54, 113
Triage, 420
Trusts
  legislation against, 174–175, 181–183
  price fixing and, 173–174
Turnover tax, 465–466

Uganda, 399
  life expectancy in, 401
  population of, 408
Underemployment
  in developing countries, 415
  discriminatory, 247–248
Unemployment. *See also* Employment; Un-
    deremployment
  in cities, 415
  in developing countries, 414, 415–417
  during Great Depression, 318, 319–320
  labor costs and, 325–326
  measurement of, 326–328
  population growth and, 408–409
  race and, 247–249
  sex and, 247–249, 251
  unions and, 325–326

Unions, *see* Labor unions
Union shop, 323
United Electrical Workers, 194
United Kingdom, *see* Britain
United States
  agriculture in, 25–27, 36–42, 46
  business in, 165–195
  capitalism in, 165–168
  cities in, 345–361
  congressional budget process, 119
  Constitution of, and capitalism, 167, 425
  defense industry in, 372–373, 442–447
  dependence of other countries on, 363–
    365
  economic planning in, 441
  educational system, 227–245
  energy policy, 254–258, 262, 265–270
  energy use, 258, 261–270
  foreign aid, 413, 417, 420
  foreign trade pattern, 376–381
  health care in, 288–309
  import duties of, 368–372
  income distribution in, 198–200
  infant mortality in, 293
  inflation in, 139–163
  labor in, history of, 312–324
  life expectancy in, 293
  military expenditures of, 420
  military exports of, 447–448
  monetary management in, 89–101
  money in, 77–78
  money supply in, 80–89
  national income management, 59–72,
    73
  national income measurement, 49–55
  poverty in, 209–224
  tax system of, 119–136
  urbanization of, 345–346
  wealth in, distribution of, 201–202, 203
  in world economy, 363–386, 393–394
United States Arms Control and Disarmament
    Agency, 446
U. S. Steel Corporation, 175
  price fixing by, 172–173
Unlimited liability, 169
Urban crisis, 347. *See also* Cities
Urbanization, 345–346, 348
  government spending and, 108
"Unregulated" industries, 433–435
Utah, mortality in, 298
Utilities. *See also* Public utilities
  governmental ownership of, 115

Value
  labor theory of, 454–456
  surplus, 455
VanBuren, Martin, 313
Vertical integration, 176
Vietnam War
  inflation and, 143
  poverty and, 216
Volcker, Paul A., 389
Volvo, 339

Wage(s)
  foreign labor and, 371–372
  minimum, 222–223, 321
  productivity and, 324–325
  in Soviet Union, 474
  unions and, 325–326
Wage controls, inflation and, 146
Wage-price spiral, 155
Wage-push inflation, 152–156
Wages and Hours bill, 321
Wagner, Adolf, 108
Wagner Act, 318–319
  modification of, 323
Waite, Morrison R., 427
War. See also specific wars
  government spending and, 109
  inflation and, 142–143
War economy, international, 446–447
War of 1812, tariffs and, 369–370
War on Poverty, 211, 216–217
Waste charge, 274
Water, as energy source, 261
Wealth
  distribution of, 197–198, 201–202, 203
  inheritance of, 205

Weisbrod, Burton A., 236
Welfare, see Public assistance
West Germany
  importance of foreign trade to, 365
  income distribution in, 201
Weston, J. Fred, 194
White-collar workers
  difficulty of organizing, 323
  dissatisfaction among, 336
Wholesale price index, 140–141
Wiseman, Jack, 109
"Wobblies," 317
Wood, as energy source, 261
Work. See also Labor; Labor unions
  attitudes toward, 312, 331–338
  job and career enrichment and, 339
  job reform and, 340–342
  participative management and, 338
Workday
  division of, under capitalism, 455
  length of, 313–314, 340
Work ethic, 332
Working conditions, improvement of, 313–314, 339–340
World War I
  inflation and, 142, 143
  Russia during, 456–457
World War II
  effect on labor, 321–324
  employment during, 251
  inflation during, 142, 149

Yellow dog contract, 315

Zero Population Growth movement, 43